Destinations in the making

New technologies and adult learning: Experience from Canada, USA and the UK

Ian Harford

niace
promoting adult learning

Published by the National Institute of Adult Continuing Education
(England and Wales)
21 De Montfort Street, Leicester LE1 7GE
Company registration no: 2603322
Charity registration no: 1002775

First published 2006
© 2006 Ian Harford

NIACE has a broad remit to promote lifelong learning opportunities for adults.
NIACE works to develop increased participation in education and training,
particularly for those who do not have easy access because of barriers of class,
gender, age, race, language and culture, learning difficulties and disabilities, or
insufficient financial resources.

For a full catalogue of NIACE's publications, please visit

www.niace.org.uk/publications

Cataloguing in Publications Data
A CIP record for this title is available from the British Library

ISBN 1 86201 274 1

Cover design by Hybert Press
Designed and typeset by Avon DataSet, Bidford-on-Avon, Warwickshire
Printed and bound in Great Britain by Ashford Colour Press

Contents

Foreword

In the summer of 1960 I encountered my first computer, a Ferranti Mercury at the UK Atomic Energy Authority's Harwell laboratory. This relic of the pre-transistor, pre-chip and pre-printed circuit board age could be reached only through tickertape input and spoke only via slow, clacking tele-printers. Each kilobit of memory was closely guarded. The new priesthood wore Jesus sandals and anoraks and like all priesthoods before them spoke a secret language intelligible only to the cognoscenti. Today I carry more computing power in my mobile phone, which instantly transmits words and images around the globe; I can buy gigabits of memory by the handful.

In the 1970s the USA's experimental project ARPANET, run by the Department of Defense, gave many scientists their first glimpse of a potential global communication network. The arrival of super computers heralded the age of Moore's Law – that the cost of computing power will halve every 18 months – and monitors and keyboards eased communication, hastening the development of distributed computing. The real revolution, however, came with point and click when suddenly everyone could access intelligent terminals, and through the world wide web and the internet share global communications and access to unimaginable amounts of information.

The digital revolution has impacted on almost every form of human activity. It has changed the way we communicate, yielding global instant access. It has transformed the way we do business and how we entertain ourselves.

No area is potentially more open to the digital revolution than the world of learning. The hype abounds; the e-this and e-that, the dot-com that failed, but beneath the hype there is a revolution taking place. Freedom in space and time to study what you want to know where and when it is convenient or needed, the world of distributed learning and the knowledge economy are now with us.

In the UK there was awareness in the 1960s that our universities needed access to the new technologies and the Computer Board was established to provide expensive main frames, which cash-strapped institutions could not afford. As the price of computing power fell and the emphasis moved to the provision of networks and support services, the Computer Board evolved into the Joint Information Services Committee. Its remit was later broadened to include all aspects of post-secondary education, including further education and adult and community learning. The different sectors grew out of different cultures and different rules of governance.

As the world shrank, the need to discuss global protocols became essential and the potential for dialogue, collaboration and partnerships grew. Ian Harford has performed a useful service in gathering together information about the uses of new technology in adult education and the range and richness of formal and informal community based learning. He has shown the links being made across sectors, not only in the UK, but also in Canada and the USA and this will benefit practitioners and managers as they grapple with the changes that are needed. His analysis and recommendations are worthy of serious consideration – the revolution is not over yet.

Maxwell Irvine
Chairman, Manchester Computing Centre 1988–91
Chairman, Joint Information Services Committee (JISC) 1998–2003

Manchester, March 2005

Preface

My interest in carrying out this comparative study on the use of digital and web-based technologies (WBT) in post-school education and community development in North America and the UK has been threefold. It stems firstly from a fascination with the process of change and the ways – both predictable and unexpected – that organisations and institutions respond to changing environments. So pervasive is the web that there is suddenly no corner of the world, no feature of our society that can avoid its reach and impact. Ignoring it is perilous.

Secondly, the research has a focus on social inclusion and links with my experience since the 1970s of working with socially and economically disadvantaged learners in adult education and community settings. Much of this has been with the Workers' Educational Association (WEA), the UK's largest voluntary organisation providing adult education and training.

Thirdly, this is a formative period for developing the use of digital and web-based technologies for learning and engaging adults and there are lessons to be learnt. It is six years since the governments of all three countries announced or commenced the funding of local information technology (IT) or community technology centres, and a whole new arena of community-based learning has rapidly emerged.

Analysis and evaluation can have an impact upon policy making and evolving practice in this context; and needs to if there is to be a return on the very significant investments that have been made in this area to support the creation of an Information Society and knowledge economy.

Much of what is included in this research relates closely to issues in the e-strategy report from the Department for Education and Skills, *Harnessing Technology: Transforming Learning and Children's Services*, and to the Cabinet Office and DTI report, *Connecting the UK: The Digital Strategy*, both of which were published in March 2005.

Whatever the country, the same crucial issues face anyone with an interest in promoting lifelong learning and adult education: How do you effectively widen participation and hook adults into learning?[1]; and, having engaged their interest, how do you provide, in a dispersed and multi-centre teaching environment, the support and resources for learning so that they can progress through staged and flexible learning programmes, which build confidence, are responsive to their needs and offer opportunities for progression, achievement and skills acquisition?

The advent of the internet and the web has brought a seismic shift of the ground. On the one hand a networked world increases the skill levels required to be an engaged citizen and an effective worker. In a world where only 10 per cent of the population has actually made a telephone call, it poses the threat of adding a layer of 'digital division' to the existing divisions of race, class, gender and income. On the other hand information and communication technologies (ICT), appropriately applied, offer great potential for the adult learner.

Instead of the 1970s book box with its well thumbed volumes humped around from class to class by the tutor, we now have at our fingertips the promise of a treasure house of resources, digitally delivered and infinitely customisable. Even the wealthiest could not have dreamt of this in the past. Control, choice and personalisation for the learner are within reach and are becoming more so as syndication technology – in the form of RSS ('really simple syndication') subscription based 'feeds' for internet users – has burgeoned in the last year.

Suddenly we have at our disposal the means of stimulating people's basic curiosities, of attracting the reluctant back into learning. Google, a search tool of great sophistication to support this, and available to anyone, could not have been equalled 12 years ago by a small army of researchers.

In the early 1990s the WEA in north-west England was involved in supporting the use of computers at the workplace and with trade unions through its Labour Telematics Centre. In 1992 it began an innovative programme of *ICT in the Community* courses, taking at first desktop PCs and later laptops into community venues for the unemployed, single parents, members of minority ethnic groups and people with disabilities.[2]

We were inundated with requests for more courses with more groups in more venues and realised how quickly computer technology had become a significant factor in motivating adults to become learners. Surprising though this may seem now, email – always quoted as the most commonly used tool of the computer revolution – remained twelve years ago a minor and obscure practice in the UK, although references to it had started to appear in the press.

With the release of the Mosaic web browser in 1993 and subsequent launching of the commercially available Netscape Navigator browser in 1995,[3] the potential for offering the motivated learner the means of independently accessing a course, retrieving information, conducting research, problem-solving and communicating with others over the Web was at hand. Connectivity and access issues of course remained very real and for a period of at least two years, laptop PCs could not be bought in the UK with built in PCMCIA cards for dial-up connections and email.

In 1996 the first broadband multimedia resource centre in the UK further and adult education sector was established in Manchester by the WEA. The culmination of a process of internal debate about the use of ICT for teaching and learning,[4] it was a good example of a cross-sector technology transfer partnership with the University of Manchester providing through Manchester Computing a 10Mb link to JANET, the higher education (HE) sector network.

At the time high-speed connectivity of this kind was beyond the reach of most companies, let alone adult education providers. There was a steady flow of tutors, learners, staff and volunteers who were able to gain experience of the internet with its global network. They learnt first-hand of its capacity to facilitate rapid information searching and communication. As a result of this some interesting ICT-based projects have developed, in several cases with the active support of Manchester

City Council[5] and there has been great willingness in the WEA to experiment.

One major initiative to flow from this was the Greater Manchester Community Grid for Learning (www.learners.org.uk) partnership. CGfL is an aggregation project, with over 32,000 unique visitors since January 2004 and 1450 registered learners in March 2006. It is creating and delivering online and blended learning materials with a strong focus on pedagogy and social inclusion. With a team of six appointed in 2003, the project aims to make a substantial contribution in support of the Government's digital inclusion and skills strategies.[6]

Despite the early start in the north-west, there remains however much more that could be done in harnessing the power of the technology to benefit our learners and improve our services. We have come to realise that transforming how we work is not an easy task. Most challenging is the threat that new technologies bring to our thinking and practice and to the culture and traditions of the organisation.

In this respect the WEA is not different from other organisations. Similar issues have arisen in the HE sector, in schools and in further education (FE). Laying down the infrastructure and providing equipment is only the beginning.

The UK adult and community learning (ACL) sector has had far fewer resources in the past than other sectors and is only now starting to address the issues. It has benefited – mostly in an indirect way – from a major government investment of over £450 million from 2001 in equipment and infrastructure for libraries and UK online centres and is gaining directly from the Learning and Skills Council's (LSC) £33 million information and learning technology (ILT) investment strategy for ACL.

New technologies are disruptive and their introduction has to be managed. They impact in different ways in different sectors. There is a lot of exaggeration about their significance when what is required is rigorous assessment and careful planning with attention to detail, training of staff and the needs of learners. It is better to evolve slowly and gain support and ownership of the process rather than adopt the 'big bang' approach.

We are at an early stage in our understanding of how their use can be optimised and about their deployment in the future. We need a philosophy of 'build and learn'. Cross-sector and international comparisons provide benefits because we can borrow from others' successes and learn from their failures. There are excellent examples of good practice to be found and modified as appropriate.

After being involved for over a decade in the development and organisation of ICT-based courses and projects in the UK, I had become intrigued about how this technology was being implemented in other countries and the extent to which it was breaking existing moulds. In this context the study will give practitioners leads and ideas that they can follow up, and provide some benchmarks against which policy makers and researchers will be able to measure change in the future.

Inevitably in this fast-moving field things are not fixed. Last year's innovation may have been superseded next year, or at any rate have been modified. This does not mean that an analysis of what has been taking place is wasted or irrelevant. Examining the process of how things have changed in organisations in the past can provide compelling insights for others as they build for their future.

Developments with mobile devices and connectivity, with desktop searching, with podcasting, with speech recognition software, with learning platforms and with the use of communication tools for tutors are all likely, however, to have an impact on the experience of adult learners; and managers and practitioners involved in working in ACL need to keep a weather eye open for these and other innovatory approaches. To assist readers, a companion website (www.digitalnations.org) and a *Transforming Learning* Blog (http://transforming.wordpress.com) have been set up. The first contains links to some of the source documents referred to in the footnotes and a photo gallery. The second will have items of interest added after the book's publication to provide updates and further links.

I am grateful to the British Academy for providing a small research grant to allow me to carry out the interviews and visit projects and organisations in Canada and the United States. I am indebted to a wide range of people in both countries for their agreeing to be interviewed and for their interest and insights into what was happening in this fascinating area of work.

In particular I would like to thank Richard Bangs, Laura Breeden, Tom Breitling, Steven Chan, Gary Closson, Sam Coghlan, Suzanne Griffin, George Gundrey, Barney Harford, Sandra Hodder, Roger Hooper, Don Irvine, Alan Joy, David Keyes, Craig Kyte, Stephen Lam, James Lau, Asfaha Lemlem, Ti Locke, Brigitte Malenfant, Kathryn McCulloch, Kelly McCune, Meredith Meywood, Peter Miller, John Moore, Raymond Provencher, Steve Ronan, David Rosen, Peter Royce, Sally Sargent, Gareth and Mae Shearman, Mahal Torres, Ryan Turner, Karia Wong, Steve Wright and David Zermeno.

I am also grateful to colleagues in the UK who have commented on drafts and discussed aspects of the work. These include Jean Barr, Richard Bolsin, Ellen Carling, Dave Carter, Alastair Clark, Alan Clarke, Ian Clifford, John Cook, Greg Coyne, Kevin Donovan, Jon Down, David Egan, Richard Evans, Ann Faulkner, Peter Fowler, Fred Garnett, Chloe Harford, Lindsay Harford, Joe Holly, Fiona Iglesias, Maxwell Irvine, Clare Killen, Graham Luccock, Fiona Parr, Barry Phillips, Bob Powell, Philip Slater, Ian Standish, Chris Swaine, Colin Thorne, Maria Toro-Troconis and Ann Walker. While I owe them a great deal, I must take responsibility for the arguments and any errors that have remained.

Introduction

There is nothing more difficult to take in hand, more perilous to conduct, or more uncertain in its success, than to take the lead in the introduction of a new order of things. (*The Prince*, Niccolò Machiavelli)

The growth of the internet and the widespread use of email and online services have brought the potential for major changes in many spheres of activity. This study focuses on how developments in digital and web-based learning and information systems and the growth of e-learning and e-government services are affecting and will impact upon:

- organisations and institutions offering lifelong learning;
- economically and socially disadvantaged communities.

As computing and telecommunications converge, an array of new personal devices and applications has been developed allowing the user to collect, manipulate and communicate data anywhere and at any time. There are daily stories or advertisements about computing power, the internet, wireless networks and so on. We learn how new technologies are being used for banking and retailing, by government departments and hospitals, and for gambling and dating; and how they will be used in the future to transform our homes into a single interconnected system. In the face of this onslaught it is easy to think that the changes being introduced are inevitable.

Making the right choices

The manner in which technology is implemented is not, however, pre-determined, nor is its impact neutral. There are many examples of useful inventions or innovative methods that have not been taken up or only slowly introduced. The private sector has been more aggressive in finding uses for new technologies than other sectors, but has provided more spectacular collapses. Making the right choices at the right time can make the difference between organisations flourishing or floundering.

In education the use of networking and the web for research and communication has been most evident in universities. This is not surprising in a sector that has been broadly responsible for creating the infrastructure, architecture, standards and protocols that sustain the myriad of networks that make up the internet world.

Since the mid- to late 1990s there has been a strong push, both in the UK and in North America to promote the use of computers and the development of computer-related skills in schools and colleges. Related to this has been a growing interest in the potential and practice of e-learning. There has, for instance, been widespread use of virtual learning environments (VLEs) in HE, FE colleges and schools in the UK, which was reflected in research findings presented to the ALT-C September 2005 Conference in Manchester.

In the world of adult education and in the voluntary and community sector (VCS), on which the research has focused, the potential is huge, but the content and scale of development and innovation is much more limited both in North America and in the UK. There is, as a result, less mature experience to draw upon. This position has been changing, and for a variety of reasons, particularly relating to government policies, which will be explored. There are excellent examples of computer- and web-based learning and pioneering work being done in informal community-based settings, which I have drawn upon in this research and from which other sectors could learn. It remains, however, a comparatively undeveloped area that would benefit from the transfer and migration of experience and skills from other sectors.

Aim and objectives of the research

The aim of the research was to explore the impact of the Information Society (IS) and new technologies on formal and informal organisations offering post-school education (PSE) and the ways they are responding to this changing environment. The key objectives were to examine:

- the significance and role of government and local State policies in promoting the IS and the use of new technologies in PSE, and the extent to which these policies require and stimulate skills acquisition and enhancement in the labour market;
- the ways and extent to which communication and web-based technologies are being used for networking, collaboration, planning and innovation, and the factors which promote and impede this;
- the manner and extent to which these technologies are transforming the organisational processes and roles being played by organisations offering PSE and the stages involved in this evolution;
- the features and strategies of those organisations which are proving most adept or capable at incorporating the new culture of the IS into their business planning, methodology and training, and at anticipating broadband and next generation applications;
- the use being made of new technologies for teaching and learning and the barriers to their deployment;
- the extent of and potential for technology transfer and migration schemes through community–university links;
- the strategies and methods being used for community capacity building, such as the use of volunteers, and for promoting IS skills acquisition by the socially excluded.

Methodology and scope

The study has been carried out by desk research and reading and by a series of semi-structured interviews during two short visits to the USA and Canada in spring and autumn 2002. These were with individuals representing organisations and institutions involved in adult education and community development or supporting its development. In several cases there has been follow-up contact and further research to check details and update. This approach has been complemented by discussions in the UK with people involved in the use of ILT in WEA networks and other organisations, including the LSC, the British Educational and Communications Technology Agency (Becta), National Institute for Adult and Continuing Education (NIACE), Learning and Skills

Development Agency (LSDA), local authorities, and community and voluntary organisations.

The bulk of the experience included in the report, reflecting the interview programme, is from North America, but comparisons are made with the UK and with the work of ACL providers like the WEA and the range of UK programmes and activities supported by the Department for Education and Skills (DfES), LSC, Becta, NIACE, JISC and its regional support centres (RSCs), UKERNA and others.

It is apparent that there is limited research available on the growth and present use of new technologies in adult and community education either for individual countries or of an international and comparative nature.

Information has had to be sought from a variety of sources, much of it web-based. To reflect this and encourage others to build on this research, extensive use has been made of endnotes for those wishing to follow up on the argument of the report. These may be omitted by readers wanting to obtain a general view of the developments in the ACL sector. Inevitably there are technical words and acronyms used in the report and a glossary is included at the end in Annexe 1.

The web and developments in connected and 'on-demand' computing are creating a complex network society. Organisations need to have clear structures and plans to integrate IT into their systems, quality improvement, staff development, training and work practices. Some aspects of this are explored in the report by looking at how the most effective organisations have been able to deploy their resources and nurture a culture of change without de-motivating staff and members or losing sight of their wider objectives.

Other aspects take us more into the terrain of enterprise application integration (EAI) and enterprise resource planning (ERP), more commonly associated with the commercial world. Questions about human and application interaction, organisational culture, complexity management, process analysis, web services and end-to-end monitoring are just as relevant to public and voluntary bodies seeking to be responsive and run efficient services for adult learners.

While some of these questions are briefly reviewed, there are issues of scale and cost involved which are beyond the reach of many of the smaller and community-based organisations interviewed. These issues need further study beyond the scope of this investigation.

Inter-organisational networks

Within the network society organisations typically find it essential to link up and collaborate with other organisations and bodies in order to achieve their objectives. The alliances and partnerships created may be short term or long term, may involve otherwise competing bodies and are often of a cross-sector nature. One of the key benefits of these organisational networks is the creation of 'social capital', the relationships among people and the shared values that grow from them.

The research looks at this phenomenon through some examples and case studies exploring the process by which value is added, and analysing the benefits that accrue to the different partners. North America is a huge continent, and with limited time available a small number of people and organisations were chosen to represent the different areas and interests.

Speed of technical developments

The speed of technical developments is rapid and the researcher can only provide a snapshot, updating wherever possible. Much of the literature, especially if published in book form, is based on work carried out at least two years earlier and it is important to keep abreast of new developments via specialist journals and articles in broadsheets and elsewhere.

Wireless networks are a case in point. During a visit to Seattle in April 2002, a story in the press of how the coffee chain Starbucks was revolutionising the experience offered to its customers looked to be worth a follow up. By introducing Wi-Fi technology, it was noted, anyone with a laptop could send emails and browse the web all day, while enjoying their *latte*. The managers of two local outlets, however, knew nothing about this, as was the case with others, and the line of enquiry was discontinued.

Yet two years later, short-range wireless networks had become widely introduced, and in 2005 over ten million US homes had a Wi-Fi base station. For UK adult learners the DfES has pioneered an £8 million wireless initiative for local areas, via the LSC and NIACE. Two hundred and sixty-four separate small projects have been set up to bring wireless laptop technology to some of the most disadvantaged communities and groups in the UK.[7] (See case study, pp. 50–52.)

By July 2003 Wi-Fi had reached two Starbucks outlets in Manchester in the UK, where an explanatory leaflet was available, while in New York and Boston the company had been able to buck the recession because unemployed white collar professionals were going daily with their laptops to the local café, which had become for them a networking and job centre.

Elsewhere English pubs have been wired up for Wi-Fi access for anyone buying a drink. The Museums, Libraries and Archives Council (MLA) in the UK announced in March 2004 a scheme allowing Wi-Fi access in ten rural libraries for local people using their own or loaned laptops, and Lufthansa began to offer an in-flight wireless service the following spring. Most significant have been developments for those who travel on the railway network. On the east coast GNER now offer a Wi-Fi service on some of their trains and the west coast routes will follow shortly. Broadreach, Virgin's technology partner, is developing an 'intelligent spoofing' system to deal with the problem of tunnels and is working with net telephony company Skype, which has pioneered the use of VOIP services (Voice over internet protocols), to offer free phone calls at any of 350 wireless hotspots.

Most recently The Cloud has announced plans to roll out by Spring 2006 blanket Wi-Fi broadband services in eight major UK cities, using lampposts and street signs. In short, the pace of new developments in this field in just four years – reflecting wider changes in the whole arena of communication and learning technologies – has been fast moving, innovative and fascinating to track.[8]

Selection of the research arena

The selection of countries for the investigation was made on both research and practical grounds. There is much interesting experience to draw upon in Europe, but most of the early innovation associated with the internet and the web has come from the USA. This is true both in technical terms and in the application and use of the technology for government and local services, for business, for community capacity building and for systems and network development.

Examples over the last 30 years include ethernet protocols established in 1973 at Xerox's Palo Alto Center for distributing data over local networks;[9] the release of the Unix operating system in 1974 by Bell Laboratories; ARPANET – precursor of the internet – devised in 1975 for the US military; the creation in the same year of Altair, the first computing box with a microprocessor and the subsequent launch of the commercial Apple 1 in 1976; IBM's creation in 1981 of the 'Personal Computer' (PC) that became a generic name; the Democrats' 'Re-invention of Government' in 1993 and the Access America Programme; the launch in 1995 of Netscape Navigator; the operation by the US government of the satellite based global positioning system (GPS) and the application of geographic information systems (GIS); the emergence in 1998 of the dotcom phenomenon and of household names like amazon.com and eBay.com and recently the growth of web services and Google's range of specialist search facilities for images, scholarly citations, items for sale and news.

Comparing government policies

By combining the US (population of 293 million) with this history of innovation with adjoining Canada (population of 32.5 million) it would be possible to draw upon a range of urban and rural experiences and also make some assessment of the impact of State policies in this area and compare this with the experience of the UK (population 60 million).

The Canadian government, for instance, has placed substantial emphasis on skills development and broadband access for remote communities, while in the USA the Federal Government has relied more on the workings of the market and the inventiveness of the private sector.

The UK government has since the 1990s had a primary focus on the educational use of new technology and over the last five years has invested substantially in the provision of ICT infrastructure and equipment in the most socially and economically disadvantaged communities as part of a strategy to tackle both the digital divide and low literacy and numeracy rates.

English as a primary language

A further practical advantage is that the primary language of both countries is English, which makes comparisons with UK experience easier. In all three countries there are sizeable minorities, of course, where English is not the primary language. The majority of the population in all three countries live in urban areas and for logistical as well as research purposes the pattern of visits and interviews reflected this.

Summary of chapter contents

The results of the research and interviews are divided into five areas.

Chapter 1 considers providers, internet populations and the digital divide, exploring definitions of the adult and community education sector and introduces the organisations surveyed. It looks at measurements of internet populations relating these to concerns about a digital divide.

Chapter 2 looks at the history and role of government intervention in relation to the knowledge economy and skills development and at issues about funding and infrastructure development.

Chapter 3 examines the responses to the information society and new technologies of mostly North American organisations providing post-school education and of other bodies involved in community-based informal learning and capacity building. It provides some examples of usage and case studies of how new technologies have been introduced.

Chapter 4 draws together findings and conclusions from the research, including some experience from the UK, and tests these against the original research objectives. It looks at the benefits and drawbacks and assesses the factors that promote and impede innovation and successful implementation planning.

Finally, a number of recommendations are made for government, LSC and funding bodies about policy development and for the WEA, ACL and other organisations about ways of working to take advantage of new technologies and the network society.

1

Providers, internet populations and the digital divide

Everyone either loves or hates the internet, but there's no question that the impact of the internet is real and profound. (Jeffrey Cole, Director, UCLA Center for Communication Policy, Los Angeles, June 1999.)

It is common to talk about the transformational nature of new technologies. We experience this in the nature of work undertaken, in the adaptations we have to make and in our personal lives. Consider the example of the mobile phone, which in Japan is taking on the character of the mobile internet. The mobile has even changed the way that people walk down the street, either with head down, thumb-clicking a pad in their palm or with head slightly inclined and a hand clamped firmly to one ear!

There are now 80 mobile phones for every 100 households[10] in the UK and we can use them anywhere and at any time as alarms, clocks, calendars, calculators, credit 'wallets', directories, stopwatches, torches and notebooks, and for taking photos, talking, reminders, games, information services, web access, voice recording and 'wireless' messaging. The portability of mobiles and the ability to track them through global positioning systems (GPS) open up whole new avenues for social organisation and cooperation, intriguingly explored by Howard Rheingold in his book *Smart Mobs*. The functions of mobiles are certain to evolve further and have potential use for adult learners. On the average day in the UK, according to the Mobile Data Association, they are used to send 93 million text messages and the fixed line telephone carriers are looking to follow suit to protect their own income streams.[11]

This process of change in the use and application of technology is mirrored in the institutions and organisations that provide post-school education and training. But the technologies available are far more extensive than the mobile phone alone. Few make use of all of them. Most could do more without major effort. Some are more flexible than others, some are losing out and the pace of change is not linear. In this new frontier world without clear ground rules new kinds of organisation are emerging, while others are losing ground or are redefining their roles to offer new opportunities for learning and skills acquisition.

Providers

A broad definition

To capture this changing scene the definition of those providing post-school education for adults and promoting capacity building in local communities has been kept deliberately wide. It includes voluntary and community-based organisations, community networking bodies, community technology centres and computer labs (similar to the UK Online centres), adult education services, community and FE colleges and libraries. Universities and other sections of municipal authorities can also play a role.

In order to limit the scope of the enquiry, however, the research has not focused on workplace-based education, although many adults undertake training and attend courses via their work, and in the UK the government encourages employers and providers to work in partnership to address the basic skills deficit. Examples include provision made through the University for Industry (UfI) and by local colleges and the WEA's 'New Pathways' courses with the NHS Workplace Confederations and UNISON.

Difficulty of mapping a complex field

Mapping exactly how much adult education is being offered in each area and by whom is very difficult as there are multiple funding sources, no common definitions and no central registers. Furthermore, work that is undertaken in the voluntary and informal sector is often not recognised or recorded. A brief survey of the landscape is outlined below, but it is not suggested that the data provided here is either comprehensive or gives an exactly comparable position for each of the three countries.

In the USA the Adult Education Act 1966 created a system for drawing providers of adult education into a common framework and this subsequently metamorphosed under the Adult Education and Family Literacy Act in 1998. The Adult Education and Literacy (AEL) System covering provision funded by the Department of Education's AEL Division over the period 1992 to 1999 had 31 million enrolled students, giving an average of 4.4 million a year.

Provision is also funded under the Elementary and Secondary Education Act (ESEA) and the figures above do not cover the work of community technology centres. The largest growth area in recent years has been through federal support for after school provision, which increased in the period 1996–2001 from $1 million to approximately $1 billion. Non-profit, community-based organisations can now apply for these funds and run courses at independent sites away from the schools provided certain conditions are met.

In terms of volume of delivery of adult education in the USA one researcher interviewed ranked the top four institutions/sectors in order as:

1   Public schools
2   Community colleges
3   Community-based organisations
4   Libraries[12]

In the third category is included the network of community technology centers and community networks which have expanded enormously over the last decade in both the USA and Canada. In the USA alone there are thought to be over 14,000 of these centers. There is in the USA no exact parallel to the UK adult education service run by the local authority (LA) – although this is far from being uniform in nature as can be seen from Table 1 below.

The pattern of providers in Canada is broadly similar to the USA and a more detailed picture of the position there can be built up from the

Canadian *Adult Education and Training Survey*. This was commenced in 1990 but the most recent data relates only to 1997.[13] The interviews carried out in the 2002 North American research covered all the categories except the public schools.

In the UK the position is also complicated with a wide range of statutory and voluntary providers. Further education colleges, funded by the LSC, make provision for over three million adults but this covers a range of courses, mostly of a vocational nature. LAs have responsibilities in this area, although not all make direct provision themselves. They constitute the largest single group in the adult and community sector, although the position with regard to the provision they manage or oversee is complex.

Data collected in 2003 for the LSC's Adult and Community Learning Information and Learning Technologies (ILT) Group for the UK LEA sector of adult education (Table 1) shows that this provision for almost 1.6 million adults[14] is organised in very different ways. This figure does not include courses run by the community and voluntary sector – unless they have been contracted out from the LA – or provision funded under the Single Regeneration Budget, other government initiatives like SureStart, or run directly by library authorities.

Table 1. LSC-funded provision via Local Education Authorities in the UK, 2002.

Type of provision	No. of providers	% of providers	No. of students	% of students
Direct	66	44%	690,200	43%
Direct via schools	14	9%	290,000	18%
Franchising	4	3%	30,100	2%
Contracted out	49	33%	327,100	21%
Thro' Community	6	4%	66,100	4%
Mixed Economy	11	7%	183,900	12%
TOTALS	150		1,587,400	

Source: AE2 Returns from LEAs to DfES. © Crown Copyright.

Research on adult learning in the UK has indicated that in any year, even if a wide definition of 'learning' is given, under 25 per cent of the population claim to be currently involved and this figure is much lower for those leaving school at 16, the unemployed and the retired. For 2004 the figure dropped to as low as 19 per cent. There is a link too with access to technology, with 53 per cent of adults with internet access being current or recent learners as against 21 per cent of those without internet access. This point is reinforced by the 2004 *Report of the Digital Inclusion Panel*, which stressed the importance of home access for technology adoption and thus learning.[15]

It shows too that unskilled and educationally disadvantaged adults are far more likely to participate in learning where they become involved through participation in other community activity. The importance of the voluntary sector – which includes the Community Networking and Technology Centers in the USA and Canada and the community-based UK Online and other ICT centres in the UK – in widening participation and creating a learning society is very significant and was recognised in the Hall Aitken final evaluation report (www.hallaitken.co.uk) of the UK Online centres.

Interviews and visits undertaken

A list of the visits and interviews undertaken can be found in Annexe 2. In all, 29 interviews were held and a breakdown by type of organisation is shown in Table 2. The number of entries is given as 33, as in four cases the respondents were judged to represent two different types of organisation because of their intermediary role or employment position.

On the West Coast visits were made to San Francisco, Seattle and Vancouver, and on the East Coast to Boston, Toronto and Montreal. Experience of some of the issues affecting more remote and rural areas was gained from visits in Canada to Vancouver Island (Comox Valley), Quebec and Ontario Province (Oxford County).

As Table 2 indicates, there were some differences in focus in the two sets of visits. On the West Coast, interviews were held with more networking groups, community-based organisations and computer labs. These included both 'traditional' ones like Vancouver Net, Victoria Community

Network, Seattle Community Network and Compumentor, set up in the early 1990s or earlier, and more recent computer labs like the Yesler Center and Chinese Center in Seattle – similar to the UK Online centres – and a Los Angeles networking project to promote disability issues.

Table 2. Interviews in the USA and Canada in 2002, by type and area.

Type of organisation	West Coast	East Coast
Voluntary networking organisation	8	3
Local community-based organisation	3	0
Government or local authority	2	3
Library service	1	3
Community college	1	1
University	1	3
Corporation	2	0
Charitable foundation	2	0
Totals	20	13

Interviews were also held with two bodies, the Gates Foundation and the Salesforce.com Foundation, both supporting the use of ICT in local communities; and with two companies, Avanade and Expedia, involved respectively in advanced networking training, and online sales and marketing in the travel industry. These provided good examples of how web-based methods were being used to advantage in the private sector.

On the East Coast more emphasis was given to contacts with university-based organisations and with the activities and perspectives of government departments like Industry Canada and the Canadian Office of Learning Technologies. The visit to Boston provided very useful information about the Community Technology Centers Network and the America Connects Consortium. On both the West and East Coasts visits were made to community colleges – in Seattle and Oakville, Toronto – and to look at the ways that Library Services were initiating new services and responding to the changing needs of their users.

Internet populations

Internet and broadband usage

The intention was to target for the research areas where there was known to be high internet usage, as these could indicate trends for the future in the UK. Data from a 2003 Nielsen survey showed that all the three US cities visited ranked in the top four for internet home usage, with Seattle (1) at 80.6 per cent, Boston (2) at 79.1 per cent and San Francisco (4) at 78.3 per cent. An AOL survey in March 2003 shows all three cities were also in the top ten US areas for high-speed broadband home usage with the order reversed. San Francisco had the highest with a 55 per cent penetration followed by Boston (3) and Seattle (10). Pew internet figures for December 2004 showed across the USA that 106 million adults had home internet access, of whom 51 per cent had broadband – a substantial increase over two years.

Exactly comparable figures for Canada and the UK are not available, but a study in January 2003 showed Canada at the time considerably further ahead of the USA overall in broadband usage with 53.6 per cent of the population committed to high speed connectivity. This compared with the overall 2003 figure for the USA of 33.8 per cent.[16] A good example of the effort needed to bring fast speed access to a rural area was provided by a visit to the Comox Valley Project on Vancouver Island.[17]

For a very large country with a relatively small population the overall picture is an impressive record, but the figure conceals the urban-rural split as a 2003 report indicated for more remote areas:

> When it comes to high-speed network services, Canada is a nation divided. Along with most rural and remote regions, the Northwest Territories is on the wrong side of the digital divide. In an area of more than one million hectares, there are 42,000 people living in 33 communities.[18]

The returns for providing broadband services in thinly populated areas are not attractive to commercial operators and result in both Canada and the USA having a de facto zonal character to high speed internet access with substantial variance particularly in the USA from state to state. This is not so surprising when it is remembered that 38 per cent of the

American continent is wilderness compared with Africa's 28 per cent.

Even within relatively small states there can be huge variations. In Franklin, Massachusetts for instance only 22 miles south-west of broadband Boston, the upmarket Marriott long-stay hotel was offering in 2002 rooms with an accompanying study, but provided only a 28k modem link for its business guests.[19]

UK experience

In general contrast to this the UK has had one of the lowest rates of home broadband usage in Europe, with a 'fragmented and highly fluid technology atlas'.[20] Just 3 per cent of households had this facility in 2001,[21] compared with Denmark with 20 per cent. Figures in April 2003 suggested that there was a faster increase in cable broadband with NTL and Telewest registering their first million users just ahead of ADSL (Asymmetric Digital Subscriber Line) connections – which are based on the traditional copper phone lines.

BT has, however, been actively upgrading its exchanges to accommodate ADSL technology and thus promote geographical 'extensiveness', one of the government's broadband targets. By autumn 2003, 80 per cent of British households had the potential of accessing broadband by cable or ADSL and BT indicated that it had recorded 'trigger levels', or website demand for broadband from potential users, for a further 10 per cent. Helped partly by investment by the Scottish Executive in infrastructure for some of the most remote areas, BT announced in 2004 that it anticipated that by July 2005, 99 per cent of UK homes would be capable of high-speed internet access.

In late 2002 broadband still represented only about 8 per cent of UK households, with rural areas as in North America being particularly disadvantaged, but by December 2003 data supplied to the Office for National Statistics by internet service providers showed that 19 per cent of connections, representing over 3 million subscribers, were broadband – more than double that of 12 months earlier.[22] One response to the problems facing rural areas has come from local authorities and development agencies, which have either set up subsidised broadband projects or supported aggregation initiatives. Examples can be seen with the East of England Development Agency (EEDA) in the north-west with the NWDA[23] and in Cornwall.[24]

The UK government indicated in 2000 that it wished to guarantee universal access to high-speed broadband and thanks to BT this has been justified, although it was unclear at the time if this meant the provision of services to the home.[25] There has been a policy of promoting competitiveness, which has led to a significant lowering of prices and a surge in demand. Despite this the UK still lagged in 2004 behind Europe for broadband penetration with only 5 per cent subscribing out of the total population, compared with the EU average of 6 per cent and figures of 12 per cent or more for Belgium, Denmark and Holland, as Figure 1 indicates.[26]

Figure 1. EU broadband take-up, 15 January 2003 – January 2004
Broadband penetration – number of subscribers as a % of population

Source: Connecting Europe at High Speed: National Broadbank Strategies. EU, 2004. © European Communities, 1995–2005.

Home internet penetration has continued to grow in the UK, although the pace has slackened. In 2002 46 per cent of households had home access, which was double that of 1999 but only 7 per cent up on the previous year; and by October 2004 the figure had reached 53 per cent.

National Statistics (ONS) now produces a valuable monthly update of internet connectivity, which showed that there had been a further 6 per cent increase in all UK subscriptions by October 2005. Significantly however broadband connections continued to increase their market share – up from 19 per cent to 59 per cent of all connections over just two years – putting the UK ahead of the US on this count for the first time (see p. 21).[27]

In the USA, with its higher internet penetration rate, a pattern of stabilisation has been emerging with 'internet drop-outs' matching the number of new users. In September 2001 the US Department of Commerce recorded that 54 per cent of Americans (143 million) were online but figures in 2003 from the Pew Research Center suggested that the number of internet users was stuck at about 60 per cent. New joiners were only compensating for leavers. Most recent 2005 Pew research figures however show a further increase, with 68 per cent of American adults using the internet and only 22 per cent saying that they had never used the web or email. The report concluded, 'In broad terms two thirds of American adults now go online and one third do not.'[28]

Charting the digital divide

Over the last decade a small industry has developed which is devoted to tracking usage and access to the internet by class, income, age, gender, racial origin and country. Surveys are being undertaken to show the time being spent online and on individual websites, the activities being foregone by the online 'surfer', the number of websites visited, the relationship between virtual encounters in chat rooms and via email and social contacts made in the real world.

The web has been a boon both to sociologists propounding views about the relationship between the individual and society and to advertisers, to whom much of the usage research is directed. Probably the most balanced picture[29] of the impact of the internet in the US can be found in the comprehensive account by Katz and Rice published in 2002.

Fault lines based upon education and income

Based upon telephone surveys between 1995 and 2000, it concluded that the internet can be used like any other tool for both harmful and beneficial purposes and that the principal fault lines of the digital divide are on income and education grounds.[30] They acknowledged that ethnicity was a factor but generally differences in access were better explained in terms of income rather than race. The experience of Latinos in California supports this view as the figures drawn from a Pew Study of 2001 show.

While overall only 47 per cent of California Latinos (CL) used the internet compared with 70 per cent of non-Hispanic whites (NHW), usage by CLs with some college education was 68 per cent compared with usage of 69 per cent by all Californian adults with similar education. For those CLs with an income below $20,000, usage was 21 per cent compared with a figure of 35 per cent for all California adults; but for those with an income of $20,000–$59,999 the respective figures were 52 per cent and 63 per cent.[31]

Updated data for the period December 1998 to September 2001 used by the US Department of Commerce for its 2002 digital divide report suggested that there was a catching up process going on. It found that for the lowest income households (with less than $15,000 per year) internet usage was increasing by 25 per cent yearly, while that for high-income households (earning more than $75,000 per year) the rate was increasing – from a higher base rate – by only 11 per cent. In the twelve-month period up to September 2001 internet use by blacks and Latinos increased by 33 per cent and 30 per cent respectively. The Pew internet research report for 2005 suggested however that, with 53 per cent of all users having high speed connectivity, a significant feature of a new US digital divide is access to broadband. This was again linked to education, income levels and age.[32]

The position in the UK provides a very similar picture in relation to income and may indicate a less promising position than the USA in terms of home access to the internet enjoyed by low-income adults. Exactly equivalent figures are not available but data from the Government's Office for National Statistics in July 2003 (See Table 3) showed that whereas 86 per cent of those in the top decile of earners were reported to have home internet access, only 12–14 percent of those in the lowest 20 per cent of the population had this facility and their take-up rate was not accelerating. These figures should be taken as indicative, but can also obscure more complex relationships.[33]

Table 3. Households in the UK with home access to the internet, by gross income decile group.

	1998–99	1999–00	2000–01	2001–02	2002–03*
Lowest ten per cent	3	6	7	11	12
Second decile group	1	3	5	13	14
Third decile group	2	4	12	15	23
Fourth decile group	3	6	17	24	32
Fifth decile group	4	15	26	34	41
Sixth decile group	7	15	32	42	48
Seventh decile group	10	22	43	50	57
Eighth decile group	16	28	49	58	68
Ninth decile group	19	38	60	67	75
Highest decile group	32	48	73	80	86
All households[1]	10	19	32	40	46

Source: National Statistics website: www.statistics.gov.uk. Based on *Family Expenditure Survey* (1998–2001); Expend. & Food Survey (April 2001). Crown copyright material is reproduced with the permission of the Controller of HMSO.
* Provisional data.

Measuring public access

Home internet usage and broadband access, though important, is only part of a much more complex issue in considering issues relating to the digital divide. The efforts of governments, municipalities and community-based bodies and networks have succeeded in creating in North America and the UK – in many urban areas at any rate – IT centres or labs where the disadvantaged and those on low incomes can get access to computers and training free of charge, but the issue of usage remains.

In Seattle, the city's Department of Information Technology has examined ways in which objective and measurable judgments can be made about progress on these fronts. It has worked with a Citizens Technology and Telecommunications Advisory Board to devise a series of indicators of what a healthy IT community would look like. One measure of public access would be the number of publicly available computers per 100 households within walking distance of one mile; another would be an indicator showing the ratio of usage to capacity.[34]

Literacy as an underlying component

More important questions, however, go beyond the issue of mere access or bandwidth. We need to consider just what the skills are that are needed for the knowledge economy, how learners develop these skills, and how they integrate them into their working and personal lives. Much of the material on the web, written by well-educated and middle class people, and selling often relatively expensive consumer items like books, travel and holidays for the affluent, are not likely to motivate adults with low incomes and limited education.

Access alone to a computer and the internet do not in themselves provide the necessary skills. Although there has been some scaling down of the claims made at the height of the dotcom boom about the high percentage of workers requiring advanced IT skills, there is no doubt that increasingly there are more and more jobs that in some way involve the collection, manipulation, evaluation, interpretation and communication of information. Indeed, research by e-skills UK in 2004 showed that more than 90 per cent of new jobs in the UK require some level of ICT ability.

These are complicated skills and, as Andy Carvin of the Benton Foundation has argued, involve a wider literacy as the key component. Without this individuals are unable to carry out the essential tasks of a knowledge worker in a professional or office environment, whatever the IT skills they have developed.[35] Carvin identifies a number of different literacy areas including functional, occupational, technological, information and adaptive and suggests that IT centres and computer labs must adapt their programmes, content and practices to this reality if they are to play an effective role in reducing the barriers thrown up by the digital divide.

ICT as a basic skill

In the UK the Post-16 e-Learning Strategy Task Force came to a similar position in 2002, but from a different direction, arguing that just as reading and writing are seen as essential for ensuring social inclusion, so likewise ICT skills – which include the skill to learn through ICT – should be added to the list as a basic skill. In 2003 the report *21st Century Skills* formally recognised ICT as a third basic skill, and in 2005 an ICT Skill for Life Core Curriculum was developed by a small team for QCA.[36] The role of government in tackling the digital divide is critical here, as are the costs associated, and in the next chapter the different approaches that have been taken in the three countries are explored in more detail.

II

History and role of government intervention

The problem is finding ways of engaging the attention of the under-achievers, those who could do much better but at present fall by the wayside. The digital revolution won't automatically bring electronic salvation to everybody. (Victor Keegan on the Labour Party Conference, *Guardian*, 5 October 1995.)

All governments are faced with the social and economic impact of globalisation and the competitiveness that accompanies it. Some aspect of this process can be seen in every developed country – local industries shrinking, older workers needing to retrain, young people unable to find jobs or forced to move to find work.

Globalisation is destabilising. It brings relocation of production, reengineering of processes, refocusing on core business and outsourcing of services; and it affects all. Although the process is complex, information technologies play a key role enabling rapid communication, virtual design teams, complex production alliances, secure financing, cost reductions, close monitoring and quality control and just-in-time supply chains.

Information has now become in the 'information society' a key resource, with raw materials taking up an increasingly small percentage of the costs of the final product.[37] The ability to capture, synthesise and repurpose data at speed is vital to wealth creation and to a country's competitiveness in the knowledge economy. More and more jobs require not only higher literacy and numeracy skills but also IT fluency.

It is not surprising therefore that governments have turned their attention to the structuring and deployment of information technologies and to promoting innovation in order to find solutions for their economic and social problems. The policies adopted fall into the four interrelated categories set out below and these are explored in this chapter with reference to the three countries. Each of these policy areas impinge directly on adult and lifelong learning and have considerable potential for driving the use of new technologies both in disadvantaged communities and in the general ACL sector.

1   Infrastructure creation and promotion via public expenditure and telecommunication regulation and policies on broadband, competition and wireless spectrum.
2   Promotion of e-commerce and e-business through a balance of incentives and regulation.
3   Establishment of coordinated e-government services at both national and local levels via public expenditure, restructuring and incentives.
4   Funding of programmes and initiatives to provide the full spectrum of IT training from basic skills to advanced programming, networking and multimedia qualifications.

The US experience

Given the focus of this study on adult learning via computer and web-based technologies, it is interesting to start a review of US government intervention in this area by referring to a little known but significant political document, *Putting People First: How We Can All Change America*. Published in 1992 by Bill Clinton and Al Gore as part of the Democrats' campaign for the presidency, the programme of reforms was clearly influenced by some of the thinking behind Osborne and Gaeler's *Reinventing Government* book published at the end of the year.

The Clinton–Gore manifesto set out in broad-brush terms the blue print for an efficient, responsive and customer-focused government that would cut red tape and cost less. Its language was populist, general and oriented to the concerns of local communities:

We cannot put people first and create jobs and economic growth without a revolution in government. We must take away power from the entrenched bureaucracies and special interests that dominate Washington.... The answer for every problem cannot always be another program or more money. It is time to radically change the way the government operates – to shift from top down bureaucracy to entrepreneurial government that empowers communities and citizens to change our country from the bottom up.[38]

The National Performance Review

Within months it was to be followed up by President Clinton's announcement of a six-month-long *National Performance Review* (NPR) to be led by the Vice-President. Their purpose was far reaching: 'We intend to redesign, to reinvent, to reinvigorate the entire national government'. The drivers behind the programme were openly acknowledged – a $4 trillion national deficit, ill-directed welfare policies, ineffective education and training programmes which undermined competitiveness, and a lack of trust in government.[39]

This intensive review was conducted by teams of officials, business experts, private citizens, and others with first hand knowledge. The outcome was a series of 1200 radical recommendations. As Gore put it: 'The federal government is filled with good people trapped in bad systems... many are now afraid to deviate even slightly from standard operating procedure... Yet innovation, by its very nature requires deviation.'

The proposals had IT at the centre. 'Public officials should view information technology as the essential infrastructure for government for the twenty first century', stated the accompanying report, *Re-engineering through Information Technology*. It further stated that integrated electronic access to governmental information and services was already possible and that 'access to government is a right of Americans.'[40] The alpha version of the Mosaic browser, commonly regarded as the precursor for mass web access, had been released just five months earlier and there was good reason for high expectations about the potential and benefits to be gained from new technology.

Moving the American state towards the digital age

The NPR has had its critics. Some of its underlying assumptions look questionable and many of its proposals have not been realised. Its vision, however, was substantially in advance of what was under consideration in any other country and much has been achieved. It is impossible to disagree overall with Fountain's considered assessment that 'the focus of reformers on leveraging cyberspace, using the internet to create a new infrastructure and "logic" for organising in the federal bureaucracy, has rapidly moved the American state towards the digital age.'[41]

It was an example of the Type 3 policy initiative listed above and raised implicit questions about how exactly 'citizens and communities' would be able to interact with the technology and gain access to the government's services. The universal right to information including for those with disabilities was enshrined in the Constitution and in legislation like the 1990 Americans with Disabilities Act and the 1996 Telecommunications Act.

Though these issues were not immediately addressed in relation to the NPR programme, the questions were by 1997 becoming more obvious when further developments in electronic services via the Access America programme were announced. As Gore put it in his introduction:

> … it calls for new ways to bring electronic options to all who want them, including those in underserved and rural areas… each of the actions… must be truly accessible to individuals with disabilities.[42]

Role of the Commerce Department

In parallel with the Vice-President's moves to implement and create support mechanisms for electronic government, the US Commerce Department, through its National Telecommunications and Information Administration (NTIA), was already playing an imaginative role in promoting the Information Society. It had been active from an early stage in supporting the growth of e-commerce and in charting the take up and penetration of the internet among different groups.

In 1994 it sponsored an online conference with the Cleveland Freenet, asking users about their ideas on how best to provide universal access to the internet;[43] and commissioned the Census Bureau to include questions on computer and modem usage in its household surveys.

In October of the same year it had provided a $697,000 Technology Opportunities Programme (TOP) grant to the United Neighborhood Houses of New York to set up a pilot information system for five non-profit settlement houses in deprived areas and, as part of the programme, computers with access to the internet were subsequently installed in 'family rooms.' This was just one of 92 IT-based projects across a range of areas approved for funding in this first year of the programme.[44] By 2003 TOP had funded 555 projects, allocating £205 million and leveraging an additional £280 million in matched funds.

Information have-nots

In 1995 NTIA published its first report on *Falling through the Net*, which headlined the emergence of information 'have-nots' in rural and urban America and the need to empower the 'Information Disadvantaged'. A pivotal role should be played by schools, public libraries and other 'community access centers' in providing 'at least for an interim period, a means for electronic access' to public services for these groups.[45]

For the first time federal recognition was being openly given to the role of community-based IT centres in tackling the digital divide. In the same year the Department of Housing and Urban Development (HUD) started a programme of creating computer learning centres in conjunction with the private sector in mostly private apartments, not public housing. Public funds, however, were not used for this programme until 2002.[46]

First federal grants made to community technology centres

A recommendation similar to that put forward in the first report was contained in the second NTIA *Falling through the Net* report[47] published three years later in 1998, and this time it was picked up by the Department of Education, which released details the following year of a $9.25 million 'community technology centers' (CTC) programme.[48]

This was to support CTCs, which were already spreading across the country supported by their own CTCNet and the wider community technology movement. The programme required matching grants of 30%–50% over the three year life of the projects and 40 were announced in September, reflecting the acceptance of the need for intervention in targeted areas with both limited infrastructure support and training aimed at the disadvantaged – the first and fourth types of policy.

By the time NTIA published its third *"Falling through the Net"* report in 1999, its message was clear – that income and education were the biggest dividers in terms of access to the internet, with a subsidiary warning that whites were more likely to be connected than Afro-Americans and Hispanics. As a reflection of this, the US government's Information Technology Research Program launched in September a 'Program Solicitation' on the 'Social and Economic Implications of IT' which would explore how to overcome barriers related to the use of IT and foster 'IT access equity and universal participation in networks…'.[49]

The following year the White House decided to pick up on the findings of the *Falling through the Net* report, emphasising the serious problems of the digital divide in President Clinton's 'New Markets Trip'. In a visit to Palo Alto he pointed to the poverty there and unequal access to technology and skills that affected Hispanics especially – despite the city being adjacent to Silicon Valley, the epicentre of 'the digital revolution that is sweeping the globe.'[50] It was a wake up call to the private sector to take its responsibilities seriously, but by the end of the year a new administration was to be in the White House with a less enthusiastic attitude to the promotion of a digitally skilled nation.

Based upon a September 2001 population census, NTIA produced its fourth report in 2002, *A Nation Online: How Americans are Expanding their Use of the Internet.* While there were improvements in penetration rates across the country, the conclusion that 'With more than half of all Americans using computers and the internet, we are truly a nation online', was hard to justify. The detailed tables showed that just 50.5 per cent of households had internet access and for those with incomes under $15,000 the figures for whites, blacks and Hispanics were at rates respectively of 27 per cent, 13 per cent and 18 per cent.[51]

Promotion of e-commerce

The other role of the Commerce Department was in analysing the growth of e-commerce and of promoting it as appropriate as a source of growth in the economy – the second type of policy as noted in the typology above. A framework for this had been comparatively late in emerging in 1997, reflecting the non-interventionist position of both the Democratic and Republican Parties. The first three principles made this very clear:

1   The private sector should lead.
2   Governments should avoid undue restrictions on e-commerce.
3   Where Governmental involvement is needed, its aim should be to support and enforce a predictable, minimalist, consistent and simple legal environment for commerce.[52]

The following two years saw the Department releasing its first *Emerging Digital Economy* report in April 1998 and its *Emerging Digital Economy II* report in 1999. The latter noted that IT-producing companies (engines of e-commerce), although only producing 8 per cent of US GDP, accounted for on average 35 per cent of real economic growth in the years 1995–1998.[53]

A key section (Chapter 4) of the 1999 report on *Labor Markets in the Digital Economy* focused on training and skills development, an example of the Type 4 policy initiative in the typology. Noting the shortage of specialist IT skills, it reported on the policy of increasing visas for high skilled foreign workers by an average of 73 per cent over the three years 1999–2001,[54] partnerships established between educational institutions, local councils and business to run training courses and the commitment of a $60 million federal budget to train IT workers in key areas.

Communications Commission: Review of regulatory tools

The operation of the private market did not meet all the requirements of the new knowledge economy, both in terms of skilling the workforce and in providing access in rural and deprived city areas. In its second report in 2000 to Congress on the availability of internet services, the Federal Communications Commission confirmed the position with rural areas – that large pockets of rural America had no access to broadband.[55]

An attempt to start remedying the situation came in December 2002 with the launch of a Notice of Inquiry seeking:

75396

comment on the effectiveness of regulatory tools it currently has in place to facilitate the delivery of wireless service to rural communities across the United States …[and asking] whether the Commission should modify its policies to promote the provision of more spectrum-based services in rural areas, what types of wireless services are being provided in rural areas, and what obstacles exist to the provision of wireless services in rural areas.

By June 2003 the Federal Communications Commission was reporting a take up of broadband by 20.6 million homes and small businesses, still substantially lower in percentage terms than Canada.

In March 2004 the issue of broadband was brought into the public arena by a widely reported speech on new technology by President Bush to Hispanic lawmakers in Albuquerque, New Mexico, a state where he narrowly lost in the 2000 presidential election. Focusing on the priority of having universal affordable access to broadband by 2007, he declared the need to 'stay on the cutting edge of technological change' but gave no indication of how this would be achieved. The issue was brought into sharp focus again by a much discussed article, *Down to the Wire*, by Thomas Bleha in Foreign Affairs (May–June 2005), which argued that the USA, to its economic detriment, has fallen far behind Japan and its neighbours in mobile phone technology and broadband deployment.[56]

Funding the programmes

An accurate survey of federal and State monies being put into the broadly defined US adult and informal community sector for ICT projects, computer technology centres and labs is difficult but important if comparisons are to be made. In many cases there was an expectation, as with the Department of Education grants to the CTCs, that there would be a matched funding if federal money was to be provided.

Some cities, as part of the settlement for opening up new cable markets, have obtained concessionary rates for broadband usage, which will benefit not for profit and educational bodies. In other areas like California special foundations have been set up following the restructuring of organisations. Two such examples are the Community Technology

Foundation of California, set up as a condition of the merging of two telecommunications companies, and the California Wellness Foundation which was created following the decision of several non-profit health trusts to go private and as a condition of the move.

Several programmes bear on the provision of training and support for the disadvantaged and include both IT skills training for teachers in low-income areas and the Department of Labor's One Stop Network which received $120 million in 2002. Table 4, however, gives figures for the two main departments involved in the support of CTCs and other computer learning centres.[57]

Table 4.

Government department	Programme	FY 2001	FY 2002	FY 2003	FY 2004
Education	Community Technology Centres	$65m	$32.5m	$32m	$10m
Commerce – NTIA	Technology Opportunities	$45m	$15m	$13.9m	$12.9m
Totals		$110m	$47.5m	$45.9m	$22.9m

NTIA – National Technology and Information Administration

Redirection of federal funding

The overall direction since the election of George Bush as President in 2000 has been a declining contribution from public funds for the CTC centers. Increasingly concerned with 'homeland security' after the events of 9/11, the administration introduced substantial cuts in 2002 to the CTC and NTIA programmes and further reductions for 2004. Additionally CTCs were expected to focus their bids on specific areas – on low achieving adults in 2003 and after school programmes for youngsters in 2004. The former target group was given priority by the Education Department for 2003 awards, in line with the *Blueprint for Preparing America's Future*, its new policy for adult basic and literacy education (June 2003). Overall, however, the Bush Administration has not made adult literacy or basic education a priority for funding.

These shifts in policy raised concerns for those existing technology centers which were seeking sustainability over the long term and have relied on federal funding. This became most apparent in 2004 where the Education Department cut its CTC allocation to $10 million, less than a third of the 2003 figure; and the NTIA Technology Program received almost 500 applications requesting £277 million for its $12.9 million grant fund.

Support from the corporate sector

It is important to recognise, however, that there has been a much stronger tradition in the USA of private and corporate support for community programmes and particularly for the promotion and support of new technology. We have already seen this with the Department of HUD developing learning centres in private housing schemes without any public monies.

Another major initiative was PowerUp – launched in November 1999 at the same time as the Department of Education grants to CTCs. This was the brainchild of AOL's chief executive and former Secretary of State Colin Powell (then an AOL board member) and involved setting up some 250 computer labs with support from the Waitt Family Foundation, run by Gateway Inc.

Role of foundations

The top ten private foundations in the US have assets of $68.4 billion and can make a big impact through their charitable policies. A $227 million support programme for wiring libraries has come, for instance, from the Bill and Melinda Gates Foundation, including a grant for the US Libraries for the Future programme and an $8.4 million grant for Ontario libraries in Canada. The Foundation has also provided substantial grants and satellite technology to connect First Nation reservations in several US states. The Gates Foundation is the largest in the world with an asset base of $32.8 billion and over the period 1994–2003 has donated $1.8 billion to educational projects.[58]

A number of substantial initiatives for computer and information society type projects across North America have come from other wealthy individuals and IT-based foundations including Gordon Moore of Intel, the Verizon Foundation, the Packard Foundation, the Hewlett Foundation, the Lucent Technologies Foundation, and the Salesforce.com Foundation.[59]

While this is only a fleeting survey of corporate sector involvement, there is evidence of wealth giving in the US which now amounts to about 1 per cent of national income. According to figures produced by the Social Welfare Research Institute at Boston College, those with $5–$10 million give away 3.8 per cent and the average in the USA is 2.2 per cent. This compares with between 0.2 per cent and 0.8 per cent in Europe.[60] This tradition of private and corporate giving applies particularly in tertiary education. US spending in this area, representing 7 per cent of its GDP, is higher than anywhere else and has a higher component (over 30 per cent) of private funding.[61]

Experience in Canada

A large country with a much smaller population and IT-producing industrial sector than its neighbour, Canada is dependent on the USA for trading and its economic development generally. The higher wages and greater opportunities offered in the USA attract some of Canada's ablest talent as well as foreign students who have graduated in the country. With its e-commerce policy it has followed a broadly similar road map. It created a Task Force on Electronic Commerce in 1997 and published its strategy in September 1998, aiming to create the best infrastructure, legal and taxation framework for e-commerce.

In other respects however the Canadian Government's approach has differed substantially from the USA. An emphasis on e-government came comparatively late – compared with the Clinton–Gore initiative in 1993 – with the announcement in late 1999 of a new Government Online strategy with a commitment to making the government the most connected to its citizens by 2004.[62] Despite this late entry, Canada has achieved an enviable reputation, ranking first in the last five years, 2001–2005, in the Accenture e-government survey, with the USA in second place in 2005, Singapore in third place and the UK in 10th place. In 2004 Ontario Province won the best public website of the world award for its health portal www.healthyontario.com.

Canada's citizen focused approach has resulted in almost a third of transactions between Government and citizens taking place online, with resulting cost savings. A Government survey has estimated the cost of an online transaction at CAN $1 compared with CAN $44 for an in-person transaction.[63]

Role of Industry Canada and Canarie

The first stages in preparing the country for the Information Society had begun, however, a good deal earlier, with Industry Canada playing a key role. It was formed in 1993 from the merger of departments separately covering industry and technology, communications, and consumer and corporate affairs.

In the same year Canarie, a not for profit body representing the private and public sectors equally, was established to develop advanced high-speed internet facilities and a robust communications infrastructure. Canarie has through a variety of initiatives played an important research and development role operating unusually across government, business, education and more widely and has been involved in moves to expand broadband facilities to remote communities, including a 1997 pilot project for Aboriginal networking.

Industry Canada continues as a dominant player in this field, placing substantial emphasis on collaborative and innovative projects, where government monies are deployed to leverage in municipal and private sector funds. A good example of this has been the Smart Communities Programme in twelve cities, funded with $60 million from Industry Canada. Recently there has been a strong push for developing broadband services to support the development of services such as telemedicine and e-learning.[64]

Connectedness and access

In 1994 the Information Highway Advisory Council (IHAC) was set up to advise on appropriate strategies and published a government-wide action plan *Building a More Innovative Economy*, which focused on the conditions needed for establishing a knowledge-based economy.

The emphasis was on 'connectedness' and Type 1 policy initiatives. From the outset there was recognition of the centrality of the access issue, which would affect the country with its huge rural areas and dispersed populations. 'Connecting Canadians' became the brand name for pulling together a wide range of imaginative federal initiatives.

Figure 2. Population of Canada in British Columbia, Ontario and Quebec.

Source: Statistics Canada's Internet site.

Figure 2 illustrates this, showing that 74 per cent of the entire population live in the three provinces visited for the research – British Columbia, Ontario and Quebec – with the remaining 26 per cent in the eight other provinces. The table is also of interest for another reason. It was generated online from data on the Statistics Canada website which can be manipulated and customised by the user as required. This is a good example of the way that the Government has sought to include information visualisation technology or 'infoviz' into its online services to improve access and usability for the public.[65]

In 1995 IHAC published its influential report *Connection, Community, Content: The Challenge of the Information Highway* with over 300 recommendations; and the Community Access Program (CAP) was launched for rural areas to create initially internet access centres for awareness raising about the information society, training, accessing services and e-learning.

The urban CAP programme for areas with populations over 50,000 followed in 1999 and there are now more than 7000 centres established – many located at local libraries. Details of these can be found on the *Industry Canada* website, which provides another example of imaginative use of technology for facilitating access. Figure 3 shows the ease with which information about any of these CAP sites can be accessed by the public, using data mining software built into the website.

Comparing the CAP and CTC programmes

The Canadian CAP programme for rural areas was initiated in the same year that in the US the report *Falling through the Net* was advocating community access centres to combat the digital divide. In the case of the USA, however, the CTC programme for local IT access did not emerge until four years later.

The CAP programme has been a pioneering and substantial investment for the country and represents approximately one access centre for every 4430 people. An exact figure for US computer access centres is not available, but estimates range from 14,000 to 20,000. At the latter figure this would give for the USA a much higher ratio of one centre for every 14,500 people. This commitment to developing IT centres universally was, however, dropped by the government in 2004 as the costs of maintaining the services were rising. In April 2004 Industry Canada announced that funding for CAP would be reduced to $25 million for each of the years 2004–05 and 2005–06 and the focus would shift from general public access to support for public access sites serving communities of greatest need (digital divide communities) as well as on

Figure 3. Illustration of data visualization technology: Web shots generated in locating the Comox Valley CAP site on Vancouver Island, Canada.

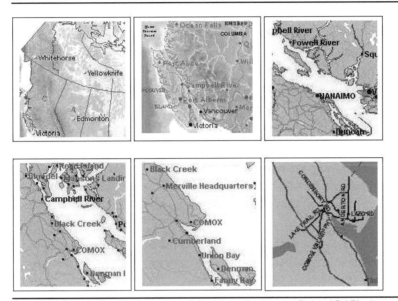

Source: Industry Canada website of Community Access Point (CAP) sites, with built in facility for data mining to locate any of 7000 centres. Clicking on the location on the map brings successively larger scale maps to the viewer's screen. Comox Valley CAP was visited during the research.

supporting access to online government services. A downsizing of the network will be inevitable. The impact of this and the similar actions being taken by the US government in relation to the CTCs is explored further in Chapter 3.

Broadband services

High speed broadband adoption has also been an important government emphasis, which is reflected in the 53.6 per cent penetration rate in Canada noted in the previous chapter. Rural areas have, however, posed continuing and persistent accessibility problems and these were identified as needing special measures in a major consultation exercise carried out with over 10,000 Canadians during 2002.

In September 2002 a $105 million 'Broadband for Rural and Northern Development Pilot' programme in two rounds was announced by the Industry Minister, and by July 2003 some 154 proposals from the two rounds had been supported with up to $30,000 grants for initial business plan development.[66]

The applications covered some 2056 communities, of which 266 were First Nation communities, where compared with the national average there are higher rates of unemployment, higher mortality rates, lower skill levels and a higher incidence of diseases like diabetes.[67] Land rights and problems affecting Aboriginal Canadians have become major political issues in recent years and the potential of broadband to deliver telemedicine, e-learning and business services to counter aspects of the digital divide in these communities is being put to thorough testing through these projects.[68]

Building Partnerships

Linked to the CAP programme was the Voluntary Sector Network Support Program (VolNet), established in 1998 to link voluntary and charitable organisations to the internet. Over 10,000 organisations benefited from this scheme, which offered internet access and support services for one year, 50 per cent of the costs of computer equipment and basic internet skills training.[69]

A further example of the Canadian Government's emphasis on partnership arrangements came in 2000 with the announcement of 12 Smart Communities Demonstration Projects. This was a $60 million programme, which required matching with local monies and was aimed at establishing in each province leading edge models for large-scale integration of new technologies into community life for education, business, health, and so on.

Human Resources Development Canada

The other key Government player has been Human Resources Development Canada (HRDC), which has been responsible for promoting training and skills as workforce development and the use of the CAPs, the fourth policy area. HRDC has now been split into two new departments,

Social Development Canada and **Human Resources and Skills Development Canada**, but in this report the former title has for simplification been retained when referring to past programmes. Following the important IHAC report in 1995, the government established the Office of Learning Technologies (OLT) in 1996 within HRDC to promote 'innovative lifelong learning opportunities.'

This early initiative in the field has led to the OLT playing a significant role in developing strategies for the use of learning technologies, monitoring research and supporting community networks for lifelong learning and capacity building using network technologies. Its Community Learning Networks (CLN) Initiative was set up in 1998 expressly to encourage innovative use of new technologies by community or voluntary organisations. It offers development phase funding of $20,000 and grants of up to $300,000 over three years. In 2003–04 almost half of its total budget of $17 million was committed to CLN projects. Canada has also been innovative in developing the use of mobile learning practice especially in the College sector. A good example of this can be seen in the work of the McGraw-Hill m-Learning consortium of post secondary institutes and educational technology companies.[70]

At a more general level a report of the Expert Panel on Skills was presented in 2000 to the Prime Minister's Advisory Council on Science and Technology. This engendered a wide ranging debate about skills and literacy levels and led to the publication of *Learning Matters: Skills and Learning for Canadians* in 2002 about appropriate skills and training strategies needed to create a knowledge-based economy. In practice these strategies have been implemented through Labour Management Development Agreements (LMDA) negotiated between the Federal Government and individual provinces; and vary widely as to the scope and scale of responsibility taken on locally for the services.

This feature can obviously impact considerably on local communities and on the way that new technologies are being developed and used by community organisations and in the ACL sector.

The UK experience

Although there are clear similarities that can be seen when comparing the development of UK policies with those of Canada and the USA, there is one major difference. In the UK the educational sector has been very much involved from an early point in spreading the use of IT, and the Department for Education was during the 1990s and earlier the most influential arm of government in promoting the use of new technologies. This has much to do with the more centrally controlled educational system in the UK, compared with the greater influence of individual states and provinces in the USA and Canada. In the UK, for instance, 95 per cent of monies spent in school are raised by national government, compared with 5 per cent in the USA.[71]

Early interest in new technologies for education

The National Council for Educational Technologies (NCET), transformed and renamed as Becta in 1998, had been promoting the use of computer-based learning systems since the 1960s,[72] and in the early 1990s there were substantial numbers of reports issued by both NCET, the Department of Education and Science and HMI on issues relating to the use of IT, especially in schools. In 1995 NCET was commissioned by the Further Education Funding Council (FEFC) to produce a report on technology and learning in further education, which found major problems in funding new technology and little evidence of the integration of IT across the curriculum.

UK higher education was more actively engaged than further education (FE) in promoting the use of IT, with the Universities Funding Council agreeing in 1992 to launch the Teaching and Learning Technology Programme (TLTP), which eventually had a total budget of £75 million from the Higher Education Funding Council for England (HEFCE). Its aim was 'to make teaching and learning more productive and efficient by harnessing modern technology'.[73]

Of greater significance for the development of networked learning and research was the support and funding from HEFCE in 1994 for the creation of the Super-JANET broadband high speed network – an example of a Type 1 infrastructure policy, promoted by HE. This was managed through JISC and UKERNA and created a high quality network capable of substantial upgrading, which was to be extended to FE following the 1996 Further Education Funding Council's (FEFC)

Higginson Report. It is now being rolled out to adult education providers through the £33 million ILT for ACL investment programme agreed by the LSC for 2003–2006.[74]

Launch of SuperHighways report

Reflecting this interest in the educational use of new technologies, the Department for Education (renamed later in the year as the Department for Education and Employment), following a consultation exercise, launched its Report *SuperHighways for Education: The Way Forward* in autumn 1995. It was the Conservative Government's first public embrace of the issues thrown up by the internet and the knowledge society.

Its emphasis, however, was on schools education and evaluation, on regulatory structures and competition and not on taking substantial action or committing resources; and unlike the US Commerce Department's NTIA first report of the same year, *Falling through the Net*, it made no mention of the digital divide or the dangers of social exclusion. The statement in the foreword by Gillian Shephard, the Education Minister, summed up the government's cautious view of the way forward: 'Real achievement in this field will not come about as a result of hasty measures designed to provide instant solutions.'

Labour Party and new technologies

The Labour Party in opposition was, by contrast, pursuing a more proactive line of thinking. At the request of the party leader Tony Blair, it had set up a Policy Forum on the Information Highway in late 1994 and sought views from a wide spectrum. In a statement accompanying the launch of the Forum, seven priority areas were stressed: economic growth, access, education and skills, social benefits, cultural life, freedom of information, and public awareness.[75]

This thrust was picked up with enthusiasm by Blair at the Party Conference in autumn 1995, where the tone was set for a much more interventionist role to be played by government in promoting the information society and ensuring that access to the technology was not limited to a privileged few. The resources to power this up were not identified, but for *The Guardian*'s Victor Keegan, who saw the approach as a way of catching up on a revolution the UK should have led, there remained the big question of motivation: 'The problem is finding ways of engaging the attention of the underachievers, those who could do much better but at present fall by the wayside. The digital revolution won't automatically bring electronic salvation to everybody'.[76]

Elected in 1997, the new Labour Government set out on a broad programme to review and reform public services, with some interesting parallels to be drawn with the new Clinton Administration's National Performance Review in the USA in 1993. The FEFC published its influential *Learning Works* report on widening participation in June 1997 and this was quickly followed by the government's Dearing report on higher education, the announcement by the Prime Minister in the autumn of proposals for a National Grid for Learning for Schools,[77] a consultation paper on lifelong learning, *The Learning Age: A Renaissance for a New Britain* and the pathfinder prospectus for the *University for Industry* (Summer 1998). This last proposal was to set up online learning programmes, aimed particularly at the workplace, and to promote ICT and basic skills through Learndirect and UK Online centres.

By 1999 the shape of much wider reform was becoming clearer. In March *A Fresh Start*, the result of the Moser investigation into basic skills was published. The report quoted research as showing that there were 7 million adults, or one in five of the adult population, who lacked the basic literacy skills of an average 11-year-old and gave an even bleaker picture for numeracy skills. It commented, 'We have found that people are staggered when one confronts them with the basic facts about literacy and numeracy, and rightly so... It is a state of affairs that cannot be allowed to continue...'. Britain was second to bottom in the European league tables.

Creating a new framework for the Information Society

Changing this position was to become a key part in the government's developing skills strategy, which was linked integrally to other key policy developments announced during 1999–2000 (see Figure 4). This has led to new curricula and standards for literacy, numeracy and language, national tests and a suite of new specialist teaching qualifications.

Although the national targets have been achieved, a report from the House of Commons Public Accounts Committee in January 2006 argued that there had been a limited impact from the £3.7 billion investment programme in raising adult literacy and numeracy levels.

In June 1999 the *Learning to Succeed* White Paper heralded a new system of planning and funding of post-16 education. In place of the FEFC and the Training and Enterprise Councils, a single new body, the Learning and Skills Council (LSC), was to be established from 2001 with an £8 billion budget, operating through a network of 47 local LSCs, which would plan and coordinate provision.

Figure 4.
The Information Society and you. UK Government policies 1999–2000

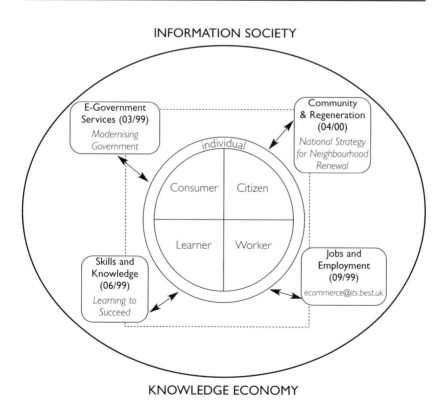

In March the *Modernising Government* White Paper had been published, providing an overview of how government services were to be improved. It gave a strong emphasis to the provision of services online and set the general framework for the delivery of e-government. It was followed up by *e. Gov – Electronic Government Services for the 21st Century* (September 2000). This later report, setting out a comprehensive strategy, was an example of the Type 3 policy initiative and anticipated that all local and central government services would be online for the consumer/citizen.

Implicit in the strategy was the assumption that every individual should be able to access these services. There were therefore important issues about the digital divide raised by the report, paralleling those confronted in the *Falling through the Net* reports of the US Commerce Department from 1995.

These remain of great relevance to the adult and community education sector in the UK. As e-government services have started to proliferate, with spending running at £14 billion in 2005, there has been increasing recognition of the need to link e-learning and e-government strategies if citizens are to have the skills to make use of the available services. This was implicitly acknowledged in the Cabinet Office's report *Transformational Government: Enabled by Technology*, published in October 2005. This set out ambitious and detailed proposals for how Government services would be brought and planned together in a holistic manner to provide personalised services to meet the needs of individual citizens.[78]

Quadrangulation and the Information Society

If skills and knowledge and public services were two nodes in the Information Society quadrangle, the third was jobs and employment, and in September 1999 came *e-Commerce@its.best.uk*, the government's consultation paper launched by the Prime Minister as part of the drive to create jobs and promote competitiveness. Blair's speech to British businesses was blunt, describing the UK as lagging behind the USA, Canada and Scandinavia: 'If you don't see the internet as an opportunity, it will be a threat ... If you are not exploiting the opportunities of e-commerce, you could go bankrupt'.[79]

Linking the UK with the digital economy in the USA

Prepared by the Performance and Innovation Unit, *e-Commerce@its.best.uk* stressed the challenge of providing access to communications and computing technology for safeguarding and creating jobs, referring specifically to the US Commerce Department's *Emerging Digital Economy II* report, published in June. It pointed to the need to fund 'successful local access centres in the long term for those who cannot afford, or choose not to have, access from home' and for subsidies on computers for low income families as part of a computer skills £450 million programme, outlined in the budget.

Neighbourhood renewal and strategic partnerships

It also set the stage for the publication in April 2000 of the Government's *communities* strategy – the *National Strategy for Neighbourhood Renewal*, the fourth node in the Information Society map. This was based on work by the Social Exclusion Unit and its 18 Policy Action Teams, made up of civil servants and outside experts, and reminiscent of the US 1993 National Performance Review. The ten-year plan to support the country's most deprived communities was based on many of the PATs' 569 recommendations. It involved setting up 88 Local Strategic Partnerships (LSPs) to manage the process and an extension of the New Deal for Communities, which would commit £1.9 billion over ten years to schemes in specific areas. The Neighbourhood Renewal Fund was fixed at £900 million over three years.[80]

The urban renewal programme was closely linked to a series of significant 'millennium' initiatives launched in early 2000, which have had an important impact on both the development of locally-based IT facilities and on the management and direction of adult and community education services in several areas.[81] The ICT Learning Centres Programme announced in January 2000 was very specifically aimed at narrowing the digital divide. Grants were to be made available under the Capital Modernisation Fund (CMF) programme for the establishment of centres (subsequently described as UK Online centres) in about 700 of the most deprived wards in the country.

Related to this £252 million, two-year programme was the National Opportunities Fund's (NOF) Community Access to Lifelong Learning (CALL) programme, which added a further £200 million to support the scheme. £100 million of these NOF monies were ring fenced for libraries, with extra funds put aside for setting up Community Grids for Learning. The proposals, taken together, represented the allocation of substantial resources for disadvantaged communities and were a significant commitment by the UK Government.

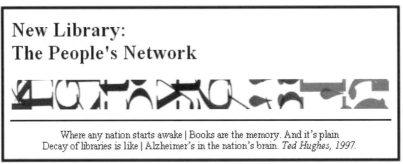

**New Library:
The People's Network**

Where any nation starts awake | Books are the memory. And it's plain
Decay of libraries is like | Alzheimer's in the nation's brain. *Ted Hughes, 1997.*

Heading from DCMS 1997 Report, with extract from Ted Hughes poem, *Hear it again.*

The following month the short-term ICT for Employability Training Programme to provide free training in ICT for 50,000 unemployed people was announced by the Chancellor in his pre-Budget speech, and was linked very clearly with the CMF programme for setting up of local ICT centres and with the Wired up Communities Programme (announced in March 2000). The proposals reflected the views of the Chancellor, Gordon Brown, expressed a year earlier in his Budget speech of 9 March 1999: 'Mastering information technology from the PC to the internet, from email to e-commerce is the newest and most decisive challenge of the 21st century.'

Further initiatives in the Labour Government's second term

With a general election in 2001 and a substantial period of discussions and planning for the local ICT centres, it was not until 2002 that more activity in this area became apparent with the launch of the report of the LSC's Distributed and Electronic Learning Group (September 2002). The DELG report was important in identifying the implications and opportunities which new technologies could bring to all working in the post-16 sector. It was centrally concerned with promoting the expansion of e-learning and made a series of recommendations on how the LSC could provide the strategic framework and funding to support the more active use of ILT. This remains a still under-explored area and as the technology and experience of its use develops, so there will be a need to revisit the issues raised in this report.

The same month as the DELG report another significant initiative, the Wireless Outreach Network (WON) project was announced to support the development of innovative practice in the ACL sector. The background to this scheme is described in the interview overleaf with Barry Phillips of the DfES e-Learning Strategy Unit. It provides a fascinating cameo of the process of governmental policy development in the fast-changing digital world.

Focus on skills, training and e-learning

The most significant report in 2003 was the DfES's *21st Century Skills – Realising our Potential.* The strategy sought to remove barriers preventing providers from delivering the training which employers wanted, set out plans for clearer targeting of funds and had a strong commitment to using ILT to support reforms in the system.[82] This report was accompanied in the same month by *Towards a Unified e-Learning Strategy*, which sought views on proposals for creating a coherent strategy for e-learning.

It had chapters looking at sustainable development, promotion of innovation, workforce development, quality standards and learner support and assessment; and addressed the issue of creating an e-learning market. The final e-strategy report, *Harnessing Technology: Transforming Learning and Children's Services*, was published in March 2005 with ambitious targets and there has been restructuring within the National Learning Network (NLN), the partnership programme which was designed to increase the use of ILT and ensure better coordination of planning and initiatives. There have been welcome moves to incorporate ACL providers within the overall programme, but there are some concerns that the reduction of dedicated e-learning staffing and restrictions in funding affecting ACL from August 2006 will result in the uptake of e-learning being accorded less priority.[83]

Setting up the DfES Wireless Outreach Network scheme

Barry Phillips, e-Learning Strategy Unit, DfES*

When I joined the National Learning Network [NLN] I wanted to drive forward ICT and ILT. I asked several people for advice: "What's the one single thing you would do?" and one or two answered "wireless networks". I thought about this and decided in the summer of 2001 to go and visit Hartpury College – it's an agricultural college which ten years before had less than 100 students.

They'd tested out a network on the campus with students using wireless laptops at a distance of well over 100 metres from the college. They had also hosted the European Young Rider Championships and captured the video footage wirelessly. They had shown this via their college website, getting more than 100,000 hits from all over the world. The whole college had become the classroom. This had confirmed for them its value. I was very impressed.

I knew that we needed to be widening the NLN remit out to adult and community learning [ACL]. But there was no money in the spending review for information and learning technologies for ACL. Then in April 2002 I was party to an email saying that there was possibly about £8 million available, which could be diverted from a scheme which had proved problematic. DfES ICT colleagues were asking for proposals for this money which was originally earmarked for reducing the digital divide.

I was warned not to get involved as there was far too much work to do, given the chances of success, and anyway it was possible to reach people via colleges. But that wouldn't help the ACL sector, I thought, and there was money available – so we decided to explore further. We needed evidence to show the Treasury that a wireless laptop plan would work. Fortunately there was the NIACE 1999 laptop loan scheme and evidence from that that none were stolen. Now we had the motive and the opportunity – a good defence against incremental policy making!

I was given lots of telephone numbers for colleges, universities and others and began ringing up about the details and how wireless works – it was all very new. Everyone was most helpful. I even got on to the University of Tennessee at Knoxville. Then I found the US traffic police had started using wireless and round the corner from our offices doctors were taking laptops onto the wards in Sheffield Children's Hospital.

By now I had enough of the facts. There were other ideas being considered in the Department but these were dropped and I had to put the bid together. It had to go through all the stages. The scheme originally was going to be for the most deprived wards only, but people were saying there was already so much kit in some places, you were falling over it when you got off the train.

So we extended it to all the local authority areas where there was a most deprived ward. Then Defra [Department for Environment, Food and Rural Affairs] came up with a report on the 'problems affecting rural areas' and suddenly we were able to incorporate this in the criteria where a particular disadvantage was identified. The 330,000 beneficiary figure we came up with was a bit tenuous but you have to give the best guess you can. Colleagues in Adult Learning and Statistics had pulled out the stops at short notice to source and analyse what little hard evidence was available at the time.

The bid had to go to all the levels as well. We had to persuade the minister that you have to get out to people where they are; and that this was not just another initiative. That would have been the last thing a minister wanted to hear. We needed to show that existing providers would be able to extend their reach. This was a way of getting deep in to communities and then drawing the learners back into colleges and centres. The minister [John Healey, appointed as Parliamentary Under Secretary of State for Adult Skills in June 2001] was just about to approve the bid when we learnt that there was to be a change of minister. Everything came to a halt and time was slipping away.

Eventually the Divisional Manager [DM] with responsibility for this policy area and I were summoned to a teleconference with the senior civil servant in Whitehall with ultimate responsibility for this work. The DM was a very important supporter of the scheme and to simplify what happened somewhat, basicaly told him: "you have to ring the new minister today or we will lose the money". And that's what he did – rang him I believe on the beach in Florida while he was on holiday. Ivan Lewis [the new Minister] agreed to approve the bid. We were able to make the announcement inviting applications in September. It was a great statement of support and show of confidence in ACL.

For me it had been a fascinating education – and perhaps if both the DM and I hadn't been relatively new to the civil service, we wouldn't have attempted to get the project started at all! It wasn't easy but now people are coming up with great ideas of what they can do with the equipment. That's the key point. The technology is there, but people are creative and we are starting to get really imaginative uses coming out of the projects.

* From an interview with the author, August 2003.

A further strand in policy development over the period 2003–04 came with the launching of four reports concerned with outreach and growing capacity in local communities, as part of the wider Neighbourhood Renewal programme. These covered widening adult participation, active citizenship, promotion of collaboration between the LSC and the VCS; and building infrastructure in the VCS via the *Futurebuilders* Programme.[84] The last one was linked in 2005 to the regionally managed *ChangeUp* programme for VCS support.

Launch of the ILT programme for ACL

However, from the ACL perspective the most pertinent event of 2003 was the launch of the ILT programme for the ACL sector. Coordinated by NIACE with the close involvement of the LSC, Becta, JISC and UKERNA, this ambitious scheme over three years has a range of component parts. It will have provided a minimum 2Mb broadband link to LA and external institution ACL services, which are funded by the LSC; and has established under the auspices of Becta a web-based Community Learning Resource (CLR), www.aclearn.net, to provide support and information for practitioners wishing to develop ILT-based resources. It has a linked APOLLO mailing list, which by January 2006 had almost 900 ACL practitioner subscribers. The CLR service has similarities with the America Connects website launched in 2001 in the USA with a $2 million Education Department grant. (Page 79)

In 2004 after an initial pilot, an e-Guides training programme was started to equip 3000 ACL staff and tutors with the skills to cascade knowledge and enthusiasm about the uses and potential of ILT to their colleagues. This has built upon the TrEACL (Technology to Enhance Adult and Community Learning) programme, which has been designed to encourage ACL providers and their staff to create and deploy innovative ILT materials for learners by offering grants of between £2,000 and £50,000.[85] There were also five pilot projects supported to explore the appropriateness for the ACL sector of different learning platforms (LP) or VLEs with the aim of providing advice for ACL services about whether, when and what kind of LP is suitable for a given set of factors. In 2006 to follow this up a further 35 ACL providers are being funded via NIACE to explore how an LP is best deployed with their staff and students.[86] From 2005 an open source application, Learning Activities Management System (LAMS), has been available for wider use and currently this is being integrated into several existing LPs.[87]

Additionally plans were put in place to commission interactive multi-media content for ACL under a new Round 4 of NLN materials creation, to be available from 2005. This has been the result of recognising the need to create appropriate educational material for the ACL sector – where the earlier Rounds 1–3 of NLN-sponsored materials had all focused on FE.[88]

Building Schools for the Future (BSF)

A further initiative of significance is the BSF programme which will involve £30 billion being spent up to 2020 on rebuilding every State secondary school in the country. This is the biggest capital programme in UK education for at least 60 years and all LAs and schools are being encouraged strongly – via a £680 million programme up to 2008 – to make their buildings and resources available to the community and in support of school-based intergenerational learning.[89]

The experience from the UK shows a proactive line being taken by educational institutions and by successive government education departments to the use of new technology, and this is in the early stages of being cascaded down to the ACL sector. The UK Government generally was initially slower than the US and Canadian Governments to take up the issues raised by the internet and the world wide web, but since Labour came into office a more interventionist approach has been taken to the issues raised by the Information Society. This is reflected in the report *Connecting the UK*, launched in April 2005,[90] although it should be noted that financial constraints led in June 2005 to the LSC reducing funding by 27 per cent to JISC for its support of ILT for FE colleges and the adult and community learning sector.[91]

III

Responding to the Information Society

We are fortunate to be living through the internet revolution . . . History will record 1999–2000 as the turning point. (Erkki Liikanen, EU Commissioner for enterprise and the IS, 6 May 2000.)

The previous chapters have given a general overview of ACL and voluntary and community organisations working in this area. They have considered how new technologies have brought the threat of a widening knowledge and skills divide and the role being played in all three countries by governments to promote the use of ICT in support of competitiveness, skills acquisition and an inclusive society. This longer chapter, drawing upon interviews from North America and discussions in the UK, provides for these broadly defined sectors:

- details of the activities of each of the organisations;
- five implementation case studies or vignettes;
- insights into how these ACL and VCS organisations are responding to the challenges and opportunities thrown up by new technologies;
- possible models for the stages involved in this process of change;
- indications of new directions arising from technological advances.

Rapid pace of change

The technologies now affecting adult and community-based learning have been introduced over a very short time scale. This is different from the past. Computers and the internet have been compared with other transforming technologies like printing and the steam engine. Both these inventions were critical turning points leading to the widespread dissemination of knowledge on the one hand, and of mechanised forms of production on the other. Neither example, however, was met with immediate and common adoption.

Watts' steam engine, for instance, was first successfully patented in 1769. By the 1870s it had transformed west Newcastle upon Tyne into the epicentre of a new phase of the Industrial Revolution, based upon coal and heavy engineering. It was teeming with factories, armaments and housing but as late as 1840 the view of the area across the River Tyne showed little impact upon the rural scene other than a few boats moving coal downstream and the occasional line of smoke from a passing locomotive.[92]

In the twenty-first century as global communication systems – integral to the computer-based revolution – inundate us with reports and images about the internet and new technologies, we need to recall just how rapid has been the speed of this change. JANET, initiated in 1983 as a UK HE networking infrastructure, only became converted to its high-speed current form of Super JANET with speeds of 10Mbs to 155Mbs per second in 1994. It was another three years before the recommendations of the Higginson Report led to the process of connecting up FE colleges to a high-speed network.

In the world outside HE and FE, when Freeserve introduced a new internet service provider (ISP) model in 1998 offering a free connection service to the internet for users in the UK, most workers in government departments and local authorities, let alone in voluntary organisations, did not have their own email address.

Early North American experience

In North America voluntary and locally based organisations were establishing an incipient community technology movement from the late 1980s, with the first freenet offering simple email facilities and bulletin boards set up in 1986 in Cleveland, USA. Users of these electronic systems tended to be 'white middle class males between the ages of 20 and 50 … employed, [with] greater than average incomes … and [with] few disabilities'.[93] Other early examples in the US include Blacksburg Electronic Village (www.bev.net), and Compumentor (1987). It was not until the mid-1990s that community-based computer labs were first set up to offer IT awareness and training and internet access to a much wider audience.

Importance of funding

Funding was the principal problem facing ACL and VCS organisations wishing to extend their work with socially excluded groups.[94] In North America the first government-financed experiments were started in 1995 through the US Commerce Department and the Canadian CAP for rural areas (See Chapter 2). In the UK the WEA was only able to establish in 1996 in Manchester the first broadband multimedia centre in the ACL and FE sectors by obtaining a European Regional Development Fund (ERDF) grant.

The European Union, through its Directorate XIII, had indeed been proactive, from 1992 at least, in promoting the development and application of telematics for education and training in member states, and funded a series of innovative programmes in which the WEA and other VCS bodies were able to participate, often with HE partners.[95]

Recent government funding programmes

Funding on a substantial scale for community-based technology centres – often involving voluntary and statutory partnerships – did not, however, receive approval until 1999 in the USA and Canada and until 2000 in the UK with the launch of the £600 million Libraries Network and Capital Modernisation Fund Programmes. This was followed up in 2003 by the LSC's £33 million programme for ILT targeted at ACL.

This latter LSC programme has recognised the complexity of issues to be addressed, but the earlier initiatives in all three countries had an implicit assumption that the key requirement is the provision of capital equipment – computers and networking infrastructure – and that effective use of this would naturally follow. This is a dubious assumption, since the infrastructure normally represents less than 20 per cent of the total costs of ownership.

Undoubtedly ownership or access to technology resources is a critical precondition and can allow ACL and VCS organisations to offer training in its use and raise awareness, but there are four other dimensions that need to be considered as the experience of the different bodies in integrating ILT across the curriculum is examined:

• Organisation and planning
• Pedagogy and staff development
• Appropriate content
• Sustainability

Embedding the technology, exploring new ways

There has been little systematic research about these issues as they affect ACL and the VCS bodies, although there is a widespread view that new technologies will lead to a restructuring of all aspects of the economy including the 'learning industry'.[96] The boxed article on page 59 (from a WEA website) shows by way of illustration some typical examples of how new technology has been practically applied in recent years by WEA tutors and groups across the UK to enhance and extend the experience of learning. There are plenty of other imaginative examples to be found in all three countries and in many different organisations, and some of these were cited in interviews in North America.

All of these are valuable and essential developments. They encourage both tutors and learners to experiment with the technology and start to understand how it can be used to do things differently and to do different things. They represent an evolutionary and appropriate model in which people start to gain a sense of ownership of the technology, rather than see it as a threat or challenge. They help to reinforce the notion of the student as the focus and controller of the learning process.

Using IT with WEA learners

The national WEA is supporting the more active use of information and learning technologies in our courses as a contribution to stimulating learners and improving quality. Listed below are some examples from different localities across the regions.

- A family history group searching the Ellis Island database on the web for details of relatives who were immigrants to the USA.
- A course for school teachers where an email and video-conferencing link was set up with a WEA group in Sweden.
- A creative writing tutor emailing another tutor to establish arrangements for students swapping examples of their work.
- Downloading of pictures from an art website to show a class.
- A class on 18th century wills transcribing details into a database.
- Creation of a list of URLs for the class to investigate at home or in a library as part of a course on Asian arts and crafts.
- Using a digital camera to email images to friends and relatives.
- An environmental tutor using a search engine in the local library for some initial research for a course.
- A local WEA branch collaborating with the local library to run a course on Egyptology using ICT facilities.
- Work with a local school to develop a family learning course to use their IT facilities with parents.
- Students on a return to learn course working with the tutor to create a website and chat forum.

IH July 2003
Source: WEA North Western website

Models for restructuring

However, these examples do not amount to a transformation or to the creation of substantially new ways of planning and organising learning, which the technology has the potential to offer. People's lives now are busier and more pressurised and learning has to be fitted in with other work, family and leisure commitments. Computer-based and online learning can here be a positive advantage.[97] To be successful ACL and VCS providers above all have to respond imaginatively to this situation because they do not have the 'captive' audience of the school, college or university. They have to entice and motivate.

For the UK FE sector, a model for the adoption of ILT by colleges has been evolved which was first developed by the Massachusetts Institute of Technology (MIT). In this model a first *evolutionary* stage (involving localised leading to coordinated action) is followed by a *transitional* stage (with transformative action) and a third *revolutionary* stage (with embedded and innovative actions). For implementing ILT at a college level Becta, with its national remit, established the Ferl Practitioners' Programme (FPP) with 26 different modules. This was piloted in 116 colleges in 2003 and was subsequently modified with a sixth strand, *Demonstrating Transformation*, added.[98] Designed specifically for senior managers, this was used in 2004 in a series of regional workshops.

Experience from this programme provided valuable insights into how a range of FE staff – teaching practitioners, coordinators, learning support staff, ILT champions and ILT developers – responded with help from a support team to the challenges posed by new technologies.[99] In the view of the FPP manager it was 'the single biggest weapon in Becta's arsenal at institutional level. It can effect organisational change, win over the hearts and minds of managers and practitioners and demonstrate significant changes in practice.'[100]

Not all of the FPP will relate directly to the ACL sector, where episodes of learning are likely to be much shorter and experienced in a more informal environment without the structures associated with institutions. Adults want 'bite-sized' learning opportunities to be accessed in different ways, at different times and in different places. It is exactly this flexibility of delivery, user control and customisation that new technologies can provide, whether it is in accessing your bank account, paying the rates, booking a holiday, buying a book or learning a new skill. How relevant is this to the ACL sector?

Experience from the non-educational sector

Some insights about this whole process can indeed be gained by looking at initial experience in non-educational sectors. In the private sector and in the area of e-government several models have been proposed to cover the stages of evolution or maturity that organisations need to go through in order to embrace the changes required by new technology and in particular the web. Typically these stages include awareness raising, obtaining internet access, strategy planning, ensuring appropriate skill levels, systems development and implementation.[101] Usually companies which have introduced e-commerce combine this with continuing existing traditional methods.

The e-commerce model has also sought to capture the relationships and underlying infrastructures that are involved in using the technology and with the advent of the internet are needed by companies to achieve the online sale to customers of a product or service. Well-known examples of large internet-based companies are Amazon (books), Dell (computers), Cisco (internet routers and switches)[102] and Expedia (air flights and hotels).

In this e-commerce model Business to Business (B2B) relationships are concerned with supply chains to ensure a predictable flow of items and services from sub-contractors to the vendor business, which need support by Business to Administration (B2A) relationships to document the transaction and allocate and meet the costs. Business to Customer (B2C) relationships cover the range of tasks involving the vendor and purchaser which are associated with the marketing, ordering, distribution and payment for the goods or services.

Relevance of e-commerce and e-business models

While some of the organisations interviewed for the research were too small or limited in their role to relate directly to this, it is possible to see the parallels with this model that could apply more generally to at least larger VCS bodies. Locality-based providers of services work with large numbers of groups and people and by combining together – and where appropriate with statutory services – could develop a sustainable e-community or e-voluntary business model to meet a wide range of individual and specific support needs at low or minimal cost to the user.

Responsive and customised services from volunteers and others could be supplied in this way, using web-based and mobile phone technology like email, mailgroups, and SMS texting[103] to senior citizens, working mothers, disabled people, tenants, families at risk, carers and so on. These services could include shopping, temporary childcare assistance, transport, housing advice, 'just in time' family support and respite breaks.

Similarly, ACL educational providers (P), employing mostly part time 'subcontractor' tutors (T), require P2T relationships to create or modify course offerings with related documentation for learners (L), supported by P2L relationships to supply these e-learning opportunities and courses to the learners. A practical example of this (see Figure 5) is the use made by the WEA Yorkshire and Humberside Region of data about venues for marketing its classes to prospective learners. The particulars, supplied by partner bodies and tutors, are inputted to a courses database – which can be regularly updated – and rendered from there to the WEA website www.wea-yn.org.uk. This provides details of the course, a map and accessibility information. This theme has now been picked up by the WEA NW Region, which has on its website, www.nw.wea.org.uk, a wide range of resources to support P2T and P2L links for both administrative and curriculum purposes.

The major departure from the e-commerce model for the educational body in MIT's transitional stage which is providing online learning (defined here as an internet-linked computer-based course, with a tutor interacting remotely for at least some of the time or simply between meetings) is that the P2L relationship is more complex. It requires in terms of process the creation of content or 'structured learning pathways', with a degree of non-

Figure 5.

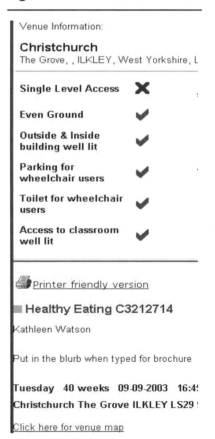

standardisation and the encouragement of a richer series of constructive interactions including tutor to learner (T2L), and ideally L2L and T2T relationships.

A provider could, for instance, allocate separate chat rooms and discussion forums on a managed learning platform to IT tutors and to arts and crafts tutors who were operating over a wide region, where they could swap materials and experience via their home PCs. The mechanism for this would be through the allocation of appropriate permissions and would allow the curriculum manager to provide focused 'telechiric'[104] support and advice to improve quality and consistency of the teaching across the curriculum. This telechiric or *handshake* (literally 'hands at a distance') feature of the technology, with potentially many components, adds a third dimension to the telephonic (speech) and televisual (eyes) elements of communication we are now used to. Its significance for learning developments is little recognised but will be substantial in the future. An illustration of this can be seen in the adoption of the *LongPen* by the novelist Margaret Atwood, which allows an author to see and **sign** a book elsewhere using a touchpad and remote robot arm.[105]

Developing an approach along these lines involves the use of the technology at different levels – at the enterprise level (for marketing, training, tutor monitoring), at the course level (for tracking, registration) and at the level of the learner (for feedback, communication). In the real world of ACL, as with businesses, a bi-modal or blended approach is likely to be dominant with learners combining elements of online and 'bundled'[106] e-learning with traditional forms of delivery. Yet increasingly tutors and learners are acquiring email addresses and mobile phones and the skills to use them; and public and private broadband take up has accelerated. The gains potentially to be made from exploiting these to deliver more cost effective provision with richer interactive content to larger numbers and with greater control for the learner – through P2L, T2L and L2L relationships – are waiting for those organisations able to adapt and change their working methods.

e-Government model

Paralleling e-business developments has been the push from the mid-1990s to develop e-government services, which again is premised upon a substantial take up of and access to the technology by individuals. The Gartner Group has proposed a four-stage model for evaluating progress from traditional legacy systems to a web-enabled e-government system – presence, interaction, transaction, transformation.[107]

The emphasis in this model is on the movement from the one-way posting of information on the web (presence) to a system enabling successively two-way communication (interaction), online procurement and payment (transaction) and, finally, seamlessly integrated government services (transformation). While this draws attention to important components such as interactivity and back office systems, it suggests a uni-linear approach, with less potency when considering the issues for e-learning facing ACL and VCS organisations, as they develop widening participation and community development strategies. However, it is interesting that the Gartner Group noted the need to drive take up of e-services through intermediation, suggesting a potential role for ACL and the VCS sectors in supporting these services as well.[108]

Towards a model for ACL

The experience of the FE, e-commerce and e-government sectors, appropriately contextualised, has therefore substantial relevance to ACL, suggesting a revised model with ten possible components:

- awareness raising;
- staff training and development;
- identification of ways of incorporating ILT into the curriculum;
- identification of partners;
- development (including re-usage) of content and structured learning pathways;
- creation of delivery models for community capacity building through ILT;
- systems development for data capture and deployment (for marketing, registration, fee payment, tracking, assessment, monitoring and funding);
- formulation of the learning blend (of online and traditional delivery);
- ensuring access and technical support;
- implementation of a sustainable plan.

Beyond this, however, there are three essential preconditions for organisations to start the process of harnessing the potential that technology and the internet offer. There must be a *clear vision and objectives* backed by the leadership of the organisation; a *change culture* that welcomes innovation and risk taking and accepts failures; and finally a *willingness to build broad partnerships and alliances* to achieve goals. Indications of how these qualities manifest are explored in the examples and case studies which follow.

Typology of organisations surveyed and evidence

The full list of 29 organisations interviewed is contained in Annexe 2. These included three government or local authority departments and two foundations active in supporting ICT in the community work, whose views are of importance for how they fund and perceive the ACL sector and VCS organisations. The remaining 24 organisations are divided into five categories as set out below and the activities and experience of each of these is initially described separately before some general conclusions are drawn in Chapter 4 in relation to the original research objectives. The fifth group of two companies provides some insights into how the private sector has been using technology in unusual and innovative ways, which are of wider relevance.

1 Local community technology centres (Total: 3)
2 Voluntary community network bodies and related organisations (Total: 7)
3 Other community and family service centres (Total: 4)
4 Public educational bodies – libraries, universities and colleges (Total: 8)
5 Private sector bodies using IT as part of core business (Total: 2)

The investigation reveals a complex picture in North America – both of *new* kinds of organisation emerging, which are effectively harnessing the potential of web-based technologies in pursuit of their objectives, and of *existing* organisations assimilating the technology within legacy systems to transform aspects of their work – described elsewhere as the 'clicks and mortar' model. Generally there was significant evidence of alliances and partnership working, while networking was recognised as essential for survival.

1. Local community technology centres

The three local CTCs were in Seattle and reflected a wide variety of management arrangements. All of them, the Yesler Learning Center (YLC), the Chinese Information and Service Center (CISC) and the New Holly Neighborhood Center (NHNC) had been set up as a result of an initiative in 2000 by the City Council's Department of Information Technology (DIT) to promote community-based computer labs in local disadvantaged neighbourhoods, which were accessible and functioned effectively with trained staff, consistent systems and internet connectivity.[109]

The project had brought together as part of the Seattle Community Technology Alliance (SCTA) nine separate centres including non-profit organisations like CISC, the YCC which had its base in a public housing development, and NHNC run by the South Seattle Community College in a neighbourhood campus. Supported by a two-year $600,000 grant to the Education Department, which paid the salaries of the coordinators and a technical assistant, SCTA held monthly planning and information sharing meetings, had accessed training provided by Seattle Libraries and used induction materials like the *CTC Instructors' Guide*. The Alliance had also been able to secure donations of software and equipment from Microsoft, Cisco and Gateway and free broadband connectivity.[110]

There were 170 IT centres in the Seattle/King County area listed by the City's DIT in 2004, for which DIT gave the following breakdown on its website:

• Schools: 20
• Libraries: 69
• Government, including community centers: 10
• Housing complexes: 22
• Other human service organizations: 49

The SCTA ones, however, were specifically aimed at low-income groups and ethnically diverse populations, including Latino, Chinese, Asian and East African and were attracting a range of users. All put on standard computer- and internet-linked courses for various ability levels, providing other facilities such as drop-in sessions and support for web authoring, and in some cases running courses on literacy and English for speakers of other languages (ESOL).

There were a number of difficult issues, which reflected the way that the initiative had been set up and the separate management arrangements for each centre. The YLC was based in a public housing estate with the coordinator responsible to the Parks and Recreation (P&R) Manager. The P&R Department did not have a clear strategy for the centre, and neither policies nor experience in providing learning opportunities. The result was that the coordinator had to take personal responsibility for developing a business plan for the centre with the help of an external non-profit specialist organisation.

In 2004 the YLC remained actively engaged in supporting classes and other activities in this downtown area of the city and received a City of Seattle Neighborhood Matching Fund grant of $8580 to develop a Virtual 3D Project. The goal of this project was for local youth and technically skilled adults to work together to create a presentation of information about Yesler Terrace using 3D modelling, audio design, and the University of Washington's cutting edge Augmented Reality technology. Through this university–community link up participants could be helped to develop an understanding of the potential of the technology for the area and in their own lives.

Sustainability was a key issue for the CISC, which was a long established multi-service agency with a prime focus on providing access to social services for non-English speaking Asian newcomers. Neither YLC nor CISC had any budgets for tutoring staff. The possibility of collaboration with local community colleges was being explored but the likelihood of low numbers was a deterrent to a long-term partnership.

Generally the centres had to rely upon volunteers to run courses and support users. This made it hard to plan programmes and determine priorities and the position was not helped by there being no outputs or targets set in advance by SCTA for each centre. In the case of YLC the coordinator had to recruit volunteers every year by going round classes at the university, while at CISC there was a lack of volunteers with bilingual skills. The city's DIT has subsequently provided a partial solution to this problem by setting up an imaginative *UWired* community technology partnership with the University of Washington's Office of Educational Partnerships and Learning Technologies to place work-study students in local CTCs.

Under the scheme the students spend 10–20 hours at the centre and receive a salary of $12.50 per hour, of which the CTC contributes 20 per cent. Continued support for them is provided by a listserv or email discussion group of peers who together have a good knowledge of problems and possible solutions. To date ten CTCs have participated in this locally developed scheme.[111]

The third Seattle centre, in the New Holly neighbourhood, was well used by local residents and a part of the Seattle Housing Authority Campus of Learners. This included also a library, small business centre, a career development centre, a Catholic Community Services youth programme and a local campus branch of the South Seattle Community College, which was able to meet from existing funding part of the coordination and tutoring costs for the activities at the computer lab. The model developed here was a more sophisticated and collaborative version of the one that has been developed in many of the Learn Direct and UK Online centres, and offers a sustainable future provided funders' criteria are met and numbers are maintained at a viable level.

Seattle City Council's role

Seattle City Council's DIT has played a very significant role in co-ordinating and finding funding for the CTC network in the city and generally in promoting community-based new technologies.[112] DIT liaised with other council departments like Housing and Libraries and with local colleges, and worked with the Seattle Community Network and the Citizens Telecommunications and Technology Advisory Board to develop the Information Technology Indicators for a Healthy Community Project (2000), which included a large survey of some 700 non-profit organisations, carried out with King County and Npower, using the email survey tool zoomerang.com.

It also conducted a survey on IT usage in Seattle itself of 316 non-profit neighbourhood bodies and reported in March 2001 that of the 30 per cent responding, 85 per cent were communicating with their members by email (a high figure for the time), that there was high interest in a council-run listserv service, and that there was substantial interest in training in how to use technology more effectively for community development activities.[113] It has been instrumental in creating links with bodies like the Gates Foundation and in bringing CTCs together across a wider metropolitan area; and since 2002 has run an online magazine *Brainstorm*[114] on CTC-related issues.

Comparable experience of centres elsewhere

In addition to the Seattle interviews, visits were made to other IT centres in North America, which were parts only of more extended activities of the organisation. These included on the West Coast computer labs run on Vancouver Island by the Comox Valley project and on the mainland by the Vancouver Community Network and the Seattle Library Service; and on the East Coast centres run by the well-funded Cambridge Community Television in Boston and by the Oxford County Library Service in Ontario province. In all these cases the work of the centres was integrated into a wider programme for which funding was being received from a variety of federal and local workplace development, unemployment and community learning programmes.

The pattern of activity found in the CTCs visited was generally similar to that described in a 1999 mail survey of 328 CTCs in the US conducted by Servon and Nelson. Of the 122 responding over 80 per cent had offered general PC access and word processing and over 70 per cent job search and email. Fifty-seven per cent of use was recreational, 47 per cent was homework help (reflecting the active use made by young people of the centres), 29 per cent involved video projects and 24 per cent was for business development. Fifty-six per cent provided adult education and literacy support.[115]

For the many smaller stand-alone CTCs or PACs in North America like the YCC and CISC the securing of effective coordination, technical support and financial stability to maintain these services is the critical question, just as it has become in the UK since the grants from the New Opportunities Fund came to an end. In Seattle the issue was already critical in 2002 and was partly dealt with through the setting up of a wider-based association, the Puget Sound Alliance for Community Technology (PSACT), in place of SCTA.

2. Community network organisations and related bodies

The Free-Nets and community networks (CN), which have deployed ICTs for community development and informal learning have a history in North America dating back to the late 1980s,[116] attracting in the early stages for the most part technologically sophisticated young white males who helped to create and use their services. There is no close equivalent to the North American CN movement in the UK. A decade or so after most of them were set up, they have needed to reassess and adapt to a different environment.

The provision of email services, web access and discussion groups as a local ISP, once innovative, is now a fairly thin offering when so many commercially-based operators act as free ISPs or offer free web-based email (Hotmail, Yahoo, Gmail, and so on).

Many of the arguments put forward by the CNs for tackling the digital divide and opening up access to low-income individuals have been met since the late 1990s by government and city council access and ICT programmes. How have the CNs responded to these changes? Have they still been able to attract the volunteers and technical and networking specialists who originally saw the Free-Nets as a way of creating new kinds of society and new ways for communicating? Where are the niches where the CNs have been able to innovate and add value for local communities?

The study has considered the experience of five CNs, all on the West Coast, ranging from Compumentor established in 1987, to Comox Valley on Vancouver Island (1996). The three others in Victoria, Vancouver and Seattle were set up respectively in 1992, 1993 and 1994. Together they provide a framework for examining the different responses of the CNs to a changing Information Society and to the need for brokering of collaborative partnerships involving government, municipal authorities, educational institutions, the private sector and non-profits.

The interviews were carried out with either the director or coordinator of the CN or in one case with a senior programme manager. Resource issues about funding and use of volunteers have been central concerns and the choices made have determined much of the direction taken. To some extent of course there have been inherent constraints based upon geography, demographic and income profiles of the areas served and government policies. The last factor was highlighted in 2004 with significant changes being introduced in priorities and funding of community-based ICT programmes and infrastructure in both the USA and Canada (see pages 34 and 38).

As Table 5 shows, the rural Comox Valley is the only Community Network which stands out quite separately from the others in total population terms, although the Victoria Telecommunity Network, also on Vancouver Island, covers a smaller and more homogeneous population than the ethnically mixed and income stratified metropolitan areas of Vancouver, Seattle and San Francisco.

Table 5. Characteristics of five community networks

	Seattle	Victoria	Vancouver	Comox Valley	Compumentor
Year founded	1994	1992	1993	1996	1987
Population (000s)	572	300	546	60	729
Use of volunteers*	5	4	4	2	1
Turnover, 2002–03	$25k	<Cn$50k	Cn$500k	Cn$150k	$6m
CTC/CAP involvement	✓	✓	✓	✓	✓
Founders still involved	✗	✓	✓	✓	✓
Training for CTCs and PACs	✗	✗	✓	✓	✓

* Assessment by author based upon interviews, data from Website and reports.

Seattle Community Network
Originally a project established by the local chapter of Computer Professionals for Social Responsibility, the Seattle CN (www.scn.org) is the only all-volunteer organisation of the five and the only one where none of the initial founder members are now active.

It celebrated its first decade in 2004 but the small operating budget of $25,000 limits the scale of its operations to community message boards, running some free computer programmes for local CTCs and carrying out PC recycling through the council's Computer Giveaway programme. The difficulties it faces in attracting new volunteers – most of whom are technical/networking professionals recruited by existing Board members – combined with its small size suggests that SCN will struggle to survive in its existing form.

Victoria Telecommunity Network (VTN)

By contrast the other four organisations have to date engaged far more actively, though in different ways, with government and State funding programmes to promote collaboration, networking and innovation for the benefit of technologically disadvantaged communities and groups. VTN on Vancouver Island continues to play a role as a low-cost traditional ISP offering internet access via a 56k dial-up modem.

This is sustained by substantial technical and management input, all provided on a voluntary basis. Value added is provided by the supply of information and a range of discussion groups. VTN also has close links with the South Island Community Access Network, supplying local information content to public access centres and libraries across the south of the island and saw this as an important area of concentration for the future.[117] VCN works closely with the British Columbia Networks Association of over 130 CNs and is a contributor to the work of the CN umbrella group, Telecommunities Canada.

Comox Valley Information Systems (CVIS)

Further north on the east coast of Vancouver Island, CVIS[118] covers a scattering of rural townships and some islands and has taken a far more interventionist developmental role. With only 25 paid-up members, the project has relied primarily on government and federal funding, especially from Industry Canada – for its five public access centres (PACs) – and from the Job Creation Program run by Human Resources Development Canada (HRDC).

This latter scheme has enabled CVIS to have 'interns' on 14-week training courses developing websites and databases, training volunteers and tutoring in the PACs. Despite the technical and other difficulties operating in a remote rural area, CVIS has with good leadership from the local director been innovative and imaginative in its programme.

It has supported projects such as a Linux Users Group, a water quality monitoring and stewardship group using GIS data (Project Watershed), a North Island Distance Education School (www.nides.bc.ca) and an open source online tutorial system facilitating learner–tutor interactions (http://tutor.valleylinks.net).

Vancouver Community Network (VCN)
Like the two CNs on Vancouver Island, VCN, the oldest ISP in the city, has benefited from the pro-active Canadian Government policies supporting the use of ICT and internet facilities. With over 6000 users, 1450 individual members and 249 affiliated bodies, its core business is:

• owning and operating a free, publicly accessible computer facility;
• creating a framework for developing VCS infrastructure through training and technical support.

By 2002 VCN's annual income had risen to about CN$500,000, of which just under 60 per cent was from the government, mostly for specialist projects. Described as the 'best example of information highway Robin Hoods', VCN has a significant number of users who are on low incomes or unemployed, speak English as a second language, or gain email access only through public access centres.

Technical capacity and use of web-based tools
With a strong in-house technical skills base, VCN has been involved in a Technical Volunteer Web (TVW) project across the city, has substantial server capacity for community usage and mail list services and was already in 2002 using an industrial grade ticketing system, Request Tracker, to monitor and manage requests from community users.[119]

It has exploited this technical capacity to play a significant part in Industry Canada's Voluntary Sector Network (VolNet) scheme by connecting 460 local voluntary organisations to the internet and by providing free training and support for over 800 individuals and 539 agencies.[120] This VolNet work has linked to VCN's support for the Lower

Midland Community Access Network of 32 non-profit bodies running internet access centres in partnership with Industry Canada.

VCN has also been involved in setting up a training and support network (http://imit.vcn.bc.ca) across British Columbia and Yukon on IM/IT (information management and IT), which has been funded under the government's Voluntary Sector Initiative.[121] The IM/IT is a good example of how aggregation of web-based services can bring wider synergies, as the project is able to offer across a broad region a call centre, online IM/IT registries and same-time meeting spaces, use of VOIP (voice over IP) technology, workshops and a range of other interactive features to support VCS bodies, based upon a content management system. The project got under way in 2004 with workshops for training providers to be followed by training events for VCS bodies later in the year.

Of all the CNs visited, VCN was the most successful in engaging volunteers. This was the result of clear strategies being agreed by the Board, an identification of different roles to be played and good levels of induction, initial pairing and ongoing support.[122] Of over 70 active volunteers, 27 were providing regular help desk support to staff ten three-hour shifts per week. Other roles included committee membership, administrative work, technical work on server development and hacker monitoring, championing public access and supporting community content development through a Community Learning Networks Project.[123]

Established with support from HRDC's Office of Learning Technologies, this innovative scheme was based upon an underlying "Asset based Community Development" model and sought to explore the effectiveness of using interactive tools – like *Sympa*, email listserv software and *WebGUI* a web development tool – to encourage local residents to become more active technology users and content developers. Despite its considerable project management skills, use of volunteers and technical experience, VCN was aware like many other CNs and CTCs of its heavy reliance on state funding and the need to build long term sustainability.

Compumentor

The fifth CN organisation was Compumentor in San Francisco and one of the earliest established in the USA. Closely involved in the networking and non-profit structures of the Bay area, Compumentor has achieved a wider recognition by virtue of the trajectory it has taken and the scale of its operation.

Compared with the other four CNs it employs eight times as many staff and has a budget 16 times bigger than the second largest, Vancouver CN. A more detailed examination of its operations follows.[124]

Technology supplier to the non-profits

Compumentor has its origins in 1987 after Daniel Ben-Horin received helpful advice after posting a message on a listserv about a printer problem. He hit on the idea of creating a non-profit technology assistance provider by tapping volunteer resources from the WELL (Whole Earth 'Lectronic Link), one of California's earliest online communities.

Ten years later it had provided support through its skilled computer experts or 'mentors' to a list of 2500 organisations and was receiving grants from funders like the California Wellness Foundation, the US Department of Education, Pacific Bell, the James Irvine Foundation and others for a range of projects. The five basic building blocks of Compumentor were now in place:
• techsoup.org, a free technical magazine for non-profits (N-Ps);
• collaboration with partners in support of technology use by N-Ps;
• training for CTCs and others and for low-income youth;
• software distribution supported by Microsoft, Cisco and others;
• consultancy services to non-profits and schools for a $175 fee.

With its specialist and wide-ranging knowledge of the N-P sector and community technology issues, Compumentor was able to expand techsoup.org magazine into a comprehensive unbiased source of information about technology and how it can help to meet N-P and VCO needs and objectives. With 16 separate sections, articles, mailing lists, message boards, tools and resources, it has been consulted by over 1.5 million unique users worldwide.

The crucial issue for a sustainability model for Compumentor was to generate an earned revenue stream from the resources invested and that has been achieved by linking techsoup.org with DiscounTech (DT), an efficient software database and distribution system with information on up-to-date product availability. Supported by 40 major software suppliers, DT combines wide coverage of 36,500 organisations for the vendors with focused advice and low costs for N-Ps, which pay a small administration fee for the service. By 2003 DT had supplied to over 10,500 N-Ps, all of which it could also support with training and consultancy services; and by 2005, it expects to have saved more than $519m for the entire N-P sector.

With a mixture of opportunism, good fortune and focused strategic thinking, Compumentor had developed a highly successful aggregation model for the N-P sector and in 2003 was one of four winners from 655 entrants, each receiving a $100,000 award in the National Business Plan Competition for N-P Organisations, sponsored by Yale School of Management, the Goldman Sachs Foundation and the Pew Charitable Trust. With a turnover of $6 million it was employing 58 staff, though ironically only two of these were devoted to supporting the voluntary mentors' scheme, from which its success had originally sprung.

Community Technology Centers' Network (CTC Net)

The CN organisations described above received their inspiration from the Free-Nets of the 1980s and in turn have influenced or become involved in the development of community-based technology centres (as described on pages 29 and 38), for which both the Canadian and US Governments have provided funding. Though varying in size, areas served and funding, the centres in the USA recognised at an early stage their common interests and organised their first national affiliates meeting in 1990 as the 'Playing to Win' Network.

Subsequently renamed the CTC Network, it was originally a project of the Educational Development Center (EDC) and received a three-year grant from the Natural Science Foundation in 1992. Ten years later it had become an incorporated non-profit body and was being supported, via the EDC, by a $500,000 Federal grant from the US Department of Education.

Rapid growth and need for support and training

Essentially a 'trade association', with its centre of operations based since 2003 in Washington, DC, CTC Net grew rapidly from the mid 1990s. From 21 centres affiliated in 1994, it had expanded to a 750-centre affiliate organisation by 2002, able to represent a whole new social movement which had rapidly shot up to champion the interests of disadvantaged communities.[125] There is no equivalent in the UK.

The need for support and training for local centres is obvious in a fast-moving technology created world and particularly because of their explosive growth from 1999–2000 and their high staff turnover. A change of administration and the events of 9/11 brought a slow down and with the inevitable consolidation has come a focus on the skills required for programme delivery and financial sustainability.

CTC Net has worked with the Association for Community Networking (AfCN) and others like Compumentor in San Francisco, UMass in Boston (see later) and Seattle's DIT to develop regional and metro-politan area networks, which can support local meetings, conferences and training events and facilitate communication with the local centres.

Use of web-based technology

CTC Net has also produced a 'center start-up' manual and toolkit for organisers and hosts an advice line for over 1500 subscribers, archiving this for reference at www.ctcnet.org/americaconnects. It runs national, regional and metropolitan mail lists[126] and organises server-based panel presentations by experts. These are all good examples of using web-based technology to pass information rapidly across a widely dispersed national network.

While a national CTC Conference is held annually for face-to-face contact and workshops, the last example, for instance, provides the opportunity for an invited panellist to post a short piece of, say, 300–800 words on a subject such as digital imaging software or community mapping and invite comments and queries on an active discussion board over two weeks for over 750 affiliates.

Network of strategic links

CTC Net has also built a network of strategic links with other national, federal educational partners, where there have been symmetrical interests. These include the Benton Foundation in Washington DC[127] (www.benton.org) – which supports the Digital Divide Network (www.digitaldividenetwork.org) – the CTC VISTA Project, sponsored by the University of Massachusetts (page 84) and the Children's Partnership, a national lobbying body. By careful partnership building and promotion of joint projects, CTC Net has nurtured these links to promote the interests of centres and channel public and foundation resources into the CTC movement.

Educational Development Center
The CTC Net has developed into an independent body as the result of actions taken initially by the Educational Development Center, which is mainly funded by the US Department of Education's Office of Vocational and Adult Education (OVAE). Based in Newton, Massachusetts, EDC has a role in relation to workforce preparation and has provided a national technical assistance centre for the CTCs. It assists the centres with data collection and analysis and in 2002 was exploring with the OVAE how it could promote the use of the web by people with limited basic education skills.

A key concern was to develop ways in which self-assessment could be undertaken and in particular via CTCs, while recognising that adults lacking these skills and self-confidence would need also face-to-face support from a tutor or learning support worker.

EDC has been closely involved with CTC Net in the creation and support of the America Connects consortium, which provides information and resources for CTCs and others wishing to support community-based adult education provision in low-income areas. Established in 2000 with a $2 million grant from the Department of Education's Office of Vocational and Adult Education, the ACC launched its website, www.americaconnects.net in April 2001. It has sections dealing with technology, evaluation and programme design, and includes a series of best practice or 'Promising Practices' briefs in community technology, one of which is on 'Project-based learning at CTCs'.

The constructivist approach of this example, drawing on the participatory methodology of Paulo Freire, stresses the integration of the technology skills with the learning, gives practical ways for the tutor to develop her ideas, and is specifically targeted at those who want to gain their GED (General Educational Diploma) or learn English as a second language.[128] It draws on the experience of *ScienceQuest* activities, which have been successful in developing inquiry, collaboration, technology and literacy skills.

CTC VISTA Project (www.cpcs.umb.edu/VISTA)

Closely connected with the CTC Network, the VISTA Project was one of a number of community technology initiatives launched by the College of Public and Community Service (CPCS) at Boston's University of Massachusetts (UMass), which include also sponsorship of the Community Technology Review and a new degree programme in Community Media and Technology.

The VISTA Project had its origins in the Domestic Peace Corps and the Corporation for National and Community Service set up in 1965, as the Americorps national volunteer programme. It was re-fashioned by the Clinton–Gore Administration to take account of some of its social policy commitments. In the UK the nearest equivalent is the HE Active Community Fund linked to the Millennium Volunteers scheme, which is intended to enhance the role played by HE institutions in their local community.[129] Under the US scheme UMass received $1.8 grant over three years to recruit, place and support 150 Americorps volunteers to work in CTCs across America. The scheme still continues although the level of funding is now lower and allows the placing of only 50 volunteers in 2005–06.

One of the most popular of the VISTA schemes available to well qualified – and mostly graduate – young people, the UMass/CTC Project was receiving 600–1000 applications a year, with the selected candidates receiving a stipend for the year of $10,000 plus training, health insurance and post-service education award or $1200 in cash. The scheme provides much needed support and some staffing continuity for the participating centres and a model for other local schemes like that devised in Seattle with the University of Washington[130] (page 68).

It also represents an example of significant commitment by an HE institute to make resources and technology know-how available to local centres and in support of the VCS and ACL.

3. Other community and family service centres

Interviews were also held with four other organisations which were of interest for the research but which did not fit neatly into the previous two categories. One was a community TV service, two were children's and family service organisations and the last was a partnership group addressing the needs of people with disabilities in Los Angeles

Cambridge Community Television (www.cctvcambridge.org)

Based in Boston, CCTV involves local residents in providing materials and programming for its three cablecast access channels. Over 13,000 hours were broadcast in 2001. Linked to this central activity are a range of training courses in TV skills, video editing, computer web design and graphics, which are run through open recruitment and with partner bodies like the Cambridge Family Literacy Unit and the Childcare Research Center.

CCTV had net revenue for 2001 of $1.26 million against expenditure of $773,000 and has benefited from the financial arrangement established as part of the franchise agreement between AT&T Broadband and the City of Cambridge. This allowed the latter to provide cable TV and telecommunications services at a fee of 5 per cent of its gross revenues to support public, educational and government access programming, plus a one-off $1 million contribution.[131] Bills filed in Congress in 2005, however, threaten CCTV and others, as they seek to dilute or remove the need for cable companies to obtain local franchises.

Many of the activities of CCTV are similar to those undertaken by the CTCs, although these are ancillary to their main objective of organising a local cable-based community television service.

The Children's Partnership (www.childrenspartnership.org/)

The US Federal Government policy over the last decade has been to direct more resources towards helping children and families. A particular focus for this has been after-school funding especially for activities between 3pm and 6pm – providing childcare in support of working families – where federal expenditure increased from $1 million to $1 billion in the period 1996–2001. Community-based organisations such as CTCs and other non-profits could previously benefit from these schemes only as contractors to schools, but can now receive funding direct for programmes organised outside school premises, provided that they have had experience already of managing a certain level of funding for activities in the past.

The Children's Partnership (CP), based in Los Angeles and Washington, has played a significant part in these developments, as a small but effective advocate for children's rights. It has achieved this by forming alliances with bodies like CTC Net and the National Christian Inter-Denominational Group, and provides information to national and state legislators on issues relating to children.

In April 2002 it was working closely with local groups in San Francisco and across California to organise a day of lobbying of senators in Sacramento to promote legislation supporting the deployment of IT resources in disadvantaged communities. Cable franchising agreements had also been the subject of substantial CP lobbying in recent years and this was helping city councils like Cambridge, Boston (see above) in their negotiations to strike the best deal for the public with cable companies over rights to lay cable and offer services.[132]

Creating content

Significant impact has also been achieved by CP in its activities to promote the creation of appropriate content on the web for and by local under-served communities. This followed the release of its study in March 2000 of 10,000 relevant websites, which reached the conclusion that only 1 per cent of content was created for adults with limited literacy and only 1 per cent in a culturally relevant manner.[133] The response was to develop a website, the Community Contentbank portal (www.contentbank.org), which provides resource-sharing facilities, knowledge about projects and new initiatives, and useful applications like a Read-Aloud utility.

Despite its advocacy of the use of ICT to support services for children, CP itself was not, in 2002, actively using web technologies for its own internal organisation. This was largely due to its small size and the comparatively high implementation costs – an important point to be considered by VCOs when determining their IT strategies.[134]

Parental Stress Service (PSS)

Based in Oakland, California PSS, with 68 mental health staff employed, is much larger than CP. It was established in 1971 as a non-profit organisation to help families in Alameda County who have abused their children or were at risk of abusing them. With an annual turnover of between $2–3 million, teams of volunteers to run 24-hour help lines, respite services, training programmes and a large caseload in an area with over 20,000 reported incidents of child abuse in 1998, PSS has the profile of an organisation where both staff and users could benefit substantially from enhanced use of IT.

In 2002, however, they were at an initial planning stage exploring how to upgrade their present limited IT facilities. Their IT specialist was hoping to install a faster TI data line connection[135] the following year and establish a mail server and web server – to which a resources database from an existing intranet could be migrated. They were using a database to track staff hours, put information about jobs on the local web-based Craig's List and provided information about their activities on their website (www.psshelps.org). The concern of PSS was therefore at a stage primarily focused on improving organisational and communication resources for staff and volunteers, rather than using ICT for training or for directly educational purposes.

Some of the work of PSS in supporting families is comparable to activities undertaken by community development practitioners and SureStart teams in the UK and PSS could at a later stage develop an e-learning dimension to their work. An online Parent Survival course recently developed by the WEA in the north-west and its Community Grid for Learning team is of relevance here – and could indeed be repurposed for use outside the UK.[136]

Living Independently in Los Angeles (LILA Project)

This pioneering project was the only one investigated during the research, which focused on the needs of people with disabilities. An online partnership initiative of the Westside Center for Independent Living and the Advanced Policy Institute of UCLA (University of California, Los Angeles), it provides a casebook example of how technology transfer from HE can be successfully combined with grassroots knowledge and action. While other UCLA activities have developed

Socially useful technology gives everyday access…

The inspiration for Living Independently in Los Angeles came from Alan Joy, himself a wheelchair user, who had completed a MA at UCLA and was unemployed. He hit on the idea of using geographical information systems (GIS) to support disabled adults in their normal lives. They needed information about everyday access issues (steps, curb cuts, entrances, availability of ramps, WCs, beach facilities, wheelchairs, and so on). He approached the Director of UCLA's Computing Department about the scheme and was given $1000, an office and a month to prepare a bid for funding with appropriate partners!

Funds came from a variety of sources including the Community Technology Foundation of California and $100,000 from Microsoft 'with no strings attached'. Central to the vision of the project was the drive to empower some of the most disenfranchised groups in any community by encouraging self-help and peer-based networks. Greater use of community assets would lead to increased mobility and more enhanced networking. Users are encouraged to become volunteer Community Access Technologists (CATs) to help build LILA by uploading their own knowledge about disability related issues on to simple forms, which can be mapped and converted into 'asset' pages on the website.

The project relies for its implementation upon GIS reference data from state, county and district databases and ironically obtaining permission to use this was one of the most difficult tasks for the project. 'If we allowed LILA the use of the data, we would have to give it to UCLA as well', was the comment of one data holder. 'Why not?' had been Joy's laconic response!

neighbourhood mapping schemes with local residents,[137] LILA has created a unique online system and 'Map-Room' – using interactive mapping technology – to provide information for the county's two million people who are living with disabilities and for those who work with them.

4. Universities, colleges and public libraries

University of Massachusetts (UMass)

We have already seen the close involvement of UMass in the work of the CTC Net, through sponsorship of the Vista Project and of the Community Technology Review. Additionally, its College of Public and Community Service (CPCS) has given support for the Greater Boston Broadband Network (www.cbcmedia.net) and its consortium of university and community partners, and in 2002 established with a wide range of other bodies the Commonwealth Broadband Collaborative (CBC).

This aims to meet the demand for local informative content, broadcast over broadband, which can form part of a public information infrastructure. Its *First Tuesday* programme offers almost full-frame live download of CBC content, using *BitTorrent* technology. This allows the transfer of files over a network as large as the number of people accessing the material. The advantage of this is that the *BitTorrent* software enables the spreading of the load by permitting the simultaneous download and upload of material from all participating computers.

The University's Graduate College of Education (GCOE) was involved in the support of adult basic education initiatives, in which Massachusetts State had made a substantial investment over the last two years. UMass was, for instance, providing the R&D and documentation for the Greater Massachusetts ABE project, involving three pilots at an annual cost of $400,000.

Through the work of David Rosen, the Adult Literacy Resource Institute at the GCOE was also providing consultancy to the Westchester County, New York public library, which led a collaboration of New York City area public libraries to create a portal of websites (www.firstfind.info) of interest to low literate adults; and was closely involved in the Student Coalition for Action in Literacy Education (SCALE), a national organisation of campus-based adult literacy organisations. Based in North Carolina, SCALE has a staff of seven and, drawing upon the community service tradition of US HE, supports campus-based programmes which attract substantial numbers of volunteers into helping with adult literacy support and coaching.[138]

Sheridan College, Oakville, Ontario (www.sheridanc.on.ca)
With an established reputation in Canada for developing students as top-rated computer animators and multimedia developers,[139] Sheridan College offered the opportunity of investigating how a community college, committed to preparing its students for the knowledge society, dealt with the issues of infrastructure development, culture change and staff training, and of exploring the role played by the senior management in this process.

Sheridan is Canada's largest college with over 10,500 full-time and part-time students enrolled on almost 100 different courses. The principal, senior management team and governors had committed themselves to spending resources on technology. The upshot had been that, remarkably, 92 per cent of students had obtained jobs within six months of graduating, but the downside had been finding the resources when the provincial government was cutting back on overall allocations and expecting 'more for less' from the sector.

DELTA³ laptop scheme

One of the most interesting features of the college was its decision to promote the use of laptop computers by students as the primary tool for all their work (see Figure 6). By 2002 five thousand, or almost half of the students, were using laptops for 35 different programmes in the DELTA³ scheme, the largest of its kind in Canada. A wide range of subject areas had been brought in, including engineering, computing, media, social service programmes and, of course, education. For Sandra Hodder, who was organising the scheme, stating the problem they faced was simple: 'It was difficult for the tutors to give up control.'

Finding the solution was more taxing. The mean age of tutors was 51 and the college needed to get them involved. The solution was firstly to take great care with the layout and redesign of the classrooms so as to facilitate group work – involving the users themselves – and secondly to make sure that the hurdles for the staff were not set too high. Thereafter the early (teacher) adopters were the key to success, because they brought in the others who did not wish to be left behind by failing to make use of the technologies available.

Young people now are more visually literate, but in the words of

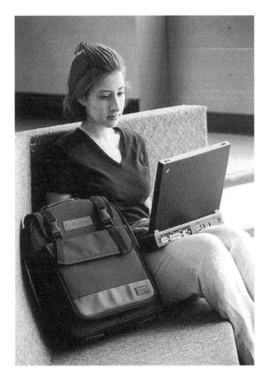

Figure 6. Student using laptop at the College.

Hodder, 'With our laptop scheme, we are finding that the ordinary "Joe teacher" can sing.' Behind the initiative, described below, was the concept of a collaborative model of learning, where redesign of the teaching space would lead to changes in teaching styles with the teachers becoming facilitators. It was linked too with an open curriculum repository and archiving project to support T2T collaboration – a feature which ironically became harder to maintain, because the less involved teachers reverted back to an 'unseen' private model of working.

South Seattle Community College (www.southseattle.edu)
South Seattle Community College was one of two colleges chosen for the study initially because it was directly involved in working in partnership with the City Council and others in developing community-based ICT facilities at the New Holly Learning Center (page 45). Its General Studies Department had increased its share of the total college population to over 25 per cent and this was supported by additional contracts of about $1 million annually, for example, for workforce development.

Integrating the laptop into learning and teaching – Canadian style

Description of the DELTA^3 scheme by Sandra Hodder, Director of Advanced Learning Technologies at Sheridan College, Ontario

In the classroom setting the laptops are used for two basic purposes – either as a portable computer lab or as a learning tool. The basic categories of use are for calculation, organization, visualization, research, communication and problem solving since those are things for which computers with their access to databases or the internet are very well suited.

Since each laptop is loaded with general communication software plus program specific software, the portable computer lab offers many possibilities. A student of architecture or interior design would use programs such as CAD and PhotoShop to create plans and drawings. They may even create virtual walkthroughs or 3D animations of a design. A student in computer studies would use the compilers associated with the various programming languages.

Business students might use an accounting or statistical analysis package. In media arts students use their laptops to edit audio and video, while in electronics they use electrical simulations and program PLCs (programmable logic controllers) with their laptops. In effect, the software application mirrors real work situation usage.

Since the laptops are taken to class, they are also a learning tool and can be used directly for a problem-solving activity when appropriate. A costing of a design for example can be done on the spot using a spreadsheet with the actual costs downloaded via the internet. This immediate access to information and applications makes the learning environment both more engaging as students are working on problems and more authentic since the information they are using is likely to be more current.

A wide variety of activities take place in classrooms. There is typically a lecture but in a laptop environment that tends to be shorter than in a non-laptop environment. Students can directly download the lecture notes or slides and annotate them during the lecture. The lecture portions tend to come in 'bursts' often limited to 15 minutes. Between the lecture 'bursts', students are engaged in learning activities. They might be researching, synthesizing, evaluating, programming, designing, presenting, discussing and so on. Essentially the idea is to have the students learn by doing whenever possible.

It ran a large variety of campus-based programmes of community education and technology-related courses, including web production, radio and music on the web and 'Washington online'. A number of courses were offered online and students were provided with internet facilities and email for which they were charged $25–35 each. A more in-depth investigation of the experience of learners on the courses and of the use of online discussions and chat rooms at the College to promote communication and sharing would be of value.

Seattle Public Libraries (www.spl.org)
The Seattle Public Libraries service (SPL) has a central library and 22 local libraries and has developed extensive ICT facilities for users. In all they had some 600 computers installed for the public, of which about 50 per cent in 2002 had internet access. These were being used to organise a programme of 25 regular classes for the public covering five defined curriculum areas of basic technical literacy – Email, Basic Computing Level 1 and Level 2, Internet Level 1 and Level 2.

This was a substantial programme of classes for adults and represented a new instructional role being played by SPL. It was seen as being linked to the library service's primary objectives of promoting information literacy and enabling users to evaluate and apply information. The service was offering a first step for their users, after which they could progress on to courses and activities elsewhere. SPL worked closely with the city's DIT and had supported the work of the Seattle Community Network, whose server they housed.

The mission of SPL is to become the best public library in the world. Having received approval from Seattle voters in 1998 for a special $196 million bond measure, the Council opened in 2004 an impressive new central library in a state of the art building with more extended IT facilities, a larger programme of courses for adults than in 2002 and a bold database-driven electronic art installation. Further details are available from the dedicated *Libraries for All* website, where there are also some intriguing gif animations of the construction process.[140]

In adjoining King County, the public library service (www.kcls.org) covering areas like Redmond and Bellevue, home of many Microsoft workers, made 8500 e-books available to borrowers and in November 2004 added a further 634 online audio books, all of which were in high demand. This scheme was expanded substantially across the US in 2005 with large cost savings.[141]

Figure 7. Top floor of Seattle's central library

Oxford County Public Library Service, Ontario (www.ocl.net)

The involvement of the Oxford County Library Service (OCL) in the development of community-based technology has stemmed directly from the Canadian Government's CAP initiative described earlier (page 38). As a large rural area in south-western Ontario experiencing the problems of population migration, shrinking villages and declining agriculture, the county has similar challenges to those affecting rural communities throughout Canada and indeed in many parts of the world including Britain. It provides an interesting contrast with the urban experience of other visits undertaken during the research.

CAP programme opens doors for local communities

Faced with community concerns in the early 1990s about a disappearing way of life OCL, though only a small service at the time, responded by committing itself to maintaining the network of local branch libraries. Often they were the only remaining centre of community life as post offices, stores, banks and petrol stations closed their doors. The scheme provided the chance to take positive action, with the vision of a county-wide IT network put forward by Chief Librarian Sam Coghlan, who wrote the original application for the 16 CAP sites.

Opened in 1996, the public access points were initially unreliable but a parallel grant from Human Resources Development Canada (HRDC) enabled OCL to establish Information Access Oxford (IAO) as OCL's Technology Section, which set up a broadband wireless link (subsequently extended) between two of the biggest towns. The effect of this was to allow OCL, now expanding its role substantially beyond library services, to establish the County of Oxford Integrated Network (COIN), a wireless network for the whole authority.

For the libraries the benefit was a reliable resource which could draw in and involve their local communities, but the critical issue was to support and build the confidence of front line staff, whom Sam Coghlan described as 'our most important partners'.[142] The 'killer application' was the provision of email links across the county with a listserv and the development of an online county-wide central catalogue of books. This allowed the staff, often with fairly small collections at their immediate disposal, to pinpoint the availability of a book elsewhere in the system.

Vision and networking

Several valuable activities have been developed by OCL, which have required a clear sense of purpose and vision. But they have had to be coupled with the ability to impress funding bodies that there is a matching of interests. As Coghlan put it, when describing his negotiations, 'HRDC want apples. We persuade them that we can do the job, but that we will produce oranges, which is what they really want.'

An example of how OCL has used its networks to attract funds can be seen from the account below of a meeting which was key in the setting up of the COOL database of local companies and services.[143]

Description by OCL's John Moore of the setting up the COOL Project, an information portal in Ontario, Canada – October 2002

We had got COIN (County of Oxford Integrated Network) set up in 1998 as a high-speed network with support from all three levels of Government, plus strong business and community support. Industry Canada (IC) wanted to see what was going on in Oxford County and look at several of the Community Access Programmes (CAP) sites. I was deputed to arrange the visit and accompany the IC representative during the day as we toured the area. Well, he turned out to be a senior member (and director) of IC who was an old friend of mine, as we had worked together several years earlier.

Doug (the IC representative) also happened to be a good friend of the President of the University of Waterloo in Kitchener, who he had arranged to meet that evening. So he said to me, 'Why don't you come along too?' Well we all met up that evening – twelve of us or so round a big table with people from the Computer Science Department and others and were yacking away about this and that.

Doug was saying what a great job we were doing in Oxford County with the CAP sites and why didn't we do something with the Computer Science people. They had been developing a web-based community directory of businesses for an urban area, but wanted to see how this could be applied in a rural setting and they started to talk about the details.

After a bit of this Doug comes back and says 'OK, so how much do you want?' We looked at each other, had a quick chat at the table, scribbled out some rough costs on the back of a napkin and came up with a figure – 100,000 dollars. 'Done' he said, 'just send me the details and we can get the contract signed.' That was it. That was the start of the COOL Project.

Moore's description shows the importance of social networks and personal contacts, and in this case HE links, in moving things forward. It does not suggest that Oxford County was an inappropriate recipient of an Industry Canada grant for the COOL project. OCL had to deliver a product (the populated database) with the support of Waterloo University and had already demonstrated competence in delivering IT projects with community support. They had succeeded in differentiating themselves from other municipal authorities and thus were able to gain access to the essential 'seed' money needed to innovate and take risks. Here a government department was playing in the public sector a similar role to that played by venture capital 'angels' in the private sector during the dotcom boom.

Responding to the needs and views of a rural community
OCL was also able to provide a service which was geared to the specific needs and priorities of a predominantly rural area with a population of only 97,000 compared with that of the nearest large city of London with 350,000, where there is a more open-minded view about IT. Like Seattle City Council and many others, OCL provides a computer training programme but it has to take account of attitudes in a traditional non-metropolitan rural community. It is an area of contrasts, according to Kathryn McCulloch the OCL Training Manager, with two distinct groups of farmers, the *hi-tec farmers* and the *technophobes*.

The former group are well educated, keen to participate, want to use computers and GIS (geographical information systems) and responded positively to OCL initiatives. An example of this was the 'Mapping your Farm' scheme in 2003. This was hosted by the COOL portal and drew upon the skills and knowledge of the staff in the County's GIS Department. Web-based map customisation facilities are offered to farmers with, for example, groundwater features, zoning and nutrient management options made available free over the Internet (see Figure 8).

Figure 8. 'Map Your Farm', from the COOL Website

Map Your Farm

The latter group of farmers are suspicious of technology and resistant to its use. This is particularly the case with the Dutch settlers who came over to Canada in the 1950s and 1960s, while those who immigrated in the 1970s and later are keen to modernise. These attitudes create difficulties, as McCulloch explained:

> There is a whole tradition built round the farm and farm life. The parents indoctrinate the children. They are not encouraged to look at new things. This is especially the case with the Dutch Reform Church and the Mennonites. I had an example with a group of five adult students. They refused to continue in one of our programmes if the teacher used the computer again. What had happened? The previous week she had used the internet to show the students examples of life in Holland and the holiday opportunities available.

Extensive computer training programme

The computer training programme run by OCL was substantial with intermediate and advanced classes, seniors clubs and monthly or fort-nightly computer clubs. There was also a large programme of IT training in Microsoft Office for 370 county employees as part of the corporate plan for the authority, although typically it was proving difficult to move this forward rapidly because of problems with release of staff.

Details of the courses are well set out on the dedicated website (http://training.ocl.net) and teachers make active use of a chat board, inviting students from the course to send questions to which replies are quickly posted. In an area with a scattered population, web-based tech-nologies were seen as evidently valuable to learners and staff also directed them to external sites (like www.actden.com) where they could obtain reinforcement of skills they were developing in the OCL class.

5. Private sector bodies

The final group visited were two private companies, both with links to Microsoft, which were interviewed to provide some benchmarks of technically advanced services and to explore their relevance to adult and community-based learning.

Avanade

Established in 1999 by Microsoft and the consultancy firm Accenture, the core business of Avanade was the provision globally of corporate solutions, such as networking and content management systems. The visit was focused exclusively on examining their advanced e-learning system which was hosted in Seattle and used for remote training of systems and solutions engineers operating anywhere in the world.

In the aftermath of the events of 9/11 in 2001, companies were looking to reduce the amount of travel undertaken by staff and e-learning solutions were considered particularly attractive. The heart of Avanade's offer was a four-hour Virtual Instructor Led (VIL) video-conferenced lecture session using high-speed bandwidth and VOIP, supported by telephone and IAM Instant Messaging. A sophisticated multiplex arrangement of servers allows ten concurrent users to access remotely ten separate servers to practice their skills in systems and network set-up, aspects of which have been introduced during the lecture. In this way interactivity and technical support can be provided to the learners who often will be located in two or three continents.

Typically three sessions of four hours each will be run over a 12-hour 'Seattle' day, from 6am–10am, 10am–2pm, and 2pm–6pm, which ensures that most people can participate in the lectures and assignments from anywhere in the world during *their* working day. Normally courses of this nature will last for up to nine days, either continuously or over a longer period. In addition to this 'high maintenance' scheme, the company was developing a blended learning option. This was a computer-based self-study (CBSS) or 'managed CBSS' scheme, which involved burning the lectures onto CDs for distribution. Users of this would be offered instructor support via email (with 24-hour turnaround responses) and lists of others doing the course to promote peer support.

Expedia and Travelscape

Expedia is an internet-based travel company, initially launched by Microsoft in 1996 as a wholly owned subsidiary before the dotcom boom took off two years later. By 2001 when USA Networks bought a 75 per cent shareholding in the company, it had grown its share of the US internet travel market to 10 per cent and by late 2002 was, unusually for internet-based companies, making a profit.

In 2004 it predicted sales of $12 billion of airline tickets in the USA, representing 5 per cent of the total.[144] The primary interest of the company for this research on ACL and new technologies lies in the way that it has grown the market, the attention it has shown to the details of developing its web-based presence and the manner in which it and Travelscape, which it purchased in 2000, have been able to scale up operations over a short timescale (see case study overleaf).

Part of the business model for Expedia's hotels business had been built up through the practice and technology developed initially by Travelscape. The company now offers via its website flights, hotels and 'dynamic' packages, which allow the user to change the components of the purchase during the shopping process. It sends millions of emails weekly to users on its databases, allowing suppliers to deliver targeted offers to customers.

Travelscape – Lessons from a dotcom flare-up?

Seventy years ago Las Vegas was little more than a dusty township beside a railroad in the Nevada desert, but technology in the shape of the giant 1935 Hoover Dam, the BBC's seventh *Wonder of the Industrial Age*, was to change all that. With 88 per cent of its water supplied by taming the mighty Colorado River, Vegas was to become by the year 2000 the single most popular tourist destination in the world and the fastest growing city in the US.

The internet age broke comparatively late in this capital of casinos and gaming, but the story of one small local company, which used computer and web technology to transform its business, has left Las Vegans breathless and may provide insights as much for non-profit and public bodies as for the private sector.

Las Vegas Reservation Systems (LVRS) began life in 1990, the brainchild of a local college graduate, Tim Poster, while he was at the University of Southern California. He built the company with Tom Breitling who joined in 1993. They recognised that in the hotel boom of the 1990s there was an underused asset – vacant rooms – and potential customers ready to take them if the price was right. The challenge was to bring the rooms and customers together and scale up the operation.

They started by securing a block of rooms which were sold through local advertisements, an arrangement the hoteliers were happy to support, as it increased their occupancy rates. A firm and growing foundation was established, but take off came when they changed the name from the forgettable LVRS to Travelscape.com and launched a website with the same name in February 1998.

This was the period of the dotcom boom and they contracted the systems engineers, Thoughtmill, to improve and consolidate their back office architecture and procedures. Integrating these with specified national airline and hotel reservation systems, they created a simple, easy-to-use DIY website bringing lower cost rooms *and* 30 per cent gross profits with Travelscape controlling the price of the inventory offered. Two hundred visitors to the site in the first week had risen to 2.5 million monthly by November 1999 with rooms available at 1600 hotels in 240 cities.

Selling more than 95 per cent of the reserved rooms, the company, in the words of Poster, 'just took off like crazy' and exactly two years after the website launch was snapped up by the internet travel company, Expedia for $95 million. By using technology and partnerships to combine pre-existing assets in a new business model, Travelscape had vaulted through to reach a huge market and create new consumer demand.

Are there parallels to be found in the area of adult and community education where private/public alliances could exploit rich archival and multimedia resources, focused on local communities, to develop interactive computer-based materials and online courses? There is potential here to motivate non-participating adults to take up more education and training, both blended and online; and in doing so to stimulate a new e-learning market, aggregate supply and promote skills and productivity. After all, with only one in five UK adults involved in learning in any one year, there is plenty of room for growing demand.

(*Sources: Red Herring; San Francisco Business Times; The View* neighborhood newspapers; *Internet News;* Land, B. and Land, M. (1999) *A Short History of Las Vegas.* University of Nevada Press; BBC 2, *Seven Wonders of the Industrial Age,* 16 October 2003; Interview with Tom Breitling, 15 September 2003.)

An airline, for example, can request that an electronic coupon is sent to each of Expedia's customers, who live in a key originating market and/or who have searched for flights between a particular place and destination over a specified period. In this way the airline can deliver targeted offers to a clearly defined customer segment and so stimulate demand in this segment. The practice does not however dilute the yield they achieve from other customers outside the targeted segment, who they consider would buy a full price ticket anyway.

Expedia has a Usability Lab to test in precise detail new user interface prototypes, which it plans to introduce. Crucial determinants in the drive to increase market share are ease of use together with the competitiveness of the inventory pricing. The importance given to the analysis of users' responses to possible interfaces over three full days of testing was very instructive.

Lessons from technology and change in the private sector

In summary, Avanade had developed supported e-learning programmes for networking staff; and Expedia with Travelscape had in just 12 years grown a travel and hotel booking service from scratch into a major force in the industry. In both cases the companies had committed substantial capital resources and had a wide range of staff with technical, program-ming and management skills to roll out and scale up the work. Although there are important differences, their experience and methods are relevant to ACL organisations for two reasons.

Firstly, some features described are transferable. There is no reason why online induction and training modules for new tutors – with less complexity to be sure – should not be created. This would be par-ticularly useful for an ACL service operating over a large dispersed area with mostly part-time tutors; and indeed is now being piloted by the WEA north-west Region (see page 115).

The second reason is more complex and speculative and relates to technological shifts, which are being described variously as Web 2.0 or Computing's 'Fifth Wave'. In the July 2005 edition of *Business 2.0*, Michael Copeland and Om Malik argue that we are on the verge of an 'epic technological transformation', which will be powered by cheap hardware (including laptops and mobile phones), ubiquitous broadband and 'technological openness'. This latter feature of a 'global tinkerer's workshop' with reusable programming code opens the door to finding creative new solutions and services at a fraction of the previous cost.[145]

It brings closer eBay founder Pierre Omidyar's vision of the web as 'a fundamental shift in power toward the bottom, toward the people as they organise themselves, and away from a small group of people who want to impose a policy top-down'. 'Social computing', as this has been called, encapsulates the notion that individuals are influenced by and prefer to link with other people, rather than with institutions and official sources.

Social computing typically involves individuals using the technology to make personal contributions, which through combination either enhance the value of the overall asset or come to represent its primary value. Examples of this can be seen with websites such as amazon (reviews of books), e-Bay (items for sale), epinions (ratings of products), zillow (data on individual houses), flickr (images and photos), blogger (weblogs), and friendsunited (personal details); and in the non-profit sector with wikipaedia.info (knowledge and information), craigslist.org (job and other adverts) and the LILA project (focused information for disabled people).

Charlene Li from Forrester Research points out that this process – of technology empowering individuals – is destabilising for companies and organisations and requires from them a very different response to their customers or users on account of its three defining characteristics where:

- innovation will shift from top-down to bottom-up;
- value will shift from ownership to experience;
- power will shift from institutions to communities.[146]

The potential of all these developments for ACL is very interesting. The utility of an educational course or activity, for example, is in inverse proportion to the cost of learner recruitment. Since the web allows the scaling of a service to a thousand at no greater cost than to one, the advantage of a policy of sharing or of 'collaborate to grow' is enormous.

An example of this can be seen with the WEA's Community Grid for Learning where *own label* CGfL sites are being piloted in Bolton and Knowsley, with library staff managing existing CGfL content and supporting its use with their own learners.

IV

Findings and conclusions

Technology is impacting on our lives and in every domain, but there still remain many unanswered questions and different views about how ACL and post-school education will be reshaped to meet the needs of the Information Society.

We do not know how mobile technologies and next generation applications will evolve, the impact of 'always on' connectivity or, most importantly, the expectations of new cohorts of adults, brought up as children in a web-connected world. The 'long shadow of the future' may affect our actions, but its shape is indistinct. In the private sector there has been major investment both in the technology and in new alliances but as the *Financial Times* has observed of large corporate internet strategies, they remain 'one giant experiment'.[147] Just how experimental some of the schemes dreamt up were can be seen in the dotcom collapse of 2000 when $725 billion was wiped off the US stock market valuations of some 363 companies.

Experiments carry risks of failure

Nor have the failures been limited to the private sector. In HE and research some of the most prestigious institutions led by Columbia University and including the London School of Economics, the British Library, Cambridge University Press, University of Chicago, the British Museum, the Victoria and Albert Museum and the Science Museum combined in a new alliance to create fathom.com in 1999 as an international service to deliver online lectures worldwide from renowned experts. Four years later it was quietly announced that the scheme was to be discontinued, as Columbia University intended to reorganise its digital media activities.[148]

Figure 9. Young people take to new technology regardless of class, income, gender or ethnicity.

In a similar vein HEFCE set up in 2001 an ambitious *UK e-Universities Worldwide* scheme, with the support of £62 million from the DfES, to create and market HE courses abroad to compete with the USA and elsewhere. By early 2004, however, with developments behind schedule and only 900 students in total and 145 of them using the £15 million e-learning platform created by Sun Microsystems, the risky nature of the venture and the failure to attract the numbers envisaged in the original business plan persuaded HEFCE to close the project down with £50 million of the original project committed.[149]

Just as Jane Fountain[150] has indicated that in the world of US bureaucracy there were no known models and no agreed jurisdictions to fall back on in the mid-1990s, so the same has applied in the heterogeneous and interconnected worlds of ACL and community development. In all three countries a process of stake claiming – and scrambling for position – has been evident. Statutory and voluntary agencies, corporate bodies and educational institutions, local and regional bodies, established groups and start ups have all been developing programmes and strategies, at times separately and at times in collaboration.

More stabilisation after initial flurry of activity

In the USA different government departments have funded similar local

ICT centres. In Canada sometimes the libraries have taken a lead role, which in other areas has been assumed by a community networking body, and in the UK there are agencies at a national and regional level which have overlapping responsibilities. History, technological developments, enthusiastic individuals and government policies have all played a part in creating this complex picture in this first stage but there are broad patterns beginning to emerge.[151]

As computerisation and the web have become normal and public access widespread, there are now signs that we are moving into a new stage where the search will be for content development, re-usage and delivery models, sustainable structures and return on investment, all linked to governments' strategies for competitiveness, innovation, upskilling and social inclusion. This will raise new issues for those working in ACL and VCS organisations and the outcomes will be influenced by the responses and developments to date. These will now be summarised in relation to the original research objectives.

1. Significance of government and local State policies

There have been considerable differences in the roads taken by the three Governments in promoting the Information Society. While the initial driver in the USA came from the Clinton–Gore concern with reducing federal expenditure and developing improved e-government services, the focus in Canada was on creating a competitive economy and in the UK on education and training.

By 2000, however, there was substantial convergence of government strategies in North America and the UK reflecting to a remarkable extent how these three English-speaking countries were drawing upon their respective experience to develop similar domestic policies on the economy, innovation, skills and public services. Although the UK had been slower off the mark than the other two countries, the Government had by 2000 published substantial and logically coherent reports and proposals on the way it planned to move forward. (See Figure 4.)

e-government and e-commerce had in less than a decade become major domestic policy areas, and there was recognition that digital economies require digital nations. Without a population with IT skills and awareness, online public services would remain marginal, new competitive industries would be slow to emerge and the economy would stagnate.

Initiation of local ICT centres and related schemes

These therefore were the key drivers which led in 1999 to the announcement or start of programmes in each of the three countries for nationwide IT access or community technology centres aimed predominantly at the socially excluded. They have been the most evident of the Type 1 policies in our classification system (page 26). They have given rise to a new segment of community-based learning activities and together with the IT expenditure that has been committed for the benefit of adults by colleges, schools and libraries represent substantial and historically unprecedented levels of investment in ACL. Only in the USA has there been the commitment of major corporate sector funding from companies such as Gateway, Microsoft and Intel.

The schemes for distributing these public funds have been flexible, have encouraged new entrants and VCS organisations and involved evaluation.[152] In many cases there have been imaginative projects like the early ones funded by NTIA in the USA and the Canadian VolNet and Community Learning Network programmes (pages 39–40). There are parallels to be found between the VolNet scheme and the *Futurebuilders* and *ChangeUp* VCS infrastructure support programmes, which the UK Home Office's Active Community Unit established in 2004. These aim to create a voluntary sector, robust enough to deliver public services for hard to reach clients at full cost recovery. ICT is a cross-cutting theme in this initiative, although not its sole focus.

In the UK the LSC-funded TrEACL content development scheme and e-Guides programmes have since 2003 stimulated considerable interest in developing the use of ILT in the ACL sector, while the Regional Development Agencies have supported a number of broadband economic regeneration schemes. In some areas there has been promotion of more community oriented projects like those supported by the North West Development Agency's (NWDA) EU-financed BRAIN programme and by the London Development Agency.[153]

Local municipalities – varying roles

At the local or district level, the role of the local council has varied, reflecting the lack of clearly defined jurisdictions in a new field. In some cases like Seattle, the city's DIT has been the central player, in others like Oxford County in Ontario it has been the Libraries Department. Neither in North America nor in the UK has the funding for IT centres been directed to local authorities so they have had to 'earn' a role as fund-raiser or coordinator.

In many cases however, particularly in the USA and Canada, where a CN movement has been active since the late 1980s or early 1990s, the knowledge and skills have resided outwith the local council. In these cases, such as Vancouver, San Francisco and Boston, there has been scope for other players like the CN or university to play a bigger role.

In Vancouver the CN has developed a model of VCS capacity building through its IM/IT training and support network scheme, which could have substantial potential in relation to the ChangeUp programme being planned by regional government offices in the UK. In Boston the push for broadband services for the community has come from a consortium of educational and CVS bodies, led by the University of Massachusetts. This has resulted in the setting up of a broadband consortium to broad-cast informative content as part of a public information infrastructure using innovative *BitTorrent* technology.

In the UK local councils have generally been significant, though not necessarily leading players; and again, as with the North American experience, the drive may have come from their economic regeneration, libraries, chief executive's or education departments. In a number of areas Local Learning Partnerships (LLPs) have been at centre stage, where FE colleges, with their experience in the use of ILT since the mid-1990s, have had significant influence.

Importance of risk capital

In the early stages government departments and agencies have been more willing to provide 'risk capital'. This has been evident in the pioneering work of the US Commerce Department from 1994, in the whole CMF programme for local ICT centres and the case study of the DfES 2002 Wireless Outreach Network scheme (see page 50) in the UK and in Industry Canada's SMART programme and its support for Oxford County's COOL Project in 1998.

This feature has been important in offering space for organisations to experiment – and for reluctant learners to have a non-threatening 'soft' landing – without the burden of having taxing output targets. As programmes have matured however, there has been a growing tendency to tie grants to specific policy objectives – for instance to the achievement of the General Education Diploma (GED) in the US or to the demonstration in the UK that participants are progressing to other qualification bearing provision or to the achievement of the Level 1 and Level 2 Adult Certificates.

Alliances and convergence over skills strategies

The importance of these kinds of priorities – Type 4 policies – should not be underestimated. Indeed in this whole area of policy development there has been a substantial convergence of interests between Governments and companies on the one hand and the VCS and ACL bodies on the other, which has commonly resulted in effective cross sectoral alliances being forged to meet the challenge of the IS. Many individuals come to IT classes because they recognise the need to enhance their employability skills to gain a job.

The *Computers in our Future* (CIOF) report describes a four year California programme, involving 11 low income Californian communities and 22,500 users and was supported by the Children's Partnership and Compumentor. With 55 per cent of the adults using the centres actively seeking employment or a better job, it concluded: 'Developing curriculum that supported measurable objectives, figuring out the best way to link participants to jobs . . . provided significant challenges but were areas where meaningful strides were made'.[154]

The emphasis on jobs and skills has been given an additional urgency in the USA, by the phenomenon of the jobless recovery, where the upturn in the improving economy in autumn 2003 had resulted in a *drop* in employment of 1.2 million over a 12 month period. This represented in terms of the anticipated upturn in the cycle, a shortfall of some 4.2 million jobs.[155]

A similar focus can be seen in the UK with the Government's *21st Century Skills* report in 2003 and in the LSC's 2004 Consultation Paper *Investing in Skills: Taking Forward the Skills Strategy*.[156] The LSC's paper proposed differentiated funding for 'learning for personal development' and 'first step and return to learning provision as an essential component of skills development', with the latter receiving priority attention. It has implications for local IT centres and those looking to use new technologies to support the broad ACL curriculum.

Need to motivate and to encourage personal development

However, the important emphasis on skills and training should not obscure the fact that local ICT centres in both North America and the UK fulfil a wider educational role. 65 per cent of the CIOF users were not involved in formal technology skills classes and the Servon and Nelson 1999 CTC survey found that 57 per cent of use was recreational (see page 69).

A key factor in bringing adults to the learning table is motivation. A major feature in many of the new ICT centres is the strong emphasis on community development and capacity building, as a way of hooking new users. People coming to the centre are encouraged to develop their interests and skills but are likely to be introduced to other activities in the centre and this may lead them to take up new directions, by involving them in voluntary work, in mentoring other learners, in setting up self-help groups or some kind of social enterprise.

There is not of course a uniform manner, in which learners learn in ICT centres, but the offer of informality, flexibility and choice contributes significantly to their success in attracting community members unwilling in the first instance to contact community colleges and further education institutions.[157] While there are people who will be keen from the outset to come to an ICT centre to learn a specific skill (word processing, spreadsheets etc.), there are many more whose motivation is about self improvement, gaining confidence, pursuing a hobby or leisure interest such as family history, accessing a municipal e-service, supporting a voluntary activity.

This kind of informal learning does not immediately lead to a qualification, but it opens up a pathway and gives confidence and choice to learners about the next leg in their journey. This view is supported by a literature survey for the Joseph Rowntree Foundation, which found that there was a consistent message that ICT training for disadvantaged adults needed to be more informal and innovative than traditional methods.[158]

From uncertainties to more direction and rationalisation

The catalyst of Government policies on skills development and funding programmes has been crucial in setting up the network of centres, but at the outset there were no obvious ways of anticipating responses. In early 2000 in the UK, when bids were being sought by the Government Office of the North West for setting up local ICT centres, one official openly admitted: 'I have no idea if we will receive 20 applications or 200, I've just no way of knowing'.[159]

Essentially in many areas of the UK the problem was one of an overwhelming number of applications. Planning and coordination was extremely difficult with a plethora of centres and access points being set up, often funded from different sources and departments. In the case of Greater Manchester an audit carried out by Ekos Consulting for the local LSC tracked down 580 publicly available centres and facilities where internet access could be obtained.[160] In the wider context however the scale and speed of infrastructure development in disadvantaged communities over the last four years in all three countries has been remarkable. It is rare now in an urban area not to have public and free access to the internet within a two to three miles radius of your home.

Extending broadband penetration

There has also been interest in all three countries from the start of this period in extending broadband penetration – another Type 1 infrastructure policy. The Canadian Government has taken a very active role, generating high take up despite the dispersed nature of the population. In the UK there has been a variety of projects set up by regional development agencies and broadband consortia; and schemes run by local authorities to have high speed connections as part of their push to supply online e-services for local residents. These latter Type 3 services, which can put at a disadvantage anyone without the skills to access them, have also been energetically pursued in the US and Canada.[161]

The UK has lagged behind in broadband take-up, with highest usage in affluent areas and cities, but 2005 witnessed a remarkable volte-face. National Statistics reported in December 2005 that broadband connections had grown from 39 per cent to 59 per cent of all UK connections in just 12 months.[162] Access to broadband has expanded largely through BT overcoming the hurdle that had limited ADSL connectivity to points less than six kilometres from the exchange. By the end of 2004 virtually all UK homes were capable of high speed internet access and this fact together with competition and reduced costs has produced the turn round. Comparative 2004 OECD figures show that only 75 per cent of US households had access although the figures for the East and West coasts are very much higher.[163]

Rationalising programmes and the geographical spread

In all three countries there are moves to rationalise levels of support and numbers of ICT centres which can be sustained through public funds in the long term.[164] Inevitably Governments and policy makers will look for returns on the investments which have been made, but at the very least, they need to recognise, as Cook and Light argue, that 'e-learning is an important precursor for e-government and e-democracy; higher level "e-gearing" cannot be accessed before lower level ICT e-learning "competency" has been acquired'.[165]

In the UK the National Learning Network (NLN) has been reorganised and according to Ivan Lewis, the Minister for Adult Skills, the Government in 2004 wanted, 'to cut bureaucracy and extend the ICT strategy to the adult and community learning sector'.[166] ACL providers, VCS bodies and IT centres will need to respond energetically and demonstrate that they can attract those who have missed out and face exclusion from the digital divide. In the UK they have to show that users are progressing from the learning they are undertaking and that as organisations they are engaged effectively in the next key stages of sustaining online learning and content development. These involve staff training, more innovative usage, integrated systems and learner support as the DfES identified in its 2003 report, *Towards a Unified e-Learning Strategy*. Its resulting e-Strategy – *Harnessing Technology: Transforming Learning and Children's Services* was published in March 2005 and sets out an ambitious programme for the next five years and beyond.[167] There remain disconnections and contradictions in policy and practice however which need addressing.

2. Extent of new technology usage and transformation

We now turn to how new technologies are being used by new and existing organisations in the informal and formal PSE sector. Care needs to be taken to avoid drawing sweeping conclusions on the basis solely of a small sample. However, the evidence of this study, combined with other research and findings from North America and the UK, gives clear indications of both the range and extent of take-up and transformation within the sector, and the relative position compared with the much better funded schools and HE sectors.

It must also be acknowledged that the PSE sector is not neatly defined and limited; and this reality was reflected in the variety of organisations surveyed. These included different ACL providers including ICT centres, community organisations, libraries, community network bodies, colleges, universities and national coordinating groups. They were united by their focus of attention on providing educational opportunities for disadvantaged or 'underserved' groups and individuals, mostly in community settings.

They were distinguished from each other by their respective visions, budgets, staffing and skill sets, which they brought to the task; and these varied substantially. The two community colleges visited in Seattle and Oakville, Ontario for instance were large and had substantial resources at their disposal and were using these in imaginative ways to promote computer-based learning and communication. Of a similar vein were the HE institutions like UCLA in California and UMass in Boston, which were able to assist not for profit bodies and local ICT centres to promote several new ICT-based services.

Lack of investment for ACL has limited developments

In general however the area of community-based post-school informal learning through ICT is not well endowed either in North America or the UK, with government emphasis being placed initially upon meeting the capital and infrastructure costs, rather than the total costs of ownership (TCO). These are the considerably higher long term revenue costs associated with maintenance, staff support, training and content creation.

Nor is there much evidence yet of the kind of organisational transformation that technology could potentially bring to the way that learning is organised and planned. To underscore this, consider the experience of e-commerce with Amazon, eBay, Dell, Yahoo and Google using the web to metamorphose traditional patterns of activity.[168] In terms of the MIT model, we have been reviewing in the PSE and ACL sector the first evolutionary stages with localised action bringing at most coordination and sharing of experience.

This is not surprising. The second transitional stage of bringing changes in culture and organisation requires investing time and resources and a refocusing of energy. ACL and VCS bodies need to meet existing commitments and targets on tight budgets. They cannot commit massive resources to build and test new parallel ICT-based systems in the way for example that Las Vegas-based MGM Mirage, a multinational leisure and casino conglomerate in the private sector, has done in the Isle of Man so that it can implement offshore online gambling.[169]

Importance of technologies for networking and support

Despite limited resources, the achievements and innovation within the sector are considerable. The most important area has been in using new technologies for networking, communication and mutual support, where 'dot-orgs' can gain considerable benefits without high risks to their financial stability.[170]

National representative bodies for technology centres have been set up in both Canada and the US. The CTC Network, supported by the Educational Development Center and its *America Connects* consortium, has brought together over 750 technology and related centres and reinforces this national affiliation with regional groupings offering training, conferences and advice.

Strong 'anchor' organisations like Compumentor in San Francisco and Seattle Council's Department of Information Technology often provide the 'glue' to ensure these are effective at sharing and promoting good practice. In Canada the Victoria and Vancouver Community Networks have been able to play a similar role in support of Telecommunities Canada and the CAP network of centres, which hold national and provincial conferences and training activities.

Compumentor's *techsoup* online technical magazine and Bay Area News-letter, Seattle's *Brainstorm*, the Commonwealth Broadband Collaborative in Boston and the CTC Net advice centre, downloadable toolkits and server-based expert demonstrations are all practical examples of this sharing of experience and information. They have helped to shape a more informed constituency of staff and volunteers, which is able to argue the case and lobby legislators about action at state and federal level – to reduce the digital divide, to put pressure on telecommunications companies to finance community ICT infrastructure in return for cable licenses and to gain corporate support for consortia proposals.

The capacity to organise and maintain web-based services of this nature – automated responses to registrations, rendering a programme of courses to a website, maintaining an online discussion forum, video-streaming live content and running a listserv or mailing list – all require sophisticated technical and networking skills. In this respect there is a stronger and more widespread 'indigenous' skills base in the informal PSE sector in North America than in the UK. This is primarily because of the longer experience of the Community Networks and because the web-based world has expanded and matured more quickly in North America and especially the USA, than anywhere else.

There can for example be few countries in the world where a company would display an advertisement like the one opposite, seen in San Francisco in 2002, in the certain knowledge that it would be understood by most who read it.[171]

Despite the lure of the dot-com boom, the non-profit and PSE sector remained an attractive and stimulating working environment for considerable numbers of 'tech-savvy' individuals; and after the dot-com collapse in 2000 was being actively targeted in San Francisco by redundant technical staff in search of work.[172]

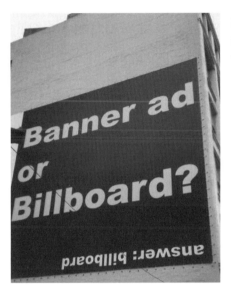

Figure 10. San Francisco hoarding in 2002.

UK comparisons and examples

Although Government policies in the UK have led to a mushrooming of ICT centres, networked libraries, digital e-learning projects and support for e-enabling the ACL sector through NIACE's e-Guides and TrEACL programmes, there remains a distance to travel to catch up with the position in North America in terms of technical and ILT skills. Nor is there an independent UK movement or membership organisation like CTC Net in the US and the CAP Net in Canada, which is able to represent and lobby for funding and policy changes. The University for Industry (Ufl) however through its promotion of Learndirect courses[173] has taken on the role of providing support for UK online centres in order to help develop them into a sustainable network. This will be reinforced through the *DirectSupport Online* website, where an *Experts Online* service is also provided, and by the *Help is at Hand* service.[174]

The other major player in the UK is Becta – an agency comparable in some respects to the US Education Development Center (see page 78) – which has a wide remit from the DfES to support the development and use of ILT across all schools, FE and ACL. Its resource exchange and aclearn.net website, together with its mailing lists – attracting by 2006 almost 1000 registered users – have played a significant role in spreading good practice within ACL.

Networking and collaboration were certainly evident in North America on cross-sector, regional and national bases, led by some of the larger bodies and Community Networks already described. It was apparent too where IT centres, neighbourhood centres, libraries and colleges planned their provision of ICT courses jointly. But cases of using web-based technologies for improving and transforming whole organisational structures and processes in post-school education and ACL were rare.

Online services point a way forward

The LILA Project in Los Angeles (see page 83) and the COOL project in Ontario (see page 92) were two interesting examples of creating collaborative communities of practice, which involved individuals or organisations inputting information to create publicly accessible registries with the former mapping this to existing GIS datasets for the benefit of disabled users across a wide area. UK parallels can be seen with work being carried out in Manchester and elsewhere.[175]

The Manchester Community Information Network (MCIN) provides training to activists from local groups to populate and update neighbourhood-based community information portals with details of their own activities.[176] In the ACL sector the WEA Community Grid for Learning (CGfL) piloted in 2004 the development of two new web-based services. Firstly, in partnership with the examinations body, Edexcel, CGfL can now offer online assessment remotely to learners for the Government's Level 1 and Level 2 Adult Certificates (see Figure 11) at any pre-designated site using a dedicated server with immediate and personalised feedback of results.[177]

Secondly, CGfL has created pilot interactive training modules on lesson planning and learner support, which new WEA tutors will have to

Figure 11. Results of first CGfL Level 2 assessment for learner on Employer Training Programme.

Passmark for this Exam (Literacy 2) = 27							
Candidate	Raw Mark (Stage 1)	Marking (Stage 2)	Indicator	Tracking Status	Candidate No.	Centre Reference	Void Status
Lucy xxxx	30	30	PASS	3	Q113xxx		---

All marks are provisional, the final result is that received by certificate from the exam board. All marks shown online are subject to correction and changes to the marking schemes.

complete online as part of their induction. In 2006 this has been linked to a 7407 tutor training programme, run nationally by the WEA across the country. These two services are very attractive to a dispersed VCS body with 600 part time tutors operating in 250 venues. They can save time, reduce administration and have the potential for wider roll out across the whole WEA.

Use of the web enables richness and reach

Like other innovatory practice described above in this chapter, these examples encapsulate the new paradigm of the web. Instead of the old model where extending operations required a thinner offer and/or higher costs, web-based technologies can provide both richness and reach *and* cost savings at the same time. As the system is scaled up, the costs and effort of deploying training for 1000 tutors is scarcely more than it is for 10 tutors.[178]

The process of introducing these changes is not however simple for existing organisations with their legacy systems and attitudes geared to traditional ways of operating. Budgets have to be managed and re-directed to invest in new infrastructure and equipment and this can have a knock-on effect on other areas of their work. This can be seen with the UK Pubic Libraries, where expenditure on IT systems has been accompanied by a reduction of spending on books. It is evident however that much can be achieved through adopting an open mind and securing advances initially through small steps, which are recognised as bringing value throughout the organisation.

Obstacles to innovation

The biggest impediment comes from the attitudes of staff and members, particularly those in a leadership or senior position. Two small but significant examples of where a positive stance was not adopted came from the UK. In the first a local authority suspended a member of staff simply for sending a personal email while at work. In the second a senior member of staff of an adult education body prevented email addresses being collected from students on the grounds that firstly it would breach the Data Protection Act – despite the fact that far more intrusive personal information was already being collected – and that secondly it would infringe equal opportunities policies. A more frequent kind of barrier experienced is indifference, fuelled often by a lack of knowledge.

These kinds of attitudes have a twofold effect: they dampen the energy and enthusiasm of the early adopters and provide comfort to those others in the organisation who wish to protect their practices against change. The message they receive is: '*Innovators keep away*'. The result if unchecked is that the former group is likely to move, leaving the organisation with less capability to tackle the tasks needed to respond to the changing external environment.

None of this should come as a surprise. It is all part of the hurly burly of organisational politics to be found in public and corporate life. The point is nicely illustrated in an article about the methods employed by Bill Bratton, New York's 'zero tolerance' Commissioner of Police to introduce innovation. As a young officer in Boston, Massachusetts, he had posted a brash sign in his office about youth and skill always winning through against age and treachery and found himself shunted into the sidelines as a result. 'He never again', the authors noted, 'forgot the importance of understanding the plotting, intrigue and politics involved in pushing through change'.[179]

In addition to these internal impediments there are numerous external obstacles. Some have been described already including the opposition to modernisation and computers in some Canadian rural communities experienced by the Oxford County Library service. There are other examples elsewhere.[180]

3. Features of the most ICT adept organisations

A variety of organisations have been covered for this study and inevitably their strategies differed. Some were part of large statutory agencies, others were small VCS bodies. Some were operating at a national or regional level, while others were small community-based organisations. Perhaps most significantly established or 'incumbent' and start up or 'insurgent' organisations were examined and compared.[181] The former, whether companies, ACL providers or VCS bodies have the disadvantage of legacy systems; those working within them, who seek change, face the 'innovator's dilemma' because most organisations resist altering what has worked well for them in the past.[182]

The start-ups do not suffer this disadvantage and can afford to embrace the new without fear of threatening any status quo. Their challenge is to raise their profile and break into new areas without the benefit of long-standing networks and without an existing base of users loyal to the brand or organisation. Most start-ups in the non-profit sector have very limited resources at initial launch.[183]

If they get the formula right, start-ups can enjoy rapid growth, as can be seen with Internet success stories in the private sector like Google, eBay[184] and Travelscape or in the community-based sector like Compumentor and Craigslist, the San Francisco-based postings service. Launched in 1995 by Craig Newmark, the latter now operates in 35 countries and monthly has six million classified ads, ten million users, one million forum postings and three billion page views.[185]

Top 10 organisational rules to maximise impact

Change is impacting upon many areas and sectors and technology developments are moving at great speed. In this environment the astute head of an adult education, library or VCS organisation needs to con-sider the internet as an opportunity and focus on how his or her organisation should engage with it to improve and transform their services to meet changing needs.

Having a vision of what that transformed future would look like and selling the need for change to the staff and members is an important early step, but more than this is required to reach a successful outcome. Whilst recognising that there will be differences in focus, we list below 10 commonalities that characterise those e-enabled organisations effective in adapting to the Information Society and harnessing the power of new technology. These features are key to effective institutional development and are expanded upon in the remainder of the subsection. In summary the adept organisation:

1   Ensures its aims and objectives are forwarded by the use of IT
2   Is aware of the broad Information Society and funding context
3   Involves itself in effective networking and alliances
4   Understands the nature and value of creating social capital
5   Has tolerance of uncertainty and is entrepreneurial in its outlook
6   Can assess and take risks in pursuit of transformation
7   Recruits, empowers and retains good staff
8   Has a strategy for supporting staff including its innovators
9   Is of relevance to the needs of the wider community
10   Has strong technical capacity to support online services

Subservience of IT to the overall mission

The initial first rule for achieving any successful implementation is to ensure that technology is subservient to the overall vision. It has to be used to support the aims and objectives of the organisation.[186] As George Gundrey from Compumentor put it: 'Always view the technology as a means to an end, rather than the end in itself'.[187] The point may seem obvious, but there are many stories of equipment purchased which remains shelf-bound or underused because this principle has not been applied. As a start the writing of a plan and strategy document helps to concentrate on the key issues and purpose. But it is apparent that an organisation has to do much more than this alone in order to deliver an effective overall ICT or ILT strategy which matches its needs.

Broad awareness of context and funding

It is essential to have a good awareness of the broad economic and social context affecting the educational and skills sector and an understanding of the thrust and shifting emphases of a range of policies, including the strong drive for individual empowerment and digital inclusion. Coupled with this is the need for up-to-date intelligence about Government programmes and alternative private sector and charitable funding with which to invest in equipment and infrastructure and in the longer term to ensure sustainability. Funding indeed was a key strategic concern of all interviewed during the research and extensive knowledge had been built up about this by the most adept.[188]

Crucial role of networking

This knowledge of a new, fast changing and complex external environment is critical. It points to the need for effective networking for those organisations aiming to plug their work into the Information Society world; and when the knowledge base is particularly hard to understand or there are emerging technologies, collaboration and alliances are even more vital. A good example of this can be seen with the DfES 2002 wireless networks initiative in the UK. Several applicants had not understood the nature of the technology and had to be rejected at the first hurdle as they did not meet the criteria.[189]

The DfES case study (page 50) is a clear illustration too of the cross-border cross-institutional nature of networking. Advice and information was being sought by the DfES from the USA and from institutions and educational bodies all over the UK because networking is as important for policy makers as it is for ACL bodies and the VCS. In her book *Building the Virtual State*, Jane Fountain relates this process to the changing nature of bureaucracy and its contemporary context and notes that studies of policy making have shown that: '. . . networks of actors across agencies and in the non-profit and private sectors are more central to policy making than formalised governance structures alone . . . and that the state is organised as policy networks'.[190]

Locking into and/or creating these kind of networks is the single most significant hallmark of the IS adept or capable organisation and illustrations can be found from those surveyed in both Canada and the US. Close links at local, provincial and national level could be seen in Canada in the case of the Community Networks and the Oxford Library Service in Ontario; and were reflected in their involvement with schemes promoted by Industry Canada and HRDC and with bodies like Canarie and the Office of Learning Technologies.

Exploring new frontiers and new terrain

In the US alliances between CTC Net, the Benton Foundation, the Children's Partnership and inter-denominational and ethnic groupings on issues affecting children, access to IT and cable franchising had had significant effects on policy and funding decisions at national level. At a city and metropolitan level there was evidence of effective networking alliances operating in the three main conurbations visited – Seattle, San Francisco and Boston. These were helping to bring public, private sector and foundation resources, skilled staff and innovatory practice into the areas but had three different types of organisation as the guiding or dominant influence – Compumentor in San Francisco, the City Council in Seattle, and the University of Massachusetts and its CPCS Department in Boston. In all these cases there was willingness to cross frontiers, explore new terrain and migrate experience between sectors.

Creating social capital

The product of this networking – described by social scientists as 'social capital' – has value and needs nurturing. Its underlying components are trust, reputation and shared values. It contributes to organisational effectiveness, improves performance and is an essential ingredient in building the economic capacity of localities, cities and regions.[191]

While social capital brings wider community benefits, organisations at the centre of networks or with most links and relationships were best able to influence and ratchet up added value; and in a similar way those individuals within organisations who have cross-professional personal contacts and inter-disciplinary networks, accrue power and the ability to broker deals and help forge new alliances. These can add value to what would otherwise be disparate elements, orchestrated separately by say a public sector institution, a university, a technology start-up, a VCS body or ICT centre. Each can bring something to the table, the value of which is augmented through collaboration.

Examples of this can be seen with the use of GIS data with farmers in Oxford County in Ontario, the provision to non-profits of low cost software by Compumentor in San Francisco, student intern schemes like the CTC Vista project, the 3-D modelling project involving youngsters from the Yesler Center in Seattle with the University of Washington and the creation of the www.contentbank.org website by the Children's Partnership.

Pursuing transformation while responding to uncertainty

Successfully innovative organisations must therefore be outward looking as they seek to change their organisational practice and culture. But there are also internal features which will predispose them towards effective engagement with the Information Society. There needs to be willingness to live with a degree of uncertainty about the future as it is impossible to predict how new technical developments and policies will impact in say 18 months time.

An entrepreneurial culture is also needed where new opportunities are sought which tie back to the overall vision and are supported by the leadership. Where the organisation in question − say a local ICT centre − is part of a larger institution, it is important that full support is gained from the parent body. This was not always the case from the experience in North America and the UK.

The ability to assess risk and the taking of calculated risk in support of innovation are key features. With this comes the possibility of failure, from which as much can be learnt as it can from success. Case studies of what has not worked are rarely written but can be valuable for others and funding bodies should be encouraged to acknowledge this.

Staffing strategies for maintaining impetus

The organisation itself has to be relatively stable, which in turn enables it to recruit, motivate and retain good staff with appropriate skills and attitudes. Empowering staff to take action within a system of trust is usually more effective than a tight system of management control. There was evidence too from the interviews of the importance of the 'enthusiastic individual' in introducing innovation and persuading others to follow. Capitalising upon these innovator assets, while offering support for other staff and gaining wider buy-in is part of a necessary management balancing act. Staff and members need to have a sense of ownership and commitment to the direction being taken.

Community relevance and support for individuals

Ensuring that the work being carried out by the ICT centre, VCS body, adult education or library service is of relevance to and meeting the needs of the wider community enhances the chances of overall success and of gaining internal support. A key component here is a focus on developing users' self-confidence and their ability to construct their own progression goals.

The place of technology and technical staff

Emphasis has been placed in this sub-section on organisational, management, staffing and cultural aspects of introducing new technology, because these are throwing up the hardest problems for educational managers and innovators to solve. The acknowledged capacity of technology to alter, subvert, extend, enrich and generally revolutionise all that we do should not however induce us to ignore it in a discussion of success factors for developing e-learning!

The core of the argument is that its use and introduction has to be managed; and the skill is to marry the technology with the learning, so that the technology serves the underlying aims. To achieve this goal, organisations need strong technical capacity either in-house or in a close partner body. Staff with the ability to apply their technical and networking skills are essential for any Information Society-capable body. They are a cornerstone feature for achieving the implementation of any technical solution to a problem, can help other staff to think laterally about issues and can help the organisation assess new developments and relate to possible technology alliances.

4. Use of new technology for teaching and learning

The focus of attention in all three countries with respect to adult learning has been since the late 1990s on laying down an infrastructure and installing equipment in community-based ICT centres. In the search to widen participation in the Information Society and address the issues of social exclusion and the digital divide, the host organisations were chosen primarily because of their being embedded in communities. They were close to local neighbourhoods and disadvantaged groups.

Experience of running courses and wider curriculum issues was not essential as it was assumed that other bodies like schools, colleges and libraries would be able to provide the staffing to support this.[192] In many cases the initial target outputs for the centres were expressed in terms of local residents attending the centre and using a computer. As programmes developed both in North America and the UK, there was greater recognition of the important link between IT skills and numeracy and literacy skills.

For the most part however the bulk of provision to be found in the majority of community technology and ICT access centres, libraries and in many colleges has been focused on acquiring basic skills of word processing, using spreadsheets and web searching. More advanced courses were being offered by some centres and colleges in webpage construction, desktop publishing and multimedia, but primarily the emphasis remained on specific PC-related or technical skills.

Integration of technology initially given low priority

Integrating technology more widely into teaching and learning across the whole curriculum has not therefore been a high priority either in North America or in the UK in this first phase, although there have been important exceptions. Nor is the position so very different in further education or higher education, where there has been far more and earlier investment in equipment than in ACL and informal community settings. This position is starting to change in the UK and is reflected in the UfI's Learndirect programme, in the widespread piloting of learning platforms in ACL and in recent JISC publications on learning platforms and effective and innovative practice with e-learning (including the use of mobile and wireless technologies).[193]

Commenting on 'the gap between the hardware heap and people's willingness and ability to use it', the Times Educational Supplement quoted the UK Minister for Adult Skills: 'If you go into schools and colleges, you will be impressed with the ICT kit – the level of investment has been substantial. But in too many institutions, it has still not been central to teaching as much of the curriculum as it should be.'[194]

Figure 12. The global café – green tea at 10,000 feet in the world's deepest gorge above the Yangtze River in SW Yunaan, China. Mobile phone, Blackberry and digital camera enable instant phone calls, emails and photo transfer from the Himalaya to London, New York and Toronto.

While it is important to develop and encourage the technical skills, embedding and innovation in their use takes much longer to achieve and requires continuing support. Generalising about the experience of UK higher education at a 2004 online conference, Grainne Conole concluded in a keynote paper: '. . . the reality is that e-learning is still marginal in the lives of most academics, with technology being used for little more than content repository and administration.'[195]

The potential of the technology to revolutionise the way teaching and learning are conducted – including its use online and at a distance – and to change the skill sets required of a tutor is huge and a glimpse of this can be seen in a 1998 future-gazing WEA-NW proposal for tutor training (see opposite). Technology poses tough challenges both to the institutions and to teachers and tutors, because old ways have to be dismantled and new ways substituted.

Planning for the use of information and communication technologies for teaching and learning

The WEA and other institutions offering lifelong learning must plan now to equip themselves and their staff for the future. The adult tutor of the 21st century must anticipate that her students will expect the same kind of ICT facilities as are now widely available to students in higher education and will be common in five years time in schools; and that there will be a percentage of students who will be wanting to access remotely online learning via in-home or community-access facilities. She will have to be conversant with these new norms and have a basic understanding of the direction and potential of digital technology. She will have to be aware of how the student can be helped to extend the frontiers of his knowledge and how she in turn can use ICT to assess his progress and provide advice and support for further study.

A model tutor of the Information Age taking a class in Manchester in the year 2002 might want to use a notebook and modem to do one or all of the following:

- search a website in Chicago or Delhi
- send an email to a research institute in Oxford
- download data from a web server in Helsinki or Harare
- mediate a web-based discussion forum from her Bolton home
- publish online material for students in Salford, Paris or Caracas
- use videoconferencing for a city-ports project with Antwerp
- file a digital photo of environmental evidence from Moston
- swap files of comparative material with a tutor in Sydney
- advise a student from a Learndirect site in London
- check out availability of a book in Edinburgh

And importantly she will show and support her students so that they can apply this same dexterity themselves and independently access net-based learning resources for their research and project assignments. But this model tutor will only be able to emulate the global networked society that we are now living in, if educational institutions provide the space to develop these new skills and ways of working.

(Extract from WEA 1998 future-gazing funding application)

In these circumstances Kevin Kelly counsels that 'letting go at the top is an act not against perfection, but against short-sightedness' and that it is often easier to start afresh because skill guilds constrain (and defend) an organisation.[196] While Kelly's advice is aimed at the corporate sector, his 'new rules' have a resonance with ACL and in particular with current theories about the role of teachers and how adults learn. Hase and Kenyon[197] for instance in an extension of the theories of Rogers (1951), Knowles (1970) and others have argued that what is important is not so much the acquiring of skills and knowledge, but developing the fundamental skill of knowing how to learn.[198]

In this heutagogical model of learning, the focus is on promoting self-determined and self-directed learning as the only way that the individual will be able to cope with the pace of change and innovation which characterises the Information Society. The Delta[3] laptop scheme introduced at Sheridan College, Ontario (page 85) was an imaginative and well-resourced programme – at the heart of a whole college re-engineering process – which was putting these principles into practice. Not only was it directly enabling the students to become active self-directed learners, but it was also changing the culture of the organisation and the role of the teacher 'at the top'.

The innovating teachers were setting new standards, to which their colleagues felt obliged to rise in order to retain their professional credibility. A parallel example of peer pressure in bringing institutional change was described by a former college lecturer in the UK over the use of Virtual Learning Environments (VLE): 'Learners at my previous institution were starting to complain when one of their teachers was making good use of a VLE, with material online and good communications, whilst another was not making any use at all.'[199]

Focus on self-directed learning

Within the informal community learning sector in North America the push to encourage self-directed learning could be seen in the Educational Center's promotion of best practice briefs like that on project-based learning and in much of the material on www.contentbank.org. This includes an online exchange on issues like e-government and usability; and has a focus on tools and application reviews for content creation software[200], diaries and blogs.[201]

In the Asian tsunami disaster in December 2004, blogs came of age as a source of breaking news and are now a big US growth area. They have potential for extended use in ACL in the UK.[202] Other good examples of the focus on student learning can be seen in the growth of podcasting and the development of toolkits like Webquest and Quandary, which can be used by tutors to encourage active engagement by students. The Webquest idea was conceived by Bernie Dodge from San Diego University, California in 1995 and is widely used in the States.[203] An ACL version was developed by Becta in 2005 and is now promoted through the aclearn.net site.[204]

The promotion of communication by and with students is an important ingredient for encouraging active and self directed learning and offers a way of testing, questioning and challenging one's own and others' views and perspectives. These are characteristics of the traditional face-to-face class or discussion group. Replicating these online through CMC (computer mediated communication) is not however easy even at undergraduate level as it requires both practical word processing skills and equally important the confidence to submit inchoate and often provisional thoughts to unknown others.

Rogers argued that for learning to take place most effectively, minimising the threat to 'self' is important. Launching a question or comment through CMC can be seen as a risky and dangerous activity, which induces many to remain as non-participating 'lurkers'. Ensuring the use of an online discussion forum requires therefore persistent prompting and encouragement by the tutor. This can be greatly assisted by the students already knowing each other through face-to-face conventional classes, as was occurring successfully with the Oxford County computer skills chat board, where answers were quickly given by the tutors to the students' questions.

Changing practice, responding to new imperatives

The research has supported evidence elsewhere of the importance of providing tutors space to change their practice. This could mean development time to explore with others how blended and 'bundled' learning could be incorporated into existing lesson planning; and how their time could be spent in other ways to the benefit of learners if their period in direct contact with current students was being reduced or the nature of the relationship was being altered.

While all will recognise the importance and value of the direct tutor-student relationship, it is bought at too high a price if it is not widely available. Brenda Gourley, Vice-Chancellor of the Open University has noted: 'We cannot provide it to millions of people who for various reasons are unable to avail themselves of it. The fact is we have to find a way to extend the real benefits of education to many, many more people.'[205] While she may have been referring in her lecture to higher education, the argument about reach applies *a fortiori* to ACL, where four out of five people in the UK in any one year do not identify themselves as learners. The task now is to embed the technology firmly in practice so that a more inclusive and flexible curriculum is offered to meet the needs of those at present outside the learning pale.

5. Potential for technology transfer and migration

The fifth research objective was established in order to assess the extent to which technology transfer schemes through university-community links and cross-sector partnerships might help to disseminate good practice and to compensate for the low level of investment in the ACL and community sector; and to explore the conditions which would favour this.

Influence of EU telematics programmes in the 1990s

In the UK in the early and mid 1990s several EU programmes like Delta (1992) and the Telematics Applications Progamme (1994) were providing opportunities for universities in particular to set up innovative leading edge e-learning and e-community projects and in a number of cases ACL and VCS bodies were drawn in as partners. Examples in which the WEA took part were the RATIO Project run by the University of Plymouth and the Dearne Valley Project run by the University of Sheffield. In the north-west the WEA received valuable support and advice from Manchester Computing at the University of Manchester for several initiatives through its involvement in a cross-European *Infocities*

Project; and subsequently from Liverpool John Moores University in the piloting of some e-learning materials in 2002 in the exploratory stages of its CGfL programme.[206]

Without exception these early 1990s initiatives were all supported through EU funding.[207] With deep pockets, high-end research skills, broadband networks and advanced technical know-how, higher education and research institutions were the key players to move these EU-inspired IS initiatives forward. They needed partners either as a condition of receiving grant or to implement the project. Thus the seeds were sown for some cross-fertilisation of ideas and practice about technology migration and application in different environments. There are now though less incentives of this nature and the level of technology transfer from UK research institutions and HE into community-based activities is declining. With a deepening funding crisis, the focus in universities has moved to science parks, incubator units and spin-offs and hi-tech alliances with the corporate sector, which promise a more lucrative return on their efforts.[208]

North American experience

How is the position different in North America where there has been no external EU funding source to encourage partnerships? The survey carried out was not comprehensive, but indicated that in many areas both in the US and in Canada, the interconnectedness of the university with the community led the former to encourage linkages and seek to transfer its experience into practical schemes of benefit to local people and businesses. This is well illustrated with the Alliance for Community Technology, established as a partnership, led by the University of Michigan with support from the Kellogg Foundation.[209] In many ways the offer of matching federal or other grants has acted in North America as a similar incentive to that found with EU monies in the UK.

The assistance of the University of Waterloo with Oxford County's COOL project and UCLA's endorsement of the LILA scheme for the disabled are good examples of this creative interaction. An interesting feature in both cases was the use of Geographical Information Systems (GIS) for community mapping projects. The potential for applying GIS for socially useful purposes like environmental surveys, hazard and pollution control, community safety and land and building usage was being explored in several areas by CTCs and other community-based organisations and could offer a rich vein for future UK community development and capacity building schemes.

In the UK use of GIS is being developed by some local authorities like Huntingdonshire District Council[210] and through some interesting work undertaken by the Orange mobile telecoms company with a think-tank Proboscis on *Urban Tapestries* in London.[211]

Integrating volunteering schemes into the HE curriculum

The most significant feature of the US scene however was the incorporation of community volunteering into the university curriculum, which could take different forms, including internships, financial assistance, local arrangements such as the one in Seattle with the University of Washington and full scale programmes like the VISTA scheme run by the University of Massachusetts.

This emphasis reflected prevailing attitudes in the US about the need for university-community links. Importantly it is also reinforced by the credit accumulation and transfer systems adopted by the HE institutions, which gives incentives to students to volunteer their time and skills to local CTCs and others by attributing specified credits for the completion of agreed commitments.

Change needed in UK attitudes to community engagement

In the UK HEFCE runs a small scheme to promote volunteering, but it is viewed as a marginal activity by most universities and commitment is limited. One notable exception to this is the University of Central Lancashire, a former polytechnic, which remains active in this area and has been closely involved in the IN2IcT project in the Pendle and Burnley area. This is a partnership with the Coldwell Activity Centre and the Edge End Hill School[212] with a focus on community cohesion through digital film-making.

The issue of volunteering was examined in the UK by the Russell Commission in 2005.[213] A recommendation from this body that universities and higher education adopt a similar credit framework to that supporting engaged volunteering in the US could have had a marked impact in fostering technology transfer for social inclusion, in raising the profile and status of community technology posts for graduate recruitment and in increasing the return on investment from the high levels of public expenditure on community-based public infrastructure. Unfortunately no such recommendation was made although consideration will be given to promoting inter alia full time volunteering similar to that developed through the US Americorps programme.

6. Strategies for community capacity building and promoting IS skills

It is twelve years since the US Commerce Department's NTIA sponsored with the Cleveland Freenet an online conference on universal internet access in support of the Clinton Administration's National Performance Review. Although major strides have been made, there remains a big lag in the extent to which the populations in all three countries have incorporated the Information Society into their thinking and the skills for it into their everyday lives.

In discussing her work on technology and human vulnerability, Sherry Turkle quotes the case of the student who describes his experience of having a portable web connected computer with him 24/7: 'I become my computer. It is not just that I know more or remember people better. I feel invincible, sociable, better prepared. I am naked without it. With it I am a better person.'[214]

Although this may accurately reflect the intense experience of a small number of over-dependent power users, for many older adults and those with lower skill levels, the description is of a world quite separate from their own experience. Yet Turkle's young student could become (with some support and training) the ideal model for the connected citizen or worker, able – whenever motivated – to take up services, access information, respond to enquiries and communicate deftly with his employer and others. He has in short both capability and choice.

Young people growing up with technology

He is not far away from a whole generation of ICT literate young people growing up with computer games and PCs wherever they turn, in a world which is constantly and rapidly evolving. The environment was portrayed in 2001 in this way: 'Kids are learning in front of technology all the time . . . TV, videos that is where things are coming from . . . kids are learning how to communicate with each other online and with staff. You can always get someone by email.'[215]

In discussing the new US online schools network directory, facebook.com, with its 3.5 million registered users, MSN's Newsweek was by 2005 describing the latest cohort of college students in these more active terms: 'They grew up digital: with PCs, broadband and cell phones at the ready. Likelier to reach for Google than for a dictionary, they live-journal their days and photoblog their snaps, trade music and swim in a sea of messages . . .'[216]

The opportunities in this context for ACL providers to reach out with new approaches and programmes, involving mobile learning or m-Learning for adults too, are substantial. In 2006 this potential was high-lighted by the announcement by Google of a deal with Motorola to make their search technology available to mobile phone users at the press of a button; and by Yahoo's plans to make their email, messaging and other services available via mobile phones and TV.[217]

In this whirlpool of activity, Turkle describes her purpose as 'to deeply understand the personal effects of the technology in order to make it better serve our human purposes'. Back in 1994 the NTIA recognised that in order for Governments to gain the fiscal and cost-cutting advantages of 'leveraging cyberspace' via online public services, which was their purpose, citizens had to be provided with opportunities to develop capability and exercise choice like these young students. As a result a raft of programmes and activities has been rolled out in neigh-bourhoods and local communities in this first phase to promote IT skills acquisition.

Spanning a continent

Examples of good work and of effective capacity building can be seen in centres and cities across North America – of initial IT skills being developed with Chinese communities in Vancouver, Horn of Africa immigrants in Seattle, First Nation groups in Canada and the US, Latinos in San Francisco, disabled groups in Los Angeles, young people in Boston, farmers in Ontario. Partnerships have been built and strategies developed by local councils and VCS bodies to generate interest and market the opportunities available. Sustaining the programmes has been difficult, but there has been commitment and enthusiasm and to date funding has mostly been found and enough staffing and volunteering to prevent centres and schemes from collapsing.

A similar position can be seen in the UK, with IT-based learning opportunities attracting new learners and spawning a new vocabulary and exciting practice in UK online centres and elsewhere. For some like the man who dropped in to a Manchester centre 14 months ago and whose experience is described in the vignette overleaf, the centres have opened up whole new personal horizons.

DirectGov services and community intermediaries

Yet as we now enter in the UK a second phase after the laying down of an infrastructure, there remain many who have little or no engagement with computers, mobile phones or other features of the IS revolution. There is a need too for individuals to be gaining more advanced net-working and netmedia skills, which can support new digital industries and generate jobs. In this new phase there will also be a major push to promote the use of Government and Council DirectGov services. There are demanding targets for participation to be met through the ODPM's Implementing Electronic Government (IEG) system as well as a require-ment for these services to be socially inclusive.

VCS bodies and ICT centres can play a key role here developing capacity and skills within local communities, as was recognised in a 2005 report on UK Online centres,[218] but the funding and support framework can only be provided by Government and public bodies. This should be linked to promoting third sector bodies as trusted intermediaries[219] to drive up the use of DirectGov services.[220] This is starting to happen in the US as a 2004 Pew internet study showed. But it revealed also that those with internet access are far more likely to make contact with Government than those without.[221]

UK policies for the Information Society were set out with clarity and logic in 1999–2000 (see Figure 4, page 45) and need now to be re-focused in a unified e-strategy for the next five years. An enabling e-democracy will bring together the worlds of work, learning, community and public services, but to achieve this Government has to orchestrate the different activities required to cope with a fast changing e-environment.

Online and e-learning will be a growing and important part of the transformation and this will intensify. There cannot be one model alone however for engaging with reluctant and disadvantaged learners as the case study below shows.

Community learning and skills for life

Tony Bowden knows where he is going and the reason for this is Gorton North UK Online Centre in East Manchester. A former postman, he's been a regular there for the last 14 months and it has changed his life. 'The more you do, the more you learn', says Tony. 'If people get interested, they will want to find out more. You can give them CLAIT or ECDL or whatever, but if they aren't interested, they won't come back.'

Life has not been easy for Tony. In 1999 he was attacked in the street – in a case of mistaken identity – by two assailants with a broken bottle and received multiple injuries to his head and back. He returned to work too early and eventually had to retire on health grounds while still in his mid-forties. He had had an interest in his family history since 1996, when he was told he was to receive a legacy via the descendant of an uncle in Australia; and had started to do some research about Manchester policemen.

When he came to the Gorton centre, he did a course on

Photoshop and a Surf Direct course and hasn't looked back. In the summer he started as a volunteer, helping people with email, internet searching and instant messaging. After he'd signed off and gone on the dole, the job shop suggested a short course on Setting up a Business, which he completed. After that he became at Gorton and two other centres a paid adviser – from the community and working in the community.

'I only learn what I need to. I haven't time for learning things which aren't relevant. The important thing is to get the people of Gorton using the computers', says Tony, but it just so happens that along the way he's learnt about image manipulation, file and document management, publishing, how to work with others in a team and how to assess the needs of new users – all significant and transferable skills for any job.

He has also negotiated via email with the Commonwealth War Graves Commission over a publicity story they have run about his students, who have been accessing the CWGC website and developing their own research skills.

It's a success story for Tony, for the Gorton North Centre and for the self-directed kind of community learning, which UK Online centres can offer. 'What's the secret?' he was asked. 'It was when I was with my daughter' he answered. 'I found then how easy it is to teach people if they are interested. You just have to find out their needs.'

Source: Tony Bowden interviewed by the author, 3 December 2004.

Work in UK online centres and targeted community provision of the type run by the WEA and ACL bodies in many areas, whilst often not resulting immediately in a Level 2 certificate, can effectively hook adults into new learning pathways and provide them with a first rung and the ICT skills needed for the Information Society. The programmes delivered play an important role in economic regeneration and skills development for the knowledge economy, but remain vulnerable to the vicissitudes of insecure and short term funding regimes.

This needs to change if the value of the work in widening participation and starting disadvantaged adults on their learning journey is to be maximised. This could be achieved by setting quality standards for this kind of provision and then funding the programmes and centres meeting the standards. Monitoring could be light for those demonstrating effective systems of quality assurance.

Integrating these community-based and VCS organisations into a wider institutional framework for learning and skills would bring substantial gains, as has been recognised to some extent by the UK Government in committing to the *Futurebuilders* and *ChangeUp* programmes in support of the sector. Capacity building in local communities is more than just providing a course for individual learning, but helps develop projects and collective solutions to problems which have a wider impact on the lives, work and opportunities of local residents.

Inclusion through innovation

In the context of current discussions about women and childcare, it is possible to see that a DirectGov/community solution could be found for the childcare challenge outlined in the case study opposite. Equally, community-based ICT centres could help to set up socially useful schemes involving transport, the local environment and the needs of disadvantaged groups. There is a rich area here for the future.

Upskilling nations is a multi-faceted long haul task. The issue of digital exclusion remains firmly on the agenda, as the Social Exclusion Unit's 2005 Final Report and Action Plan on New Technologies, *Inclusion through Innovation* indicated,[222] because changing cultures takes time. We need to learn from and transfer good practice and take account of cultural differences. The North America experience shows that a range of imaginative schemes for community renewal and developing skills can provide space for innovation and motivating individuals. The process of change has to be sustained and funded over the long term if we are to avoid a growing divide between those able to grasp the shape of an Information Society future and those resisting it without any alternative. This is a challenge to all of us.

A technology challenge for community capacity building

Women, IT and childcare – if not now, then when?

In February 1888 Jane Davies, a Manchester woman from Newton Heath with young children, won a small skirmish in the struggle for the rights of working women. Fined 14 shillings – the equivalent of two weeks wages – for not notifying her employer that she was ill, she challenged the decision. In reviewing her case, which was at bottom about balancing the needs of the economy and the family, the magistrates judged that she had been unfairly treated. At 5.30 in the morning her husband, who needed to get to work, could only have concentrated on arranging care for their children.

The problems faced by Jane Davies have not disappeared. Could technology play a significant part in helping to meet the needs of both employers and working women in areas like Manchester, where almost 40 per cent of children are brought up in single parent households? Margaret Grieco has argued that it could. A networked PC would enable a single mother to send an email to her employer and book a stand-by worker from a replacement worker service.

Could alternative childcare also be arranged when a child was sick? This would be difficult if the carer was unknown to the child but could small groups of parents be linked together with SMS texts sent from the PC asking if assistance could be given? None of these arrangements exist now, but they could be put in place. Given the current interest in meeting the needs of working women, what would need to be done to create a viable scheme?

Sources: Harford, I. (1994) *Manchester and its Ship Canal Movement: Class, Work and Politics in Late-Victorian England*, Keele University Press, p.116; Grieco, M. (1998) *'Intelligent Development': Technical Organisation and Social policy in the New Millennium*. Lecture at University of North London.

Recommendations

This study has explored how new technologies are being deployed in North America and the UK to promote adult learning and skills for the Information Society and to develop capacity in local communities. It has considered the actions being taken by Governments, educational institutions and VCS bodies to tackle the issues of the digital divide. Much has been achieved, but technology moves fast and disrupts, often making obsolete equipment and practice only two or three years old.

Next generation applications will throw up new uses, which we have not anticipated. They also have the potential of solving real problems affecting significant numbers of people, of impacting with real benefit on disadvantaged groups and individuals. We need the will and resources to bring about change and specifically the willingness to cross borders, migrate experience, admit mutual ignorance and share good practice. The following recommendations are made in a spirit of cooperative endeavour.

Recommendation	Agency/Body
ACL – support and funding	
1 Create toolkits and guidance for ACL providers to show how new technologies could be introduced to improve and make more efficient and effective a range of functions like tutor training, course planning and marketing.	DfES, Becta, LSC, NIACE, QIA
2 Expand the staffing and resources available regionally to support ACL in its use and development of ILT.	DfES, LSC, JISC, RDAs
3 Explore mechanisms for creating regional and	DfES, LSC,

sub-regional agencies and e-repositories focusing
on support for content development and delivery,
personalisation and repurposing by ACL in pursuit
of skills and regeneration strategies.

RDAs, JISC,
QIA

4 Consider what changes are needed to existing
LSC and other funding regimes to ensure that
there are incentives for ACL and VCS providers
to create and offer short or 'bundled' e-learning
modules as part of a digital inclusion programme.

LSC, DfES,
NIACE, Becta

Libraries and digital literacy – linking with ACL

5 Promote more active collaboration between
local libraries and WEA and ACL providers over
use of equipment and digital resources, staff
training and curriculum development in context
of the DCMS Framework for the Future.

WEA, ACL,
DCMS, MLA,
Becta, Big
Lottery

Growing the Voluntary and Community Sector

6 Provide seed money for some pilot projects into
how VCS bodies and Community Grids for
Learning could act as trusted intermediaries in
promoting take up of DirectGov services in
association with local councils.

ODPM,
Treasury,
Big Lottery

7 Set up a scheme similar to the Canadian VolNet,
linked to the ChangeUp programme to
encourage small VCS bodies to obtain internet
connectivity, train staff and explore its use.

Treasury,
Home Office,
ACU, NCVO

UK online and community-based ICT work

8 Strengthen links between UK online centres and
WEA regions and ACL providers and encourage
the running of IT enhanced courses across the
curriculum.

WEA, ACL,
Ufl

9 Develop a kite-mark quality system for those
UK online and neighbourhood ICT centres and
Community Grids for Learning, which offer
community learning opportunities. Once assured,
these bodies could receive LSC and other funding

LSC, DfES,
ODPM, Becta,
NIACE, QIA

against agreed WP outputs and be subject to lighter monitoring.

10	Explore potential for volunteer IS gap or fellowship year akin to the US Vista scheme for graduates and others to support UK online and other centres – to be supported by a combination of Government, Foundation and corporate funding.	DfES, Home Office, Big Lottery, Foundations, SEU

Role for the WEA

11	Seek funding for a three year VCS 'think-tank' for promoting next generation content creation, organisational transformation and the application of ICT for Community Learning and Community Development in support of the Government's e-strategy and policies for skills development, digital inclusion and active citizenship.	WEA, HO/ACU, Big Lottery, NIACE SEU
12	Use the experience and networks of the WEA as a national provider to promote the learner's voice in this area; and actively to encourage the use of ILT in ACL through WEA practice, through encouraging research into its impact and heutagogical principles and through WEA alliances with other VCS bodies.	WEA, NIACE, NCVO, ALT-C, ESRC

Community development and capacity building

13	Promote more active deployment of GIS for community development activities (e.g. for disabled access, community safety, environmental support), drawing upon North American experience; and fund some CGfL or VCS led pilot schemes.	ODPM, Home Office, Big Lottery, SEU
14	Examine with the corporate sector, including IT companies, how they can work with ACL and the VCS to develop community capacity and more advanced IT skills acquisition for the IS; and help sustain local ICT and UK online centres.	DfES, Ufl, ODPM, Alliance for Digital Inclusion

HE and links with community learning

15 Investigate with ACL and the VCS how they can contribute to Government widening participation policies and relate to the Aim Higher HE programme; and establish targets and performance indicators for this.

DfES, LSC, WEA, ACL, NIACE, HEFCE

16 Encourage HE institutions to include student volunteering in community ICT centres and as community technologists as part of their credit frameworks for degrees.

Home Office, HEFCE, Russell Commission

Annexe I

Glossary

Acronym	Full title	Description
ACL	Adult and Community Learning	
Becta	British Educational and Communications Technology Agency	Becta has a remit to support the adoption of ILT across the schools and post 16 educational sector
CAP	Community Access Programme/Point	The Canadian scheme for IT centres
CGfL	Community Grid for Learning	The Greater Manchester CGfL was set up by the WEA and has a website www.learners.org.uk
CMS	Content Management Systems	
CRM	Customer Relationship Management	
CTC	Community Technology Center	The US term for IT centres
DEFRA	Department for Environment, Food and Rural Affairs	
DfES	Department for Education and Skills	
ECDL	European Computer Driving License	Qualification covering a wide range of IT skills
ERDF	European Regional Development Fund	Monies made available to member States for areas of economic and social need

FE	Further Education	
GIS	Geographical Information Systems	
HE	Higher Education	
HEFCE	Higher Education Funding Council for England	
HRDC	Human Resources Development Canada	
ICT	Information and Communication Technologies	
IS	Information Society	
ITLT	Information Technology for Learning and Teaching	
JISC	Joint Information Services Committee	Originally set up by HEFCE to oversee the provision of IT infrastructure and services for the HE sector. It now has FE representation as well.
LA	Local Authority	
LP	Learning Platform	See description for VLE below
LSC	Learning and Skills Council	47 local bodies (LSCs) are responsible for planning and funding post 16 learning
LSDA	Learning & Skills Development Agency	
MLA	Museums, Libraries and Archives Council	
NIACE	National Institute for Adult and Continuing Education	National body actively promoting the interests of adult learning and the use of new technologies
NLN	National Learning Network	Set up to promote the development of e-learning
NOF	New Opportunities Fund	

NTIA	National Telecommunications and Information Administration	Key US body set up in the early 1990s as part of the Commerce Department
PCMCIA	Personal Computer Memory Card International Association	This is a standard set for small credit card-sized devices called pc cards
PLC	Programmable logic controller	A device used to automate monitoring and control of industrial plants
PSE	Post-School Education	
QIA	Quality Improvement Agency	
RSC	Regional Support Centre	Set up by JISC to support regional ILT teams
RSS	Really Simple Syndication	A format used to syndicate content such as news or blog posts (RSS 'feeds') to another website or application – e.g. to a user's personalised webpage
SEU	Social Exclusion Unit	
UKERNA	United Kingdom Education and Research Networking Association	The body set up in 1994 by HEFCE to develop networking programme and services
URL	Universal Resource Locator	This is the address needed to locate a website
VCS	Voluntary and Community Sector	
VLE	Virtual Learning Environment	A Learning Platform, offering a range of functions, including hosting of interactive materials, tracking and monitoring
VOIP	Voice Over Internet Protocols	An emerging technology for communication
WEA	Workers' Educational Association	National charitable body providing ACL
WBT	Web-based technologies	
WWW	World Wide Web	

Annexe II

List of organisations visited as part of North America ICT research

City or Area	Name of organisation	Vol N/wrking Org	Community Based ICT	Govt/Semi-Quango	LA	Library Service	College	Univ	Corp	Funding Trusts
CANADA – West										
Vancouver	Vancouver Net	–								
Vancouver Isl	Comox Valley,Vancouver I	–								
Vancouver Isl	Victoria Com Net	–								
USA – West										
Seattle	Yesler Community Center		–		–					
Seattle	Chinese Inf & Service Center		–							
Seattle	Seattle Community Network	–	–							
Seattle	S. Seattle Community College						–			
Seattle	Seattle City Council				–					
Seattle	Seattle Libraries Dept					–				
Seattle	Avanade Inc								–	
Seattle	Gates Foundation									–
Seattle	Expedia Inc								–	
San Francisco	Compumentor	–								
San Francisco	Parental Stress Service	–								
San Francisco	Salesforce.com Foundation									–
Los Angeles	Children's Partnership	–								
Los Angeles	LILA Project (UCLA)	–						–		
USA – East										
Boston	Univ Mass/David Rosen							–		
Boston	Univ Mass/ABE/R Hooper							–		
Boston	Vista Project	–						–		
Boston	CTC Net	–								
Boston	Cambridge CCTV	–								
Newton, MA	America Connects Cons'tium			–						
CANADA – East										
Oakville	Sheridan College						–			
Ontario	Oxford County Library					–				
Ontario	OCL Training					–				
Ontario	OCL Cool					–				
Toronto	Industry Canada			–						
Toronto	Office of Learning Technologies			–						
Totals = 33		11	3	3	2	4	2	4	2	2

Annexe III
Photo gallery from North America
ICT research visits 2002–2004

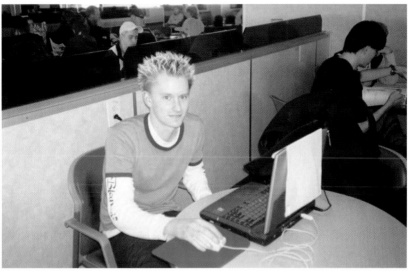

Students in Canada using laptops for their studies as a way of life while travelling by ferry between Vancouver Island and the mainland.

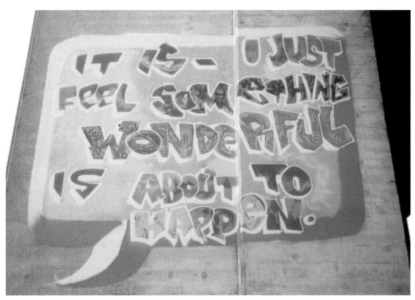

Street art in San Francisco's South of Market area. In the dotcom boom the area had the highest concentration of domain registrations of anywhere in the world.

Vancouver Island

- Travelling by ferry is a way of life for those living on Vancouver Island.
- Tele-working Canadian style! Ships have facilities for using laptops as a norm.
- Girls in Comox Valley try recording themselves with a camera and linked monitor.
- Don Irvine, Comox Valley Project (CVP) coordinator, with a student volunteer.

Seattle

- Highway 5, the major route to Canada as it carves its way past the city centre.
- David Keyes, Seattle ICT Officer, with staff at the New Holly Neighborhood Center.
- Dragon mural in Chinatown, with the Chinese Information and Service Center behind.
- Top floor of Seattle's central library.

Boston

- Street side distribution box for Creative Writing classes in the city.
- Man with hi-tech mobile sandwich bar offering breakfast to building workers.
- Offices of CTC Net with sign in Harvard.
- Detail from a memorial in a central Boston park, showing volunteer 'Americans of African descent' who supported the Union cause in the 1860s.

San Francisco

- Offices in Embarcadero area south of Market Street. New jobs had dried up in 2002.
- Speakers at a Conference on ILT for the Disadvantaged.
- Offices of Compumentor, a body promoting collaboration amongst CTCs.
- In-line roller blader passes ads for the city's renovation plans for the seafront.

- Looking southeast from the landing stages with the wider Bay area beyond.
- Manhole cover for one of the telecommunications companies.
- Bus stop advertisement for Java software.
- Hoarding advertisements assume a very IT and web literate community!

Ontario

- Pumpkins lying in the field at harvest time.
- John Moore, COIN Manager from Oxford County Library Service.
- Student with laptop at Sheridan College, Oakville, Ontario.
- Typical rural scene in the big plains of Ontario with farm and silo behind.

Note: Photos can be viewed in large format in the Picture Gallery at www.digitalnations.org/

Convergence through technology – from the world's deepest gorge in China to the world's best public library in Seattle!

Halfway café in the Himalaya at 10,000 feet in China's Tiger Leaping Gorge – mobile kit offers instant access and data transmission across the globe.

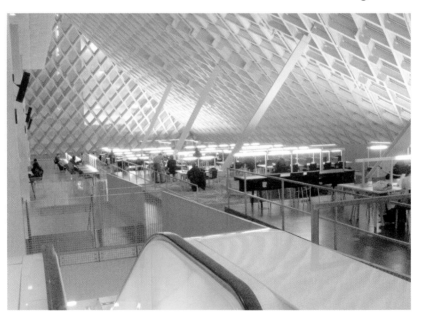

Seattle's new central library, completed in 2004 with a special $196 million bond measure, approved by the city's voters.

Endnotes

1. In 1987 UNESCO funded the European Centre for Leisure and Education to run an international conference in Prague on comparative approaches to adult and workers' education. Practice varied substantially in the 13 countries represented, but on one issue all were agreed – the difficulty of motivating adults who had slipped through the net after school and were no longer involved in learning activities. For a discussion about motivation, see contributions from Rogers, A. and Illeris, K. (2003) 'How do adults learn?', *Adults Learning*, November 2003, pp. 23–27.

2. For an example of the work carried out by the LTC, see WEA/LTC Report on Conference held in Manchester, WEA/LTC (1995) *Working on the Infobahn: Teleworking and the Labour Movement*, WEA; and Gosling, P. (1995) 'Cheap labour at the end of a phone line', *Independent*, Section 2, 3 July 1995, p. 13. WEA staff who were involved in the LTC were John Atkins, Gary Herman, Dave Spooner and Joe Holly. See http://www.digitalnations.org/ithist.htm for a 1999 interview with Lynda Haworth, WEA Tutor Organiser giving details of the *ICT in the Community* programme. A 1994 WEA ICT proposal to the EU for economic and cultural regeneration can be seen at http://www.digitalnations.org/archer.doc

3. For a video recording of an event for the 10th anniversary celebration of the launch of Mosaic, including a talk by Vin Cerf, widely regarded as 'one of the founders of the internet', see http://realvideo.ncsa.uiuc.edu/asxfiles/MosaicAnniversary.asx.

4. See for instance WEA North Western District (1994) *Report of the 50+ Voluntary Members Commission*, WEA; and Discussion Document (1996) *Developing an Information Technology Strategy for Teaching & Learning*. 6 September 1996. http://www.digitalnations.org/itstrat3.doc

5. Manchester City Council's Economic Initiatives Group (EIG), through the

coordinating work of its director, Dave Carter, has played an important role particularly in attracting regional and European funding for ICT work and projects in the city. In 2004 EIG was transformed into the Manchester Digital Development Agency, supported by the North West Development Agency.

6. Examples of experimentation in the north-west can be seen from the following documents which are all available at http://www.digitalnations.org – 'Online to ease poverty' (1999) *Times Educational Supplement*, Further Education Focus, 3 September 1999, p. 33; Harford, I. (2000) 'The Net Show: lessons for lifelong learning?' *Webtalk northwest* 2000(1); Adshead, J. (2001) 'An Arts Project for adults with learning difficulties' *Webtalk northwest*; 'Fifteen years of innovation and change: WEA learners and new technology'; WEA Web News No 1, July 2000 (The WEA's first 'technology-push' email newsletter). See also Note 206 for more information about CGfL.

7. www.niace.org.uk/Research/ICT/WON.htm For the details of the technical development of Wi-Fi, the significance of the decision in 1999 to establish common standards and the likely impact of a new technical standard Wi-Max (a wide-area version of Wi-Fi operating over a range up to 50 kilometres) see 'A brief history of Wi-Fi' (2004) *Economist, Technology Quarterly*, 12 June 2004, p. 22. For details of US home take up of Wi-Fi see 'Growth of wireless internet opens new path for thieves', (2005) *New York Times*, 19 March 2005, http://www.nytimes.com/2005/03/19/technology/19wifi.html?

8. *Guardian Online* 22 May 2003 and 29 May 2003. See 'Make mine a latte' (2003) *Economist*, 14 June 2003, p. 48, for details of Starbucks which had succeeded by 2003 in setting up Wi-Fi access in several UK coffee bars. In 2006 most of their outlets have Wi-Fi, while The Cloud plans to provide its ubiquitous wireless access system for mobile devices in London, Edinburgh, Birmingham, Leeds, Liverpool, Manchester, Oxford and Cambridge. BBC News, 3 January 2006, http://news.bbc.co.uk/1/hi/technology/4578114.stm For the libraries see MLA press release, 16 March 2004. For developments with GNER and Virgin trains and Broadreach's partnership with Skype see http://news.zdnet.co.uk/communications/wireless/0,39020348,39164154,00 .htm (20 August 2004) and http://news.bbc.co.uk/1/hi/technology/4312101.stm (3 March 2005); and 'Wails on the rails' (2005) *Economist*, 2 June 2005 for update on London's underground. For the expansion of VOIP services see http://www.nytimes.com/2005/09/01/technology/circuits/01basics.html?th &emc=th (1 September 2005).

9. See 'The big three-O' (2003) *Economist*, 24 May 2003, p. 83; and 'Out of

the ether'. (2003) *Economist Technology Quarterly*, 6 September 2003, p. 26 for a good case history of the development of Ethernet.

10. Oftel Statistics. http://www.oftel.gov.uk/publications/research/2003/q11mobr0103.htm#chapterthree See also 'A spiritual connection' (2005) *Economist Technology Quarterly*, 12 March 2005, p. 13 for a fascinating account of how the mobile phone, a uniquely personal form of technology, 'has burrowed its way into popular consciousness'. It notes that even Alexander Bell, the inventor of the telephone, was interested in using it to make contact with the dead.

11. Rheingold, H. (2002) *Smart Mobs: The Next Social Revolution*, Basic Books; for use of mobiles in the UK see Mobile Data Association press release 20 December 2005 at http://www.text.it/mediacentre/default.asp?intPageId=881 and for US details see article, 'Carriers push text messaging' (2003) *Wall Street Journal Europe*, 30 May 2003, p. A9.

12. Sticht, T. (2001) *Reforming Adult Literacy Education*. http://www.nald.ca/fulltext/sticht/reformin/cover.htm Information on the US AE system is compared with those in the UK and Canada. The estimates about providers are from an interview with David Rosen, University of Massachusetts, Boston, September 2002. He is also Director of the Boston Adult Literacy Resource Institute.

13. Statistics Canada, Adult Education and Training Survey. http://www.statcan.ca/

14. These figures cover enrolments for the full year. The Observer ('Adults drop out of education despite £663m boost for courses', 8 June 2003) reported that between 1998 and 2002, the number of enrolments on adult education courses had fallen from 1,115,000 to 1,042,000. These latter figures relate to enrolments at 1 November each year; they are not full year figures.

15. NIACE (2002) *Briefing note on Adult Participation and Learning*, NIACE (www.niace.org.uk); NIACE (2001) *National Adult Learning Survey*, NIACE; Lifelong Learning News, May 2002 (www.lifelonglearning.co.uk); Aldridge, F. and Tuckett, A. 'Business as usual?' *Adults Learning*, May 2004, pp. 22–23; Report of the Digital Inclusion Panel (2004) *Enabling a Digitally United Kingdom*, Cabinet Office.

16. http://www.internet.com (Report May 8, 2003). For the 2004 US figures, see http://www.pewinternet.org/PPF/p/1026/pipcomments.asp

17. The Comox Valley Project established a partnership with a local telephone company to bring high speed wireless connectivity to its five Public Access Centres. In April 2002 the plan was to extend this to two of the outlying islands. See http://www.valleylinks.net

18. NWT struggles to leap digital divide (2003) *Globe and Mail*, 6 June 2003.

19. Interview with Michael Miller, National WEA Director of Administration and IT, June 2003.

20. 'Restricted access to new technology will widen digital divide' (2000) *Financial Times*, 15 July 2000.

21. See http://www.net-value.co.uk/presse/

22. 'The country switches on' (2003) *Guardian Online*, 4 December 2003.

23. See http://www.nwda.co.uk/broadband for some north-west projects.

24. 'Surfing Cornwall, new style', *Guardian Online*, 26 June 2003. This gives information about the *Actnow Broadband Cornwall* EU-financed project for ADSL directed at small and medium enterprises (SME).

25. 'UK seeks universal broadband access' (2000) *Financial Times*, 28 August 2000.

26. Commission of the European Communities (2004) *Connecting Europe at High Speed: National Broadband Strategies*, p. 15; UK Online Annual Report, 2003.

27. Report of the Digital Inclusion Panel, 2004. http://www.cabinetoffice.gov.uk/reports/digital/index.asp

Internet Connectivity October 2005, ONS. http://www.statistics.gov.uk/pdfdir/intc1205.pdf

28. Pew Research Centre, quoted in Guardian Online 24 April 2003. www.pewinternet.org/reports/toc.asp?Report=88; Fox, S. (2005) Digital Divisions, Pew Internet and American Life Project. 5 October 2005. http://www.pewinternet.org/PPF/r/165/report_display.asp

29. Much that is written about the internet is not balanced. The case of the unfortunate 12 year-old girl from Wigan, Greater Manchester abducted to

Germany before returning home to safety shows how the tabloid press fans stories involving the internet. Front and extensive back-up pages with headlines such as 'Pervert Marine lured her with emails' (*The Sun*) and 'Internet Sex Monster' (*Daily Express*) took advantage of the name of the US abductor (later convicted) being known. See treatment of the story on 15 and 17 July 2003. Compare this with the limited coverage given a fortnight later to the account of extensive child slavery and trafficking in many UK cities uncovered by a UNICEF UK report. *Guardian* 30 July 2003 and www.endchildexploitation.org.uk

30. Katz, James E. and Rice, Ronald E. (2002) *Social Consequences of Internet Use: Access, Involvement and Interaction*, Cambridge, MA: MIT Press. The most recent analysis of the use of the internet by Americans has been carried out by the Stanford Institute for the Quantitative Study of Society and can be found at www.stanford.edu/group/siqss See Markoff, J. *New York Times*, 30 December 2004.

31. Pew Research Centre Survey, February 2001, quoted in 'California's Digital Divide', an information sheet from the Public Policy Institute of California – www.ppic.org

32. *A Nation Online: How Americans are expanding their use of the internet.* February 2002. http://www.ntia.doc.gov/ntiahome/dn/; Fox, S. (2005) *Digital Divisions. op. cit.*

33. http://www.statistics.gov.uk/StatBase/ssdataset.asp?vlnk=6937&Pos=&Col Rank=1&Rank=128
In Sheffield for instance Barry Phillips, the city's e-Learning Strategy Manager, reported that in an area targeted by one of the cable companies, 'one of our large secondary schools, with a mixed but predominantly white non-aspirational blue-collar catchment area, recently found from a rough survey of pupils that 90% had broadband at home'. Email to the author, 22 February 2005.

34. City of Seattle (2000) *Information Technology Indicators for a Healthy Community*. See http://www.cityofseattle.net/tech/indicators The one mile measure is now commonly used in the UK by authorities such as Cambridgeshire County Council.

35. Carvin, A. (2000) 'More than just access: fitting literacy and content into the digital divide equation', *Educause Review*, November 2000. See www.educause.edu/pub/er/ Carvin is one of the coordinators of the Digital Divide Network. Information about the 2004 UK e-Skills report on ICT

skills can be found at http://www.e-skills.com/cgi-bin/go.pl/%7Breferer%3Dx%7D/press/press-release.html?uid=305

36. Post 16 E-Learning Task Force (2002) *Get on with IT*, July 2002. The final core curriculum document for ICT as a third Skill for Life became available from the QCA in September 2005.

37. The percentage of raw materials used for the production of goods in developed countries has been shrinking dramatically year by year. Peter Drucker pointed out that Japan in 1986 was only consuming 60 per cent of the materials for a given unit of production that it had been using just 11 years earlier. One of the key reasons for this is the advent of new technology industries; with semi conductors for instance, he argues, raw materials were representing only 1–3 per cent of total costs and this trend has accelerated since the 1980s. Drucker, P. (1986) 'The Changed World Economy', *Foreign Affairs*, Spring 1986, p. 773.

38. Clinton, W. and Gore, A. (1992). *Putting People First: How we can all change America*. pp. 23–24. Times Books. Gore's knowledge of technology and its implications for the economy and wider society is considerable. See for instance Gore, A. (1994) 'Plugged into the world's knowledge' *Financial Times*, 19 September 1994. Osborne, D. and Gaeler, T. (1992) *Reinventing Government. How the Entrepreneurial Spirit is Transforming the Public Sector*.

39. National Performance Review, 7 September 1993.

40. Re-engineering through Information Technology, September 1993. http://govinfo.library.unt.edu/npr/librar/reports/reports/it.html

41. Fountain, Jane E. (2001) *Building the Virtual State: Informational Technology and Institutional Change*, p. 18. Brookings Institution Press.

42. The Vice President's Introduction to Access America. February 1997. http://clinton4.nara.gov/WH/New/html/Access.html

43. Ronda Hauben, email to David Farber, 5 October 1999. Established in 1986, the Cleveland Freenet was probably the oldest freenet in the world. See http://www.interesting-people.org/archives/

44. Maxine Rockoff, case study quoted in Katz, James E. and Rice, Ronald E. (2002) *Social Consequences of Internet Use: Access, Involvement and Interaction*, p. 88.

45. US Department of Commerce, (National Telecommunications and Information Administration), July 1995.
http://www.ntia.doc.gov/ntiahome/fallingthru.html

46. Clines, Francis X. (2001) 'Wariness yields to motivation in Baltimore Free-Computer experiment', *New York Times Technology Section*, 24 May 2001.

47. US Department of Commerce, (National Telecommunications and Information Administration), July 1998.
http://www.ntia.doc.gov/ntiahome/net2/falling.html

48. Department of Education, CTC Program, Notice inviting applications for Fiscal Year 1999. 28 April 1999.
http://www.ed.gov/legislation/FedRegister/announcements/1999-2/042899a.html See also for first grant announcements
http://www.senate.gov/~dodd/press/Releases/99/0928.htm

49. US Information Technology Research, September 1999.
http://www.nsf.gov/pubs/1999/nsf99167/nsf99167.htm

50. The White House, *The President's New Markets Trip: From Digital Divide to Digital Opportunity*, April 17–18 2000.

51. *A Nation Online: How Americans are expanding their use of the internet*. NTIA. 2002. op.cit.

52. *A Framework for Global Electronic Commerce*. (1997) The White House.
http://www.technology.gov/digeconomy/framewrk.htm

53. *The Emerging Digital Economy II*. (1999) US Department of Commerce.

54. Increases were from 65,000 to 115,000 for financial years 1999 and 2000, dropping to 107,500 in 2001. The UK 2003 Budget also introduced steps to encourage migration as a source of skills. An overseas student graduating from a UK institution in technology, engineering, science or mathematics would be entitled to work in the UK for 12 months following graduation. Source: Office of the E-Envoy, 6 May 2003.

55. 'Broadband builds base in US: access lags in rural areas' (2000) *Wall Street Journal Europe*, 7 August 2000, p 22.

56. 'Prophet of American technodoom' (2005) *Economist*, 22 April 2005, p.80.

For the 2003 position see Federal Communications Commission website http://www.fcc.gov/cgb/rural/

57. I am indebted to Ryan Turner for information on 2001 and 2002 figures provided in his article: Turner, R. (2002) 'A Mixed Picture – Telecom Policy Update and Analysis', *CTC Review*, Winter-Spring 2002, p36. http://www.comtechreview.org/ The Housing and Urban Development Department (HUD) through its Neigborhood Networks programme provided grants of £20 million in FY 2002, but information for FY 2003 was not available.

58. For details of PowerUp see Klein, A. (2000) 'Closing the Digital Divide', *New York Times*, 16 August 2000, p. E01. For details of the Gates Foundation's work in both education and health see *New York Times*, 13 July 2003, Financial Times 22 September 2003, pp. 6, 15 and http://www.lff.org/ for Libraries for the Future project. Additional information was supplied to the author by Sally Sargent, a consultant to the Gates Foundation in an interview on 9 April 2002.

59. For some foundation and corporate details see selected sites at www.gatesfoundation.org/, http://www.lucent.com/news/foundation/, http://www.salesforcefoundation.org/ and http://foundation.verizon.com/ Steve Wright of the Salesforce.com Foundation, which gives substantial support for community-based ICT programmes in San Francisco, provided useful insights for this study on the use of new technology by VCS bodies in an interview with the author on 4 April 2002.

60. 'In praise of the unspeakable' (2002) *Economist*, 20 July 2002, p. 42.

61. 'Who pays to study? Special Report on Financing Universities' (2004) *Economist*, 24 January, 2004, p. 23.

62. See http://communication.gc.ca/gol_ged/gol_history.html

63. Society Guardian, Epublic, 23 November 2005, p.7; 'Global E-government efforts weaken' (2005) *Government Technology*, 8 April 2005. http://www.govtech.net/magazine/channel_story.php?channel=24&id=93630 For healthy Ontario see 'Turning the tables' (2004) *Government Computing*, p. 46. July/August 2004.

64. The details in this section are substantially drawn from a 26 page Industry Canada report on Milestones 1993–2000. See http://www.ic.gc.ca/cmb/welcomeic.nsf/ICPages/Milestones The publication

of this narrative is itself symptomatic of the very focused and transparent manner in which the Canadian Government has approached the use and deployment of new technologies. Additional information was supplied by Raymond Provencher, Senior Director at Industry Canada in an interview with the author on 10 October 2002.

65. Information visualisation involves the use of graphics to improve the presentation of data and build in real time interactivity. For an account of how this technology is being developed by mostly American companies, see 'Grokking the infoviz' (2003) *Economist Technology Quarterly*, 21 June 2003 p. 28.

66. For details of the schemes to set up broadband services for Northern and First Nation communities see http://www.ic.gc.ca/cmb/welcomeic.nsf/261ce500dfcd7259852564820068dc 6d/85256a220056c2a485256d5f0055fff2!OpenDocument

67. A similar position applies in the US reservations. For details for the Navajo Indians at Crownpoint in New Mexico, where unemployment in 2001 was 67 per cent and per capita incomes were under $13,500, see the website of the Gates Foundation, from whom they received a grant in 2001 for computer equipment. http://www.gatesfoundation.org/Libraries/

68. An example of the way that business support is being given to First Nation communities can be seen with the Aboriginal Business Canada website, http://strategis.ic.gc.ca/epic/internet/inabc-eac.nsf/vwGeneratedInterE/home

69. For other services available to local communities, see http://www.connect.gc.ca/index.htm

70. Email from Brigitte Malenfant, Office of Learning Technologies, HRDC 9 June 2003. See also OLT website at http://olt-bta.hrdc-drhc.gc.ca/ourprogram/index_e.html For m-Learning examples see http://www.mcgrawhill.ca/college/mlearning.

71. 'No City Left Behind', p. 2. Speech by David Miliband, MP, Minister of State for School Standards, to London Conference, 18 March 2004.

72. NCET (1969) *Computer-based learning systems, report of a feasibility study to outline an advanced programme of research and development to apply computers to education and training.* Coventry: NCET.

73. Details are in the TLTP Newsletters. Although substantial public monies were spent by universities on this programme, the resulting digital materials were not available to educational bodies outside HE. As Brian Fender, Chief Executive of HEFCE put it: '… whilst we do, of course, wish to see wider use of such materials the UK higher education funding bodies do not have ownership of the materials developed under TLTP; … although we required every TLTP project to make their materials available at cost to UK higher education… we cannot stipulate any other arrangement.' Letter to the author, 26 August 1997.

74. The report NLN Adult and Community Learning Information and Learning Technologies Strategy was published by the LSC in December 2003. It was produced by the Adult and Community Learning ILT Working Group, of which the author was a member. Copies of the strategy document are available in pdf format from www.lsc.gov.uk.

75. WEA (1995) 'The Future of Work; Labour's Policy Forum moves into gear', *Labour Telematics News*.

76. 'Labour on net' (1995) *Guardian*, 5 October.

77. Funding of £700 million for this National Grid for Learning programme was announced by the Prime Minister on 6 November 1998. More details of these and some 29 other reports and initiatives over the seven years of the existing Labour Government's period of office 1997–2004 can be found in Harford, I. (2004) *New Directions: Labour and Lifelong Learning* at http://www.digitalnations.org/lifelong.htm

78. Cabinet Office (2005) *Transformational Government: Enabled by Technology*. http://www.cio.gov.uk/index.asp

79. 'Blair puts finger on the e-problem' (1999) *Guardian*, 14 September 1999. p. 23.

80. http://www.socialexclusionunit.gov.uk/

81. Trafford and Salford LAs for instance have started to run provision directly, instead of contracting this out to other providers and ICT courses have been a central part of their offer. Their decisions will also have been influenced by the availability of resources from the LSC.

82. This built upon the *Success for All Report* of the previous year. Further details of the 21st Century Skills Report can be found at http://www.dfes.gov.uk/skillsstrategy/

83. See http://www.nln.ac.uk for more details about the NLN Transformation programme. From August 2006 ACL providers will be expected to raise a higher percentage of their resources from students and will receive a consequent decrease in LSC funding. For 2006–2007 the Government has allocated £210 million for personal development and community learning. (Source: Speech by Phil Hope, Minister for Skills, DfES Conference on Testbed Learning Communities, 18 January 2006. http://www.dfes.gov.uk/speeches/latest.cfm)

84. The first two reports, *Successful Participation for All* (2003) and *Working Together – a Strategy for the VCS and the LSC* (2004) were published by the LSC. The third and fourth reports, *Active Learning for Active Citizenship* (2004) and *Futurebuilders* (2004) were produced by the Home Office.

85. Reports about the TrEACL materials are at http://www.aclearn.net/display.cfm?page=951

86. Powell, B. and Minshull, G. (2004) *Choosing and using a learning platform in adult and community learning.* NIACE/JISC. This work was coordinated by the Joint Information Services Committee (JISC) and involved the trialling of different learning platforms (LP) including a commercial one, an open source LP and an 'own build' LP, being created by the WEA Community Grid for Learning; and a communication and conferencing system used by the Open University. The report on the trials can be found at http://www.aclearn.net/leadership/learning-platforms Of the 35 ACL providers being supported in 2006 by NIACE with the use of learning platforms, 22 are, or will be, using the Moodle platform, which the UK's Open University has also decided to adopt for its students.

87. The LAMS has been developed by James Dalziel at Macquarie University, Sydney. It provides the opportunity for non-technical staff and tutors to create structured and sequenced learning resources with simple drag and drop techniques. The software was tested in late 2004 by a number of FE Colleges, by the WEA CGfL and in Sheffield as part of a pilot being run by JISC.

88. A condition for successful tendering for the creation of this NLN material was that there should be significant involvement of ACL providers with those creating the resources.

89. Details of the *Building Schools for the Future* programme can be found at http://www.bsf.gov.uk See also 'Schools to become public ICT centres', 14 June 2005, http://www.egovmonitor.com/node/1350

90. 'Connecting the UK: the digital strategy' (2005) Cabinet Office and DTI. This was launched by the Prime Minister on 1 April 2005. http://www.strategy.gov.uk/work_areas/digital_strategy/index.asp

91. JISC Funding Announcement, 21 June 2005. http://www.egovmonitor.com/node/1464; and 'E-learning under threat' (2005) in *Education Guardian*, 5 July 2005, p. 15. The cut has amounted to £6.5 million p.a.

92. See Benwell Community Project (1978) *The Making of a Ruling Class*, CDP; and *Sunset over the River Tyne*, a painting by Robert F Watson, circa 1840. The view of Elswick and Benwell, which became the location of the huge engineering company W.G. Armstrong, is from the Gateshead side of the river. http://www.digitalnations.org/tyne-sun.jpg

93. Schuler, D. (1996) *New Community Networks: Wired for Change*, p. 273.

94. Financial constraints did not affect the US Community Colleges, which were starting at this time to equip their main campuses with substantial infrastructure and computers. Report of NILTA Study Visit to American Association of Community Colleges Convention (AACC), Atlanta, April 1996.

95. Notable among these initiatives were the DELTA Programme (1992), the Telematics Applications Programme (1994) and schemes established by the IT Programme Directorate. MUSENET, a project with media trade unions, run by the WEA Labour Telematics Centre in the North West was an example.

96. See Arnsten, R. (1998) 'Restructuring the learning industry', in *Building the National Grid for Learning: Access for Adult Learners*. National WEA Report on Conference in Manchester.

97. 29 per cent of UK learners in a national survey had received some kind of course based on computer delivery and respondents were generally happy with this and found it useful. National Centre for Social Research (2003) *Pathways in Adult Learning Survey* (PALS), p. 131. National Centre for Social Research.

98. http://ferl.becta.org.uk/fpp6

99. Becta (2003) *The Ferl Practitioners Programme: Pilot Evaluation Report*, Becta.

100. Clare Killen, FPP Manager, Becta. Interview with the author, 10 January 2005. In August 2005 LSDA announced that it would take over FPP from Becta.

101. Grant, S. (1999) *E-commerce for small business.*
http://www.simongrant.org/pubs/iec99/small.html

102. Castells, M. (2001) *The Internet Galaxy*, pp. 68–72. Castells describes Cisco as the pioneer of the 'networked business model' and 'a concrete image of the transformation underway'.

103. See *Guardian Online*, 1 May 2003, p 17. LiquidDrop.com allows users to send email messages from their PCs to any mobile phone by just typing in the number followed by @www.LiquidDrop.com/ See also 'E-mailing a cellphone by the numbers' (2004) *New York Times*, 5 February 2004, about a similar US email service from Teleflip.com.

104. The word 'telechiric', an engineering term describing a machine able to grasp and manipulate objects at a distance, is transferred here to indicate the power offered by the web for people to combine to manipulate remotely words, images and ideas from a PC synchronously with others. See Cooley, M. (1980) *Architect or Bee? The Human/Technology Relationship*, p. 73.

105. At a Community Networking conference in Montreal in 2002, attended by the author, a group of five young Canadian students with their tutor collaborated on a joint project with a similar group at RMIT in Melbourne Australia over 10,000 miles away, using a communication software package, Centra. All of them were totally absorbed for two hours by the immediacy of the experience (using VOIP) of verbal presenting, highlighting and altering diagrams on a shared space. 'Atwood sign of the times draws blank' in *Guardian*, 6 March 2006. http://www.guardian.co.uk/print/0,,32947283-103681,00.html

106. The term 'bundled' is used to denote short 1–2 hour online activities and structured programmes, which first step adult learners can undertake independently, within a supported environment and with the possibility of receiving at least asynchronous online assistance from a qualified tutor. This kind of material has been developed by the WEA's Community Grid for Learning (www.learners.org.uk/), but at present this does not attract funding through the LSC's funding framework. See recommendation 4 from this research (page 140).

107. Hubbs, Norman P. III. (2001) 'Next generation government', *eAI Journal*, July 2001, p 54.

108. DiMaio, A. (2004) 'E-Government hype cycle: where does local government stand?', *Local e-government now*, 2004, Socitm. p. 5. DiMaio, an

analyst with Gartner, argues that intermediation – allowing a role in delivering public services to be played by other organisations – and the use of new channels to engage citizens in democratic debates have been trailing behind.

109. Before this welcome initiative was taken, residents in Seattle wishing to access the internet in any of the city's 35 CTCs would be likely to 'find the lights out, the doors locked and the computers sitting idle', according to a correspondent writing in the *Community Technology Review*, Summer-Fall 2001, p 33.

110. For more information on SCTA see www.cityofseattle.net/tech/scta/partners.html

111. See http://cityofseattle.net/tech/ctc/uwired.htm

112. David Keyes, the city's Community Technology Manager has played a key part here and has been a representative of the Community Technology Centers on the National CTC Net.

113. http://www.cityofseattle.net/tech/indicators/neighborhoodsurvey.htm

114. http://www.cityofseattle.net/tech/brainstorm/

115. Quoted in Davies, S., Pinkett, R.D., Servon, L.J. and Wiley-Schwartz, A. (2003) *Community Technology Centres as Catalysts for Community Change: A Report to the Ford Foundation*, p. 35.

116. Schuler, D. (1996) ibid.

117. See http://sican.tc.ca/locations.php and http://victoria.tc.ca

118. http://www.valleylinks.net

119. See www.bestpractical.com/rt The company Best Practical has since 2002 successfully developed this Request Tracker system as an open source product with additional features in conjunction with UKERNA, the UK Educational Network Agency. See UKERNA News, No 28, September 2004, p. 16.

120. The scheme ended in March 2002, having met the 10,000 connections target.

121. Details of this Government scheme can be found at http://www.vsi-isbc.ca/

122. See http://www.vcn.bc.ca/vcn/volunteer/

123. See http://www.vcn.bc.ca/vcn/overview/ The interview was held on 22 March 2002 with Steve Chan, one of the founding members of VCN and Peter Royce.

124. In the UK the software distribution role taken by Compumentor has been played by Eduserve a charity initially set up by the JISC for the Higher Education sector. This runs the CHEST scheme. For additional details about Compumentor see http://ventures.yale.edu/competition_archives_May2003.asp and http://www.techsoup.org/news/news_article.cfm?newsid=1278&btcfile=new s_article

125. Miller, P. (1998) 'CTCNet and AFCN: the shared future of community technology centers and community networking', *CTC Review*, January 1998.

126. A good metropolitan example is the one for the Bay Area in San Francisco, where local stories and news are posted.

127. See article by Shapiro, P. (2001) 'Stopping by Benton', *CTC Review*, Summer – Fall 2001, p. 35. http://www.comtechreview.org

128. Education Development Center (2003) 'Promising practices in project based learning at CTCs' (2003) Education Development Center. Available for download at www.americaconnects.net/research/PBL.pdf

129. The HEFCE scheme supports volunteering by staff and volunteers, but on a smaller scale. The budget for 2004–06 is up to £10 million.

130. See 'Highlighting CTC Vista's Experiences' (2002) *Community Technology Review*, Winter 2002, p. 33.

131. CCTV Annual Report (2001) *Journey* 2001. CCTV was forced to take legal action in 2001 against A.T.&T. for payment of these monies and the matter was settled. In November the City of Cambridge agreed to provide CCTV 3 per cent of A.T.&T. gross revenue to support CCTV and $½ million for equipment up to 15 December 2005.

132. Cleveland for instance secured $3 million and Seattle $10 million from

cable companies, which had to be spent by the cities supporting local ICT facilities.

133. Only 20 per cent of the sites posted information in a variety of languages. See Lazarus, W. and Mora, F. (2000) *Online Content for Low-Income and Underserved Americans: The Digital Divide's new frontiers*, The Children's Partnership.

134. The example given by James Lau was of not installing MS Exchange for email. The installation cost of $5,000 and subsequent maintenance was hard to justify for an organisation with only 8 staff.

135. A T1 Connection is a dedicated high-speed data line or phone that can support the transfer of up to 1.544Mbits of data per second.

136. The WEA/CGfL course was developed with tutors who were running a traditional course for parents facing difficulties in coping with their children's behaviour. It uses real parents and children in real situations to provide video clips, around which the course is built. It can be used for self-guided study, as a refresher or as part of a blended course. See http://www.learners.org.uk for further details. Funding for creating the course came from the NIACE TrEACL 2003 programme.

137. For details of other schemes see Pitkin, B. and Rattray, N. (2002) 'Community mapping for neighborhood knowledge in Los Angeles', *Community Technology Review*, Winter-Spring 2002, pp. 15–1. The LILA scheme can be found at http://lila.ucla.edu/

138. David Rosen is the Chair of the SCALE National Board of Advisors. Details of SCALE can be found at http://www.readwriteact.org/

139. 'School for Digital Wizards' (2001) *Financial Post, IT Monthly Section*, 16 July 2001, p. 3.

140. See Structural Steel Erection Sequence at http://www.spl.org/lfa/index.html

141. 'Libraries reach out, online', (2004) *New York Times*, 9 December 2004. Details are at the KCLS site. By 2005 Overdrive and OCLC's NetLibrary were supplying online books, between them to 1200 library services at a cost of $7 pa per book. See 'Libraries offering audiobook downloads' (2005) in MIT's *Technology Review*, 29 August 2005. http://www.technologyreview.com/articles/05/08/ap/ap_082905.asp?trk=nl

142. Information in this account is based upon interviews with Sam Coghlan, Chief Librarian, John Moore, Manager of Information Access Oxford, Kathryn McCulloch, Training Coordinator and Meredith Maywood, COOL coordinator, 3–4 October 2002. Coghlan and McCulloch have now moved to other posts.

143. In 2005 over 2000 local companies can be accessed, with responsibility placed on the business to maintain the accuracy of the data. Details can be found at www.cooloxford.ca./portalnews

144. Expedia is now a wholly owned subsidiary of IAC/InterActiveCorp, the world's biggest online travel company. See interview with Barry Diller, CEO of IAC, 'Toughing it out in the travel industry' (2004) *Financial Times*, 6 December 2004, p. 29.

145. http://wade.trblogs.com/archives/2005/07/computings_fift.html?trk=nl The term Web 2.0 is not precise. For a fascinating discussion of how the term has been evolving since 2004, see O'Reilly, T. (2005) What is *Web 2.0?* http://www.oreillynet.com/pub/a/oreilly/tim/news/2005/09/30/what-is-web-20.html

146. 'Social Computing: How Networks Erode Institutional Power, And What To Do About It.' Forrester Research. 16 February 2006. http://blogsforrester.com/charleneli/2006/02/forrsters_socia.html For details of a potential social computing killer application see 'New Social Networking Technology Packs a Wallop', *Technology Review*, 4 May 2006. http://www.technologyreview.com/read_article.aspx?id=16773&ch=infotech

147. 'Alliances with grand designs' (2000) *Financial Times*, 7 August 2000, p. 6.

148. Much of the material has been archived at www.fathom.com and remains accessible.

149. 'The online revolution, mark II' (2004) *Guardian Education, Higher*, 13 April 2004, p.18.

150. Fountain, Jane, E. (2001) *Building the Virtual State, op.cit.*

151. There are many powerful local forces, which impact on how technologies are developed around the world and affect adult learning programmes. What matters most depends upon where you are (http://www.technologyreview.com/articles/05/04/issue/feature_gp.asp?trk=nl). *Technology Review.com*, April 2005. This gives a perspective on how seven

countries are pursuing policies which relate to domestic concerns – from Brazil seeking to develop bio-diesel to Holland's concerns with coastal water control. US policy, it notes, is now 'bluntly militaristic' with R&D focused on short-term 3–5 year projects. For 2006 the US plans to commit $1 billion to the Homeland Security Advanced Research Projects Agency.

152. See Hall Aitken Associates (2002) *Evaluation of CMF-funded UK online centres: initial report.* (Research Report No 368) and http://www.ntia.doc.gov/otiahome/top/research/research.htm for details of the evaluation of the US NTIA programme.

153. See NWDA (www.nwda.co.uk) and London Development Agency (http://www.lda.gov.uk/) for more details of the projects being presently funded.

154. Fowells, L. and Lazarus, W. (2001) *Computers in our Future: What works in closing the technology gap?* p. ii. www.ciof.org/

155. Claudio Gutiérrez, email to David Farber, 'Blame India for that jobless recovery', 1 October 2003. See http://www.interesting-people.org/archives/ ; 'The new geography of the IT industry' (2005) *Economist*, 19 July 2003, pp. 53–55. The article describes the growing tendency for offshore outsourcing of IT work. For a detailed examination of this issue and its impact upon working families, see Mishel, L., Bernstein, J. and Allegretto, S. (2005) *The State of Working America, 2004/2005.* This is summarised at http://digitalcommons.ilr.cornell.edu/cgi/viewcontent.cgi?article=1001&context=books

156. Learning and Skills Council (2004) *Investing in Skills: Taking Forward the Skills Strategy – Reforming the Funding and Planning Arrangements for First Steps, Personal Development and Community Learning for Adults.* Consultation Paper, LSC.

157. Cook, J. and Smith, M. (2002) *Study of UK Online Centres.* LTRI/Becta; Cook, J. and Smith, M. (2004) *Enabling Learner 'Progression' in a Community Setting with e-learning.* Paper to BERA Conference, Manchester, September 2004.

158. Loader, B. and Keeble, L. (2004) *Challenging the Digital Divide? A literature review of community informatics initiatives.* p. 14. The review covered ICT projects and work in Europe and North America.
http://www.jrf.org.uk/bookshop/eBooks/1859351980.pdf

159. Interview with the author, 27 March 2000.

160. *E-Skills Mapping in Greater Manchester* (2004) Ekos Consulting.

161. For details of e-Government activities in the UK, see
http://www.egovmonitor.com/

162. See 2005 map of England and Wales from consultants Point Topic. *e-Gov Monitor*, 22 April 2005. http://www.egovmonitor.com/node/670 Cardiff was highest in the table and rural areas generally lowest. Internet Connectivity October 2005, ONS.

163. 'Broadband: Another surprising success' (2004) *Economist*, 11 September 2004, p. 28.

164. In the UK the DfES indicated in 2005 that the ICT centres programme was at the end of its 3 year funding. The new aim was to encourage centres to find income to become self-sustaining. For 2004–05 the Ufl managed an allocation of £13 million to support some 500 ICT centres in deprived wards, with grants of up to £24,000. £2 million of this came from the Big Lottery Fund's underspent CMF funds.

165. Cook, J. and Light, A. (2006) New Patterns of Power and Participation? Designing ICT for Informal and Community Learning. *E-Learning Special Issue of ICE2 Symposium*, 3(1), 51–61. Available from http://www.wwwords.co.uk/ELEA/content/pdfs/3/issue3_1.asp

166. 'New Waves: Report on post-16 e-learning' (2004) *Times Educational Supplement*. 12 November 2004. p. 2.

167. The DfES e-Strategy report, published on 15 March 2005 can be downloaded from http://www.dfes.gov.uk/publications/e-strategy/

168. Google and Yahoo are developing sophisticated visualisation tools to enhance the results of linking initial locational data with mapping and graphics data, undermining 'traditional' companies like Yellow Pages. Google Local was launched in the UK on 19 April 2005 and Google Earth on 28 June 2005.

169. 'MGM Mirage seeks to allure the gamblers of cyberspace' (2002) *New York Times, Business Day*, 28 September 2002, p. B1. It is illegal to offer online gambling to US residents so the company is developing the use of geo-location technology to identify the country of origin of users. This is then

checked against publicly available databases. The $15 million Isle of Man development costs for MGM Online are small compared with the $1 billion costs of setting up another Las Vegas casino.

170. For an interesting discussion of this and some more American and UK examples, see 'Dot-org models: organising the net to network' (2002) *Financial Times, IT Review*, 6 February 2002, p. v.

171. The ad reads: *'Banner ad or Billboard? answer: billboard'*. Banner Ads at the top of web pages were very popular with advertisers in the dot-com boom. It was thought they would yield a good return as everyone swarmed to use the internet and make online purchases. With the collapse of the boom, they became much more difficult to sell to companies. Search technologies and 'click-on' have in the four years since 2002 transformed advertising.

172. Interview with George Gundrey, Compumentor, 5 April 2002.

173. The Ufl was established by the Government in 1998, following the publication of a report, *University for Industry: Creating a National Learning Network*, by the Institute of Public Policy Research in 1996. As of 1 January 2005, 1.5 million people had enrolled on nearly 3.5 million Learndirect courses, run by Ufl. In April 2003 Ufi accepted responsibility from the DfES for the support of UK online centres to help develop them into a sustainable network.

174. Ruralnet, set up by Warwickshire Rural Enterprise Network (WREN), provides this service and an additional *Experts online* service on behalf of a consortium of agencies. The UK Online centres are viewed by Ufl as 'gathering pools' for learners, who may progress to Learndirect courses.

175. Examples in other parts of the country include WREN and Brixton Online in London. The former has had an annual turnover of £1 million for the last two years, the latter (http://www.bolts.org.uk) supports a range of activities, including INTO, a £4 million regeneration programme in the Elephant and Castle area (http://www.into.org.uk/aboutus.cfm). Both WREN and Brixton Online offer support to small businesses. See also Shearman, C. (1999) *Local Connections: Making the net work for neighbourhood renewal.*

176. See www.mcin.net and www.mymanchester.net for an example of a local information site.

177. See Evans, R. (2004) *Online Testing in Remote Centres.* WEA Innovations

in Practice case study. WEA. http://www.digitalnations.org/edexcel-test.doc

178. Evans, P. and Wurster, T.S. (2000) *Blown to Bits: How the new economics of information transforms strategy*, Chapter 3, p. 23. Harvard Business School Press.

179. Kim, W.C. and Mauborgne, R. (2003). 'Tipping point leadership', *Harvard Business Review*, April 2003, p.10

180. The OCL example in Canada is certainly not unique. In Southern Ireland after a wireless network was set up in 2004 on Sherkin Island and two adjoining islands, the project became embroiled in a feud between traditionalists and modernists, resulting in the co-ordinator being given '48 hours to remove the network operations centre'. The project had to be reorganised with the loss of use by the islanders, who had been benefiting from the service. Some details of this *Intelligent Islands Pilot Project*, funded by the Innovative Actions Program of the EU are at http://www.sherkinisland.ie/nlet.htm

181. See Evans, P. and Wurster, T.S. (2000) *op.cit.* p. 115. Although the analysis is about change and competition affecting different kinds of organisation in the private sector, the insights in *Blown to Bits* have relevance to ACL and VCS bodies, as Government and funding bodies seek greater efficiency in meeting targets and increasing outputs.

182. Christensen, C.M. (1997) *The Innovator's Dilemma. When new technologies cause great firms to fail.* Boston, Mass. http://www.businessweek.com/chapter/christensen.htm The book is based on a study of the disc drive industry and explores the concept of sustaining and disruptive innovation.

183. Only a few in the non-profit sector are like Cambridge Community Television, who had an assured income of over $1 million pa from a cable franchisee.

184. Google handles over 45 million web searches daily. eBay had nearly 50 million visitors in December 2003 and sold $7 billion of goods in the last quarter of 2003. *New York Times*, 25 November 2004.

185. 'Craigslist: Honouring nerd values' (2004) *Economist*, 14 October 2004. Interview with Craig Newmark, *Media Guardian*, 16 January 2006, p.5. Many of the not for profit bodies in the Bay area use the service offered to advertise jobs, for which they pay. All other listings are free. In 1997 the offer by Microsoft to pay a large sum to run banner ads on the site was turned down.

Craig's List is estimated to have an annual income in 2006 of between US$10 million and US$20 million.

186. There is symmetry here with the views of David Bell, head of the UK's Ofsted Inspection team, on the consistent similarities between the most successful institutions they have inspected: 'All have a clear understanding of the particular nature of their mission and pursue its realisation single-mindedly.' 'More colleges fail in the south' (2004) *Education Guardian*, 30 November 2004, p. 15. For an interesting discussion of introducing change in the private sector, see Kotter, J.P. (1995) 'Leading change: why transformation efforts fail', *Harvard Business Review*, March–April 1995.

187. CTC Net Experts Panel, 12 April 2001 – http://www.ctcnet.org/americaconnects/panel4/0002.htm

188. An indication of the complexities of funding to support ILT and adult learning can be seen with the WEA's Community Grid for Learning. Its £850,000 budget for 2003–2005 was built up from 11 separate funding sources.

189. Because of the short range of a wireless link using the 802.11b protocol, applicants needed to show how the initial link to the internet would be achieved through a physically connected access point.

190. Fountain, J. (2000) op.cit. p. 66.

191. For a discussion of this issue in relation to the development of the semi-conductor and computer-based industries in California see Granovetter, M. et al. (2002) ;Social Networks in Silicon Valley'. http://www.sscnet.ucla.edu/soc/faculty/kollock/classes/entrepreneurship/reso urces/Castilla+%202000%20-%20Social%20Networks%20in%20Silicon%20Valley.pdf

192. In the NOF Information for CALL applicants in England in 2000, projects had to target social exclusion, have marketing, delivery and financial plans and meet technical specifications. The key educational criteria were that they should fit in with the plans of the Local Learning Partnerships and allow progression to other learning opportunities. New Opportunities Fund (2000) *Community Access to Lifelong Learning: Information for applicants*, pp. 16–19.

193. Powell, B. and Minshull, G. (2004) *Choosing and using a Learning Platform in Adult and Community Learning*; and (2004) *Effective Practice with e-Learning: A*

Good Practice Guide in Designing for Learning, JISC; and (2005) *Innovative Practice with e-Learning: A Good Practice Guide to Embedding Mobile and Wireless Technologies into everyday Practice*, JISC; and (2006) *Designing Spaces for Effective Learning*, JISC.

194. 'New Waves: Report on post-16 e-learning' (2004) *Times Educational Supplement*, 12 November 2004. p. 2.

195. Grainne Conole, quoted in Minshull, G. (2004) *VLEs: Beyond the fringe and into the mainstream*, p. 5. NLN and Becta.

196. Kelly, K. (1998) *New Rules for the New Economy: 10 ways the network economy is changing everything*. pp. 87–89. 1998.

197. http://ultibase.rmit.edu.au/Articles/dec00/hase2.htm#heutagony; Hase, S. and Kenyon, C (2000). From Andragogy to Heutagogy.

198. Rogers, C.R. (1969) *Freedom to Learn*; Knowles, M. (1970) *The Modern Practice of Adult Education: Andragogy versus Pedagogy*.

199. Paul Brown, Becta quoted in Minshull, G. (2004) op.cit. p. 21.

200. A good source for a wide and evaluated range of downloadable software is www.tucows.com

201. See www.contentbank.org and details at www.diaryland.com and http://www.sixapart.com/movabletype/ For an informative review of new participatory media like blogs, wikis and podcasting and their wider significance, see 'Among the audience: A survey of new media' (2006) *The Economist*, 22 April 2006.

202. By the end of 2004, 8 million US adults had created a blog and 27 per cent of US internet users read them. Pew internet survey 2 January 2005. http://www.pewinternet.org/PPF/r/144/report_display.asp

203. For podcasting sources see http://www.podcast.net/ See http://webquest.sdsu.edu/ and http://www.ozline.com/learning/index.htm for links to other materials like Filamentality.

204. http://www.aclearn.net/ To register click on the toolkits section. See http://www.halfbakedsoftware.com/quandary.php for US details of the Quandary activity.

205. Gourley, B. (2004) *Moving Open and Distance Learning to Centre Stage.* The Geoffrey Hubbard Memorial Lecture. 17 June 2004. p. 7.

206. The Greater Manchester Community Grid for Learning had its origins in a WEA proposal, *D2L (Direct to Learn): Putting content on the network*, discussed in November 1999 with the heads of the Library services of Manchester, Salford, Tameside and Trafford. See http://www.digitalnations.org/D2L.doc A bid to NOF for CGfL was made in 2000 and additional monies were secured from the ERDF, the LSC and NWDA. The team of six took up their posts in Spring 2003. The staff have included David Egan, Maria Toro-Troconis, Tracy Burrell, Richard Evans, Fiona Iglesias, Rochelle Gunter and Danielle Lowy. A summary of its 2003–2006 programme and current services, *The WEA CGfL–e-learning in practice for adults* is available from WEA, 4th Floor, Crawford House, Oxford Road, Mancester, M13 9GH.

207. These EU funds are mostly coming to an end now and will diminish still further with the accession of other East European countries from 2006. Some ICT initiatives remain like the Minerva projects under the Socrates Education and Culture programme. See http://www2.britishcouncil.org/socrates

208. 'Spin-outs: universities into business. Special report' (2004) *The Observer*, 4 April 2004, 8 pp.

209. See http://www.communitytechnology.org/

210. 'Building on Success' (2004) *Local e-government now 2004*, p. 7. Socitm and I&DeA.

211. See http://proboscis.org.uk/soma/ and http://urbantapestries.net/

212. See www.coldwellcentre.co.uk This imaginative digital film making project with groups of young people exploring multiculturalism, has received strong support from the school and was funded by the NWDA's BRAIN scheme. This was an innovative EU-supported programme directed by Peter Fowler, former Head of the International Centre for Digital Content at Liverpool John Moores University.

213. www.russellcommission.com The Commission was established by the Treasury and the Home Office.

214. Conversation with Sherry Turkle from the Massachusetts Institute of Technology, in *Harvard Business Review*. September 2003, p. 43. The

contemporary version of this is the Blackberry, Research In Motion's phone and email PDA, which now has two million users worldwide. Its addictive nature has led to it being described as a 'Crackberry'. See 'Blackberry becomes addictive' (2004) *The Washington Times*, 23 November 2004. See also Turkle, S. (1995) *Life on the Screen: Identity in the Age of the Internet*.

215. Quoted in Conole, G. and Bull, J. (2001) *Pebbles in the Pond: Evaluation of the CAA Centre*, p. 69.

216. Schwartz, J. High-Tech Hot Spots. (2005) *Newsweek Education*, 22 August 2005. http://www.msnbc.msn.com/id/8941034/site/newsweek/

217. For a good summary of issues in relation to m-Learning, see http://www.aclearn.net/display.cfm?page=958/ For 2006 news stories see: 'Web giants show the way in Vegas', 9 January 2006, http://news.bbc.co.uk/1/hi/technology/4594290.stm; 'Google says hello Moto', 6 January 2006, http://networks.silicon.com/mobile/0,39024665,39155422,00.htm For the significance of search technologies see Battelle, J. (2005) *The Search: How Google and its Rivals Rewrote the Rules of Business and Transformed our Culture*.

218. UK Online Centres and E-Government. (2005) *DfES Research Report No 632*. SQW Limited and Mori Social Research Institute.

219. Intermediaries have been defined by the Office of the e-Envoy as 'organisations from the private or voluntary sectors offering services targeted at groups of customers'. See Office of the e-Envoy (2003) Policy *Framework for a Mixed Economy in the Supply of E-Government Services*, 2003.

220. An Invest to Save Budget Round 8 was announced in June 2005, which sought to encourage Third Sector Bodies to apply for funding to deliver public services in specified priority areas in partnership with other public and VCS bodies. £40 million was available under the scheme. See http://www.isb.gov.uk/

221. Horrigan, J.B. (2004) *How Americans Get in Touch with Government: Internet users benefit from the efficiency of e-Government, but multiple channels are still needed for citizens to reach agencies and solve problems*. http://www.pewinternet.org

222. *Inclusion through Innovation: Tackling Social Exclusion through New Technologies* (2005) ODPM. See also: Report of the Digital Inclusion Panel (2004) *Enabling a Digitally United Kingdom*. Cabinet Office.

Index

Note

US and Canadian organisations are indicated by the suffix [US] and [Canada], e.g. Adult Literacy Resource Institute [US]

Page numbers followed by 'Fig.' or 'Table' are for references to figures or tables; page numbers followed by 'n.' and a number are for endnotes; italicized page numbers are for illustrations, e.g.: Comox Valley Community Access Project [Canada] 17, 39Fig.3, 69, 70, 71Table 5, 148, *150*, 156n.17

Hyphenated words starting with 'e-' are filed as whole words, as in the following example: eBay, e-books, e-business, education, e-democracy

OXFORD WORLD'S CLASSICS

THE INTERPRETATION OF DREAMS

SIGMUND FREUD was born in 1856 in Moravia, but was brought to Vienna by his parents at the age of 4 and lived there until his flight to England after the German annexation of Austria in 1938. Having received a broad classical education, he trained as a doctor at the Vienna Medical School. He worked initially on the nervous system, then became interested in the therapeutic uses of cocaine, in speech disorders, and in using hypnosis in treating psychological afflictions. His *Studies in Hysteria* (1895), written jointly with his older colleague Josef Breuer, maintained that 'hysterics suffer mainly from reminiscences' which could be recalled and discharged by the 'talking cure'. In 1897, however, Freud concluded that hysterical and neurotic patients most often suffered from fantasies stemming from their relations with their parents in childhood. He embarked on the investigation of unconscious fantasy-life which produced *The Interpretation of Dreams* (1899), *The Psychopathology of Everyday Life* (1901), and *Jokes and their Relation to the Unconscious* (1905). His *Three Essays on the Theory of Sexuality* (1905) argued that patterns of sexual development, involving such mechanisms as identification and repression, were central to the unconscious forces shaping the personality. From there he developed psychoanalysis as a therapeutic technique and a theory of the unconscious which underwent many mutations, both in Freud's work and in that of followers, from Jung onwards, who successively established independent schools of psychoanalytic thought and treatment. Freud died in exile in Hampstead in 1939.

JOYCE CRICK was, until her retirement, Senior Lecturer in the Department of German at University College London. Previous translations include texts by Hamann, Herder, Friedrich Schlegel, Novalis, and Solger selected for Cambridge University Press's volumes of *German Aesthetic and Literary Criticism*. She has edited the German material for the Princeton edition of Coleridge's *Notebooks* and (forthcoming) his translation of Schiller's *Wallenstein*. Interest in translation theory took her to the problems raised by Freud's texts. She has also written on Thomas and Heinrich Mann, Christa Wolf, Bertolt Brecht, and Günter Grass.

RITCHIE ROBERTSON is Reader in German at Oxford University and a Fellow of St John's College. He is the author of *Kafka: Judaism, Politics, and Literature* (OUP, 1985), *Heine* (Peter Halban, 1988), and *The 'Jewish Question' in German Literature, 1749–1939* (OUP, 1999), ar⸏⸏⸏⸏⸏⸏⸏⸏⸏ German. He has edited *The Ger⸏⸏⸏⸏⸏⸏⸏⸏⸏*rld's Classics.

OXFORD WORLD'S CLASSICS

*For almost 100 years Oxford World's Classics have brought
readers closer to the world's great literature. Now with over 700
titles—from the 4,000-year-old myths of Mesopotamia to the
twentieth century's greatest novels—the series makes available
lesser-known as well as celebrated writing.*

*The pocket-sized hardbacks of the early years contained
introductions by Virginia Woolf, T. S. Eliot, Graham Greene,
and other literary figures which enriched the experience of reading.
Today the series is recognized for its fine scholarship and
reliability in texts that span world literature, drama and poetry,
religion, philosophy and politics. Each edition includes perceptive
commentary and essential background information to meet the
changing needs of readers.*

OXFORD WORLD'S CLASSICS

SIGMUND FREUD

The Interpretation of Dreams

Translated by
JOYCE CRICK

with an Introduction and Notes by
RITCHIE ROBERTSON

OXFORD
UNIVERSITY PRESS

OXFORD
UNIVERSITY PRESS

Great Clarendon Street, Oxford OX2 6DP

Oxford University Press is a department of the University of Oxford.
It furthers the University's objective of excellence in research, scholarship,
and education by publishing worldwide in

Oxford New York

Athens Auckland Bangkok Bogotá Buenos Aires Calcutta
Cape Town Chennai Dar es Salaam Delhi Florence Hong Kong Istanbul
Karachi Kuala Lumpur Madrid Melbourne Mexico City Mumbai
Nairobi Paris São Paulo Shanghai Singapore Taipei Tokyo Toronto Warsaw

with associated companies in Berlin Ibadan

Oxford is a registered trade mark of Oxford University Press
in the UK and in certain other countries

Published in the United States
by Oxford University Press Inc., New York

Translation © Joyce Crick 1999
Editorial material © Ritchie Robertson 1999

The moral rights of the author have been asserted

Database right Oxford University Press (maker)

First published as an Oxford World's Classics paperback 1999

British Library Cataloguing in Publication Data

Data available

Library of Congress Cataloging in Publication Data

Data available

ISBN 0–19–210049–1 (hbk.)
0–19–282352–3 (pbk.)

3 5 7 9 10 8 6 4 2

Typeset by RefineCatch Limited, Bungay, Suffolk
Printed in Great Britain by
Cox & Wyman Ltd., Reading, Berkshire

CONTENTS

INTRODUCTION

Freud's Work Before The Interpretation

The Interpretation of Dreams (*Die Traumdeutung*), a slimmer volume than the much-expanded version that has hitherto been available, was published in November 1899, though postdated by the publisher to 1900. Its muted but respectful reception by reviewers disappointed Freud's hopes and led him to complain unjustly that it had been ignored.[1] For Freud, it was and remained the central book of his prolific career. In 1932 he wrote, in the preface to the third English edition: 'It contains, even according to my present-day judgement, the most valuable of all the discoveries it has been my good fortune to make. Insight such as this falls to one's lot but once in a lifetime' (SE iv. p. xxiii).[2]

When the book came out, however, Freud was more sombre. Writing to his medical colleague, confidant, and fellow-Jew Wilhelm Fliess (1858–1928), he compared the effort of writing it to the struggle with the angel which left the biblical Jacob permanently lame: 'When it appeared that my breath would fail in the wrestling match, I asked the angel to desist; and that is what he has done since then. But I did not turn out to be the stronger, although since then I have been limping noticeably. Yes, I really am forty-four now, an old, somewhat shabby Jew . . .'[3] Behind the wry self-disparagement lies a desperate need for professional success, understandable in a member of the upwardly mobile Jewish middle class of the Habsburg Empire. Freud's parents, Jacob Freud, a wool-merchant, and Amalia Nathansohn, twenty years his junior, both came from Galicia (now the Western Ukraine, then the north-easternmost Habsburg province). They settled first in Freiburg (now Příbor) in Moravia, where their eldest child, Sigmund, was born in 1856, then moved in 1859 to

---

[1] On the book's reception, see Frank J. Sulloway, *Freud, Biologist of the Mind: Beyond the Psychoanalytic Legend,* 2nd edn. (Cambridge, Mass., and London, 1992), 448–53.

[2] References in this form are to *The Standard Edition of the Complete Psychological Works of Sigmund Freud,* ed. James Strachey, 24 vols. (London, 1953–74).

[3] Letter of 7 May 1900, in *The Complete Letters of Sigmund Freud to Wilhelm Fliess, 1887–1904,* tr. and ed. J. M. Masson (Cambridge, Mass., and London, 1985). Future quotations from this book are identified in the text by the date of the letter.

Leipzig and in 1860 to Vienna, where Sigmund was to live until his escape from National Socialism in 1938.

Freud's medical training at Vienna University was stamped by the scientific, positivistic spirit of the later nineteenth century. The Romantic approach to natural science, which sought to disclose a harmonious universal order and saw in it the expression of an indwelling world-soul, was now outdated. Freud's own belief in the unity of nature was based on Darwin, whose *Origin of Species* (1859) explained how one living species changes into another and thus made human beings continuous with all other organisms. Freud tells us in his *Autobiography* (1925) that 'the theories of Darwin, which were then of topical interest, strangely attracted me, for they held out hopes of an extraordinary advance in our understanding of the world' (SE xx. 8). In his first year at university he chose to attend Carl Claus's lectures on 'General Biology and Darwinism'. However, his principal mentor was Ernst von Brücke, who was in turn a follower of the great physiologist and physicist Hermann von Helmholtz, and, like him, was intent on explaining organisms entirely by physical and chemical forces. Occult forces like vital energy were to be excluded. Darwinian evolution, operating through conflict without any animating purpose, suited this hard-nosed approach. Freud adhered to the Helmholtz school's tenets in his early neurological work. Beginning with publications on the nervous systems of fish, he moved on to the human nervous system, exploring the anaesthetic properties of cocaine, speech disorders, and cerebral paralyses in children. He was thus a reputable neurologist before psychoanalysis was ever thought of. It is not surprising, therefore, that his first attempt at devising a psychological theory was thoroughly materialist.

This was the 'Project for a Scientific Psychology', which Freud wrote at great speed in September and October 1895 and never published.[4] Its assumptions and method, however, are still visible in *The Interpretation of Dreams* and indeed underlie much of his later psychoanalytic thought. Briefly, Freud, like the Hehmholtz school, supposes that nervous or mental energy is analogous to physical energy. It works on particles, called neurones (posited by

---

[4] For an introduction, see Ernest Jones, *Sigmund Freud: Life and Work*, 3 vols. (London, 1953–7), i. 422–31; a fuller analysis in Richard Wollheim, *Freud* (London, 1971), ch. 2.

H. W. G. Waldeyer in 1891), which it fills like an electrical charge. This energy circulates within a closed system, occasionally inhibited by contact barriers. Within this system, wishes arise which seek satisfaction. Satisfaction takes the form of discharging energy. At the same time, the system is governed by a principle of constancy which seeks to keep the amount of energy constant. The system is in contact with the external world through the self or ego (*Ich*), imagined as an organization of neurones constantly charged with energy, and able to receive or inhibit stimuli from the outside world. When energy remains unconnected with the outside world, as in dreaming, it flows freely; when connected with the outside world via the ego, its flow is weakened and inhibited. This distinction between the free-flowing energy of the primary process, where desire takes no account of reality, and the hesitant flow of the secondary process, where desire has to compromise with reality, will meet us again at the end of *The Interpretation of Dreams*, and will reappear in Freud's later writings as the contrast between the id and the ego; while the circulation of energy will also appear later as the movement of libido among objects of desire. And it is in the 'Project' that Freud first states that dreams 'are *wish-fulfilments*—that is, primary processes following upon experiences of satisfaction' (SE i. 340).[5]

Also in 1895, Freud and his fellow-physician Josef Breuer published a book, *Studies in Hysteria*, which inaugurates the interactive therapy soon to be known as psychoanalysis. Breuer had in 1880 met a young Viennese woman with a bizarre and varying range of symptoms: she could not drink water, she could speak only English, she had a squint, visual disturbances, partial paralyses. Under hypnosis she related the events that had initiated these afflictions: for example, she had been unable to drink water since seeing a dog drinking out of a glass. Freud applied Breuer's 'talking cure' to other unfortunate women. A British governess, Miss Lucy R., suffered from a depression made worse by a continual smell of burnt pudding.[6] Freud traced this olfactory illusion back to an occasion when, as she was cooking pudding with her charges, a letter arrived from her mother and was seized by the children; during this tussle the pudding got burnt. Not

---

[5] See also Freud's letter to Fliess, 4 March 1895.
[6] Freud describes her as 'English', but as her mother lived in Glasgow, she was presumably Scottish.

satisfied with this explanation, Freud probed further and elicited from Miss R. the admission that she was in love with her employer and distressed by a scene in which he reprimanded her. Having got this off her chest, she regained her good cheer and her sense of smell. Their case studies led Breuer and Freud to maintain, in their preface to *Studies in Hysteria*, that '*Hysterics suffer mainly from reminiscences*' (SE ii. 7). Hysterical symptoms, apparently bizarre, did have a meaning: they were displaced recollections of experiences too painful to remember consciously. Freud makes the further, tacit, assumption that those experiences are always sexual; and he did not scruple to confirm his assumption by asking Miss R. leading questions.

On this basis, Freud theorized that the buried memory tormenting hysterics was of sexual abuse in childhood. He attached huge importance to this theory, equating it with discovering the source of the Nile. Slowly, however, it crumbled, till on 21 September 1897 he confided to his friend Wilhelm Fliess that he no longer believed his own theory. It did not help him cure his patients; it implied that child abuse must be implausibly widespread; and it ignored his patients' tendency to confuse reality with fantasy (especially, perhaps, when Freud was prompting them). Freud was not denying that child abuse often really occurred, though he may have underestimated its frequency.[7] He was accepting—with a cheerfulness that puzzled him—a major defeat to his ambitions.

While gradually abandoning this theory, Freud was also reacting to his father's death on 23 October 1896. Grief, overwork, and worry brought on what has plausibly been called a creative illness.[8] It was a painful spell of inner isolation, following his intense preoccupation with his ideas, and resulting in the exhilarating conviction that he had discovered a great new truth. Freud worked through his illness by probing his own past. He recollected his sexual arousal in infancy by his nurse; he remembered seeing his mother naked during a train journey when he was two and a half; and he acknowledged hostility towards his father. 'Being totally honest with oneself is a good exercise,' he told Fliess on 15 October 1897. 'A single idea of general value dawned on me. I have found, in my own case too,

[7] See J. M. Masson, *The Assault on Truth: Freud's Suppression of the Seduction Theory* (London, 1984), which overstates the case against Freud.

[8] Henri F. Ellenberger, *The Discovery of the Unconscious: The History and Evolution of Dynamic Psychiatry* (London, 1970), 447.

[the phenomenon of] being in love with my mother and jealous of my father, and I now consider it a universal event in early childhood.' The expression of these primordial emotions, he continued, might explain the power of Sophocles' *Oedipus Rex* and Shakespeare's *Hamlet*.

This is the germ of the famous 'Oedipus complex', an idea whose power consists in representing ordinary life as tragic. To become a man—that is, to become like one's father—every man must oppose and overcome his father, paying in guilt the price of maturity. The objections are obvious. *Is* this universal? What about women? What about non-European cultures? Is the 'Oedipus complex' perhaps a self-aggrandizing masculine myth, a generalization from Freud's personal myth of the hero?[9] Whatever the answers, this notion at any rate helped Freud through his personal crisis, in which the main therapeutic activity was writing *The Interpretation of Dreams*. After the book's completion, Freud even overcame what he considered the neurotic travel phobia that had prevented him, despite many Italian trips, from visiting Rome, and spent twelve days in the Holy City in September 1901. *The Interpretation of Dreams* is, among other things, a disguised autobiography, drawing on the dreams that provided Freud with material for self-analysis. But before exploring that dimension, let us examine the argument and structure of the book itself.

Freud's Argument

In summarizing Freud's argument, it will be convenient to stay reasonably close to the structure of *The Interpretation of Dreams*. For although the book is composed with the rhetorical skill, the attention to the reader, characteristic of Freud, its structure is not wholly clear. As the book's guiding metaphor, that of a journey, indicates, it follows in some measure the process by which Freud devised and developed his theories. Thus the key concepts on which the theory is based, the primary and secondary processes, are explained only near the end; and certain nagging problems, like the place of anxiety-dreams in his theory, are not dealt with once and for all, but are treated at different points with solutions that are not always consistent.

[9] See Sulloway, *Freud*, 476–80.

Freud knew that he had to convince his readers of his scholarly respectability by reviewing previous studies of dreams, and he accomplishes this laborious task in a lengthy survey which shows his skill in abstracting the essential points from voluminous and only intermittently rewarding authors. In keeping with his own classical education and the cultural standards of his milieu, he also quotes what classical authors said about dreams. Aristotle is quoted as differing from his predecessors by assigning dreams a physiological rather than a divine origin; Lucretius and Cicero testify to the view that people dream about the things that concern them in waking life. These references, along with the book's epigraph from Virgil, signal that Freud is not writing a narrowly medical treatise but placing the problem of dreams in the mainstream of cultural tradition.

After these preliminaries, which need not detain readers for long, the real substance of the book begins in Chapter 2. Here, preparing to illustrate his own method of dream-interpretation by means of a specimen dream, Freud gives his work yet another genealogy by referring to the symbolic dream-interpretations carried out by Joseph in Genesis 41, to the ancient dream-book of Artemidorus of Daldis (second century AD), and to the popular dream-manuals which circulate at the present day. The folk-belief that dreams have a meaning is nearer the truth than the scepticism of scientists; Freud proposes to place this belief on a scientific footing. To do so, he employs the method of free association, already practised with hysterical patients, in which one relaxes one's concentration and waits for ideas to enter one's mind spontaneously. He first recounts a dream relating to his professional life, that of 'Irma's injection', then reports the associations that occur to him, and finally extracts the desire that gave rise to the dream—the desire that a mistaken diagnosis should be a colleague's fault instead of Freud's. The dream shows how recollections of one's everyday life can be worked into a structure where one person can be substituted for another, where unacknowledged feelings like envy and guilt can find expression, where ideas can be linked by verbal similarities, and where the laws of logic can be suspended. We may wonder that the concealed wish should be a petty piece of professional rivalry, and suspect that the interpretation of the dream could be extended much further even than Freud hints. For the moment, however, the dream has neatly served its purpose of showing that dreams are the fulfilments of wishes.

Having made this point, Freud invites us to pause on our journey and consider the next step. For even if all dreams are wish-fulfilments, very few are obviously so. When thirsty, one may dream of drinking. Children may dream of forbidden food or desirable outings. But in most dreams the manifest content differs from the latent content, and the latter can only be discovered by undoing the mechanisms of censorship and dream-distortion that have hidden it. Often the latent content is unflattering to our vanity. Freud disarms us by recounting a dream in which his ostensible affection for a friend disguised latent malice. Thus we are prepared to accept malevolent motives as the explanation in cases where a wish is apparently *not* fulfilled. A lady's ostensible disappointment at being unable to give a supper-party conceals her wish to prevent a rival from becoming plump and attractive. Another lady's dream, apparently contradicting Freud's theory, is said to stem from a desire to contradict Freud's theory. Another lady, who is distressed by a dream that her daughter is dead, has her dream attributed to long-past wishes, during her unwanted pregnancy, that the embryo might die. A young man's unpleasant dream of being arrested for infanticide turns out to mask the yet more unpleasant fear that his mistress might get pregnant. And in anxiety-dreams—a tough challenge for the theory of dreams as wish-fulfilments—the anxiety is explained as a transformation of unused libido and hence as revealing the presence of inadmissible sexual desires.

As these examples show, Freud's theory is resourceful, perhaps dangerously so, in incorporating apparently recalcitrant counter-examples. His argument proceeds by confronting difficult cases, including many remarkable dreams of his own, absorbing them into the theory, and expanding the theory more and more in the process. Faced with the objection that dreams are mostly trivial, Freud replies that trivial recollections from the previous day (*Tagesreste*, 'day's remainders' or 'residues') are used by the dream to encode its latent content. Hence, although they use trivial material, no dreams are themselves trivial. Somatic stimuli, like physical discomfort while in bed, are similarly employed by the dream as part of its material. Dreams are not bound by our conceptions of time. They have access to material from our childhood, so that embarrassing dreams of being naked in public can be explained as harking back to children's pleasure in nakedness, with the embarrassment introduced by the censorship. And dreams about the deaths of our loved ones point to the emotional ambivalence felt most intensely in childhood, when children may feel intense antagonism towards their siblings and their parents. Here Freud inserts the argument that love for one parent and hostility to the other form a universal pattern illustrated in Sophocles' *Oedipus* and, in more veiled form, in Shakespeare's *Hamlet*. The reader may feel that by introducing this portentous theory of emotional conflict and illustrating it by the masterpieces of Western literature Freud risks bursting the bounds of his dream-book. But for readers sceptical of Freud's theory, there could hardly be more powerful witnesses than Shakespeare and Sophocles. And by citing the classics Freud again conveys his ambition. He wants to show that dreams are central to psychic life, and therefore central to the themes of human culture.

Having led the reader thus far through a large number of dreams and suggested a link between dreams and literature, Freud adopts a more systematic approach. Labelling the activity of the dream 'the dream-work', he discusses the four ways in which a latent dream-thought is reshaped into a dream. One is condensation, in which different dream-elements are fused. Different people may be identified; different ideas may be linked by a pun, as when Freud found at least four ideas combined in the dream-word 'Autodidasker'. At the same time, the dream-work practises displacement, transferring emotional intensity from the centre of the dream-thought to its marginal components. Meanwhile, the dream-thought must be adapted to fit the representational resources of the dream. For example, the dream cannot express logical relations like 'because' or 'either/or'. Hence the illogicality which Freud noted in his dream of Irma's injection. The dream excels, however, in turning thoughts into pictures. It uses visual images that are also found in relatively primitive forms of expression like proverbs, jokes, and songs. However, the absurdity of dreams is limited by a fourth activity which Freud is uncertain whether or not to assign to the dream-work. This is 'secondary revision', which censors the exuberance of the dream, reassures the dreamer by introducing thoughts like 'It's only a dream', and fills in gaps in the dream's structure so as to make it more logical and coherent. Hence the final form of the dream is fully determined, with nothing owed to chance, but at first glance indecipherable. It is like a hieroglyphic inscription, consisting partly of pictures and partly of verbal symbols, which has been distorted, blurred, and defaced.

The last chapter, grandiosely entitled 'The Psychology of the Dream-Processes', does not offer the final clarification we might expect. Instead, Freud warns us that our journey will descend once more into darkness, uncertainty, and speculation. Dealing apparently with several separate topics, he restates some of the assumptions underlying his dream-theory and opens up more mysterious perspectives, indicating the place of his dream-theory within a wider, still half-obscure theory of the mind.

One of these assumptions, operative throughout *The Interpretation* but now reaffirmed, is that all psychical activity is determined by the pursuit of an unconscious purpose. None of it is arbitrary or haphazard. Even the manner in which one recounts one's dreams is shaped by an extension of the dream-work: so there is no need to fear that dreamers give mistaken accounts of their dreams. For the purposes of interpretation, the account of the dream *is* the dream. Hence, though some dreams will in practice elude us, all dreams can in principle be interpreted by Freud's method.

Another assumption is labelled 'regression', and here the reader encounters strange diagrams purporting to represent the direction of psychical energy within the mind. Freud gave these conceptions spatial form because he still thought, as in his 'Project', that it would eventually be possible to locate them within the brain as described by neurology. The normal sequence is that energy is prompted at the perceptual system, passes into consciousness, and thence to the motor system, where it is discharged by action. (I feel an unpleasant sensation, realize that I have been bitten by a mosquito, raise my hand, and swat the insect.) But in dreaming energy flows the other way. Barred by the censor from consciousness, and hence from discharge through action, wishes flow back, collecting unconscious memories on their way, and present themselves once again, now transformed by the dream-work, to the sleeper's lowered consciousness. In this scheme, the 'unconscious' and the 'preconscious' are agencies or authorities (*Instanzen*) which the wish has to satisfy; the unconscious is more tolerant, and helps the wish to smuggle its past the censorship of the preconscious. As a result, psychical en is discharged without disturbing sleep.

Even if we prefer to set aside these schemes as residues of Freud's misplaced neurological ambitions, we need to realize how lasting such ambitions were, for the concept of regression leads on to Freud's account of the primitive character of dream-thought. He prepares for this description by likening the unsatisfied wish underlying the dream to the Greek Titans, the giants overthrown by the Olympian gods and buried under mountains which still quake when the prisoners move their huge limbs. Then he formulates the distinction between two kinds of thinking: the rational, realistic kind that is supposedly normal in waking life, and the irrational kind, found in hysterical patients, which denies unacceptable facts and takes refuge in fantasies. Freud calls the latter kind the primary process. Infants, with their imperious desires, think only in this manner. As one matures, one learns to adjust one's wishes to reality, to repress many infantile desires into the unconscious recesses of the mind, and to replace irrational, associative thinking with logical reasoning. But since Freud still conceives the mind as a closed system, desires are not expelled but only hidden away. They reassert themselves most riotously in dreams, where the primary process engages in conflict with the censor; but they also manifest themselves in neurotic symptoms, and, as Freud would argue in his next books, in jokes, slips of the tongue, and seemingly casual but in fact deeply significant mistakes. And in later works, Freud would relate the childhood of the individual to the early stages of humanity, and seek the origins of art and religion in the supposedly irrational thought-processes of primeval man.

Arguing with Freud

What Freud offers as a scientific theory looks more like an imaginative vision. With its scale and sweep, and its revelation of profound and unwelcome truths about human life, the theory invites an awed suspension of disbelief. We are, it seems, embedded in the organic world and in thrall to the past more deeply even than Darwin had envisaged. The violently ambivalent emotions of our childhood still shape our adult experiences and are themselves shaped in a structure inherited, as Freud would later contend, from the primitive past of humanity.

> Archaic fevers shake
> Our healthy flesh and blood
> Plumped in the passing day
> And fed with pleasant food.
> The fathers' anger and ache
> Will not, will not away
> And leave the living alone . . .[10]

And this archaic heritage makes itself known both in the master-pieces of our literature and in the seemingly nonsensical productions of our dreaming minds. Freud has delivered a rebuke to our vanity.

Still, we should respect Freud's intellectual ambitions by arguing with his theory. We should also remember that the passage of a century will inevitably have revealed the flaws in this, as in any thesis, and will also have disclosed its underlying presuppositions. What Freud took for granted may now strike us as dated, implausible, or absurd, insofar as we inhabit a different cultural world and follow a different intellectual paradigm. But that difference itself is partly of Freud's making.

We may wonder, first, whether the theory is too powerful for its own good. As Freud's theoretical apparatus rolls onward, it chews up all the counter-evidence in its path, at the risk of rendering the theory unfalsifiable and vacuous. For if no counter-evidence were conceivable, the theory could not be tested and could not be developed. As we have seen, the theory that all dreams are wish-fulfilments finds it hardest to cope with dreams of fear and punishment. Having claimed that anxiety in dreams comes from transformed libido, Freud finally adopts another, evasive strategy by saying that anxiety-dreams concern him only insofar as they illustrate the dream-work and really belong to the psychology of the neuroses. As for punishment-dreams, they express the desire to be punished for indulging a forbidden wish. In any case, every successful dream is a wish-fulfilment because it fulfils the wish to sleep. To Freud's credit, he resorts to this desperate argument—for the wish to sleep can hardly be the latent dream-thought—only once and in passing, while his explanation of punishment-dreams is clearly an interim solution which he will worry away at until, in *The Ego and the Id* (1923), he proposes the concept of the superego.

---

[10] Edwin Muir, 'The Fathers', in his *Collected Poems* (London, 1984), 139.

Turning to particular instances, Freud's interpretations reveal a gender-bias that is both comical and discreditable. As with his hysterics, he assumes that his female patients are unconsciously obsessed with sex and reveal their obsession through involuntary puns. A 'reserved' young woman dreams that she goes to market, cannot buy butcher's meat, but is offered strange-looking vegetables (p. 140). The 'butcher' makes Freud think of a vulgar expression, 'to shut the butcher's shop' (=to button one's fly), while the vegetables are identified as black radish (*schwarzer Rettich*) and decoded as 'Schwarzer, rett' Dich!' (Black, save yourself!). Apparently Freud is imputing both sexual and racial fantasies to his patient.[11] A footnote mentions that she accused him of sexually provocative behaviour: whatever happened in the consulting-room, the atmosphere must have been highly charged, and Freud's interpretations might well have been felt as sexual aggression. Another woman patient dreams about Italy (p. 179); since she has never been there, Freud interprets as 'Genitalien' (genitals) the phrase 'gen Italien' (Italy-wards) which, be it noted, is so obsolete that the woman is highly unlikely to have actually used it. Freud's double standard becomes obvious when he fails to see any sexual meaning in his own dream about riding a horse through a narrow passage between two carts (p. 177).

Freud's weakness for doubles entendres illustrates a striking feature of his dream-interpretations: their heavy reliance on word-play. He draws freely on colloquial expressions, as when a basket in a dream evokes the standard expression 'einen Korb geben' (to give someone a basket, i.e. to reject a suitor). A dream about a box evokes the English word 'box' and hence the sexual connotations of *other* German words for box. Freud's own dream about Count Thun brings in English, Latin, and Spanish. His dreams often turn on invented portmanteau words like 'norekdal' and 'Autodidasker'. This reliance on puns gives Freud an interpretative freedom which might often be considered licence. It anticipates the verbal bias of *Jokes and their Relation to the Unconscious* (1905), which deals with witticisms rather than humour in general, and of *The Psychopathology of Everyday Life* (1901), which deals with many

[11] The 'black' may have been suggested by the Ashanti village from West Africa, complete with inhabitants, which was displayed in the Prater in Vienna in 1896 and attracted innumerable visitors. See Andrew Barker, *Telegrams from the Soul: Peter Altenberg and the Culture of fin-de-siècle Vienna* (Columbia, SC, 1996), 63–74.

kinds of mistake but especially with the verbal parapraxes now famous as 'Freudian slips'.

Evidently Freud, like many writers, was under the spell of words. This is not surprising if we consider his multilingual education. Although his family, as Jews intent on assimilation, had provided him only with perfunctory Hebrew teaching, his education had given him a solid grounding in the Greek and Latin classics. As a school-boy he corresponded with a friend in Spanish; he translated several books by John Stuart Mill from English; his French was good enough for him to study in Paris. The effect of his classical education should be underlined. He wrote that his classical learning had brought him 'as much consolation as anything else in the struggle of life' (SE xiii. 241). Throughout his life he astonished people by his familiarity with classical philology.[12] His theory of parapraxes has been most searchingly criticized by a classical scholar, who compares them to textual errors.[13] Indeed Freud's preferred analogy for dream-interpretation is decipherment, suggesting how a philologist tries to restore the original sense of an inscription blurred by time or a text corrupted by a succession of inaccurate copyists. In philology, as in dream-analysis, the original may be remote from the text, as in the example quoted by A. E. Housman from a German critic: 'If the sense requires it, I am prepared to write *Constantinopolitanus* where the MSS. have the monosyllabic interjection *o*.'[14]

The extremely verbal character of Freud's mind leads him to underestimate visual imagery in dreams. Freud admits that his own dreams are not very visual: 'my own dreams have in general fewer sensory elements than I have to reckon with in the dreams of others' (p. 358). Punning dreams are apparently not uncommon, though seldom as lapidary as the dream-declaration 'Iona Cathedral'.[15] But most people report dreaming principally in visual images. Freud, however, assumes that dreams start from a dream-thought that is best expressed in words and translate it into a picture-language

---

[12] See Ernest Jones, *Free Associations: Memories of a Psycho-Analyst* (London, 1959), 35.

[13] See Sebastiano Timpanaro, *The Freudian Slip*, tr. Kate Soper (London, 1974).

[14] Housman, 'The Application of Thought to Textual Criticism', in his *Selected Prose*, ed. John Carter (Cambridge, 1962), 142.

[15] See Charles Rycroft, *The Innocence of Dreams*, 2nd edn. (London, 1991), 124–5.

which is intellectually inferior because it cannot convey logical connections; the analyst restores to the dream its verbal character. However, the first edition of *The Interpretation of Dreams* at least stops short of the crude doctrine of sexual symbolization with which Freud's dream-theory is popularly but misleadingly associated. It was only in later editions that Freud, influenced by his colleague Wilhelm Stekel, added all the mechanical equivalences—staircases signify the sexual act, tables represent women, losing one's hair or teeth symbolizes castration, etc.—which have given so much satisfaction to the simple-minded and done so much to bring Freudian analysis into disrepute. Freud revelled in linguistic play, but, despite his appreciation of painting and especially sculpture, he did not know what to make of visual imagery in dreams. Freud's own dream-theory is, in this respect, seriously skewed and unfaithful to most people's experience.

As a scientific rationalist, Freud distrusts the manifest content of dreams. But his distinction between the meaningless manifest content and the all-important latent content has been questioned by Jung and others. Why should not the manifest content be meaningfully related to problems and tensions that preoccupy the dreamer? If, as surveys suggest, American blacks dream more often than whites about loss, injury, and violence, this is presumably not because they suffer more from castration-anxiety but because they are more exposed to violence. The astonishing dreams collected by Charlotte Beradt during the Third Reich show how the atmosphere of terror penetrated into people's unconscious minds.[16] Many dreams can make sense without Freud's tortuous decipherments.

In assigning dreams to the primary process, the mode of thought that refuses to acknowledge reality as an obstacle to its desires and regresses from logic to images, Freud seems to distrust the imaginative activity by which dreams are shaped. The shortcomings in his theory of dreams are linked to his inability to account for artistic creation. He thought that both activities were forms of day-dreaming, fantasies in which the censorship is relaxed, desire is allowed to roam, the constraints of reality are temporarily ignored, and infantile experience again comes to the fore. In his essay 'Creative Writers and Day-Dreaming' (1908) he maintained that the

---

[16] Beradt, *The Third Reich of Dreams*, tr. Adriane Gottwald (Chicago, 1968).

creative artist indulged such fantasies by softening their egoistic character so that the reader could share the vicarious pleasure of overcoming obstacles and gaining love and fortune. But this notoriously inadequate essay does nothing to explain the power of great art, although or because it deals with painful material, to give us a feeling of satisfaction, harmony, and uplift; nor the power of even simple stories and pictures to give shape to our experience and make us feel more at home in the world. The idea that some dreams at least may be like imaginative creations, restoring our psychic balance and helping us towards wholeness, was again left to Jung.[17]

Another deficiency in Freud's account of dreams is his downplaying of their emotional power. For him, emotion in dreams shows that the censorship has failed in its normal task of reducing the affective strength of dream-material. Unlike Jung, he shows no interest in those 'big dreams' which tend to come at important thresholds in one's life—puberty, early middle age, the approach of death—and can give one's life a new direction. A famous example is the symbolic dream which the philosopher Descartes dreamt on the night of 10–11 November 1619 and associated with an intellectual breakthrough.[18] In other cultures such dreams can be accommodated within a meaningful pattern. They may be understood as revelations by the gods or as initiating the dreamer into a preordained role as seer or shaman. Thus young Ojibwa boys in North America used to undergo a 'dream fast' to induce dreams of the animals or birds that would become their guardian spirits. When the culture disintegrates under colonial pressure, however, such 'culture pattern' dreams vanish and only 'individual' dreams remain.[19] One of Freud's later patients, the young Russian who has gone down in psychoanalytic history as the Wolf Man, brought him an extraordinary childhood dream about seven white wolves sitting in a tree outside the dreamer's bedroom window (SE xvii. 29). By dubious reasoning, Freud traced the dream back to a speculative episode in which the dreamer saw his parents

---

[17] See C. G. Jung, 'On the Nature of Dreams', *The Collected Works*, ed. Herbert Read, Michael Fordham, and Gerhard Adler, tr. R. F. C. Hull, 2nd edn. (London and Princeton, 1970), viii. 281–97.

[18] See Stephen Gaukroger, *Descartes: An Intellectual Biography* (Oxford, 1995), 106–11; Marie-Louise von Franz, 'The Dream of Descartes', in her *Dreams* (London and Boston, 1998), 107–91.

[19] See Jackson Steward Lincoln, *The Dream in Primitive Cultures* (London, 1935).

copulating.[20] But its analogues in Russian folklore, and some unusual features of the patient, suggest that it was an initiatory dream; the Russian was Westernized enough to have lost the key to its meaning, and Freud's analysis ensured that he never found it.[21]

The Interpretation *as Autobiography*

Although the applicability of Freud's theory may be limited, it enabled him to make sense of his own dreams, many of which are recounted and analysed in great detail. Freud tempered his indiscretion by prudently withholding much further material, some of which researchers have since brought to light. With their help, we can see how far *The Interpretation of Dreams* is a semi-disguised autobiography. Carl Schorske, who explores this dimension in his inspiring study of fin-de-siècle Vienna, remarks: 'Imagine St Augustine weaving his *Confessions* into *The City of God*, or Rousseau integrating his *Confessions* as a subliminal plot into *The Origins of Inequality*: such is the procedure of Freud in *The Interpretation of Dreams*.'[22]

Many autobiographical elements are of course present on the surface. We learn much about Freud's dealings with his father, other relatives, and colleagues, about his medical training, his daily life, his health, his holidays with his family. The book also incorporates much of 1890s Vienna, from its politics to its sexuality and its slang; as a contemporary document, it should be read alongside the early chapters of Stefan Zweig's *The World of Yesterday* and Arthur Schnitzler's recently published diaries for the 1890s. Our present concern, however, is with what remains half-concealed in Freud's major dreams.

Professional ambition and anxiety play an important role. We should remember that in 1899, when Freud published *The Interpretation of Dreams*, he was more than halfway through a long life which had hitherto brought many disappointments. His appointment as

---

[20] For a tart summary of Freud's argument see Roy Porter, *A Social History of Madness: Stories of the Insane* (London, 1987), 223–8 (with further references, p. 251); on Freud's rhetoric, Stanley Fish, 'Withholding the Missing Portion: Psychoanalysis and Rhetoric', in his *Doing What Comes Naturally* (Oxford, 1989), 525–54.

[21] See Carlo Ginzburg, 'Freud, the Wolf-Man, and the Werewolves', in his *Myths, Emblems, Clues*, tr. John and Anne C. Tedeschi (London, 1990), 146–55.

[22] Schorske, *Fin-de-siècle Vienna: Politics and Culture* (Cambridge, 1981), 183.

lecturer in neuropathology at Vienna University enabled him in 1886
to marry Martha Bernays, to whom he had been engaged for four
years, but in order to support a family he had also to open a private
medical practice. Despite his prolific research, his promotion to professor was delayed till 1902, partly by anti-Semitism. In 1897, when
his name was unavailingly put forward, he had a dream identifying
another Jewish colleague, R., with his Uncle Josef. Since this uncle
had been sentenced to ten years' imprisonment for handling forged
banknotes, Freud's dream equates Jewishness with criminality as
professional handicaps and displaces them onto a colleague.

Despite his frequent disclaimers, Freud was intensely ambitious.
He hoped to make his name by an epoch-making scientific discovery.
In 1884 he narrowly failed to win credit for discovering the anaesthetic properties of cocaine. Although Freud published an article on
this topic, the crucial research was done just afterwards by his friend
Carl Koller. Freud's resentment finds expression in the dream of the
botanical monograph, dating from early March 1898. The dried
plant specimen in the monograph is associated, via the leaves of an
artichoke, with the pages that Freud and his sister were encouraged
by their father to tear out of an illustrated book. Thus books here are
consigned to desiccation and destruction, implying Freud's own
failure as a writer. His father, who had died some sixteen months
earlier, is cast here as an enemy of books and thus covertly blamed
for Freud's failure. To atone for this hostile thought, however, Freud
recalls how in 1885 his father's glaucoma was operated on, with
Koller administering the cocaine anaesthesia, and he puts himself in
his father's place by imagining how he too might undergo such an
operation.

The friend who restores Freud's sight by supervising his glaucoma operation is the Berlin ear, nose, and throat specialist Wilhelm
Fliess, who makes many covert appearances in *The Interpretation of
Dreams*. After their first meeting in autumn 1887, when Fliess, visiting Vienna, attended Freud's lectures, they soon became close
friends. Freud's letters to Fliess, an invaluable source for his personal and intellectual biography, have embarrassed Freudians by
showing how their hero temporarily accepted Fliess's eccentric-
sounding theories. Fliess maintained, for example, that the female
menstrual cycle of twenty-eight days corresponded to a male cycle of
twenty-three days and that these two periodicities governed much of

life; that all human beings were essentially bisexual; and that many nasal disorders could be explained by positing a physiological link between the nose and the genitals. As Frank Sulloway has shown, these theories were neither unique to Fliess nor lacking in physiological evidence.[23] The theory of universal bisexuality powerfully influenced Freud's later theory of sexual development and is highly relevant to present-day debates in gender theory.[24]

Freud's acceptance of Fliess's naso-genital theory led to the events that underlie his specimen dream of Irma's injection. In March 1895 Freud treated a young woman called Emma Eckstein for hysteria.[25] Assuming that her hysteria was sexual in origin, he thought Fliess might cure it by operating on her nose. After the operation Emma kept having nosebleeds, till a fortnight later a massive and near-fatal haemorrhage obliged Freud to call in another doctor, who removed from her nasal cavity half a metre of gauze left there by Fliess. Deeply distressed by Fliess's incompetence, Freud assured him that he was not to blame for this 'minimal oversight' (13 March 1895) and that Emma's nosebleeds were really motivated by her desire for the doctor's love (4 May 1896). In the dream, Freud defends himself against similar charges of professional incompetence by illogically blaming his colleagues. But his self-defence is made harder by other guilty associations. He recalls how a dear friend hastened his own death by cocaine abuse. This friend was Ernst Fleischl von Marxow (1846–91), a physiologist in Brücke's laboratory, whom Freud greatly admired. Fleischl had a painful infection in his right hand which required repeated surgery. To dull the pain, he took morphine, and became addicted to it. Freud, who had helped pioneer cocaine as an anaesthetic, encouraged him to overcome his morphine addiction by switching to cocaine, which was then thought to be normally nonaddictive. Thus a dream which, according to the discreet interpretation Freud gave his readers, deals only with professional rivalry, turns out to encode some of Freud's most searing experiences of guilt. It also reveals the intense, almost homosocial bonds linking male colleagues. Emma Eckstein is blamed for her own

---

[23] Sulloway, *Freud*, ch. 5.
[24] See Marjorie Garber, *Vice Versa: Bisexuality and the Eroticism of Everyday Life* (London, 1995).
[25] For a detailed narrative of the Eckstein affair, see Masson, *The Assault on Truth*, 55–72.

haemorrhages and serves as a channel for affection between Freud and Fliess, while Irma in the dream, surrounded by doctors who examine, percuss, and inject her, seems almost to be the passive victim of male group sexuality.

Freud's dreams not only express his own frustration at finding his career apparently blocked by scientific failure and anti-Semitic prejudice; they reveal much about his feeling of isolation in an Austro-Hungarian Empire that was falling under the sway of dema-gogic nationalism. As Austrian Jews, Freud and his family identified strongly with the central Imperial government which had gradually extended civil liberties to the Jews, beginning in 1781 with the Tol-eration Patents of the enlightened despot Joseph II and ending in 1867 with complete emancipation as part of the constitutional com-promise (*Ausgleich*) between the Austrian and Hungarian halves of the Empire. They were loyal to the German language and culture and often cast longing eyes northwards to Germany, where political Liberalism seemed to have more effective spokesmen. Freud himself, as a student at Vienna University, belonged to the radical and German-nationalist Leseverein der deutschen Studenten Wiens (Reading Club for German Students at Vienna). This placed him at one extreme of the Liberal camp. The heyday of Liberalism in Austria began in 1868, when the Emperor Franz Joseph appointed a cabinet led by the liberally inclined aristocrat Prince 'Carlos' Auersperg and consisting mainly of middle-class ministers. Freud refers to this 'Bourgeois Ministry' in connection with his dream about his uncle, saying that it seemed to assure Jews that they could scale the heights of political power, and thus explaining the ambition in his dream as the residue of youthful hopes. From this, Schorske and others have concluded that the young Freud held political ambi-tions which were displaced into science; but the evidence is slight.[26]

By the 1890s, when Freud dreamt the dreams analysed in *The Interpretation*, the political outlook was much bleaker. The Liberals had fallen from power in 1879: their free-market economics led to financial scandals and failed to help the growing number of indus-trial workers, who turned instead to the Socialists and to the welfare

---

[26] Schorske, *Fin-de-siècle Vienna*, 189. Seminal though his book has been, Schorske, who is also the historian of German Social Democracy, tends to assume that political activity forms the whole duty of man and that cultural activity is only a substitute or sublimation.

policies of the Christian Social Party, founded by Dr Karl Lueger
and others. Lueger, who presented himself as defender of the common man against Jewish capitalism, alarmed Freud and many others
by his distasteful anti-Semitism. He was elected Mayor of Vienna
five times before the Emperor consented to let him assume office in
April 1897. Meanwhile, conservative governments were anxious
to conciliate the increasingly powerful nationalist movements
elsewhere in the Empire. In April 1897 the Prime Minister, Count
Badeni, issued two language decrees requiring all public employees
in Bohemia and Moravia to know both German and Czech. The
Germans replied by rioting throughout the summer in Prague, other
Bohemian towns, and Vienna. They also borrowed the Czechs' tac-
tics of parliamentary obstruction: it was on this occasion that the
Liberal deputy, Dr Lecher, spoke for thirteen hours, and, more
amazingly still, always stuck to the point. On 28 November Franz
Joseph accepted Badeni's resignation. These turbulent events inter-
ested Freud all the more since his family were German-speaking
Jews who had come to Vienna via Moravia, one of the areas where
German culture was retreating before militant Czech nationalism.

This is the background to Freud's 'revolutionary dream' of early
August 1898, inspired by seeing the Prime Minister, Count Thun—
successor to the unfortunate Badeni, and himself obliged to resign
the following year—setting off to consult with the Emperor in the
summer resort of Bad Ischl (p. 160) Freud's conscious rebelliousness,
shown by whistling the aria in which Mozart's Figaro challenges
Count Almaviva, is strengthened in the dream by recalling his early
German nationalism and the revolution of 1848, eight years before
his own birth. He brings in his reading of Zola's revolutionary novel
Germinal and the defeat of the Spanish Armada by England, a nation
to which Freud was so attached that he named one of his sons Oliver
after Oliver Cromwell. His dream-rebellion, however, extends to the
lower bodily stratum. Zola's description of a farting competition
provides a link with the wind that dispersed the Armada, while the
French word *pissenlit* (dandelion, literally 'piss-in-bed') is connected with holding the glass for an old, half-blind man to urinate
into, with Freud's early bed-wetting, and with his desire to prove to
his father (the blind man) that he has achieved something in life.
Associating urine with childhood megalomania, Freud thinks also of
Rabelais's giant Gargantua, who floods the city of Paris with his

urine. In his unconscious, then, Freud imagines himself as a giant who can mobilize his prodigious powers of pissing and farting against the over-polite aristocracy. Although historians have made much of this dream's revolutionary content, it might more aptly be called Freud's Rabelaisian dream.

A different kind of rebellion is suggested in Freud's many dreams concerned with Rome. Despite his fondness for Italy, some inhibition prevented him from visiting Rome until September 1901. In the dreams Rome appears as an object of both enmity and desire. Freud associates it with the Roman Catholic Church, which represented for him the stronghold of religious obscurantism in contrast to his own scientific enlightenment. To a German nationalist, who undoubtedly sympathized with Bismarck's campaign against the political power of the Church in the 1870s, Rome would also represent a deadly political enemy. And when Freud recalls how his father, as a young man, meekly submitted to the insults of a 'Christian' (i.e. a Gentile), Rome comes also to typify the anti-Semitism which was indeed rife, often with clerical support, in Freud's Vienna. Against this Rome, Freud casts himself as a military assailant. He identifies himself with Hannibal, the Carthaginian and hence Semitic general who defeated the Romans but failed to take Rome, and with Napoleon's marshal Masséna, who was popularly but wrongly supposed to be Jewish, and who fought, unsuccessfully, against British forces in the Peninsular War.

Why, however, does Freud identify only with unsuccessful assailants? Why does he not think of Alaric the Goth, who conquered Rome in AD 410, or the Imperial forces that sacked Rome in 1527? To Freud, Rome is also an object of desire. He wants to get there one day; he does not want it to be destroyed. More than that: it is precisely Catholic Rome that Freud desires. For he associated the Catholic Church with the Czech nanny who, as he told Fliess, took him to church as a child, aroused his sexual desires, and was then dismissed for stealing (letters of 3, 4, 15 October 1897). The anxiety caused by her loss may, as Paul Vitz has argued, underlie the taboo on visiting Rome which he only overcame after working through his fears by writing *The Interpretation of Dreams*.[27] And on his many visits to Rome from 1901 onwards, it was not classical but Christian

---

[27] Vitz, *Sigmund Freud's Christian Unconscious* (New York, 1988), 22.

Rome that fascinated him, particularly of course Michelangelo's statue of Moses in the church of San Pietro in Vincoli, about which he wrote an essay in art history (SE xiii. 209–36).

If we accept the terms of Freud's theory, the historical and cultural material that Freud's unconscious shapes into dreams is always based on the template of early family relations. His professional friendships and rivalries correspond to the model he describes late in *The Interpretation of Dreams*: 'An intimate friend and a hated foe have always been necessary to my emotional life' (p. 314). Thus his friend Fliess and his rival Koller fit into the model of his ambivalent childhood relationship with his nephew John, who was one year older. His rebellion against Count Thun is ultimately directed against his father. And his ambivalence towards Rome is based on his early attitude to those two contrasting mother-figures, his taboo-breaking nurse and his dominating mother. If we were to adopt Jung's theory of dreams, however, we would want to turn things round and say that individual relationships fit the mythical templates of the collective unconscious. We need to bear both these interpretive possibilities in mind as we approach the dream which, of all those in this long book, has the best claim to rank as a 'big dream', that of the Three Fates (p. 157).

In itself, this dream may not seem impressive, but Freud's associations to it introduce, via far-fetched puns, a dense thematic network. He identifies the three women in the kitchen as the three Fates. The first, who seems to be making dumplings, is a mother providing nourishment. Freud then recalls how his mother proved that we are made of earth by rubbing her hands together, as though making dumplings, and producing black scales (a result not easy to reproduce experimentally, by the way). Thus the dumplings suggest also our eventual return to the earth in death. In his strange mythographic essay of 1913, 'The Theme of the Three Caskets', Freud connects the three caskets in *The Merchant of Venice* and the three daughters in *King Lear* with 'the three forms taken by the figure of the mother in the course of a man's life—the mother herself, the beloved one who is chosen after her pattern, and lastly the Mother Earth who receives him once more' (SE xii. 301). Returning to the dream, we note how Freud's puns and quotations introduce repeated motifs of food (fish, flesh, milk) and of earth ('dirt' and 'dust' in the quotations from Herder and Goethe). Shakespeare is significantly misquoted: Prince Hal's words in *2 Henry IV*, 'Thou owest God a death', turn into 'You owe Nature a death', supporting Freud's naturalistic myth of man's passage from birth to burial. The third Fate, the beloved, is vestigially present in the name 'Pélagie'. Alexander Grinstein has traced it back to Charles Kingsley's novel *Hypatia* (1853), where Pelagia is a seductive dancer and sister to the ascetic monk Philammon.[28] In this haunting dream, therefore, the father, otherwise ubiquitous in Freud's theories, has yielded to the ambivalent, archetypal figure of the mother who dispenses nourishment, love, and finally death.

Freud's Disputed Legacy

In its reception, *The Interpretation of Dreams* shares the curious fate that Freud's work as a whole has encountered. Nowadays, anyone who studies psychology at university may never be required to read anything by Freud or his followers. But anyone who studies literature will almost certainly find that the course has a theoretical component in which knowledge of Freud and recent Freudian thinkers is mandatory. The scientific study of the mind can proceed with little reference to Freud, but for the study of literature, and more generally for the study of culture, the approaches first developed in *The Interpretation of Dreams* are indispensable.

The failure of psychoanalysis to demonstrate its scientific status has been the starting-point for some wide-ranging critiques of Freud and his thought. We may distinguish two versions of such critiques. The scientific version, represented especially by Adolf Grünbaum, judges Freud's work by the standards of scientific method and finds it wanting.[29] It especially points out that the analytic session cannot provide objective and testable clinical data, because the psychoanalytic method depends on emotional interaction between analyst and analysand, and because it is thus all too easy for the analyst to suggest to the analysand the emotional connections which the latter is supposed to discover. Such critics also doubt the effectiveness of

[28] Grinstein, *On Sigmund Freud's Dreams* (Detroit, 1968), 179–86.
[29] See Adolf Grünbaum, *The Foundations of Psychoanalysis: A Philosophical Critique* (Berkeley, Los Angeles, and London, 1984); for a reply, David Sachs, 'In Fairness To Freud', in Jerome Neu (ed.), *The Cambridge Companion to Freud* (Cambridge, 1991), 309–38.

psychoanalysis as a therapy, on the grounds that there are no clear criteria by which its success can be measured. The more polemical version of anti-Freudian criticism is represented especially by Frederick Crews, who was once a distinguished Freudian literary critic but who now calls himself a 'Freud-basher'. In this account, Freud was not only unscientific in his methods: he was a charlatan who browbeat his patients, falsified his findings, tyrannized his followers, and (for good measure) cheated on his wife.[30] And despite his constant hostility to all religion, expressed most uncompromisingly in *The Future of an Illusion* (1927), he has even been pilloried as an impostor who sought to found a false religion.[31]

What are we to make of these critiques, and what is really at stake? Often, Freud's critics are stating the obvious. Psychoanalysis does not and cannot conform to the objective and experimental model of science. Although Freud drew up guidelines to minimize the analyst's influence on the analysand, the analytic session is very different from a laboratory experiment. Psychoanalysts and psychotherapists constantly try to revise the clinical models which help them to understand their patients, and they have produced a rich and varied body of reflection. But such revision should be seen as the refinement of analytic and therapeutic techniques rather than the construction of hypotheses to be tested experimentally. Many psychoanalysts accept that their work is 'a craft rather than a science'.[32]

In other respects, Freud's detractors show a strange tunnel vision. They make many valid points about Freud's therapeutic blunders and his undoubted tendency to steer patients in the direction he wanted. They show an irreproachable concern for reason and evidence, but they seldom present any positive purpose to which these intellectual tools should be applied. In their obsession with Freud himself, they forget that psychoanalysis has developed into a variety

[30] See especially Frederick Crews *et al.*, *The Memory Wars: Freud's Legacy in Dispute* (New York, 1995), and, in reply, Jonathan Lear, 'On Killing Freud (Again)', in his *Open Minded: Working out the Logic of the Soul* (Cambridge, Mass., 1998), 16–32. On Freud's relations with his sister-in-law, see Lisa Appignanesi and John Forrester, *Freud's Women* (London, 1992), 50–3.

[31] See Richard Webster, *Why Freud Was Wrong: Sin, Science and Psychoanalysis* (London, 1995), which incorporates numerous earlier critiques.

[32] Anthony Bateman and Jeremy Holmes, *Introducing Psychoanalysis: Contemporary Theory and Practice* (London, 1995), 243.

of schools of thought engaged in healthy competition. Beyond that, psychoanalytic theories have been absorbed into the common-sense understanding with which we approach other people and ourselves. Psychoanalysis has helped us to understand the psyche as deep, complex, and mysterious. Hence psychoanalysis is not, as its detractors often imply, an alternative to treatment by mind-altering drugs like Prozac, nor to self-help manuals that offer us useful knowledge—but, too often, only knowledge—about one another. It approaches people, not as essentially transparent beings who can be studied, adjusted, and manipulated, but as creatures who have—to use a word Freud would not have liked—souls, and who are characteristically enigmatic to themselves and to others.

Like any healthy intellectual and spiritual movement, psycho-analysis, despite the constant dangers of orthodoxy and funda-mentalism, has been rich in creative heresy. One development, associated with Jung, places more trust than Freud did in the mani-fest content of dreams and visions, taking them as guides to the individual's spiritual development, and thus reasserting the Roman-tic heritage of psychoanalysis.[33] Another, associated with the maverick Jacques Lacan, builds on Freud's conception of the verbal character of unconscious processes, combines it with structural linguistics, and proclaims that 'the unconscious is structured like a language'.[34] Yet a third development in psychoanalytic reflection places the emphasis on the act of interpretation and argues that psychoanalysis is less a scientific theory of the mind than a hermeneutic, a technique of understanding, and hence a branch of the humanities like biography and philology.[35] Like any classic, *The Interpretation of Dreams* has retreated into the past while fructifying the present.

Within dream research, *The Interpretation of Dreams* anticipates both the major directions of subsequent study: the inquiries into the *function* and into the *meaning* of dreams. Neurophysiologists have found that our sleep alternates between deep sleep, with slow breath-ing and heartbeat, and light sleep in which rapid eye movements

---

[33] See Polly Young-Eisendrath and Terence Dawson (eds.), *The Cambridge Companion to Jung* (Cambridge, 1997), esp. Douglas A. Davis, 'Freud, Jung, and Psychoanalysis', 35–51.

[34] See David Macey, *Lacan in Contexts* (London and New York, 1988), ch. 5.

[35] See Jürgen Habermas, *Knowledge and Human Interests*, tr. J. J. Shapiro (Boston, 1971).

(hence REM-sleep) suggest that we are following interior events in our mind's eye. Dreams occur in the latter state, which occupies about a quarter of our sleeping time. If repeatedly woken during REM-sleep, we become anxious, irritable, sometimes distressed. It is likely, therefore, that in addition to the physiological function of maintaining our sleep, dreams often have the psychological function of helping our minds to process and eliminate trivial or threatening material. The dreamer by definition does not know about this function, just as, in Freud's view, the latent dream-thoughts could be disclosed by the analyst but not by the dreamer. At least some dreams, however, may have not only a function but also a meaning, which may be apparent in the manifest content. There need be no universal key, no system of symbols, to explain this meaning; a dream has been successfully interpreted when its meaning suddenly clicks for the dreamer. The dream may be a message from one part of the self to another, seeking, as in Jung's theory, to restore psychic balance. The message may be shaped by the individual's creative and artistic capacities. Some imaginative people may have a special talent for dreaming, as for singing, drawing, or storytelling.

Despite Freud's commitment to scientific rationalism, he created a psychology which, in Lionel Trilling's words, 'makes poetry indigenous to the very constitution of the mind'.[36] Freud himself made an over-sharp distinction between the irrationality of the primary process, which produces the absurd manifest content of the dream, and the rational reflection which restores the latent content. But what if we see 'irrational', or (more politely) symbolic thinking, not as the antithesis to rational reflection but as the basis from which conceptual thinking develops?[37] A dream-interpretation would then take dream-symbolism seriously and educe from it a conceptual meaning, just as the interpretation of a poem accepts symbolism as a valid mode of expression and gingerly educes conceptual implications from it, while taking care not to substitute the interpretation for the poem. Hence the importance of *The Interpretation of Dreams* for the study of culture. Freud and the other early psychoanalysts were highly cultured people who wanted to apply their theories to literature, art, and history: Ernest Jones wrote about *Hamlet*,

---

[36] Trilling, 'Freud and Literature', in *The Liberal Imagination* (London, 1951), 52.

[37] See Jonathan Lear, *Love and its Place in Nature: A Philosophical Interpretation of Freudian Psychoanalysis* (London, 1990), 8.

Theodor Reik about Schnitzler, Marie Bonaparte about Edgar Allan Poe, Otto Rank about the representation of incest in world literature and mythology, while Lou Andreas-Salomé was herself a writer of fiction. Psychoanalysis seemed potentially able to bridge the division between the 'two cultures'.

The impact on creative literature of *The Interpretation of Dreams*, and of Freudianism in general, is less than is sometimes assumed. As Freud was the first to admit, creative writers anticipated his findings by their own psychological intuition. Writers do not create by anxiously following the instructions of a psychological theorist; and insofar as writers do absorb the psychological theories of their time, the early twentieth century offered many others besides Freudianism. The greatest psychological novelists—Marcel Proust, Robert Musil, Virginia Woolf—took little interest in Freud.[38] The dreamlike fluidity of stream-of-consciousness narrative antedates Freud: its earliest practitioner, Édouard Dujardin (*Les Lauriers sont coupés*, 1888), was inspired by Wagner's 'continuous melody'. On the other hand, Franz Kafka, recording what had passed through his mind while writing his 'breakthrough' story 'The Judgement' in 1912, wrote: 'Thoughts about Freud, naturally', and it is possible that first- or even second-hand acquaintance with Freud's early works helped him to make a confident and concentrated use of images, especially in his haunting story 'A Country Doctor'.[39] A more deliberate use of Freud's dream-theory was made by the Surrealists, who in poetry and painting tried to abandon rational control and juxtapose images from the unconscious. Above all, the verbal character that Freud imputed to the unconscious formed the foundation for Joyce's epic in dream-language, *Finnegans Wake*, where an archetypal narrative emerges through a multilingual swirl.

It is not in literature, but in literary criticism, that Freudianism has had a lasting impact. The great critics of the mid-twentieth century, like William Empson, W. H. Auden, Edmund Wilson, and Lionel Trilling, absorbed psychoanalysis as part of the intellectual equipment that enabled them to relate literature to the emotional,

---

[38] See 'Freudian Fictions' (1920), in *The Essays of Virginia Woolf*, ed. Andrew McNeillie, vol. 3 (London, 1988), 195–8.

[39] See Edward Timms, 'Kafka's Expanded Metaphors: A Freudian Approach to *Ein Landarzt*', in J. P. Stern and J. J. White (eds.), *Paths and Labyrinths: Nine Papers from a Kafka Symposium* (London, 1985), 66–79.

social, and philosophical fabric of human existence. Criticism that ignored psychoanalysis would nowadays look naive; but criticism that relies exclusively on psychoanalysis can easily be tiresome and sectarian. Freud's conception of interpretation as the disclosure of a hidden dream-thought is a doubtful precedent. Most critics would rather agree with Conrad's Marlow, for whom 'the meaning of an episode was not inside like a kernel but outside, enveloping the tale which brought it out only as a glow brings out a haze'.[40] Even in his pro-Freudian period, Frederick Crews conceded: 'It must be admitted that Freudian criticism too easily degenerates into a grotesque Easter-egg hunt: find the devouring mother, detect the inevitable castration anxiety, listen, between the syllables of verse, for the squeaking bedsprings of the primal scene.'[41] Crews's own study of Nathaniel Hawthorne's fiction inquires subtly and astutely into the buried fantasies of guilt, incest, parricide, and sadism which he presents as the real meanings concealed beneath Hawthorne's moral and theological surface meanings. In dealing with Hawthorne's inquiry into New England's Puritan heritage, however, Crews himself risks narrowness by insisting that Hawthorne was not really interested in the Puritans, who simply represent the repressive side of the author, and that Hawthorne's sense of the past refers only to symbolic family conflict.[42] Here, and still more in some post-Freudian criticism, we see the danger that a single-minded use of psychoanalytic theory to illuminate literature ends up presenting literature as an expression of psychoanalytic theory.

The Interpretation of Dreams has been fruitful for literary study by developing the hermeneutic principle illustrated in Freud's explorations of dreams: that interpretation and analysis are interminable. Freud says repeatedly that the latent content of a dream always exceeds its interpretation. Later he was to declare that psychoanalytic treatment could never really reach a final conclusion. Similarly, the implications of an imaginative work reach

---

[40] Joseph Conrad, *Heart of Darkness*, in *Youth, Heart of Darkness, The End of the Tether*, Collected Edition (London, 1947), 48.

[41] Crews, *Out of My System: Psychoanalysis, Ideology, and Critical Method* (New York, 1975), 166.

[42] Crews, *The Sins of the Fathers: Hawthorne's Psychological Themes* (New York, 1966), 31, 60.

down into the buried regions of our imagination, so that the meaning of a literary masterpiece is inexhaustible. There cannot in practice be a single, conclusive interpretation, though such a concept may be necessary as a regulative idea to direct our interpretative efforts and save them from mere vacuous subjectivity. The exploration of a work of literature must be undertaken afresh by each reader and involves an element of (perhaps unwitting) self-exploration.

Psychoanalytic criticism most successfully avoids becoming an Easter-egg hunt when it transfers its attention from the supposed latent content to the mechanisms of condensation and displacement through which a text can communicate, and when psychoanalysis is integrated with formalist and social approaches. The literary genre where psychoanalysis has proved most rewarding is Gothic fiction, in which surface realism is fractured by half-hidden terrors and obsessions.[43] Unacknowledged impulses may be displaced onto a Doppelgänger, as in Robert Louis Stevenson's *Dr Jekyll and Mr Hyde*; meanings may be forcefully condensed into a single figure, as when the monster in Mary Shelley's *Frankenstein* embodies the guilty, self-punishing fears of its creator, the nemesis of overweening science, and the reckless resentment of victims of injustice. A critical eye thus sharpened can find mechanisms of doubling, displacement, and mirroring even in the most ostensibly solid works of realism.[44] One can also understand fictional characters, like those in dreams, as being formed on the templates of parents and siblings, and hence as revenants. Thus, in *David Copperfield* the father whom the orphan David never knew has a sinister revenant in Mr Murdstone and a benign, ineffectual counterpart in Mr Micawber, while sibling conflict emerges with the admired Steerforth and the hated Uriah Heep, both of whom appear as sexual rivals.

The wider legacy of Freud's early work is too all-enveloping to be readily visible. It is the interpretive approach to culture, and the understanding of much social life *as* culture, that currently domin-

[43] For an exemplary study, see David Punter, *The Literature of Terror: A History of Gothic Fictions from 1765 to the Present Day*, 2nd edn., 2 vols. (London and New York, 1996).

[44] For a critically agile and eclectic example, see Andrew J. Webber, *The Doppelgänger: Double Visions in German Literature* (Oxford, 1996).

ates the humanities. It has been influentially formulated by Clifford
Geertz: 'Believing . . . that man is an animal suspended in webs of
significance he himself has spun, I take culture to be those webs, and
the analysis of it to be therefore not an experimental science in
search of law but an interpretive one in search of meaning.'[45] If we
want to historicize this search for meaning, a good starting-point
would be Darwin's study, *The Expression of the Emotions in Man and
Animals* (1872), which shows how bodily actions that originally
served some practical purpose survive by finding a new use as
means of expression. Freud extended this approach to the hysterical symptoms which had previously been thought meaningless.
'All these sensations and innervations', he wrote, 'belong to the
field of "The Expression of the Emotions" which, as Darwin has
taught us, consists of actions which originally had a meaning and
served a purpose' (SE ii. 181). Freud went on to disclose meaning
in other unconsidered trifles of everyday life: in dreams, jokes,
slips of the tongue, and seemingly casual lapses of memory.
Thanks to Freud, vast areas of social life became intelligible: they
formed a text which could be read. But while Freud provided a
vocabulary for the social text, it also needed a syntax, and that was
supplied by his contemporary, the Swiss linguist Ferdinand de
Saussure, who showed how far language depends not on reference
to non-linguistic realities but on its internal systematic character.
Understood as a system of signs, language could provide the
model for 'a science that studies the life of signs within society', to
which Saussure gave the name 'semiotics'.[46] When Saussure's conception of a semiotic system is combined with Freud's extension
of its potential scope, the way lies open for the transformation of
the humanities into a study of meanings, their construction, perception, and interpretation. We now have semiotic and cultural
studies not only of the arts, but of gesture, clothes, food, manners,
ritual, and all forms of social classification.[47] We have learnt to
apply to ourselves the distant, half-perplexed gaze which an
anthropologist turns on another culture, and it is no accident that

---

[45] Geertz, *The Interpretation of Cultures* (New York, 1973), 5.

[46] Saussure, *Course in General Linguistics*, tr. Wade Baskin (London, 1974), 16.

[47] For a concise example, dealing with American classifications of domestic animals,
clothes, and colours, see Marshall Sahlins, 'La Pensée Bourgeoise: Western Society as
Culture', in his *Culture and Practical Reason* (Chicago, 1976), 166–204.

the 'cultural turn' in the humanities was pioneered by anthropologists like Geertz.[48]

What, finally, enabled Freud to see his society with the detached gaze of the anthropologist? Like many middle-class German and Austrian Jews of his time, he was deeply and intimately imbued with Western culture, from the Greeks to Mark Twain. But this profound acculturation was not accompanied by full social integration. Much as Freud admired many Gentiles among his teachers and colleagues, including especially Brücke and Fleischl von Marxow, he felt most at ease among fellow-Jews with whom he shared, as he told the B'nai B'rith Society in Vienna, 'a clear consciousness of an inner identity, the safe privacy of a common mental construction' (SE xx. 274). Freud's sense of marginality has been claimed as an important spur to his creativity.[49] Not only did he feel obliged to prove himself, but he sought to construct a universal science which would submerge Jewish difference within an all-embracing account of the irrational, hidden, often shameful forces that governed the mind.[50] Thus he looked at his society from a position partly within, partly outside it, the classic position of the participant observer, and from his standpoint on its margins he revolutionized its self-understanding.

[48] As one particularly influential example, see the early work of Mary Douglas, especially *Purity and Danger: An Analysis of the Concepts of Pollution and Taboo* (London, 1966) and *Natural Symbols: Explorations in Cosmology* (London, 1970).

[49] In the English-speaking world, many anthropologists have been either Jewish émigrés or Roman Catholics (e.g. E. E. Evans-Pritchard and Mary Douglas); in a Protestant-dominated society the latter can easily occupy a marginal position analogous to Freud's.

[50] See Stanley Rothman and Phillip Isenberg, 'Sigmund Freud and the Politics of Marginality', *Central European History*, 7 (1974), 58–78; Sander L. Gilman, *Freud, Race, and Gender* (Princeton, 1993); id., *The Case of Sigmund Freud: Medicine and Identity at the Fin de Siècle* (Baltimore and London, 1993).

NOTE ON THE TEXT

The text presented here is translated from the first edition of *Die Traumdeutung*, published in November 1899 with the date '1900'. It was hardly an instant bestseller: the initial print run of 600 copies took eight years to sell out. A sign of the importance Freud nevertheless attached to this book is that he kept it up to date by adding new material in each subsequent edition. Since the additions themselves were not always dated, the contours of Freud's original dream theory became increasingly blurred. The first collected edition of Freud's works, the *Gesammelte Schriften* (published at Vienna from 1924 to 1934), reprinted in 1925 the first edition of *Die Traumdeutung* as volume 2 and the additions separately in volume 3. Later, however, the *Gesammelte Werke*, published in London by the Imago Publishing Company from 1940 to 1952, reverted to a single text, that of the eighth (1930) edition, and reprinted it with all its additions. The English translation by James Strachey which forms part of the Standard Edition of Freud's works was based on this eighth edition, but Strachey, by indicating when each of the additions had been made, provided a variorum text which could enable a diligent reader to reconstruct how Freud elaborated his dream theory from the original edition onwards.

The main difference between the original edition, translated here, and the eighth edition which Strachey worked from, consists in the inclusion of a long section on symbolism as part of Chapter VI. Under the influence especially of Wilhelm Stekel, Freud came to think that dreams relied heavily on a repertoire of symbols whose meanings were partially at least independent of their context, and some such notion has passed into popular currency. One effect of making the first edition available in English should be to dispel this misconception by showing that the original dream theory is based on a much more flexible and sensitive interpretation of dream imagery.

Freud scholars have often wished for a critical edition which would retrace how Freud composed his work. In the case of *The Interpretation of Dreams*, and of most of the texts Freud wrote before the First World War, such an edition is impossible, because the manuscripts do not survive. In 1936, when Abraham Schwadron of the Hebrew University of Jerusalem asked Freud to donate his papers to the University Library, Freud replied: 'I have a probably unjustifiable antipathy to personal relics, autographs, collections of handwriting specimens, and everything that springs from these. This goes so far that I have, for example, handed all my manuscripts before 1905 into the wastebasket, among them that of the *Interpretation of Dreams*.'[1] Not till about 1913 did Freud realize that his manuscripts could have monetary value. He bequeathed a large number of them to his daughter Anna, and they are now stored in the Library of Congress in Washington. The scholar most familiar with Freud's manuscripts, Ilse Grubrich-Simitis, makes no great claims for the surprises that a critical edition might bring.[2]

However, an annotated edition which went beyond Strachey's useful notes in elucidating the cultural references and the conceptual changes in Freud's work would be an extremely valuable project. The present edition provides more annotations than Strachey's, thanks in part to the endeavours of subsequent scholars, though a few of Freud's references remain obscure; but we can at least see how steeped Freud was in literature, including the classics, and how much *The Interpretation of Dreams* reflects the professional and domestic life of a highly cultured medical academic in turn-of-the-century Vienna, not least his trips with his family to the environs of Vienna, to holiday resorts in southern Austria, and to Italy and the Adriatic.

R.R.

---

[1] Letter of 12 July 1936, quoted in Peter Gay, *Freud: A Life for our Time* (London, 1988), 612.

[2] Ilse Grubrich-Simitis, *Zurück zu Freuds Texten* (Frankfurt, 1993), 315.

NOTE ON THE TRANSLATION

Although the basis of this text is the first edition of Freud's *Die Traumdeutung*, as a translation it is a latecomer, and enters a much-ploughed field that has been the scene of some controversy. The first version was done in 1913, after Freud's third edition, by A. A. Brill, the Austro-Hungarian follower of Freud who settled in New York. This was replaced in 1953 by James Strachey's monumental variorum edition, which became volumes IV and part of V of the *Standard Edition of the Complete Psychological Works of Sigmund Freud*.[1] As such, it has become part of the memorializing and institutionalizing of Freud's life's work that was Ernest Jones's grand project.[2] It has become a classic and a touchstone. But, also as such, it has of recent years come under fire both ideologically and linguistically. Notoriously—by now—many of its linguistic solutions (and hence its conceptualization) to the problems posed by Freud's professional terminology fall in with Jones's avowed intentions of reinforcing the claims of psychoanalysis to scientific status and of making the controversial new science acceptable to the medical establishment. By now, Strachey's Greek- and Latin-based neologisms are deeply embedded in the language of English psychoanalysis. So are his much-debated rendering of 'Seele' by 'mind', and his general tendency to use terms implying structure rather than process for the workings of the—mind? soul? psyche? Moreover, his great editorial achievement in the Standard Edition as a whole in doing just that—*standardizing*, making an evolving and often contradictory oeuvre coherent over many years and topics and writings—has not entirely escaped the danger of a retrospectively induced uniformity. His own language, though perhaps rather dated now, is graceful and idiomatic; he is often interventionist, but his interventions are mainly in the interests of greater clarity and consistency (often greater, that is, than Freud's). But *Die Traumdeutung*,

[1] This translation is made from Freud's first edition: *Die Traumdeutung* (Leipzig und Wien: Franz Deuticke 1900).

[2] See Riccardo Steiner, '"To explain our point of view to English readers in English words"', in *Translation in Transition: The Question of the Standard Edition, The International Review of Psycho-Analysis*, 18 (1991), 351–92.

especially in its first form, is an early work—a founding work, it is true, but one in which terms and ideas are still provisional aids—'scaffolding' was Freud's metaphor—not yet set in stone, not yet subject to Jones's glossaries.[3]

Nothing can replace Strachey's *The Interpretation of Dreams*, just as nothing will replace the Authorized Version. It is, quite simply, THERE. It has for half a century belonged to that rare category of translations which Goethe described as read not instead of the original, but in their place. Many of its inventions are ingenious and necessary and have entered the language ('unpleasure' for 'Unlust', for example). Where they are successful and uncontroversial, it would seem perverse not to adopt them. There is no starting all over from scratch, no going back to 1899. The present translator has had admiring recourse to Strachey again and again. Nevertheless, in the light of so many objections, and with the imminent prospect of a Revised Standard Edition,[4] it may be timely to risk another version, a variant made on rather different principles (though, in the agony of the workshop, principles have a way of yielding to expediency). It is not done from inside the psychoanalytic profession, but by a Germanist with, it is hoped, an ear for the literary and cultural resonances of Freud's German, and an eye on the lay reader prepared to tackle a work which is in any case demanding enough without having to enter the arcanum of a specialized terminology. The advantage, and the opportunity, of being 'Not the SE' is that the criticisms can be listened to, tested in the active workshop of practical translation, and followed up—or not. It may be possible to go behind the interventionist nature of the SE and approach Freud's text more closely. This is not so much a matter of being more literal (though the present version probably is that—but these are matters of degree), as of attempting to render Freud's varying registers, listening for latent metaphors as well as his grand elucidatory analogies, and for not freezing uniform renderings when he is still thinking his way into new areas of thought.

[3] As early as 1918, Jones drew up a *Glossary for the Use of Translators of Psycho-Analytical Works* (Supplement 1 to *The International Journal of Psycho-Analysis*). He notes (p. 2) by way of introduction that it is 'to be regarded purely as a useful aid to translators, in no sense a lexicon of psycho-analytic terms, though conceivably it may later form the basis of one'. It did.

[4] Announced by the Institute of Psycho-Analysis in London in conjunction with the Hogarth Press for publication from 2000.

It is not only a matter of terminology, but of register, syntax, and the dynamics of German grammar that enable Freud to think in the way he does.[5] In the workshop, one wrestles with more than the concept-carrying noun, but also with sentence-structure and emphasis, with verbs and their modes. How to render these in the inevitable mismatch, which one can only hope to mitigate, of another language, and another mindset? What follows is a catalogue of some of the difficulties encountered on this secondary journey, and of the decisions they called forth. They may, negatively, as it were, serve to characterize some selective aspects of Freud's style in this treatise-cum-autobiography for the English speaker, at least those that emerged in the workshop. What strikes one in retrospect is how many of them are problems not only of Freud's language but of the German language *überhaupt*, as they say in German.

Broadly, this text is written in at least three main modes: theoretical, narrative, and analytic-exploratory, with fine-tuned registers within them. There is first the discursive, formal language of the argued treatise, presenting evidence, argument, rebuttal, qualification, inference. (The pace is stately, but will quicken as a point is clinched or an authority—'Autor'—refuted.) Now in German, the logical connectives necessary for such discourse—'daher', 'dennoch', 'also', 'doch', 'allerdings', 'zwar . . . aber', and so on—are comfortably current in everyday speech. Their unobtrusiveness helps to give formal argument a certain ease, apparent in much of Freud's prose. Not so their English equivalents, the hences and thuses, the nonethelesses and notwithstandings, which are the first steps into the arcanum. I have not been able to avoid them entirely, but I have reduced, simplified where possible ('all the same' instead of 'nevertheless', for example).

One of the main criticisms levelled at the SE is that this same everydayness characterizes many of Freud's apparently technical terms. Here too, Freud is following the habit of his own language: medical and scientific German has no alternative learned Latinate idiolect, as English has—or at least to a lesser extent. German patients are in a position to understand the language of their

[5] See Ilse Grubrich-Simitis, 'Reflections on Sigmund Freud's Relationship to the German Language and to Some German-Speaking Authors of the Enlightenment', *The International Journal of Psycho-Analysis*, 67 (1986), 287–94, quoted by Patrick Mahoney in *Translating Freud*, edited by Darius Ornston (New Haven and London, 1992), 24–5.

diagnosis. To convey this accessibility, the challenge for the late translator is how to surmount Strachey's technical renderings. It may be easy enough to replace 'coenaesthesia' (Gemeingefühl) by the more immediate 'general vital feeling', but other terms are more problematic. In *Die Traumdeutung* Freud had not yet fully developed the language of psychoanalysis; it was still in the making. All the same, the famously ordinary 'Besetzung' ('occupation', 'investment', 'charge', with their latent military or electrical metaphors) expresses a concept essential to its arguments, as its notoriously medical rendering by 'cathexis' also does, that contentious coinage which by now has become deeply established in English analytic discourse.[6] I have dispensed with it and opted for 'charge' and its cognates (though this sometimes requires silent extension into 'charge [of energy/intensity]'). That is something a variant translation can allow itself. On the other hand, other neurological terms—'stimulus', 'excitation'—appear incorrigible.

So, on the whole, does another characteristic of German which is also an essential characteristic of Freud's German—in this work in particular. That is its ease in making word-combinations, specifically combinations with 'Traum': 'Traumarbeit', 'Trauminhalt', 'Traumgedanke', 'Traumvorstellung', 'Traummaterial', and many, many more besides. On the whole such combinations sit uneasily in English, and there are small strategies for getting round them. But these five indicate fundamental theoretical concepts. Indeed, the distinction between 'Trauminhalt' and 'Traumgedanke' is essential to the analysis of dreams (or to 'dream-analysis'?). Freud explicates the terms with the adjectives 'manifest' and 'latent' quite early, but develops his argument using the less lucid noun-combinations, making his way towards clarification as he rediscovers 'manifest' and 'latent'. So in these instances in particular, and in a number of others, I have gone against the grain of English idiom, and rendered the combinations literally. They are in fact all-pervasive, and contribute to the general character of Freud's text. But they do signal that this English text is translated.

---

[6] See Darius Ornston, 'The Invention of "Cathexis" and Strachey's Strategy', *International Review of Psycho-Analysis*, 12 (1985), 391–9. Ornston (see note 5) has been a leading advocate of rethinking the SE. As far as this particular word is concerned, however, John Forrester bows to the reality-principle: 'It is much too late to suggest an alternative translation [for 'Besetzung'], even if one were to find one that was satisfactory.' *Language and the Origins of Psychoanalysis* (London, 1980), 224.

The debate reached a wider public with criticism of a range of words designating aspects of the inner life where Freud simply employed terms long familiar and in popular use, having rich, older, theological or philosophical resonances: first of all with 'Seele', and its cognates 'seelisch' and 'Seelenleben'.[7] I have rendered these by 'psyche' and 'psychical', moving into more literary language by rendering the third as 'inner life'. I have used 'soul' on occasion when Freud quotes one of his older authorities. 'Das Ich', too, for the figure seen in one's dreams, or even for the dreamer herself, I have rendered in more literary fashion as 'the self', for when he wrote *Die Traumdeutung* Freud had not yet undertaken a sharper conceptualization of what became 'the ego' in English. However, that term was current in philosophical and psychological discourse, and I have sometimes used it, once again, when Freud quotes from others— from Meynert, for example.

In the course of translating Freud's theoretical language, I let myself be guided but not constricted by the rule-of-thumb of using the same rendering for the same term; but I also let myself be deflected by the occasional intractability of English idiom, by context, and by the growing sense that Freud himself was exploring possible ways of saying what was on the brink of the unsayable: hence those frequent verbal forms of 'stirring', 'emerging', 'arising'—'regen', 'entstehen', 'hervorgehen', 'auftauchen'—to express the dynamics of the strictly *Un*conscious; hence the obscurity of some of his formulations—which I have often left obscure,[8] so that there might perhaps be some virtue, not in *in*consistency, but in not forcing consistency. For example, Freud uses 'Bildung' both statically, as 'a formation', and dynamically as a transitive process of 'forming', related to 'shaping', 'producing', 'creating'; and he uses 'Gebilde' mainly as 'structure'. But the distinction is not clear-cut, and on occasion (p. 80) the two words are even interchangeable. Such fluidity raises even greater problems in the workshop in rendering the philosophical/psychological term 'Vorstellung' and its cognate 'vorstellen', both of which are terms in common usage

---

[7] See Bruno Bettelheim, *Freud and Man's Soul* (New York, 1983).

[8] An example, which will also illustrate SE's elucidatory approach: 'Das seelisch Unterdrückte, welches im Wachleben durch die *gegensätzliche Aufhebung der Widersprüche* . . .' (1st edn., Chapter VII (e), p. 262, Freud's italics). JC: 'by the removal of contradictions by their opposite'; SE: 'the fact that the contradictions present in it are eliminated—one being disposed of in favour of the other.'

too (as 'idea' and 'to imagine', i.e. 'to generate ideas'). Initially, the translator has a choice between the traditional philosophical terms of 'idea' and 'representation', with a possible preference for the second.[9] But as Freud goes on to argue that the dream-content consists of disguises, substitutions, and stand-ins for the dream-thoughts, in terms of 'vertreten' and 'darstellen'—that is, of 'representing' in a quite different sense—that word-of-all-work had to be co-opted for a different office, and I had on the whole to return to 'idea'. It is not entirely satisfactory; not because the word is normally also used to render 'Einfall', for there are ways of getting round that little hurdle; but because of the occasional overlap in Freud's usage of 'Vorstellung' with 'Bild', rendered by 'image'. The two words are further apart in English than 'image' and 'representation'. (Confusion is greatest where Freud quotes his authorities, who have their own uses for the term.) So, in cases where greater clarity is required, I have found two ad hoc strategies useful: in contexts where there is no danger of confusing 'Vorstellung' with 'Darstellung' I have sometimes recalled 'representation' into service; and to guard against 'ideas' by itself being misunderstood as formulated conceptions, I have more often used 'imagined ideas'. This may rouse objections as not being a standard philosophical formulation, or perhaps even as being tautological, but I would defend it as being relatively close to what I think is Freud's meaning and register—and it rescues 'imagine' for the simple 'vorstellen', which I will not translate as 'generate representations'. Once again we are moving in a field where German terms of art are closer to everyday usage than English ones.

As a last item in discussing Freud's theoretical language, there is one specific psychoanalytic concept—'Nachträglichkeit'—where Strachey's rendering (as 'deferred action') has been disputed. I would not dream of entering this difficult debate, but I find that rendering the cognate adjective as 'retrospective', varied in context on occasion as 'retroactive', seems to serve Freud's argument, at least in this early text.

---

[9] 'Classical term in philosophy and psychology for that which one represents to oneself, that which forms the concrete content of an act of thought' and 'in particular the reproduction of an earlier perception'. Quoted in the entry on 'Idea (or Representation or Presentation)', in J. Laplanche and J.-B. Pontalis, *The Language of Psycho-Analysis*, tr. Donald Nicholson-Smith (London, 1973), 200–1. They go on to point out that to Freud, the 'act of thinking' can be unconscious.

But his theoretical mode is not his only mode. Another major register is to be found in the accounts of dreams, his own and others. His own are told in more lively fashion, and though he responds to a colourful dream from a patient (his words of praise are 'witty', 'ingenious', 'beautiful'), the narrative language is plain, even bald, and the storyline appropriately full of gaps. Importantly, Freud conveys the immediacy of the dream's experience by using the present tense. The present indicative is also the appropriate verb-form for the dream's sense of time and actuality: the past is present and the wish is realized. So I have followed him in this.

The narrative present also characterizes the third major mode of *Die Traumdeutung*, which I have called the exploratory-analytical. This is to be found mainly in the dream-analyses. Here the tense conveys the immediacy of process, the excitement of making discoveries on the hoof, sometimes the sudden 'Aha!' To use the past tense in translating would close the whole adventure. The analyses are by far the most varied writing in the text, in pace, material, and colour. The importance Freud ascribes to 'ordinary linguistic usage' as the 'Urtext' of dream-images, the reliance of many of his analyses on the picturesque suggestiveness of poetry—or Viennese slang—and his fondness for verbal play and punning, which is put to full use here, are the despair of the translator, who can only refer the reader to the explanations in the notes,[10] for to fabricate equivalents would be to negate the authenticity of the dreams. However, in their inventiveness and variety, their finely modulated ironies (so difficult to capture without exaggeration), their conversations and their ventriloquism, these analyses have given one translator a great deal of pleasure.

From declaring that dreams have a meaning which can be interpreted, Freud went on to compare the operation of the dream-work in transposing the text of the dream-thoughts into the new language of the dream-content to an act of translation. But that kind of transposition takes place unconsciously. Not this.

My warm thanks are due to Dr Ritchie Robertson for reading this text so closely and carefully; his comments and suggestions were

---

[10] I owe a debt of gratitude to Strachey's elucidation of a number of the grosser plays on words.

always constructive, and saved me from a number of errors, while his historical knowledge of Freud's social world—which enters Freud's dreams so palpably—made a context for a work which has itself become historical. My thanks too to Judith Luna for spur and encouragement, and to Jeff New for his patience and editorial labours. And not least to the strong predecessor. As one of Freud's favourite poets wrote: 'Mach's einer nach, und breche nicht den Hals.'

J. C.

SELECT BIBLIOGRAPHY

Biography

Anzieu, Didier, *Freud's Self-Analysis*, tr. Peter Graham (London, 1986).

Appignanesi, Lisa, and John Forrester, *Freud's Women* (London, 1992).

Clark, Ronald W., *Freud: The Man and the Cause* (London, 1980).

Gay, Peter, *Freud: A Life for our Time* (London, 1988), with an invaluable bibliographical essay.

Jones, Ernest, *Sigmund Freud: Life and Work*, 3 vols. (London, 1953–7).

Krüll, Marianne, *Freud and his Father*, tr. Arnold J. Pomerans (London, 1987).

Margolis, Deborah P., *Freud and his Mother: Preoedipal Aspects of Freud's Personality* (Northvale, NJ, 1996).

Roazen, Paul, *Freud and his Followers* (New York, 1975).

Vitz, Paul C., *Sigmund Freud's Christian Unconscious* (New York, 1988).

General Studies

Fisher, Seymour, and Roger P. Greenberg, *The Scientific Credibility of Freud's Theories and Therapy* (New York, 1977).

Grubrich-Simitis, Ilse, *Back to Freud's Texts: Making Silent Documents Speak*, tr. Philip Slotkin (New Haven and London, 1996), on Freud's manuscripts.

Grünbaum, Adolf, *The Foundations of Psychoanalysis: A Philosophical Critique* (Berkeley, Los Angeles, and London, 1984).

Laplanche, J., and J.-B Pontalis, *The Language of Psycho-Analysis*, tr. Donald Nicholson-Smith (London, 1973).

Lear, Jonathan, *Love and its Place in Nature: A Philosophical Interpretation of Freudian Psychoanalysis* (London, 1990).

Mitchell, Juliet, *Psychoanalysis and Feminism* (London, 1974).

Rieff, Philip, *Freud: The Mind of the Moralist* (Chicago, 1959).

Stevens, Richard, *Freud and Psychoanalysis* (Milton Keynes, 1983), a good introduction.

Webster, Richard, *Why Freud Was Wrong: Sin, Science and Psychoanalysis* (London, 1995), the most comprehensive negative critique.

Wollheim, Richard, *Freud* (London, 1971).

On The Interpretation of Dreams

Forrester, John, 'Dream Readers', in his *Dispatches from the Freud Wars* (Cambridge, Mass., and London, 1997), 138–83.

Grinstein, Alexander, *On Sigmund Freud's Dreams* (Detroit, 1968).

Hopkins, James, 'The Interpretation of Dreams', in Jerome Neu (ed.), *The Cambridge Companion to Freud* (Cambridge, 1991), 86–135, a sympathetic philosophical critique.

Schorske, Carl E., 'Politics and Patricide in Freud's *Interpretation of Dreams*', in his *Fin-de-siècle Vienna: Politics and Culture* (Cambridge, 1981), 181–207.

Steiner, George, 'The Historicity of Dreams', in his *No Passion Spent: Essays 1978–1996* (London, 1996), 207–23, an imaginative and stimulating critique.

Intellectual and Historical Contexts

Beller, Steven, *Vienna and the Jews, 1867–1938: A Cultural History* (Cambridge, 1989).

Buhle, Mari Jo, *Feminism and its Discontents: A Century of Struggle with Psychoanalysis* (Cambridge, Mass., and London, 1998).

Ellenberger, Henri F., *The Discovery of the Unconscious: The History and Evolution of Dynamic Psychiatry* (London, 1970).

Forrester, John, *Language and the Origins of Psychoanalysis* (London, 1980).

Gay, Peter, *Freud, Jews and Other Germans* (New York, 1978).

Geehr, Richard S., *Karl Lueger, Mayor of Fin de Siècle Vienna* (Detroit, 1990).

Gilman, Sander L., *et al.* (eds.), *Reading Freud's Reading* (New York and London, 1994).

Gresser, Moshe, *Dual Allegiance: Freud as a Modern Jew* (Albany, NY, 1994).

McGrath, William J., *Freud's Discovery of Psychoanalysis: The Politics of Hysteria* (Ithaca and London, 1986).

Micale, Mark S., *Approaching Hysteria: Disease and its Interpretations* (Princeton, 1995), with extensive recent bibliography.

Price, S. R. F., 'The Future of Dreams: From Freud to Artemidorus', *Past and Present*, 113 (Nov. 1986), 3–37.

Ritvo, Lucille, *Darwin's Influence on Freud* (New Haven and London, 1990).

Ryan, Judith, *The Vanishing Subject: Early Psychology and Literary Modernism* (Chicago, 1991).

Sulloway, Frank J., *Freud, Biologist of the Mind: Beyond the Psychoanalytic Legend*, 2nd edn. (Cambridge, Mass., and London, 1992).

Wistrich, Robert S., *The Jews of Vienna in the Age of Franz Joesph* (Oxford, 1989), including a thorough study of Freud's Jewish identity.

Freud's Legacy

Beharriell, Frederick J., 'Psychoanalysis and Literature: The Freud-Denial Syndrome', in Karl Konrad Polheim (ed.), *Sinn und Symbol: Festschrift für Joseph P. Strelka zum 60. Geburtstag* (Berne, 1987) 593–610.

Collier, Peter, and Judy Davies (eds.), *Modernism and the European Unconscious* (Cambridge, 1990).

Crews, Frederick, *Out of My System: Psychoanalysis, Ideology, and Critical Method* (New York, 1975).

Hoffman, Frederick J., *Freudianism and the Literary Mind* (Baton Rouge, La., 1945).

Metz, Christian, *Psychoanalysis and Cinema: The Imaginary Signifier*, tr. Celia Britton *et al.* (London, 1982).

Trilling, Lionel, 'Freud and Literature', in his *The Liberal Imagination* (London, 1951).

Wright, Elizabeth, *Psychoanalytic Criticism*, 2nd edn. (Cambridge, 1998).

Dreams

Béguin, Albert, *L'Âme romantique et le rêve* (Marseilles, 1937).

Burke, Peter, 'The Cultural History of Dreams', in his *Varieties of Cultural History* (Cambridge, 1997), 23–42, with many further references.

Engel, Manfred, '"Träumen und Nichtträumen zugleich": Novalis' Theorie und Poetik des Traumes zwischen Aufklärung und Hochromantik', in Herbert Uerlings (ed.), *Novalis und die Wissenschaften* (Tübingen, 1997), 143–67.

Franz, Marie-Louise von, *Dreams: A Study of the Dreams of Jung, Descartes, Socrates, and other Historical Figures* (Boston and London, 1998).

Hobson, J. Allan, *The Dreaming Brain* (London, 1990), combining neurological with interpretive approaches.

Jung, C. G., *Dreams*, tr. R. F. C. Hull (London, 1985), a handy collection of Jung's essays on dreams.

Rycroft, Charles, *The Innocence of Dreams*, 2nd edn. (London, 1991), on dreaming as imaginative activity.

Stevens, Anthony, *Private Myths: Dreams and Dreaming* (London, 1995), broadly Jungian.

Freud as a Writer

Frankland, Graham, *Freud's Literary Culture* (Cambridge, 1999).

Hyman, Stanley Edgar, *The Tangled Bank: Darwin, Marx, Frazer and Freud as Imaginative Writers* (New York, 1959).

Mahony, Patrick, *Freud as a Writer* (New Haven and London, 1987).

Schönau, Walter, *Sigmund Freuds Prosa: Literarische Elemente seines Stils* (Stuttgart, 1968).

Translating Freud

Bettelheim, Bruno, *Freud and Man's Soul* (London, 1983).

Gilman, Sander L., 'Reading Freud in English: Problems, Paradoxes, and a Solution', in his *Inscribing the Other* (Lincoln, Nebr., and London, 1991), 191–210.

Ornston, Darius Gray (ed.), *Translating Freud* (New Haven and London, 1992).

Timms, Edward, and Naomi Segal (eds.), *Freud in Exile: Psychoanalysis and its Vicissitudes* (New Haven and London, 1988).

A CHRONOLOGY OF SIGMUND FREUD

This chronology focuses mainly on the period up to and soon after the publication of *The Interpretation of Dreams*.

1856	6 May: Sigismund (later Sigmund) Freud born at Freiberg (now Příbor) in Moravia.
1860	The Freud family settles in Vienna, after a stay in Leipzig.
1873	Freud enters Vienna University as medical student.
1876–82	Works under Ernst Brücke at the Institute of Physiology in Vienna.
1881	Graduates as Doctor of Medicine.
1882	Becomes engaged to Martha Bernays.
1882–5	Works in Vienna General Hospital, concentrating on cerebral anatomy.
1884	Begins research on the clinical uses of cocaine. July: publishes his paper 'On Cocaine'.
1885	Appointed *Privatdozent* (university lecturer) in neuropathology.
1885	October: begins studies under J. M. Charcot at the Salpêtrière (hospital for nervous diseases) in Paris (until February 1886); becomes interested in hypnosis.
1886	Marries Martha Bernays.
1886–93	Continues work on neurology at the Kassowitz Institute in Vienna.
1887	Birth of eldest child, Mathilde.
	Gets to know the Berlin physician Wilhelm Fliess; their intellectual relationship, intense throughout the 1890s, cools by 1902.
1888	Begins to follow Josef Breuer in using hypnosis for cathartic treatment of hysteria.
1889	Birth of eldest son, Martin.
	Foundation of Austrian Social Democratic Party.
1891	Birth of second son, Oliver.
1892	Birth of youngest son, Ernst.
1893	Birth of second daughter, Sophie.

1895   Birth of youngest child, Anna (later a distinguished psycho-analyst in her own right).

       Publication with Breuer of *Studies on Hysteria*.

1896   Death of Freud's father Jakob, aged 80.

1897   Freud's self-analysis and 'creative illness', leading to the theory of the Oedipus complex.

       Appointment of Gustav Mahler as director of Imperial Opera in Vienna; his informal analysis with Freud took place in 1910.

       April: appointment of the anti-Semite Karl Lueger as Mayor of Vienna; only after his fifth electoral victory would the Emperor confirm him in office.

       August: First Zionist Congress organized in Basle by Theodor Herzl.

       November: 'Badeni language riots' in response to proposals by the Prime Minister, Count Badeni, for appeasing nationalists by giving Czech and other languages equal status with German in Austrian provinces.

1899   Founding of Karl Kraus's satirical periodical *Die Fackel* (*The Torch*).

1899   November: publication of *The Interpretation of Dreams*.

1901   Publication of *The Psychopathology of Everyday Life*.

       Freud's first visit to Rome.

1902   Appointed Professor Extraordinarius.

1903   Publication of Otto Weininger's notorious *Sex and Character*, which shares with Freud and Fliess a theory of bisexuality.

1905   *Three Essays on the History of Sexuality*.

1906   Contact with C. J. Jung, whose adherence to psychoanalysis Freud particularly values; close relationship till their final breach in 1914.

1913   *Totem and Taboo*, in which Freud applies psychoanalysis to explain the origins of culture.

1914   Assassination of heir to the Austrian throne, Archduke Franz Ferdinand, at Sarajevo and outbreak of First World War, in which Austrian troops suffered heavy losses especially on the Russian and Italian fronts.

1915   Freud responds to the War with 'Thoughts for the Times on War and Death'.

1916   21 November: death of Emperor Franz Joseph I of Austria.

1918   Dissolution of Austro-Hungarian Empire; November: proclamation of Austrian Republic.

1920   Death of Freud's daughter Sophie.

1923   *The Ego and the Id*: the conscious/unconscious/preconscious triad of *The Interpretation* is finally replaced with the division of the mind into ego, id, and superego.

1930   *Civilization and its Discontents*, perhaps the greatest of Freud's sociological works.

            Awarded the Goethe Prize for his literary and scientific achievement by the City of Frankfurt.

            Death of Freud's mother Amalie, aged 95.

1933   After Hitler's seizure of power in Germany, books by Freud are burnt in Berlin.

1938   Hitler's annexation of Austria; Freud leaves Vienna for London.

1939   23 September: death in London.

THE INTERPRETATION
OF DREAMS

*Flectere si nequeo superos, Acheronta movebo**

CONTENTS

FOREWORD

In making this attempt at presenting an interpretation of dreams I do not think I have gone beyond the bounds of neuro-pathological interests. For under psychological scrutiny the dream turns out to be the first item in the series of abnormal psychical formations, whose further members—hysterical phobia, obsession, and delusion—are bound to occupy the physician in his practice. Although, as we shall see, the dream cannot claim a comparable significance for practice, its theoretical value as a paradigm is all the greater for that, and if we are not able to explain how dream-images originate, we will also labour in vain to understand and possibly treat the phobias, obsessions, and delusions.

However, the same connection that makes our subject so important can also be held responsible for the shortcomings of the present work. The disjunctions to be found so frequently in this account correspond to those points of contact where the problem of dream-formation intervenes in wider problems of psychopathology. These could not be dealt with here, but if time and strength allow and further material presents itself, later revisions will be devoted to them.

The peculiarities of the material I use to elucidate the interpretation of dreams have also made this publication difficult for me. It will become apparent from the work itself why for my purposes I could make no use of any of the dreams related in the literature or of any I might have collected from strangers. The only choice I had was between my own dreams and those of my patients under psychoanalytic treatment. I could not use the latter material, as the processes of the dream were undesirably complicated here by interference from neurotic characteristics. Reporting my own dreams, however, turned out to be inextricably tied to revealing more of the intimacies of my psychical life than I could wish or than usually falls to the task of an author who is not a poet, but a scientist. This was painful and embarrassing, but unavoidable; I have bowed to it then, so that I should not entirely do without presenting the evidence for my psychological conclusions. But of course I have been unable to resist the temptation to take the sting out of many an indiscretion by omitting or substituting certain material; though whenever I did this, it was definitely detrimental to the value of my examples. I can only express the hope that readers of this work will put themselves in my difficult position and be forbearing with me; and further, that all those who find that the dreams related here allude to them personally in any way, will not wish to deny freedom of thought—at least to the life of dreams.

Freud

THE SCIENTIFIC LITERATURE ON
THE PROBLEMS OF DREAMS

In the following pages I shall provide proof that there is a psychological technique which allows us to interpret dreams, and that when this procedure is applied, every dream turns out to be a meaningful psychical formation which can be given an identifiable place in what goes on within us in our waking life. I shall further try to explain the processes that make the dream so strange and incomprehensible, and infer from them the nature of the psychical forces in their combinations and conflicts, out of which the dream emerges. Having got so far, my account will break off, for it will have reached the point at which the problem of dreaming opens out into more comprehensive problems which will have to be resolved on the basis of different material.

I shall begin with a survey both of what earlier authorities have written on the subject and of the present state of scientific inquiry into the problems of dreams, as I shall not often have occasion to return to it in the course of this treatise. In spite of being concerned with the subject over many thousands of years, scientific understanding of the dream has not got very far. This is admitted by the writers so generally that it seems superfluous to quote individual authors. In the writings I list at the end of my work many stimulating observations and a great deal of interesting material can be found relating to our subject, but little or nothing touching the essential nature of the dream or offering a definitive solution to any of its riddles. And of course, even less has passed into the knowledge of the educated layman.

The first work to treat the dream as an object of psychology seems to be Aristotle's* *On Dreams and Dream Interpretation* [1]. Aristotle concedes that the nature of the dream is indeed daemonic, but not divine—which might well reveal a profound meaning, if one could hit on the right translation. He recognizes some of the characteristics of the dream-life, for example, that the dream reinterprets slight stimuli intruding upon sleep as strong ones ('we believe we are passing through a fire and growing hot when this or that limb is only being slightly warmed'), and he concludes from this that dreams could very well reveal to the physician the first signs of impending changes in the body not perceptible by day. Lacking the requisite knowledge and teaching and without informed assistance, I have not been in a position to arrive at a deeper understanding of Aristotle's treatise.

As we know, the ancients prior to Aristotle regarded the dream not as a product of the dreaming psyche, but as an inspiration from the realm of the divine, and they already recognized the two contrary trends which we shall find are always present in evaluations of the dream-life. They distinguished valuable, truth-telling dreams, sent to the sleeper to warn him or announce the future to him, from vain, deceptive, and idle dreams intended to lead him astray or plunge him into ruin. This pre-scientific conception of the dream held by the ancients was certainly in full accord with their world-view as a whole, which habitually projected as reality into the outside world what had reality only within the life of the psyche. Their conception also took account of the main impression made on the waking life by the memory of the dream remaining in the morning, for in this memory the dream is opposed to the other contents of the psyche as something alien, coming as it were from another world. It would be wrong, by the way, to think that the theory of the supernatural origin of dreams has no followers in our own day. Quite apart from all the pietistic and mystical writers—who do right to occupy the remains of the once extensive realm of the supernatural, as long as it has not been conquered by scientific explanation—we also encounter clear-sighted men averse to the fantastic who use this very inexplicability of the phenomena of dreams in their endeavours to support their religious belief in the existence and intervention of superhuman powers. The high value accorded to the dream-life by many schools of philosophy, for example, by Schelling's* followers, is a distinct echo of the undisputed divinity accorded to dreams in antiquity; and the divinatory, future-predicting power of dreams remains under discussion because the attempts at a psychological explanation are not adequate to cope with all the material gathered, however firmly the feelings of anyone devoted to the scientific mode of thought might be inclined to reject such a notion.

The reason why it is so difficult to write a history of our scientific knowledge of the problems of dreams is that, however valuable our knowledge may have become under single aspects, no progress along a particular line of thought is to be discerned. No foundation of confirmed results has been constructed on which the next researcher might have built further, but every new author tackles the self-same problems afresh as though from the very beginning. If I were to discuss the writers in chronological sequence and summarize what each of them had to say on the problems of dreams, I would have to abandon any clear overall survey of the current state of our knowledge of dreams. That is why I have chosen to construct my account according to topics rather than authors, and in dealing with each dream problem I shall cite whatever material for its solution exists in the literature.

However, this literature is very scattered and encroaches upon many other subjects, and I have not been able to cope with it all: so I must ask my readers to rest content as long as no fundamental fact or significant point of view has escaped my attention.

Until recently, most writers have felt obliged to deal with sleep and dreams within the same context, as a rule also linking to this their evaluations of analogous states extending into psycho-pathology, and their assessments of occurrences similar to dreams (such as hallucinations, visions, etc.). The most recent work, on the other hand, endeavours to restrict the subject and take some single question from the field of the dream-life as its object of inquiry. This change of emphasis is, I believe, an expression of the conviction that in such obscure matters enlightenment and agreement may only be reached by a set of detailed investigations. It is a detailed investigation of this kind, specifically of a psychological nature, that I am able to offer here. I have had little occasion to occupy myself with the problem of sleep, for this is essentially a problem of physiology, though a characterization of the sleeping state has to include changes in the conditions under which the psychical apparatus functions. So in my account I have disregarded the literature on sleep.

Scientific interest in the phenomena of dreams as such leads to the following, partly overlapping, questions:

(a) *The Relationship of Dreams to Waking Life*

The naive judgement of someone who has just woken up assumes that the dream—even if it does not come from another world—has still transported the sleeper to one. The old physiologist Burdach [8], to whom we owe a scrupulous and sensitive description of the phenomena of dreams, has expressed this conviction in a celebrated passage (p. 474): '. . . the life of the day, with its exertions and pleasures, its joys and sorrows, is never repeated: the dream is rather bent on freeing us from it. Even when our entire soul has been engrossed with one object, when our heart has been riven with a deep sorrow or some task has exercised all our mental powers, the dream either gives us something completely alien, or takes for its combinations only individual elements from reality, or only enters into the key of the mood we are in and symbolises reality.'

In his justly acclaimed study of the nature and origin of dreams, L. Strümpell [66] expresses a similar view (p. 16): 'The dreamer has turned away from the world of waking consciousness . . .' (p. 17): 'In dreams our memory of the ordered content of waking consciousness and its normal behaviour is as good as completely lost . . .' (p. 19): 'The almost memory-less isolation of the soul in dreams from the routine content and course of waking life . . .'

But the great majority of writers have taken the opposite viewpoint. Haffner [32] writes as follows (p. 19): 'At first the dream continues the waking life. Our dreams always follow the ideas present in our consciousness not long before. Meticulous observation will almost always discover a thread in which the dream links up with the experiences of the previous day.' Weygandt [75] (p. 6) directly contradicts Burdach's assertion quoted above, 'for apparently it can often be observed in the great majority of dreams that, rather than freeing us from ordinary life, they lead us right back into it'. Maury [48] (p. 56) says in a succinct formula: 'Nous rêvons de ce que nous avons vu, dit, désiré ou fait.'* In his *Psychologie* of 1855 (p. 530), Jessen [36] puts it at rather greater length: 'The content of dreams is always more or less determined by the individual personality, by age, sex, class, level of education, mode of life and by all the events and experiences of our lives hitherto.'

The ancients shared this idea of the dependence of the content of dreams on life. To cite Radestock [54] (p. 134): about to begin his campaign against Greece, Xerxes* was dissuaded from this decision by sound advice, but was spurred on to it again and again by his dreams; at this, the rational old dream-interpreter of the Persians, Artabanos, told him quite rightly that dream-images usually contain what the dreamer already thinks when awake.

In Lucretius'* didactic poem, *De rerum natura*, we find the passage (IV. v. 959):

> Et quo quisque fere studio devinctus adhaeret,
> aut quibus in rebus multum sumus ante morati
> atque in ea ratione fuit contenta magis mens.
> in somnis eadem plerumque videmur obire;
> causidici causas agere et componere leges,
> induperatores pugnare ac proelia obire, etc. etc.

Cicero* (*De Divinatione*, ii) says exactly what Maury said so much later: 'Maximeque reliquiae earum rerum moventur in animis et agitantur, de quibus vigilantes aut cogitavimus aut egimus.'

The contradiction between these two views of the relationship between dream-life and waking life seems to be indeed irresolvable. So this is a good place to recall F. W. Hildebrandt's [35] discussion. He takes the view that the peculiarities of the dream cannot be described at all except as a 'series of opposites which seem to intensify to the point of becoming contradictions' (p. 8). 'The *first* of these opposites is the *strict seclusion or isolation* of the dream from real, true life on the one hand, and on the other the continual *encroachment* of the one on the other, the constant dependence of the one on the other.—The dream is something altogether separate from the reality we experience when awake; one might call it an existence hermetically closed within itself, cut off from real life by an unbridgeable chasm. It frees us from reality, extinguishes our normal recollection of it, and places us in another world and in a quite different life-story, which has fundamentally nothing to do with our real one . . .' Hildebrandt then explains how, when we fall asleep, our whole being, with the forms of its existence, disappears 'as though beneath an invisible trap-door'. Then perhaps we dream we are making a sea-voyage to St Helena in order to offer the imprisoned Napoleon something special by way of Moselle. We are received by the ex-Emperor in the friendliest fashion and are almost sorry to see the interesting illusion disrupted by our awakening. But then we compare the situation in the dream with reality. We have never been a wine-merchant, and have never wanted to be one. We have never been on a sea-voyage, and St Helena is the last place we would choose to take one to. For Napoleon we feel no kind of sympathy, but on the contrary harbour a fierce patriotic hatred towards him. And on top of all that, the dreamer was not yet even among the living when Napoleon died on his island; to enjoy any personal relationship with him was beyond the bounds of possibility. Thus the dream-experience appears as something alien interpolated between two divisions of our life which otherwise fit into each other perfectly and continuously.

'And yet,' Hildebrandt goes on, 'the apparent *opposite* is just as true and correct. In my view, the most intimate relationship and connection nevertheless goes hand in hand with this isolation and seclusion. We may even say: whatever the dream may present, it acquires its material from reality and from the intellectual life which goes along with this reality ... However strangely the dream may employ it, it can never actually get free from the real world: its most sublime and its most farcical phenomena alike must always borrow their raw material either from what has appeared before us in the world of the senses or from what has somehow already found a place in our waking thoughts—in other words, from what we have already experienced, outwardly or inwardly.'

(b) *The Dream-Material—Memory in Dreams*

That all the material composing the content of the dream derives in some way from our experience, and so is reproduced, *remembered*, in the dream—this at least we may count as undisputed knowledge. But it would be an error to assume that such a connection between the dream-content and waking life is bound to emerge effortlessly as the obvious result of comparing the two. It has rather to be attentively sought, for in a large number of cases it is capable of concealing itself for a long time. The reason for this lies in a number of peculiarities shown by our powers of memory in dreams, and which, although they have been generally remarked, have so far resisted every attempt at an explanation. It will be worth our while to examine these characteristics in detail.

The first thing to emerge is that material appears in the dream-content which, when subsequently awake, we do not recognize as part of our knowledge or experience. We may well remember that we dreamed this or that, but not that we ever experienced it. We are then in a quandary as to what source the dream has drawn on, and may well be tempted to believe that the dream possesses the power of independent production, until, often after a long interval, a new experience restores the memory of the earlier experience and so reveals the source of the dream. We then have to admit that we had known and remembered something in our dream which had escaped our powers of recollection when awake.

A particularly impressive example of this kind is told by Delboeuf [16] from his own dream-experience. In his dream he saw the yard of his house covered in snow and found two little lizards half-frozen and buried under the snow. Being an animal-lover he took them up, warmed them, and restored them to the little hole in the wall intended for them. In addition he gave them a few leaves from a little fern-plant growing on the wall which he knew they were very fond of. In his dream he knew the name of the plant: *Asplenium ruta muralis.*—The dream then continued, after an interval returned to the lizards, and to Delboeuf's astonishment showed him two new little lizards which had set upon the remains of the ferns. Then he turned and looked into the distance, saw a fifth and a sixth lizard making their way to the hole in the wall, until finally the whole road was covered with a procession of lizards all moving in the same direction, etc.

In his waking life, Delboeuf was familiar with the Latin names of only a few plants, and the *Asplenium* was not among them. So he was greatly astonished to discover that a fern of this name actually existed: its correct designation was *Asplenium ruta muraria*, which the dream had slightly distorted. It seemed hardly credible that the name had occurred by coincidence; but where his knowledge of it in his dream had come from, remained a mystery to him.

The dream took place in 1862. Sixteen years later the philosopher was visiting a friend when he noticed a little album containing dried flowers of the sort that are sold as souvenirs to visitors in many parts of Switzerland. A memory arose within him, he opened the herbarium, found in it the *Asplenium* from his dream, and recognized his own handwriting in the Latin name added to it. Now the connection could be made: in 1860—two years before the dream of the lizards— a sister of this friend had visited Delboeuf while on her honeymoon. She had had this album with her, intending it for her brother; and

Delboeuf had taken the trouble to write its Latin name, at a botanist's dictation, beside each of the little dried plants.

A happy accident, of the sort that make this example so very much worth relating, allowed Delboeuf to trace yet another part of the content of this dream back to its forgotten source. One day in 1877 an old volume of an illustrated magazine came into his hands, and there he saw a picture of the entire procession of lizards as he had dreamed it in 1862. The volume bore the date 1861, and Delboeuf was able to recall that he had been a subscriber to the magazine from the time of its appearance.

The fact that the dream has at its disposal recollections which are inaccessible to the waking person is so remarkable and theoretically significant that I should like to reinforce it by recounting some more 'hypermnestic' dreams. Maury [48] relates that for some time the word *Mussidan* kept coming into his mind during the day: he knew it was the name of a French town, but nothing more. One night he dreamed of a conversation with a certain person, who told him she came from *Mussidan*, and when he asked where the town was she replied that *Mussidan* was the main town in the *Département de la Dordogne*. When he awoke, Maury gave no credence to the information in the dream. But from the gazetteer he learned that it was perfectly correct. In this case the dream's superior knowledge is confirmed, but the forgotten source of this knowledge has not been traced.

Jessen [36] relates (p. 551) a very similar event in a dream from older times: 'Among these is the dream of the elder Scaliger* (Hennings p. 300), who wrote a poem in praise of the famous men of Verona. A man calling himself Brugnolus appeared to him in a dream, complaining that he had been forgotten. Although Scaliger could not recall ever having heard anything of him, he composed lines about him all the same, and his son afterwards learned in Verona that a Brugnolus had indeed once been famous there as a critic.'

In a publication unfortunately not available to me (*Proceedings of the Society for Psychical Research*), Myers is said to have produced a collection of such hypermnestic dreams. In my view, anyone engaged in the study of dreams is bound to recognize that it is a very common phenomenon for a dream to bear witness to knowledge and recollections which the waking person does not believe he possesses. In my psychoanalytic work with nervous patients, which I shall refer to later, I find myself several times every week in the position of proving to my patients from their dreams that they really do know certain quotations, obscene words, and the like very well, and that they use them in dreams even though they have forgotten them in waking life. I should like to add here a further innocuous case of dream-hypermnesia, for in this instance the source that gave rise to the knowledge accessible only to the dream is very easy to detect.

As part of a lengthy dream a patient dreamed that in a coffee-house he had ordered a 'Kontuszowka'. But after relating the dream he asked what it could be: he had never heard the name. I was able to reply that 'Kontuszowka' was a Polish schnapps which he could not have invented in his dream, as the name had long been familiar to me from posters. At first the man would not believe me. A few days later, after he had made his dream come true in a real coffee-house, he noticed the name on a poster, and what is more, on one at a street corner which he must have passed at least twice a day for several months.

One of the sources that dreams draw upon for material for reproduction, some of it not remembered or employed in the mental activity of waking life, is the life of childhood. I shall cite only a few of the writers who have noticed this and emphasized it:

Hildebrandt [35] (p. 23): 'It has already been expressly conceded that dreams faithfully bring quite remote and even forgotten events from the distant past back to our minds, sometimes with a marvellous power of reproduction.'

Strümpell [66] (p. 40): 'The issue becomes even more complex when we remark how sometimes dreams draw forth images of individual places, things, and persons quite unscathed and in all their original freshness, as it were out from under the deepest and most massive accumulations deposited by later years on the earliest experiences of our youth. This is not confined merely to those impressions which we were vividly conscious of when they first arose, or were associated with strong psychical values and now recur later in a dream as actual recollections in which the wakened consciousness takes pleasure. Rather, the depths of the dream memory also include those images of people, things, places, and experiences from our earliest years which either impressed themselves only slightly on our consciousness, or possessed no psychical value, or have long since lost both, and so, both in the dream and after we have woken up, they appear quite alien and unfamiliar to us until their early origin is discovered.'

Volkelt [72] (p. 119): 'It is particularly remarkable how easily recollections of childhood and youth enter dreams. The dream never tires of reminding us of things we have long since ceased to think about, things which have long since lost all importance to us.'

The dream's command of childhood material, most of which, as we know, falls through the gaps in our conscious power of recollection, occasions interesting hypermnestic dreams, a few of which I would again like to relate.

Maury [48] tells us (p. 92) that as a child he often travelled from his home town of Meaux to the nearby town of Trilport, where his father was directing the construction of a bridge. One night a dream transported him to Trilport and set him playing again in the streets of the town. A man approached him wearing a kind of uniform. Maury asked him what his name was; the man introduced himself as C., and said he was a watchman at the bridge. After he woke, Maury still doubted the truth of this recollection, so he asked an old servant who had been with him since childhood whether she could remember a man of this name. Certainly, came her reply, he was the watchman at the bridge your father was constructing at that time.

Maury reports another example, just as satisfyingly confirmed, of the reliability of childhood recollection as it appears in dreams. It came from a Montsieur F., who had grown up as a child in the town of Montbrison. Twenty-five years after he had left it, this man decided to revisit his home town as well as old friends of the family whom he had not seen since. In the night before his departure he dreamed that he had arrived, and in the vicinity of Montbrison encountered a man unknown to him by sight, who told him he was Monsieur T., a friend of his father's. The dreamer knew that as a child he had known a man of this name, though when awake he could no longer remember what he looked like. A few days later, now actually arrived in Montbrison, he found the locality of his dream again, which he had thought was unfamiliar to him, and encountered a man whom he promptly recognized as the T. of his dream. Only that the real person was much older than the dream had represented him.

At this stage I can relate a dream of my own, in which the impression to be recalled is replaced by an association. In a dream I saw a person who I knew in the dream was the doctor of my home town. His face was not clear, but was blended with the impression of one of my teachers at the *Gymnasium*, whom I occasionally still meet today. After I woke, I could not make out what association linked these two people. But when I asked my mother about this doctor from my earliest years, I learned that he had had only one eye—and the schoolteacher whose figure in the dream had covered that of the doctor also has only one eye. I had not seen the doctor for thirty-eight years, and to my knowledge I have never thought about him in my waking life.

It sounds as if there was an intention to set up a counterweight to the overly great role played by childhood impressions in dreams, when several authorities maintain that most dreams can be shown to contain elements from the days most recently preceding the dream. Robert [55] (p. 46) even asserts that in general the normal dream is concerned only with the days just past. We shall in any event discover that the theory of dreams Robert has constructed makes it imperative for him to push back the oldest impressions and bring forward the most recent. I can, however, confirm from my own investigations that what Robert says in this respect is a fact. An American writer, Nelson [50], takes the view that what most often happens is that the dream makes use of impressions from the day before the day of the dream or from the third day before, as though the impressions from the day immediately preceding the dream were toned down, not remote enough.

Several writers who would not doubt the intimate connection between the content of dreams and waking life have observed that impressions that occupy the waking thoughts intensely appear in dreams only when they have to some extent been pushed to one side by the thinking activity of the day. Thus we do not as a rule dream of a dead person dear to us in the time right after their death, while the survivor is still filled with grief (Delage) [15]. Meantime, however, one of the most recent observers, Miss Hallam [33], has collected examples of the opposite behaviour, and in this regard claims for each of us the right to our psychological individuality.

The third, most remarkable and incomprehensible characteristic of memory in dreams is to be seen in the choice of material reproduced. For what is considered worth remembering is not, as in waking life, only the things that are of most significance, but also on the contrary the most trivial and nondescript things. At this point I shall cite those authors who have expressed their amazement most forcefully.

Hildebrandt [35] (p. 11): 'For the remarkable thing is that as a rule the dream takes its elements not from the important and far-reaching events, not from the great and motivating interests of the previous day, but from the trivial extras, from the worthless scraps, as it were, of the recent or more remote past. A distressing death in the family, whose impressions send us late to sleep, is blotted from our memory until our first waking moment brings it back to us vividly in all its sadness. On the other hand, a wart on the forehead of a stranger we encountered and did not give a moment's thought to after we had passed him by—this plays a part in our dream . . .'

Strümpell [66] (p. 39): '. . . cases where the analysis of a dream discovers elements which, though it is true they derive from the experiences of the previous day or the day before that, were so worthless and insignificant to the waking consciousness, that they sank into oblivion soon after they were experienced. Experiences of this kind are for instance words heard by accident, someone else's actions scarcely noticed, fleeting perceptions of things or persons, brief passages from our reading, and the like.'

Havelock Ellis [23] (p. 727): 'The profound emotions of waking life, the questions and problems on which we spread our chief voluntary mental energy, are not those which usually present themselves to dream consciousness. It is so far as the immediate past is concerned mostly the trifling, the incidental, the "forgotten" impressions of daily life which reappear in our dreams. The psychic activities that are awake most intensely are those that sleep most profoundly.'

Binz [4] (p. 45) takes these very peculiarities of memory in the dream as the occasion for expressing his dissatisfaction with the explanations of the dream he himself supports: 'And the natural dream raises similar questions. Why is it that we do not always dream the memory-impressions of the most recent day we have spent, but often plunge without any recognizable motive into a past that lies far behind us, almost obliterated? In dreams why does the consciousness so often receive the impression of *trivial* recollections, while the brain-cells, the very place where the most sensitive register of our experience is lodged, mostly lie still and silent, unless they have been freshly aroused in waking hours shortly before?'

It is easy to see how the strange preference of the dream-memory for trifling and hence unnoticed things among the experiences of the day was largely bound to lead to a general failure to understand the dream's dependence on the life of the day, or at least to making this very difficult to demonstrate in individual cases. Consequently, in Miss Whiton Calkins's [12] statistical analysis of her (and her companion's) dreams, it was possible for her to be left with 11 per cent of the total in which no relation to the life of the day was perceptible. Hildebrandt is certainly right in maintaining that all dream-images could be explained genetically, if we spent sufficient time and concentration on tracing their origin. True, he calls this 'an extremely laborious and thankless task. For it would mostly amount to tracking down all sorts of things with no psychical value in the remotest corners of the chamber of memory, and bringing to light all sorts of utterly trivial impulses from times long past from depths where they had been buried perhaps the very hour after they had occurred.' But I must express my regret that this penetrating writer failed to pursue this path from this modest beginning; it would have led him straight to the centre of the explanation of dreams.

The way the memory behaves in dreams is certainly most important for any theory of memory in general. It teaches us that 'nothing that is once mentally our own can ever be entirely lost' (Scholz [59] p. 34). Or, as Delboeuf [16] puts it, 'que tout impression même la plus insignifiante, laisse une trace inaltérable, indéfiniment susceptible de reparaître au jour',* a conclusion which so many other—pathological—phenomena of the psychical life likewise force us to make. Now if we keep this extraordinary capability of the dream-memory in mind, we will be keenly aware of the contradiction which certain dream-theories, referred to later, are bound to set up, as they try to explain the absurdity and incoherence of dreams by the partial forgetting of what is known to us by day.

It might perhaps occur to us to reduce the phenomenon of dreaming entirely to that of remembering and regard the dream as the expression of a reproductive activity, unresting even at night, which is an end in itself. Accounts such as that given by Pilcz [51] would accord with this, for he claims that firm connections can be demonstrated between the time of dreaming and the content of the dream, such that in deep sleep the dream reproduces impressions from the earliest times, but reproduces recent ones towards morning.

But such a conception is made improbable from the outset by the way the dream deals with the material to be remembered. Strümpell [66] rightly points out that in the dream repetitions of experiences do not occur. True, the dream makes a start at it, but the next link is missing; it appears in altered form, or something entirely strange appears in its place. The dream presents only fragmentary reproductions. Certainly, this is so often the rule that we can make theoretical use of it. However, exceptions do occur in which a dream will repeat an experience just as completely as our waking recollection can. Delboeuf tells of how in a dream one of his university colleagues (who teaches at present in Vienna) repeated a dangerous coach journey in all its detail, where he escaped an accident only as if by a miracle. Miss Calkins [12] mentions two dreams whose content consisted of the exact reproduction of an experience from the previous day, and I myself will later take the opportunity of relating an instance known to me of the return in a dream, unaltered, of a childhood experience.

(c) *Dream-Stimuli and Dream-Sources*

What we are to understand by dream-stimuli and dream-sources can be clarified by referring to the popular saying, 'dreams come from the stomach'. Behind these concepts there is concealed a theory which regards the dream as the consequence of a disturbance of sleep; we would not have dreamed if something to disturb us had not stirred in our sleep—and the dream is the reaction to this disturbance.

Discussion of the causes that generate dreams occupies more space than any other topic in the writings about them. It goes without saying that the problem could only arise after the dream had become an object of biological inquiry. The ancients, who regarded the dream as divine inspiration, had no need to seek for its source; the dream proceeded from the will of the divine or daemonic power, its content from their knowledge or intention. For science, the question arose straight away whether the incentive to dreaming was always the same, or whether there might be several incentives—which brought with it the need to consider whether the explanation for the causes of dreams fell to psychology or to physiology. Most authorities seem to assume that there can be many kinds of cause for disturbances of sleep, that is, for the sources of dreaming, and that both somatic stimuli and psychical excitations can act as causative agents of dreams. But there is wide disagreement in privileging the one or the other among the sources of dreams, and in establishing a hierarchy among them according to their importance for the genesis of the dream.

With a complete enumeration of the sources of dreams it emerges that there are ultimately four kinds, which have also been used for the classification of dreams:

1. *External (objective) sensory excitation;*
2. *Internal (organic) sensory excitation;*
3. *Internal (organic) somatic stimulus;*
4. *Purely psychical sources of stimulus.*

1. External sensory stimuli

Strümpell the younger, son of the philosopher whose work on dreams has already served us several times as a guide to the problems of dreams, has, as we know, reported on his observation of an invalid afflicted with general anaesthesia of the skin and paralysis of several of the higher sensory organs. When this man's few remaining sensory gateways were cut off from the outside world, he fell asleep. When we want to go to sleep, we all try to attain a situation similar to the one in Strümpell's experiment. We close the most important sensory gateways, our eyes, and try to protect our other senses from any stimulus or change in the stimuli acting on them. We then go to sleep, though we are never completely successful in carrying out our aim. We can neither isolate our sensory organs entirely from the stimuli, nor wholly neutralize their excitability. The fact that we can always be woken by stronger stimuli may be taken as proof 'that even in sleep the psyche has remained in constant contact with the world external to the body'. The sensory stimuli that reach us in sleep could well become sources for dreams.

Now among such stimuli there are a great number, ranging from the unavoidable ones entailed in the sleeping state itself or occasionally admitted to it, to the chance stimulus to waking which is likely or intended to put an end to sleep. A rather strong light can penetrate the eyes, a sound become audible, or an odour agitate the nasal membrane. While we are asleep, involuntary movements may uncover parts of our body and in this way expose them to the sensation of getting colder, or by changing our position we may produce sensations of pressure or contact. A fly may sting us, or a slight nocturnal accident assail several of our senses at once. Attentive observers have collected a large number of dreams in which the stimulus established on waking and a part of the dream-content coincide so closely that the stimulus could be recognized as the source of the dream.

I shall cite here from Jessen [36] (p. 527) a collection of dreams of this kind which derive from objective—more or less accidental—sensory stimulation. Each indistinctly heard sound arouses corresponding dream-images: the rumble of thunder transports us to the midst of a battle; the crowing of a cock can be transformed into a human cry of fear; the creaking of a door call forth dreams of burglars breaking in. If we lose our bedclothes at night, we might dream that we are walking about naked or that we have fallen into the water. If we are lying at an angle in bed and our feet project over the edge, we might dream that we are standing at the edge of a terrible abyss, or that we are falling from a steep cliff. If by accident our head gets under the pillow, there is a great rock hanging over us about to bury us beneath its weight. Accumulations of semen produce lascivious dreams, localized pains the idea of abuses we have suffered, hostile attacks or the infliction of bodily injuries . . .

'Meier (*Versuch einer Erklärung des Nachtwandelns*, Halle: 1758, p. 33) once dreamed that he was set upon by a number of people who stretched him out on the ground on his back and drove a stake into the ground between his big toe and the one next to it. As he was imagining this in his dream, he woke and felt a straw sticking between his toes. On another occasion, according to Hennings (*Von den Träumen und Nachtwandlern*, Weimar: 1784, p. 258), Meier had fastened his shirt rather tightly around his neck, and dreamed he was being hanged. Hoffbauer dreamed as a young man that he was falling from a high wall, and discovered when he woke that the bedstead had come apart and that he really had fallen . . . Gregory reports that he once laid a hot-water bottle at his feet when he went to bed and then dreamed he had made a journey to the top of Mount Etna, where he found the heat of the ground almost unbearable. Another dreamed after he had had a poultice applied to his head that he was being scalped by Red Indians. A third, who went to sleep in a damp shirt, dreamed he was being dragged through a river. An attack of gout while he was asleep led an invalid to believe he was in the hands of the Inquisition and was being tortured (Macnish).'

The argument from the similarity between stimulus and dream-content is strengthened if by this systematic application of sensory stimuli it is possible to produce in the sleeper dreams corresponding to the stimulus. According to Macnish, Giron de Buzareingues had already tried such experiments. 'He left his knee uncovered, and dreamed that he was travelling by post-chaise at night. He observes in his account that travellers would certainly know how cold the knees would become in a coach at night. At another time he left the back of his head uncovered and dreamed that he was attending a religious ceremony in the open air. For in the country where he lived, it was the custom to keep the head covered, except on such occasions as the one just mentioned.'

Maury [48] reports a number of new observations of dreams he himself had produced. (A further series of experiments proved unsuccessful.)

1. He is tickled on the lips and tip of the nose with a feather.— Dreams of a terrible torture; a mask of pitch is placed on his face, then torn away, taking the skin with it.

2. A pair of scissors is sharpened against a pair of tweezers.—He hears bells pealing, then warning-bells, and is transported to the June days of 1848.*

3. He smells eau de Cologne.—He is in Cairo in the shop of Johann Maria Farina. There follow wild adventures which he is unable to reproduce.

4. He is squeezed gently in the neck.—He dreams that he is having a poultice applied, and thinks of a doctor who treated him in childhood.

5. A hot iron is held to his face.—He dreams of the 'stokers'[1] who have crept into the house and are forcing the inhabitants to hand over their money by thrusting their feet into a brazier. Then the Duchess of Abrantés, whose secretary he is in the dream, appears on the scene.

8. A drop of water is poured on to his forehead.—He is in Italy, perspiring heavily and drinking the white wine of Orvieto.

---

[1] 'Chauffeurs' was the name given to bands of robbers in the Vendée using this form of torture.

9. The light from a candle, filtered through a red paper, is made to fall on him repeatedly.—He dreams of storms, of heat, and finds himself once again in a storm at sea which he once experienced in the English Channel.

Other attempts at producing dreams experimentally have been made by d'Hervey [34], Weygandt [75], and others.

Many have noticed the 'striking skill of the dream in weaving sudden impressions from the sensory world into its creations in such a way that they come to form a catastrophe whose onset has already been gradually prepared and ushered in' (Hildebrandt [35]). 'When I was younger,' this author relates, 'in order to get up regularly at a certain hour in the morning, I sometimes used the familiar alarm usually attached to clocks. It must have happened a hundred times that the sound of this alarm fitted into an apparently very long and coherent dream, as if the whole dream were directed towards it as its logically indispensable point and natural goal.'

I shall refer to three more of these alarm-clock dreams in another connection.

Volkelt (p. 68) relates: 'A composer once dreamed that he was giving a class and wanted to make something clear to his pupils. He had just done so and turned to one of the boys with the question: "Did you understand me?" The boy shouted like a madman "O ja" ["Oh yes"]. Annoyed at the shouting, he reprimanded the boy. But the whole class was already shouting "Orja". Then: "Eurjo". And finally "Feuerjo!" ["Fire! Fire!"]. And then he was awakened by real cries of "Fire! Fire!" in the street.'

Garnier (*Traité des Facultés de l'âme*, 1865), quoted by Radestock [54], reports that Napoleon I was awakened from a dream while he was sleeping in his carriage by the explosion of an infernal machine,* and that in the dream he once again experienced the crossing of the Tagliamento* and the Austrian bombardment, until he woke with a start, crying: 'We have been undermined.'

A dream Maury [48] once had has become famous (p. 161). He was unwell and lay in bed in his room. His mother was sitting beside him. He dreamed of the Reign of Terror at the time of the Revolution, took part in dreadful scenes of murder, and was finally brought before the court himself. There he saw Robespierre, Marat, Fouquier-Tinville,* and all the sombre heroes of that terrible epoch, addressed them, after all kinds of incidents which escaped his recollection was condemned, and then, accompanied by an enormous crowd, led to the place of execution. He mounts the scaffold, the executioner fastens him to the plank; it tips up; the guillotine blade falls; he feels his head being severed from his body, wakes in a torment of fear—and discovers that the headboard of the bed has collapsed and, just like the blade of a guillotine, struck the back of his neck.

This dream gave rise to an interesting discussion, set off in the *Revue philosophique* by Le Lorrain [45] and Egger [20], as to whether and how it was possible for the dreamer to concentrate such an apparently full and abundant dream-content in the brief interval between waking-stimulus and waking.

Examples of this kind make objective sensory stimuli appear to be the most firmly established among the sources of dreams. Such stimuli are also the only ones that play any part in the knowledge of the layman. If you ask an educated man otherwise unfamiliar with the literature of dreams how dreams come about, he will no doubt reply by referring to a case he has heard of, in which a dream was explained by an objective sensory stimulus recognized after waking. Scientific inquiry cannot stop there; it becomes the occasion for it to question further why the stimulus acting upon our senses while we are asleep should appear in the dream in nothing like its true form, but be represented by some other imagined idea, which stands in some kind of relationship to it. But the relationship linking the dream-stimulus and the dream it produces is, in Maury's [47] words, 'une affinité quelconque, mais qui n'est pas unique et exclusive'* (p. 72). Take, for example, Hildebrandt's three alarm-clock dreams. We shall have to raise the question why the same stimulus produced such differing dreams, and why exactly these dreams, as its consequence.

(p. 37) 'So I am taking a walk one spring morning and strolling through the early green of the fields as far as a neighbouring village. There I see a crowd of villagers in their best clothes, their hymnbooks under their arms, making their way in droves towards the church. Of course! It is Sunday, and morning service is due to begin soon. I decide to take part, but first, because I am rather hot and out of breath, I decide to cool off in the churchyard that surrounds the church. While I am reading some of the inscriptions on the gravestones there, I hear the bell-ringer climb the tower, and then see the little village bell at the top which will give the signal for the service to begin. For a while it still hangs there motionless, then it begins to swing—and suddenly its strokes ring out loud and clear—so loud and clear that it puts an end to my sleep. But the sound of the bell comes from the alarm-clock.

'A second connection. It is a bright winter's day. The streets are deep with snow. I have agreed to take part in a sleigh-ride, but I have to wait a long time before the message comes that the sleigh is standing at the door. There follow the preparations for getting in—the fur rug is spread out, the foot-muff brought out—and at last I am sitting in my seat. But the departure is still delayed until the reins let the waiting horses feel the signal to start. Then the horses move off. The sleigh-bells, vigorously shaken, strike up their familiar janissary music with such force that in a moment the cobweb of the dream is torn apart. Again it is nothing but the shrill tone of the alarm-clock.

'Now a third example! I see a kitchen-maid walking along the corridor to the dining-room carrying several dozen plates piled up. The column of china in her arms seems to me to be in danger of toppling over. "Take care", I warn her, "the whole load is going to fall." The usual contradiction is, of course, forthcoming: she is used to carrying such things, etc., while I still follow her progress with concern. Sure enough, at the threshold she stumbles—the fragile crockery falls and clatters and shatters in a hundred pieces over the floor. But—the endlessly unceasing sound is, as I soon notice, not really a clattering, but a proper ringing;—and, as I now recognize as I wake, the ringing is only the alarm-clock doing its duty.'

The question why in the dream the psyche fails to recognize the nature of the objective sensory stimulus has been answered by Strümpell [66]—and almost to the same effect by Wundt [76]—by supposing that the stimuli encroaching upon the psyche in sleep place it under conditions which enable an illusion to be created. We *recognize and correctly interpret* a sensory impression, that is, we place it in the class of memories where, according to all our previous experience, it belongs, if the impression is strong, clear, and long-lasting enough, and if we have sufficient time to reflect on it. If these conditions are not met, we fail to recognize the object that gives rise to the impression; instead we use it as the basis of an illusion. 'If someone goes for a walk in the open country and perceives a distant object indistinctly, it can happen that at first he takes it to be a horse.'

Observing it more closely, he may be urged to interpret it as a cow lying down, until finally the sight resolves itself with certainty into a group of seated people. Now, the impressions which the psyche receives in sleep from external stimuli are of a similar indefinite nature. These stimuli are the basis on which the psyche creates illusions, for the impression summons up a greater or smaller number of remembered images, through which it acquires its psychical value. Which of the many relevant spheres of memory the appropriate images are summoned up from, and which of the possible associative connections thereby come into play, even Strümpell regards as indeterminable and left as it were up to the arbitrary will of the psyche.

We have a choice here. We can admit that the laws governing the formation of dreams cannot really be pursued any further, and so refrain from asking whether our interpretation of the illusion produced by the sensory impression may not be determined by other factors. Or we can speculate that the objective sensory stimulus encroaching upon sleep plays only a modest part as a source for dreams, and that other factors determine which images from our store of memories we chose to be aroused. In fact, if we examine Maury's experimentally produced dreams—which I have related in such detail for just this purpose—we are tempted to say that the experiment set up really covers the origin of only one of the elements of the dream, and that the rest of the dream-content seems rather too independent, too definite in its details, to be explained by the one requirement that it has to be consistent with the element introduced experimentally. Indeed, one even begins to have doubts about the illusion-theory and the power of the objective impression to shape the dream when one learns that on occasion in the dream it undergoes the strangest, most far-fetched interpretation. For example, M. Simon [63] recounts a dream in which he saw gigantic figures seated at table and distinctly heard the fearful gnashing of their jaws as they chewed. When he woke, he heard the hoofbeats of a horse galloping past his window. If in this case the sound of horses' hooves roused ideas from a cluster of recollections from *Gulliver's Travels,** of sojourns with the giants of Brobdingnag and the virtuous Houyhnhnms—as, without any support from the author, I would be inclined to interpret it—would not the choice of this sphere of memories so remote from the stimulus have been more easily motivated by different factors?

2. Internal (subjective) sensory excitation

Despite all the objections, we have to concede that the part played by objective sensory excitations during sleep in initiating dreams is indisputable, and if the nature and frequency of these stimuli seem perhaps inadequate to explain every dream-image, this indicates that we should be looking for other sources of dreams which are different from these but analogous in their effect. I do not know where the idea first arose of enlisting internal (subjective) excitations of the sensory organs as well as external sensory stimuli; but it is in fact done in all the more recent accounts of the aetiology of dreams. 'In the production of dream-illusions,' says Wundt [76], 'I believe an essential role is played by those subjective visual and aural perceptions familiar to us when we are awake, such as dazzling light on a dark field of vision, ringing or buzzing in the ears, etc., among them especially subjective excitations of the retina. This would explain the remarkable tendency of the dream to conjure up large numbers of similar or wholly identical objects before our eyes. We see countless birds, butterflies, fishes, many-coloured beads, flowers, and the like spread out before us: here the scattered light of the dark field of vision has assumed fantastic shapes, and the numerous particles of light which go to make it up are embodied by the dream in as many individual images. Because the shimmering light is so mobile, these are perceived as *moving* objects. Probably this is also at the root of the great inclination of the dream to form such a variety of animal figures, whose inventiveness of form adapts easily to the particular form of the subjective light-images.'

As a source of dream-images, subjective sensory excitations have the obvious advantage that, unlike objective ones, they are not dependent on external chance. They are as it were available for service whenever an explanation requires them. But they take second place to objective sensory stimuli as explanations, for it is either difficult or impossible to confirm their role as instigators of dreams in the way observation and experiment can do for objective stimuli. The main proof of the dream-arousing power of subjective sensory excitations is provided by what are called hypnagogic hallucinations, described by Johann Müller as 'fantastic visual phenomena'. These are images, often very vivid and fluctuating, which habitually appear—with many people quite regularly—while we are falling asleep, and which can also persist for a time after we have opened our eyes. Maury [48], who was very prone to them, has examined them in detail and maintains they are related, indeed identical, to dream-images (a view also held by Müller). For them to emerge, Maury says, a certain psychical passivity, a relaxation of attention, is required (p. 59 f.). But if we are in the right mood, a second of such lethargy is enough to make a hypnagogic hallucination appear, after which perhaps we reawaken, until the often-repeated performance is brought to an end by sleep. If we then wake up again after not too long an interval, we are, according to Maury, often able to establish that we have experienced the same image in our dream as hovered before us as a hypnagogic hallucination before we fell asleep (p. 134). It once happened in this way to Maury with a hallucination of a number of grotesque figures with distorted features and strange hair-styles who were harassing him with incredible persistence while he was falling asleep. After he woke, he remembered that he had also dreamed of them. Another time, when he had put himself on a diet and so was feeling hungry, he had a hypnagogic vision of a dish, and of a hand armed with a fork which took some of the food in the dish. In his dream he found himself at a well-laden table and heard the sounds the diners were making with their forks. Another time, when he had fallen asleep with sore and painful eyes, he had the hypnagogic hallucination of microscopically small signs which he had to strain to decipher one by one: an hour after he had woken he recalled a dream in which there was an open book, printed in very small letters, which he had to read through laboriously.

In just the same way as these images, auditory hallucinations of words, names, etc., can also appear hypnagogically and then be repeated in dreams, forming the overture, as it were, announcing the leitmotifs of the opera to follow.

The same path as the one followed by Johann Müller and Maury has been taken by a more recent observer of hypnagogic hallucinations, G. Trumbull Ladd [40]. By practising he was able to wrench himself suddenly awake two to five minutes after gradually falling asleep, but without opening his eyes: he then had the opportunity of comparing the sensations on his retina as they were just fading with the dream-images as they survived in his memory. He affirmed that a close relationship was recognizable between the two each time, for the luminous particles and lines of the retina's own light made as it were the outline sketch, the diagram, of the figures perceived in the dream. For example, a dream in which he saw before him clearly printed lines, which he read and studied, matched an arrangement of parallel lines of luminous particles in the retina. As he put it himself: the clearly printed page he read in his dream resolved itself into an object which appeared to his waking perception like part of a real printed page seen through a small hole in a piece of paper from too far away to make out anything distinctly. Ladd, who does not underestimate the central part played by the phenomenon in other respects also, takes the view that hardly a single dream unfolds within us which does not depend on the material of the inner excitations of the retina. This applies especially to dreams shortly after falling asleep in a darkened room, whereas in morning dreams when we are close to waking, he suggests, the objective light penetrating to the eyes in the brightened room supplies the source of the stimulus. The fluctuating character of the excitations of light in the retina, with their endless changeability, corresponds exactly to the restless flow of images which our dreams present to us. If we regard Ladd's observations as significant, we cannot doubt that this subjective source of stimulus is most productive in the creation of dreams, for as we know, visual images constitute the main component of our dreams. The contribution of the other senses, apart from that of hearing, is slighter and irregular.

3. Internal, organic somatic stimulus

As we are still looking for sources of dreams not outside but within the organism, we must remind ourselves that when they are in a state of health almost all our internal organs give us hardly a sign of their existence, but that when they are irritated—as we put it—or when we are ill, they become a source of mainly painful sensations for us, which must be put on the same footing as those external agencies which arouse excitations of pain or feeling. These are very ancient experiences, prompting Strümpell [66], for example, to say (p. 107): 'The psyche attains in sleep to a much more profound and wide-ranging sensory consciousness of its bodily nature than it does when awake, and cannot but receive and be affected by impressions of certain stimuli that originates in parts of the body and in changes there, which it was unaware of when awake.' Even as early a writer as Aristotle [1] declared it might very well be possible that in dreams our attention might be drawn to incipient illnesses whose traces we have not noticed when awake (by virtue of the magnification the dream gives to the impressions, see p. 1); and medical writers who were certainly very far from believing in the prophetic powers of dreams have granted them this importance at least as heralds of illness. (See M. Simon [63] (p. 31) and many earlier authors.)

There appear to be plenty of authenticated instances of success in diagnosis by dreams from more recent times too. For example, Tissié [68], following Artigues (*Essai sur la valeur séméiologique des rêves*), reports the story of a woman of forty-three who was afflicted by anxiety-dreams over several years of apparently perfect health, and who then, under medical examination, displayed an incipient heart condition to which she soon succumbed.

Advanced disorders of the internal organs clearly act in quite a large number of people as initiators of dreams. The frequency of anxiety-dreams among those suffering from diseases of the heart or lungs has been generally remarked: indeed, many authors have brought this association of the dream-life so much to the fore that I can content myself here with merely referring to the literature (Radestock [54], Spitta [64], Maury, M. Simon, Tissié). Tissié even considers that diseased organs impose a particular character on the dream-content. The dreams of someone with a heart condition are usually very brief and end with his awakening in terror; the situation of death under frightful circumstances almost always plays a part in their content. Sufferers from lung disease dream of suffocation, crowding, and fleeing, and a striking number are prey to the familiar nightmare—which Börner [5] has also been able to produce experimentally by lying on his face and covering the respiratory organs. Indigestion evokes in the dream ideas from the field of enjoyment and disgust. The influence, finally, of sexual arousal on the content of dreams will be comprehensible to every one of us from our own experience and provides the whole theory that dreams are initiated by organic stimulus with its strongest support.

As we work our way through the literature on dreams, it also becomes unmistakable that some of the authors concerned (Maury [48], Weygandt [75]) were led to their interest in the problems of dreams by the influence of their own illnesses on the content of their dreams.

However, although these undoubtedly established facts increase the sources of dreams, this is not as significant as one might like to think: for after all the dream is a phenomenon occurring in those in good health—perhaps to everyone, perhaps every night—and organic disease is obviously not one of its indispensable conditions. But for us, the issue is not where exceptional dreams come from, but what the source of stimulation for the ordinary dreams of normal people might be.

Meanwhile it requires only one step further for us to come upon a source of dreams that flows more abundantly than any of the previous ones and really shows no prospect at all of drying up. If it has been established that the interior of the body in a state of sickness becomes a source of dream-stimuli, and if we concede that, in a sleeping state, diverted from the external world, the psyche is able to devote greater attention to the body's interior, then we are tempted to assume that the organs do not first have to become sick for excitations—which somehow turn into dream-images—to reach the sleeping psyche. What we dimly apprehend when we are awake only in its quality as a general vital sense, to which in medical opinion all the organ-systems contribute, would, when working powerfully at night and with its individual components active, supply the strongest and at the same time the most common source for the arousal of representations.

We have touched here on that theory of the genesis of dreams which has become the favoured one among all medical authors. The darkness in which the core of our being, the 'moi splanchnique', as Tissié [68] calls it, is shrouded from our knowledge, and the darkness in which dreams originate correspond too well not to be brought into association with one another. The train of ideas which makes the vegetative sensations of our organs into makers of dreams has this further appeal to the physician that it also enables us to make the dream and mental disturbance, which have so much in common in their manifestations, compatible in their aetiologies as well; for changes in the general vital sense and in the stimuli which proceed from the internal organs are also accorded far-reaching importance in the genesis of psychoses. So it is not surprising if the theory of physical stimulation can be traced back to more than one first thinker who proposed it independently.

The line of thought developed by the philosopher Schopenhauer*

[60] in 1851 has become definitive for a number of authors. Our conception of the world arises in us as our intellect recasts the impressions it receives from without into the forms of time, space, and causality. The stimuli from the interior of our organism, communicated by the sympathetic nervous system, manifest by day at most an unconscious influence on our mood. At night, however, when the deafening effect of the impressions of the day has ceased, those impressions surging from within are able to call attention to themselves—just as at night we can hear the murmuring of the stream which the noise of the day made inaudible. But how else is the intellect to react to these stimuli but by fulfilling its distinctive function? It will transform the stimuli accordingly into figures occupying space and time and moving on the connecting thread of causality, and that is how the dream comes into being. On this assumption, Scherner [58], and after him Volkelt [72], attempted to go deeper into the relationship between physical stimuli and dream-images. However, we shall reserve consideration of their work until the section on theories of dreams.

In a particularly rigorous inquiry the psychiatrist Krauss [39] derived the origin of dreams as well as of hallucinations and delusions from the same element, *sensations caused organically*. In his view, there is scarcely a place in the organism conceivable which cannot become the starting-point for a dream or a delusion. The organically caused sensation 'can, however, be divided into two groups: 1. those of the overall temper of feeling (general vital feelings), 2. the specific sensations immanent in the main systems of the vegetative organism, in which we have distinguished five groups, (*a*) muscular sensations, (*b*) respiratory, (*c*) gastric, (*d*) sexual, and (*e*) peripheral' (p. 33 of the second article).

Krauss assumes that the emergence of dream-images on the basis of physical stimuli takes the following course: in accordance with some associative law the awakened sensation arouses an imagined idea related to it and combines with it into an organic formation. However, the way the consciousness acts towards this is different from its normal behaviour. It does not heed the sensation itself, but turns its attention entirely to the accompanying imagined ideas—which is also the reason why this fact could remain unrecognized for so long (pp. 11 ff.). Krauss also coins the special term *transubstantiation* of the sensations into dream-images for this process.

The influence of organic physical stimuli on the formation of dreams is almost universally accepted today, but the question as to what law governs the relationship between the two gets very different and often obscure answers. Accordingly, when dream-interpretation is based on the theory of physical stimulus, it has the particular task of tracing the content of a dream back to the organic stimulus which caused it; and if we do not accept the rules for interpretation devised by Scherner [58], we are often faced with the awkward fact that the only way the organic source of stimulation reveals itself is precisely by means of the very content of the dream.

However, a degree of agreement has been reached in the interpretation of various forms of dreams which have been designated 'typical' because they recur with very similar content in so many people. These are the familiar dreams of falling from a height, of the teeth falling out, of flying, and of the embarrassment of finding oneself naked or ill-clad. This last dream is supposed to derive simply from our awareness while asleep that we have thrown off the bedclothes and are now lying uncovered. The dream that our teeth are falling out is attributed to a 'sensitivity of the teeth'—which does not, however, need to imply that the excitation is due to bad teeth. The dream of flying, according to Strümpell [66], is the appropriate image used by the psyche to interpret the quantum of stimulus proceeding from the rise and fall of the lungs when the cutaneous sensation of the thorax has simultaneously sunk into unconsciousness. The latter condition is responsible for the sensation associated with the idea of floating. The cause of falling from a height is supposed to be that as we lose consciousness of the feeling of pressure on the skin, we either let an arm sink from the body or suddenly straighten a bent knee; as we do so we become conscious once more of the feeling of pressure on the skin, but this transition to consciousness is psychically embodied in the dream of falling (Strümpell, p. 118). The weakness of these plausible attempts at explanation clearly lies in the fact that without offering any further grounds for doing so, they allow this or that group of organic sensations to disappear from psychical perception or to force themselves upon it, until the constellation favourable to the explanation is produced. I shall, by the way, have occasion later to return to typical dreams and their genesis.

By comparing a number of similar dreams, M. Simon [63] has

attempted to deduce some rules for the influence of organic stimuli in determining their ensuing dreams. According to him (p. 34), if in sleep any organic apparatus normally involved in the expression of an affect is put by some other cause into the state of arousal into which it is usually placed by that affect, the dream arising will contain imagined ideas which are appropriate to that emotion.

According to another rule (p. 35), if in sleep an organic apparatus is in a state of activity, arousal, or disturbance, the dream will introduce imagined ideas related to the exercise of the organic function which that apparatus performs.

Mourly Vold [73] has undertaken to demonstrate the influence on the production of dreams assumed by the theory of physical stimulus by experiment in one particular field. He has done so by changing the position of the sleeper's limbs, and then comparing the consequent dreams with the changes he had made. He reports his findings in the following propositions:

1. The position of a limb in a dream corresponds roughly to its position in reality, i.e. we dream of a static condition of the limb corresponding to the real one.

2. If we dream of a limb moving, it is always the case that one of the positions taken in the course of the movement corresponds to the real position.

3. In the dream, we can also ascribe the position of our own limb to another person.

4. We can also dream that the movement in question is impeded.

5. In the dream, the position in question can also appear as an animal or a monster, setting up a certain analogy between the two.

6. In the dream, the position of a limb can call up thoughts which have some sort of connection with the limb. Thus, for example, if the fingers are involved, we dream of numbers.

I would conclude from such results that even the theory of physical stimulus cannot entirely extinguish our apparent freedom in determining the dream-images to be awakened.

4. Sources of stimulation in the psyche

In discussing the connections between dreams and waking life, and the origin of dream-material, we found that both the most ancient and the most recent inquirers into dreams held the view that people dream of what they do by day, and of what interests them when they are awake. This interest continuing from waking life into sleep is, they claim, not only a psychical bond linking the dream to life, but it also provides us with a source of dreams not to be underestimated. This, in addition to the interests developing during sleep—the stimuli affecting us while asleep—should be sufficient to explain the origin of all dream-images. However, we have also heard the objection to this claim: that the dream withdraws the sleeper from the interests of the day, and that we—mostly—dream of the things that have moved us most intensely by day only when they have lost their immediate relevance to our waking life. Thus at every step in the analysis of the dream-life, we get the impression that it is inadmissible to set up general rules unless we anticipate reservations with an 'often', an 'as a rule', or a 'usually', and provide for the validity of exceptions.

If the interests of our waking lives together with the internal and external stimuli acting upon sleep were sufficient factors in the aetiology of dreams as a whole, we ought to be in a position to give a satisfactory account of the origin of all the elements in a dream. The riddle of where dreams have their sources would be solved, and all that would be left would be the task of distinguishing the respective shares of the psychical and the somatic dream-stimuli in any particular dream. In reality, there has been no case as yet in which this complete resolution of a dream has been successful, and anyone who has attempted it has been left with—usually very many— components whose origin could not be accounted for. The interests of the day are clearly not such influential psychical sources of dreams as confident assertions that in dreams we all continue the business of the day would lead us to expect.

No other sources in the psyche for dreams are known. All the explanations of dreams represented in the literature—with the possible exception of Scherner's [58], which we will discuss later—thus leave a great gap when it comes to tracing back to source the material for the images most characteristic of dreams. In this embarrassing situation, most of the authors tend as far as possible to minimize the share of psychical factors, so difficult of approach, in the arousal of dreams. It is true, they distinguish major categories of *dreams aroused by nervous stimuli* and *dreams aroused by association*, the latter having its source exclusively in reproduction (Wundt [76]), but they cannot rid themselves of the doubt 'whether they ever appear without the impetus from a physical stimulus' (Volkelt [72] p. 365). Even the description of the pure association-dream does not work: 'In true association-dreams, there can no longer be a question of such a firm core. Here, the looseness of the grouping enters even the centre of the dream. In this kind of dream, the life of the imagined ideas, in any case released from sense and reason, is no longer held together even by the more substantial excitations of body and psyche, and so is left to its own variegated devices and desires, its own confusions and contortions' (Volkelt, p. 118). Wundt too attempts to reduce the share of the psyche in initiating dreams by arguing that it is probably wrong to regard the phantasmagoria of dreams as pure hallucinations. Probably most dream-images are in reality illusions, arising from faint sense-impressions which are never extinguished in sleep (pp. 359 f.). Weygandt [75] has adopted this view and applied it generally. He maintains that all dream-representations 'have their immediate cause in sensory stimuli, to which reproductive associations only then attach themselves' (p. 17). Tissié [68] (p. 183) goes even further in repressing the sources in psychical stimuli: 'Les rêves d'origine absolument psychique n'existent pas', and elsewhere (p. 6): 'les pensées de nos rêves nous viennent de dehors . . .'*

Those authors who take a middle position, like the influential philosopher Wundt, make a point of remarking that in most dreams somatic stimuli work together with psychical initiators of dreams, whether unknown or recognized as coming from the interests of the day.

We shall find out later that the riddle of how dreams are formed can be solved by the discovery of an unsuspected source of stimulus in the psyche. For the moment, let us not be surprised at the over-estimation of those stimuli to dream-formation which do not derive from the life of the psyche. It is not just that these are the only ones easy to detect, and even to confirm by experiment; the somatic conception of the origin of dreams is also in complete accord with the prevailing line of thought in psychiatry today. True, the dominance of the brain over the organism is given great emphasis, but anything possibly showing that the life of the psyche might be independent of demonstrable organic changes, or could act spontaneously, fills the psychiatrist of today with alarm, as if to acknowledge this would inevitably mean a return to the days of Natural Philosophy and the metaphysics of the soul. This mistrust on the part of the psychiatrist has placed the psyche as it were under the supervision of a guardian, and demands that it should make no movement that might reveal that it possesses a competence of its own. Yet what this attitude in fact implies is a lack of trust in the causal chain extending between the body and the psyche. Even where investigation shows the primary cause of the phenomenon to be psychical, if we go deeper, we shall one day discover that the way continues until it reaches the organic basis for the psychical. But where in the present state of our knowledge, we cannot but regard the psychical as the end of the road, that is no reason for denying it.

(d) *Why Do We Forget Our Dreams After We Wake?*

It is proverbial that a dream 'fades' in the morning. Of course, it can be remembered. For after all we only know of its existence from our recollection of it after waking; but we very often believe that we are remembering it only imperfectly, that there was more of it present in the night; we can observe how a recollected dream, still vivid in the morning, will vanish in the course of the day, leaving only fragments behind; we often know that we have dreamed, but not *what* we have dreamed, and we are so accustomed to knowing that dreams can be forgotten that we do not even reject as absurd the possibility that we could have been dreaming in the night, but know nothing in the morning of either the content of the dream or the fact that we have been dreaming. On the other hand, it does happen that dreams can retain an extraordinary hold on the memory. I have analysed dreams of my patients which occurred twenty-five or more years previously, and I can remember a dream of my own which happened at least thirty-seven years ago, but which is still as fresh as ever in my memory. All this is very remarkable, and at first impossible to understand.

The most detailed treatment of forgetting dreams has been provided by Strümpell [66]. This forgetting is clearly a complex phenomenon, for Strümpell traces it back not to a single cause but to a whole set of them.

In the first place, all the reasons for forgetting in our waking life are also operative in forgetting dreams. When we are awake we habitually forget a vast number of sensations and perceptions straight away, because they were too weak, because the degree of psychical arousal connected with them was too slight. The same applies to many of our dreams. They are forgotten because they were too weak, while stronger images close to them are remembered. However, the element of intensity is not in itself decisive for the retention of dream-images; Strümpell as well as other authors (Calkins [12]) concedes that we often forget very quickly dreams that we know were very vivid, while very many shadowy, faintly perceived images are to be found among those retained in our memory. Moreover, when we are awake it is usually easy for us to forget what has only happened once, and easier for us to remember what we have been able to perceive repeatedly. Most dreams, however, are once-and-for-all experiences.[2] This will contribute to some extent to all dreams and their forgetting. There is a third reason for forgetting which is far more important. For sensations, images, thoughts, etc. to attain a certain degree of memorability, it is necessary that they should not remain isolated, but enter into connections and associations of an appropriate kind. If we break up a little line of poetry into its single words and shake them up together, it will become very hard to remember. 'Neatly ordered and in proper sequence, one word aids another, and the whole makes sense and remains firmly in our memory. In general it is as difficult and as rare for us to remember the absurd as it is to retain the confused and disordered.' Now in most cases dreams have no intelligibility or order. Dream-compositions are essentially devoid of any possible memory themselves, and are forgotten because they usually merge into one another from one moment to the next. However, these observations are not entirely in accord with what Radestock [54] claims to have observed: that the strangest dreams are the very ones we retain best.

It seems to Strümpell that other elements deriving from the relationship between dreams and waking life are still more effective as factors in forgetting dreams. The ease with which the waking consciousness can forget dreams is plainly just the counterpart to the fact we discussed earlier that the dream (almost) never borrows ordered recollections from waking life, but only details, which it tears out of their accustomed psychical connections where they are remembered when we are awake. This means that the dream-composition has no

---

[2] Dreams recurring periodically have often been noted. See those collected by Chabaneix [11].

place in the community of the ordered series with which the psyche is filled. It has nothing that would help us to remember it. 'In this way the dream rises up from the ground of our inner life, as it were, and floats in our psychical space like a cloud in the sky, which any fresh breeze will quickly blow away' (p. 87). The same tendency is furthered by the fact that when we wake the onrush of the sensory world occupies our attention so fully that only very few dreams can withstand its force. They retreat before the impressions of the new day, as the brightness of the stars gives way to the light of the sun.

Finally, it has to be considered that forgetting dreams is aided by the fact that most people show little interest in their dreams anyway. Anyone who is interested in dreams for a certain time, for example, for scientific inquiry, will also dream more during that period than usual, which probably means that he remembers his dreams more easily and more often.

Two other reasons for forgetting dreams which Bonatelli (cited by Benini [3]) adds to Strümpell's are probably already covered by the latter: (1) that the change in general vital feeling which takes place between sleeping and waking makes it unfavourable for one to reproduce the other, and (2) that the different arrangement of the material of the imagined ideas in the dream makes it impossible for the waking consciousness to translate, as it were.

After all these reasons for forgetting, it really is strange, as Strümpell himself emphasizes, that we still retain so much of our dreams in our memory. The continual efforts of our authors to formulate rules for remembering dreams amount to an admission that here too there is something enigmatic and unsolved. Some particular aspects of the remembrance of dreams have rightly been noted of late, for example, that a dream which in the morning we thought we had forgotten can return to our memory in the course of the day, triggered by some perception which chances to touch on the—forgotten—content of the dream (Radestock [54], Tissié [68]). However, the entire issue of dream recollection is open to an objection calculated to reduce its value substantially in critical eyes. We may very well doubt whether our memory, which retains so little of the dream, might not falsify what it does retain.

Strümpell too expresses doubts of this kind as to whether we can reproduce our dreams exactly: 'It happens so easily that the waking consciousness involuntarily introduces many things into its recollection of the dream: we imagine we have dreamed all kinds of things which the actual dream did not contain.'

Jessen [36] is particularly emphatic on this point (p. 547): 'But in investigating and interpreting coherent and consistent dreams, we should also consider very carefully a circumstance which has, it seems, so far received little attention: there is always the tricky problem of truth. For when we call to memory a dream we have had, without noticing or intending it we fill out the gaps in our dream and add to it. Rarely and perhaps never has a coherent dream been as coherent as it appears to us in recollection. However much a man may love truth it is scarcely possible for him to relate a remarkable dream he has had without adding to it or embellishing it: the human mind's endeavour to see everything in coherent connection is so great that when it remembers a relatively incoherent dream it involuntarily makes good the flaws in the coherence.'

Egger's [20] remarks on the subject sound like a translation of these words of Jessen's, though he will certainly have arrived at them independently: '. . . l'observation des rêves a ses difficultés spéciales et le seul moyen d'éviter toute erreur en pareille matière est de confier au papier sans le moindre retard ce que l'on vient d'éprouver et de remarquer; sinon, l'oubli vient vite ou total ou partiel; l'oubli total est sans gravité; mais l'oubli partiel est perfide; car si l'on se met ensuite à raconter ce que l'on n'a pas oublié, on est exposé à compléter par imagination les fragments incohérents et disjoints fournis par la mémoire . . .; on devient artiste à son insu, et le récit périodiquement répété s'impose à la créance de son auteur, qui, de bonne foi, le présente comme un fait authentique, dûment établi selon les bonnes méthodes . . .'*

A very similar observation is made by Spitta [64] (p. 338), who seems to assume that we only introduce order at all into the loosely associated elements of the dream simply when we try to reproduce the dream, attempting—'out of mere juxtaposition to create succession and development, that is, to introduce the process of logical connection which the dream lacks'.

Now, as we do not have another control to act as an objective check on the fidelity of our recollection—which in any case is impossible in the case of a dream, as it is our own personal experience and we have only our memory as its known source—what value is left in our recollection of it?

(e) *The Distinctive Psychological Features of Dreams*

In the scientific consideration of dreams, we start from the assumption that they are the products of our own psychical activity; yet the finished dream seems to us something alien, and we feel so little disposed to admit to its authorship that we are just as happy to say 'a dream came to me' as 'I dreamed'.* Where does this 'psychical strangeness' come from? After our discussion of the sources of dreams, we ought not to think that it is determined by the material that enters the content of the dream, for this is for the most part common to both the dream life and the waking life. We can ask ourselves whether this impression is not produced by modifications brought about by the psychical processes in the dream, and in this way attempt a characterization of the dream in psychological terms.

No one has emphasized the essential difference between dream and waking, or used it to draw such far-reaching conclusions, as G. T. Fechner [25] has (in some observations in his *Elemente der Psychophysik*, part II, p. 520). In his view, 'neither simply the reduction of the conscious life of the psyche below the main threshold' nor the withdrawal of attention from the influences of the external world is sufficient to explain the particular characteristics of the dream-life in contrast to waking life. He suspects rather that the *location of the dream is different from that of waking mental life*. 'If the location of psycho–physical activity during sleep were the same as during waking life, the dream could in my opinion merely be a continuation of waking mental life at a lower degree of intensity, and would, moreover, have to share the same material and the same form. But that is not how things are.'

What Fechner means by such a relocation of psychical activity is by no means clear; nor, as far as I know, has anyone else gone further along the path he indicated in these remarks. We will no doubt have to reject an anatomical interpretation in the sense of localization in different parts of the brain, or even with reference to the histological stratification of the cerebral cortex. But the idea may perhaps one day prove useful and fruitful if it is applied to a psychical apparatus made up of several agencies set up one behind the other.

Other writers have contented themselves with emphasizing one or other of the more tangible psychological features that distinguish the dream-life and making it the starting-point, say, for further attempts at explanation.

It has rightly been observed that one of the chief peculiarities of the dream-life already enters the scene while we are in the state of falling asleep, and can be described as the phenomenon introducing sleep. According to Schleiermacher [61] (p. 351), what characterizes the waking state is that thinking takes place in *concepts* and not in *images*. Now the dream thinks mainly in images, and it can be observed that as sleep approaches, to the degree that voluntary activity becomes more sluggish, so *involuntary ideas emerge*, which all belong to the class of images. This incapacity for the kind of thinking that we feel is intentional, and the emergence of images that is regularly associated with this absent state of mind are two features which persist in the dream, and which psychological analysis compels us to recognize as essential characteristics of the dream-life. These images—the hypnagogic hallucinations—are, as we have learned, even as regards content identical with the images in dreams.

Dreams, then, think mainly in visual images, but not exclusively. They also work with auditory images, and to a lesser extent with impressions from the other senses. A great deal is also simply thought or imagined in dreams (probably represented by the residual representations left from words) just as it is in waking life. But what are really characteristic of dreams are only those elements in the content that behave like images, that is, they are more like perceptions than remembered representations. Disregarding all those discussions familiar to the psychiatrist on the nature of hallucinations, we can state that the dream *hallucinates*, that it replaces thoughts with hallucinations. In this respect there is no difference between visual and acoustic representations. It has been observed that the recollection of a sequence of musical notes heard as we fall asleep is transformed into a hallucination of the same melody as we sink further into sleep, but that whenever we wake in the course of nodding off, alternating as these frequently do as we drowse, the hallucination gives way to the softer and qualitatively different remembered (acoustic) representation.

The dream's transformation of representations into hallucinations is not the only way it differs from the waking thought that might correspond to it. The dream creates a situation out of these images, it enacts something as immediately present, it *dramatizes* an idea, as Spitta [64] (p. 145) puts it. However, the description of this aspect of the dream-life will not be complete until we add that when we dream—as a rule, that is, for exceptions require a separate explanation—we believe not that we are thinking, but that we are experiencing, that is, we accept the hallucinations in good faith. Criticism of this belief—that we have not been experiencing anything, but have only been thinking in a peculiar form, dreaming— arises only when we wake up. This characteristic distinguishes the true dream in sleep from day-dreaming, which is never confused with reality.

Burdach [8] has summarized the characteristics of the dream-life so far observed as follows (p. 476): 'The essential features of the dream include (a) that the subjective activity of our psyche appears as objective, for the faculty of perception regards the products of the imagination as though they were apprehended by our senses; . . . (b) in sleep our autonomy is suspended. Hence falling asleep requires a certain passivity . . . Images called up in slumber are determined by a reduction in our autonomy.'

The point now is to try to explain why the psyche places such faith in these dream-hallucinations, which can appear only after a certain independent activity on our own part has been put on hold. Strümpell [66] argues that in doing this the psyche is behaving correctly and according to its own mechanism. According to him, the elements of the dream are not at all mere presentations, but *real and genuine experiences of the psyche*, such as occur when we are awake through the mediation of our senses (p. 34). Whereas the psyche thinks and imagines in verbal images and language when awake, in dreams it imagines and thinks in real sensory images (p. 35). In addition, there is a consciousness of space present in the dream, for sensations and images are transported into an external space, as they are when we are awake (p. 36). So we have to concede that with regard to its images and perceptions, the psyche is in the same position in dreams as it is in waking life (p. 43). If nevertheless it goes astray in dealing with them, this is because in sleep it lacks the criterion able to distinguish between sense-perceptions coming from without and those coming from within. It cannot subject its images to the only tests that can demonstrate their objective reality. It *also* disregards the distinction between images which are *arbitrarily* interchangeable and others where this arbitrariness does not exist.

It goes astray because it is unable to apply the law of causality to the content of its dreams (p. 58). In short, the psyche's act of turning away from the external world also holds the grounds for its belief in the subjective world of the dream.

The same conclusion is reached, after a partly different psychological argument, by Delboeuf [16]. According to him, we believe in the reality of the images in our dreams because in sleep we are removed from the external world and so have no other impressions to compare them with. But surely this is not why we believe in the truth of our hallucinations, for in sleep we have lost the possibility of applying tests. The dream can create the illusion of all these tests: it can, for instance, show us that we are touching a rose we see, and yet we are still dreaming. According to Delboeuf there is no valid criterion whether something is a dream or waking reality except—and this only in practice and in general—the sheer fact of awakening. I declare everything I have experienced between going to sleep and waking up to be an illusion when I notice on awakening that I am lying on my bed undressed (p. 84). While asleep I took my dream to be true on account of the *habit of thought*, which is itself not to be lulled asleep, and assumes an external world with which I contrast my self.[3] If

---

[3] Like Delboeuf, but describing the condition in rather different words, Haffner [32] has attempted to explain the activity of dreaming by the modification which is bound to result from introducing an abnormal condition to the otherwise correct functioning of the psychical apparatus. According to him, the dream is primarily characterized by the absence of any location in place or time, i.e. by the emancipation of the dream-idea from the dreamer's position in time and place. This is connected with the second fundamental feature of the dream: its confusion of hallucinations, products of the imagination and combinations of the fantasy with external perceptions. 'As all the higher powers of the psyche, in particular the powers of conceptualization, judgement, and inference on the one hand and free self-determination on the other, are attached to imaginary sensory images and always have these as their foundation, it follows that these activities also have their part in the uncontrolled irregularities of the dream-images. They have their part, we say, for in itself our power of judgement, like our will, is by no means altered. These activities are just as keen and just as free as when we are awake. In our dreams too we cannot contravene the laws of thought, i.e. we cannot propose that the image represented is identical with its opposite etc. In our dreams too we can only desire what we imagine to be a good (*sub ratione boni*). But in thus applying the laws of thinking and willing, the human mind is led astray in the dream by confusing one idea with another. Thus it happens that in dreams we propose and perform the wildest contradictions, while on the other hand we can reach the most clear-sighted judgements, draw the most logical conclusions, and make the most virtuous and saintly decisions. *Lack of orientation* is the entire secret of the flight of our imagination in dreams, and *lack of critical reflection*, as well as of communication with others, is the chief source of the boundless extravagances in our dreams of our judgements, our hopes, and our desires' (p. 18).

the psyche's act of turning away from the external world is given prominence in this way as one of the determining factors in shaping the most striking features of the dream-life, it is worth citing some subtle observations made by Burdach [8] long ago, which throw light on the relationship between the sleeping psyche and the external world and are calculated to restrain us from overestimating the conclusions we have just been discussing. 'Sleep occurs', says Burdach, 'only under the condition that the psyche is not roused by sensory stimuli ... but the condition for sleep is not so much a lack of sensory stimuli as a lack of interest in them; some sensory impressions are even necessary in so far as they serve to soothe the psyche, for instance, when a miller can go to sleep only when he hears the sound of his mill, or when someone who needs a night-light as a precaution cannot get to sleep in the dark' (p. 457).

'In sleep the psyche isolates itself from the external world and draws back from its periphery ... At the same time, connection is not entirely broken off: for if we did not hear and feel while we were asleep, we could not be woken up at all. The continuation of sensation is demonstrated even more strongly by the fact that we are not always woken by the mere sensory strength of an impression, but by its psychical associations; an insignificant word will not wake the sleeper, but if you call him by name he will wake up ... which means that in sleep the psyche distinguishes between sensations ... So it appears that we can also be woken by the lack of a sensory stimulus if this relates to something we regard as important; in this way we wake when the night-light is put out, as the miller does when his mill ceases grinding, that is to say, when the sensory activity comes to a stop. That assumes that this activity has been perceived, but as something indifferent, or rather as satisfying, without disturbing the psyche' (pp. 460 ff.).

Even if we disregard these not inconsiderable objections, we still have to concede that the strangeness of the dream cannot fully be accounted for by those characteristics of the dream-life we have discussed so far, which derived from a turning away from the external world. For otherwise it ought to be possible to transform the hallucinations of the dream back into ideas and the situations of the dream back into thoughts, and in that way resolve the task of the interpretation of dreams. This, in fact, is what we do when we reproduce a dream from memory after we awake, and whether this back-translation is wholly or only partly successful, the dream retains its enigmatic quality undiminished.

All our authors also assume without a second thought that in dreams other and profounder changes have occurred to the ideational material of waking life. Strümpell [66] attempts to unearth one of them in the following discussion (p. 17): 'With the cessation of active sensory perception and normal awareness of life, the psyche also relinquishes the ground in which its feelings, desires, interests and actions are rooted. Even those mental states, those feelings, interests, value-judgements which still cling to the remembered images when we are awake, are subject to . . . an obscuring pressure, with the result that their link with the images is dissolved. The perceptual images of the things, people, places, events, and actions of waking life are reproduced in great numbers individually, but none of them carries with it its *psychological* value. This has been removed from them, and so they hover around in the psyche on their own resources . . .'

According to Strümpell, stripping the images of their psychical value in this way—a process which again is itself traced back to the subject's turning from the external world—accounts to a large extent for the impression of strangeness that the dream leaves in our memory by contrast with waking life.

We have heard that even in the act of falling asleep we relinquish one of our psychical activities, the direction by our will of the course of our ideas. In this way we are forced to the suspicion, obvious in any case, that the sleeping state may also extend to the operations of the psyche. One or other of these operations is perhaps entirely suspended; the question then is whether the remainder work on undisturbed, whether they are able to perform their normal work under such circumstances. The thought arises that it might be possible to explain the peculiarities of the dream by the reduced performance of the psyche in the sleeping state—and the impression which the dream makes on our waking judgement does support such an idea. The dream is incoherent, without compunction it unites the grossest contradictions, permits impossibilities, sets aside the knowledge that influences us by day, and exposes us as ethically and morally obtuse. Anyone who behaved while awake in the way the situations in the dream present him would be regarded as insane; anyone who while awake uttered or sought to communicate the kind of things that occur in the content of dreams would gives us the impression of being confused or weak-minded. Accordingly we believe we are only stating a fact when we express a very low opinion of psychical activity in dreams, and in particular declare the higher intellectual capacities to be in suspension, or at least seriously impaired, in them.

With rare unanimity—the exceptions will be discussed else-where—our authors have passed judgements on the dream that also lead directly to a particular theory or explanation of the dream-life. It is time for the summary I have just made to give way to a collection of statements made by various writers—philosophers and physicians—on the psychological characteristics of the dream.

According to Lemoine [42] the incoherence of the dream-images is the one essential characteristic of the dream.

Maury [48] agrees with him: he says (p. 163): 'il n'y a pas des rêves absolument raisonnables et qui ne contiennent quelque incohérence, quelque anachronisme, quelque absurdité.'*

According to Hegel (cited by Spitta [64]) the dream lacks all intel-ligent objective coherence.

Dugas [19] says: 'Le rêve, c'est l'anarchie psychique, affective et mentale, c'est le jeu des fonctions livrées à elles-mêmes et s'exerçant sans contrôle et sans but; dans le rêve l'esprit est un automat spirituel.'*

Even Volkelt [72], whose theory regards psychical activity during sleep as not in the least purposeless, admits to the 'loosening, dis-solution, and confounding with one another of ideas held coherently together in waking life by the central ego's force of logic' (p. 14).

The *absurdity* of the connections between ideas occurring in dreams could hardly be more severely condemned than it was long ago by Cicero (*De divinatione*, ii): 'Nihil tam praepostere, tam incondite, tam monstruose cogitari potest, quod non possimus somniare.'*

Fechner [25] says (p. 522) it is as if psychological activity had been transferred from the brain of a rational man to that of a fool.

Radestock [54] (p. 145): 'It does in fact seem impossible to recog-nize any firm laws in these crazy antics. Evading the attention of that stern policing power, the rational will, which directs the course of our waking ideas, the dream whirls everything madly together like a kaleidoscope.'

Hildebrandt [35] (p. 45): 'What strange escapades the dreamer permits himself, for example, in the rational conclusions he draws! With what unconcern he sees the most familiar empirical laws stood on their heads! What ludicrous contradictions to the rules of nature and society he can endure before, as we say, it all gets too much for him and the extremity of the nonsense wakes him up! Occasionally we will multiply three by three and in all innocence make twenty; we are not in the least surprised if a dog recites poetry, a corpse walks to its own grave, a rock floats on water; in all seriousness we go on a mission to the Duchy of Bernburg or the Principality of Liechtenstein to inspect their navies, or let Charles XII enlist us as a volunteer just before the battle of Pultava.'*

Binz [4] (p. 33), referring to the theory of dreams founded on these impressions: 'Out of every ten dreams, the content of at least nine is absurd. We couple together in them people and things which have absolutely nothing to do with one another. As in a kaleidoscope, one grouping is the next moment changed into another, if possible into one crazier and more senseless than its predecessor; and so the interplay within the imperfectly sleeping brain goes on until we wake up, clutch our brow, and ask ourselves whether we are still in possession of the faculty of rational thought.'

Maury [48] discovers a comparison for the relationship between dreams and waking thoughts which a physician will find very impressive: 'La production de ces images que chez l'homme éveillé fait le plus souvent naître la volonté, correspond, pour l'intelligence, à ce que sont par la motilité certains mouvements que nous offrent la chorée et les affections paralytiques . . .' For the rest, the dream is to him 'toute une série de dégradations de la faculté pensante et raisonnante' (p. 27).*

It is hardly necessary to cite those writers who repeat Maury's proposition with respect to the various higher functions of the psyche.

According to Strümpell [66], in the dream all the logical operations of the psyche based on relations and connections withdraw— also, of course, where the irrationality is not immediately obvious (p. 26). According to Spitta [64] (p. 148), in the dream the ideas seem to be completely detached from the law of causality. Radestock [54] and others emphasize the weakness of the powers of judgement and deduction characteristic of the dream. According to Jodl [37]

(p. 123), in the dream there is no criticism or correction of a set of perceptions by reference to the content of the total consciousness. The same writer maintains: 'All kinds of conscious activity occur in dreams, but incompletely, impeded, isolated from one another.' Stricker [77, 78] (together with many others) explains the ways in which the dream contradicts our waking knowledge as deriving from the fact that in dreams events get forgotten, or the logical relations between ideas get lost (p. 98), etc. etc.

Those authors who pass such a generally unfavourable judgement on the performance of the psyche in dreams still concede that a certain amount of psychical activity remains in the dream. Wundt [76], who has become an authority in the theory of dream-problems for so many others who have dealt with them, expressly admits as much. We could ask what the nature of this remnant of normal psychical life in dreams might be. It is fairly generally agreed that the faculty of reproduction, the memory, seems to have suffered least, indeed, it is even able to show a certain superiority over the same function in waking life (see p. 12 above), even though part of the absurdity of dreams is supposed to be explained by the very forgetfulness of the dream-life. According to Spitta [64], it is the *emotional life* of the psyche which is not affected by sleep and which directs the dream. He defines 'emotion' as 'the unfluctuating concentration of feelings that make up the innermost subjective nature of man' (p. 84).

Scholz [59] sees the 'allegorizing reinterpretation' which the dream-material undergoes as one of the activities of the psyche expressing itself in dreams. Siebeck [62] also detects in the dream 'that activity of supplementary interpretation' (p. 11) of the psyche which it practises on everything it perceives and experiences. A special difficulty in assessing dreams is presented by the role of our supposedly highest psychical function, consciousness. Since consciousness is our only means of knowing, there can be no doubt that consciousness is maintained; however, Spitta takes the view that only consciousness is maintained in dreams, but not *self*-consciousness. Delboeuf [16] confesses he is unable to grasp this distinction.

The laws of association according to which ideas combine also apply to dream-images; indeed, their rule is expressed more clearly and strongly there. Strümpell [66] (p. 70): 'The dream runs its course, it seems, either governed exclusively by the laws of bare ideas, or by those of organic stimuli together with such ideas, that is to say, neither reflection nor reason, aesthetic taste nor moral judgement is able to affect the process.' The authorities whose views I am reproducing here imagine dreams to be formed rather as follows: the sum of sensory stimuli arising from the various sources already discussed operates during sleep first of all to arouse a number of ideas in the psyche which present themselves as hallucinations (according to Wundt as genuine hallucinations, because they derive from internal and external stimuli). These combine with one another according to the known laws of association, and, in accordance with the same rules, call up a fresh set of ideas (images). The entire material is then processed by the active remnant of the organizing and thinking powers of the psyche as best it can (see for instance Wundt [76] and Weygandt [73]). All they have not yet succeeded in discovering are what motives decide whether the images that do not come from outside are aroused according to one law of association or another.

However, it has often been observed that the associations linking the dream-ideas with one another are of a quite distinctive sort, and quite different from those active in waking thoughts. As Volkelt [72] says (p. 15): 'In dreams, ideas chase and catch one another on the basis of chance similarities and barely perceptible connections. Every dream is permeated by such casual, haphazard associations.' Maury [48] sets great store by this way of connecting ideas, for it allows him to draw a close analogy between the dream-life and certain forms of mental disturbance. He recognizes two main features in 'délire': '(1) une action spontanée et comme automatique de l'esprit; (2) une association vicieuse et irrégulière des idées' (p. 126).* Maury himself supplies two excellent examples of dreams in which mere similarity in the sound of words is sufficient to link the dream-ideas together. He once dreamed he undertook a pilgrimage (*pélerinage*) to Jerusalem or Mecca. Then, after many adventures he found himself with the chemist *Pelletier*, who, following a conversation, gave him a shovel (*pelle*) made of zinc, which at a later stage in the dream became his great sword of battle (p. 127). In another dream, he went out on to a country road and read the *kilo*metres on the milestones, after which he found himself in the shop of a grocer who had a huge pair of scales, and a man placed *kilo*-weights on the scales in order to weigh Maury; then the grocer said to him: 'You aren't in Paris, you are on the island of *Gilolo*.' There followed several episodes in which he saw the *lobelia* flower, then General *Lopez*, whose death he had read of shortly before; finally he woke, playing a game of *lotto*.

But we are not surprised to find that this low opinion of the psychical powers of the dream has not gone uncontradicted by others—though contradiction on this point seems difficult. It also does not mean very much when one of the detractors of the dream-life (Spitta [64], p. 118) assures us that the same psychological laws that govern us when we are awake also rule over the dream, or when another (Dugas [19]) says: 'Le rêve n'est pas déraison ni même irraison pur',* if neither of them takes the trouble to reconcile this judgement with the anarchy and dissolution of all functions they have described in the dreaming psyche. But the possibility does seem to have dawned on others that the madness of the dream may not be without method, may perhaps be only pretence, like that of the Prince of Denmark, referred to in this perceptive judgement. Either these authors must have refrained from judging by appearances, or the appearance presented by the dream looked different to their eyes.

Accordingly, without wishing to dwell on its apparent absurdity, Havelock Ellis [23] recognizes the dream as being 'an anarchic world of vast emotions and imperfect thoughts', whose study might teach us something of the primitive stages in the development of the psychical life. A thinker like Delboeuf [16] maintains—though without producing the evidence to counter the material that contradicts him, and so really without good reason: 'Dans le sommeil, hormis la perception, toutes les facultés de l'esprit, intelligence, imagination, mémoire, volonté, moralité, restent intactes dans leur essence; seulement, elles s'appliquent à des objets imaginaires et mobiles. Le songeur est un acteur qui joue à volonté les fous et les sages, les bourreaux et les victimes, les nains et les géants, les démons et les anges' (p. 222).* The most energetic opponent of the detractors of the psyche's performance in dreams appears to have been the Marquis d'Hervey; Maury [41] argues vigorously against him, but despite every effort, I have been unable to get hold of his work. Maury says of him (p. 19): 'M. le Marquis d'Hervey prête à l'intelligence, durant le sommeil, toute sa liberté d'action et d'attention et il ne semble faire consister le sommeil que dans l'occlusion des sens, dans leur fermeture au monde extérieur; en sorte que l'homme qui dort ne se distingue guère, selon sa manière de voir, de l'homme qui laisse vaguer sa pensée en se bouchant les sens; toute la différence qui sépare alors la pensée ordinaire de celle du dormeur c'est que, chez celui-ci, l'idée prend une forme visible, objective, et ressemble, à s'y méprendre, à la sensation déterminée par les objets extérieurs; le souvenir revêt l'apparence du fait présent.'*

Maury adds, however: 'qu'il y a une différence de plus et capitale à savoir que les facultés intellectuelles de l'homme endormi n'offrent pas l'équilibre qu'elles gardent chez l'homme l'éveillé.'*

Estimations of the dream as the product of the psyche cover a wide gamut in the literature: they extend from the deepest disdain of the kind we have become familiar with, through the presentiment of a value not yet revealed, to an overestimation which places the dream far above the achievements of waking life. Hildebrandt [35], as we know, represents the psychological characteristics of the dream-life in three antinomies, and the third of his antitheses finally sums up this set of judgements (p. 19): 'They lie between *an intensification*, an *enhancement* which not rarely rises to the point of *virtuosity*, and on the other hand a decided *reduction* and *enfeeblement* of the life of the psyche, often to a level below the human.

'As to the first, which of us could not confirm from his own experience that in the working and weaving of the spirit of the dream there is sometimes a profundity and warmth of feeling, a clarity of vision, a subtlety of observation, a quickness of wit, which we would modestly disclaim as our own in waking life? The dream possesses a marvellous poetry, a capacity for allegory, an incomparable sense of humour, a delicious irony. It beholds the world in an idealizing light unique to it, and intensifies the effect of its manifestations often by the aptest understanding of their fundamental nature. It presents earthly beauty to us in truly heavenly splendour, the sublime in the height of majesty, our ordinary fears in the most frightful form, the ridiculous with ineffably graphic comedy. Sometimes we are so full of one of these random impressions when we wake that it seems to us that the real world has never offered us anything to compare with it.'

We may well ask ourselves whether the contemptuous remarks and the enthusiastic praise are really referring to the same thing. Has the one overlooked the idiotic dreams and the other the profound and subtle ones? And if both kinds occur—dreams deserving the one judgement and dreams deserving the other—does it not seem idle to look for a psychological description of the dream? Is it not enough to say that in dreams everything is possible, from the lowest degradation of our psychical life to an intensification of it rare when we are awake? Attractive though this solution would be, it has this one thing against it: the efforts of all those investigating the dream seem to be based on the assumption that a characterization of the dream does exist, universally valid in its essential features, which would reconcile these contradictions.

It is indisputable that the psychical achievements of the dream were given readier and more positive recognition in the intellectual period, now behind us, in which philosophy and not the exact sciences, dominated the mind. Views such as Schubert's,* that the dream is a liberation of the mind from the power of external nature, a release of the soul from the fetters of sensuality, and similar judgements by the younger Fichte[4]* and others, which all represent the dream as an ascent of the inner life to a higher level, seem hardly comprehensible to us today; nowadays they are repeated only by mystics and religious fanatics. The rise of the scientific mode of thinking is accompanied by a reaction in the appreciation of the dream. Medical writers in particular are most inclined to brand psychical activity in dreams as insignificant and valueless, while philosophers and observers outside the profession have mostly clung to the psychical value of dreams—amateur psychologists whose contribution is not to be neglected in this of all fields. Anyone inclined to disdain the performance of the psyche in dreams understandably favours somatic sources of stimuli as their aetiology; naturally, those who consider that the dreaming psyche has left most of its abilities behind in the waking world also have no motive for granting the inner life any stimulus of its own to dreaming.

Among the great achievements which we are tempted to ascribe to the dream-life even in sober comparisons, that of memory is the most striking; we have dealt in detail with the—quite frequent—experiences demonstrating it. Another distinction enjoyed by the dream-life often commended by older writers, its sovereign ability to transcend space and time, is easily recognized as an illusion. This distinction, as Hildebrandt [35] remarked, is just that: illusory. Dreaming transcends space and time in just the same way that waking thought does, simply because it is no more than a form of thought. Dreams are also supposed to enjoy a further distinction

---

[4] Cf. Haffner [32] and Spitta [64].

with regard to temporality, that of being independent of the passage of time in another sense. Dreams like the one related above by Maury [48] (pp. 24–5) of his execution by the guillotine seem to demonstrate that dreams are capable of compressing far more perceptions into a very short space of time than our psychical activity can cope with in our thoughts while we are awake. However, various arguments have disputed this inference: since the essays of Le Lorrain [45] and Egger [20] 'on the apparent duration of dreams', an interesting discussion has developed which has probably not yet reached a clarification of this profound and difficult question.

That the dream is capable of continuing the intellectual work of the day and bringing it to a conclusion which had not then been reached; that it can resolve doubts and problems and be the source of fresh inspiration for poets and composers—in the light of many different accounts, and after the collection made by Chabaneix [11], this seems to be incontestable. But though the fact may admit of no doubt, we must have many reservations touching matters of principle about the way it is understood.

Finally, the alleged divinatory powers of the dream form an object of contention where a scepticism very hard to overcome encounters assurances obstinately repeated. There is a reluctance—no doubt justified—to reject the notion outright, because in many cases we may be on the threshold of a natural psychological explanation.

(f) *Ethical Feelings in Dreams*

For reasons which will become apparent only after I have presented my own investigations into dreams, I have separated the specific problem of whether or how far the moral dispositions and feelings of waking life extend into our dream-life from the general topic of the psychology of dreams. Here too we are dismayed to see the same contradictions we have observed with surprise and exasperation in the accounts we have already noted of all the other achievements of the psyche. The certainty with which one writer asserts that the dream knows nothing of moral demands is matched by the assurance with which another affirms that mankind's moral nature also holds good in our dream-life.

Appeal to our dream-experience every night seems to put the first assertion beyond all doubt. Jessen [36] says (p. 553): 'We do not grow better or more virtuous in sleep; rather, the conscience seems to be silent in dreams, for we feel no pity, and we are able to commit the gravest crimes, stealing, murdering, and killing with perfect indifference, and without any subsequent remorse.'

Radestock [54] (p. 146): 'It has to be considered that in dreams associations run on and ideas are linked together without any part being played by reason or reflection, aesthetic taste or moral sense; the judgement is extremely weak and what predominates is *ethical indifference.*'

Volkelt [72] (p. 23): 'In dreams, as everyone knows, sexual behaviour is especially unrestrained. Just as the dreamer himself is shameless to the last degree and devoid of all moral feeling or judgement, so he also beholds everyone else, including even the most respected, caught up in the performance of acts he would shrink from associating them with in waking life, even in his thoughts.'

The sharpest contrast to these views is provided by assertions such as Schopenhauer's that in dreams everyone acts and speaks wholly in accordance with his character. R. P. Fischer[5] maintains that subjective feelings and efforts, or affects and passions, are revealed in the arbitrary acts of the dream-life and that people's individual moral peculiarities are reflected in their dreams.

Haffner [32] (p. 25): 'Apart from rare exceptions . . . a virtuous man will also be virtuous in dreams; he will resist temptation and be invulnerable to hatred, envy, wrath, and every vice; the man of sin, however, will as a rule also find in his dreams the images he has before him when awake.'

Scholz [59] (p. 36): 'In the dream there is truth, in spite of all the disguising; in dignity or degradation we recognize our own self . . . The honest man could not commit a crime that would dishonour him, even in a dream, or if he does he is horrified at it as something alien to his nature. So the Roman Emperor who had one of his subjects executed because the latter had dreamed he had had the emperor's head cut off was not altogether wrong when he justified this by saying that whoever dreamed of such a thing was bound to have similar thoughts in mind when awake. It is telling that we say of something that is totally foreign to our nature: "I wouldn't even dream of it."'

---

[5] *Grundzüge des Systems der Anthropologie* (Erlangen: 1850), cited after Spitta.

Pfaff[6] says outright, varying a familiar proverb: 'Tell me your dreams for a while and I will tell you what you are really like.'

Hildebrandt's [35] little book, which I have already quoted so many times—formally the most perfect contribution to the inquiry into the problems of dreams, and the most fertile in ideas I have found in the literature—places this very problem of morality in dreams at the centre of its interests. For Hildebrandt too it is a firm rule that the purer the life the purer the dream, the more impure the one, the more impure the other.

The moral nature of man persists even in dreams: 'But whereas no error in arithmetic however obvious, no reversal of science however romantic, no anachronism however comic ever offends us or even arouses our suspicions, we never lose our sense of the difference between good and evil, right and wrong, virtue and vice. However much of what accompanies us by day may fade during the hours of slumber, Kant's categorical imperative* has clung to our heels so firmly as our inseparable companion that we cannot get rid of him, even in sleep . . . However, this fact can only be explained by supposing that the fundamental basis of human nature, the moral being, is too firmly constructed to have any part in the effects of the kaleidoscopic shake-up which imagination, reason, memory, and other faculties of the same order undergo in dreams' (pp. 45 ff.).

In the wider discussion of the subject some remarkable inconsistencies and evasions can be observed in both groups of writers. Strictly speaking, for all those who believe that the moral personality of man disintegrates in dreams, any interest in immoral dreams would come to an end with this statement. They could reject the attempt to make the dreamer responsible for his dreams, and from the wickedness of his dreams conclude the existence of an evil tendency in his nature with as much composure as they would the apparently equivalent attempt to demonstrate from the absurdity of his dreams the worthlessness of his intellectual attainments when awake. The others, for whom the 'categorical imperative' extends even into dreams, would have to assume responsibility for immoral dreams without reservation: it is only to be hoped that if they themselves have dreams of a reprehensible kind this does not oblige them to lose faith in the soundness of their own morals.

---

[6] *Das Traumleben und seine Deutung* (1868), in Spitta, p. 192.

However, it seems that no one can really know how far he is good or wicked, and that no one can deny the memory of his own immoral dreams. For beyond these opposing judgements on the morality of dreams, the writers of both groups endeavour to explain the origin of immoral dreams, and a new opposition develops according to whether the origin is sought in the functioning of the psychical life or in impairments to it from some somatic cause. The compelling power of the facts then enables the advocates of both responsibility and irresponsibility in the dream-life to meet in acknowledging that the immorality of dreams has a distinctive psychical source.

All the same, all those who would have morality persist in dreams still guard against assuming full responsibility for their dreams. Haffner [32] says (p. 24): 'We are not responsible for dreams, because our thinking and willing have been deprived of the sole basis on which our life has truth and reality . . . That is why no willing or acting in dreams can be virtue or sin.' Yet man is responsible for sinful dreams insofar as he is their indirect cause. As in waking, so quite particularly before going to sleep he has the duty of morally purifying his soul.

Hildebrandt's analysis of this mixture of rejection and recognition of responsibility for the moral content of dreams goes much deeper. After explaining that the dream's dramatic mode of presentation, its compression of the most complicated thought-processes into the briefest periods of time, and what he too concedes is a devaluation and confusion of the ideational elements in the dream all have to be allowed for and discounted when it comes to the dream's appearance of immorality, he admits that all the same we should have the gravest reservations about denying altogether our responsibility for sins and crimes committed in dreams.

'When we want to deny an unjust accusation emphatically, especially one that touches on our fundamental views and beliefs, we will probably use the expression: I wouldn't think of it even in my dreams. However, when we say that, we are stating that we regard the domain of the dream as the furthest and remotest domain in which we would have to vouch for our own thoughts, for there our thoughts are connected with our real being so loosely that they can hardly be considered still our own; on the other hand, by feeling obliged to deny the presence of such thoughts even here, we indirectly concede that our justification would not be complete if it did not reach as far as this. And I believe that here, even if unconsciously, we are speaking the language of truth' (p. 49).

(p. 52) 'For there is not a deed can be imagined in our dreams whose primary motive has not in some way previously passed through our soul when awake, as wish, desire, or impulse.' We would have to say of this primary impulse that the dream did not invent it—the dream only imitated it and expanded it, only adapted in dramatic form a scrap of historical material it had discovered in us; it enacts the saying of the Apostle that whosoever hateth his brother is a murderer.* Aware of our moral probity, we can smile at the extended recollection of a sinful dream, but we do not find anything to laugh at in the original material from which the dream was formed. We feel ourselves responsible for the aberrations of the dreamer: not for their sum, but for a certain percentage. 'In short, if we understand Christ's saying: "Out of the heart proceed evil thoughts"* in this indisputable sense, then we shall hardly be able to resist the conviction that every sin committed in dreams brings with it at least an obscure minimum of guilt.'

Hildebrandt, then, discovers the source of the immorality of dreams in the germs and hints of evil impulses passing through our soul during the day as thoughts of temptation, and he does not hesitate to include these immoral elements in the moral evaluation of the personality. It is these same thoughts, and the same judgement of them, which have, as we know, led the pious and saintly of every age to lament that they are miserable sinners.

There can surely be no doubt that these *utterly contrasting* ideas occur universally, in most people and in other fields besides the ethical. Judging them has on occasion been treated less seriously. Spitta [64] quotes a relevant passage from A. Zeller's article 'Irre' ['Lunatics'] in Ersch and Gruber's *Encyklopädie der Wissenschaften* (p. 144): 'A mind is rarely so fortunately organized that it possesses full authority over itself at all times, and is not interrupted again and again in the clear and steady course of its thoughts by ideas which are not only uncharacteristic but altogether grotesque and nonsensical; indeed, the greatest thinkers have had cause to complain of this dreamlike, teasing, and embarrassing rabble of ideas, as it disturbs their profoundest meditations and most solemn and serious intellectual work.'

More light is cast on the psychological position of these contrasting ideas by a further remark of Hildebrandt's that the dream sometimes allows us to see into the depths and crevices of our nature which are mostly still barred to us when we are awake (p. 55). Kant* reveals the same insight in a passage in his *Anthropologie* when he says that the dream no doubt exists to disclose to us our hidden dispositions and reveal, not what we are, but what we could have become if we had had a different upbringing; Radestock [54] (p. 84) does the same when he says that often the dream reveals to us what we do not want to admit to ourselves, and that we are wrong to call it a liar and a deceiver. Our attention is drawn to the fact that the emergence of these impulses alien to our moral consciousness is only analogous to what the dream does with other ideational material lacking or playing only a minor role in waking life, processes already familiar to us from observations such as those made by Bernini [3]: 'Certe nostre inclinazioni che si credevano soffocate e spente da un pezzo, si ridestano; passioni vecchie e sepolte rivivono; cose e persone a cui non pensiamo mai, ci vengono dinanzi'* (p. 149), and by Volkelt [73]: 'Even ideas which have entered the waking consciousness almost unnoticed and which perhaps have never again been recalled to memory often have the habit of making their presence in the psyche known to the dream' (p. 105). Finally, this would be the place to remind ourselves that according to Schleiermacher [61] even the act of falling asleep is attended by the emergence of *involuntary* ideas (images).

We may, then, sum up all this ideational material whose occurrence in immoral as well as in absurd dreams arouses our surprise and displeasure as '*involuntary ideas*'. The only important difference is that in the moral domain the involuntary ideas can be recognized as the opposite of our normal feelings, while the others seem to us merely alien. So far no advance has been made in dealing with the problem which might enable us to resolve this distinction by deeper understanding.

What significance, then, has the emergence of involuntary ideas in dreams? What conclusions can be drawn for the psychology of the waking and dreaming soul from this nightly appearance of contrasting ethical impulses? Here we have to note a fresh difference of opinion and yet another regrouping among the writers on the subject. The line of thought taken by Hildebrandt and others sharing his views can surely continue only in the direction of recognizing that the immoral impulses have a certain power in waking life too, though this power is inhibited from going as far as action; also of supposing that something is suspended in the state of sleep which, likewise operating as an inhibition does, has prevented us from noticing the existence of this impulse. The dream would thus exhibit the real, if not the whole, nature of man, and is one of the means of making the hidden interior of the psyche accessible to us. It is only on the basis of such assumptions that Hildebrandt can assign to the dream the role of *warning voice* drawing our attention to hidden moral defects in our soul, just as according to physicians it can alert our consciousness to previously unnoticed physical illness. And Spitta [64] too must be adopting the same view when he points to the sources of arousal which enter the psyche at the period of puberty, for example, and when he reassures the dreamer that he has done everything in his power if he leads a strictly virtuous life when awake and tries to suppress sinful thoughts whenever they appear, preventing them from maturing into action. According to this view, we could call the *involuntary* ideas the ideas *suppressed* by day, and would have to regard their emergence as a genuine psychological phenomenon.

Other writers would deny us the right to this last conclusion. For Jessen [36] the involuntary ideas—in dreams as in waking, in the delirium of fever as well as in other kinds—have 'the quality of a volitional activity laid to rest and of *a more or less mechanical* procession of images and ideas caused by motions within' (p. 360). An immoral dream would demonstrate nothing further of the dreamer's inner life than that he had at some time acquired knowledge of its ideational content, but certainly not that it revealed an impulse of his own psyche. Another writer, Maury [48], leaves us in doubt as to whether he too does not ascribe to the dream-state the ability to dismantle psychic activity into its component parts rather than unsystematically to destroy it. He says of those dreams where we put ourselves outside the bounds of morality: 'Ce sont nos penchants qui parlent et qui nous font agir, sans que la conscience nous retienne, bien que parfois elle nous avertisse. J'ai mes défauts et mes penchants vicieux; à l'état de veille, je tâche de lutter contre eux, et il m'arrive assez souvent de n'y pas succomber. Mais dans mes songes j'y succombe toujours ou pour mieux dire j'agis par leur impulsion, sans crainte et sans remords . . . Évidemment les visions qui se déroulent devant ma pensée et qui constituent le rêve, me sont suggérées par les incitations que je ressens et que ma volonté absente ne cherche pas à refouler' (p. 113).*

If we believed in the capacity of the dream to disclose a real but suppressed or hidden moral disposition on the part of the dreamer we could not express this opinion more plainly than in these words of Maury's (p. 115): 'En rêve l'homme se révèle donc tout entier à soi-même dans sa nudité et sa misère natives. Dès qu'il suspend l'exercice de sa volonté, il devient le jouet de toutes les passions contre lesquelles, à l'état de veille, la conscience, le sentiment de l'honneur, la crainte nous défendent.' In another passage he observes acutely (p. 462): 'Dans le rêve, c'est surtout l'homme instinctif qui se révèle . . . L'homme revient pour ainsi dire à l'état de nature quand il rêve; mais moins les idées acquises ont pénétré dans son esprit, plus les *penchants en désaccord* avec elles conservent encore sur lui l'influence dans le rêve.'* Then as an example he cites the fact that his dreams often show him to be a victim of that very superstition which in his writings he has combated most vigorously.

But the value of all these insights of Maury's for our knowledge of the psychology of the dream-life is diminished when he insists on regarding the phenomena he has so correctly observed only as proofs of the 'automatisme psychologique' which in his view dominates the dream-life. This automatism he conceives as being the absolute antithesis to psychical activity.

A passage in Stricker's [77] studies of consciousness states that dreams do not consist solely and wholly of delusions. For example, if we are afraid of robbers in a dream, the robbers are certainly imaginary, but the fear is real. This draws our attention to the fact that the development of affects in dreams is not amenable to the judgement we make of the rest of the dream-content, and we are faced with the problem of what part or aspect of the psychical processes of the dream may be real, that is, what can lay claim to being included among the psychical processes of waking life.

(g) *Theories of Dreams and the Function of Dreams*

A proposition about the dream which attempts to explain as many of its observed features as possible from a single standpoint, at the same time determining the position of the dream in relation to a more comprehensive field of phenomena, may be called a theory of the dream. Particular theories of the dream are distinguished from one another according to which of its features they elevate into its essential characteristic and treat as the point of reference for the explanations and connections they set up. That dreams have a function, that is a use or other capacity, does not necessarily have to be inferred from the theory, but, as we are accustomed to thinking teleologically, we are still likely to be attracted to those theories which include an insight into a function for dreams.

We have already met several views of the dream which more or less deserved the name of dream-theories in this sense. The belief of the ancients that the dream was a gift of the gods for the purpose of directing the actions of men was a complete theory of the dream which provided information about everything worth knowing about it. Since then the dream has become an object of biological research, and a large number of dream-theories have appeared, though many of them are far from complete.

Without making any claim to comprehensiveness, we can perhaps attempt the following loose grouping of dream-theories according to their fundamental assumptions about the degree and kind of psychical activity present in the dream.

1. Theories such as Delboeuf's, which propose that the full psychical activity of waking life continues in dreams. According to these, the psyche does not sleep; its apparatus remains intact; but under the conditions of sleep, which differ from those of the waking state, in normal functioning it is bound to produce different results from those of the waking state. With these theories the question is whether they are in a position to derive all the differences between dreams and waking thought from the conditions of the sleeping state. Moreover, they have no means of explaining the function of the dream: we cannot understand to what end we dream, or why the complex mechanism of the psychical apparatus carries on working even when it is placed in a situation which it does not seem to be intended for. To sleep without dreaming, or, on the intervention of disturbing stimuli, to wake up, remain the only appropriate reactions, rather than the third, of dreaming.

2. Theories which on the contrary assume a lowering of psychical activity in the dream, a loosening of connections, an impoverishment

of usable material. These theories would entail an entirely different psychological description of sleep from Delboeuf's, for instance. Sleep would extend over the entire psyche; it would not merely shut off the psyche from the external world, but rather would penetrate into its mechanism and render this temporarily unusable. If I may draw a comparison with material from psychiatry, I would say that the former theories construe the dream as a form of paranoia, the latter make of it a model of mental deficiency, or amentia.

The theory that in the dream-life only a fragment of our psychical activity finds expression, as it has been largely paralysed by sleep, is by far the most favoured among medical authors and by the scientific world at large. As far as we may assume a more general interest in the explanation of dreams, this must certainly be called the *dominant* theory of the dream. It has to be emphasized how easily this theory above all is able to get over the worst hurdle in the way of any explanation of dreams—that is, coming to grief over one of the contradictions embodied by the dream. As it regards the dream as the product of a partially waking state ('a gradual, partial and at the same time very anomalous waking state', Herbart's *Psychologie* says of the dream), it is able to explain the entire gamut—from the dream's defective performance as displayed in absurdities up to fully concentrated thinking—by a series of states from ever-increasing wakefulness up to full waking alertness.

Those who cannot dispense with physiological terms of description, or who think them more scientific, will find this theory of dreams outlined by Binz [4] (p. 43): 'This condition [of numbness], however, draws an end only gradually in the early morning hours. The fatigue-producing agent accumulated in the brain-protein grows sparser and sparser and more of it is dissipated or carried away by the restlessly active bloodstream. Here and there particular clusters of awakened cells are already brightening, while all around everything is still in repose. The *isolated action of the individual clusters* now appears before our clouded consciousness, and they lack control by the other parts of the brain that direct association. That is why the images created, most of which correspond to material impressions of the recent past, come about in a wild and unruly manner. The number of liberated brain-cells continually increases, the irrationality of the dream continually diminishes.'

We shall certainly find this conception of dreaming as an

imperfect, partial waking among all modern physiologists and philosophers—or at least traces of its influence. Maury [48] presents it in its fullest form, and here it often seems as if the author imagined that being awake or being asleep could be shifted to different regions of the anatomy—though this entails his thinking that a particular anatomical province and a particular psychical function are apparently connected to each other. However, I would merely suggest here that if the theory of partial waking were confirmed, a great deal of discussion would have to be spent on differentiating it more finely.

This conception of the dream-life naturally fails to show what function the dream might have. Rather, its judgement on the status and significance of the dream is put quite consistently by Binz (p. 357): 'As we see, all the facts urge us to characterize the dream as a *physical* process, one which is in every instance useless and in many instances downright pathological . . .'

The expression 'physical' in connection with the dream, emphasized by the author himself, surely has a very wide range of reference. It refers first of all to the aetiology of dreams, which, of course, was particularly important for Binz when he was studying the experimental production of dreams by the administration of poisons. For this kind of dream-theory is related to the argument which would have the stimulus to dreaming proceed if possible solely from the somatic side. To put it in its most extreme form: after we have lapsed into sleep through the removal of stimuli there would be no need or occasion for dreaming until morning, when our gradual awakening through newly arriving stimuli could be reflected in the phenomenon of dreaming. But we cannot succeed in keeping sleep free from stimuli; just as Mephisto* complains of the germs of life constantly stirring, stimuli which the sleeper has paid no heed to when awake now approach him from all directions, from without, from within, from every region of the body. Thus sleep is disturbed, the psyche is shaken awake, tweaked at the corners now here now there, then functions with its wakened part for a little while, glad if it can go back to sleep again. The dream is the reaction to this disturbance of sleep caused by the stimuli, though it is of course a perfectly superfluous reaction.

However, there is a further significance to calling the dream, which after all is still an activity of the psyche, a physical process. The dream is denied the *dignity* of being a process of the psyche.

Perhaps the best illustration of what valuation the exact sciences mostly place on the activity of dreams is that metaphor, already applied long ago to the dream, of the 'ten fingers of someone wholly ignorant of music strumming on the keys'. Viewed in this way, the dream becomes something altogether uninterpretable: for how should the ten fingers of an unmusical player produce a piece of music?

From very early on there have been plenty of objections to the theory of partial waking. In 1830 Burdach [8] wrote: 'When we say that the dream is a partial waking, in the first place this explains neither waking nor sleeping, and in the second all it does say is that some forces of the psyche are active in the dream, while others are at rest. But such an imbalance occurs throughout our entire life . . .' (p. 483).

There is a further, very interesting conception of the dream dependent on the prevailing dream-theory which regards the dream as a 'physical' process. It was first put forward by Robert [55], and is especially attractive because it is able to propose a function, a beneficial outcome, for dreaming. As the basis for his theory, Robert takes two observed facts which we have already dwelt on in our assessment of the dream material (see p. 17): that we so often dream of the most trivial impressions of the day, and so rarely carry over its major interests into our dreams. Robert insists that things we have fully thought through never become the impulses of our dreams, but always and only those which lie in our mind unfinished or have only fleetingly touched our thoughts (p. 10). The reason why we usually find a dream inexplicable is that its causes are '*those sensory impressions of the previous day which the dreamer has not been sufficiently aware of*'. Thus the condition for an impression to become part of a dream is either that its processing was disturbed or that it was too insignificant to be worth processing.

So Robert represents the dream 'as a physical process of elimination and excretion which we become aware of in our mental reaction to it'. *Dreams are the excretion of undeveloped thoughts, thoughts nipped in the bud.* 'A man deprived of the ability to dream would in time go insane, because a mass of unfinished, incomplete thoughts and superficial impressions would accumulate in his brain, and what should have been incorporated in his memory as a finished whole would be stifled under their weight.' The dream serves the over-burdened brain as a safety-valve. *Dreams possess the power to heal and to relieve* (p. 32).

It would be a misunderstanding to ask Robert how generating ideas in a dream can bring relief to the psyche. The author clearly concludes from those two peculiarities of the dream-material that during sleep this evacuation of worthless impressions is carried out *somehow* as a somatic course of events, and that dreaming is not a distinct psychical process but only the information reaching us that this elimination is occurring. Moreover, excretion is not the only thing going on in the psyche at night. Robert himself adds that in addition the stimulations of the day are being processed, and that 'anything from the thought-material lying undigested in the mind which cannot be excreted is bound into a rounded whole with *threads of thought borrowed from the imagination* and so becomes part of the memory as a harmless imaginary picture' (p. 23).

However, in its evaluation of the sources of the dream, Robert's theory stands in the starkest opposition to the one now prevailing. Whereas in the latter dreaming would not occur at all if the psyche were not repeatedly awakened by external and internal sensory stimuli, in Robert's theory the impulse to dreaming lies within the psyche itself, in the overloading which it desires to have relieved, and he judges, quite consistently, that the causes of the dream lying in our physical condition have a subordinate place and could in no way give rise to dreaming in a mind which held no raw material from the waking consciousness to form its dreams upon. All he concedes is that the fantasy-images developing in the dream out of the depths of the psyche may be influenced by nervous stimuli (p. 48). So, according to Robert, the dream is not so very dependent on somatic factors after all; true, it is not a psychical process, has no place among the psychical processes of waking life: it is a nightly somatic process operating on the apparatus of psychical activity, and it has a function to fulfil, to protect this apparatus from overload or, to vary the metaphor, to clear out the stables for the psyche.

The same characteristics of the dream apparent in its selection of material provide support for the theory of another writer, Yves Delage [15], and it is instructive to observe how only a slight change in the way the same things are conceived produces a result with quite different implications.

On the death of someone dear to him, Delage observed from his own experience that one does *not* dream of what has filled one's thoughts during the day, or does so only when it begins to give way during the day to other interests. His researches with other people confirmed to him how universal this was. He makes a nice observation of this kind, should it turn out to be universally true, on the dreaming of young married couples: 'S'ils ont été fortement épris, presque jamais ils ont rêvé l'un de l'autre avant le mariage ou pendant la lune de miel; et s'ils ont rêvé d'amour c'est pour être infidèles avec quelque personne indifférente ou odieuse.'* But what *do* people dream of, then? Delage recognizes that the material occurring in our dreams consists of the fragments and remains of impressions from recent days and earlier times. Everything appearing in our dreams which we may at first be inclined to regard as created by our dream-life turns out on closer inspection to be unrecognized reproduction, 'souvenir inconscient'. But all this ideational material has one feature in common: it originates in impressions which have probably affected our senses more powerfully than our mind, or in impressions from which our attention was diverted very soon after they arose. The less conscious and at the same time the more powerful an impression, the greater its prospect of playing a role in our next dream.

These are essentially the same two categories of impression—the trivial and the unprocessed—which Robert [55] emphasizes, but Delage gives a different turn to the connection in his opinion that these impressions are capable of generating dreams not because they are trivial, but because they are unprocessed. The trivial impressions, too, have to a certain extent not been fully processed, they too are by their nature new impressions, 'autant de ressorts tendus',* which will be relaxed during sleep. A powerful impression whose processing has been accidentally halted or deliberately suppressed will be even more entitled to a role in the dream than one that is weak or almost unnoticed. The psychical energy accumulated through the day by inhibition and suppression becomes the mainspring of the dream at night. What appears in the dream is what has been psychically suppressed.

Unfortunately Delage breaks off his train of thought at this point: he can concede only the most minor role to the independent activity of the psyche in the dream, and so with his theory of the dream he promptly returns to the prevailing doctrine that the brain is only partly sleeping: 'En somme le rêve est le produit de la pensée errante, sans but et sans direction, se fixant successivement sur les souvenirs, qui ont gardé assez d'intensité pour se placer sur sa route et l'arrêter au passage, établissant entre eux un lien tantôt faible et indécis, tantôt plus fort et plus serré, selon que l'activité actuelle du cerveau est plus ou moins abolie par le sommeil.'*

One can create a third group of dream-theories out of those which ascribe to the dreaming psyche the capacity and inclination for exceptional psychical achievements that are either beyond its powers or that it can only carry out imperfectly when awake. On the whole the exercise of these capacities produces a beneficial function for the dream. The evaluations of the dream made by earlier writers on psychology mostly belong in this group. However, instead of quoting them, I shall content myself with referring to an observation of Burdach's [8], to whom dreaming 'is the natural activity of the soul, which the power of the individual does not restrict, self-consciousness does not disturb, self-determination does not direct, but is the vitality of our centres of sensibility revelling in free and uninhibited play' (p. 486).

Burdach and others clearly envisage this indulgence in the free use of its own powers as a state in which the psyche refreshes itself and gathers new energy for the day's work, rather like taking a holiday. That is why Burdach also quotes in acknowledgement the winning words in which the poet Novalis praises the free run of the dream: 'The dream is a defence against the ordinary regularity of life, a recreation for the fettered fantasy, a place where it can throw all the images of life into confusion and interrupt the earnestness of grown men with joyful children's play; without dreams we would certainly grow old sooner, and so we can regard the dream, if not as a direct gift from above, still as a delightful task, a friendly companion on our pilgrimage to the grave.'*

The refreshing and healing action of the dream is described even more forcefully by Purkinje [53] (p. 456): 'Productive dreams especially would convey these functions. They are effortless products of the imagination in free play, unconnected with the events of the day. The psyche does not wish to continue the tensions of waking life, but to resolve them, recover from them. First and foremost it produces states that are the very opposite of those in our waking state. It cures sadness with joy, care with hope and cheerful diverting images, hatred with love and kindness, fear with courage and confidence; doubt it soothes with conviction and firm faith, vain expectations with fulfilment. Many sore places in the heart, which the day would keep ever open, are healed by sleep, which covers them over and keeps them from fresh irritation. This is what the healing effect of time in part depends upon.' We all feel that sleep is a benefaction to our psychical life, and the obscure awareness of the popular mind is clearly unwilling to be robbed of its prejudice that the dream is one of the ways in which sleep confers its benefactions.

The most original and far-reaching attempt to explain the dream as an activity peculiar to the psyche which can develop freely only in sleep is the one undertaken in 1861 by Scherner [56]. Scherner's book, written in a heady, florid style, exhibits an almost intoxicated enthusiasm for its subject and, if it does not sweep us along with it, is bound to put us off. It resists analysis to such an extent that we turn readily to the clearer and briefer account of Scherner's theories as the philosopher Volkelt [72] presents them. 'A mysterious appearance of sense does flash and gleam out of the mystical conglomerations, out of all the surging splendour, only it fails to illuminate the philosopher's path.' Such is the judgement passed on Scherner's mode of presentation even by a follower.

Scherner is not one of those writers who permit the psyche to take its capacities with it into the dream-life undiminished. He even explains how the centrality, the spontaneous energy, of the ego becomes enervated in dreams, how as a result of this decentralization cognition, feeling, willing, and the generation of ideas are altered, and how the remnants of these psychical forces no longer possess the true character of mind but only the nature of a mechanism. But instead, the activity of the psyche which we may call the *imagination*, free of all control by reason and so, too, free of all restraint, soars to absolute domination in the dream. True, it does take its ultimate building-blocks from waking memory, but it uses them to construct buildings vastly different from the structures of waking life; in dreams it is not only reproductive, it is *productive* as well. These peculiarities are what lend the dream-life its particular character. It has a preference for what is *unrestrained, exaggerated, monstrous*. At the same time, however, its liberation from the inhibiting categories of thought gives it a greater suppleness, agility, flexibility of shifting shape; it is highly sensitive to the delicate stimuli that arouse moods of tender warmth or emotions that disturb; straight away it gives the inner life the vividness of outwardly perceived forms. The dream-imagination *lacks a conceptual language*: what it has to say it has to paint visibly, and since it is not weakened by the presence of concepts, it paints it with all the richness and power of the thing seen. But clear though this language is, its visual nature also makes it rambling, awkward, clumsy. Its clarity is especially impeded because it is reluctant to express an object by its own image and prefers a *different image* as long as this is capable of expressing the aspect of the object the imagination wants to present. This is the *symbolizing activity* of the imagination . . . It is also very important that the dream-imagination does not reproduce objects exhaustively but only in outline, and very freely at that. Its paintings thus seem like brilliant improvisations. However, the dream-imagination does not stop at merely representing an object; it is under an inner compulsion to involve the dreaming self with it more or less deeply and so produce a dramatic action. A dream roused by a visual impression, for example, paints pieces of gold in the street: the dreamer gathers them up, rejoices, and carries them off.

The material which the dream-imagination takes for its artistic powers to work upon is, according to Scherner, mainly that offered by the stimuli of the bodily organs so dimly perceived by day. So, though otherwise poles apart, in this respect—in their assumptions about what the sources and instigators of dreams may be—Scherner's all-too-fantastical theorizing and the perhaps overly sober theses put forward by Wundt and other physiologists are in entire agreement. Now according to the physiological theory, the psyche's reaction to the inner bodily stimuli is over and done once the ideas somehow appropriate to them are aroused; by way of association these ideas then call others to their aid, and at this stage the course of the psychical processes in dreams seems to be concluded. According to Scherner, on the other hand, the bodily stimuli only offer the psyche material it can make use of for its imaginative purposes. For Scherner the formation of dreams is only beginning at the stage where in the eyes of others it has come to an end.

Of course, we cannot regard what the dream-imagination does with the bodily stimuli as exactly purposeful. It plays a teasing game with them and imagines the organic sources from which the stimuli in a particular dream originate in some kind of palpable form. Indeed, Scherner believes—though Volkelt and others do not follow him here—that the dream-imagination has a certain favourite way of representing the whole organism, and that is as a *house*. Fortunately, though, it does not seem to confine itself to this subject-matter for its representations: contrariwise, it can use large numbers of houses to designate one particular organ, for instance, a very long street of houses for the stimulus from the intestines. At other times particular parts of the house represent in reality particular parts of the body; for example, in a headache dream the ceiling of a room (which the dreamer sees covered with disgusting, toad-like spiders) represents the head.

Quite apart from the house symbolism, all kinds of other objects are employed to represent the parts of the body sending out a stimulus to dreaming. 'Thus the respiring lung finds its symbol in the fiery oven with its breathlike roar, the heart in empty baskets and chests, the bladder in pouch-shaped objects or hollowed-out objects generally. The male sexual dream has the dreamer find the upper part of a clarinet in the street, beside it the same part of a tobacco pipe, and beside that again a fur coat. The clarinet and the pipe represent the approximate form of the male member, the fur coat the pubic hair. In the female sexual dream the crotch of the thighs can be symbolized by a narrow courtyard enclosed by houses, the vagina by a very narrow, slippery soft footpath leading across the middle of the yard which the dreamer has to cross, perhaps to deliver a letter to a gentleman' (Volkelt, p. 39). It is especially important that at the end of a physically stimulated dream of this kind the dream-imagination as it were throws off its mask and presents the arousing organ or its function unconcealed. Thus a 'toothache dream' usually concludes with the dreamer taking a tooth out of his mouth.

But the dream-imagination can do more than turn its attention only to the form of the arousing organ; it can just as well take the substance contained in it as the object of symbolization. Thus, for example, a dream stimulated by the intestines leads the dreamer through muddy streets, a dream stimulated by urine leads him beside foaming water. Or the stimulus itself, the nature of its excitation, the object it desires, are represented symbolically; or the dream-self enters into a concrete connection with the symbolizations of its own condition; for example, when aroused by pain we struggle in desperation with snapping dogs or raging bulls, or when in a sexual dream a woman sees herself pursued by a naked man. Quite apart from the abundance of its possible forms of representation, the central force in every dream is still a symbolizing activity of the imagination. Volkelt [72] then attempted to penetrate more closely into the nature of this imagination and assign a place in a system of philosophical thought to the psychical activity. His book is written beautifully and with ardour, but it is too difficult to understand for anyone whose early training has not prepared him for an intuitive grasp of the conceptual schemes of philosophy.

There is no useful function attached to the activation of Scherner's symbolizing imaginaton in dreams. As it dreams, the psyche plays with the stimuli it is offered. We might even surmise that it plays with them mischievously. But we could also be asked whether our own detailed consideration of Scherner's theory of dreams could possibly lead to anything useful, for its arbitrariness and disconnection from all the rules of scientific research seem only too obvious. If so, it would be proper to register a veto against the arrogance of rejecting Scherner's theories before scrutinizing them. This theory is built on the impression made on someone by his dreams; he has paid great attention to them and he seems to have a strong personal aptitude for pursuing the dark aspects of the psyche. Moreover, this theory deals with a subject which for thousands of years mankind has certainly found mysterious, but rich in content and associations, and which rigorous science has on its own admission done little to elucidate beyond attempting, wholly counter to popular feeling, to deny it any meaning or importance. Finally, let us frankly admit that it does seem that our attempts to explain the dream cannot easily avoid the fantastic. Even the ganglion-cells are subject to it: the passage quoted on p. 64 from so sober and exact a scientist as Binz [4], which describes how the aurora of awakening passes across the sleeping cell-clusters of the cerebral cortex, is no whit less fantastic—and improbable—than Scherner's attempts at interpretation. I hope to be able to show that behind the latter something real does exist, though it has been recognized only vaguely and is not characterized by the universality which a theory of dreams may claim. For the present, Scherner's theory of dreams, by its contrast to the medical theory, for instance, shows us clearly the extremes between which explanations of the dream still fluctuate today.

(h) *The Relations Between Dreams and Mental Illnesses*

In speaking of the relation of dreams to mental disturbances we can mean three different things: (1) aetiological and clinical relationships, as when a dream takes the place of a psychotic condition, inaugurates it, or is left over after it; (2) changes the dream-life undergoes in the case of mental illness; and (3) inner relationships between dreams and psychoses, analogies indicating essential similarities. These various relationships between the two sets of phenomena were a favourite theme of medical writers in earlier ages of medicine—and have been again more recently, as we learn from the literature on the subject collected by Spitta [64], Radestock [54], Maury [48], and Tissié [68]. Not long ago Sante de Sanctis [56, 57] turned his attention to them. It will be sufficient for the interests of our own account if we merely touch on the subject.

As to the clinical and aetiological relations between dreams and psychoses, I propose to refer to the following observations as model examples. Hohnbaum (cited in Krauss [39]) reports that the first outbreak of madness was often ascribed to origins in a terrible anxiety-dream, and that the predominant idea was connected with this dream. Sante de Sanctis presents similar observations of paranoiacs, and says that in individual cases the dream was the 'vraie cause déterminante de la folie'.* Psychosis can spring to life at a stroke with the operative dream containing the explanation, or it can develop slowly through further dreams which still have to struggle with doubts. In one case of de Sanctis's, the disturbing dream was followed by mild attacks of hysteria, and then further by a melancholy-anxious condition. Féré (cited by Tissié) reports a dream which resulted in a hysterical paralysis. In these instances the dream is presented to us in terms of the aetiology of mental disturbance, although we can account for the facts of the case just as well if we say that the mental disturbance first manifested itself in the dream-life, or broke out first of all in the dream. In other examples the dream-life contains the pathological symptoms, or the psychosis remains restricted to the dream-life. Thus Thomayer [70] draws attention to *anxiety-dreams* which must be regarded as equivalent to epileptic attacks. According to Radestock, Allison has described cases of 'nocturnal insanity' in which individuals are apparently quite healthy throughout the day, while hallucinations, fits of rage, and the like regularly appear at night. Similar observations can be found in de Sanctis (a dream equivalent to paranoia in the case of an alcoholic—voices accusing his wife of infidelity), and in Tissié. Tissié presents a wealth of recent observations in which actions of a pathological nature (based on delusory assumptions, obsessive compulsions) derive from dreams. Guislain describes a case in which sleep was intermittently replaced by insanity.

There can be no doubt that one day physicians will also concern themselves with a psychopathology of dreams as well as their psychology.

In cases of recuperation after mental illness it often becomes particularly clear that, although the patient may be functioning soundly by day, his dream-life can still be in the grip of the psychosis. According to Krauss [39], Gregory is said to be the first to have drawn attention to this phenomenon. Macario (cited by Tissié) tells of how a manic patient, a week after his full recovery, experienced over again in his dreams the flight of ideas and the passionate impulses belonging to his illness.

Up to now only very few studies have been made into what changes the dream-life undergoes in permanent psychotics. On the other hand, the deep affinity between dreams and mental disturbance, revealed in the general correspondence between the phenomena of both, was noticed from the first. According to Maury [47], Cabanis was the first to draw attention to it in his *Rapports du physique et du moral*; after him came Lélut, J. Moreau, and especially the philosopher Maine de Biran. Comparison between the two certainly dates from before this, however. Radestock [54] introduces the chapter in which he deals with it with a collection of quotations drawing an analogy between dreams and madness. Kant says in one place: 'The lunatic is one who dreams while awake.' Krauss: 'Madness is a dream with waking senses.' Schopenhauer calls the dream a brief madness and madness a long dream. Hagen describes delirium as dream-life brought about not by sleep but by illness. Wundt says, in his *Physiologische Psychologie*: 'Indeed, in our dreams we are able to experience ourselves almost all the phenomena we encounter in lunatic asylums.'

The individual correspondences which provide the basis for accepting this kind of equivalence are listed by Spitta [64] (very much as Maury did) in the following series: (1) Abolition or at least retardation of self-consciousness, consequently ignorance of the condition as such, hence impossibility of surprise at it, lack of moral consciousness. (2) Modified perception by the sense-organs, in dreams reduced, in madness generally very much intensified. (3) Connection of ideas with one another merely in accordance with the laws of association and reproduction, thus the automatic construction of sequences, hence disproportionate relationships between the ideas (exaggerations, fantasies) and everything resulting from them. (4) Changes or reversal of the personality, and occasionally character-changes (perversions).

Radestock adds a few other features, analogies in the material: 'most hallucinations and illusions are to be found in the domain of the senses of sight and hearing and in the general vital feeling. As in dreams, the fewest elements are provided by the senses of smell and taste. The deliriums of fever and the recollections of dreams both rise out of the remote past: what the waking and the healthy seem to have forgotten, the sleeping and the sick remember.' The analogy between dream and psychosis achieves its full force, however, only when it extends like a family resemblance to the subtler gestures and to the distinctive individual features of facial expression.

'To the man who is tormented by physical or mental suffering the dream grants what reality has denied: well-being and happiness; so too there arise for the mentally ill bright images of happiness, greatness, grandeur, and wealth. The supposed possession of goods and the imaginary fulfilment of desires whose refusal or loss was in fact a cause of the madness usually make up the main content of the delirium. A woman who has lost a dear child experiences the joys of motherhood in her delirium, someone who has suffered a loss of property considers himself extraordinarily rich, the deserted girl sees herself tenderly loved.'

(This passage from Radestock is an abridgement of a sensitive account by Griesinger [31] (p. 111), which reveals, with all possible clarity, that *wish-fulfilment* is one of the forms of imagining common to the dream and the psychoses. My own investigations have taught me that this is where the key to a psychological theory of the dream and of the psychoses is to be found.)

'Bizarre combinations of ideas and weakness of judgement are what chiefly characterize dreams and madness.' The *overestimation* of one's own intellect, which to the sober judgement seems only to produce absurdities, occurs in both; the *rapid succession of images* in the dream corresponds to the *rapid flight of ideas* in the psychoses. Both lack any *measure of time*. The *splitting of the personality* in dreams, where for instance our own knowledge is divided between two people, with the alien figure correcting our own ego, is exactly equivalent to the division of the personality in hallucinatory paranoia: the dreamer, too, hears his own thoughts uttered by alien voices. Even persistent delusory ideas find their analogy in stereotypically recurring pathological dreams (le rêve obsédant).—After recovering from a delirium sufferers quite often say that the entire period of their sickness seems like a dream to them, and often a not unpleasant one; they tell us, indeed, that during their illness they have occasionally felt that they were only trapped in a dream, just as often happens in dreams occurring in sleep.

After all this, it is not surprising when Radestock sums up his own views and those of many others by saying that 'madness, an abnormal, pathological phenomenon, is to be regarded as an intensification of the normal, periodically recurring, state of dreaming' (p. 228).

Krauss [39] has sought to establish a relationship between dream and madness, more intimate perhaps than the analogy between the two overt phenomena will really admit, by grounding it in their aetiology (or rather in their sources of excitation). In his view the basic element common to both is, as we have heard, the organically caused sensation, the somatic sensation, the general vital feeling to which all the organs together contribute (see Peisse, in Maury [48], p. 52).

The undeniable correspondence between dreams and mental disturbance, which extends even to characteristic individual details, offers one of the strongest supports to the medical theory of the dream-life, according to which the dream presents itself as a useless and disturbing process and as the expression of a reduced psychical activity. We cannot, however, expect to arrive at a definitive explanation of dreams by reference to psychical disturbance so long as our insight into the course of these latter disorders is still, as we well know, in such an unsatisfactory state. On the other hand, it seems probable that a revised conception of the dream is bound to influence our view of the inner mechanism of mental disturbance; and so we may say that we are also working towards an explanation of the psychoses when we seek to cast light on the mystery of the dream.

THE METHOD OF INTERPRETING DREAMS

Analysis of a Specimen Dream

The title I have given my treatise makes it clear which tradition I would like to take up in the way dreams are understood. I propose to show that dreams are capable of yielding an interpretation; and any contribution this may make towards elucidating those problems of dreams we have just been discussing, will in my eyes turn out to be merely a by-product gained in the course of carrying out my own task. This assumption that dreams are interpretable brings me at once into opposition to the prevailing theory of dreams, indeed to every dream-theory except Scherner's, for 'to interpret a dream' means to determine its 'meaning', to substitute for it something that fits into the chain of our psychical acts as a full and equally valid member. However, as we have learned, the scientific theories of the dream have no room for a problem of dream-interpretation, for to them the dream is not a psychical act at all but a somatic process which makes its occurrence known by indications in the psychical apparatus. Popular opinion has at all times thought differently. It exercises its right to inconsistency, on the one hand admitting that dreams are incomprehensible and absurd, but on the other unable to bring itself to deny them all significance. A dim presentiment seems to lead it to assume that the dream does possess a meaning, though a hidden one, that it stands as a substitute for another mode of think-ing, and that it is only a matter of finding the right way to reveal this substitute for the hidden significance of the dream to be disclosed.

So it is that popular opinion has always endeavoured to 'interpret' dreams, and in doing so has tried two essentially different methods. The first procedure takes the dream-content as a whole and seeks to replace it with a different, intelligible, and in certain respects analo-gous content. This is *symbolic* dream-interpretation: it comes to grief from the start, of course, with those dreams which appear not only incomprehensible but also confused. An example of this procedure might be the interpretation Joseph provides for Pharaoh's dream in the Bible. Seven fat kine followed by seven lean kine which consume them—that is a symbolic substitute for the prophecy of seven years of famine in the land of Egypt which will consume all the surplus created by seven years of plenty. Most of the artificial dreams invented by the poets are intended for this kind of symbolic interpretation, for they render the author's thoughts in a disguise found to match those characteristics of our dreaming familiar to us from experience. The view that dreams are mainly concerned with the future, having a premonition of what form it will take—a remnant of the prophetic significance once accorded to dreams—then becomes the motive for transposing the meaning of the dream discovered by symbolic interpretation into the future tense by means of an 'it will'.

There are of course no instructions for discovering the route to such symbolic interpretation. Success remains a matter of inspiration, of sudden intuition, and that is how the interpretation of dreams by means of symbolism was able to raise itself to the practice of an art which seemed to be bound up with an especial gift.[1] The other popular method of dream-interpretation is very far from making any such claim. It might be called the 'decoding method', as it treats the dream as a kind of secret writing in which every sign is translated by means of a fixed key into another sign whose significance is known. I have had a dream of a letter, for example, but also of a funeral or the like; I now consult a 'dream-book' and discover that 'letter' is to be translated as 'ill humour', 'funeral' as 'betrothal'. It is then up to me to make some connection between the catchwords I have deciphered, which I then accept as lying in the future. An interesting variant of this decoding procedure, which to some extent corrects its character as a purely mechanical transposition, appears in the treatise on dream-interpretation by Artemidorus* of Daldis [2]. Here not only the content of the dream but also the personality and the circumstances of the dreamer are taken into account so that the same element in the dream has a different meaning for the rich man, the married man, or the orator from the meaning it has for the poor man, the unmarried man, or, say, a merchant. The essential thing about this procedure is that the work of interpretation is not

---

[1] After I had completed my manuscript, I had access to a work by Stumpf [65], which is in agreement with my own in its aim to prove that dreams have a meaning and can be interpreted. But he interprets according to an allegorizing symbolism without any guarantee that the procedure is universally valid.

directed towards the dream as a whole, but at each piece of the dream-content by itself, as if the dream were a conglomerate in which each little fragment of rock required a separate definition. It is certainly the incoherent and confused dreams that provided the first impetus to the creation of the decoding method.

There is not a moment's doubt that neither of the popular methods of dream-interpretation is of any use in the scientific treatment of the subject. The symbolic method is limited in its application and incapable of being stated in general terms. As for the decoding method, everything would depend on whether the 'key', the dream-book, is reliable. And of that there is no guarantee whatever. We might be tempted to agree with the philosopher and the psychiatrist, and join them in dismissing the problem of the interpretation of dreams as a chimaera.

But I have come to learn better. I have had to realize that here is another of those not infrequent cases where an ancient, stubbornly held popular belief seems to have come closer to the truth of things than the judgement of contemporary science. I have to maintain that dreams really do possess a meaning, and that a scientific method of dream-interpretation is possible. I came to my knowledge of this method in the following way.

For many years I have been occupied with unravelling certain psychopathological structures, hysterical phobias, obsessional ideas, and the like, for therapeutic purposes—in fact ever since I learned from an important contribution by Josef Breuer that for these formations, experienced as symptoms of illness, the unravelling and the cure, solution, and resolution, amount to the same thing.[2] If one has been able to trace a pathological idea of this sort back to the elements in the patient's inner life which produced it, then it will disintegrate and the patient will be freed from it. Given the inadequacy of our other attempts at therapy, and considering the puzzling nature of these conditions, I was tempted, despite all the difficulties, to go further along the path pioneered by Breuer all the way to a complete solution. How this technique has ultimately developed, and what the results of this endeavour have been, are things I shall have to report on in detail another time. In the course of these psychoanalytical studies I came upon the interpretation of dreams. Patients who had

[2] Breuer and Freud, *Studien über Hysterie* [*Studies on Hysteria*], Vienna, 1895.

undertaken to inform me of all the thoughts and ideas that beset them on a certain subject told me their dreams, and in this way taught me that a dream can be interpolated into the psychical chain which, starting from a pathological idea, can be traced backwards in the memory. This suggested that the dream itself might be treated as a symptom, and that the method of interpretation developed for symptoms might be applied to dreams.

Now, for this the patient's psyche requires a certain preparation. I want him to do two things: to pay attention to his psychical perceptions more intently, and to switch off the critical faculty he normally uses to sift the thoughts arising in him. In order to give all his attention to self-observation, it is helpful for him to lie down and close his eyes; he must be expressly bidden to abstain from any critical judgement of the thoughts he forms and becomes aware of. He is told, that is, that the success of the psychoanalysis depends on his paying attention to everything that passes through his mind, reporting it, and on not allowing himself to be tempted, for instance, to suppress one idea occurring to him because it appears to him unimportant or irrelevant to the subject, another because it appears nonsensical. He has to be wholly impartial towards the ideas that come to him; for it was just this critical judgement that was to blame for any earlier failures to find the solution to the dream, the obsessional idea, or whatever.

In the course of my psychoanalytical work I have noticed that the psyche of a man engaged in reflection is in a very different frame of mind from that of someone who is observing his own psychical processes. In reflection, one psychical activity comes into play more than in even the most attentive self-observation, as the tense expression and creased brow of a man occupied in reflection shows, by contrast to the expression of repose in someone engaged in self-observation. In both cases a concentration of attention must be taking place. But the man who is reflecting is exercising a critical activity as well. Consequently, once he has become aware of the ideas arising within him, he rejects some and cuts others off short so that he does not pursue the paths of thought they might open up for him. Towards still other thoughts he acts in such a way that they never become conscious at all, that is, they are suppressed before they are perceived. On the other hand, the only trouble the self-observer has to take is to suppress this critical activity. If he is successful, a tremendous number of thoughts which he would otherwise have been unable to grasp enter his consciousness. It is with the aid of this new-found material for his self-awareness, that the interpretation of both pathological ideas and dream-formations can be carried out. As we see, it is a matter of producing in the psyche a condition sharing a certain similarity in distribution of psychical energy (mobile attention) with the condition present just before falling asleep (and certainly with the hypnotic state too). As we fall asleep, the 'involuntary ideas' emerge on account of the reduction of a certain willed (and certainly also critical) operation which we allow to affect the course of our ideas; the cause of this reduction we usually call 'tiredness'; the involuntary ideas emerging are transformed into visual and acoustic images. (Compare the remarks of Schleiermacher [61] and others, p. 60.) In the condition we employ for the analysis of dreams and pathological ideas we deliberately and voluntarily abstain from that critical activity and use the psychical energy saved (or part of it) for the attentive pursuit of the involuntary thoughts now emerging, which retain their character as ideas (this being the distinction between this condition and the one that attends falling asleep). *We thus turn the 'involuntary' ideas into 'voluntary' ones.*

In general it is not difficult to transport oneself or someone else into the required state of uncritical self-observation. Most of my patients manage it after their first instruction. I myself can achieve it very completely by the help of writing down the thoughts that occur to me. This reduces the critical activity by a certain amount of psychical energy, which can then be used to heighten the intensity of the self-observation. It varies considerably, however, according to the subject which is to be the focus of attention.

Now, the first step in employing this procedure teaches us that the object of attention has to be not the dream as a whole, but only the separate parts of its content. If I ask an unpractised patient: 'What does this dream make you think of?', as a rule there is nothing within his mental horizon he can call to mind. I have to present him with his dream bit by bit, and then for each bit he will provide me with a series of ideas occurring to him which can be called the 'ulterior motives' of this part of the dream. With this first important condition, then, the method of dream-interpretation I practise already departs from the popular method of interpretation by symbols, famous in history and legend, and it approaches the other method, the 'decoding method'. Like this, it is an interpretation *en detail*, not *en masse*; like this, it conceives the dream from the first as something put together, as a conglomorate of psychical formations.

In the course of my psychoanalyses of neurotics I have probably interpreted more than a thousand dreams at least, but I would rather not use this material here as an introduction to the technique and theory of dream-interpretation. Quite apart from the fact that I would expose myself to the objection that these are, after all, the dreams of neuropaths which do not allow any conclusions to be drawn about the dreams of those of sound mind, there is another reason why I am compelled to reject them. The subject-matter these dreams are aiming for, of course, is always the clinical history lying at the root of the neurosis. This would require an over-lengthy pre-amble for each dream, going deep into the nature and aetiological conditions of the psychoneuroses. These are things which are in themselves novel and highly disturbing, and so they would distract attention from the problem of dreams. My intention is rather to make the unravelling of the dream a preliminary to elucidating the more difficult problems of the psychology of neuroses. But if I dis-pense with the dreams of neurotics, my main material, I cannot be too nice in my dealings with the remainder. All that is left are the dreams which have occasionally been told me by persons of sound mind from among my acquaintance, or which I have found described as examples in the literature on the dream-life. Unfortunately I have no analysis for any of these dreams, and lacking this, I am unable to discover their meaning. For my procedure is not so easy to practise as the popular decoding method, which translates the given dream-content according to a fixed key; rather, I expect to find that with different people and in different contexts the identical dream-content might well conceal a quite different meaning. So I have to rely on my own dreams, resorting to them as an abundant and con-venient fund of material coming from a more-or-less normal person and relating to a variety of occasions in daily life. The reliability of such 'self-analyses' will certainly be called into question. There is a risk of arbitrary conclusions, it will be said. Rather, in my judge-ment, the conditions for self-observation are more favourable than the conditions for the observation of others. At any rate, we can try to see how far self-analysis will take us in the interpretation of dreams. There are other difficulties which I will have to overcome within myself. There is an understandable diffidence about exposing so many intimate things in one's psychic life, knowing too that others might well misinterpret them. But this is something one has to be able to go beyond. 'Tout psychologiste', says Delboeuf [16], 'est obligé de faire l'aveu même de ses faiblesses s'il croît par là jeter du jour sur quelque problème obscure.'* And I trust I may assume that in the reader, too, an initial interest in the indiscretions I shall have to commit will very soon give way to an absorption solely in the psychological problems they serve to illuminate.

I shall therefore take one of my own dreams and use it to explain my method of interpretation. Every dream of this sort requires a preliminary statement. But now I must ask the reader to make my interests his own for some little time, and immerse himself with me in the minutest details of my life, for our interest in the hidden significance of dreams absolutely demands a transference of this kind.

Preamble: In the summer of 1895 I had been giving psychoanalytic treatment to a young lady who was a very close friend of my family and myself. It will be understood that mixed relationships of this kind can become the source of various perturbations for the physician, especially for the psychotherapist. The physician's personal interest is greater, his authority less. A failure is a threat to his friendship with his patient's relatives. The course terminated in partial success: the patient lost her hysterical anxiety but not all her somatic symptoms. At the time I was not yet quite certain of the criteria which would indicate that a hysterical illness had been definitively cured, and I suggested to my patient a solution which seemed to be unacceptable to her. It was in this state of disagreement that, on account of the summer holidays, we broke off the treatment.—One day I was visited by a younger colleague, one of my closest friends, who had also visited my patient—Irma*—and her family where they were staying in the country. I asked him how he had found her, and received the answer: She is better, but not entirely recovered. I know I was annoyed by these words of my friend Otto,* or by the tone in which they were spoken. I thought I heard a criticism in them, perhaps that I had promised my patient too much, and—rightly or wrongly—I attributed Otto's apparent opposition to me to the influence of her relatives, who, so I assumed, had never really approved of my treating her. In any case, the unpleasant feeling I had was unclear to me, nor did I give expression to it. That same evening I wrote out Irma's clinical history, in order to give it to Dr M.,* a friend we had in common and the dominant personality in our circle at that time, as though to justify myself. During the night after this evening (or more probably in the early morning) I had the following dream, which I set down immediately after waking.

Dream of 23–24 July 1895

A large hall—many guests, whom we are receiving.—Among them Irma, whom I take aside at once, as it were to answer her letter and reproach her for not having yet accepted the 'solution'. I say to her: If you are still having pain it is really only your own fault.—She replies: If only you knew what pain my throat and stomach and abdomen are giving me. I feel I am choking.—I am startled and look at her. She looks pale and puffy; I think perhaps I have overlooked something organic after all. I take her to the window and examine her throat. At this she shows some reluctance, like women who wear dentures. I think to myself: but she has no need to. Her mouth then opens wide and I discover to the right a big white patch, and elsewhere I see large, greyish-white scabs set on remarkable curled structures clearly modelled on the nostrils.—I quickly call Dr M. over, who repeats the examination and confirms it . . . Dr M. looks quite different from usual; he is very pale, walks with a limp, and his chin has no beard . . . My friend Otto is now also standing beside her, and my friend Leopold* is percussing her through her bodice, saying: She has an attenuation low to the left, also pointing out an infiltrated part of the skin on the left shoulder (which like him I felt, in spite of her dress) . . . M. says: No doubt about it, it is an infection, but it doesn't matter; dysentery will set in and the poison will be eliminated . . . We also know directly where the infection originated. Not long before, when she felt unwell, my friend Otto gave her an injection of a propyl preparation, propylene . . . propionic acid . . . trimethylamine (I see its formula before me printed in bold type) . . . Such injections are not to be given so lightly . . . Probably the syringe was not clean, either.*

This dream has one advantage over many others. It is immediately clear which events of the previous day it is connected to and what subject it deals with. The preamble supplies the details. The news from Otto about Irma's condition and the clinical history I had written far into the night were still engaging the activity of my psyche, even in sleep. All the same, no one knowing the preamble and the content of the dream could have any idea of what the dream means. I myself do not know. I am surprised at the symptoms Irma complains of to me in the dream, for they are not the same as those I have been treating her for. I smile at the nonsensical idea of giving an injection of propionic acid, and at the consolation Dr M. offers. Towards its conclusion the dream seems to me more obscure and condensed than it is at the start. To discover the meaning of all this I have to resolve on a detailed analysis.

Analysis

The hall—many guests, whom we are receiving. That summer we were living at Bellevue, a house standing by itself on one of the hills adjoining the Kahlenberg. The house was once intended to be a dance-hall, hence the unusually lofty, hall-like rooms. I had the dream at Bellevue a few days before the celebration of my wife's birthday. During the day my wife had said that she expected that several friends, including Irma, would becoming to us as guests on her birthday. So my dream anticipates this occasion: it is my wife's birthday and many people, Irma among them, are being received by us in the large hall at Bellevue.

I reproach Irma for not having accepted the solution I had suggested; I say: If you are still having pain, it is really only your own fault. I could also have said this to her in waking life, or I did in fact say it to her. I was then of the opinion (which I later recognized to be incorrect) that my task did not go beyond informing my patients of the hidden meaning of their symptoms; whether or not they accepted this solution, on which the success of the treatment depended, was no longer my responsibility. I am grateful to this error, now happily overcome, for having lightened my existence at a time when, with all my unavoidable ignorance, I was supposed to be producing successful cures.—But I note from the sentence I speak to Irma in my dream that above all I am refusing to be blamed for all the pain she still has. If it is Irma's own fault it cannot be mine. Is the intention of the dream to be sought for in this direction?

Irma's complaining; pains in her throat, abdomen, and stomach, a feeling of choking. Stomach pains were among my patient's symptoms, although they were not very prominent: she complained rather of sickness and nausea. Pains in the throat and abdomen, choking sensations, scarcely featured. I wonder why I decided on this choice of symptoms in my dream, but for the moment cannot find an answer.

She looks pale and puffy. My patient was always rosy-cheeked. I suspect that here another person is being foisted on her.

I am startled to think I have overlooked an organic illness after all. This is, as one may well believe, a perpetual anxiety on the part of a specialist who sees almost no one but neurotics and is used to ascribing to hysteria so many phenomena other physicians treat as organic. On the other hand, a faint doubt steals over me—I do not know where it comes from—as to whether my alarm is entirely genuine. If Irma's pains are organic in origin, again I am not responsible for curing them, for after all, my course of treatment removes only hysterical pains. So it actually seems to me as if I wanted my diagnosis to be faulty: for then the reproach of failure would also be removed.

I take her to the window to examine her throat. She shows some reluctance, like women who wear false teeth. I think to myself: but she has no need to. I never had occasion to inspect Irma's mouth. The event in my dream reminds me of an examination some time previously of a governess who had at first given the impression of youthful beauty, but on opening her mouth took some measures to hide her denture. This instance recalls other medical examinations and the other little secrets they reveal—to the pleasure of neither party.—'But she has no need to' is in the first place, no doubt, a compliment to Irma: but I also suspect a another meaning as well. In carrying out an analysis attentively one gets a feeling whether the ulterior motives expected are exhausted or not. The way Irma is standing at the window suddenly reminds me of another experience. Irma has a close woman friend I regard very highly. When I visited her one evening I discovered her at the window in the situation reproduced in the dream, and her physician, the same Dr M., was explaining that she had a diphtheritic membrane. In fact, the person of Dr M. and the membrane recur in the continuation of the dream. It occurs to me now that in recent months I have had every reason to suppose that this other lady was also a hysteric. Indeed, Irma herself betrayed this to me. But what did I know about her condition? Only this very thing, that like my Irma in the dream she suffers from hysterical choking. So in the dream I have replaced my patient by her friend. Now I recall I have often played with the thought that, like Irma, this lady too might make a claim on me to free her from her symptoms. But I thought it was very unlikely myself, for she has a very reserved nature. She *shows reluctance*, as the dream indicates. Another explanation might be *that she has no need to*: in fact she has so far shown herself strong enough to control her condition without the help of others. Then there are a number of other traits which I could attach to neither Irma nor her friend: pale, puffy, false teeth. The false teeth led me to that governess; I feel inclined to settle for bad teeth. Then another person occurs to me to whom these traits could allude. She too is not my patient, and I would not like to have her as one, as I have observed that she is shy in my presence, and I do not think she would make a compliant invalid. She is usually pale, and on one occasion when she had had a good time she was puffy.[3] So I have been comparing my patient Irma with two other people who would be equally reluctant to submit to treatment. What can be the sense in my having exchanged her in my dream for her friend? Perhaps it is that I would like to exchange her: either the other woman rouses stronger feelings of sympathy in me or I have a higher opinion of her intelligence. For I regard Irma as foolish because she does not accept my solution. The other would be wiser and so would give way the sooner. *Her mouth then opens wide*: she would tell me more than Irma.[4]

What I see in the throat: a white patch and nostrils with scabs. The white patch reminds me of diphtheritis and thus of Irma's friend, but it also reminds me of the serious illness my eldest daughter suffered from nearly two years before and of all the fear we went through in that terrible time. The scabs on the nostrils bring to mind a problem I once had with my own health. At that time I frequently used cocaine to suppress bothersome swellings in my nose and a few days ago I had heard that a woman patient who did the same had contracted an extensive necrosis of the nasal mucous membrane. My recommendation of cocaine, which I made in 1885,* also brought

---

[3] Irma's unexplained complaints in the dream of abdominal pains can also be traced back to this third person. I am referring, of course, to my wife; the abdominal pains remind me of one of the occasions when I noticed her shyness. I have to confess that in my dream I do not treat Irma or my wife very kindly. But in excuse be it noted that I am measuring them both against the ideal of the good, compliant patient.

[4] I have the feeling that the interpretation of this part is not taken far enough to follow all its hidden meaning. If I were to pursue the comparison of the three women, I would digress too far. Every dream has at least one place where it is unfathomable, the navel, as it were, by which it is connected to the unknown.

severe criticism upon me. A dear friend, who was already dead in 1895, had hastened his death by misuse of this remedy.

I quickly call Dr M. over, who repeats the examination. This would simply correspond to the position M. held among us. But the 'quickly' is sufficiently striking to require a special explanation. It reminds me of an unhappy experience I had as a doctor. I had once produced a severe toxic state in a woman patient by the repeated prescription of a remedy which was then still considered harmless (sulphonal), and rushed to my experienced elder colleague for assistance. That this really is the case I have in mind is substantiated by another detail: the patient who succumbed to the poisoning had the same name as my eldest daughter. Until now I had never thought of the fact: now it seems to me almost like the retribution of fate. As though the substitution of persons were continued here in a different sense; this Mathilde for that Mathilde; an eye for an eye and a tooth for a tooth. It is as though I were seeking out every occasion which could be turned into grounds for accusing myself of a lack of medical conscientiousness.

Dr M. is pale, with a clean-shaven chin, and a limp. Of this so much is true, that his friends are often concerned at how unwell he looks. The other two characteristics must belong to another person. My elder brother occurs to me; he lives abroad, is clean-shaven, and, if I recall correctly, on the whole bore a resemblance to the M. of the dream. A few days previously news came of him that on account of an arthritic affliction in his hip he has a limp. There must be a reason for me to merge the two into one in my dream. I actually remember that I was out of humour with both of them, and for a similar reason. Both had rejected a certain suggestion I had recently made to them.

My friend Otto is now standing beside the patient and my friend Leopold is examining her and indicating an attenuation low to the left. My friend Leopold is also a physician, a relative of Otto's. As they both practise the same specialization fate has made of them rivals who are constantly being compared with one another. They both assisted me for years when I ran a surgery for children with nervous disorders. Scenes such as the one reproduced in the dream often took place there. While I was debating the diagnosis of a case with Otto, Leopold had made a fresh examination of the child and produced an unexpected contribution to our decision. There existed between them a difference of character similar to that between

Inspector Bräsig and his friend Karl.* The one was distinguished by his 'quick thinking', the other was slow, deliberate, but thorough. When I contrast Otto with the cautious Leopold in my dream, I am clearly doing so in order to praise Leopold. It is an act of comparison similar to the one between Irma the disobedient patient and her—in my view—wiser friend. I notice now another track on which the thought-connections of the dream are moving: from the sick child to the children's clinic. From the attenuation low to the left I get the impression that it corresponds to the details of a particular case where Leopold struck me by his thoroughness. In addition, I have vaguely in mind something like a metastatic affection, but it might also relate to the patient I would like to have in place of Irma. For, as far as I can judge, this lady imitates a tubercular condition.

An infiltrated part of the skin on the left shoulder. I know straight away that this is my own rheumatic shoulder, which I regularly feel if I have stayed awake deep into the night. The wording of the dream, too, sounds ambiguous: 'which like him I *feel* . . .' 'To feel in oneself' is a common expression. It occurs to me, incidentally, how curious the description 'an infiltrated part of the skin' sounds. 'Infiltration in the upper left back' is a more familiar phrase: it would refer to the lung, and so again to tuberculosis.

In spite of her dress. This is certainly no more than a parenthesis. When we examined children at the children's clinic they were naturally undressed; it is one of the contrasts to the way we have to examine adult female patients. It used to be said of an excellent clinician that he only ever conducted a physical examination of his patients through their clothes. The rest is in the dark to me, and, to speak frankly, I have no inclination to probe any deeper.

Dr M. says: It is an infection, but it doesn't matter. Dysentery will set in and the poison be eliminated. At first this seems ludicrous to me, but like everything else it still has to be carefully taken apart. Considered more closely, a kind of meaning does appear. What I discovered in the patient was a localized diphtheritis. From the time my daughter was ill I recall a discussion of diphtheritis and diphtheria: the latter is the general infection which starts with the localized diphtheritis. Leopold has indicated from the attenuation a general infection of this kind, which leads one to think of metastatic foci. I believe, it is true, that metastases of this kind do not occur in diphtheria. They remind me, rather, of pyaemia.

It doesn't matter is a consolation. I believe it fits in as follows. The last part of the dream has for its content the idea that the patient's pains derive from a serious organic infection. I sense that all I want with this too is to shift the blame from myself. The psychological treatment cannot be held responsible for the persistence of a diphtheritic condition. But I still feel troubled at having invented for Irma a serious illness wholly and solely to exonerate myself. It seems so cruel. So I need some assurance that all will be well, and it does not seem to me to be a bad choice to put this consolation into the mouth of Dr M. himself. But in this I am putting myself in a superior position to the dream, which itself requires explaining.

But why is this consolation so nonsensical?

Dysentery: some remote theoretical idea that diseased matter can be removed through the bowels. Am I trying to make fun of Dr M.'s wealth of far-fetched explanations and unusual pathological linkages? With regard to dysentery something else comes to mind. A few months before I had taken on a young man who had very remarkable difficulties with defecating, and whom other colleagues of mine had treated as a case of 'anaemia with under-nourishment'. I recognized that it was a case of hysteria, wanted to try my psychotherapy out on him, and sent him on a sea voyage. Now, a few days previously I received a desperate letter from him in Egypt telling me he had had a new attack there, which the doctor declared was dysentery. True, I suspect that the diagnosis is only an error on the part of an ignorant colleague who is letting himself be deceived by the hysteria, yet I could not spare myself the reproach of putting my patient into a situation in which to his hysterical bowel affection he may have added one that was organic. Furthermore, dysentery was reminiscent in sound to diphtheria,* a name under taboo which was not mentioned in the dream.

Yes, it must be that with the consoling prognosis 'Dysentery will set in, etc.' I am making fun of Dr M., for I remember that he once told me, laughing, something quite similar of another colleague years before. He had been called by this colleague to a consultation over a seriously sick patient, and felt induced to reproach his colleague, who had seemed very hopeful, with the fact that he had found albumen in the patient's urine. But the colleague refused to be disconcerted, and calmly replied: '*It doesn't matter*, my dear colleague, the albumen will be eliminated, you'll see!'—So I am no longer in any doubt that this part of the dream contains mockery at the expense of those of my colleagues ignorant of hysteria. As though to confirm this, the thought now passes through my mind: Does Dr M. know that the symptoms shown by his patient, Irma's friend, which are giving rise to fears of tuberculosis, also derive from hysteria? Has he recognized this hysteria, or has he been 'taken in' by it?

But what motive can I have for treating my friend so badly? It is very simple: Dr M. disagrees with my 'solution' for Irma every bit as much as Irma herself does. So in this way I have already taken revenge on two people in this dream: on Irma with the words: 'If you are still having pain it is really only your own fault', and on Dr M. with the wording of the nonsensical consolation I have put in his mouth.

We know immediately where the infection originated. This immediate knowledge in the dream is very curious. Just previously we did not know, as the infection was only pointed out by Leopold.

When she felt unwell, my friend Otto gave her an injection. Otto had actually told me that during the short time he had stayed with Irma's family he was called to a nearby hotel to give an injection to someone who suddenly felt unwell. The injections again remind me of my unhappy friend who poisoned himself with cocaine. I had advised him to take the drug only orally during withdrawal of morphia, but he started injecting it immediately.

Of a propyl preparation . . . propylene . . . proprionic acid. How on earth do I get on to these? On the evening when I had later worked on the clinical history, and then had the dream, my wife opened a bottle of liqueur on which the word 'Ananas' [pineapple][5] could be read. It was a gift from our friend Otto. For he has the habit of giving presents on every possible occasion. I hope one day he will have a wife who will cure him of this. This liqueur gave out such an odour of cheap alcohol, of fusel oil in fact, that I refused to taste it. My wife said: 'We'll give this bottle to the servants', but even more prudently I forbade it with the philanthropic remark that the servants ought not to be poisoned either. The odour of alcohol (Amyl . . .) clearly stirred in me the recollection of the entire series: propylene, methyl, etc. . . . which supplied the dream with the propyl preparation. True, I made a substitution. I dreamed 'propyl' after having smelled

[5] 'Ananas', by the way, contains a curious echo of my patient Irma's family name.

'amyl': but such substitutions are perhaps permissible in organic chemistry more than anywhere else.

Trimethylamine. In my dream I see the chemical formula for this substance, which at any rate witnesses to a considerable effort of memory; actually, I see it printed in bold type, as though I wanted something of quite special importance to stand out strongly from its context. But with my attention thus drawn to it, what is trimethylamine leading me to? To a conversation with another friend* who has followed the development of my work for years, as I have his. On that occasion he had told me about certain ideas of his concerning a chemistry of sexuality, and mentioned among other things that he believed he recognized trimethylamine to be one of the products of sexual metabolism. So this substance leads me to sexuality, that factor to which I attribute the greatest significance in the origin of the nervous afflictions I want to cure. My patient Irma is a young widow; if my concern is to find an excuse for the failure of the treatment I gave her, my best course will surely be to appeal to this state of affairs, which her friends would be very glad to alter. How strangely, by the way, a dream like this is put together! The other woman, who is my patient in the dream instead of Irma, is also a young widow.

I sense why the formula for trimethylamine has taken up so much of the dream. So many important things come together in this one word: trimethylamine is an allusion not only to the overwhelming factor of sexuality but also to a person whose approval, at a time when I felt myself alone and deserted, I remember with gratification. Was it likely that this friend, who played so great a role in my life, might not make any further appearance in this dream's chain of ideas? He does so, of course: he is an expert in the effects that proceed from the affections of the nose and the cavities adjacent to it, and has revealed to science some very remarkable connections between the nostrils and the female sexual organs. (The three curled structures in Irma's throat.) I had Irma examined by him to see whether her stomach pains might have a nasal origin. He himself, however, suffers from nasal abscesses which cause me concern, and the pyaema called to mind by the metastases in the dream probably alludes to these.

Such injections are not to be given so lightly. Here the charge of rashness is flung directly at my friend Otto. I believe I thought something of the kind on the afternoon when, by word and glance, he seemed to be opposing me. It was something like: how easily he can be influenced; how quickly he comes to a decision.—Also, the sentence quoted above again points to my dead friend, who had so rashly decided to inject himself with cocaine. As I said, I had in no way intended the drug to be injected. With my criticism of Otto for treating those chemical substances lightly, I note that again I am touching on the story of that unfortunate Mathilde which provoked the same accusation against me. It is clear that I am collecting examples of my conscientiousness here, but also of its opposite.

Probably the syringe was not clean, either. Another criticism of Otto, but one with its origin elsewhere. Yesterday I happened to meet the son of a lady of eighty-two to whom I have to administer two injections of morphia daily. She is at present staying in the country, and I learned that she is suffering from phlebitis. I thought at once that there must have been an infiltration caused by a contaminated syringe. It is my pride that over a period of two years I have not introduced a single infiltration; I take constant care, to be sure, to see that the syringe is clean. I am, simply, conscientious. From phlebitis I come back to my wife, who suffered from a blockage of the veins during a pregnancy. And now three similar situations surface in my memory—involving my wife, Irma, and the dead Mathilde—the identity of these situations has clearly given me the right to substitute these three people for one another in my dream.

I have now completed the interpretation of the dream. During this work I had trouble in keeping at bay all the many ideas which were bound to be set going by the comparison between the dream-content and the dream-thoughts concealed behind it. In the course of the work, the 'meaning' of the dream also became clear to me. I noticed an intention which was realized by the dream and which must have been the motive for dreaming. The dream fulfilled a number of wishes which had been aroused in me by the events of the previous evening (Otto's news, writing down the clinical history). For the outcome of the dream is that I am not to blame for the pain Irma continues to suffer, and that Otto is to blame for it. Otto annoyed me by his comments on Irma's incomplete recovery, and the dream takes revenge on him for me as it turns the criticism back onto him. The dream exonerates me of responsibility for Irma's condition in tracing it back to other factors (a whole series of reasons). The dream represents a certain state of affairs as being as I would wish it to be: *its content is thus a wish-fulfilment, its motive a wish.*

So much leaps to the eye. But many of the details of the dream, too, become comprehensible to me when seen in terms of wish-fulfilment. I take my revenge on Otto not only for his having rashly opposed me by ascribing to him an equally rash medical treatment (the injection), but also for having given me a bad liqueur which smelled of fusel oil. And I find an expression in my dream which unites both charges: the injection with a propyl preparation. Even then I am not satisfied, but carry on my revenge by contrasting him with his more reliable rival. In doing so I seem to be saying: I prefer him to you. But Otto is not the only one who has to feel the weight of my wrath. I also revenge myself on my disobedient patient by exchanging her for a wiser, more compliant one. Nor do I quietly accept Dr M.'s disagreement with me, but clearly insinuate to him that in my view he is incompetent to judge the matter in hand ('Dysentery will set in, etc.'). Indeed, it seems to me that I am appealing over his head to someone else of greater competence (the friend who told me of the trimethylamine), just as I turned away from Irma to her friend, and from Otto to Leopold. Get rid of these people, replace them with three others of my own choice, then I shall be free of the accusations which I don't believe I have deserved! How baseless these accusations are is demonstrated to me in the dream in the most detailed fashion. Irma's painful condition cannot be charged to me, for she herself is to blame for it in rejecting the solution I had offered. Irma's illness has nothing to do with me, for it is organic in nature and in no way curable by a course of psychical treatment. Irma's illness can be satisfactorily explained by her widowhood (trimethylamine!), which of course I can do nothing to alter. Irma's illness has been caused by an incautious injection on Otto's part with an inappropriate substance, a thing I would never have done. Irma's illness comes from an injection with a dirty syringe, like the phlebitis contracted by my elderly patient, whereas nothing of the kind occurs when I give injections. I note, to be sure, that these explanations of Irma's illness, which unite to relieve me of blame, are not consistent with one another, but on the contrary are mutually exclusive. The entire plea—for the dream is nothing but just that—vividly recalls the defence offered by the man accused by his neighbour of returning a kettle to him in a damaged condition: in the first place the kettle wasn't damaged at all, in the second it already had a hole in it when he borrowed it, and in the third he had never borrowed a kettle from his neighbour. But so much the better: if only one of these three defences is acknowledged to hold good, the man has to be acquitted.

Other subjects are woven into the dream whose relevance to exonerating me from responsibility for Irma's illness is not so transparent. My daughter's illness and that of my patient with the same name, the harmful effect of cocaine, the illness that affected my patient on his travels in Egypt, concern for the health of my wife, my brother, Dr M., my own bodily ailments, concern for my absent friend who suffered from nasal abscesses. Yet when I take a good look at it, all these things are linked together to form a single sphere of ideas, perhaps with the label: concern for health, my own and others', the physician's conscientiousness. I recall having a vaguely disagreeable feeling when Otto brought me the news of Irma's condition. From the sphere of ideas which played a part in my dream I think I can find words retrospectively to describe this momentary feeling. It is as if he had told me: 'You don't take your duties as a physician seriously enough, you aren't conscientious, you don't perform what you promise.' As a consequence, that sphere of ideas would have placed itself at my disposal so that I could demonstrate how very conscientious I am, how much I have at heart the health of my relations, friends, and patients. Remarkably enough, this ideational material also includes painful recollections calculated rather to support the accusation ascribed to my friend Otto than to vindicate me. The material does not take sides, as it were, but there is still an unmistakable connection between the broader raw material on which the dream was based and the narrower subject of the dream, out of which my wish to be innocent of blame for Irma's illness emerged.

I do not claim that I have uncovered all the meaning of this dream or that its interpretation is without any gaps.

I could linger much longer over this dream, extract from it further elucidations and discuss fresh puzzles which it has thrown up. I myself know the passages from which fresh connections among the thoughts can be pursued; but considerations of the sort that apply to all dreams of one's own deter me from this work of interpretation. Anyone who is prepared to censure me for this reserve is welcome to try being franker than I have been. For the moment I shall content myself with this one newly gained insight: if we follow the method of dream-interpretation indicated here, we discover that dreams really do have a meaning and are in no sense an expression of brain-activity in a state of fragmentation, as the authorities on the subject would have it. *After the work of interpretation has been completed the dream reveals itself as a wish-fulfilment.*

III

THE DREAM IS A WISH–FULFILMENT

After passing through a narrow defile and suddenly arriving at the top of a rise where the paths divide and the most fertile prospect opens out in all directions, one may pause for a moment and consider where to make for next. A similar situation confronts us now that we have got through this first dream-interpretation. We are standing in the clear light of a sudden insight. The dream cannot be compared to the random resonation of a musical instrument struck not by the hand of a player but by the impact of an external force; it is not meaningless, not absurd, it does not assume that one part of our store of ideas slumbers while another begins to wake. It is a fully valid psychical phenomenon, in fact a wish-fulfilment; it is to be included in the series of intelligible psychical acts of our waking life; it has been constructed by a highly elaborate intellectual activity. But just as we are about to rejoice in this knowledge, we are assailed by a host of questions. If, as the dream-interpretation would have it, the dream represents a fulfilled wish, what is the source of the striking and disconcerting form in which this wish-fulfilment is expressed? What change has taken place in the dream-thoughts for them to assume the shape of the manifest dream as we recall it on waking? In what way has this change come about? Where does the material come from that has been fashioned into the dream? What is the origin of the peculiarities we noticed in the dream-thoughts, for example, that they might quite acceptably contradict one another? (The comparison with the kettle, p. 95.) Can the dream teach us anything new about our inner psychical processes, can its content rectify opinions we have held during the day? I propose to leave all these questions aside for the present and to pursue one particular path. We have learned that the dream represents a wish as fulfilled. Our next concern must be to find out whether this is a general characteristic of dreams or only the chance content of the dream our analysis began with ('the dream of Irma's injection'): for even if we prepare ourselves to expect that every dream has a meaning and psychical value, we still have to leave the possibility open that this meaning may not be the same in every dream. Our first dream was a wish-fulfilment; another may perhaps turn out to be the fulfilment of a fear; a third may have a reflection for its content, a fourth simply reproduce a recollection. Are there any other wishful dreams, or are wishful dreams perhaps the only dreams there are?

It is easy to show that dreams frequently display the features of wish-fulfilment without disguise, so that one may wonder why their language has not been understood long ago. There is, for example, a dream I can produce for myself by way of experiment, as it were, whenever I wish to. If I eat anchovies, olives, or some other strongly salted dish in the evening, I develop a thirst at night which wakes me up. But the awakening is preceded by a dream which always has the same content, which is that I am drinking. I gulp down water in deep draughts, and it tastes as delicious as only a cool drink can be when one is parched, and then I wake up and have to drink in reality. The occasion for this simple dream is the thirst, which of course I become aware of when I wake up. It is this sensation that produces the wish to drink, and the dream shows me this wish as fulfilled. In doing so it serves a function which I can quickly guess. I am a good sleeper, not used to being awakened by some need. If I manage to quench my thirst by dreaming that I am drinking, I shall not need to wake up to satisfy it. So the dream is a dream of convenience: dreaming replaces action, as it also does in other areas of life. Unfortunately, the need for water to quench my thirst is not to be satisfied by a dream, as my thirst for revenge on my friend Otto and Dr M. was, but the will and wish to do so are the same. Not long ago the same dream appeared in modified form. I was thirsty even before I went to sleep, and drank up the glass of water standing on the table beside my bed. A few hours later I was again assailed by thirst and by the inconveniences that attend it. To get water for myself I would have to get up and fetch the glass that stood on my wife's bedside table. So I dreamed, appropriately, that my wife was offering me a drink out of a vessel; this vessel was an Etruscan urn which I had brought home from a trip to Italy and had since given away. But the water it contained tasted so salty (obviously from the ashes), that I had to wake up. One sees how conveniently the dream can arrange things: since its only objective is wish-fulfilment it can be completely egotistical. Love of comfort is really not compatible with consideration for others. The involvement of the urn is probably another wish-fulfilment: I am sorry I no longer own this vessel, just as the glass on my wife's side, for that matter, is also inaccessible to me. The cinerary urn is also appropriate to the increasing sensation of a salty taste which I knew would compel me to wake up.[1]

When I was young, I had dreams of convenience like this very frequently. Accustomed to working late into the night, I always found it difficult to wake betimes; then I used to dream that I was out of bed and standing at the washstand. After a while I was unable to ignore the fact that I had not got up yet, but in the meantime I had slept a while longer. A young colleague* who seems to share my fondness for sleep told me of a similar sloth-dream which took a particularly clever form. The landlady he lodged with close to the hospital had strict orders to wake him punctually every morning, but she always had a hard time doing so. One morning his sleep was especially sweet. The woman called into his room: 'Get up, Herr Pepi, you've got to get to the hospital.' Straight away the sleeper dreamed of a room in the hospital, a bed where he was lying, and a headboard on which was written: 'Pepi H . . . . medical student, age 22.' He said to himself in his dream: 'If I am already in hospital, I don't have to go there,' turned over, and carried on sleeping. In doing so he had openly admitted to himself what was motivating his dreaming.

Here is another dream where the stimulus again produces its effect during sleep itself: one of my female patients had been obliged to undergo an operation on her jaw which turned out to be unsuccessful. Her physicians required her to wear a cooling appliance on her ailing cheek day and night, but she was in the habit of flinging it off as soon as she fell asleep. One day I was asked to reprove her for this; she had flung the appliance to the floor again. The invalid made her excuses: 'This time I really can't help it; it was the result of a dream I had in the night. In my dream I was in a box at the opera, taking a lively interest in the performance. But Herr Karl Meyer was

---

[1] The existence of thirst dreams was also familiar to Weygandt [75], who wrote (p. 41): 'The sensation of thirst is perceived most precisely of all: it always produces the idea of quenching it. The dream represents quenching thirst in various ways, which take their special form from some close memory. Here too it is a general phenomenon that after imagining that his thirst is quenched, the dreamer is promptly disappointed by the very slight effect of the supposed refreshment.' But Weygandt fails to see the universal validity in the reaction of the dream to the stimulus. — If others are overcome by thirst at night and wake up without having dreamed beforehand, this is not an objection to my experiment, it only indicates that they are not such good sleepers.

lying in the sanatorium and complaining fearfully of pains in his jaw. I said to myself: since I don't have the pains, I don't need the appliance; that is why I threw it off.' This dream of the poor sufferer's sounds like the representation of a phrase one might find oneself uttering in an unpleasant situation: 'I could think of more agreeable ways to pass the time.' The dream shows this more agreeable way. Herr Karl Meyer, on whom the dreamer had foisted her pain, was the least attractive young man of her acquaintance she could think of.

It is no less easy to detect the wish-fulfilment in several other dreams I have collected from people in good health. A friend who is familiar with my dream-theory and told his wife about it says to me one day: 'My wife has asked me to tell you that yesterday she dreamed she had started her period. You will know what that means.' Indeed I do; if the young woman has dreamed she is having her period, then she is missing it. I can imagine she would have liked to enjoy her freedom a little longer before the difficulties of motherhood begin. It was a clever way of announcing her first pregnancy. Another friend writes that his wife dreamed recently that she saw spots of milk on the front of her blouse. This too is the announcement of a pregnancy, but not of a first one; the young mother is wishing she might have more nourishment for her second child than she had for her first.

A young woman whose child had an infectious illness and who was cut off from social life for several weeks while she was caring for it dreams after the child's recovery that she is attending a party at which Alphonse Daudet, Bourget, Marcel Prévost,* and others are present, and that they are all very charming to her and entertain her most delightfully. In her dream these authors have the same features as their portraits; Marcel Prévost, whose portrait she has never seen, looks like—the disinfection man who had come to fumigate the sick-room the previous day and had been the first visitor to enter it for a long time. I think I can translate the dream perfectly: now at last, she thinks, it is time for something more entertaining than this everlasting nursing.

This selection will perhaps be enough to demonstrate that dreams of the most various kinds are very frequently found which can only be understood as wish-fulfilments, and which display their content undisguised. Most of these are short and simple dreams—which makes a pleasant contrast to the confused and extravagant dream-compositions which have attracted the attention of the authors on the subject. But it would be worth our while to linger for a time with these simple dreams. We may well expect the simplest forms of dreaming of all to be children's dreams, for their psychical attainments are certainly less complex than those of adults. Child psychology is in my opinion destined to perform a service for the psychology of adults similar to what has been done for the study of the structure of the highest classes of animals by the investigation into the anatomy or development of the lower animals. Until now not many purposeful steps have been taken to make use of the psychology of children to this end.

The dreams of small children are simple wish-fulfilments and so of no interest at all compared with the dreams of adults. They present no puzzles to solve, though they are of course invaluable as proof that in its innermost nature the dream signifies a wish-fulfilment. I have been able to collect a number of such dreams from what my own children have told me.

It is to an excursion from Aussee to the beautiful village of Hallstatt* in the summer of 1896 that I owe two dreams, one from my daughter, who was then eight and a half years old, the other from a boy of five and a quarter. By way of preamble I must explain that this summer we were staying on a hill near Aussee from which we could enjoy a glorious view of the Dachstein* when the weather was fine. With a telescope it was easy to pick out the Simony mountain lodge. The children repeatedly tried to view it through the telescope, though with what success I do not know. Before the outing I had told the children that Hallstatt lay at the foot of the Dachstein. They were greatly looking forward to the day. From Hallstatt we walked along the vale of E[s]cher,* and its changing prospects delighted the children. Only one of them, the five-year-old boy, gradually grew fractious. Whenever a new mountain came into sight he asked: 'Is that the Dachstein?' to which I had to reply: 'No, only a foothill.' After the question had been repeated several times he fell completely silent; and he frankly refused to climb the path up to the waterfall. I thought he had become tired. But next morning he came up to me radiantly happy, and said: 'Last night I dreamed we were at the Simony lodge.'* Now I understood him: when I talked about the Dachstein he had expected that on the excursion to Hallstatt we were going to climb the mountain and get to see the lodge the children had talked about so much when they were looking through the telescope. Then, when he noticed he was being fobbed off with foothills and a water-fall, he felt cheated and became cross. The dream compensated him for this. I tried to find out the details of his dream, but they were meagre. 'You walk up steps for six hours,' as he had been told.

Wishes also stirred in the eight-and-a-half-year-old girl which had to be satisfied by a dream. We had taken the twelve-year-old son of our neighbours with us to Hallstatt, a perfect little gentleman whom, it seemed to me, the little lady already found very attractive. The next morning she related the following dream: 'Just think, I dreamed that Emil is one of us, calls you Papa and Mama, and sleeps with us in the big room the same as our boys. Then Mama comes into the room and throws a handful of big chocolate bars wrapped in blue and green paper under our beds.' Her brothers, who have not, it would seem, inherited any skill in interpreting dreams, declared, just like our authorities on the subject, 'This dream is nonsense'. The girl defended part of the dream at any rate, and it is useful for the theory of neuroses to learn which part: that Emil was one of us, that was nonsense, but not the bit about the chocolate bars. Now, I was in the dark about this very part. Their mother gave me the explanation. On the way home from the railway station the children had stopped at the vending-machine and had wanted chocolate bars of just this sort, wrapped in shiny metallic foil, which they knew the machine had for sale. Their mother had rightly decided that they had had enough wishes fulfilled for one day, and left this wish to their dreams. I had missed the little scene. The part of the dream my daughter had dismissed I understood without further ado. On the road I had myself heard our well-mannered guest asking the children to wait for Papa or Mama to catch up. The child's dream had turned this temporary kinship into permanent adoption. Other forms of companionship than those mentioned in her dream, which she had drawn from her relation to her brothers, were as yet unknown to her affections. Why the bars of chocolate were thrown under the beds could not be explained, of course, without questioning the child.

A dream very similar to my boy's was told me by a friend of mine. It concerned a girl of eight. Her father had taken several children on a walk to Dornbach* with the intention of visiting the Rohrer moun-tain lodge, but because it had grown too late he had turned back, promising the children to make up for it some other time. On the way back they passed a sign pointing the way to the Hameau. The children now wanted to be taken to the Hameau, but again for the same reason had to be put off with the promise of the trip for another day. The next morning the eight-year-old girl told her father contentedly: 'Papa, today I dreamed you were with us at the Rohrer lodge and on the Hameau.' So it was that her impatience had anticipated the fulfilment of her papa's promise in her dream.

Just as straightforward is another dream which the beauty of the Aussee scenery roused in my daughter, then aged three and a quarter. The little girl had crossed the lake for the first time and the voyage had been all too brief for her. When we reached the landing-stage she did not want to leave the boat and wept bitterly. The next morning she said: 'Last night I went on the lake.' Let us hope the length of time this dream-voyage lasted gave her greater satisfaction.

My eldest son, then eight years old, is already dreaming the realization of his fantasies. He has been riding in a chariot with Achilles, and Diomedes was the charioteer. The previous day, of course, he was fired with enthusiasm for the legends of Greece, which his elder sister had been given as a present.

If I am right that when children talk in their sleep this also belongs to the sphere of dreaming, in what follows I can relate one of the youngest dreams in my collection. My youngest daughter, nineteen months old at the time, vomited one morning and for that reason was given nothing to eat for the rest of the day. During the night that followed this day of fasting, we heard her cry excitedly in her sleep: '*Anna F.eud, Er(d)beer, Hochbeer, Eier(s)peis, Papp* [strawberry, wild strawberry, scrambled eggs, mash]'. At that time she used her name to express taking possession of something; the menu no doubt included everything that would have seemed to her a desirable meal; the strawberries' appearance in two variations was a demonstration against the domestic policing of her diet and originated in the fact—which she had very likely noticed—that the children's nurse had ascribed her indisposition to eating too many strawberries; so that is how she took her revenge in her dream for this annoying report.[2]

---

[2] Shortly afterwards her grandmother, whose age added to the little girl's would come close to seventy, had a dream which achieved the same feat as her youngest grandchild's. After the disturbance of a floating kidney had compelled her to go without food for a day, she dreamed—evidently carried back to her happy prime as a young woman—that she was 'invited out' to both the main meals of the day, and both times was offered the most delicious morsels.

If we consider childhood a happy time because it does not yet know sexual desire, we should not forget what a rich source of disappointment, renunciation, and so of dream-arousal the other great vital drives can be for it. Here is a second example. On my birthday my twenty-two-month-old nephew was given the task of congratulating me and presenting me with a little basket of cherries, which at that time of year are still counted among the earliest fruits. He seems to find it difficult to do, for he says repeatedly: 'There's cherries in it,' and cannot be persuaded to let go of the basket. But he is able to compensate for this. Every morning until then he was in the habit of telling his mother that he had dreamed of the 'white soldier', a guards officer in a cloak whom he once admired in the street. On the day after the birthday sacrifice he wakes with the joyful announcement, which can only have derived from a dream: '*Hermann ate all the cherries!*'

What animals dream of I do not know. There is a proverb, mentioned to me by one of my students, which claims to know, for it asks the question: *What does a goose dream of?* and answers: *Corn.* The entire theory that the dream is a wish-fulfilment is contained in these two sentences.

We observe now that we would have found the shortest route to our theory of the hidden meaning of dreams if we had only looked to linguistic usage. Proverbial wisdom often speaks scornfully enough of dreams, it is true—it seems to want to admit that science is right when it judges: *Träume sind Schäume* [dreams are froth]—but in linguistic usage the dream is nevertheless the sweet fulfiller of wishes. 'I wouldn't have imagined it in my wildest dreams,' we cry in delight when we find our expectations surpassed in reality.

IV

DREAM-DISTORTION

Now if I make the assertion that wish-fulfilment is the meaning of *each and every* dream, and hence that there can be no other dreams besides wishful dreams, I am sure in advance that I shall encounter the strongest opposition. It will be objected: 'That there are dreams which can be understood as wish-fulfilments is nothing new: authorities on the subject have long recognized the fact.' (See Radestock [54] (pp. 137–8), Volkelt [72] (pp. 110–11), Purkinje [53] (p. 456), Tissié [68] (p. 70), M. Simon [63] (p. 42 on Baron Trenck's hunger-dreams in prison), and the passage in Griesinger [31] (p. 111).) But that there are no other kinds of dream besides wish-fulfilling dreams is just another of those unjustified generalizations with which you have been pleased to draw attention to yourself of late.* There are in fact plenty of dreams which have the most painful and embarrassing content but no trace of wish-fulfilment. The pessimist philosopher Eduard von Hartmann is perhaps most firmly opposed to the theory of wish-fulfilment. In his *Philosophie des Unbewussten*, Part II (stereotype edition p. 344), he says:

'As for dreams, all the little miseries of our waking life also pass over with them into the state of sleep, but not the one thing that can at least partly reconcile the cultivated person to life: the enjoyment of science and art ...' But less discontented observers too have emphasized that in dreams pain and unpleasure occur more frequently than pleasure. Scholz [59] (p. 33), Volkelt [72] (p. 80), and others do so. Indeed, the ladies Sarah Weed and Florence Hallam have given a numerical term, based on a study of their own dreams, to the preponderance of unpleasure in dreams: they identify 58 per cent of dreams as being distressed and only 28.6 per cent as positively pleasant. Apart from these dreams, which extend the various disagreeable feelings of our life into sleep, there are also anxiety-dreams, when this most terrible of all unpleasurable feelings holds us in its grip until we wake. And it is anxiety-dreams like this that afflict children above all, whose dreams we have found to be wishful dreams undisguised (see Debacker [17] on the *pavor nocturnus*).

Anxiety-dreams really do seem to make it impossible to make a generalization of the principle we have drawn from the examples in the previous section, that the dream is a wish-fulfilment. Indeed they seem to brand it as an absurdity.

All the same, it is not very difficult to get round these apparently compelling objections. One should merely bear in mind that our theory does not rest on a consideration of the manifest content of the dream, but refers to the thought-content which the work of interpretation enables us to recognize behind the dream. Let us compare the *manifest dream-content* and the *latent content* with each other. It is true that there are dreams whose manifest content is of the most distressing kind. But has anyone tried to interpret these dreams, to reveal their latent thought-content? If not, these two objections no longer apply to us: it is still possible all the same that once interpreted, even distressing dreams and anxiety-dreams will be revealed as wish-fulfilments.

In scientific work, when there are difficulties in solving one problem it is often helpful to add another, in much the same way as it is easier to crack two nuts against one another than to crack each separately. In this way we not only confront the question: how can distressing dreams and anxiety-dreams be wish-fulfilments? but from our previous discussions of the dream we can also raise a second question: why is it that dreams with a neutral or trivial content which turn out to be wish-fulfilments do not reveal this meaning of theirs undisguised? Take the dream of Irma's injection which we treated in such detail: its nature is not in the least distressing, and through the interpretation it can be recognized as a flagrant wish-fulfilment. But why does it require an interpretation at all? Why does it not say straight out what it signifies? In fact, even the dream of Irma's injection does not at first give the impression of representing a wish of the dreamer as fulfilled. The reader will not have received this impression, but I too failed to grasp it before I undertook the analysis. If we call this tendency of the dream to require explanation the *fact of dream-distortion*, then the further question arises: Where does this dream-distortion come from?

First thoughts on the subject may suggest a variety of possible answers, for example, that during sleep there is an inability to create an appropriate expression for our dreaming thoughts. But the analysis of certain dreams compels us to admit a different explanation of dream-distortion. I would like to demonstrate this with a second dream of my own: again, it will require a number of indiscretions, but a thorough clarification of the problem will compensate for this personal sacrifice.

Preamble: In the spring of 1897 I learned that two professors of our university had proposed me for appointment as *professor extraordinarius*.* This news came as a surprise to me, and gave me great pleasure as an expression of recognition from two outstanding men which was not to be accounted for by any personal connections. However, I told myself at once that I should not expect anything to come of this occurrence. The ministry had in recent years ignored proposals of this kind, and several colleagues who were older than I and at least my equal in merit were still waiting in vain for their appointments. I had no reason to suppose I should fare any better. So I decided privately to reconcile myself to this. I am not, as far as I know, ambitious; I pursue my medical practice with gratifying success, even without the recommendation of a title. Besides, it was not a question of my calling the grapes sweet or sour, for undoubtedly they hung too high for me.

One evening a colleague paid me a visit, a friend who was one of those whose fate I had allowed to serve as a warning to me. For some time a candidate for promotion to professor—a title which in our society raises a physician to a demigod in the eyes of a patient—and less resigned than I was, he was in the habit of appearing at the offices of the ministry from time to time in order to advance his case. He came to me straight from one of these visits. He told me that this time he had driven the high official into a corner and asked him straight out whether the delay in his appointment was not really due to—considerations of religion.* The reply had been that, to be sure—given the present tendency—His Excellency was for the moment not in a position to, etc. 'Now at least I know where I stand,' my friend concluded. His tale told me nothing new, though it was bound to strengthen me in my attitude of resignation. For the same religious considerations also apply to my own case.

On the morning after this visit I had the following dream, which was also remarkable in respect of its form. It consisted of two thoughts and two images, in such a way that one thought and one image gave way to the other. However, I shall put down only the first half of the dream, as the other has nothing to do with my purpose in reporting it.

I. *My friend R. is my uncle.—I feel great affection for him.*

II. *I see his face before me, rather altered. It is as though elongated; a yellow beard framing it is emphasized with particular clarity.*

Then there follow the two other parts, again a thought and an image, which I shall ignore.

The interpretation of this dream proceeded as follows:

When the dream occurred to me in the course of the morning, I laughed aloud and said: 'The dream is nonsense.' I could not get rid of it, however; it pursued me all day, until in the evening I finally reproached myself with the words: 'If one of your patients had nothing to contribute to the interpretation of a dream but "It is nonsense", you would reprimand him and assume that the dream conceals an unpleasant history which he wants to spare himself the pain of acknowledging. Deal with yourself in the same way: your view that the dream is nonsense signifies only an inner resistance to interpreting it. Don't be deterred.' So I set about the interpretation.

'R. is my uncle.' What could that mean? For I have only one uncle, my Uncle Josef.[1] His story was a sad one.* More than thirty years earlier his desire for gain had misled him into an act severely punishable by the law, and he was punished accordingly. My father, whose hair turned grey with grief in a few days, always used to say that Uncle Josef had never been a bad man, he had been a numbskull: that was the expression he used. So if my friend R. is my Uncle Josef, what I want to say is: R. is a numbskull. Hardly credible and very unpleasant! But there it is, that face I see in my dream, with the elongated features and the yellow beard. My uncle really had a face like that, longish, framed by a fine, fair beard. My friend R. was extremely dark, but when the dark-haired start to go grey they have to pay for the splendour of their youth. Their dark beards pass, hair by hair, through a disagreeable succession of colours: first reddish-brown, then yellowish-brown, and only then definitely grey. My friend R.'s beard has now reached this stage, and so, by the way, has my

---

[1] It is remarkable how my—waking—recollection is reduced here for the purposes of the analysis. I have known five of my uncles, and one of them I have loved and honoured. But the moment I overcame my resistance to interpreting my dream, I said to myself: I have really only had one uncle, the one who is meant in the dream.

own, as I note with chagrin. The face I see in my dream is at the same time both my friend R.'s and my uncle's. It is like a composite photograph by Galton,* who had several faces photographed on the same plate in order to trace family likenesses. So there is no possible doubt: I really think my friend R. is a numbskull—like my Uncle Josef.

At first I have no idea what purpose I have in producing this identification, which I feel I have to resist constantly. But it does not go very deep, for my uncle was a criminal and my friend R. has not a stain on his character, if we except the penalty imposed on him for knocking down an apprentice with his bicycle: but could this misdeed be what I meant? That would reduce the comparison to the ludicrous. But then I call to mind another conversation I had a few days earlier with another colleague, N., about the same subject, in fact. I met N. in the street. He too was proposed for a professorship, knew of my own honour, and congratulated me on it. I rejected his congratulations firmly. 'You of all people should not make that kind of joke, for you have learned yourself what such proposals are worth.' He replied, probably not seriously: 'You never know. And there is a black mark against me. Don't you know that a woman once made a legal complaint against me? I don't need to tell you that the investigation was called off: it was a low attempt at blackmail, and I had my work cut out to save the blackmailer from being prosecuted herself. But perhaps the ministry is holding this affair against me so as not to approve my appointment. But you haven't a stain on your character.' There, indeed, I have the criminal, and at the same time the interpretation and tendency of my dream as well. My Uncle Josef represents to me both my colleagues who have not been appointed to professorships, the one because he is an idiot, the other because he is a criminal. I also know now why I need this representation. If 'religious' considerations are decisive in the delay experienced by my friends R. and N. in securing appointments, then my own appointment is also called into question; but if I can ascribe their rejection to other grounds which do not apply to me, my hopes will remain undisturbed. This is what my dream is doing: it makes a numbskull of one, R., and a criminal of the other, N. But I am neither the one nor the other; the common ground between us is cut away; I can look forward to my appointment as professor, and I have avoided the distress of having to apply to myself R.'s news of what the high official told him.

I have to continue further with the interpretation of my dream. I do not feel that I have dealt with it satisfactorily as yet. I am still perturbed by the ease with which I degrade two respected colleagues in order to keep my way open to a professorship. True, I am less dissatisfied with my behaviour now that I know how to assess the value of the statements made in the dream. I would dispute with anyone that I really regard R. a numbskull or that I do not believe N.'s account of the blackmailing affair. Nor, of course, do I believe that Irma was dangerously infected* by Otto with a propyl preparation: here as there, what my dream is expressing is only my *wish that that is how it might be.* The assertion in which my wish is realized sounds less absurd in the second dream than in the first: in the second it is formed by an adroit use of a basis in fact, rather like a well-made slander where 'there is something in it', for my friend R. had the vote of a specialist professor against him at the time, and my friend N. unsuspectingly handed me the material for blackening his character himself. Nevertheless, I repeat, the dream still seems to me to need further elucidation.

Now I recall that the dream contains a further element which the interpretation has not heeded so far. Once it occurred to me that R. was my uncle, I feel a warm affection for him in my dream. Where am I to place this feeling? For my Uncle Josef, I have naturally never had any affectionate feelings. My friend R. has for years been very dear to me, but if I were to go up to him with words expressing an affection close to the degree of fondness I felt in the dream, he would certainly be astonished. My fondness for him appears false and exaggerated to me, much like my judgement of his intellectual qualities as I expressed it when I merged his personality with my uncle's, though exaggerated in the opposite sense. But then a new fact dawns upon me. The affection in the dream does not belong to the latent content, to the thoughts behind the dream, it stands in opposition to this content; it is calculated to hide the true interpretation of the dream from me. Probably this is its very purpose. I recall how reluctantly I approached interpreting it, how long I wanted to put it off, declaring the dream to be sheer nonsense. From my psycho-analytic practice I know how such a dismissive judgement is to be interpreted: it has no value as knowledge but merely as the expression of an affect. When my little daughter does not want an apple she has been offered, she maintains that the apple tastes sour, without having even tried it. If my patients behave like the little girl, then I know they have been confronted with an idea they want to *repress*. The same applies to my dream: I do not want to interpret it because the interpretation will contain something I am baulking at. The interpretation once completed, I learned what it is I baulked at: it is the assertion that R. is a numbskull. I cannot trace the affection I felt for R. back to the latent thought of the dream, but I can trace it back to this resistance of mine. If my dream is distorted on this point when compared with its latent content, into its opposite in fact, then the affection manifest in the dream serves this distortion, or in other words, the distortion and deformation here turn out to be intentional, a means of *pretence*. The thoughts in my dream contain a defamation of R.: so that I might not notice this, the opposite, a feeling of tenderness towards him, makes its way into my dream.

This insight could be a generally valid one. As the examples given in Chapter III have shown, there are indeed dreams which are undisguised wish-fulfilments. Where the wish-fulfilment is unrecognizable, disguised, there must have been a tendency to defensiveness against this wish, and as a consequence of this defensiveness the wish was only able to express itself in distortion. I propose to seek a parallel in social life to this event in the inner life of the psyche. Where in social life do we find a similar distortion of a psychical act? Only in the case of two people where the one possesses a certain power and the other has to take this power into account. This second person then distorts his psychical acts or, as we can also put it, he *pretends*. The politeness I practise every day is to a large extent a pretence of this kind; when I interpret my dreams for the reader I am compelled to resort to such distortions. The poet too laments the need for such distortion:

Das Beste, was du wissen kannst, darfst du den Buben doch nicht sagen.*
['The best that you can know, you cannot tell to boys.']

The political writer who has unpleasant truths to tell to those in power finds himself in a similar position. If he utters them openly the ruler will suppress his words—retrospectively if it is a question of words spoken, preventatively if they are to be made known in print. The writer has the *censorship* to fear: and so he moderates and distorts the expression of his opinion. According to the degree of severity and sensitivity of this censorship, he will find himself forced either just to hold back on certain forms of attack or to speak allusively instead of in plain statement, or he will have to conceal his objectionable views behind a harmless-seeming disguise—he may, for example, tell of incidents involving two mandarins of the Middle Kingdom, whereas he has the bureaucrats of the Fatherland in mind. The stricter the censorship, the more far-reaching the disguise and often the cleverer the devices which nevertheless put the reader on the track of what is really meant.

The correspondence, traceable down to the last detail, between the phenomena of censorship and dream-distortion justifies us in assuming similar preconditions for both. Accordingly we would assume two psychical forces (currents, systems) to be the originators of dream-formation in the individual; one of these forms the wish uttered by the dream, while the other imposes a censorship on the dream-wish and by this censorship distorts its expression. Only the question arises: 'What is the nature of the authority empowering this second agency to impose its censorship?' If we bear in mind that prior to analysis the latent thoughts of the dream are not conscious, but that the manifest dream-content they generate is recalled as being conscious, then it is a short step to assuming that the prerogative of this second agency consists simply in permitting access to consciousness. We might say: nothing from the first system can become conscious which has not previously been passed by the second agency, and the second agency lets nothing pass without exercising its rights and making whatever changes it thinks fit to the applicant for consciousness. Saying this reveals a quite distinct conception of the 'nature' of consciousness: in our view, the entry of something into consciousness constitutes a specific psychical act, different from the process by which ideas are generated or imagined and independent of it; and we regard consciousness as a sensory organ perceiving a content given from elsewhere. It can be shown that psychopathology simply cannot do without this basic assumption. We may reserve a more detailed discussion of this for later.

If I hold on to the idea of two psychical agencies and their relationship to consciousness, then the striking affection I felt in my dream for my friend R., who was so much disparaged in the interpretation, turns out to have a wholly congruent analogy in the political life of mankind. According to this, I imagine myself in a society where a ruler jealous of his power and a lively public opinion are in conflict with each other. The people rise up against an unpopular official and want him removed; to show that he does not have to take account of the popular will, the tyrant chooses just this moment to bestow a high distinction on the official, though there is no other reason for doing so. In this way my second agency, which rules over access to consciousness, bestows a distinction on my friend R. by an outpouring of excessive affection, because the wishful endeavours of the first system, in their own particular all-absorbing interest, would slander him as numbskull.

Perhaps at this point we have a presentiment that the interpretation of dreams is capable of providing us with information about the structure of our psychical apparatus which till now we have sought in vain from philosophy. However, this is a track we shall not follow: now that we have explained distortion in dreams we shall return to the problem from which we started. The question was how dreams with a distressing content can be resolved as wish-fulfilments. We see now that this is possible if a distortion of the dream has taken place, if the distressing content serves only to disguise a desired content. Taking into account our assumptions about the two psychical agencies, we can now also add that distressing dreams in fact do contain something which is distressing to the second agency but at the same time fulfils a wish of the first agency. They are wishful dreams insofar as every dream does indeed come from the first agency, while the second only acts defensively, not creatively, towards the dream. If we confine ourselves to assessing what the second agency contributes to the dream we shall never be able to understand the dream. All the puzzles of the dream noticed by the authorities will still remain.

That the dream really does have a secret meaning which turns out to be a wish-fulfilment still has to be demonstrated by analysis for each case in turn. So I shall select a number of dreams with a distressing content and attempt to analyse them. Some of them are the dreams of hysterics, requiring a lengthy preamble and in places an intrusion into the psychical events that attend hysteria. But this is a difficulty in reporting I cannot avoid.

As I have already mentioned, when I undertake the analysis of a psychoneurotic his dreams are regularly the subject of our discussions. In the course of these I have to inform him of all the psychological explanations which helped me to reach an understanding of his symptoms, and as I do so I get criticism as unsparing as any I might expect from my professional colleagues. What my patients object to with great regularity is the proposition that all their dreams are wish-fulfilments. Here are a few examples of evidence to the contrary which have been held up to me.

'You always say the dream is a fulfilled wish,' a bright woman patient begins. 'Well, I will tell you a dream which was just the opposite, in which a wish I had was *not* fulfilled. How will that fit your theory?' This is the dream:

'*I am going to give a dinner-party but I have nothing in the house except some smoked salmon. I think of going shopping, but I remember it is Sunday afternoon and all the shops are shut. Then I want to 'phone the delivery people but the 'phone is out of order. So I have to give up my wish to give a dinner party.*'

Of course I reply that only an analysis can decide the meaning of this dream, though I do concede that at first glance it does appear rational and coherent and looks like the opposite of a wish-fulfilment. 'But what is the material this dream proceeded from? You know the stimulus to a dream is always to be found in the experiences of the previous day.'

Analysis: The patient's husband, a worthy and capable wholesale butcher, told her the previous day that he was getting too fat and intended to start losing weight. He would get up early, do exercises, keep to a strict diet, and above all accept no more invitations to dinner parties.—Of her husband she said further, laughing, that on his regular evening out with his friends he had made the acquaintance of a painter who had insisted he wanted to paint him because he had never seen such an expressive head. However, her husband replied in his coarse way that he thanked him very much but he felt sure that the painter would prefer a piece of a pretty young girl's backside to the whole of his face.[2] She tells me she is now very much in love with her husband and teases him a lot. She has also asked him not to give her any caviare.—What can that mean?

For a long time, she says, she has wanted a bread-roll with caviare every morning, but has grudged the expense. She would, of course, have got the caviare from her husband at once if she had asked for it,

---

[2] To sit for a portrait. Goethe:* 'Und wenn er keinen Hintern hat, | Wie kann der Edle sitzen?' ['And if he hasn't a backside, | How can the lord be seated?']

but on the contrary she asked him not to give her any caviare, so that she could go on teasing him about it.

(This explanation strikes me as flimsy. Such unsatisfying information usually conceals unacknowledged motives. Consider Bernheim's* experiments in hypnotism in which the subjects hypnotized carry out post-hypnotic instructions, and when asked about their motives do not reply: 'I don't know why I did that' or some such answer, but have to invent a palpably inadequate reason. It is likely to be something of the sort with my patient's caviare. I note that she needs to create an unfulfilled wish for herself in waking life. Her dream also shows a wish failing or refusing to come true. But why does she want an unfulfilled wish?)

The ideas coming to her mind so far are inadequate for interpreting the dream. I press her for more. After a short pause, congruent with overcoming a resistance, she goes on to say that the previous day she paid a call on a friend she is actually jealous of because her husband always speaks so well of her. Fortunately this woman is very thin and skinny and her husband is fond of the buxom type. What was it this skinny friend had talked about? Naturally, about her wish to put on some weight. She also asked her: 'When are you going to invite us over again? One eats so well at your table.'

Now the meaning of the dream is clear. I can tell my patient: 'It is exactly as if you had said to youself when you heard this suggestion: "Of course I'll invite you so that you can eat plenty at my house, get fat, and be even more attractive to my husband. I'd rather never give a dinner party again." The dream then tells you that you cannot give a dinner party, and in this way it fulfils your wish to contribute nothing to filling out your friend's figure. Indeed, your husband's intention to accept no more invitations to dinner parties in the interest of slimming already informs you that we get fat from the food set before us on social occasions.' All that is still lacking is some kind of connection that will confirm this solution. And the smoked salmon is still unaccounted for. 'What made you think of the salmon referred to in the dream?' 'Smoked salmon is this friend's favourite dish,' she replies. I happen to know the lady as well, and can confirm that she is as fond of salmon as my patient is of caviare.

The same dream also admits of a different, and subtler, interpretation, which a minor circumstance even makes necessary. The two interpretations do not contradict each other; they coincide and present a splendid example of how dreams, like all other psychopathological formations, carry more than one meaning. We have heard how at the same time as dreaming of a wish refused my patient took the trouble to provide herself in real life with a wish denied (the bread-roll with caviare). Her friend too had expressed a wish—to get plumper, that is—and it would not surprise us if our lady had dreamed that a wish of her friend's would not be fulfilled. It is in fact her own wish that her friend's wish—to put on more weight—should not be fulfilled. Instead of this, however, she dreams that she herself has not had a wish fulfilled. The dream is given a new interpretation if in her dream she means not herself but her friend, if she has put herself in the place of her friend, or, as we may say, she has *identified* herself with her.

In my view this is what she really did, and as an index of this identification, in real life she created for herself the wish refused. But what is the sense of this hysterical identification? To explain this we need a fuller exposition. Identification is an extremely important factor in the mechanism of hysterical symptoms: it is the means which enables patients to express in their symptoms the experiences of a large number of people, not just their own, to suffer as it were for a whole host of others, and to play all the roles in a drama solely out of their own personal resources. It will be objected that this is the hysterical imitation we are already familiar with, the ability of hysterics to imitate all the symptoms belonging to other sufferers which have made an impression on them, an empathy, as it were, intensified to the point of reproduction. But this only indicates the path run by the psychical process in the case of hysterical imitation; the path is one thing, the psychical act that takes it is another. The latter is a little more complicated than the imitation of hysterics is usually imagined to be: it corresponds to an unconscious inferential process, as an example will make clear. A physician who has a patient with a certain kind of convulsion in the same hospital room with other patients will not be surprised if he discovers one morning that this particular hysterical attack has found imitators. He will simply say to himself: 'the others have seen it and imitated it; this is what we call psychical infection.' That is so: but psychical infection proceeds more or less in the following way. As a rule the patients know more about one another than the physician does about any one of them, and they are concerned for one another after the physician has paid his visit. Today one of them has had an attack: the others soon learn that a letter she has received from home, revival of lovesickness, or the like, is the cause of it. Their empathy is aroused, and the following inference is made within them, without its reaching consciousness: if one can get attacks like this from causes like this, then I too can get them, for I have the same occasions for them. If this inference had the potential to become conscious, it would perhaps result in the *anxiety* that one might get a similar attack; however, it takes place on different psychical terrain, and therefore ends in a realization of the dreaded symptom. The identification is thus not simple imitation but *appropriation* on the basis of a claim to the same aetiology: it expresses a 'just like' and refers to some factor held in common which remains in the unconscious.

In hysteria the common factor most frequently expressed is sexual. The hysterical woman identifies herself in her symptoms most readily—though not exclusively—with those people with whom she has had sexual intercourse, or who have sexual intercourse with the same partners as she herself has. Language also acknowledges a view of this kind: two lovers are 'one'. In hysterical fantasies, as in dreams, it is sufficient for the identification that sexual relations are thought of: it is not necessary to assume they are real. So my patient is merely following the rules of hysterical thought-processes when she expresses her jealousy of her friend (which, by the way, she herself recognizes to be unjustified) by putting herself in her friend's place in the dream, and when she identifies with her by creating a symptom (the wish refused). One might clarify the process with a play on words: she is putting herself in the friend's place in the dream because the friend is putting herself in her place in the eyes of her husband, because she—the friend—would like to occupy her place in her husband's affections.[3]

The objection to my dream-theory was resolved in the case of another of my patients, the cleverest of all my female dreamers—more simply, but still in conformity with the pattern that the non-fulfilment of one wish signifies the fulfilment of another. I had been arguing with her one day that the dream was a wish-fulfilment; the

---

[3] I myself regret the inclusion of such examples from the psychopathology of hysteria; represented in such a fragmentary way and torn out of all context, they cannot after all be very illuminating. If they are able to indicate the close connections between my subject of the dream and the psychoneuroses, then they will have fulfilled my intention in using them.

following day she brought me a dream in which she was travelling with her mother-in-law to the house they were to share in the country. Now, I knew that she had vehemently resisted spending the summer in the company of her mother-in-law, and also knew that in recent days she had happily succeeded in avoiding this dreaded companionship by renting a house in the country a long way from her mother-in-law's residence. Now the dream cancelled this desired solution: was this not the very opposite of my theory of wish-fulfilment through dreams? Certainly, I only had to pursue the logic of the dream to reach its interpretation. According to this dream I was wrong: *so it was her wish that I should be wrong, and the dream showed her that her wish was fulfilled.* However, the wish that I should be wrong, which was fulfilled by using the theme of the house in the country, referred in reality to a different and more serious object. At this time I had concluded from the material provided by her analysis that something important for her illness must have taken place at a certain period in her life. She had denied it because there was nothing she could recollect. We soon discovered that I was right. Her wish that I might be wrong, transformed into the dream that she was travelling to the country with her mother-in-law, thus corresponded to the justified wish that those things, which I was only then beginning to suspect, might never have happened.

Without analysis, but only by supposition, I allowed myself to interpret a little incident that occurred to a friend who had been a fellow-pupil of mine through the eight classes of the Gymnasium. He once attended a lecture I gave to a small circle on the novel thesis that the dream was a wish-fulfilment, went home, dreamed *he had lost all his cases*—he was a lawyer—and complained to me about it. I availed myself of the excuse 'You can't win every case,' but privately I thought: since I was top of the class for eight years, while he moved about somewhere in the middle, might the wish from those school years that I would for once make a thorough fool of myself be still not so far from his mind?

Another dream of a darker nature was told to me by a patient—again as an objection to the theory of wishful dreams. My patient, a young girl, began: 'You will recall that my sister now has only one boy, her Karl; she lost her elder son, Otto, while I was still living with her. Otto was my favourite, and I was the one who really brought him up. I am fond of the little one, but naturally not nearly as much as I was of the one who died. Well last night I dreamed *that I saw Karl lying dead before me. He is lying in his little coffin, his hands folded, candles all around—in short, just like little Otto, whose death was such a blow to me.* Now tell me, what does that mean? You know me well enough: am I so wicked as to wish that my sister should lose the only child she still has? Or does the dream mean that I wish Karl were dead instead of Otto, whom I so much preferred?'

I assured her that she could discount this latter interpretation. After brief reflection I was able to tell her the correct interpretation of the dream, which I then got her to confirm. I was able to do this because I was familiar with her entire previous history.

Orphaned young, the girl had been brought up by her much older sister, and among the friends and visitors who came to the house she met a man who made an enduring impression on her heart. For a while it seemed that this relationship, though not openly declared, would end in marriage, but this happy outcome was thwarted by her sister from motives that never became entirely clear. After they had broken with each other, the man our patient loved avoided the house; some time after the death of little Otto, on whom she had meanwhile turned her affection, she herself left to make an independent life. However, she failed to free herself from the dependency she had fallen into in her love for her sister's friend. Her pride bade her avoid him; but she found it impossible to transfer her love to other suitors who subsequently appeared on the scene. Whenever the man she loved, a man of letters, announced a lecture anywhere, she was unfailingly to be found among the audience, and she would also seize any opportunity that arose of seeing him elsewhere from a distance. I recalled that the previous day she had told me that the professor was going to a certain concert and she wanted to go too, so as to enjoy the sight of him once again. This was the day before the dream: the concert was to take place on the day on which she told me the dream. Knowing this, I found it easy to construct the correct interpretation, and I asked her if she could remember an event of any kind that had happened after the death of little Otto. She replied at once: 'Certainly, the professor came back after he had stayed away a long time, and I saw him again standing beside little Otto's coffin.' It was just as I expected. So I interpreted the dream in the following way: 'If the other boy were to die, the same thing would be repeated. You would spend the day with your sister, the professor would certainly come along to offer his condolences, and under the same circumstances as before you would see him again. The dream signifies nothing but this wish of yours to see him again, which inwardly you are fighting against. I know you have a ticket for today's concert in your purse. Your dream was a dream of impatience: it put seeing him again, which is to take place today, forward by a few hours.'

To conceal her wish, she had obviously chosen a situation in which such wishes are usually suppressed, a situation in which one is so full of sadness that one gives no thought to love. And yet it is quite possible that even in the real situation, which the dream so faithfully copied, beside the coffin of the first boy whom she had loved more, she had been unable to suppress her tender feelings for the visitor she had missed for so long.

A different explanation was given to a similar dream by another patient, one who had shone in her earlier years with her quick wit and a cheerful disposition, and who still showed these qualities at least as far as the ideas occurring to her during her treatment were concerned. In the context of a lengthy dream it seemed to this lady that she saw her only daughter, a girl of fifteen, lying dead in a box. She was minded to use this dream as an objection to the theory of wish-fulfilment, but suspected herself that the detail of the box must point the way to a different understanding of the dream.[4] In the course of the analysis it occurred to her that the previous evening the company had fallen to discussing the English word 'box' and the many ways it could be translated into German: as *Schachtel* [case], *Loge* [box in a theatre], *Kasten* [chest], *Ohrfeige* [box on the ear], etc. From other components of the same dream it emerged that she guessed the connection between the English 'box' and the German '*Büchse*' [tin can] and was then plagued by the recollection that '*Büchse*' is also used as a vulgar term for the female genitals. So making allowances for her knowledge of anatomical topography I could assume that the child in the 'box' signified a child in the womb. Enlightened to this extent, she now no longer denied that the dream really did represent a wish of hers. Like so many young women she was by no means happy when she found herself pregnant, and had more than once admitted to herself that she wished the child might die in her womb; indeed, in an outburst of anger after a violent scene

---

[4] As the smoked salmon did in the dream of the thwarted dinner-party.

with her husband she had beat her body with her fists so as to strike the child within it. The dead child was thus truly a wish-fulfilment, but the fulfilment of a wish abandoned fifteen years previously, and it is not to be wondered at that when it arrives so late a wish-fulfilment is no longer recognized. Too much has changed in the meantime, after all.

The group to which the last two dreams belong, having the death of a dear relative as their content, will be considered again among the typical dreams. I shall be able to show there by means of fresh examples how all these have to be interpreted as wish-fulfilments, despite their unwished-for content. I am indebted not to a patient but to an intelligent jurist of my acquaintance for the following dream, which again was told me with the intention of restraining me from rashly generalizing my theory of wishful dreams. '*My dream*', says my informant, '*is that I am arriving at my house with a lady on my arm. A closed carriage is waiting there, a man comes up to me, identifies himself as a police agent, and invites me to follow him. I ask only for time to put my affairs in order.*—Do you believe that it is perhaps a wish of mine to be arrested?' Certainly not, I have to admit. Do you know what you were being arrested for?—'Yes, I believe it was for infanticide.'—Infanticide? But you know that this is a crime that only a mother can commit against her newborn child?—'That is so.[5]—And what were the circumstances of your dream: what happened the evening before?—'I would rather not tell you, it is a delicate matter.'—I need it, however, or we must forgo the interpretation of the dream.—'Well then, listen. I spent the night not at home but with a lady who means a lot to me. When we woke in the morning we again did something together. Then I went back to sleep and dreamed what I told you.'—Is the lady married?—'Yes.'—And you don't want to have a child by her?—'No, no, that could give us away.'—So you don't practise normal coitus?—'I take care to withdraw before ejaculating.'—May I assume you had performed this feat several times that night, and after repeating it in the morning you were a little uncertain whether or not you had succeeded?— 'That may well be so.'—Then your dream is a wish-fulfilment. You

---

[5] It often happens that a dream gets related incompletely and the recollection of the parts omitted only surfaces in the course of analysis. As a rule it is these elements inserted retrospectively that yield the key to the interpretation of the dream.

received from it a reassurance that you have not begotten a child, or, what is almost the same thing, that you had killed a child. I can easily demonstrate the connecting links to you. You will recall that a few days ago we were talking about the distress of marriage, and of the inconsistency which permits coitus in ways which avoid pregnancy, although once ovum and semen have met and formed a foetus, any kind of interference is punished as a crime. In connection with this we also considered the medieval dispute over the point in time when the soul enters into the foetus, since it is only from that moment that the concept of murder becomes admissible. You are also sure to know Lenau's* ghastly poem in which infanticide and contraception are equated.—'Remarkably enough, I happened to think of Lenau only this morning.'—That too is an echo of your dream. And now I shall demonstrate to you a little subsidiary wish-fulfilment in your dream. You are arriving at your house with the lady on your arm: you are therefore *taking her home*, instead of spending the night at her house, as you did in reality. That the wish-fulfilment forming the core of the dream should conceal itself in such an unpleasant form has perhaps more than one cause. From my essay on the aetiology of anxiety neurosis you could learn that I claim that coitus interruptus is one of the causal factors in the creation of neurotic anxiety. It would accord with this if, after several acts of coitus of this kind, you were left with a feeling of unease which then became an element in the composition of your dream. You also use this ill-humour to conceal the wish-fulfilment from yourself. By the way, doesn't this also explain your reference to infanticide? How is it you hit upon what is specifically a woman's crime?—'I will confess that some years ago I was once involved in an affair like this. It was my fault that a girl tried to save herself from the consequences of a relationship with me by having an abortion. I had nothing at all to do with carrying out the intention, but for a long time, as you will understand, I was anxious lest the matter might be discovered.'—I understand; this recollection provided a second reason for being troubled by your suspicion that you might have failed in your usual practice.

A young physician who heard this dream related in my course of lectures must have felt personally affected by it, for he hastened to dream a similar dream, applying the form of its thinking to a different subject. The previous day he had submitted his income-tax return: it was an entirely honest return, for he had little income to declare. He then dreamed that an acquaintance came from a meeting of the tax commissioners and told him that all the other tax returns had been approved, but his had aroused general mistrust and he would incur a severe penalty. The dream is the barely concealed fulfilment of a wish to be accounted a physician with a large income. By the way, it recalls the familiar tale of the young girl who is advised to reject her suitor because he has a violent temper and would certainly beat her when they were married. The girl replies: 'If only he would beat me!' Her wish to be married is so intense that she is prepared to accept the trouble it was suggested would go with the marriage, and even comes to wish for it.

I hope that these examples will—pending any further objections—be enough to make it seem plausible that even dreams with a painful content can be resolved as wish-fulfilments. Nor is anyone likely to think it a matter of chance that, when these dreams are interpreted, we should always light upon subjects one would prefer not to speak of or think about. No doubt the disagreeable feeling aroused by these dreams is simply identical with the aversion which would keep us, mostly with success, from dealing with such subjects or from discussing them, and which each of us has to overcome if we find ourselves nevertheless obliged to tackle them. However, this feeling of unpleasure which recurs thus in dreams does not exclude the existence of a wish: everyone has wishes he would not like to communicate to others, and wishes he prefers not to admit to himself. On the other hand, we consider we are justified in connecting the unpleasure that characterizes all these dreams with the fact of dream distortion; and we are also justified in concluding that these dreams are distorted in the way they are, and the wish-fulfilment in them disguised to the point of unrecognizability, because an aversion exists towards the subject of the dream or towards the wish derived from it, together with an intention to repress it. Dream-distortion thus proves to be in fact an act of censorship. But we will have taken into account everything our analysis of unpleasurable dreams has brought to light if we alter our formula for the nature of the dream to read: *The dream is the (disguised) fulfilment of a (suppressed, repressed) wish.*

There now remain anxiety-dreams as a special sub-species of dreams with a distressing content, which the unenlightened will be least willing to accept as being wishful dreams. All the same, I can deal with anxiety-dreams very briefly here, for what is involved is not some new aspect of the problem of dreams but an understanding of neurotic anxiety in general. The anxiety we feel in dreams is only apparently explained by the content of the dream. If we subject the dream-content to interpretation we notice that the anxiety in the dream is not justified by the content of the dream any more than, say, the anxiety of a phobia is by the idea to which the phobia clings. It is perfectly true, for example, that one can fall out of a window and so have reason to exercise a certain caution when standing next to one: but that does not explain why in the corresponding phobia the anxiety is so great and pursues its victim far beyond its occasions. The same explanation then proves to be valid both for the phobia and for the anxiety-dream. In both instances the anxiety is only *soldered on* to the idea that attends it, and originates from a different source.

On account of this intimate connection between dream anxiety and neurotic anxiety, in discussing the former I must at this point refer to the latter. In a little essay on 'Anxiety Neurosis' (*Neurolog. Centralblatt*, 1895 [SE iii. 87]) I maintained a while ago that neurotic anxiety originates in the sexual life and corresponds to a libido deflected from its purpose and unable to find employment. Since then this formula has proved increasingly sound, and from it one can derive the proposition that anxiety-dreams are dreams with a sexual content whose accompanying libido has undergone a transformation into anxiety. We shall have an opportunity later to support this assertion with the analysis of some of the dreams of neurotics. In the course of my further attempts to approach a theory of dreams, I shall also return to the causes of anxiety-dreams and their compatibility with the theory of wish-fulfilment.

V

THE MATERIAL AND SOURCES OF DREAMS

When we gathered from our analysis of the dream of Irma's injection that the dream is a wish-fulfilment, our interest was first captured by whether this discovery had led us to identify a universal characteristic of dreams, and for the time being we silenced any other kind of scientific curiosity which might have arisen in our mind in the course of that interpretive work. Now that we have reached our goal by the one route, we may go back and choose a new starting-point for our expeditions through the problems of dreams, even though for a while we may lose sight of the subject of wish-fulfilment, which we have certainly not finished with for good.

Now that applying our method of dream interpretation has enabled us to uncover the existence of a *latent* dream-content which is far more significant than the *manifest* dream-content, it becomes pressing for us to take up the separate problems of the dream afresh in order to see whether puzzles and contradictions which appeared insuperable as long as we only knew the manifest content of the dream may not now resolve themselves to our satisfaction.

What the authorities have said about the connection between dreams and waking life, and about the provenance of the dream-material, has been reported fully in the introductory section. We may also remind ourselves of those three distinctive features of the dream-memory which have been remarked on so often but never explained:

1. that the dream clearly prefers the impressions of the days immediately past (Robert [55], Strümpell [66], Hildebrandt [35], and Weed-Hallam [33]);
2. that it selects according to different principles from those applied by our waking memory, remembering not what is vital and important, but what is trivial and unnoticed (see p. 18);
3. that it has at its disposal our earliest childhood impressions, and even fetches forth details from this period of our life which again

seem to us trifling and in our waking life were thought to have been forgotten long ago.[1]

These peculiarities in the selection of dream-material were of course observed by the authorities in the manifest dream-content.

(a) *Recent and Insignificant Material in Dreams*

If at this point I consult my own experience with regard to the provenance of the elements appearing in the dream content, I must first of all affirm the proposition that a reference to the events of the *day just past* is to be discovered in every dream. Whatever dream I choose, one of my own or someone else's, will confirm this experience every time. Knowing this fact, I can begin the dream-interpretation perhaps by first looking for the daytime experience which has set the dream off; in many cases, indeed, this is the shortest route. In the two dreams I subjected to close analysis in the previous section (the dream of Irma's injection and the dream of my uncle with the yellow beard) the connection with the day is so obvious that it requires no further elucidation. But to show how regularly this connection can be demonstrated, I should like to examine some items from my chronicles of my own dreams with this in view. I shall report the dreams only to the extent needed to uncover the dream-source we are looking for.

1. I am visiting a house where I am admitted only with difficulty, etc.; in the meantime I keep a woman *waiting* for me.
Source: Conversation with a relative in the evening, who said she would have to *wait* for a purchase she wished to make until, etc.

2. I have written a *monograph* on a certain (unclear here) species of plant.
Source: In the morning I saw a *monograph* on the genus cyclamen in the window of a bookshop.

3. I see two women in the street, *mother and daughter*, the latter a patient of mine.
Source: A patient I was treating told me in the evening what

---

[1] Clearly Robert's view that the dream is intended to relieve our memory of the trivial impressions of the day is no longer tenable if often quite trivial images recalled from childhood appear in the dream. We would have to conclude that the dream habitually fulfils its appointed task in a most inadequate way.

difficulties her *mother* was placing in the way of continuing the treatment.

4. At the bookshop of S. and R. I take out a subscription for a periodical costing 20 florins a year.

Source: My wife reminded me during the day that I still owed her 20 florins in housekeeping money.

5. I receive a *letter* from the Social Democrats' *committee* treating me as though I were a member.

Source: I received *letters* at the same time both from the Liberal electoral committee and from the board of the Humanitarian Society, of which I really am a member.

6. A man standing on a *steep rock in the middle of the sea*, in the style of Böcklin.*

*Source: Dreyfus** on *Devil's Island*, at the same time news of my relatives in *England*, etc.

One might ask whether the dream invariably relates to the events of the preceding day, or whether the connection can extend to impressions from a longer period of the immediate past. The issue is probably not a matter of principle, but for my part I would plump for the exclusive privilege of the last day before the dream (the dream-day). Whenever I thought that an impression from two or three days previously was the source of a dream, closer examination was able to convince me that I had recalled this impression on the previous day, that a demonstrable reproduction of it had thus been interpolated between the day on which the event occurred and the time I had the dream; and what is more, I was able to establish the recent occasion which could have prompted my recollection of the earlier impression.

So it is my view that for every dream there is a stimulus drawn from those experiences 'we have not yet slept on'.

Thus the relationship to the dream-content of impressions from the immediate past (except the day before the night of the dream) is no different from that of other impressions from any time more remote. The dream can choose its material from any period of our life, provided only that a train of thought extends from the experiences of the day of the dream (the 'recent' impressions) back to these earlier experiences.

But why do we prefer recent impressions? This point will be

clarified to some extent if we submit one of the dreams referred to above to a more detailed analysis. I shall choose the dream about the monograph.

Dream-content: *I have written a monograph on a certain plant. The book is lying in front of me, I am just turning to a coloured plate inserted into it. Each illustration has a dried specimen of the plant affixed to it, in the manner of a herbarium.*

Analysis: During the morning I saw a new book in the window of a bookshop entitled *The Genus Cyclamen*, obviously a monograph on this plant.

Cyclamen is my wife's *favourite flower*. I am reproaching myself for so rarely thinking of *bringing her flowers*, which would please her. On the subject of *bringing flowers*, I recall a story I told to some of my friends not long before and have used to support my assertion that forgetting is very often the execution of an intention of the Unconscious, and at all events allows us to make an inference about the secret sentiments of the one who forgets. A young woman who was accustomed to finding a bouquet from her husband on her birthday misses this expression of his affection one birthday and bursts into tears. The husband arrives and cannot understand why she is crying until she tells him: 'Today is my birthday.' Then he strikes his forehead, exclaiming: 'I'm sorry, I completely forgot,' and makes to go off and get *flowers* for her. But she is inconsolable, for she sees in her husband's forgetfulness a proof that she no longer plays the same part in his thoughts she once had.—Two days ago, my wife met this Frau L., who told her she was in the best of health, and asked after me. Some years earlier I had been her physician.

A fresh approach: I once really did write something rather like a *monograph* on a plant, an essay on the *coca plant*, which drew the attention of K. Koller to the anaesthetizing property of cocaine. I had referred to this use of the alkaloid myself in my publication, but was not thorough enough to take the matter further. In this connection it occurs to me that on the morning of the day following the dream (I only found time for its interpretation in the evening) I was thinking about cocaine in a kind of daytime fantasy. If I were ever to get glaucoma I would go to Berlin and be operated on there incognito in my Berlin friend's* surgery by a physician he has recommended. The surgeon, not knowing who his patient is, would speak highly of how easy these operations had become since the introduction of cocaine; I would not betray by the slightest word or gesture that I myself had a part in this discovery. This fantasy was followed by thoughts of how awkward it is for a physician to claim medical treatment for himself from his colleagues. I would be able to pay the Berlin eye specialist, who does not know me, like anyone else. It is only after recalling this daydream that it strikes me that the memory of a particular experience is hidden behind it. Shortly after Koller's discovery, my father contracted glaucoma. He was operated on by my friend the eye specialist Dr Königstein; Dr Koller attended to the cocaine anaesthesia and remarked that on this occasion all three people who had a part in the introduction of cocaine found themselves together.

My thoughts now move on to when I was last reminded of this story of the cocaine. It was a few days previously, when I received the *Festschrift* with which grateful students had celebrated the fiftieth birthday of their teacher and head of their laboratory. Listed among the laboratory's claims to fame I also found it mentioned that K. Koller discovered the anaesthetizing property of cocaine there. Suddenly I notice that my dream is connected with an event on the previous evening. I had accompanied home none other than Dr *Königstein* himself and had been discussing a matter with him which always rouses intense interest in me whenever it is broached. As I was lingering in the hallway with him, Professor *Gärtner* and his young wife came up, and I could not resist congratulating them on how *blooming* they looked. Now Professor *Gärtner* is, as it happens, one of the authors in the *Festschrift* I have just spoken of, and probably caused me to recall it. Frau L., whose birthday disappointment I have just related, had also been mentioned in my conversation with Dr *Königstein*, though in another connection.

I shall try to interpret the other determinants of the dream-content as well. A *dried specimen* was included in the monograph, as though it were a *herbarium*. I have a recollection from my schooldays connected with a herbarium. Our headmaster once called the pupils in the top classes together and gave them the task of checking and cleaning the institution's herbarium. Little *worms* had been found in it—*bookworm*. He does not seem to have placed much trust in the assistance I could give, for he gave me only a few leaves out of it to deal with. I can remember even now that they contained *cruciferae*. I was never much interested in botany. At my botany examination I was again given a *crucifera* to identify and failed to recognize it. I would have done badly if my theoretical knowledge had not helped me out. From the *cruciferae* I move on to the *compositae*. Actually, the artichoke is a *composita* too, and in fact the one I might call my *favourite flower*. More thoughtful than I, my wife often brings me these favourite flowers home from the market.

I *see* the monograph I have written *lying before me*. This too is not without relevance. My friend in Berlin, a strong visualizer, wrote to me yesterday: 'I am very much engaged with your dream-book. *I can see it lying finished before me and I am leafing through the pages.*' How I have envied him this prophetic gift! If only I could see it lying finished before me!

The folded-in coloured plate: When I was a medical student I suffered a great deal from the impulse to learn only from *monographs*. Despite my limited means I possessed runs of several medical journals whose *coloured plates* were my delight. I was proud of this inclination to thoroughness. When I myself began to publish I had to draw the plates for my treatises myself, and I know that one of them came out so poorly that a well-disposed colleague laughed at me on account of it. On top of that, I do not know why, a memory comes to me from my very early years. My father once amused himself by handing over a book with *coloured plates* (an account of travels in Persia) to me and my eldest sister for us to destroy. Hardly justifiable as a way of educating the young. I was then five years old, and my sister not yet three, and the picture of us children blissfully pulling this book to pieces (*like an artichoke*, leaf by leaf, I must add) is almost the only clear memory of this period of my life I still retain. Then, when I became a student I developed a decided preference for collecting and owning books (analogous to my inclination to study from monographs, a hobbyist's enjoyment of the kind that is already apparent in my dream-thought about cyclamen and artichokes). I became a *bookworm* (cf. *herbarium*). Ever since I began to reflect on myself, I have always traced this first passion of my life back to this childhood impression, or rather, I recognized that this childhood scene was a 'screen memory' for my later bibliophilia.[2] Naturally I learned very early that passions today can mean sorrow tomorrow.

---

[2] See my essay 'Über Deckerinnerungen' ['On Screen Memories'] in the *Monatschrift für Psychiatrie und Neurologie*, 1899 [SE iii. 301].

When I was seventeen I had a considerable account with a bookseller and no means of meeting it, and my father was unwilling to accept it as an excuse that my inclinations had not been for anything worse. However, mentioning this experience from my later youth brings me back at once to the conversation with my friend Dr Königstein. For the same reproach as before—that I devoted myself too much to the *enjoyment of my hobbies*—was also the subject of our conversation on the evening of the dream-day.

For reasons that have no place here I shall not pursue the interpretation of this dream, but merely indicate the path leading towards it. During the work of interpretation I am reminded of my conversation with Dr Königstein, of more than one part of it, in fact. If I keep in mind the things that were touched on in this conversation, the meaning of the dream will become intelligible to me. All the trains of thought it set going—my wife's particular enjoyments and my own, cocaine, the difficulties of medical treatment by one's colleagues, my preference for monographs, and my neglect of such subjects as botany—all these continue and converge into one of the many ramifications of our wide-ranging conversation. The dream again acquires the character of a justification, a plea on my own behalf, like the dream just analysed of Irma's injection; indeed, it was a continuation of the theme begun in that dream, airing it in terms of new material which had ensued in the interval between the two dreams. Even the seemingly neutral form of expression of the dream acquires a certain tonality. Now the implication is: 'But I am the man who wrote the valuable and successful treatise (on cocaine)', just as in the earlier dream I protested: 'But I am an excellent and industrious student'; in both cases, then: 'I am justified in claiming this.' However, I can dispense with completing my interpretation of the dream at this point, for my only intention in relating it was to use it as an example with which to investigate the relationship between the dream-content and the experience of the previous day which prompted it. As long as I know only the manifest content of this dream, all I am able to notice is a relationship between the dream and one daytime impression; after I have done the analysis, it turns out that the dream has a second source in another experience from the same day. The first of the impressions to which the dream relates was an indifferent matter, a triviality: I see a book in the bookshop window whose title I notice only fleetingly and whose contents could hardly interest me. The second experience was of great psychical value: I engaged my friend, the eye specialist, in eager conversation for what must have been an hour, made suggestions to him that were bound to affect us both, and roused memories in myself which led me to notice a great range of disturbances within me. What is more, this conversation was broken off when acquaintances approached. Now, how are these two daytime impressions related to each other and to the dream that occurred that night?

In the dream-content I can find only one allusion to the trivial impression, and this enables me to confirm that dreams have a preference for taking unimportant elements from our lives into their content. In the dream-interpretation, on the contrary, everything leads to the significant experience which had rightly stirred me. If I assess the meaning of the dream according to the latent content brought to light by the analysis—the only correct way of doing so— all of a sudden I come upon a new and important insight. The puzzle of the dream's preoccupation with worthless fragments of daily life dissolves before my eyes; I must also contradict the assertion that the waking life of the psyche does not not continue into the dream, and that the dream squanders its psychical activity on foolish material instead. The opposite is true: what has claimed our attention by day also governs the thoughts of our dream, and we put ourselves to the trouble of dreaming only on the basis of material such as would have given us occasion for thought in the daytime.

There is an obvious explanation of why I persist in dreaming of trivial and unimportant impressions from the day, even though the one that truly stirred me is what actually set me dreaming: it is likely that here again we are looking at a manifestation of dream-distortion, which we have already traced back to a psychical force exercising its power as a censorship. My recollection of the monograph on the genus cyclamen is put to use as though it were an *allusion* to the conversation with my friend, very much as, in the dream of the thwarted dinner-party, a reference to the friend is represented by the allusion to 'smoked salmon'. But the question is: what are the intermediary links by which the impression of the monograph could come to constitute an allusion to the conversation with the eye specialist, for such a relationship is not immediately apparent. In the example of the thwarted dinner-party the relation-ship is given from the outset: it goes without saying that, as her friend's favourite dish, 'smoked salmon' belongs to the sphere of ideas which the person of her friend is able to suggest to the dreamer. In our new example we have a case of two separate impressions which at first have nothing in common except that they happen on the same day. The monograph catches my attention in the morning; then I have the conversation in the evening. The answer offered by the analysis goes like this: connections between the two impressions of this kind, which were not present at first, are passed on retro-actively from the ideas contained in the one impression to the ideas contained in the other. I have already identified the links in question in my account of the analysis. Without some influence from else-where it is likely that the idea of the monograph on cyclamen would only have attached itself to the thought that this was my wife's favourite flower, and also perhaps to a recollection of the bouquet Frau L. had not received. I do not believe that these ulterior thoughts would have been sufficient to produce a dream.

> There needs no ghost, my lord, come from the grave
> To tell us this,

as it says in *Hamlet*.* But behold, in the analysis I am reminded that the man who interrupted our conversation was called *Gärtner* [gardener] and that I thought his wife 'blooming'; indeed, I only now remember in retrospect that one of my patients with the lovely name of *Flora* was for a while the main subject of our conversation. What must have happened is that these intermediaries from the botanical sphere of ideas effected a linkage between the two experiences of the day, the unimportant one and the one that initiated the dream. Then further relationships emerged, involving cocaine, which can quite appropriately mediate between the person of Dr Königstein and a botanical monograph I wrote, and they consolidate this merging of the two spheres of ideas into one, so that one element from the first impression could be used as an allusion to the second.

I am prepared for this explanation to be challenged as being arbi-trary or forced. What would have happened if Professor Gärtner and his 'blooming' wife had not appeared, if the patient we discussed had not been called Flora, but Anna? And yet the answer is easy. If these thought-connections had not presented themselves, others would probably have been chosen. It is so easy to create connections of this kind, as indeed the riddles and conundrums we amuse ourselves with during the day amply demonstrate. The scope of wit and humour has no bounds. To go a step further: if intermediate connections of sufficient range and variety could not be created between these two impressions of the day, then the dream would have just turned out differently: some other trivial daytime impression—of the sort that impinge on us in droves and are forgotten by us—would have taken the place of the 'monograph' in the dream, contrived some connection with the content of the conversation, and would have stood in for it in the dream-content. Since the impression of the monograph alone met this fate, this must have been the one most suited to establishing the linkage. We have no need to be amazed, like Lessing's Hänschen Schlau,* 'that it is only the wealthy of this world who possess the most money'.

The psychological process by which, as we explain it, the trivial experience comes to stand for the psychically valuable one must still strike us as surprising and disconcerting. In a later section we shall be faced with the task of reaching a closer understanding of the peculiarities of this apparently irrational operation. But at this point we are concerned only with the outcome of the process, which we are urged towards treating as our basic assumption by countless experiences recurring regularly in the course of dream-analysis. But as for the process itself, it is as if a *displacement*—of psychical emphasis, shall we say—were taking place by way of intermediaries, until ideas initially weak in intensity, by borrowing from those initially more intensely charged, attain a degree of power which enables them to force an entry into consciousness. We are not at all surprised by displacements of this kind when it is a matter of finding an attachment for quantities of affect, or a question of motor actions in general. The lonely spinster who transfers her affections to animals, the bachelor who becomes a passionate collector, the soldier who defends a strip of coloured cloth, the flag, with his life's blood, the feelings of ecstasy roused in a love affair by a handclasp lingering for a second, the outburst of rage engendered in Othello by a lost handkerchief—these are all examples of psychical displacements which seem to us incontestable. But that the same means and the same principles should decide what enters our consciousness and what is withheld from it—in other words, what we think—that strikes us as pathological; and when it occurs in waking life, we call it a flaw in reasoning. Let us reveal the outcome of later discussions at this point and say that the psychical process we have recognized in dream-displacement will prove to be, not a pathologically disturbed process, but rather one differing from the normal, a process of a more *primary* nature.

Accordingly, we interpret the fact that the dream-content admits remnants of trivial experiences as a manifestation of *dream-distortion* (through displacement), and we recall that we recognized dream-distortion to be the result of a censorship controlling the transit between two psychical agencies. In doing so we expect that the analysis of the dream will invariably uncover for us the real, psychically significant source of the dream in the life of the day, though our recollection of the real source has displaced its emphasis onto the unimportant one. This conception has brought us into complete conflict with Robert's [55] theory, which for us has become quite unusable. For the fact Robert wanted to explain simply does not exist; the assumption that it does rests on a misunderstanding, on a failure to put the real meaning of the dream in the place of the apparent dream-content. There is a further objection to Robert's theory: if the dream really had the task of removing the 'dross' of our recollections of the day by means of a particular psychical activity, our sleep would have to be more disturbed and put to more strenuous work than we could claim for it in our waking mental life. For it is obvious that the number of indifferent daytime impressions which we would have to shield our memory from is immeasurably large; the night would be too short for us to cope with such a sum. It is far more likely that we forget trivial impressions without any active engagement of our psychical powers.

All the same something warns us not to dismiss Robert's ideas without further consideration. We have left unexplained the fact that one of the trivial impressions of the day—of the most recent day, that is—invariably makes a contribution to the dream-content. The relationships between this impression and the actual dream-source in the Unconscious do not always exist from the outset; as we have seen, they are produced only retroactively, during the dream-work, in the service of the intended displacement as it were. So there must be present some pressure to develop connections in the particular direction of the recent, though trivial, impression; this impression must have some quality that makes it especially suitable for this, for otherwise it would be just as easy for the dream-thoughts to displace their emphasis onto an insignificant component from their own sphere of ideas.

At this point the following experiences may help us on our way to clarification. If a single day has brought us two or more experiences suitable to initiate a dream, the dream will unite reference to them both into a single whole; it obeys a *compulsion to form a unity out of them*. For example, one summer afternoon I got into a train compartment where I encountered two acquaintances who were, however, strangers to one another. One was an influential colleague, the other a member of an aristocratic family which I attended as a physician. I introduced the two gentlemen to each other; but throughout the long journey they conducted their conversation through me, so that I had to converse now with the one, now with the other. I asked my colleague to recommend to others an acquaintance we had in common who had just started up in medical practice. My colleague replied that he was convinced that the young man was a good doctor, but his unprepossessing appearance would make it difficult for him to gain an entry into better-class houses. I replied: 'That is exactly why he needs recommendation.' I inquired of my other travelling companion soon after how his aunt was doing—she was the mother of one of my patients and was at that time seriously ill. During the night following this journey I had a dream: the young friend on whose behalf I had asked for patronage is in an elegant salon in a select company I had assembled of all the distinguished and wealthy people I knew, and with all the poise of a man of the world he delivers a funeral oration in their presence on the old lady who was the aunt of my travelling companion—and who for the sake of the dream had already died. (I confess frankly that I was not on good terms with her.) So again my dream had made out connections between two daytime impressions and with them had composed a unified situation.

On the basis of many similar experiences I am led to put forward the proposition that some kind of compulsion exists for the dream-work to put together all the sources of dream-stimuli present into a unity in the dream itself.[3]

---

[3] The inclination of the dream-work to merge all items of interest occurring at the same time into one operation has already been observed by several writers on the subject, e.g. Delage [15] (p. 41), Delboeuf [16]: rapprochement forcé (p. 236).

I would now like to discuss the question whether the dream-initiating source to which the analysis leads us must always be a recent (and significant) event, or whether some inner experience, that is to say, the memory of a psychically valuable event, can assume the role of initiator of the dream. The very definite answer provided by numerous analyses is the latter: the initiator of the dream can be an inner process which has, as it were, become recent if the dreamer has been actively thinking about it during the day. This is probably the right moment to set out a table of the various conditions which can be recognized as the sources of dreams.

The source of a dream can be:

(a) A recent and psychically significant experience which is represented directly in the dream.[4]

(b) Several recent, significant experiences which are combined into a unity by the dream.[5]

(c) One or more recent and significant experiences which are represented in the dream-content by reference to an— unimportant—experience occurring at the same time.[6]

(d) A significant inner experience (a memory, train of thought) which is then represented in the dream by reference to a recent but trivial impression.[7]

As we see, for the interpretation of dreams one condition always holds good: one constituent of the dream-content is a repetition of a recent impression from the previous day. This part, meant to act as the proxy in the dream, can either belong to the sphere of ideas of the actual initiator of the dream itself—either as an essential or as an unimportant component of it—or it will derive from the field of some trivial impression which has been drawn into into relationship with the sphere of the dream-initiator by a more or less dense web of connections. The apparent number and variety of conditions only arises as a consequence of whether *a displacement has or has not occurred*, and we may note here that these alternatives offer us the same easy explanation of the array of contrasts possible between dreams as the range from partial to fully awakened

---

[4] Dream of Irma's injection; dream of the friend who is my uncle.

[5] Dream of the young doctor's funeral oration.

[6] Dream of the botanical monograph.

[7] Most of my patients' dreams during analysis are of this kind.

states of the brain cells does for the physical theory of dreams (see p. 64).

What is also to be noted about this list is that for the purposes of dream-formation the element that is psychically valuable but not recent (the train of thought, the memory) can be replaced by a recent but psychically trivial element, as long as the two conditions obtain: (1) that the dream-content retains a reference to the recent experience, and (2) that what initiates the dream is still a psychically valuable occurrence. In only one case, (a), are both conditions fulfilled by the same impression. And if we consider further that the same trivial impressions which the dream employs for as long as they are recent will forfeit their suitability as soon as they have grown a day (or at most several days) older, we must be prepared to assume that the very freshness of an impression in itself lends it a certain psychical value for dream-formation which is somehow on a par with the value of memory or trains of thought imbued with affects. Only in the course of certain later psychological reflections shall we be able to discern what the basis for this value of *recent* impressions for dream-formation can be.[8]

In addition, our attention is drawn here to important changes which the material of our memories and ideas can undergo at night and without our being conscious of them. The demand that we should sleep on a thing before coming to a final decision about it is plainly quite justified. But we note that at this point we have left the psychology of dreaming and are encroaching upon the psychology of sleep—a step which we shall have occasion to take later from time to time.

Now there is an objection which threatens to upset the conclusions we have just drawn. If trivial impressions can enter the dream-content only as long as they are recent, how is it that in the dream-content we also find elements from early periods of our life which, when they *were* recent, as Strümpell put it, possessed no psychical value, and so ought to have been forgotten long ago—elements, that is, which are neither fresh nor psychically significant?

This objection can be dealt with fully if one refers to the results of the psychoanalysis of neurotics. The solution runs as follows: the displacement which substitutes unimportant matter for psychically

---

[8] Cf. the passage in Chapter VII on 'transference'.

valuable material (in dreaming just as in thinking) has in their case already taken place in those early periods of life and has been fixed in their memory ever since. For those originally trivial elements are no longer trivial once they have assumed by means of displacement the value of psychically significant material. What has remained really trivial can no longer be reproduced in a dream.

It will rightly be concluded from this discussion that I maintain there are no trivial initiators of dreams, and thus no innocuous dreams. This is my strict and single-minded opinion, excepting the dreams of children and perhaps brief dream-reactions to nocturnal sensations. Apart from these, either what we dream is manifestly recognizable as having psychical significance, or it is distorted and can only be assessed after a dream-interpretation has been carried out, when it too will reveal its significance. The dream never wastes its time on trifles; we do not allow a mere nothing to disturb our sleep. The apparently innocuous dreams turn out to be pretty bad when we take the trouble to interpret them: if I may be permitted the expression, the dream 'wasn't born yesterday'. As this is another point where I may anticipate contradiction, and as I am glad to seize the opportunity to demonstrate dream-distortion at work, I shall now subject a number of 'innocuous' dreams from my collection to analysis.

I

A clever and refined young lady who is, however, even in her daily dealings, one of the reserved, one of the 'still waters', relates her dream: '*I arrive at the market too late and can get nothing either from the butcher or the vegetable woman.*' An innocuous dream, to be sure, but dreams do not look like this: I get her to tell it to me in detail. Then her account runs as follows: *She goes to the market with her cook, who is carrying the basket. The butcher tells her, after she has asked for something: 'That is no longer available', and makes to give her something else, with the remark: 'This is good too'. She refuses it and goes to the vegetable woman, who wants to sell her a peculiar vegetable tied up in bundles but black in colour. She says: 'I don't recognize that. I won't have it.'*

The daytime connection of this dream is simple enough: she really had gone to the market too late and had got nothing. *The butcher's shop was already shut* strikes one as a description of the experience. But wait: is that not a rather vulgar phrase which refers—or rather its opposite does—to a certain kind of carelessness* in a man's dress? The dreamer, by the way, did not use these words; perhaps she avoided them; let us look for an interpretation of the individual details contained in the dream.

When something in a dream has the character of speech, that is, when it is said or heard and not merely thought—a distinction which is usually perfectly clear—it derives from something that has been said in waking life, though this has been treated as raw material, broken up, slightly altered, but above all wrenched from its context.[9] We can take such spoken words as our starting-point in the work of interpretation. So where do the butcher's words '*That is no longer available*' come from? In fact, from myself: a few days previously I had explained to her 'that the earliest experiences of childhood as such *are no longer available*, but are replaced in the analysis by "transferences" and dreams'. So I am the butcher, and she is rejecting these transferences of earlier modes of thought and feeling to the present day.—Where do her dream-words come from: '*I don't recognize that. I won't have it*'? For the purpose of analysis this has to be divided up. '*I don't recognize that*' she said herself to her cook the previous day when she had a quarrel with her; but then she added: '*Behave properly*'. A palpable displacement is emerging here: of the two sentences she used towards her cook, she took the insignificant one into her dream; the one she suppressed, however—'Behave properly!'—is the only one appropriate to the remainder of the dream-content.* It is what one might exclaim to someone who had made an improper demand and omitted to 'shut the meat shop'. That we were really on the track of the interpretation is then demonstrated by the similarity between this and the allusions present in the scene with the vegetable woman. A vegetable sold tied together in bundles (and long and narrow, as she adds in retrospect), and at the same time black, what can that be but a dream-merging of asparagus and black radishes? Asparagus I have no need to interpret to any knowledgeable person; but the other vegetable too—as a warning shout: 'Black, look out!' [*Schwarzer, rett' dich!*, cf. *schwarzer Rettich*, black radish]—seems to me to point to the same sexual theme as

---

[9] Cf. the passage on speech in dreams in the section on the dream-work. Only one of the authorities on the subject seems to have recognized the origin of utterances in dreams, Delboeuf [16] (p.226), who compares them with 'clichés'.

we divined at the beginning when we wanted to substitute 'the meat-shop was shut' for the dream-narrative. There is no need to understand the meaning of this dream in its entirety: what has been established is that it is meaningful and in no sense innocuous.[10]

II

Another innocuous dream by the same patient, in some respects a counterpart to the preceding one: *Her husband asks: Shouldn't we have the piano tuned? She: It's not worth while, and besides the hammers need re-leathering.* Again a repetition of a real event from the previous day: her husband asked this question and she replied along these lines. But what does it mean, that she should dream this? True, she says of the piano that it is a *disgusting* chest with a *dreadful tone*, something her husband owned before they were married,[11] etc., but the key to the solution is only provided by her words: '*It's not worth while*'. This has its origin in a visit she paid to a friend the day before. She was invited to take off her jacket and declined with the words: 'No thanks, *it's not worth while*, I have to go soon.' As she tells me this, it occurs to me that while we were engaged in the work of analysis the previous day, she suddenly grasped at her jacket, where a button had come undone. It is as though she wanted to say: 'Please, don't look, it's not worth while.' Thus the *chest* [Kasten] is amplified to *her chest* [Brustkasten], and the interpretation of the dream leads directly to the time when she was developing physically, when she began to be dissatisfied with her figure. It is likely it could lead to even earlier times if we take account of the '*disgusting*' and the '*dreadful tone*', and recall how frequently the smaller hemispheres of the female body stand in—as opposite and as substitute—for the large ones in allusions and dreams.

III

I shall interrupt this series to interpolate the brief innocuous dream

---

[10] For the curious I would note that the patient's dream conceals a fantasy of indecent, sexually provocative behaviour on my part, which she repulses. This may seem incredible to some, but I would remind them of the numerous cases where physicians have been accused in this way by hysterical women, in whom the same fantasy does not appear in distorted form and in their dreams, but has become undisguisedly conscious in the form of a delusion.

[11] A substitution by its opposite, which will become clear after the interpretation.

of a young man. He dreamed *that he was putting on his winter coat again, which was terrible*. According to him, the occasion for this dream is the cold snap that has suddenly set in. However, a subtler judgement will notice that the two brief parts of the dream do not suit each other very well, for what could be 'terrible' about wearing a thick or heavy coat in the cold? It also does no good for the innocuousness of this dream that the first idea occurring to the young man during analysis is the recollection that on the previous day a lady confessed to him in confidence that her latest child owed its existence to a burst condom. He now reconstructs what he thought on this occasion: a thin condom is risky, a thick one is no good. The condom was the 'overcoat' [*Überzieher*]—rightly, for one puts it on [*zieht ihn über*]; a lightweight coat also has the same name. An event such as the one the lady related would certainly have been 'terrible' for this unmarried man.—And now back to our female dreamer of innocuous dreams.

IV

She is putting a candle into the candlestick; but the candle is broken, so that it does not stand very well. The girls at school say she is clumsy; but the mistress says it is not her fault.

Here too there is a real occasion: she really did put a candle into the candlestick the previous day; but it was not broken. A transparent symbolism is being employed here. A candle is an object that rouses the female genitalia; if it is broken, so that it does not stand very well, this signifies the impotence of the man ('*it is not her fault*'). But, carefully raised as she is, and a stranger to everything ugly, does this young woman know of this use of the candle? As it happens she is able to quote the experience through which in fact she acquired this knowledge. During a trip on the Rhine in a rowing-boat, a boat passes them by in which a group of students are sitting and singing, or rather bellowing with great gusto, a song that goes: 'When the Queen of Sweden, with the window-shutters shut, takes Apollo candles . . .'*

She fails to hear or understand the last words, and her husband has to enlighten her. In the dream-content these lines are replaced by the innocuous recollection of a task she once performed *clumsily* at her boarding-school, doing so, indeed, under the same circumstances: *with the window-shutters shut*. The connection between the theme of masturbation and impotence is clear enough. 'Apollo' in the latent dream-content links this dream to an earlier one in which the virginal Pallas was referred to. Indeed, not at all innocuous.

v

In case it may be imagined that drawing inferences from the dream about the life the dreamer really leads is all too easy, I shall add another dream which seems equally innocuous and comes from the same person. *I have dreamed of something*, she said, *which I really did during the day, that is, I was filling a little trunk so full of books that I had trouble in closing it, and I dreamed it just as it really happened*. Here the narrator herself places the emphasis on the correspondence between dream and reality. Now, although they have created a place for themselves in waking thought, all such judgements of the dream or comments on it nevertheless invariably belong in the latent dream-content, as later examples will confirm. So, then, we are told that what the dream relates really happened on the previous day. It would take us too far afield to describe the route by which in the course of the interpretation we hit upon the idea of calling on English to assist us. It is enough to say that again we are dealing with a little *box* (compare the dream of the dead child in the box, pp. 119–20) which was filled so full that nothing more would go in. This time at least nothing bad.

In all of these 'innocuous' dreams, it is the sexual element which thrusts itself forward so conspicuously as the motive for censorship. But this is a topic of fundamental importance which we shall have to set aside.

(b) *Material from Infancy as a Source of Dreams*

As the third distinctive characteristic of the content of dreams, like all the writers on the subject (except Robert), we have indicated that impressions from the earliest years of our life can appear in our dreams, which do not seem to be at the disposal of our memory when we are awake. How rarely or how often this occurs is understandably hard to judge, because the origins of these elements in the dream cannot be recognized after we wake. So proof that we are dealing with impressions from childhood has to be produced by means of objective evidence, and the conditions for this come together only rarely. A. Maury [48] tells a story for its particular value as evidence of a man who decided to visit his home town after having been away for twenty years. The night before he left, he dreamed he was in a village quite unfamiliar to him and in the street he met a man he did not know, with whom he had a conversation. When he did return to his home, he was able to assure himself that this unfamiliar village really existed in the vicinity of his hometown, and the unknown man of his dream turned out to be a friend of his late father's who lived there. A compelling proof, certainly, that he had seen both, man and village, in his childhood. In addition, the dream can be interpreted as an impatience-dream, like that of the girl who had a ticket for the concert in her purse (pp. 120–1), or of the child whose father had promised him an excursion to the Hameau, and others of the kind. The motives for reproducing just this impression from the dreamer's childhood rather than any other, of course, cannot be uncovered without analysis.

Someone attending my lectures, who boasted that his dreams were only very rarely subject to dream-distortion, told me that a while ago he dreamed he saw *his former tutor in the bed of the maid* who had been employed in the house up to his eleventh year. The locality of this scene occurred to him while he was dreaming. His interest aroused, he told the dream to his older brother, who laughed and confirmed the reality of what he had dreamed. He remembered it very well, he said, for he was six years old at the time. The loving couple used to get him, the elder boy, drunk on beer when circumstances were favourable to nocturnal dalliance; the younger child, then three years old—our dreamer—who slept in the maid's room, was not regarded as an inconvenience.

There is a further instance where it can be determined with certainty and without the aid of dream-interpretation that a dream contains elements deriving from childhood and that is when the dream is what we call a *recurrent* one, that is, one first dreamed in childhood, which repeatedly reappears from time to time in the sleep of the adult. To the familiar examples of this kind of dream I can add some I have been told, though I have never had a recurrent dream of this sort myself. A physician in his thirties told me that from the earliest years of his childhood up to the present day, a yellow lion which he is able to describe exactly has made frequent appearances in his dream-life. Now this lion, familiar to him only in his dreams, turned up one day *in natura* as a long-lost porcelain object, and the young man then heard from his mother that this object had been his best-loved toy during his early childhood, though he himself could no longer remember it. One of my women patients had dreamed four or five times in the course of her thirty-eight years the same frightening scene: she is being pursued, flees into a room, shuts the door, then opens it again in order to take out the key, which is in the outside lock; then, with the feeling that something dreadful will happen if she does not succeed, seizes the key to lock the door from the inside; after which she breathes a sigh of relief. I am unable to say at what early age this little scene could have taken place, which of course she only witnessed.

If we now turn from the manifest dream-content to the dream-thoughts disclosed only after analysis, we are astonished to find the active involvement of childhood experiences in dreams whose content would in no way lead us to suspect it. I owe an especially charming and instructive example of a dream of this kind to my honoured colleague of the 'yellow lion'. After reading Nansen's* account of his polar expedition, he dreamed that on an icefield he was giving galvanic treatment to the intrepid explorer on account of a sciatica which the latter was complaining of! In the analysis of this dream he recalled an incident from his childhood without which the dream would certainly have remained incomprehensible. One day when he was three or four years old he was listening intently to the grown-ups talking about journeys of discovery, and then asked his father if that was a serious illness. He had clearly confused 'journeys' [*Reisen*] with 'aches' [*Reissen*], and the laughter of his brothers and sisters made sure he did not forget the embarrassing experience.

Something rather similar is involved in the analysis of the dream about the monograph on the genus cyclamen when I come upon the memory of my father giving the five-year-old boy a book with coloured plates to destroy. It may perhaps be doubted whether this memory really did play a part in forming the dream-content, or whether the work of analysis is not rather creating a connection only in retrospect. But the wealth of associations, and the way they were intertwined together vouch for the former idea. (Cyclamen— favourite flower—favourite food—artichoke; pull to pieces like an artichoke, leaf by leaf (an expression one hears every day in connection with the division of the Chinese Empire*);—herbarium—

bookworm, whose favourite food is books.) Moreover, I can testify that the ultimate meaning of the dream, which I have not given in full here, is very intimately connected with the content of that childhood scene.

In the case of another set of dreams, we learn from analysis that the very wish that initiated the dream, and whose fulfilment the dream represents, has its origin in childhood, so that to our surprise we *find the child, with its impulses, living on in the dream.*

At this point I shall continue the interpretation of a dream from which we have already learned much that is new; I mean the dream in which my friend R. is my uncle (p. 109). We have pursued its interpretation to the point when the wishful motive to be appointed professor came palpably to meet us; and we explained the affection I felt for my friend R. in the dream as a defiant creation made in opposition to the slander of my two colleagues in my dream-thoughts. The dream was my own, so I may continue its analysis by saying that the solution I had reached still failed to satisfy my feelings. I knew that my judgement of the colleagues who were so ill-used in my dream-thoughts was quite different in waking life, and the strength of my wish not to share their fate with regard to the academic appointment seemed to me inadequate to explain fully the contrast between my opinion of them when awake and that of the dream. If my need to be addressed by a different title was so strong, it pointed to a pathological ambition which I do not recognize in myself and which I believe is quite foreign to me. I do not know how others who think they know me would judge me in this matter: perhaps I really have been ambitious; but if so, my ambition has long since been aimed at other goals than the rank and title of a professor extraordinarius.

So where, did the ambition that inspired my dream come from? Suddenly there comes to my mind mind a tale I was told so often in my childhood, how at my birth an old peasant woman made a prophecy to my mother as she rejoiced in her first-born child, that she had given the world a great man. Such prophecies must be very frequent: there are so many mothers full of expectations for their children, and so many old peasants or other old women who have lost what power they had on earth and so have turned their attention to the future. Nor will such a prophecy have been to the disadvantage of the prophetess. Could this be the source of my desire for greatness?

But just at this point I recall another impression from the later years of my childhood which might offer an even better explanation: one evening, in one of the hostelries on the Prater* where my parents would often take me to when I was eleven or twelve, we noticed a man going from table to table and for a small sum improvising verses on any subject he was given. I was sent to invite the poet to our table, and he showed his gratitude to the messenger. Before he asked what his subject was to be, he devoted a few rhymes to me and declared in his inspiration that one day I would probably become a 'minister'. I can still remember very clearly the impression this second prophecy made on me. It was during the period of the Bourgeois Ministry;* shortly before, my father had brought home portraits of those middle-class academics Herbst, Giskra, Unger, Berger, and others, and we had illuminated the house in honour of these gentlemen. There were even Jews among them: which meant that every industrious Jewish boy carried a ministerial portfolio in his satchel.* It must even have something to do with the effect of those times that until shortly before I enrolled at the university I intended to read law, and changed course only at the last moment. For a ministerial career is certainly not open to a medical man! So then, what of my dream? I notice only now that it is transporting me back from the troubled present to the hopeful period of the Bourgeois Ministry and is doing its best to fulfil the wish I nurtured *then*. In treating my two learned and worthy colleagues so badly because they are Jews—one as if he were a numbskull, the other as if he were a criminal—in acting in this way, I am behaving as though I were the minister, I am putting myself in the minister's place. What a thorough revenge on His Excellency! He declines to appoint me professor extraordinarius, and in return, in my dream I put myself in his place.

In another instance I was able to note that the wish that initiated the dream, though belonging to the present, was all the same powerfully reinforced by memories reaching deep into childhood. It concerns a set of dreams which have their basis in my longing to go to *Rome*.* I anticipate that for some time yet I shall have to satisfy this desire only in my dreams, for at the time of year when I am free to take a holiday, a stay in Rome is inadvisable for reasons of health. So I dream on one occasion that I am seeing the Tiber and the Ponte Sant'Angelo through a train window; then the train starts moving, and it occurs to me that I have not even set foot in the city. The view

I saw in the dream was copied from a familiar engraving which I had noticed briefly the previous day in the drawing-room of one of my patients. Another time someone is leading me to a hill and showing me Rome, half-veiled in mist and still so far away that I wonder at the clarity of the view. The content of this dream is richer than I would wish to go into here. The motif 'to see the Promised Land from afar' is easy to recognize. The city I first saw thus hidden in mist is *Lübeck*;* the model for the hill is—*Gleichenberg*.* In a third dream I am in Rome at last, or so the dream tells me. But to my disappointment what I see is not city scenery at all: *a little river with dark waters, one side of it black rocks, on the other meadows with large white flowers. I notice a Herr Zucker* (whom I know slightly) *and decide to ask him the way to the city.* It is obvious that I am labouring in vain to see in my dream a city I have not seen in waking life. When I break up the dream's landscape into its elements, the white flowers indicate *Ravenna*, a town I know, which had for a time at least taken precedence over Rome as Italy's capital. In the marshes around *Ravenna* we found the most beautiful water-lilies in the midst of dark waters; the dream has them growing in meadows, like the narcissi in our own Aussee, because in *Ravenna* it was so difficult to gather them from the water. The dark rocks, so close to the water, remind me vividly of the vale of *Tepl*, near *Karlsbad*.* 'Karlsbad' now puts me in a position to explain the strange feature of asking Herr Zucker the way. In the material from which the dream was spun I was able to recognize two of those comic Jewish anecdotes which conceal so much profound and often bitter wisdom, and which we always enjoy quoting in conversation and letters. One is the story of the 'constitution', which tells of how a poor Jew steals onto the express train to Karlsbad without a ticket, is then caught out, at every ticket-inspection told to get off and treated worse and worse, until, when asked by an acquaintance who encountered him at one of the stations of his suffering, where he is travelling to, he replies: 'If my *constitution* holds out—to *Karlsbad*.' Close to this my memory holds another story of a Jew who does not know any French and who has it drummed into him that in *Paris* he must ask the way to the Rue Richelieu. *Paris* too was for many years a goal of my desire, and the joy I felt when I first set foot there I took as a guarantee that I should also see the fulfilment of my other wishes. Moreover, asking the way is a direct allusion to Rome, for it is well known that all roads lead to

Rome. The name *Zucker* [sugar] also points to *Karlsbad*, for that is where we send all those suffering from the *constitutional* complaint of diabetes [*Zuckerkrankheit*]. What occasioned this dream was a suggestion of my Berlin friend that we should meet in Prague at Easter. The things I intended to discuss with him there would give rise to a further connection with *sugar* and diabetes.

A fourth dream, shortly after the last one, again takes me to *Rome*. I see a street-corner before me and am surprised that so many German posters have been put up there. On the previous day I had written prophetically to my friend that probably *Prague* would not be a very comfortable place for Germans* to take a walk in. The dream thus expressed at the same time both the wish to meet him in *Rome* rather than in a Bohemian city, and the desire, probably originating in my student days, that the German language might be treated with greater toleration in Prague. In any case, in the earliest years of my childhood I must have understood the Czech language, for I was born in a little town in Moravia with a Slav population. A Czech children's poem which I heard in my seventeenth year* imprinted itself so effortlessly on my memory that I can repeat it even today, though I have no idea what it means. So these dreams too are not without multiple connections to the impressions of my earliest years.

On my last visit to Italy, which among other things took me along *Lake Trasimene*, I saw the *Tiber*, but with sadness in my heart I was obliged to turn back 80 kilometres from Rome: it was then at last that I discovered that my longing for the Eternal City was reinforced by impressions from my youth. I was just working out a plan to travel to *Naples* via *Rome* one year quite soon when I recalled something I must have read in one of our classic writers:* 'It is a nice question who paced his room more restlessly after he had conceived the plan to go to *Rome*—*Winckelmann*,* the headmaster's deputy, or *Hannibal*,* the general.' And there I was, following in *Hannibal's* footsteps; like him, I had not been granted a sight of *Rome*; he too had moved to *Campania* when all the world had expected him in *Rome*. But *Hannibal*, whom I had managed to resemble so much, had been my favourite hero when I was at the Gymnasium: like so many of that age, my sympathies in the Punic Wars did not lie with the Romans but with the Carthaginians. Then, in the upper school, when I first became aware of the consequences of being descended from an alien race, and the stirrings of anti-Semitism among my schoolfellows urged me to take up a position, the figure of the Semitic general rose even higher in my eyes. *Hannibal* and *Rome* symbolized to me the opposition between the tenacity of Jewry and the organization of the Catholic Church. The significance which the anti-Semitic movement has since acquired for our emotional life later helped to fix the thoughts and feelings of that early period. Thus the wish to go to *Rome* became for my dream-life a cloak and symbol for several other fervent wishes; and I would work with all the endurance and single-mindedness of the Carthaginian for their realization, even though their fulfilment seems for the time being to be as little favoured by fate as *Hannibal's* lifelong wish to enter *Rome*.

And this is the moment when I hit on the experience from my youth which is still exerting its power in all these dreams and feelings even today. I must have been ten or twelve years old when my father began to take me with him on his walks and in conversation tell me his views on the things of this world. In this vein, to show me how I had been born into better times than he had, he once told me: 'When I was a young man I went for a walk on a Saturday in the town you were born in, wearing my best clothes and with a new fur cap on my head. Then a Christian comes along, knocks my cap in the mud with a single blow, and shouts: "Jew, get off the pavement!"'—'And what did you do?'—'I stepped into the road and picked up my cap,' came the impassive reply. That did not seem to me very heroic of the big, strong man who was leading me by the hand. I compared this situation, which I was not happy about, with another more suited to my feelings: the scene where *Hannibal's* father, *Hasdrubal*,* makes his son swear before the domestic altar to take revenge on the Romans. From that time on, Hannibal had a place in my fantasies.

I believe I can trace this enthusiasm for the Carthaginian general even further back into my childhood, so that here too all that may be involved is the transference to a new bearer of an affective relationship that had already been formed. One of the first books that came into my hands once I could read was Thiers's* *History of the Consulate and the Empire*; I recall that I had stuck little labels onto the flat backs of my wooden soldiers, bearing the names of the Napoleonic marshals, and that *Masséna** (as a Jew: *Menassa*) was my declared favourite even then. *Napoleon* himself was connected with *Hannibal* by his crossing of the Alps. And perhaps the evolution of

this warrior ideal can be pursued even further back into childhood—
back to the wishes which the company, during my first three years, of
a boy a year older, friendly one moment, belligerent the next, must
have aroused in the weaker of the two playmates.

The deeper we descend into the analysis of dreams, the more
frequently we are put on the track of childhood experiences which
act as dream-sources in the latent dream-content.

We have heard (p. 20) that the dream very rarely reproduces
recollections in such a way that they form the only manifest dream-
content, unabbreviated and unchanged. All the same, some examples
of this occurrence have been confirmed, and to these I can add some
new ones which again relate to scenes of infancy. In the case of
one of my patients, a dream once presented a barely distorted reproduction of a sexual incident which he immediately recognized as a
faithful recollection. Its memory had never been completely lost in
waking life, it is true, though it had become much obscured, and its
revival was the result of the preceding work of analysis. At twelve
years old the dreamer had visited a schoolfriend confined to his bed,
and by making some movement, probably quite accidentally, his
friend exposed himself. Seized by a kind of compulsion at the sight
of his friend's genitals, he exposed himself also, and took hold of the
other's member; but his friend looked at him with surprise and
indignation, and he grew embarrassed and desisted. A dream
repeated this scene twenty-three years later, together with all the
feelings that had attended it, except that now the dreamer assumed
the passive instead of the active role, and the person of the
schoolfriend was replaced by someone from the present.

As a rule, it is true, the scene from infancy is represented in the
manifest dream-content only by an allusion, and has to be developed
out of the dream by means of interpretation. The report of such
examples cannot be very conclusive as evidence, because of course
there is usually no other guarantee that these are in fact childhood
experiences: if they occur at an early age they will no longer be
acknowledged by the memory. The justification for inferring them at
all from the evidence of dreams is provided by a large number of
factors arising during the work of psychoanalysis which, operating in
combination, seem sufficiently dependable. Torn out of context for
the purpose of dream-interpretation, these derivations of dreams
from childhood experiences will not perhaps seem very impressive,

especially as I am not even reporting all the material on which the interpretation is based. But this will not deter me from reporting them.

I

All the dreams of one of my women patients have the character of 'being rushed' [*gehetzt*]: she rushes to be on time so as not to miss the train, and so forth. In one of her dreams she is to visit a friend of hers; her mother has told her to go by transport, not to walk; *but she runs, — and as she does so she keeps falling down.* — The material emerging in the analysis allows me to recognize a recollection of romping and rushing about in childhood [*Kinderhetzereien*]—of the sort the Viennese call '*eine Hetz*' [a bit of fun]—and in the specific case of this dream I can trace it back to the joke children are fond of, the sentence 'Die Kuh rannte bis sie fiel' [the cow ran until she fell] said as quickly as if it were a single word, which again is a 'rush' [*Hetzen*]. All these innocuous rushings with her little friends are recalled because they take the place of other, less innocuous, ones.

II

Another patient has the following dream: *She is in a big room in which all kinds of machines are standing, as she imagines an orthopaedic institution to be. She hears that I have no time and that she will have to receive treatment at the same time as five others. But she baulks at this, and refuses to lie in the bed—or whatever it was—intended for her. She stands in a corner and waits until I say it isn't true. In the meantime the others are laughing at her and saying she is fooling around.* — Besides this, *as though she were going to make a lot of little squares.*

The first part of this dream's content is a connecting link to her treatment and a transference to me. The second contains the allusion to the childhood scene; with the reference to the bed the two parts are soldered together. The orthopaedic institution could be traced back to a remark of mine in which I had compared her treatment, as regards both its nature and its duration, to an *orthopaedic* treatment. When I began it, I had to tell her *that for the moment I had little time for her*, but that later I would devote a whole hour to her every day. This aroused in her the old sensitivity which is one of the main character traits of children heading for hysteria. They are insatiable for love. My patient was the youngest of six siblings (hence *five others*) and as such her father's favourite, though even so she seems to have found that her beloved father devoted too little time and attention to her.—Her waiting until I say it isn't true has the following derivation: a little tailor's boy had brought her a dress, and she had given him the money for it. Then she asked her husband if she would have to pay again if the boy lost the money. To *tease* her, her husband assured her 'yes' (the *teasing* in the dream-content), and she asked him again and again *and waited for him finally to say it wasn't true.* So for the latent dream-content, this thought can be construed as wondering whether she may have to pay me double if I devote double the time to her, a thought that is mean or *dirty*. (Dreams very often replace the uncleanliness of childhood with meanness over money: the word 'dirty' forms the bridge.) If all the business of waiting until I say, etc., is intended in the dream to be a circumlocution for 'dirty', then *standing in a corner* and *not lying in bed* correspond to it as constituents of a childhood scene in which she has dirtied the bed, and is *sent to stand in the corner* as a punishment, with the threat that her father won't love her any more, her brothers and sisters will laugh at her, etc. The little squares pointed toward her little niece, who showed her the arithmetical trick of writing numbers in, I think, nine squares in such a way that in whatever direction you add them up, they come to 15.

III

The dream of a man: *He sees two boys who are scrapping; they are cooper's boys, as he concludes from the tools lying around; one of the boys has knocked the other down, the boy on the ground has earrings with blue stones. He runs after the miscreant, his stick raised with the intention of beating him. The boy flees to a woman standing beside a wooden fence, as though she were his mother. She is a labouring woman, with her back to the dreamer. At last she turns round and looks at him with a horrible gaze, so that he runs away in fear. The red flesh of her lower eyelids can be seen protruding.*

The dream made full use of trivial events from the previous day. He really did see two boys in the street that day, one of whom knocked the other down. When he ran up to settle the quarrel they both took flight.—'Cooper's boys' is explained only by a subsequent dream; in the course of its analysis he used the phrase *dem Faß den Boden ausschlagen* [to knock the bottom out of the barrel—to be the absolute limit].—He has observed that earrings with blue stones are mostly used by *prostitutes*. In this way the familiar line of doggerel about *two boys* was added: 'The other boy, he was called Marie' (i.e. he was a girl).—The standing woman: after the scene with the two boys he went for a walk along the Danube and took advantage of the solitude there to urinate *against a wooden fence*. As he walked on, a decently dressed older woman smiled at him in a very friendly way and tried to hand him her visiting card.

As the woman in the dream is standing as he had done when urinating, what is involved is a urinating woman, and the horrible '*sight*' also belongs to this, the protrusion of red flesh, which can only relate to the genitals gaping when a woman crouches down and which, seen in childhood, reappeared in the later recollection as '*proud flesh*', as a 'wound'. The dream unites two occasions on which the little boy was able to see the genitals of little girls, that is, when they were *knocked down* and when they *urinated*, and, as the other context indicates, it preserves the memory of a beating or a threat from his father on account of the sexual curiosity shown by the boy on these occasions.

IV

A large number of childhood recollections, combined in a rough and ready fashion, lies behind the following dream of an elderly lady.

She is rushing out to do some shopping. Then on the Graben* she sinks to her knees as if she has collapsed. Lots of people gather around her, especially the cab-drivers; but no one helps her up. She makes many vain attempts; finally she must have succeeded, for she is put into a cab which is supposed to take her home; through a window a large, heavily laden basket (similar to a shopping-basket) is thrown in after her.

This is the same patient who is being rushed in her dreams, just as she rushed about in play as a child. The first situation in the dream is clearly derived from the sight of a fallen horse, just as the 'collapse' indicates a horse-race. In her early years she was a *horsewoman*, and earlier still probably a *horse*. Falling down belongs to her earliest childhood memory of the seventeen-year-old son of the caretaker, who was seized in the street with epileptic convulsions and taken home in a carriage. Of course, she only heard of this, but the idea of epileptic convulsions, of 'someone falling', gained great power over her imagination and later influenced the form assumed by her own hysterical attacks.—When a woman dreams of falling, it almost always has a sexual significance, she becomes a '*fallen woman*'; in the case of the present dream this interpretation will hardly admit of any doubt at all, for her fall is on the *Graben*, the place in Vienna well known as a parade for prostitutes. The *shopping-basket* allows of more than one interpretation: as a basket it recalls the many *baskets* [colloquial: 'refusals'] she once handed to her suitors, and later, as she thought, she received herself. That *no one will help her up* also belongs here: she herself interprets it as being spurned and rejected. The *shopping-basket* further recalls fantasies, already familiar from the analysis, in which she married far below her station and now has to go and do the shopping herself. Finally, however, the shopping-basket can be interpreted as a symbol for a *servant*. Then further childhood recollections appear of a *cook* who was dismissed because she stole: she too *sank to her knees* and pleaded. The dreamer was twelve years old at the time. Then the memory of a housemaid who was dismissed because she consorted with the *coachman* [*Kutscher*] of the house, who, by the way, later married the girl. This recollection thus supplies us with the source for the *cab-drivers* [*Kutscher*] in the dream (who, unlike the real one, refused to look after the fallen woman). But what still remains to be explained is throwing the basket in after her, specifically *through the window*. This reminds her of dispatching luggage on the railway, of the country practice of '*Fensterln*' [visiting a girl by climbing in through her window], of little impressions from a stay in the country, when a man threw *blue plums* into a lady's room through her window, and how her little sister was afraid because a passing idiot looked into the room through the window. And then behind these there surfaces an obscure recollection from her tenth year of a maid in the country who was engaged in love-scenes with a servant of the house, which the child could have noticed something of, and who was '*dispatched*', '*thrown out*' (in the dream the opposite: '*thrown in*') together with her lover. Now in Vienna, the luggage, the suitcase of a servant is described as her '*sieben Zwetschken*' [seven little plums—bits and pieces]: 'Pack' deine sieben Zwetschken zusammen und geh' [Pack your bits and pieces together and go].

Of course my collection of dreams has plenty of dreams supplied by my patients, which, when analysed, lead back to dim or altogether forgotten childhood impressions, often from the first three years of life. But it is difficult to draw conclusions from these which are to hold good for dreams in general, for as a rule the dreamers are neurotics, hysterics especially, and the role ascribed in these dreams to childhood scenes could well be determined by the nature of the neurosis and not by the character of the dream. All the same, it happens just as often when I interpret my own dreams—which I do not undertake on account of any gross pathological symptoms—that in the latent dream-content I come unexpectedly upon a scene from infancy, and that all at once a whole series of dreams leads on to paths which have their beginnings in a childhood experience. I have already given examples of this, and shall give more when occasion arises. Perhaps I cannot conclude this section better than by relating some of my own dreams in which recent occasions and long-forgotten childhood experiences appear together as dream-sources.

I

After I sought my bed, tired, hungry, and weary from travel, I am visited in sleep by the great vital needs, and I dream: *I am going into a kitchen for a pudding. Three women are standing there, one of whom is the landlady, and she is turning something in her hand as though making dumplings* [Knödel]. *She answers that I must wait until she is finished (not clearly as speech). I grow impatient and go away offended. I put on an overcoat: but the first one I try is too long for me. I take it off again, rather surprised that it is trimmed with fur. A second that I put on has a long stripe with Turkish markings on it. A stranger with a long face and a short pointed beard comes up and prevents me from putting it on, declaring it is his. Then I show him that it is covered all over with Turkish embroidery. He asks: 'What are the Turkish (markings, stripes . . .) to you?' But then we are quite friendly with one another.*

In analysing this dream there comes quite unexpectedly to my mind the first novel I ever read, when I was perhaps thirteen years old, beginning it, that is, at the end of the first volume. I never knew the name of the novel, nor that of its author, but I can remember its conclusion very vividly: the hero declines into madness, and continually calls out the names of the three women who brought him the greatest happiness and the greatest misfortune in his life. One of these names is Pélagie.* I still don't know what I can do with this recollection in the analysis. Then the three women are joined in my thoughts by the three Fates who spin man's destiny, and I know that one of the three women, the landlady in the dream, is the mother who gives life, and sometimes, as in my case, the earliest nourishment. At the woman's breast love and hunger meet. An anecdote tells how a young man, who became a great admirer of female beauty, once said, when the conversation turned to the pretty nurse who had suckled him as an infant, that he regretted that he had not used the opportunity to greater advantage. It is my habit to use this anecdote to elucidate the element of retrospective action in the mechanism of the psychoneuroses.—One of the Fates is rubbing the palms of her hands together as though making *dumplings*: a strange occupation for a Fate and in urgent need of explanation! This comes now from another, and earlier, childhood memory. When I was six years old and enjoying my earliest instruction from my mother, I was supposed to believe that we are made of earth and must therefore return to earth. I did not like this idea, however, and expressed my doubts of it. At this my mother rubbed the palms of her hands together— just as though making dumplings, except that they held no dough— and showed me the blackish *epidermis* scales she had rubbed off as a sample of the earth of which we are made. My astonishment at this demonstration *ad oculos* was boundless, and I resigned myself to what I was later to hear expressed in the words: you owe Nature a death.*[12] So it really is the Fates I am visiting in the kitchen, then, as I did so often as a child when I was hungry, and from the stove my mother would tell me to wait until lunch was ready. And now for the dumplings! At least one of my university teachers, in fact the very one to whom I owe my *histological* knowledge (*epidermis*), will be reminded by the name Knödl of a person he was forced to sue because he had *plagiarized* his writings. To plagiarize, to appropriate what one can get even if it belongs to someone else, plainly leads to the second part of the dream, in which I am treated like the *overcoat thief* who was up to his thieving tricks for a time in the lecture halls. I have written the word *plagiarism* down without any particular purpose, just because it occurred to me, and now I see that it must belong to the latent dream-content because it is able to serve as a bridge between the various parts of the manifest dream-content.

---

[12] Both affects belonging to these childhood scenes, the astonishment and the acceptance of the inevitable, were to be found in a dream I had shortly beforehand, which first restored the memory of this childhood experience to me.

The chain of associations—*Pélagie*—*plagiarism*—*plagiastomes* [large fish, sharks][13]—*fish's bladder*—link the old novel with the Knödl affair and with the overcoats [*Überzieher*], which obviously signify a piece of sexual equipment (cf. *Maury's* dream of *Kilo*—*Lotto*, p. 51). An utterly forced and nonsensical connection, it is true, but all the same one that I could not have created when awake if it had not already been created by the dream-work. Indeed, as if nothing were sacred to my urge to create connections by force, the well-loved name of Brücke* [bridge] (word-bridges, see above) now serves to remind me of the institution where I passed my happiest hours as a schoolboy without any further needs ('So wird's Euch an der Weisheit *Brüsten* mit jedem Tage mehr gelüsten'* ['Suck on at Wisdom's *breasts*, you'll find| She daily grows more sweet and kind.']), in total contrast to the desires which *plague* me while I am dreaming. And finally, there arose the recollection of another dear teacher whose name, *Fleischl** [from *Fleisch*—flesh, meat], like Knödl, again sounded like something to eat, and of a sad scene in which *epidermis scales* played a role (the mother—landlady), and disturbance of mind (the novel), and a substance for reducing *hunger*, from the pharmacy, or 'Latin Kitchen' [Küche], cocaine.

I could pursue the intertwined trains of thought further in this way and explain fully the part of the dream which I have neglected in this analysis, but I must refrain from doing so, as the personal sacrifices it would demand are too great. I shall take up only one of the threads, which is able to lead directly to one of the dream-thoughts lying behind the tangle. The stranger with the long face and pointed beard who tries to prevent me from putting on the overcoat has the features of a merchant in Spalato* from whom my wife purchased a great quantity of *Turkish* cloth. He was called *Popović*, a suspicious name [Popo = bottom] which has also given the humorist *Stettenheim** the occasion for a suggestive remark. ('He told me his name and blushed as he shook my hand.') The same misuse of names, by the way, as with *Pélagie, Knödl, Brücke, Fleischl.* Of course, playing games with names in this way is a bad habit of children—so much I can say without contradiction; but if I am indulging in it myself, it is an act of retribution, for my own name has fallen victim countless

---

[13] The plagiastomes are not an arbitrary addition; they recall a vexatious occasion when I disgraced myself before the same teacher.

times to such idiotic joking [Freud(e) = joy]. *Goethe* once remarked
about how sensitive we are about our names, which we feel as closely
attached to as we do to our *skin*: the occasion for his remark was
Herder's play upon his name in the lines:

> 'Der Du von *Göttern* abstammst, von *Gothen* oder vom *Kothe*'—*
> ['Thou who art descended from Gods, from Goths or from dung'—]
> 'So seid ihr *Götterbilder* auch zu *Staub*.'*
> ['You godlike figures too have turned to dust.']

I note that this digression on the misuse of names was intended
only to prepare the way for my own complaint. But let us break off
here.—The purchase in Spalato reminds me of another one, in Cattaro,* when I was much too cautious and missed the opportunity of a
bargain. (See above: the missed opportunity with the nurse.) For one
of the dream-thoughts which hunger inspires in the dreamer is:
*Don't miss a thing, take what you can, even if it involves doing a little
wrong; don't let any opportunity slip by, life is so short, death inevitable.*
Since it is also meant sexually, and since desire will not stop at doing
wrong, this '*carpe diem*' has the censorship to fear, and has to hide
behind a dream. And then all the thoughts countering the desire
make their presence felt as well: recollection of the time when *spiritual nourishment* alone satisfied the dreamer, all the restraints and even
the threats of repellent sexual punishments.

II

A second dream requires a lengthier preamble:

I have arrived at the Westbahnhof to set off for my holiday at
Aussee, but I reach the platform while the train for Ischl,* due to
leave earlier, is still there. There I see Count *Thun** on the platform,
who for his part is bound for Ischl to see the Emperor. In spite of the
rain he arrived in an open carriage, getting out and going straight
through the entrance for local trains; when the ticket-collector, who
did not know him, made to take his ticket, he waved him away
without explanation with an abrupt gesture. After he has departed
on the train for Ischl, I am supposed to leave the platform again and
go back to the stifling waiting-room, but with some difficulty I succeed in being allowed to stay. I pass the time watching out for anyone
coming along and claiming the patronage of the great to get a compartment allocated to them: if that happens, I intend to kick up a

fuss, that is, demand equality of treatment. Meantime I am singing to myself something which I then recognize as an aria from *The Marriage of Figaro*:*

> Will der Herr Graf ein Tänzelein wagen, Tänzelein wagen,
> Soll er's nur sagen,
> Ich spiel ihm eins auf.
> [If milord Count should want to go dancing
> He'll pay the piper,
> I'll call the tune.]

(I doubt if anyone else would have recognized the melody.)

I had been in an exuberant, aggressive mood the whole evening, and had needled waiters and cab-drivers—without offending them, I hope; now all kinds of impudent and revolutionary thoughts are going through my mind, appropriate to Figaro's words and reminiscent of Beaumarchais's comedy, which I had seen at the Comédie Française. His remark about the great lords who took the trouble to be born; the *droit du seigneur* the Count tries to exercise on Susanna; the jokes which our wicked journalists from the opposition make on the name of Count Thun by calling him Count Nichtsthun [*Thun* = do, *Nichtsthun* = do-nothing]. Truly, I don't envy him; he is now on his way to a difficult visit to the Emperor, and *I* am really Count *Nichtsthun*: I am going on holiday. With all sorts of enjoyable plans for my holiday into the bargain. Along comes a gentleman who is familiar to me as the government representative at examinations for medical students, and whose performance in this role has earned him the flattering epithet of the 'Government Sleeping-partner'. On the strength of his official status he demands half a first-class compartment, and I hear one official say to another: 'Where shall we put the gentleman with the half first-class ticket?' A nice piece of preferential treatment: I pay my first-class fare in full. But then I do get a compartment to myself, though it is in a coach without a corridor, so that I will have no use of a lavatory the whole night long. I complain to the official, but to no avail, and I revenge myself by suggesting that he should have a hole made in the floor of the compartment in case travellers might have need of it. And at 2.45 in the morning I really do wake up from the following dream with the desire to urinate:

A crowd of people, a students' assembly.—*A count (Thun or*

Taaffe*) *is speaking. Called upon to say something about the Germans,
he declares derisively that their favourite flower is the coltsfoot* [Huflat-
tich], *and then sticks something resembling a torn leaf in his buttonhole,
actually the crumpled skeleton of a leaf. I flare up in indignation,*[14] *so I
flare up in indignation, but all the same I wonder at being in this state of
mind.* Then, less clearly: *it was as though it were the main hall* [Aula]
*of the university, the entrances crowded, and I would have to escape. I
force my way through a series of handsomely furnished rooms, obviously
rooms belonging to the administration, with furniture of a colour between
brown and mauve, and at length I arrive in a corridor where a housekeeper, a fat, elderly woman, is sitting. I avoid speaking to her; but she
clearly considers I have a right to get past, for she asks whether she should
accompany me with a lamp. I indicate, or tell her, that she should remain
on the stairs, and as I do so feel how cunning I am in finally eluding
inspection as I leave. In this way I get below and find a narrow, steeply
rising path, which I follow.*

Again unclear . . . *As if I now have the second task of getting out of
the city, just as earlier I got out of the house. I am riding in a hansom-cab
and tell him to drive to a railway station. 'I can't drive with you on the
railway line itself,' I say, after he raised an objection, as though I had
tired him out. At the same time it is as though I had already driven with
him on a stretch one usually travels by train. The stations are crowded; I
reflect whether I should go to Krems or Znaim,* but think that the Court
might be there and decide for Graz* or somewhere like that. Now I am
sitting in the carriage, which resembles a city tram, and I have in my
buttonhole a strangely entwined, long thing, with mauve-brown violets on
it made of a stiff material, which attracts a lot of attention.* Here the
scene breaks off.

*I am again in front of the railway station, but in the company of an
older man; I devise a plan for remaining unrecognized, but also see that
this plan has already been carried out. Thinking and experiencing are
here, as it were, one. He is pretending to be blind, at least in one eye, and I
am holding out a male urine-bottle to him (which we had to buy, or have
bought, in the city). I am his male nurse, then, and have to give him the
bottle because he is blind. If the ticket-collector sees us like this he is bound
to let us pass, as we are quite inconspicuous. At the same time the posture*

---

[14] This repetition slipped into my written account of the dream, presumably from
absent-mindedness. I retain it, as the analysis shows that it has its significance.

of the man in question and his urinating member can be seen very vividly. This is when I wake up with a desire to urinate.

The entire dream makes something of the impression of a fantasy transporting the dreamer to the revolutionary year of 1848. My memories of this had in fact been renewed by the anniversary celebration of 1898, as they had been by a little excursion to the *Wachau*.* Here I had got to know Emmersdorf,* the place where Fischhof,* the student leader, had retired, who might be indicated by certain features of the manifest dream-content. My train of thought then leads me to England, to the home of my brother, who had the habit of teasing his wife with 'Fifty years ago',* after the title of a poem by Lord *Tennyson*, which the children would always correct to '*fifteen* years ago'. But this fantasy, which is linked to the thoughts that had been called up by the sight of Count *Thun*, is only like the façade on Italian churches, placed in front of a building with no organic connection to it, being full of gaps, confused, and with components from the interior protruding in many places. The first situation in the dream is concocted from several scenes which I can separate out. The Count's arrogant posture in the dream is copied from a scene at the Gymnasium which occurred during my *fifteenth year*. We had formed a conspiracy against an unpopular and ignorant teacher. Its moving spirit was a fellow-student* who seems since then to have taken *Henry VIII of England* as his model. It fell to me to direct the principal assault, and a discussion of the importance to Austria of the Danube (*the Wachau!*) was the occasion when it came to open rebellion. One of our fellow-conspirators was the only aristocrat* in our year, called 'the *giraffe*' on account of his strikingly tall stature: summoned to explain himself by the school tyrant, the professor of *German*, he stood there before him like the Count in my dream. The declaration of the favourite flower and sticking in the buttonhole something that again must be a flower (which recall the orchids I had given a woman friend on the same day, and also a rose of *Jericho*), is strikingly reminiscent of the scene in *Shakespeare* which inaugurates the civil wars of the *white* and *red* roses;* the reference to Henry VIII paved the way to this recollection. Then, it was not far from the roses to the red and white carnations. (Between these the analysis interpolates two little verses, one *German*, the other *Spanish*: *Rosen, Tulpen, Nelken, alle Blumen welken.* [Roses, tulips, carnations, all flowers wither].—*Isabelita*, no llores que se marchitan las flores

[Little Isabel, do not weep because the flowers wither]. The Spanish comes from *Figaro*.) Here in Vienna the white carnation has become the emblem of the *anti-Semites*, the red that of the *Social Democrats*. Behind it a recollection of an anti-Semitic challenge during a railway journey through the beautiful land of Saxony (*Anglo-Saxon*s). The third scene contributing elements to the first dream situation comes from my earliest student days. In a *German* students' union there was a discussion of the relationship between philosophy and the natural sciences. Green youth that I was, full of materialist theories, I pushed myself forward to advocate an extremely one-sided point of view. A colleague,* my senior and my better, who has subsequently proved his ability to lead men and organize the masses, and, by the way, also has a name from the animal kingdom, then rose and gave us a sound drubbing; he too, he said, had in his youth tended swine and then returned repentant to his father's house. I *flared up in indignation* (as in the dream), became *swinishly* offensive [*saugrob*], and replied that now that I knew he had tended *swine, I was no longer surprised* at his manner of speech. (In the dream I am *surprised* at my nationalistic German state of mind.) Uproar followed; I was urged from many directions to retract my words, but I remained steadfast. The offended party was too sensible to accept the suggestion that he should offer a *challenge*, and let the matter rest.

The remaining elements of the dream-scene have their origin in deeper strata. What could the Count's proclamation of the 'coltsfoot' mean? Here I must ask my chain of associations: *Huflattich* [coltsfoot]—*lattice* [lettuce]—*Salat* [salad]—*Salathund* [the dog-in-a-manger who grudges others what he nevertheless does not eat himself]. Here one can see a stock of insults showing through these expressions: *Gir-affe* [ape], *Schwein, Sau, Hund*; by the roundabout way of a name I can also arrive at an *ass*, and thereby again at mockery of an academic teacher. In addition I translate—I do not know whether correctly or not—*Huflattich* as *pisse-en-lit*. I learned this from *Zola*'s *Germinal*,* in which the children are invited to bring salad leaves of this sort with them. Dog—*chien* contains in its name an echo of the greater bodily function (*chier*, as *pisser* was used for the lesser). Before long we will have all three kinds of indecency together, for in this same *Germinal*, which has plenty to do with the coming revolution, a singular contest is described relating to the production of gaseous excretions called *flatus*.[15] And now I am bound to see that the path to this 'flatus' has been laid down for a long time, from the '*flowers*' via the *Spanish* verse, *Isabelita* to *Isabella* and *Ferdinand*, via *Henry VIII*, the sailing of the Armada against England, after whose defeat the English had a commemorative medallion struck bearing the inscription '*Flavit* et dissipati sunt',* for the tempest had scattered the Spanish fleet. But I intended, only half in jest, to use this inscription as the title of the chapter 'Therapy', if ever I were to get round to writing a detailed account of my conception and treatment of hysteria.

As for the second scene, I am not able to analyse it in such detail—for reasons of censorship. For in this scene I am putting myself in the position of one of the great of that revolutionary period who also had an adventure with an *eagle* and is said to have suffered from *incontinentia alvi** and the like, and *I believe I would not be justified in getting past* the censorship here, even though a *Hofrat* [lit: Court Councillor, senior civil servant] (*Aula*, consilarius *aulicus*) told me the greater part of that story. The series of rooms [*Zimmer*] in the dream owe their inspiration to His Excellency's Pullman car, into which I was able to glance for a moment; as so often in dreams, however, they signified *women* [*Frauenzimmer*] (public women). In the figure of the housekeeper I am repaying a clever elderly lady most ungratefully for her hospitality and for the many enjoyable stories I have been told at her house.—The feature of the lamp goes back to *Grillparzer*,* who noted a charming experience of similar tenor and then used it in his play about *Hero* and *Leander* (Des *Meeres* und der Liebe *Wellen* [The *Waves* of the *Sea* and of Love]—the Armada and the *storm*).

I must also withhold a detailed analysis of the two remaining parts of the dream; I shall pick out only those elements leading to the two childhood scenes which are my reason for considering the dream at all. It will rightly be supposed that it is sexual material that obliges me to make this suppression: but one does not need to be entirely satisfied by this explanation. For there are many things which are no secret to ourselves but which we are nevertheless obliged to keep secret from others, and what is at issue here is not the reasons for concealing the solution to the dream, but the motives of inner

---

[15] Not in *Germinal* but in *La Terre*, an error I only noticed after the analysis. In addition, I would draw attention to the identical letters in *Hu*flat*tich* and Flat*us*.

censorship which hide the actual content of my own dream from myself. I have to say, therefore, that the analysis reveals these three parts of the dream to be impertinent boasting, the issue of a ludicrous megalomania long since suppressed in my waking life, which even ventures at particular points into the manifest dream-content (*I feel how cunning I am*), and in any event offers an excellent explanation of my exuberant mood on the evening before the dream. Boasting in every field: thus the reference to *Graz* alludes to the saying: '*What does Graz cost?*' which we are fond of repeating when we feel we have more than enough money. Anyone who recalls Master *Rabelais's** unsurpassed account of the life and deeds of *Gargantua* and his son *Pantagruel* will be able to include the implied content of the first part of the dream among the instances of boasting. What follows belongs to the two scenes of childhood I promised to relate: I had bought a *new* suitcase for this journey, whose colour, a *brownish-mauve*, appears several times in the dream (*mauve-brown* violets made of a stiff material beside a thing they call a 'girl-catcher'—the furniture in the administration's rooms). It is a well-known childhood belief that something *new* will *attract attention*. The following scene from my childhood was told me, and my memory of it has been replaced by the recollection of that account. Before the age of two I am supposed to have occasionally still *wet the bed*, and when I was rebuked for this, so I am told, I *consoled* my father with the promise that in N. (the nearest town of any size) I would buy him a lovely *new, red* bed. (Hence the parenthesis in the dream that *we bought* the bottle *in the city, or had to buy it*: what we have promised we *have* to perform.) (Notice, too, the combination of the male bottle and the female case, *box*.) The child's entire megalomania is contained in this promise. We have already been struck, in the course of an earlier dream-interpretation, by the significance for the dream of the problems children experience over urination (compare the dream on p. 154).

Then there was another domestic incident when I was seven or eight which I remember very well. One evening before going to bed I broke the rule that one must not relieve oneself in one's parents' bedroom in their presence, and in the course of rebuking me for this, my father let fall the remark: 'Nothing will come of the boy.' It must have been a terrible blow to my ambition, for allusions to this scene recur in my dreams again and again and are invariably connected with enumerations of my successes and achievements, as though I wanted to say: 'You see, something did come of me.' This childhood scene also provided the material for the last image in the dream, in which, of course, the roles were reversed in revenge. The older man, plainly my father, since the blindness in one eye signifies the glaucoma he suffered in one eye,[16] is now urinating in front of me as I once did in front of him. With the glaucoma I am reminding him of the cocaine which had been of help to him during his operation, as if thereby I had fulfilled my promise. Besides this, I am making fun of him: because he is blind, I have to hold the bottle out to him, and I am revelling in allusions to my knowledge of the theory of hysteria, which I am proud of.[17]

[16] Another interpretation: he has one eye, like *Odin*, father of the gods. *Odhin's Consolation**—The *consolation* I offer my father that I will buy him a new bed.

[17] Some of the material on which the interpretation is based: holding out the bottle [*Glas*] recalls the story of the peasant at the optician's who tries glass after glass but still cannot see.—Bauern*fänger* [peasant-catcher = con-man]—Mädchen*fänger* [girl-catcher] in the previous part of the dream.—The treatment of the weak-minded father by the peasants in Zola's *La Terre*.*—The unhappy satisfaction of seeing how in the last days of his life my father dirtied his bed like a child; hence in the dream I am his male nurse.— 'Thinking and experiencing are here, as it were, one' recalls a violently revolutionary literary drama by Oscar Panizza* in which God the Father is treated pretty shamefully as a paralysed old man; it says there: 'Will and deed with him are one,' and his archangel, a kind of Ganymede, has to restrain him from scolding and cursing, as these imprecations would instantly be fulfilled.—The *devising of plans* is a criticism of my father, originating from a later period, just as the entire rebellious content of the dream, full of *lèse-majesté* and mockery of the authorities as it is, goes back to rebellion against the father. The prince is called *Landesvater* [father of his country], and the father is the oldest, first, and sole authority for the child, from whose absolute power the other social authorities have proceeded in the course of the history of human culture (insofar as 'Matriarchy' does not impose limits on this proposition).—The version in the dream, 'Thinking and experiencing are one', points to the explanation of hysterical symptoms, to which the *male bottle* also related. A Viennese would not need me to explain the meaning of the principle of 'Gschnas': it consists in producing objects of a rare and valuable appearance out of trivial, preferably ludicrous and worthless material, e.g. arms and weapons out of cooking-pots, straw, and salt-sticks, as our artists do on their social evenings. Now, I had noticed that hysterics do the same; beside what has actually happened to them, they unconsciously create for themselves horrible or extravagant fantasy events which they construct from the most innocuous and banal material of their experience. It is on these fantasies, and not on the recollection of actual events, that their symptoms depend, and this is so, whether the symptoms are serious or equally innocuous. This explanation had helped me over many difficulties and given me much pleasure. I was able to use it to explain the dream-element of the '*male bottle*' because I had been told at the last 'Gschnas' evening that a poison chalice of Lucretia Borgia's had been put on display, which had as its centre-piece and main component a *urine bottle* for men of the sort customarily used in hospitals.

If the two urinating scenes from childhood are in any case closely linked in my history to the theme of megalomania, their arousal on the journey to Aussee is helped by the circumstance that my compartment had no WC, and I had to be prepared for an embarrassing situation in the course of the journey, which is just what did happen in the morning. I then woke with the sensations of a call of nature. One might be inclined to attribute the role of actual initiator of the dream to these sensations, but I would rather give precedence to a different idea: that it was the dream-thoughts which first called forth the desire to urinate. It is very unusual for me to be aroused from sleep by a need of any kind, least of all at the time I woke on this occasion, quarter to four in the morning. I would counter a further objection by saying that on other journeys under more comfortable conditions, I hardly ever felt a desire to urinate after waking too early. In any case, it will not matter if I leave this point undecided.

My experience in the analysis of dreams has, further, made me aware that even dreams whose interpretation at first seems complete because both the source of the dream and the initiator of the wish are easily demonstrable—even these dreams set vital trains of thought reaching out which go back to earliest childhood: and so I have had to ask myself whether this feature too does not constitute an essential condition of dreaming. If I might generalize this idea: in its manifest content, every dream would be characterized by a connection with what has been experienced recently; in its latent content, however, by a connection with the experiences from our earliest years—which, as I really can demonstrate from my analyses of hysteria, have remained in a strict sense still recent, right up to the present. However, this supposition still seems very difficult to prove; I shall have to return in another context to the probable part played by our earliest childhood experiences in the formation of dreams (Chapter VII).

Of the three peculiarities of the dream-memory we considered at the start, we have explained one satisfactorily—its preference for the trivial in the dream-content—by tracing it back to dream-distortion. We have been able to confirm the existence of the other two—the special choice made of recent and of infantile material—but we have not been able to account for them by the motives for dreaming. Let us keep these two characteristics in mind, for their explanation and utility remain to be dealt with: they are bound to find their place elsewhere, either in the psychology of sleep, or in those considerations of how the psychical apparatus is constructed, which we shall have to undertake later once we have noted that the interpretation of dreams enables us, like a window, to cast a glance into its interior.

However, I should like to emphasize one other result of these last dream-analyses before going on. The dream frequently appears *to have several meanings*; not only can several wish-fulfilments be united in it alongside one another, as we have seen; but one meaning, one wish-fulfilment can overlay another, until right at the bottom we come upon the fulfilment of a wish from earliest childhood; and here again we are bound to wonder whether in this sentence 'frequently' should not be replaced by 'invariably'.

(c) *The Somatic Sources of Dreams*

If we try to interest an educated layman in the problems of dreaming, and with this in mind ask him what sources he thinks dreams might flow from, we usually find that he believes he is quite sure of this part of their solution. He recalls at once the influence on the formation of dreams exercised by a disturbed or overburdened digestion ('dreams come from the stomach'), or by the position the body happens to take, or by little eventualities while we are asleep, and he seems quite unaware that after all these motives have been taken into consideration there still might be something left that needs explaining.

What part the scientific literature has assigned to somatic sources of stimulus in the formation of dreams has already been discussed in detail in the opening chapter (pp. 30–5), so all we need do here is recall the results of this review. We heard that three kinds of somatic stimulus-source are to be distinguished: objective sensory stimuli proceeding from external objects; purely subjective excitations of the sensory organs; and physical stimuli originating from within the body. And we noted that, in contrast to somatic sources, the authorities tended to push any possible psychical sources of dreams into the background, or even exclude them entirely (p. 36). In testing the claims made in favour of these groups as somatic sources of stimulus we learned that the significance of objective excitations of the sense-organs—partly chance stimuli during sleep, partly those which the psyche is unable to ward off even in sleep—is confirmed by numerous observations and corroborated by experiment (pp. 23–4). We found that the role of subjective sensory excitations appears to have been proved by the recurrence of hypnagogic sensory images in dreams (p. 28). And we learned that—although it cannot be demonstrated that the entire range of images and ideas occurring in our dreams is traceable to internal physical stimuli—this widely assumed derivation can be supported by the influence patently exerted on the content of our dreams by the excitations of the digestive, urinary, and sexual organs.

'*Nervous stimulus*' and '*physical stimulus*' then, it is claimed, are the somatic sources of dreams, that is, according to several authorities, the only sources there are.

On the other hand, we have also paid heed to a number of doubts which seem to attack not so much the correctness as the adequacy of the somatic stimulus theory.

However certain all its advocates must have felt about its factual basis—especially with regard to accidental and external nervous stimuli, which can be recognized in the dream-content with no trouble whatever—still, not one of them was unaware of the likelihood that the sheer abundance of ideas contained in dreams might not be derived from external nervous stimuli alone. Miss Mary Whiton Calkins [12] examined her own dreams and those of a second person from this point of view over six weeks, and found only 13.2 per cent and 6.7 per cent respectively in which the element of external sense-perception could be demonstrated; only two instances in her collection could be traced back to organic sensations. On this point, statistics confirm what a superficial survey of our own experiences had led us to expect.

Many have settled for giving prominence to the 'nervous-stimulus dream' over other forms of dream, as being a well-researched sub-species. Spitta [64] divided dreams into those aroused by *nervous-stimulus* and those by *association*. However, it was clear that this solution could not be considered satisfactory as long as it failed to demonstrate the bond linking the somatic dream-sources to the ideas contained in the dream.

Accordingly, as well as the first objection—the insufficient frequency of external stimuli—there is now a second, the inadequate elucidation of the dream that is reached by introducing this kind of dream-source to explain it. The advocates of this theory owe us two explanations in this respect: first, why we do not recognize the external stimulus as we dream for what it is, but invariably misunderstand it (compare the alarm-clock dreams, p. 25); and second, why the reaction of the perceiving psyche to this misunderstood stimulus can vary so unpredictably in its outcome. By way of answer to this question we have heard from Strümpell [66] that, as a consequence of its withdrawal from the external world in sleep, the psyche is not in a position to offer the correct interpretation of the objective sensory stimulus, but is obliged to create illusions on the basis of this stimulus with its range of indeterminate potentialities. As he puts it himself (p. 108):

'As soon as an external or internal nervous stimulus produces in the psyche a sensation or a complex of sensations, a feeling, a psychical event of any kind, and as soon as this is perceived by the psyche, this event summons up sensory images left there from the sphere of its waking experience, from earlier perceptions, that is, either naked or clad in the appropriate psychical values. It gathers around itself, as it were, a larger or smaller number of such images, which are the means by which the impression deriving from the nervous stimulus acquires its psychical value. Here too we usually say, as we do of waking behaviour, that when asleep the psyche *interprets* the impressions produced by the nervous stimuli. The outcome of this interpretation is what we call the *nervous-stimulus dream*, that is, a dream whose constituents are determined by a nervous stimulus producing its effects in the life of the psyche in accordance with the laws of reproduction.'

Wundt's [76] view is identical in all essentials to this theory; he maintains that the ideas appearing in dreams proceed in the main at least from sensory stimuli, including especially stimuli of our general vital feeling. So they are mainly illusions of the fantasy, and probably only to a minor extent pure remembered ideas intensified into hallucinations. To express the relation between the dream-content and the dream-stimuli according to this theory, Strümpell hits on the excellent comparison (p. 14): it is 'as though the ten fingers of a player wholly ignorant of music are running up and down the keyboard'. In this view the dream would appear to be not a psychical phenomenon arising from psychical motivations but the consequence of a physiological stimulus expressing itself in psychical symptoms, because the apparatus affected by the stimulus is incapable of any other form of expression. A similar assumption lies, for example, behind the explanation of obsessional ideas which Meynert put forward in his famous comparison with a dial on which certain numbers stand out more strongly than others.

However popular this theory of somatic dream-stimuli has become, and however attractive it may appear, it is nevertheless easy to point out its weak point. Every somatic dream-stimulus that requires the sleeping psychical apparatus to interpret it by constructing an illusion can arouse countless such attempts at interpretation, that is, can get itself represented in the dream-content in a tremendous variety of different ideas. However, the theory put forward by Strümpell and Wundt is unable to suggest any motive which would govern the relation between the external stimulus and the dream-idea selected for its interpretation, that is, which would explain the 'strange selection' that the stimuli 'make often enough in their reproductive activity' (Lipps, *Grundthatsachen des Seelenlebens*, p. 170). Other objections can be raised against the assumption at the basis of the entire theory of illusion, which holds that the sleeping psyche is not capable of recognizing the real nature of objective sensory stimuli. The physiologist Burdach [8] showed us long ago that even in sleep the psyche is perfectly capable of interpreting correctly the sense-impressions reaching it, capable too of reacting in accordance with the correct interpretation, for he argues that we are able to exclude sense-impressions that seem important to us (nurse and child) from the oblivion into which we fall when asleep, and that we are much more certain to be wakened by our own name than by some indifferent impression on the ear—which of course presupposes that even in sleep the psyche distinguishes between sensations (Section I, p. 36). Burdach concludes from these observations that what should be assumed is not our inability to interpret sensory stimuli while asleep, but *our lack of interest in them*. The same arguments as Burdach was using in 1830 recur unaltered in 1883 in Lipps's criticism of the theory of somatic stimulus. According to this, the psyche appears to be like the sleeper in the anecdote: when asked 'Are you asleep?', he replies 'No', but in response to the request that follows, 'Then lend me ten guilders', takes refuge behind the excuse 'I'm asleep'.

The inadequacy of the theory of somatic dream-stimuli can also be demonstrated in other ways. Observation shows that I am not compelled by the external stimuli to dream, even though these promptly appear in the dream-content in the event of my dreaming. I can react in a number of ways to a stimulus that comes over me in sleep, to the skin, say, or to one caused by pressure. I can simply not notice it, and then discover on waking up that, for instance, a leg has been uncovered or an arm squashed; indeed, pathology shows me countless examples of the most various and violent stimuli from sensations or movements during sleep which have failed to produce any effect at all. I may feel a sensation during sleep—penetrating my sleep, as it were—which is usually the case with painful stimuli, but without weaving the pain into a dream; and I may, thirdly, wake in response to the stimulus in order to remove it. It is only as a fourth possible reaction that the nervous stimulus might cause me to dream; but the other possibilities will be realized at least as often as that of forming a dream. This could not happen if the *motivation for dreaming did not lie outside the somatic sources of stimulus.*

A fair assessment of these gaps in the explanation that dreams are due to somatic stimuli has been made by other writers—Scherner [58], joined by the philosopher Volkelt [72]; they have attempted to determine more precisely the psychical activities which create such varied and colourful dream-images out of the somatic stimuli, that is, they have moved dreaming essentially back into the inner realm again, and into an activity of the psyche. Scherner not only gave a vivid and imaginative poetic description of the psychical characteristics revealed in the formation of dreams, he also believed he had divined the principle governing the psyche's treatment of the stimuli presented to it. According to Scherner, as the dream-work bestirs the imagination, soaring freely and unburdened by the fetters of the day, it strives to represent *in symbolic form* the nature of the organ that gives rise to the stimulus and the kind of stimulus it may be. In this way a sort of dream-book develops containing instructions for the interpretation of dreams and enabling us to make inferences from the dream-images about our bodily feelings, the condition of our organs, and the nature of the stimuli. 'Thus the image of a cat will express a mood of ill-humour, the image of a smooth, shining loaf of bread, bodily nudity. The human body as a whole is represented by the dream-imagination as a house, the separate bodily organs as parts of the house. In "toothache dreams" a high-vaulted entrance-hallway corresponds to the mouth, and a flight of stairs to the descent from the throat to the gullet; in "headache dreams" the ceiling of a room covered with disgusting toad-like spiders is chosen to designate the top of the head' (Volkelt, p. 39). 'A wide selection of these symbols is used by the dream to represent the same organ; thus the breathing lung finds its symbol in a blazing, roaring stove, the heart in empty chests and baskets, the bladder in round, bag-shaped, or generally hollowed-out objects. It is especially important that at the conclusion of the dream the organ producing the stimulus, or its function, is often presented undisguised, in fact, mainly as it affects the dreamer's own body. Thus the "toothache dream" usually ends with the dreamer's drawing a tooth out of his mouth' (p. 35). This theory of dream-interpretation cannot be said to have found much favour with the authorities on the subject. More than anything, it seemed so far-fetched; and there has even been some reluctance to recognize the morsel of justification which in my judgement it can claim. As we see, it leads to a revival of dream-interpretation by means of *symbolism* such as the ancients employed, except that the sphere from which the interpretation is drawn is limited to the extent of the human body. The applicability of Scherner's theory is bound to be seriously restricted by the absence of a scientifically comprehensible technique of interpretation. Arbitrariness in the dream-interpretation is certainly not to be discounted, especially as here too a stimulus can express itself in the dream-content in several forms of representation; thus, even Scherner's follower Volkelt was unable to confirm the representation of the body as a house. It is bound to cause offence, too, that here again the psyche has the dream-work foisted on it as a useless and purposeless activity, for according to this theory the psyche is content to generate fantasies about the stimulus engaging it without even the remotest prospect of removing it.

But there is one objection which deals a heavy blow to Scherner's theory of the dream's symbolization of physical stimuli. These physical stimuli are present at all times, and it is generally assumed that the psyche is more accessible to them during sleep than when we are awake. So it is difficult to understand why the psyche does not dream continually the whole night through, indeed, why it does not dream every night about all the organs. If this objection is met by stipulating that to arouse dream-activity special excitations would have to proceed from the eye, ear, teeth, gut, etc., then there is still the difficulty of demonstrating that these intensifications in the stimuli are objective—which is possible only in a small number of cases. If the dream of flying symbolizes the rise and fall of the lungs while breathing, then, as Strümpell already observed, either this dream would have to be dreamed much more frequently, or one ought to be able to demonstrate an increase in breathing activity during the dream. Yet a third case is possible, the most probable of all, that is, that special motives may be intermittently operative to draw attention to visceral sensations uniformly present—but this case already takes us beyond Scherner's theory.

The value of Scherner's and Volkelt's views lies in the fact that they draw our attention to a number of characteristics of the dream-content which need explanation and seem to obscure further insight. It is quite correct that dreams contain symbolizations of bodily organs and functions, that in dreams water often indicates a stimulus from the bladder, that the male member can be represented by an upright staff or a column, and so forth. One can hardly reject the interpretation of dreams displaying a very mobile field of vision and brilliant colours as 'visual-stimulus dreams', in contrast to the pallid colouring of others, nor dispute the contribution of illusion-formation in dreams containing noise and a babble of voices. A dream such as Scherner's, in which two rows of fine fair-haired boys stand facing one another on a bridge, attack one another, and then take up their former positions again, until finally the dreamer sits down on a bridge and draws a long tooth from his jaw; or a similar dream of Volkelt's, which involves two rows of cupboard-drawers and which again ends with pulling out a tooth: dream-images of this kind, described in great detail by both writers, will not allow us to cast Scherner's theory aside as idle invention without first investigating the core of truth it contains. Our task will then be to produce an alternative explanation for the supposed symbolization of the alleged toothache.

All the time we have been engaged with the theory of somatic dream-sources I have refrained from advancing any argument based on our dream-analyses. If we have been able to show, by a procedure which other authorities have not applied to their material on dreams, that the dream possesses a value of its own as a psychical act, that a wish is the motive for its formation, and that the experiences of the previous day provide the immediate material for its content, then every other dream-theory that neglects such an important investigative procedure, and consequently makes the dream seem a useless and puzzling psychical reaction to somatic stimuli, stands condemned even without any specific criticism. Otherwise—most improbably—there would have to be two quite different kinds of dream, of which we have encountered only one, and the earlier judges of the dream only the other. All that remains for us to do now is to find a place within our own theory of dreams for the facts on which the current theory of somatic dream-stimuli is based.

We have already taken the first step in this direction by putting forward the proposition that the dream-work is under the compulsion to process into a unity all the initiators to dreaming that are present at the same time (p. 137). We saw that when two or more experiences capable of producing an impression are left from the previous day, the wishes arising from them are united in a dream; we also saw that the psychically valuable impression and the trivial experience come together to form the material of the dream, provided that ideas mediating between the two can be generated. Hence the dream appears as a reaction to everything that is simultaneously present and currently active in the sleeping psyche. As far as we have analysed the dream-material up to now, we have recognized it as being a collection of psychical remnants, memory-traces, to which (on account of the preference for recent and childhood material) we had to ascribe a psychologically—as yet—indeterminable characteristic of current activity. It will not be very difficult for us now to predict what will happen if these active memories are joined during sleep by new material from the senses. These excitations in turn become important for the dream because they are current and active; they are combined with the other factors currently active in the psyche to provide material for forming the dream. In other words, the stimuli occurring during sleep are processed into a wish-fulfilment whose other constituents are the familiar psychical remains of the day. This combination does not *have* to take place; indeed, we have heard that more than one kind of response is possible towards bodily stimuli in our behaviour when asleep. Where it does take place is in those dreams where it has been possible to find representational material for the dream-content able to express both kinds of dream-source, the somatic and the psychical.

The essential nature of the dream is not changed if the psychical sources of the dream are supplemented by somatic material: it remains a wish-fulfilment, no matter how its expression is deter-mined by the current material.

At this point I should like to make room for a number of distinct-ive factors which can shape the importance of external stimuli for the dream in variously shifting ways. I imagine that a combination of individual, psychological, and fortuitous elements working together in any given circumstances will decide how we behave in particular instances of more intense objective stimulation during sleep; the habitual or accidental depth of our sleep, combined with the inten-sity of the stimulus, will in one instance make it possible to suppress the stimulus in such a way that it does not disturb our sleep, in another force us to wake up, or support our efforts to overcome the stimulus by weaving it into a dream. In accordance with the diversity of these constellations, external objective stimuli will find expression more frequently or more rarely in one person's dreams than in another's. In my own case, as I am an excellent sleeper and stub-bornly resist any attempt to disturb me while I am asleep, external causes of excitation very rarely intrude into my dreams, whereas psychical motives evidently cause me to dream very easily. In fact I have recorded only one single dream in which an objective, painful source of stimulus can be recognized, and this dream in par-ticular will be most instructive for us to see what effect the external stimulus had in shaping it.

I am riding a grey horse, at first timidly and clumsily, as though I were only holding on. Then I encounter a colleague, P., who is sitting high in the saddle, dressed in a suit of loden cloth, and warning me of something (probably that I have a bad seat). Now I gradually find that I am sitting more and more easily and comfortably on my highly intelligent horse, and I note that I feel quite at home up here. For a saddle I have a kind of cushion which completely fills the space between the horse's neck and crupper. Thus saddled, I ride through the narrow space between two heavy waggons. After I have ridden some distance down the road, I turn round and make to dismount, at first before a little chapel with open door, built as part of the street frontage; but then I really dismount in front of one very near it; my hotel is in the same street; I could let the horse go on there alone, but I prefer to lead it there myself. It is as if I were ashamed to arrive at the hotel on horseback. A hotel-boy is standing in front of it. He shows me a note of mine which has been found, and laughs at me over it. On the note, underlined twice, is written: 'Nothing to eat', and then a second instruction (unclear) *something like: 'No work'; in addition a vague idea that I am in a strange town, where I am not doing any work.*

At first one cannot tell from the dream that it arose under the influence, or rather under the compulsion, of a painful stimulus. But the day before I had been suffering from boils that made every movement a torment, and finally a boil at the base of the scrotum had grown as big as an apple, causing me the most unbearable pain with every step. Feverish fatigue, lack of appetite, carrying on in spite of it all with the day's hard work, all combined with the pain to distress me. I was not really capable of pursuing my duties as a physician, but the nature and location of the trouble raised the thought of a different activity—the one for which I would certainly have been more unfit than for any other, and that is *riding*. Now this is the very activity my dream sets me doing; it is the most energetic denial of my complaint that can be imagined. I cannot ride in any case; apart from this once, it never enters my dreams; I have only ever sat on a horse once, and then it was without a saddle, and I did not enjoy it. But in this dream I am riding as if I had no boil on the perineum, *no, I am riding for the very reason that I do not want to have one.* To judge from its description, my saddle is the poultice which made it possible for me to sleep. Protected by it, I probably felt nothing of my pain in the early hours of sleep. Then the painful sensations made themselves felt and tried to wake me up, whereupon the dream came and said soothingly: 'Sleep on still, you won't wake up anyway! You haven't got a boil, look, you're riding a horse after all, and you can't ride if you've got a boil.' And the dream succeeded. The pain was numbed and I slept on.

But the dream was not content with 'suggesting away' the boil by obstinately clinging to an idea incompatible with my complaint—in this respect behaving like the hallucinatory delusions of the mother who has lost her child[18] or the merchant whose losses have destroyed his fortune. In addition, the details of the sensation denied in the dream and the image used to repress it also serve the dream as material to link other material currently active in the psyche to the dream-situation, and to find a way of representing it. I am riding a *grey* horse; the colour of the horse matches exactly the *pepper-and-*

[18] Compare the passage in *Griesinger* [31] and the observation in my second paper on the psychoneuroses of defence, *Neurologisches Zentralblatt*, 1896 [in fact in his first paper, SE iii. 43].

salt-coloured suit my colleague P. was wearing when last I encountered him in the country. *Highly spiced food* has been suggested to me as the cause of my boils, in any case preferable as an aetiology to *sugar*, which one might think of in connection with boils. My friend P. is fond of *getting on his high horse* with me ever since he took over a woman patient of mine with whom I had performed great *feats* [*Kunststücke*] (in my dream I am sitting on the horse crosswise at first, like a *circus-rider* [*Kunstreiter*]), but who really led me, like the horse in the anecdote leading the Sunday rider,* whither she would. So symbolically the horse comes to signify a patient (in my dream it is *highly intelligent*); '*I feel quite at home up there*' goes back to the position I occupied in her house before I was replaced by P. '*I thought you were firmly in the saddle there*' was a remark made to me recently about my connections with the same house by one of my few well-wishers among the great physicians of this city. It was also a great *feat* to practise psychotherapy for eight to ten hours a day in such pain, but I know that unless I am physically well, I cannot carry on my particularly difficult work for long, and the dream is full of dark allusions to the situation that is bound to arise (the note, of the sort neurotics keep and show their physician): '*Nothing to eat and no work*'. Interpreting further, I see that the dream-work has contrived to find the route from the wish-fulfilling situation of riding to very early scenes of childhood quarrels which must have taken place between myself and a nephew, only a year older than I by the way, who now lives in England. In addition, it has taken up elements from my travels in Italy; the street in my dream is made up of impressions from Verona and Siena. Interpretation going still deeper leads to sexual dream-thoughts, and I recall what dream-allusions to this beautiful country were thought to mean in a woman patient of mine who had never been in Italy (*gen Italien — Genitalien* [to Italy — genitals]); at the same time this has some connection with the house where I preceded my friend P. as physician, and with the place where my boil was located.

Among the dreams mentioned in earlier sections there were already several which could serve as examples of processing nervous stimuli, as they are called. The dream of drinking water in great draughts is one of these; in this case the somatic stimulus is apparently the sole source of the dream, and the wish deriving from the sensation — thirst — its only motive. It is similar in other simple dreams, if the somatic stimulus by itself is capable of creating a wish. The dream of the invalid who cast the cooling appliance off her cheek at night shows an unusual way of reacting to painful stimuli with a wish-fulfilment. It seems that the invalid had temporarily contrived to numb her own sensations, and in doing so she foisted her pain onto someone else.

My dream of the three Fates is obviously a hunger-dream, but it contrives to push the need for nourishment back to the infant's longing for the mother's breast, and to use this harmless desire as a screen for a more serious one which may not express itself so openly. The dream about Count *Thun* showed us the paths by which a fortuitous physical need can be linked with the most powerful—but also with the most powerfully suppressed—emotions of the inner life. And when, as in the case reported by Garnier, the First Consul weaves the noise of an exploding infernal machine into a dream of battle before it wakes him, this reveals very clearly the nature of the only aim served at all by the psyche's activity as it engages with sensations during sleep.

Let us compare this dream by Napoleon I, who was, by the way, an excellent sleeper, with the dream of the lie-abed student woken by his landlady to get to the hospital, who dreamed he was in a hospital bed and then slept on with the motivation: 'If I am already at the hospital, I don't need to get up in order to go there.' The latter is an obvious dream of convenience. The speaker frankly admits his motive for dreaming, but in doing so, he reveals one of the secret motivations for dreaming at all. In a certain sense all dreams are *dreams of convenience*: they serve the purpose of continuing sleep instead of waking up. *The dream is the guardian of sleep, not its disturber.* We shall produce the arguments to justify this view at a later point, contrasting it with those psychical factors which wake us from sleep; at this stage we are already able to establish that it is applicable to the part played by objective external stimuli. Either the psyche does not concern itself at all with the causes of sensations during sleep, if it is able to do this despite the intensity of the stimuli and despite understanding very well what they signal; or it uses the dream to deny these stimuli; or, thirdly, if it *has* to acknowledge them, it seeks out that interpretation which presents the currently active sensation as a constituent of a situation which is both wished-for and compatible with sleeping. The actual sensation is woven into a dream *in order to* *rob it of reality.* Napoleon may go on sleeping: for all that is trying to disturb him is a dream-recollection of the rumble of cannon at Arcole.*[19]

Thus the wish to sleep must always be included among the motives for the formation of dreams, and every successful dream is a fulfilment of this wish. How this universal, invariably present, and constant wish to sleep relates to the other wishes fulfilled in their turn by the dream-content, will be the subject of another discussion. However, in the wish to sleep we have uncovered the factor that is able to fill the gap in the Strümpell–Wundt theory and explain the oddity and capriciousness of the way the dream interprets the external stimulus. The correct interpretation—which the sleeping psyche is perfectly capable of making—would make claims on our active interest and demand an end to sleep; so out of all the interpretations possible only those are admitted which are compatible with the absolute censorship exercised by the wish to sleep. As who should say: it is the nightingale* and not the lark. For if it is the lark, our night of love is at an end. From among the interpretations now admissible, the one then selected will be the interpretation that is able to make the best link with the wishful impulses lurking in the psyche. Thus everything is unambiguously determined, and nothing left to arbitrary choice. The misinterpretation is not illusion but—if you like—evasion. But again, as in the case of substitution by displacement at the behest of the dream-censorship, we have to concede that here too is an act which puts the normal psychical process out of joint.

If the external nervous and internal somatic stimuli are sufficiently intense to compel the attention of the psyche, then—always provided that they result in dreaming and not in waking up—they represent a firm point for the formation of the dream, a nucleus in the dream-material, for which a corresponding wish-fulfilment can be sought much as mediating ideas (see above) are sought between two psychical dream-stimuli. It is in so far true of a number of dreams that in them the somatic element is in command of the dream-content. In this extreme case, in order to create the dream even a wish that is not actively present will be roused. However, all the dream can do is represent a situation in which a wish appears as fulfilled; it is, as it were, faced with the task of seeking out the wish

[19] The two sources from which I learned of this dream do not agree in their accounts.

that can be represented as fulfilled by the sensation actively present. Even if this active material is painful or distressing in character, that does not make it useless for forming a dream. The life of the psyche also has at its disposal wishes whose fulfilment arouses unpleasure— which seems a contradiction, but can be explained if we take into account the presence of the two psychical agencies and the censor-ship prevailing between them.

As we have heard, there are in the life of the psyche *repressed* wishes belonging to the first system whose fulfilment the second system resists. When I say 'there are', I do not mean it historically, as if to say that these wishes once existed and have been abolished; on the contrary, the theory of repression, which the study of the psy-choneuroses requires, maintains that such repressed wishes still con-tinue in existence, but at the same time so does the burden of an inhibition. Language has hit upon the right term when it speaks of the 'suppression' of such impulses. The psychical organization enabling these wishes to break through to their realization remains intact and in working order. But if it happens that such a suppressed wish is in fact realized, then the inhibition set up by the second system (which is capable of consciousness) and now overcome, expresses itself as unpleasure. To conclude this discussion: when unpleasurable sensations from somatic sources are present in sleep, this constellation is utilized by the dream-work, maintaining the censorship to a greater or lesser degree, to represent the fulfilment of an otherwise repressed wish.

One set of anxiety-dreams is made possible by this state of affairs, while another set of these dream-formations unfavourable to the wish-theory displays a different mechanism. For anxiety in dreams can be psychoneurotic, originating in psychosexual excitations, and in their case the anxiety corresponds to repressed libido. In such instances, this anxiety has the significance of a neurotic symptom, as the entire anxiety-dream does, and we are standing on the border where the dream's wish-fulfilling intention breaks down. But there are other anxiety-dreams where the feeling of anxiety has a somatic origin (for instance, with breathing difficulties experienced by invalids with lung or heart trouble), and then it is exploited to assist energetically suppressed wishes towards their fulfilment in a dream, though their dream, had it arisen from psychical motivations, would have resulted in the same release of anxiety. It is not difficult to reconcile the two apparently disparate cases. If either of two factors belonging intimately together in the psyche—an inclination towards an affect together with a representational content—is currently active and given, it will evoke the other, even in a dream; in the one instance the somatically given anxiety will call up the suppressed ideas contained in the psyche; in the other, these ideas, freed from repression and accompanied by sexual excitation, will call up the release of anxiety. We can say of the one case that a somatically given affect receives a psychical interpretation; in the other, though everything is psychically given, the content, which had been suppressed, is easily replaced by a somatic interpretation appropriate to the anxiety. The difficulties our understanding has with this have little to do with dreams: they arise because with this discussion we are touching on the problems of how anxiety develops, and of repression.

The stimuli from within our body which command our dreams undoubtedly include our general physical feeling. Not that it is able to provide the content of the dream, but it does compel the dream-thoughts to select from the material which is to act as representation in the dream-content, as it brings one part of this material close to mind as appropriate and keeps another distant. Moreover, it is very likely that this general feeling from the life of the day is linked to the psychical residue important for the dream.

When the somatic sources of stimulus during sleep—that is to say, the sensations felt in sleep—are not unusually intense, their part in the formation of dreams is similar, in my view, to that played by the recent but trivial impressions of the day. I think that they are brought into play in the formation of a dream only when they are suitable for combination with the ideas contained in the psychical source of the dream, but otherwise not. They are treated like a cheap material always available and put to use whenever needed, rather than a precious material itself prescribing how it should be used. The case is rather as if a patron brought an artist a rare stone, an onyx, for him to make into a work of art. The size of the stone, its colouring and flaws, will help to decide what head or scene is to be represented in it, whereas in the case of uniform and abundant material such as marble or sandstone the artist only follows the idea which has formed in his mind. It is only in this way, it seems to me, that we can understand why the content of our dreams provided by bodily stimuli of ordinary intensity nevertheless does not appear in every dream, nor every night.

Perhaps I can best explain my view by an example which will also take us back to dream-interpretation. One day I was struggling to understand the significance of the sensation we sometimes have of inhibited movement, of being unable to stir, unable to have done with something, and the like, which appears so often in dreams, and which is so similar to the feeling of anxiety. That night I had the following dream: *I am going, very incompletely dressed, from an apartment on the ground floor up a flight of stairs to a floor higher up. As I go I jump three steps at a time, pleased that I can climb stairs so nimbly. Suddenly I see a maidservant coming down the steps, that is, towards me. I feel embarrassed, try to hurry, and then that sensation of inhibition appears. I am stuck to the steps and cannot move.*

Analysis: The situation in the dream is taken from everyday reality. I have two flats in an apartment-building in Vienna which are connected only by the main flight of stairs outside them. My consulting-room and study are on the upper ground floor, the living rooms on the floor above. When I have finished my work in the lower apartment late in the evening, I go up the flight of stairs to my bedroom. On the evening before the dream I had in fact gone this short distance in rather dishevelled dress, that is, I had taken off my collar, tie and cuffs; in the dream this had become a greater degree, as usual vague, of undress. Jumping the steps is my customary way of going upstairs, though here it was a wish-fulfilment as well, already recognized as such in the dream, for my ease in performing this feat reassured me as to the condition of my heart. Moreover, this way of going upstairs is the effective opposite to the inhibition in the second half of the dream. It shows me what needs no proof: that the dream has no difficulty in imagining motor actions being performed to perfection: think, for instance, of flying in dreams!

However, the flight of stairs I am going up is not that of my own house; at first I do not recognize it and only the person coming towards me enlightens me as to the place intended. This person is the maidservant of the old lady I visit twice a day to give her injections; the flight of stairs is also quite similar to those I have to climb there twice a day.

How have these stairs and this woman got into my dream? The embarrassment at not being fully dressed is undoubtedly sexual in character; the maidservant I dreamed about is older than I, surly and not at all attractive. The only answer I can think of to these questions is the following: whenever I make my morning visit to this house, I usually have to clear my throat; the product of my expectoration lands on one of the steps. For there is no spittoon on either of these two floors, and I take the view that keeping the stairs clean ought not to be at my expense, but aided by the provision of a spittoon. The housekeeper, likewise an elderly and surly person, but, I willingly grant, with an instinct for cleanliness, takes a different point of view from mine over this matter. She lies in wait for me to see if I will again permit myself this liberty, and when she has established that I have, I hear her grumbling audibly. Then for days she will deny me the usual marks of respect when we encounter each other. On the day before my dream, the housekeeper acquired an ally in the maid. I had completed my visit to the invalid, hurriedly, as always, when the maidservant stopped me in the hallway and uttered the pronouncement: 'Doctor, you might have wiped your boots today before you came into the room. Your feet have made the red carpet all dirty again.' This is the entire claim the flight of stairs and the maid-servant can make for appearing in my dream.

Between my flying over the stairs and spitting on the steps there is a close connection. Throat catarrh and heart trouble are both supposed to represent a punishment for the vice of smoking, which of course has given me as low a reputation for cleanliness with the lady in charge of domestic affairs in my own house as in the other; the dream had fused both into a single structure.

I must postpone further interpretation of this dream until I can explain the origin of the typical dream of being incompletely clothed. As a provisional conclusion to be drawn from the dream, I shall say only that the dream-sensation of inhibited movement is always called up wherever a certain context requires it. The cause of this dream-content cannot have been any particularly immobile condition of mine while asleep, for not a moment before I had seen myself leaping light of foot up steps as though to reassure myself on this question.

(d) *Typical Dreams*

In general we are unable to interpret someone else's dream if the person concerned is unwilling to yield us the unconscious thoughts behind its content—which is a serious restriction on the practical utility of our method of interpreting dreams. But, quite in contrast to the individual's usual freedom to trick out his dream-world in his own peculiar way and so make it inaccessible to others, there are a certain number of dreams which almost everyone has dreamed in the same way, and which we usually assume have the same meaning for everyone too. These typical dreams are also particularly interesting because they presumably derive from the same sources in all dreamers and so they seem particularly well suited to provide us with information about the sources of dreams.

In dealing with these typical dreams, I find I am hampered by the chance circumstance that I have not had access to enough of them in my own experience. So I shall do no more than give a fuller assessment of some model examples in this category, and to do this I shall select what we call the embarrassment-dream of being naked, and the dream of the death of relatives dear to us.

Dreams of being naked or ill-clad in the presence of strangers also occur with the added feature of not being ashamed of this, and the like. But we are interested in dreams of nakedness only when the dreamer feels shame or embarrassment in this kind of dream, wants to run away or hide, and then is subject to the peculiar inhibition of being unable to move from the spot and feeling incapable of doing anything to alter the embarrassing situation. It is only in this combination that the dream is typical; in other respects its content may be involved at its core in all sorts of other connections and shot through with additional elements personal to the individual. What is essential is the embarrassing sensation of shame, of wanting to hide one's nakedness, usually by mobility, and of being unable to do so. I believe that most of my readers at some time will have found themselves in this situation in their dreams.

Usually the nature and kind of undress is not very distinct. We hear it said, for instance, 'I was in my shirt', but this is rarely a clear image. Mostly the unclad state is so indefinite that when it is related an alternative is given: 'I was in my shirt or underwear.' As a rule the deficiency in dress is not so bad that the shame associated with it would seem justified. For someone who has worn the Emperor's uniform, nakedness is often replaced by incorrect dress: 'I am in the street without my sabre and I can see a group of officers coming towards me', or 'without my necktie', or 'I am wearing checked civilian trousers', and the like.

The people in whose presence one feels ashamed are almost always strangers, their faces left indefinite. It never happens in a typical dream that they raise objections or draw attention to the form of dress which is so embarrassing to oneself. On the contrary, these people are indifferent or, as I could see from one particularly clear dream, stiff and solemn in demeanour. This is worth reflecting on.

Between them the shame and embarrassment of the dreamer and the indifference of the other people produce a contradiction of the kind that often occurs in dreams. After all, the only thing appropriate to the dreamer's feeling would be for the strangers to gaze at him with astonishment and laugh at him, or be indignant at the sight. But as I see it, this offensive feature is removed from the dream by wish-fulfilment, while the other, sustained by some power or other, remains in place, and in this way the two parts are out of harmony with each other. We have interesting testimony that this dream, partly distorted as it is by wish-fulfilment, has not been rightly understood. It has, of course, become the basis of a fairy-tale familiar to us all in the version by Hans Andersen,[20]* and has recently been put to poetic use by L. Fulda* in his *Talisman*. Andersen's tale tells of two deceivers who weave a precious garment for the Emperor which is supposed to be visible only to the virtuous and loyal among his subjects. The Emperor goes forth clad in this invisible garment, and, for fear of the power of the raiment as a touchstone of their loyalty, everyone pretends not to notice that the Emperor is naked.

But this is the very situation in our dream. We do not have to be very bold to assume that as the dream-content was not understood, this provided a spur to inventing a guise in which the situation on the brink of memory makes some sense. The situation is thereby robbed of its original meaning and put at the service of other purposes. But we shall hear that a misunderstanding of this kind—of the dream-content by the conscious thinking of a second psychical system—occurs frequently and is to be acknowledged as a factor in the final form of the dream; and further, that similar misunderstandings—also within the same psychical personality— play a major part in the creation of obsessions and phobias. As for our dream, it is also possible to say where the material for this reinterpretation is taken from. The deceiver is the dream, the

[20] 'The Emperor's New Clothes'.

Emperor the dreamer himself, and the moralizing tendency betrays an obscure awareness that what is involved in the latent dream-content are forbidden wishes which have been sacrificed to the power of repression. In fact, the context in which dreams of this kind appear in the course of my analyses of neurotic cases leaves no room for doubt that what lies at the bottom of the dream is a memory from our earliest childhood. It is only in our childhood that we are seen in inadequate clothing by our relatives, as well as by strange nurse-maids, servant-girls, and visitors, and in those days we were not ashamed of our nakedness.[21] With many children we can observe that even in later years being undressed has an exhilarating effect on them rather than inducing shame. They laugh, leap around, and slap themselves, and their mother or whoever else is by reprimands them and says: 'Stop it! That's naughty! You mustn't do that.' Children often display exhibitionist pleasure in the wish to show themselves off: you can hardly walk through a village in the countryside around here without encountering a two- or three-year-old who lifts his little shirt to the traveller, perhaps in his honour. One of my patients has preserved a conscious memory of a scene from his eighth year in which, after undressing before going to bed, he tried to dance out in his shirt to his little sister in the next room, and the maidservant who was looking after him prevented it. Exposure before children of the opposite sex plays a large part in the early lives of neurotics; in paranoia the illusion of being observed while dressing and undressing is to be traced back to this experience; among adults remaining in the perverse stage there is a class in whom this infantile impulse has been raised to the point of becoming a symptom: the class of *exhibitionists*.

When we look back, this childhood where shame is absent appears to us as a paradise, and Paradise itself is nothing but the mass fantasy of the childhood of the individual. This is why in Paradise too human beings are naked and feel no shame in each other's presence, until a moment comes when shame and anxiety awaken and sexual life and the work of culture begins.* Now, dreams can take us back to this Paradise every night. We have already raised the supposition that impressions from our earliest childhood (the prehistorical

---

[21] The child also makes an appearance in the fairy-tale, for in it a small child suddenly calls out: 'But he has nothing on.'

period up to about the end of our third year) demand reproduction for their own sake, perhaps regardless of their content, and that their repetition is a wish-fulfilment. Thus nakedness-dreams are *exhibition-dreams.*

The heart of the exhibition-dream is formed by one's own figure, seen not as a child's, but as it is in the present, and by the inadequate clothing, which looks indistinct, overlaid as it is by so many later recollections of undress or to please the censorship; then there are also the persons in whose presence one feels ashamed. I know of no instance in which the actual spectators of these infantile exhibitions reappear in the dream: for the dream is hardly ever a simple recollection. Curiously enough, the people in whom we did have a sexual interest when we were children are left out of all the reproductions found in dreams, hysteria, and obsessive neurosis: it is only paranoia which restores the spectators, deducing with fanatical conviction that although they have remained invisible, they are really present. What the dream puts in their place, 'a lot of strangers' who take no notice of the spectacle offered them, is virtually the *wishful opposite* to the one familiar person in front of whom one exposed oneself. Incidentally, 'a lot of strangers' frequently appear in dreams in any number of other contexts: as wishful opposites, they always signify 'secrets'. It is noticeable that the restoration of the earlier state of affairs occurring in paranoia also takes this opposite into account. One is no longer alone, one is certainly being observed, but the observers are 'a lot of strangers, left curiously indefinite'.

Moreover, in the exhibition-dream repression finds a voice. The embarrassing feeling in the dream is, after all, the reaction of the second psychical system to the fact that the content of the exhibition scene which it repudiated has nevertheless contrived to reach representation. To spare it this, the scene should not have been brought to life again.

We will deal with the feeling of inhibition again later. In dreams it is an excellent means of representing the *conflict of will*, the *No*. The unconscious intention is to continue the exhibition, the demand of the censorship is to break it off.

The relationships of our typical dreams to fairy-tales and other poetic materials are certainly neither isolated nor accidental. The poet is normally the instrument of the transformation process, but on occasion the keen poet's eye has understood it analytically and pursued it backwards, tracing the poem back to the dream. A friend has drawn my attention to the following passage from G. Keller's *Green Henry*: 'It is not my wish, my dear Lee, that you should ever learn from experience the exquisitely piquant truth in Odysseus' situation when he appears naked and covered with mud before Nausicaa and her companions! Do you want to know what is going on in it? Some time, when you are separated from your homeland and all you hold dear, roaming in foreign lands, and when you have seen much and experienced much, when you are acquainted with grief and sorrow, are wretched and deserted, then at night you are sure to dream that you are drawing near your homeland. You will see it shining, radiant in the loveliest colours. Fair and gracious figures come to meet you. Then you suddenly discover that you are walking in rags, naked and covered in dust. A nameless shame and fear take hold of you. You try to cover yourself, to hide, and you wake bathed in sweat. As long as mankind has existed, this has been the dream of the sorrowful, storm-tossed man, and thus it is that Homer has taken that situation from the depths of man's eternal nature.'*

The depths of mankind's eternal nature, which the poet invariably counts on arousing in his listeners, are made of those motions of our inner life rooted in that time of our childhood which later becomes prehistoric. From behind the irreproachable wishes of the homeless man which are suitable for consciousness, infantile wishes break out which have become impermissible, and that is why the dream externalized in the legend of Nausicaa invariably turns into an anxiety-dream.

My own dream, referred to on p. 184, of running up the stairs, which turned soon afterwards into being rooted to the spot, is also an exhibition-dream, as it shows the essential elements of its kind. So it should be traceable back to childhood experiences, and knowledge of these should enlighten us as to how far the maidservant's behaviour towards me, her objection that I dirtied the carpet, helps her to the position she has in the dream. In fact I can supply the desired explanation. In a psychoanalysis one learns to reinterpret closeness in time as closeness in subject-matter. Two ideas, apparently unconnected, following immediately upon each other, belong to a unity which is to be inferred, just as an 'a' and a 'b' which I write down one after the other have to be spoken as a syllable, 'ab'. Likewise in relating elements to one another in dreams. The dream of the stairs referred to is taken from a series of dreams, and I am familiar with the interpretation of the other items in it. This dream, surrounded by the others, must belong in the same context. Now at the basis of the other dreams around it there was the memory of a nursemaid who looked after me from some date when I was still being breast-fed until I was two-and-a-half years old. According to information I recently gathered from from my mother, she was old and ugly, but very intelligent and competent. From what I may conclude from my dreams, she did not always treat me with the most loving care, and had harsh words for me if I failed to respond satisfactorily to her upbringing in cleanliness. So, in taking it on herself to continue this work of education, the maidservant earns the right to be treated as an incarnation of the prehistoric old nurse in my dream. We may assume that, despite her ill-treatment, the child was fond of this tutelary figure.[22]

Another group of dreams which may be called typical are those in which a dear relative, a parent, or brother or sister, a child, and so on, has died. We must immediately distinguish two classes of these dreams: those where the dreamer remains untouched by sorrow, so that on waking he wonders at his lack of feeling; and the others, in which the dreamer feels profound grief at the death, indeed, express-ing it even by weeping passionately in his sleep.

The dreams of the first group we may put aside. They have no claim to be regarded as typical. On analysis we find that they mean something different from what they contain, that they are intended to conceal some other wish. Take the dream of the aunt who sees her sister's only son before her in his coffin (p. 120). That does not mean that she wishes her little nephew were dead but, as we learned, it means the wish to see a certain much-loved person again after a long parting, the same person she had once seen again after a similar long interval at the dead body of another nephew. This wish, which is the true content of the dream, offers no occasion for grief, and that is why no grief is felt in the dream either. We note here that the affect contained in the dream does not belong to the manifest but to the

---

[22] An over-interpretation of this dream would run: spitting [*Spucken*] on the steps would lead—since *Spuken* [haunting] is an activity of spirits—by way of rough transla-tion to '*esprit d'escalier*'. *L'esprit d'escalier* means much the same as lack of ready wit [*Schlagfertigkeit* = (lit.) readiness with a blow]. That is a fault I really must admit to. Or was the nursemaid not ready enough with her blows, perhaps?

latent dream-content, and that the emotional content of the dream has remained free of the distortion that affected its representational content.

The case of dreams where the death of a dear relative is represented is different when emotions of sorrow are also felt. These mean what their content says: the wish that the person concerned might die. And as I may expect that all my readers' feelings and those of everyone who has had a dream of this kind will baulk at my interpretation, I must attempt to prove it on the broadest of foundations.

We have already explained one dream which taught us that the wishes that are represented as fulfilled in our dreams are not always current wishes. They can also be wishes that are past, over and done, overlaid or repressed, but which we are still obliged to credit with a kind of continued existence only because they surface again in our dreams. They are not dead as we conceive the dead, but are like the shades in the *Odyssey** who wake to a kind of life once they have drunk blood. That dream (p. 121) of the dead child in the box is concerned with a wish that was active fifteen years before and frankly admitted to be from that time. It is perhaps not unimportant for the theory of dreams if I add that at the basis even of this dream there lies a memory from earliest childhood. As a little girl—it cannot be said for certain when—the dreamer had heard that during the pregnancy of which she was the product her mother had fallen into a deep depression and with all her heart had wished the child in her womb dead. Now an adult and pregnant herself, she was only following her mother's example.

If anyone has a dream filled with grief that their mother or father, brother or sister has died, I never take this dream for evidence that the dreamer wishes them dead *now*. The theory of dreams does not make so great a demand; it is content to conclude that—some time in childhood—he *has* wished them dead. But I am afraid this qualification will still do little to pacify my critics; they may dispute just as energetically the possibility that they ever had such a thought, just as they feel sure that they do not nurse such wishes at the present time. That is why I have to restore a part of the lost inner life of childhood, according to the evidence that the present still has to show.

Let us first look at the relationship children have to their brothers and sisters. I do not know why we assume that it must be a loving one, for there are insistent examples of hostility between adult siblings in everyone's experience, and we are so often able to establish that these quarrels began in childhood or have always existed. But very many adults too, who are very close to their siblings today and support them, lived in a state of scarcely interrupted enmity with them during childhood. The older child has mistreated the younger, told tales about him, stolen his toys; the younger, in helpless rage at the older, admires him, envies him, and fears him, or turns his first conscious stirrings for freedom and justice against the oppressor. The parents say the children don't get on well, and cannot find the reason for it. It is not difficult to see that even the character of a good child is different from what would be desirable in an adult. Children are absolutely self-centred, they feel their needs intensely and aim quite ruthlessly at their satisfaction, particularly at the expense of their rivals, other children, and above all their brothers and sisters. But that does not make us call the child 'wicked'; we call him 'naughty'; he is not responsible for his bad deeds, neither in our judgement nor before the law. And rightly so. For we may expect that within the lifespan we ascribe to children, stirrings of altruism and a sense of morality will awaken, and that, as Meynert puts it, a secondary ego will overlay the primary and inhibit it. Morality probably will not develop at the same time in every child; also, the length of the amoral childhood period is different in different individuals. If this morality fails to develop, it pleases us to speak of 'degeneration', though obviously it is a matter of hampered development. Where the primary character has already been overlaid by later development, it can still come to the surface again at least partially, if the subject falls ill with hysteria. The similarity of what we call the hysterical character with that of a naughty child is really quite striking. Obsessional neurosis, by contrast, corresponds to an excessive morality, reinforcing the burden on the primary character as this begins to stir again.

Thus many people who love their brothers and sisters today, and would feel bereft at their death, carry ill wishes towards them in their unconscious from long ago, which can be realized in dreams. But it is particularly interesting to observe small children of up to three years old or a little more in their behaviour towards their younger siblings. Until now, the child was the one and only. Now he is told that the stork has brought a new baby. The child inspects the new arrival and declares firmly: 'The stork can take it away again.' It is my entirely serious opinion that the child has the measure of the disadvantage it has to expect from the stranger. I was told by a lady close to me, who gets on very well today with her sister, four years her junior, that when she heard the news of the new arrival, she answered with the reservation: 'But I won't give her my red cap.' Even if the child did not reach this insight until later, the arousal of her hostility would still date from that moment. I know of a case in which a little girl not yet three years old attempted to strangle the baby in its cradle, sensing that no good would come of its further presence. Children of about this age are capable of jealousy, intensely and unmistakably. Or it can happen that the baby really does disappear quite soon, and once again the child is the centre of all the tenderness in the house. But then a new one arrives, sent by the stork. Is it not quite reasonable that our darling should generate within him the wish that his new competitor might meet with the same fate as the earlier one, so that things go as well again for him as they did before and in the interim? Of course, in normal circumstances this behaviour of the child to the later infant is a simple function of the difference in their ages. If the interval in age is greater, motherly instincts towards the helpless newborn baby will already begin to stir in the older girl.

Feelings of hostility towards siblings must be far more frequent in childhood than the imperceptive adult may observe.

In the case of my own children, who followed quickly on one another, I missed the opportunity to make observations of this kind. I am catching up on them now with my little nephew, whose sole reign was disturbed after fifteen months by the appearance of a rival. True, I am told that the young man behaves very chivalrously towards his little sister, kisses her hand, and strokes her. But I am becoming convinced that even before he is two years old he is using his ability to talk to criticize a creature who does, after all, appear superfluous in his eyes. Whenever the talk turns to her, he joins in the conversation and exclaims with displeasure: 'Too little, too little.' In recent months, weaned away from this contemptuous attitude by his excellent development, he has found different grounds for his admonition that she does not deserve so much attention. He reminds us on every occasion that offers: 'She hasn't got any teeth.' We all recall the story of the eldest daughter of another sister: six years old at the time, for half an hour she kept asking all her aunts to reassure her: 'Lucie can't understand that yet, can she?' Lucie was her rival, two-and-a-half years her junior.

I have come upon the dream of a sibling's death appropriate to this intensified hostility in every one of my women patients, for example. I found only one exception, which could easily be interpreted as proving the rule. Once during a consultation I was explaining this state of affairs to a lady whose symptoms seemed worth considering under this aspect. To my astonishment she responded that she never had dreams of this kind. Another dream occurred to her which ostensibly had nothing to do with it. It was a dream she first had when she was four years old, as the youngest child at the time, and had then dreamed many times. *A flock of children, all her brothers, sisters, and cousins, were romping in a meadow. Suddenly they grew wings, flew up in the air, and were gone.* She had no idea what the dream meant. It will not be hard for us to recognize it as a dream of the death of all her brothers and sisters in its original form, very little affected by the censorship. I will venture to replace it with the following analysis. At the death of one of the flock—in this case the children of two brothers were brought up together as brothers and sisters—our little mourner, not yet four years old, will have asked a wise grown-up: 'What happens to children when they are dead?' The answer will have been: 'Then they grow wings and become little angels.' In the dream, in accordance with this explanation, all the brothers and sisters have wings like angels and—and this is the main thing—they fly away. Our little angel-maker* is left alone—think of it!—the only one left after such a great flock! The children romping in a meadow and then flying away from it is surely an unmistakable reference to butterflies, as if the child were drawn by the same combination of ideas as moved the ancients to picture the psyche with butterflies' wings.

Now perhaps someone will interject: 'Granted the hostile impulse of children towards their siblings, but how could a tender infant disposition reach such heights of wickedness as to wish its rivals or sturdier playfellows dead, as if every offence were only to be expiated by the death penalty?' Anyone who says this is not taking into account the child's idea of 'being dead', which has only the word and very little else in common with ours. The child knows nothing of the horrors of decomposition, of freezing in the cold grave, of the terror of endless Nothingness which the adult's imagination cannot bear to contemplate, as all the myths of the world to come bear witness. The fear of death is unknown to the child; that is why he will play with the terrible word and threaten another: 'If you do that again, you'll die, like Franz!'—which makes his poor mother shudder, for she may be unable to forget that the greater part of mankind born on this earth will not outlive the years of childhood. Even at the age of eight, back from a visit to the Science Museum, a child can say to his mother: 'Mama, I love you so much; when you die I'll have you stuffed and set you up here in this room so that I can see you for ever and ever!' That is how little the child's idea of being dead resembles ours.

To the child, who is, after all, spared the scenes of suffering before death, being dead is much the same as 'being away', no longer disturbing the survivors. The child does not distinguish how this absence comes about, whether on account of a journey, an estrangement, or death. If in the prehistoric years his nurse is sent away and his mother dies a while later, the two events as they are uncovered in the course of analysis overlay each other in his memory. That the child does not miss them very intensely in their absence is something many a mother has learned to her sorrow on returning home after a summer trip of several weeks, when, in response to her enquiries she has to hear: 'The children haven't asked after their mama, not once.' But if she really has made the journey to 'That undiscovered country from whose bourne | No traveller returns',* the children will seem to have forgotten her at first and they will begin to remember her only *in retrospect*.

So if the child has motives for wishing another child away, there is nothing to stop him giving this wish the form of wanting him dead, and the psychical reaction to the wishful dream of death is evidence that, despite all the differences in content, the child's wish is nevertheless somehow the same as the consonant wish in the adult.

But if this wish for his brothers or sisters to die is explained by the child's self-centredness, which makes him see them as rivals, how are we to explain his death-wish towards his parents, who are for the child the givers of love and fulfillers of his needs, and whose preservation he should wish for simply from selfish motives?

We are led to a solution of this difficulty by our experience that dreams of a parent's death most frequently concern the parent who shares the same sex as the dreamer, so that a man mostly dreams of his father's death, a woman of her mother's. I cannot set this up as the rule, but the predominance of the pattern I have indicated is so distinct that it requires to be explained by a factor of general significance. Put crudely, it is as though a sexual preference were established very early, as though the boy saw a rival for love in his father, and the girl in her mother, and removing them could only be of benefit to the child.

Before this idea is rejected as monstrous, let us take a good look at the real relationships between parents and children. We have to distinguish what the cultural demand to honour our parents requires of this relationship from what daily observation tells us is the case. There is more than one occasion for hostility hidden in the relationship between parents and children; the conditions for creating wishes which will not pass the censorship are present in abundance. Let us dwell first on the relation of father and son. It is my opinion that the sanctity we have accorded the Ten Commandments blunts our perception of reality. Perhaps we do not dare to notice that the greater part of mankind put themselves above obeying the Fourth Commandment.* At the lowest levels of human society as much as at the highest, parental respect habitually yields to other interests. The dark tidings that reach us in myth and legend from the primeval days of human society give us some idea of the power of the father and the ruthlessness with which he wielded it that is most disagreeable. Cronos devours his children, rather as the boar devours the mother-sow's farrow, and Zeus castrates his father and takes his place as ruler. The more absolute the father's rule in the ancient family, the more the son as rightful successor is forced into the position of enemy, and the greater his impatience to come to power himself through the death of the father. Even in our middle-class families, by refusing his son his independence and the wherewithal to support it, the father is helping to develop the natural seeds of enmity in him. The physician is often enough in a position to notice that in his grief at the loss of his father, the son cannot suppress his satisfaction at gaining his freedom at last. The father habitually keeps a rigid grip on the remnants of the dreadfully antiquated *potestas patris familias* in our society today, and every writer is sure of making an impact if, like Ibsen, he pushes the ancient battle between father and son to the foreground in his plot. The occasions for conflict between daughter and mother arise when the daughter grows up and sees her mother as her wardress while she herself desires her sexual freedom; on the other hand, as her daughter blossoms the mother is reminded that the time has come for her to give up her own claims to sexuality.

All these relationships are plain for everyone to see. But they do not take us any further in our aim to explain the dreams of a parent's death in persons whose honour for their father and mother has long been something sacrosanct. Moreover, our previous discussions have prepared us to expect that the death-wish towards the parents will derive from earliest childhood.

This assumption is confirmed by our analyses in the case of psychoneurotics with a certainty that excludes any doubt. We learn from them that sexual wishes in the child—insofar as they can be called that at such an early stage—develop very early, and that the girl's first affection is for her father, and the boy's first infant desire is for his mother. Thus the father becomes an intrusive rival for the boy, as the mother does for the girl, and we have already explained in the case of siblings how little the child needs for this feeling to lead to a death-wish. As a rule their sexual choice is already determined by the parents' preferences. A natural inclination sees to it that the husband will spoil his little daughter, the wife take her son's part, while both of them—as long as the magic of sex does not upset their judgement—will be strict in their influence on the little ones' upbringing. The child is quite aware of the preference and rebels against the parent who opposes it. To be loved by the grown-ups means for him not only the satisfaction of a particular need, but also that he will get his way in all other respects too. Thus the child follows his or her own sexual impulses and at the same time perpetuates what the parents initiated by choosing between them along the same lines as they did.

The signs of these infantile affections in children are, most of them, usually overlooked; a few can be noticed even after the first childhood years. An eight-year-old girl of my acquaintance took advantage of the opportunity offered when her mother was called away from table to proclaim herself her successor: '*I*'ll be mama now. Karl, do you want more vegetables? Do help yourself, please,' and so on. A particularly gifted and lively girl, not yet four years old and particularly transparent with regard to this aspect of child psychology, declared point-blank: 'Mummy can go away now. Then daddy will have to marry me and I'll be his wife.' In the life of children this wish does not in the least exclude the child's tender love for her mother. If the little boy is allowed to sleep close to his mother when his father is away, and when his father returns he has to go back to the nursery to someone far less to his liking, then a wish could easily form that his father should always be absent so that he can keep his place near his dear, sweet mama, and one means of achieving this wish is obviously if his father were dead. For one thing his experience has taught him: 'dead' people, like grandpapa, for example, are always absent, and never come back.

Although such observations of small children neatly fit the interpretation I have suggested, still they do not have the same persuasive power that the psychoanalyses of adult neurotics have to convince the physician entirely. When neurotics tell me their dreams in this respect, they do so with introductory material of a kind that makes interpreting them as wishful dreams inescapable. I discover a lady one day in low spirits with eyes red from weeping. She says: 'I don't want to see my relatives again; the sight of me must fill them with horror.' Then, almost without transition, she tells me that she remembers a dream but of course she doesn't know what it means. She dreamed it when she was four, and it goes as follows: *A lynx or a fox is going for a walk on the roof, then something falls down, or she falls down, and then her mother is carried out of the house dead,* at which she weeps bitterly. I have scarcely informed her that this dream must mean a wish from her childhood to see her mother dead, and that this dream must be why she thinks her relations are filled with horror at her, when she promptly offers some material to explain the dream. 'Lynx-eyes' is a rude name she was once called by a street urchin when she was a very small child; when she was three years old, a tile fell from the roof onto her mother's head, so that she bled heavily.

I once had the opportunity to make a close study of a young girl who was going through a variety of psychical conditions. In the state of raving confusion with which her illness began, the patient showed a particular revulsion from her mother, struck her and swore at her whenever she came near her bed, while at the same time she remained loving and obedient towards a much older sister. There followed a lucid but apathetic condition, with very disturbed sleep;

in this phase I began her treatment and analysed her dreams. A vast number of them dealt, in more or less disguised form, with the death of her mother; in one dream she was attending the funeral of an old woman; in another she saw herself and her sister sitting at table in mourning. There was no doubt as to the meaning of these dreams. As she improved further, hysterical phobias made an appearance; the most tormenting was that something had happened to her mother. Then, wherever she might be, she had to hurry home to convince herself that her mother was still alive. This case, in combination with what I had learned elsewhere, was very instructive. It showed the variety of ways the psychical apparatus has of reacting to the same initiating idea, translated, as it were, into many languages. In her confused condition, when, as I see it, the second psychical agency was overwhelmed by the normally suppressed first, her unconscious hostility towards her mother powerfully affected her motor activity; then, as she first grew calmer, and her turmoil was suppressed and the power of the censorship restored, this hostility had only the field of dreaming left open to it to realize the wish for her mother's death; as this state of normality grew still stronger, it created the excessive concern for her mother as a hysterical counter-reaction and defensive phenomenon. In this connection, it is no longer inexplicable why hysterical girls so often cling to their mothers with such extravagant tenderness.

Another time I had the opportunity to see deep into the unconscious inner life of a young man whose obsessional neurosis had made him almost incapable of living; he could not go out into the street because he was tormented by the fear that he might kill every passer-by. He spent his days sorting out the evidence for his alibi in case he should be accused of any murder that occurred in town. It goes without saying that he was as moral a person as he was highly cultured. The analysis—which, by the way, led to his recovery—revealed the basis of this painful obsession to be murderous impulses towards his rather too severe father, which to his astonishment had expressed themselves consciously when he was seven years old, though of course they derived from much earlier childhood years. After his father's painful illness and death, when he was thirty years old the obsessional accusation appeared, transferred to strangers in the form of this phobia. Anyone capable of wanting to hurl his own father from a mountain-peak into the abyss below cannot, to his way of thinking, be trusted to spare the lives of those less close to him; so he is quite right to lock himself up in his room.

In my experience, which is already very extensive, parents play the main parts in the inner life of all children who later become psychoneurotics. Being in love with the one parent and hating the other belong to the indispensable stock of psychical impulses being formed at that time which are so important for the later neurosis. But I do not believe that in this respect psychoneurotics are to be sharply distinguished from other children of Adam with a normal development in their capacity to create something absolutely new and theirs alone. It is far more likely—and this is supported by occasional observations of normal children—that with these loving and hostile wishes towards their parents too, psychoneurotics are only revealing to us, by magnifying it, what goes on less clearly and less intensely in the inner life of most children. In support of this insight the ancient world has provided us with a legend whose far-reaching and universal power can only be understood if we grant a similar universality to the assumption from child-psychology we have just been discussing.

I refer to the legend of King Oedipus* and the drama of that name by Sophocles. Oedipus, son of Laius, King of Thebes, and Jocasta, is abandoned as an infant because an oracle had proclaimed to his father that his son yet unborn would be his murderer. He is rescued and grows up as a king's son at a foreign court, until he himself consults the oracle about his origins, and receives the counsel that he should flee his home city, because he would perforce become his father's murderer and his mother's spouse. On the road from his supposed home city he encounters King Laius and kills him in a sudden quarrel. Then he arrives before Thebes, where he solves the riddle of the Sphinx as she bars his way, and in gratitude he is chosen by the Thebans to be their king and presented with Jocasta's hand in marriage. He reigns long in peace and dignity, and begets two sons and two daughters with his—unbeknown—mother, until a plague breaks out, occasioning fresh questioning of the oracle by the Thebans. At this point Sophocles' tragedy begins. The messengers bring word that the plague will end when the murderer of Laius is driven from the land. But where is he?

> . . . Where shall we hope to uncover
> The faded traces of that far-distant crime?*

The action of the play consists now in the gradually intensified and skilfully delayed revelation—comparable to the work of a psychoanalysis—that Oedipus himself is Laius' murderer, but also that he is the son of the murdered king and Jocasta. Shattered by the abomination he has in his ignorance committed, Oedipus blinds himself and leaves his homeland. The oracle is fulfilled.

Oedipus the King is what we call a tragedy of fate; its tragic effect is supposed to depend on the contrast between the all-powerful will of the gods and the vain struggles of men threatened by disaster. What the deeply moved spectator is meant to learn from the tragedy is submission to the will of the divinity and insight into his own powerlessness. Consequently, modern dramatists have tried to achieve a similar tragic effect by weaving the same contrast into a plot of their own invention. But the spectators have looked on unmoved as, despite all the efforts of innocent humans, some curse or oracle is fulfilled. The later tragedies of fate* have failed in their effect.

If *Oedipus the King* is able to move modern man no less deeply than the Greeks who were Sophocles' contemporaries, the solution can only be that the effect of Greek tragedy does not depend on the contrast between fate and human will, but is to be sought in the distinctive nature of the subject-matter exemplifying this contrast. There must be a voice within us that is ready to acknowledge the compelling force of fate in *Oedipus*, while we are able to reject as arbitrary such disposals as are to be found in *Die Ahnfrau* or other tragedies of fate. And a factor of this kind is indeed contained in the story of King Oedipus. His fate moves us only because it could have been our own as well, because at our birth the oracle pronounced the same curse upon us as it did on him. It was perhaps ordained that we should all of us turn our first sexual impulses towards our mother, our first hatred and violent wishes against our father. Our dreams convince us of it. King Oedipus, who killed his father Laius and married his mother Jocasta, is only the fulfilment of our child-hood wish. But, more fortunate than he, we have since succeeded, at least insofar as we have not become psychoneurotics, in detaching our sexual impulses from our mothers and forgetting our jealousy of our fathers. We recoil from the figure who has fulfilled that ancient childhood wish with the entire sum of repression which these wishes have since undergone within us. As the poet brings Oedipus' guilt to light in the course of his investigation, he compels us to recognize our own inner life, where those impulses, though suppressed, are still present. The contrast with which the chorus takes its leave:

> . . . behold: this was Oedipus,
> Greatest of men; he held the key to the deepest mysteries;
> Was envied by all his fellow-men for his great prosperity;
> Behold, what a full tide of misfortune swept over his head. (p. 68)

this admonition refers to us too and our pride, who have grown so wise and powerful in our own estimation since our childish years. Like Oedipus we live in ignorance of those wishes, offensive to morality and forced upon us by Nature, and once they have been revealed, there is little doubt we would all rather turn our gaze away from the scenes of our childhood.

There is an unmistakable indication in the text of Sophocles' tragedy itself that the legend of Oedipus sprang from that ancient dream material which contains the painful disturbance of our relations with our parents by the first stirrings of our sexuality. Jocasta consoles Oedipus at a stage where he has not yet learned the truth, but is troubled by the memory of what the oracle proclaimed. She refers to a dream which many indeed do dream, but without—or so she thinks—its having any significance:

> Nor need this mother-marrying frighten you;
> Many a man has dreamt as much. Such things
> Must be forgotten, if life is to be endured. (p. 53)

The dream of having sexual intercourse with the mother is dreamed by many today as it was then, and they recount it with indignation and amazement. It is clearly the key to the tragedy and the complement to the dream of the father's death. The Oedipus story is the imagination's reaction to these two typical dreams, and just as the dreams of the adult are filled with feelings of revulsion, the legend too is bound to include the horror and self-punishment in its content. Its further revision derives from a misleading secondary revision of the subject-matter, which seeks to make use of it for theological ends. (Compare the subject-matter of the exhibition-dream, p. 186.) (The attempt to reconcile divine omnipotence with human responsibility, of course, is bound to be defeated by this material, as by any other.)[23]

I cannot leave the typical dreams of the death of dear relatives without adding some words to elucidate their general significance for the theory of dreams. These dreams present the very unusual

---

[23] Another great creation of tragic poetry is rooted in the same soil as *Oedipus the King*: Shakespeare's *Hamlet*. But the change in treatment of the same material reveals the difference in the inner life of these two cultural periods so remote from each other: the advance of repression over the centuries in mankind's emotional life. In *Oedipus* the child's wishful fantasy on which it is based is out in the open and realized—as it is in dreams; in *Hamlet* it remains repressed, and we learn of its existence—as we learn of a neurosis—only through the inhibiting effects it produces. Curiously, *Hamlet* has shown that the overwhelming power of modern drama is compatible with the fact that we can remain quite unclear about the hero's character. The play is based on Hamlet's hesitation in fulfilling the task of revenge laid upon him; what the reasons or motives are for this hesitation the text does not say; the most various attempts at interpretation have not been able to identify them. According to the view argued by Goethe and still dominant today, Hamlet represents the type of human being whose power of action is paralysed by the over-development of the activity of thought ('sicklied o'er with the pale cast of thought').* According to others, the poet has attempted to portray a pathological, irresolute character close to neurasthenia. However, the drama's plot tells us that Hamlet should certainly not appear to be entirely incapable of action. We see him in action twice, once in sudden passion, when he stabs the eavesdropper behind the arras, the second time purposefully, indeed cunningly, when with all the insouciance of a Renaissance prince he dispatches the two courtiers to the death intended for himself. So what inhibits him from fulfilling the task laid upon him by his father's ghost? Here again we have at our disposal the knowledge that it is the particular nature of this task. Hamlet can do anything—except take revenge on the man who removed his father and took the latter's place beside his mother, the man who shows him his own repressed infant wishes realized. The revulsion that should urge him to revenge is thus replaced by self-recrimination, by the scruples of conscience which accuse him of being, quite literally, no better than the sinner he has to punish. I have translated into conscious terms what is bound to remain unconscious in the hero's psyche; if anyone wants to call Hamlet a hysteric, I can only acknowledge that it is an inference my interpretation admits. The sexual revulsion which Hamlet expresses in the dialogue with Ophelia is congruent with it—the same sexual revulsion which was to take increasing hold of the poet's psyche in the following years, reaching its extreme in *Timon of Athens*. Of course it can only have been the poet's own inner life that confronts us in *Hamlet*; I note from the work on Shakespeare by Georg Brandes* (1896) that the drama was written immediately after his father's death (1601), that is, when Shakespeare's mourning for his father was still fresh, and when presumably his childhood feelings towards him were revived. It is also known that Shakespeare had a son called Hamnet* (identical with Hamlet) who died young. Just as *Hamlet* deals with the relationship of the son to his parents, so *Macbeth*, written in much the same period, deals with the theme of childlessness.* Incidentally, just as every neurotic symptom, even the dream, is capable of over-interpretation, indeed demands it, if we are to understand it fully, so every truly poetic creation will have arisen from more than one motive and more than one impulse in the poet's psyche, and will admit of more than one interpretation. What I have attempted here is only an interpretation of the deepest layer of the impulses in the psyche of the creative poet.

instance of a dream-thought formed by a repressed wish escaping any censorship and entering the dream unaltered. There must be quite special conditions to make this fate possible. I think these dreams are encouraged by the following two factors. First, we cannot think of a wish more remote from us than this one; we believe that to wish *that* 'would not occur to us in our wildest dreams', and that is why the dream-censorship has no weapons against this monstrous thing, rather as Solon's laws were unable to decree any punishment for parricide. Secondly, however, it is just here that a remnant of the day very frequently comes halfway to meet the suppressed and unsuspected wish in the shape of a *care and concern* for the life of the dear person. The only way this concern can enter the dream and leave its mark is by making use of the congruent wish; but the wish is able to mask itself with the care and concern which has come to life during the day. If we take the view that all this happens more simply, that we are only continuing at night and in our dreams what we are concerned about by day, then we are just cutting off these dreams of the death of someone dear from their explanation, and holding on unnecessarily to an easily soluble puzzle.

It is also instructive to pursue the relation of these dreams to anxiety-dreams. In the dreams of the death of someone dear the repressed wish has found a way of escaping the censorship—and the distortion it imposes. Then it is unfailingly accompanied by feelings of pain or grief in the dream. Similarly, an anxiety-dream only comes about if the censorship has been entirely or partially overcome, while on the other hand the censorship is overcome the more easily if anxiety is already present as a current sensation deriving from somatic sources. In this way it becomes obvious what tendency the censorship pursues in exercising its office and practising dream-distortion: it is *in order to prevent the development of anxiety or other forms of distressing affect.*

In the previous discussion I spoke of the self-centredness of the child's psyche. I shall pick up on this with the aim of suggesting a connection: that dreams have preserved this characteristic too. They are all of them absolutely self-centred; in all of them the self, our own dear self, makes an appearance, even though disguised. The wishes fulfilled in them are invariably this self's wishes. Any dream said to have been called forth by interest in another is only a deception and a show. I shall submit to analysis a few examples contradicting this assertion.

I

A boy not yet four years old relates: *he saw a big dish, with veget-*
ables and a big joint of roast meat on it, and all of a sudden the meat was
eaten up whole, all in one piece—not cut up. He did not see the person
who ate it.[24]

Who can the stranger be, whose sumptuous repast of roast meat
fills our little one's dream? What the boy experienced on the day of
the dream is bound to enlighten us on this score. For some days he
has been on a milk diet prescribed by the physician; but on the
evening of the day of the dream he was naughty and as a punishment
he was not given any supper. He had endured a fast of this kind once
before and behaved very bravely throughout. He knew that he would
get nothing to eat, but he also did not dare to give the slightest
indication that he was hungry. Upbringing is beginning to have its
effect on him. It is already expressed in his dream, which shows the
beginnings of dream-distortion. There is no doubt that he himself is
the person whose wishes were directed at such a lavish meal, of roast
meat in fact. But since he knows that this has been forbidden him, he
does not dare, as hungry children do in their dreams (compare my
little daughter Anna's dream of the strawberries, p. 104), to sit down
to the meal himself. The person remains anonymous.

II

I dream on one occasion that I see displayed in a bookshop a new
volume of a particular series in binding for connoisseurs, which I
usually buy (monographs on art, world history, places famous for
their art, etc.). *The new collection is called: 'Famous Speakers' (or*
*'Speeches') and the first volume bears the name 'Dr Lecher'.**

In the analysis, it seems improbable to me that the fame of Dr
Lecher, the never-ending speechmaker of the German Obstruction
in Parliament, should concern me in my dreams. It is in fact the case
that a few days ago I took on new patients for psychological treat-

---

[24] The sheer size too, the excessive abundance, scale, and exaggeration of dreams,
could be an infantile characteristic. The most ardent wish of children is to grow up and
get as big a share of everything as the grown-ups; they are hard to satisfy; do not know
the meaning of 'enough'; insatiably demand the repetition of anything that has given
them pleasure or tasted nice. They only learn to moderate their demands, restrain
themselves, and give in to others though the cultural process of their education. It is
well known that the neurotic is also inclined to immoderation and excess.

ment, and am now compelled to speak for ten or eleven hours a day. So I am that kind of never-ending speechmaker myself.

III

Another time I dream that a teacher of my acquaintance at the University says: *My son, the myope.** Then there follows a dialogue consisting of brief remarks and replies. But then there follows a third part of the dream in which I and my sons are present, and as for the latent dream-content, father and son and Professor M. are only straw men corresponding to myself and my eldest son. On account of another peculiarity, I shall deal further with this dream later on.

IV

The following dream gives an example of really base egoistic feelings hiding themselves behind tender care.

My friend Otto is looking ill; he is brown in the face and has protruding eyes.

Otto is my family doctor, and I am still hopelessly in his debt because for years he has watched over the health of my children, treated them successfully when they were ill, and on top of that given them presents on every occasion that offered a pretext. He paid a visit on the day of the dream, and my wife remarked that he looked tired and under stress. At night my dream comes and lends him some of the symptoms of Basedow's disease.* Anyone who discards my rules in analysing dreams will understand this dream to mean that I am worried about my friend's health, and that this worry is realized in the dream. This would contradict not only the proposition that the dream is a wish-fulfilment, but also the other proposition that it is only accessible to egoistic impulses. But I would ask anyone who takes this line to explain my fears that Otto might be suffering from Basedow's disease, when his appearance does not give the slightest occasion for such a diagnosis. My analysis, on the other hand, provides the following material drawn from an event that took place six years ago. We were travelling, a small group of us, which also included Professor R., in deep darkness through the forest of N., a few hours from the place where we were spending the summer. Our driver, not entirely sober, tumbled us together with the carriage down a hillside, and it was fortunate that we all escaped unhurt. But we were forced to spend the night at the nearest inn, where the news of our accident aroused great sympathy for us. One gentleman, showing the unmistakable symptoms of *Morbus Basedowii*—but only browning of the facial skin and protruding eyes, by the way, just as in the dream, no sign of struma—placed himself entirely at our disposal and asked what he could do for us. Professor R., in his forthright way, replied: 'Just lend me a nightshirt.' 'So sorry, I can't,' rejoined the noble fellow, and went his way.

In continuing the analysis, it occurs to me that Basedow* is not only the name of a physician but also of a famous educator. (Now that I am awake I do not feel entirely sure of this knowledge.) But my friend Otto is the person I have asked to take care of my children's physical welfare, particularly during puberty (hence the nightshirt), if anything were to happen to me. In seeing my friend Otto in my dream with the symptoms of our noble helper, I obviously mean to say: 'If anything happens to me, I can expect just as little from him for the children as from Baron L. on that occasion, despite his obliging offers.' The egoistic thread in this dream now seems to be revealed.

But where is the wish-fulfilment here? Not in my revenge on my friend Otto, who is fated to be badly treated in my dreams, but in the following association. In representing Otto as Baron L. in my dream, I have at the same time identified my own person with someone else, that is, with Professor R., for of course I am demanding something of Otto, just as on that occasion R. demanded something of Baron L. And there we have it. Professor R., with whom I would not otherwise dare to compare myself, is like me in one respect: he made his way independently outside the university and only late in life attained the title he had long merited. So once again, I want to become a professor! Even that 'late in life' is a wish-fulfilment, of course, for it means that I shall live long enough to see my boys through puberty myself.

I have no knowledge from my own experience of other typical dreams in which the dreamer is flying at his ease, or falling filled with feelings of anxiety, and everything I have to say about them I owe to my psychoanalyses of patients. From the information gathered from them, one is bound to conclude that these dreams too repeat impressions from childhood, and relate to the motion-games children find so enjoyable. What uncle is there who has not made a child fly by rushing through the room with him, arms outstretched, or played 'falling' by bouncing the child on his knees and then suddenly stretching out his legs, or by lifting the child up high and then suddenly pretending to take away his support? The children shout with pleasure and never tire of wanting it repeated, particularly when some fear and giddiness are involved. Then, years afterwards, they create the repetition in their dreams, but in their dreams they leave out the hands that held them, so that now they hover and fall freely. The pleasure all small children take in games such as swinging and bouncing is well known; when they see acrobatic tricks in the circus their memory is renewed. In many young boys a hysterical attack is made up of reproducing tricks of this kind, which they perform with great skill. Not infrequently in these motion-games, innocuous in themselves, sexual feelings will be aroused.[25] To use a common word covering all these games, it is the 'romping' [*Hetzen*] of childhood that is repeated in these dreams of flying, falling, growing giddy, and the like, but its feeling of pleasure is now turned into its opposite, changed into anxiety. But as every mother knows, the romping of childhood too ends often enough in quarrels and tears.

Thus I have good reason for rejecting the explanation that dreams of flying and falling are called up by the state of our tactile feelings during sleep or sensations of the movement of our lungs. As I see it, these sensations are themselves reproduced from the memory to which the dream relates, that is, they are the content of the dream and not its source.

Everyone who has finished his senior years at school with the final matriculation examination complains how persistently he is pursued by the dream that he has failed, has to repeat a year, and the like. For someone who possesses an academic degree, this typical dream is replaced by another, which offers the prospect of not holding his own at the viva for his doctorate, though he may object in vain in his sleep that he has been practising medicine for years, is a university

---

[25] Apropos, a young colleague, entirely free of nervous troubles, told me: 'I know from my own experience that when swinging as a child, and at the very moment when the downward movement had the greatest impact, I had a peculiar feeling in the genitals which, though it was not really very agreeable, I have to describe as a feeling of pleasure.'—I have often heard from patients that the first pleasurable erections they remember appeared in boyhood when they were climbing.—It emerges from psycho-analyses with great certainty that the first stirrings of sexuality frequently have their roots in childhood scuffling and wrestling.

lecturer, or head of a government department. These are the ineradicable memories of punishments we suffered in childhood for our misdeeds stirring within us again, attaching themselves to the two decisive stages of our studies, the 'dies irae, dies illa'* of these strict examinations. The 'examination-fear' of neurotics, too, is reinforced by this infantile anxiety. Once we have ceased to be schoolchildren, it is no longer our parents and nurses, or later our teachers, who see to our punishment, as once they did; the implacable causal chain of life has taken over our further education and now we dream of the matriculation or the viva—and which of us has not trembled at undergoing them, even the righteous?—whenever we expect that the outcome will punish us because there is something we have not done right, or have not finished properly, or whenever we feel the pressure of some responsibility.

But I certainly do not deceive myself that I can produce a full explanation for this set of typical dreams. In my attempts to do so, my material really has left me in the lurch. I must hold on to the general viewpoint that all the sensations of movement and tactile feeling in these typical dreams are roused as soon as some psychical motive requires them, and they can be ignored if a need of this kind does not come halfway to meet them. The relation to infantile experiences also seems to me to emerge with certainty from the indications I have received in the analysis of psychoneurotics. But what other meanings may have attached themselves in the course of life to the memory of those sensations—different in each individual perhaps, despite the typical appearance of these dreams—I cannot say, and I would very much like to be in a position to fill this gap by careful analysis of good examples. To anyone who is surprised that I should complain of the lack of good material, despite the frequency of dreams of flying, falling, drawing teeth, and the like, I owe the explanation that I have not had such dreams in my own experience since I have been giving my attention to the topic of dream-interpretation. Moreover, the dreams of neurotics which are otherwise at my disposal are not all of them interpretable, and often not into the last nook and cranny of their hidden intentions; a certain psychical force that had a share in constructing the neurosis and is reactivated in resolving it resists being interpreted down to the last riddle.

THE DREAM-WORK

Until now every other effort to solve the problems presented by dreams has latched directly on to the dream's manifest content as it is present in the memory, and has attempted to use this as the basis of an interpretation; or, if it dispensed with an interpretation, it sought to substantiate its judgement of the dream by reference to its content. We are alone in confronting a different state of affairs; as we see it, there is a new kind of psychical material intervening between the content of the dream and the results of our reflections: the *latent* dream-content reached by our procedure, or the dream-thoughts. It is from this latent content, not the manifest, that we worked out the solution to the dream. This is why a new task faces us which did not exist before, the task of investigating the relationship of the manifest dream-content to the latent dream-thoughts, and of tracing the processes by which the latter turned into the former.

The dream-thoughts and the dream-content lie before us like two versions of the same content in two different languages, or rather, the dream-content looks to us like a translation of the dream-thoughts into another mode of expression, and we are supposed to get to know its signs and laws of grammatical construction by comparing the original and the translation. Once we have learnt what these are, the dream-thoughts will be easy for us to understand without any further ado. The content of the dream is given as it were in the form of hieroglyphs whose signs are to be translated one by one into the language of the dream-thoughts. We would obviously be misled if we were to read these signs according to their pictorial value and not according to their referentiality as signs. Suppose I have a picture-puzzle, a rebus, before me: a house with a boat on its roof, then a single letter of the alphabet, then a running figure with his head conjured away, and the like. Now I could fall into the trap of objecting that this combination and its constituent parts are non-sense. A boat does not belong on the roof of a house and a person without a head cannot run; besides, the person is bigger than the house, and if the whole is supposed to represent a landscape, then single letters of the alphabet do not fit in there, as they certainly do not occur in Nature. Obviously the correct solution to the rebus can only be reached if I raise no such objections to the whole or to the details, but take the trouble to replace each picture by a syllable or a word which, through some association, can be represented by the picture. The words connected in this way are no longer nonsense, but can yield the most beautiful and meaningful poetic saying. The dream is a picture-puzzle of this kind, and our predecessors in the field of dream-interpretation made the mistake of judging the rebus as if it were a pictorial composition. As such, it seemed to them to have no meaning or value.

(a) *The Work of Condensation*

The first thing the investigator comes to understand in comparing the dream-content with the dream-thoughts is that *work of condensation* has been carried out here on a grand scale. The dream is scant, paltry, laconic in comparison to the range and abundance of the dream-thoughts. Written down, the dream will fill half a page; the analysis containing the dream-thoughts will require six, eight, twelve times as much space. The ratio varies for different dreams; as far as I can check, it never changes its intent. As a rule, in taking the dream-thoughts brought to light to be all the dream-material there is, one is underestimating the degree of compression that takes place, whereas further work of interpretation is able to reveal fresh thoughts hidden behind the dream. We have already had to note that actually one is never certain of having interpreted a dream in its entirety; even when the solution seems satisfying and complete, it is always possible for a further meaning to announce its presence through the same dream. *The quota of condensation* is thus, strictly speaking, indeterminable. One conclusion to be drawn from this disproportion between dream-content and dream-thoughts might be that a wholesale condensation of the psychical material takes place during the dream's formation. However, one could raise an objection to this which at first sight seems very tempting. After all, we so often have the feeling that we have dreamed a great deal all through the night and then forgotten most of it. Accordingly, the dream we remember when we wake would be just a remnant of the total dream-work, which would probably equal the dream-thoughts in extent, if only we were able to remember the dream in its entirety. This is certainly correct in part; it is evident that a dream is reproduced most faithfully when we try to recollect it soon after waking, and that its memory becomes more and more sketchy towards evening. On the other hand, however, it emerges that the feeling that we have dreamed a great deal more than we can reproduce very often rests on an illusion, whose origins will be explained later. Moreover, the assumption that condensation is operative in the dream-work is not affected by the possibility of forgetting our dreams, for its activity is proven by the masses of ideas belonging to the separate bits of the dream that *are* retained. If a great deal of the dream is in fact lost to memory, this more or less cuts off our approach to a fresh set of dream-thoughts. There is nothing to justify any expectation that the lost parts of the dream would only have related to the thoughts already known to us from our analysis of the parts that *have* been retained.

In face of the vast number of ideas analysis can offer for every element in the dream-content, many readers will feel the stirrings of doubt as to whether all the things coming into someone's mind retrospectively in the course of analysis may in principle be counted as the dream-thoughts, that is, whether it may be assumed that all these thoughts were already active during sleep and played their part at the time in forming the dream. Or rather, whether fresh thought-associations might not arise in the course of analysing which had no part in forming the dream. I can only give qualified assent to this doubt. It is certainly correct that particular thought-associations do arise only during the analysis; but on each occasion one can satisfy oneself that fresh associations of this kind only come about between thoughts which are already associated in some other way in the dream-thoughts; the new associations are, as it were, parallel connections, short-circuits made possible by the existence of other and deeper connecting paths. As for the greater mass of the thoughts revealed in the analysis, it has to be recognized that they were already active in forming the dream, for after working through a chain of these thoughts, which seem to be quite unconnected to the formation of the dream, one suddenly comes upon one which is represented in the dream-content and which is essential to its interpretation, but which was only accessible by way of that chain. In this respect, see the dream of the botanical monograph, for example, which appears to be the result of an astonishing feat of condensation, even though I have not reported its analysis in full.

But how, then, are we to imagine the conditions prevailing in the psyche during the sleep which precedes dreaming? Are all the dream-thoughts present side by side, or will they follow one after the other, or are there several simultaneous trains of thought formed from different centres, which then converge? I do not think it is necessary to make an imaginary picture of the psychical conditions prevailing in the process of dream-formation. However, we should not forget that this is a matter of unconscious thinking, and that the process could easily be very different from the one we are aware of in ourselves in the course of purposeful reflection accompanied by consciousness.

However, the fact that the formation of dreams is based on condensation is established beyond question. Now, how does this condensation come about?

When one considers that only very few indeed of the dream-thoughts discovered by the analysis are represented in the dream by one of their ideational elements, one might suppose that condensation proceeds by way of *exclusion*, for the dream is not a faithful translation or point-by-point projection of the dream-thoughts, but an exceedingly incomplete and fragmentary reproduction. But, as we shall soon discover, this is a most inadequate view. All the same, let us use it as a basis to start from and go on to ask ourselves: if only a few elements of the dream-thoughts reach the dream-content, what are the conditions that determine their selection?

For light on this question we shall turn our attention to those elements in the dream-content which must in fact have fulfilled the conditions we are seeking. The most suitable material for this inquiry will be a dream which has been formed by a particularly strong process of condensation. I shall choose the dream of the botanical monograph reported on p. 129.

I

Dream content: *I have written a monograph on a species (which kind is left open) of plant. The book is lying in front of me. I am just turning over a folded colour plate. Bound into the copy is a dried specimen of the plant.*

The most immediately striking element in this dream is the *botanical monograph*. This derives from the impressions of the dream-day.

I had in fact seen a *monograph on the species 'cyclamen'* displayed in the window of a bookshop. The dream does not mention species, retaining only the monograph and its reference to botany. The 'botanical monograph' promptly shows its connection to the *work on cocaine* which I once wrote. From cocaine the train of thought moves on the one hand to the *Festschrift* and to certain events in a university laboratory, on the other hand to my friend, the eye specialist *Dr Königstein*, who had a share in the medical application of cocaine. The figure of Dr K. links up with my recollection of the interrupted conversation I had with him the previous evening, and to my various thoughts on payment for medical services among colleagues. Now, it is this conversation which is actually the active initiator of the dream. The monograph on cyclamen is also an agent, but an unimportant one. As I see it, the *botanical monograph* in the dream turns out to be a *mediating common factor* between the two experiences of the day, taken over unchanged from the unimportant impression, but linked by a wealth of associative connections with the psychically significant experience.

But not only the composite idea *botanical monograph*, but also each of its elements separately, *botanical* and *monograph*, enters by way of multiple connections deeper and deeper into the maze of the dream thoughts. *Botanical* is the link to my recollections of the figure of Dr *Gärtner*, of his *'blooming'* wife, of a patient of mine who was called *Flora*, and of the lady with the forgotten flowers whose story I recounted. *Gärtner* leads again to the laboratory and to my conversation with *Königstein*; the reference to both patients belongs in the same conversation. The dream-thoughts branch along one path from the woman with the flowers to my wife's *favourite flowers*, and their other route ends in the title of the monograph seen fleetingly during the day. In addition, *botanical* recalls an episode at school and an examination from my university days, and a fresh theme broached in that conversation, that of my favourite hobbies, is linked via what I call in jest my *favourite flower*, the artichoke, to the train of thoughts that started out from the forgotten flowers. Behind 'artichoke' there is hidden the recollection of Italy on the one hand and a scene from childhood on the other, where I inaugurated my relationship to books which has since become so intimate. So *botanical* is a real point of intersection, where very many trains of thought contributing to the dream converge; and I can vouch for it that these were all brought quite fittingly into connection with one another in that conversation. This is where we find ourselves in the middle of a thought-factory where, as in the weaver's masterpiece,

> Ein Tritt tausend Fäden regt,
> Die Schifflein herüber, hinüber schiessen,
> Die Fäden ungesehen fliessen,
> Ein Schlag tausend Verbindungen schlägt.*

> ['One thrust of his foot, and a thousand threads
> Invisibly shift, and hither and thither
> The shuttles dart—just once he treads
> And a thousand strands all twine together.']

Monograph in the dream touches again on two themes: how specialized my studies were and how expensive my hobbies.

This first examination suggests that the elements 'botanical' and 'monograph' have been admitted into the dream because they are able to show the widest range of contacts with the most dream-thoughts, that is, they represent *points of intersection* where a great number of the dream-thoughts converge; and because they have *many meanings* with respect to the interpretation of the dream. The fact at the basis of this explanation can also be put differently: each element of the dream-content turns out to be *over-determined*, to be represented many times and in many ways in the dream-thoughts.

We shall learn more if we scrutinize the remaining components of the dream for their appearance in the dream-thoughts. The *coloured plate* I unfold refers to a fresh theme (see p. 131), my colleagues' criticism of my work; and to one already represented in the dream, my hobbies; besides these, to the childhood memory in which I pull apart the leaves of a book with coloured plates; the dried specimen of the plant touches on my experience at school with the herbarium and gives particular emphasis to this recollection. So I perceive what kind of relationship this is between the content and the thoughts of the dream: it is not only that the elements of the dream are determined *many times over*, but also that the individual dream-thoughts are represented in the dream by several elements. The path of associations leads from one element of the dream to several dream-thoughts; and from one dream-thought to several dream-elements. Thus, the formation of a dream does not come about by a process of one dream-thought or a group of them supplying a shorthand term for the dream-content, and then by the next dream-thought providing a further shorthand term as its deputy, much as representatives are elected from the population for Parliament. Rather, the entire mass of the dream-thoughts undergoes a certain procedure whereby those elements with the most and best support are best qualified for admission to the dream-content, rather like election by means of the list system. Whatever dream I submit to this kind of analysis, I always find the same principles confirmed: the elements formed into the dream are drawn from the entire mass of the dream-thoughts, and in its relation to the dream-thoughts each one of the elements seems to be determined many times over.

It is certainly not idle to demonstrate this relationship of dream-content and dream-thoughts with a fresh example, one which is remarkable for the particularly intricate way it intertwines its interacting associations. The dream comes from a patient I am treating for claustrophobia. It will soon become apparent why I feel occasioned to give this exceptionally clever feat of dreaming the heading of:

II. 'A Pleasant Dream'

He is travelling in a large private party to X Street, where a modest hostelry is located (which is not the case). *A play is being performed in its rooms; one moment he is a spectator, the next an actor. Finally someone says they will have to change their clothes to return to town. Some of the party are directed to the rooms on the ground floor, others to those on the first floor. Then a quarrel ensues. The ones up above are annoyed that those down below are not yet ready, so that they cannot come down. His brother is up above, he himself down below, and he is annoyed at his brother that he is being hurried so.* (This part is unclear.) *In any case, it was already decided and disposed on their arrival who should be up above and who should be down below. Then he is walking by himself up the rise made by X Street towards the town, and his steps are so heavy, so laborious, that he cannot stir from the spot. An elderly gentleman joins him and rails against the King of Italy. Then at the end of the rise he walks with much greater ease.*

The difficulties he had in climbing the rise were so distinct that when he woke he wondered for a while whether it was dream or reality.

The manifest content scarcely moves one to praise this dream. Against the rules, I shall begin with that part described by the dreamer as the most distinct.

The difficulty dreamed of and probably felt as it was dreamed, the laborious climb accompanied by dyspnoea,* is one of the actual symptoms my patient had displayed years ago, which was then attributed, together with other symptoms, to tuberculosis (probably in hysterical imitation). We are already familiar with this peculiar sensation of inhibited movement from exhibition-dreams, and here again we find it as material present and always available to be used for any other representational purpose. The part of the dream-content describing how difficult climbing was at the beginning and how easy the rise became at the end, reminded me as he recounted it of the well-known, masterly opening of Alphonse Daudet's *Sappho*.* There, a young man is carrying his beloved up the staircase; at first she is light as a feather; but the further he climbs, the more heavily she weighs in his arms, and this scene is a model for the course of their relationship; in describing it thus, Daudet intends to warn young men not to squander their more serious affections on girls of low origin and doubtful past. Although I knew that my patient had recently had a love affair with a lady from the theatre and had broken it off, I really did not expect to find my idea for the interpretation confirmed. In any case, the situation in *Sappho* was the reverse of the one in the dream; in the dream, the climb was difficult at the start and became easier later; in the novel, the symbolism was only served if what was taken easily at first turned out to be a heavy burden at the end. To my astonishment my patient remarked that the interpretation chimed very well with the content of the play he had seen the previous evening in the theatre. The play was called *Rund um Wien* [*Round about Vienna*], and dealt with the life of a young woman who begins as a good girl, but then enters the *demi-monde*, has affairs with highly placed personages, and so '*rises high up*', but finally sinks '*down lower and lower*'. The play had reminded him of another one performed years before, entitled *Von Stufe zu Stufe** [*From Step to Step*], with advertisements showing a flight of stairs made up of several steps.

Now for further interpretation. The actress with whom he had had this latest affair, so full of associations, lived in X Street. There is no inn in the street. However, he spent part of the summer in Vienna on account of the lady, and *put up* [*abgestiegen*; lit: *got down*] at a small hotel nearby. As he left the hotel, he said to the cabby: 'At least I haven't caught any vermin, I'm glad to say'—another of his phobias, by the way. The cabby replied: 'But how can anyone stay there! That's not a proper hotel, it's only a *hostelry*.'

The inn links up at once in his memory with a quotation:

> Bei einem Wirthe wundermild
> Da war ich jüngst zu Gaste.
> ['Not long ago I was a guest,
> My host was wond'rous kind.']

But the host in Uhland's* poem is an *apple-tree*.

Now a second quotation continues the train of thought:

> *Faust* (mit der Jungen tanzend).
>
> Einst hatt ich einen *schönen Traum*;
> Da sah ich einen *Apfelbaum*,
> Zwei schöne Aepfel glänzten dran,
> Sie reizten mich, ich *stieg hinan*.

> *Die Schöne*
>
> Der Aepfelchen begehrt ihr sehr
> Und schon vom Paradiese her,
> Von Freuden fühl' ich mich bewegt,
> Daß auch mein Garten solche trägt.*

> [*Faust* (dancing with the young witch).
>
> A *pleasant dream* once came to me:
> I saw a lovely *apple-tree*,
> And two fine apples hanging there;
> I *climbed to pick* that golden pair.

> *The Fair One*
>
> You men were always apple-mad;
> Adam in Eden was just as bad.
> I've apples in my garden too—
> How pleased I am to pleasure you!]

There is not the slightest possible doubt about what is meant by the apple-tree and the apples. A beautiful bosom was high among the charms binding my dreamer to his actress.

The interrelations revealed by the analysis gave us every reason to assume that the dream goes back to an impression from childhood. If this was correct, it was bound to relate to the wet-nurse of this nearly thirty-year-old man. For a child the nurse's breast is indeed the hostelry. The nurse, as well as Daudet's Sappho, appears to be an allusion to the lover he had recently broken with.

My patient's (elder) brother also appears in the dream-content, the brother being *up above* and he himself *down below*. This is again a *reversal* of their real relationship, for the brother, to my knowledge, has lost his social position, and my patient has maintained his. In recounting the dream-content, the dreamer avoided saying his brother was 'up above' and he himself 'on the ground floor'. That would have been much too explicit a declaration, for here in Vienna we say of persons who have lost wealth and position that they are '*on the ground floor*', that is, we are using a similar metaphor to saying 'they have *come down in the world*'. There must be some meaning to the representation of something *in reverse* at this point in the dream. The reversal must also apply to another connection between dream-thoughts and dream-content. There is an indication as to where this reversal is to be found. Clearly it is at the end of the dream, where a similar *reversal* applies to climbing as to *Sappho*. Then it easily emerges what reversal is meant: in *Sappho* the man is carrying the woman who has a sexual relationship with him; in the dream the situation is *reversed* and it is the woman who is carrying the man; as this can only happen in childhood, the reference is again to the nurse, who finds it hard to carry the baby she is breast-feeding. The end of the dream sums it up in representing *Sappho* and the nurse by the same allusion.

Just as the name of *Sappho* as chosen by the poet is not without reference to a lesbian disposition, so those parts of the dream in which figures are involved *above* and *below* point to the dreamer's being preoccupied by fantasies with a sexual content which, being suppressed desires, are not unconnected with his neurosis. The interpretation of the dream does not itself indicate that these are fantasies and not recollections of actual events; it only provides us with the content of the thought and leaves it to us to decide what it is worth as reality. Actual and imaginary events appear at first to be of equal value here—and not only here, but also in the creation of more important psychical formations than dreams. A large social gathering, as we already know, signifies a secret. The brother is nothing but the representative, introduced into the childhood scene by 'imagining back', of all his later rivals for women. The episode of the gentleman who railed against the King of Italy relates again, mediated by a recent experience of slight importance, to the intrusion by persons of the lower orders into higher society. It is as if, alongside Daudet's warning to the young man, a similar one was meant for the suckling child.[1]

As a third example to hand for studying condensation in the formation of dreams, I shall report the partial analysis of another dream which I owe to an elderly lady under psychoanalysis. In accordance with the grave anxiety-state from which this patient suffered, her dream thoughts contained a wealth of sexual material which disconcerted as much as alarmed her when she came to learn of it. As I am not able to pursue the interpretation of her dream to the end, the dream material appears to break up into a number of groupings without visible connection.

III

Dream content: *She recalls that she has two may-beetles* in a box which she must set free or else they will suffocate. She opens the box; the beetles are exhausted; one of them flies up out of the opened window, but the other is squashed by the casement as she is closing the window, which someone wants her to do (expression of disgust).*

Analysis: Her husband is away on a journey. Her fourteen-year-old daughter sleeps in the bed next to her. In the evening the girl draws her attention to a moth which has fallen into her water-glass; but she neglects to rescue it and next morning she feels very sorry for the poor little beast. The book she had been reading that evening told how some boys threw a cat into boiling water, and described the animal's convulsions. These are the two intrinsically unimportant occasions for the dream. The theme of *cruelty to animals* continues to engage her. Years before, when they were staying in a certain district for the summer, her daughter had been very cruel to all kinds of

---

[1] The imaginary nature of the situation relating to the dreamer's nurse is demonstrated by the objective circumstance that the wet-nurse in this case was his mother. I recall, moreover, the regret referred to on p. 158 of the young man in the anecdote that he had not made better use of the situation with his wet-nurse—which is probably the origin of this dream.

creatures. She made a collection of butterflies and asked her mother for *arsenic* in order to kill them. On one occasion a moth flew around the room for a long time with a pin through its body. Another time some caterpillars which were being kept till they developed to the chrysalis stage were left to starve. While still very young the same child was in the habit of pulling off the wings of *beetles* and butter-flies. Today she would recoil in horror at all these acts of cruelty; she has grown so tender-hearted.

My patient's thoughts are occupied by this contradiction. It reminds her of another one, between *appearance* and attitude, as it is presented by [George] Elliot [*sic*] in *Adam Bede*.* A girl who is beautiful but vain and very stupid, beside her one who is plain but high-minded. The *aristocrat* who seduces the silly little thing; the working-man of noble feeling who behaves accordingly. You can't tell that from *looking at* people's appearance, she thinks. Who could tell from looking at *her* that she was tormented by desires of the senses?

The same year as the little girl made her butterfly collection, the region suffered badly from a plague of *may-beetles*. The children waged war on the beetles, *squashed* them mercilessly. She saw a man tear off their wings and then eat the bodies. She herself was born in *May* and had been married in *May*. Three days after the wedding she wrote a letter home to her parents saying how happy she was. But she was not in the least happy.

On the evening before the dream she had been looking through old letters and had read out various serious and amusing letters to her family, including one most ridiculous letter from a piano-teacher who had paid court to her as a girl, and also one from an *aristocratic* admirer.[2]

She reproaches herself that one of her daughters had got hold of a bad book by Maupassant.[3]* The *arsenic* demanded by her small daughter reminds her of the *arsenic pills* that restored his youthful powers to the Duc de Mora in *Le Nabab*.*

Regarding 'setting free', the passage from *The Magic Flute** occurs to her:

---

[2] This is the actual initiator of the dream.

[3] To develop the point: in her view, reading-matter of this kind is *poison* for a young girl. She herself had learned a great deal as a girl from forbidden books.

Zur Liebe kann ich Dich nicht zwingen,
Doch geb ich Dir die *Freiheit* nicht.
[I cannot force you to love,
But I will not give you your *freedom*.]

Regarding the may-beetles, there is also the line from Kleist's *Das Käthchen von Heilbronn*:*

Verliebt ja wie ein *Käfer* bist Du mir.[4]
[You are as much in love with me as a may-*beetle*.]

And between them Tannhäuser:* 'Weil Du von *böser Lust* beseelt—' ['Because your soul is filled with *evil desire*—'].

She lives in a state of worry and anxiety about her absent husband. The fear that something should *happen* to him on the journey is expressed in numerous daytime fantasies. Shortly before, in the course of the analysis, she had discovered a complaint in her unconscious thoughts about his 'senility'. The wishful thought disguised by this dream can perhaps best be guessed at if I relate that several days before the dream, going about her daily business, she was suddenly alarmed at the imperative she had aimed at her husband: '*Go hang yourself.*' It emerged that a few hours previously she had read somewhere that a powerful erection sets in when a man is hanged. It was the wish for this erection returning from its repressed state in this alarming disguise. 'Go hang yourself' says as much as 'Get an erection at all costs'. Dr Jenkins's arsenic pills in *Le Nabab* belong here; but my patient also knew that the strongest aphrodisiac, *cantharides* ('Spanish flies', as it is called), is prepared by crushing beetles. This is the meaning that the main component of the dream-content is getting at.

Opening and closing the *window* is an issue of constant dispute with her husband. She herself needs fresh air to sleep, her husband dislikes it. The main symptom she was complaining of in these days is *exhaustion*.

In reporting all three of these dreams I have used italics to highlight the points where one of the dream-elements recurs in the dream-thoughts. But since none of these dreams is analysed through to the end, it will probably be more rewarding to look at a dream

---

[4] A further train of thought leads to the same poet's *Penthesilea*:* *cruelty* to the beloved.

where the analysis is reported more fully, and use that to demonstrate the over-determination of the dream-content. To do so I shall select the dream of Irma's injection. It will not be difficult for us to see from this example that the work of condensation employs more than just one device in the formation of dreams.

The main figure in the dream-content is my patient Irma, who is seen with the features belonging to her in real life, and so in the first place represents herself. However, her posture as I examine her at the window is taken from my recollection of someone else, the lady for whom I would like to exchange my patient, as the dream-thoughts indicate. Insofar as Irma displays a diphtheritic attenuation recalling my concern for my eldest daughter, she comes to stand for this child of mine, behind whom there is hidden the figure of the patient I lost from the severe toxic condition, linked to her by having the same name. As the dream proceeds, the meaning of Irma's person changes (without any alteration in her visible image); she turns into one of the children we are examining in the public surgery at the children's clinic, when my friends demonstrate the difference in their intellectual gifts. The transition was obviously made by way of my little daughter. By her reluctance to open her mouth this same figure of Irma turns into an allusion to another lady whom I once examined, and, in the same context, to my own wife. In the pathological changes I discover in her throat, moreover, I gathered together allusions to further persons still.

All these persons whom I came upon in my pursuit of 'Irma' do not appear in the dream in their own form; they are hidden behind the dream-figure of 'Irma', which in this way becomes a collective image, though endowed, it is true, with contradictory features. Irma becomes the proxy for these other persons sacrificed in the process of condensation, in which I have her go through everything, item for item, that reminds me of them.

I can also create a *collective figure* for the dream-condensation in a different way by combining the actual features of two or more persons into a dream-image. This is how the figure of Dr M. in my dream came about; he bears the name of Dr M.; he speaks and acts like him; his physical build and his illness belong to someone else, to my eldest brother; one single characteristic, his pallor, is doubly determined, being shared by both persons in real life. In the dream of my uncle, Dr R. is a similar composite figure. But here the dream-image was created in another way again. I did not combine features belonging to the one with features of the other, thereby reducing the remembered image of each by certain features; rather, I adopted the procedure Galton used in making his family portraits, that is, I projected both images onto each other; in this way the features they have in common emerge more prominently, and those that do not match obliterate each other, and become blurred in the image. In the dream of my uncle the reinforced characteristic that stands out among blurred facial features—blurred because they belong to two people—is the *yellow beard*, which also contains an allusion to my father and to myself, by way of the association with growing grey.

The production of collective and composite figures is one of the main methods of condensation in dreams. We shall soon have occasion to deal with them in a different context.

Similarly, the idea of 'dysentery' in the dream of the injection is determined several times over, on the one hand by the resemblance of its sound to 'diphtheria', on the other by its association with the patient I sent to the Near East whose hysteria goes unrecognized.

The reference to '*propyls*' in the dream turns out to be an interesting case of condensation. The dream-thoughts did not have '*propyls*' in them, but '*amyls*'. One might think that a simple displacement had been effected in the formation of the dream. That is so; however, this displacement also serves the purposes of condensation, as the following addition to my analysis will show. If my attention pauses for a moment at the word '*propyls*', what occurs to me is the similarity of its sound to the word '*Propylea*'.* But there are *Propylea* not only in Athens but also in Munich. This was the town where a year before my dream I visited the friend—who was very ill at the time—unmistakably referred to by the *trimethylamine* following hard upon *propyls*.

I shall pass over the striking circumstance that, here and elsewhere in the analysis of dreams, associations of the most varying quality are used in connecting thoughts as if they were of equal value, and I shall yield to the temptation to imagine, as it were visually, the process by which *amyls* was replaced by *propyls* in the dream-thoughts.

Suppose, on the one hand, there is the group of ideas around my friend Otto, who does not understand me, puts me in the wrong, and gives me a liqueur smelling of amyl; on the other, connected by contrast, there are the ideas relating to my Berlin friend, who does understand me, would say that I am in the right, and to whom I owe so much valuable information, including his thoughts on the chemistry of sexuality.

From Otto's group, what ought especially to arouse my attention is determined by the recent events occasioning the dream; *amyls* belongs to these distinctive elements, predestined to enter the dream-content. The wealth of ideas in the 'Wilhelm' group virtually draws its life from its contrast with 'Otto', and it is the elements in it alluding to those already aroused in 'Otto' that are given prominence. Indeed, in this entire dream I move to and fro from one person who annoys me to another whom I can contrast with him at will; point for point, I can call up my friend against my adversary. Thus, 'amyls' from the Otto group wakes memories from the sphere of chemistry in the other group too; trimethylamin, supported from many sides, enters the dream-content. '*Amyls*' too might be able to enter the dream-content unchanged; however, it is subject to the influence of the 'Wilhelm' group, as out of the entire range of memories covered by this name, one element is picked out that is capable of yielding a double determination for amyls. '*Propyls*' is close to '*amyls*' for this association; it is met half-way by Munich and the *Propylea* from the 'Wilhelm' sphere. In *propyls-Propylea* both fields of ideas come together. As though by compromise, this middle element then enters the dream-content. A *mediating common factor* is created here admitting of multiple determination. This makes it utterly clear that if an element is determined many times over, its entry into the dream-content is bound to be made much easier. For this mediating factor to be formed, our attention is displaced from what is actually meant to something closely associated with it.

Studying the injection-dream has already given us an insight into the processes of condensation in dream-formation. We have been able to identify as particular functions of the work of condensation: its selection of elements occurring many times in the dream-thoughts; its formation of new unities (collective figures, composite structures), and its production of mediating common factors. What the larger purpose of condensation may be, and what helps to bring it about, are questions we shall not raise until we come to deal with the psychical processes of dream-formation in relation to one another. For the moment, let us be content with affirming that *condensation* in dreams constitutes a remarkable relationship between dream-thoughts and dream-content.

The work of condensation in a dream can most easily be grasped if it has selected words and names for its objects. Words are often treated as things in dreams, and then they go through the same combinations, displacements, substitutions and also condensations as the representations of things.

I

A colleague once sent me an article he had written in which, in my judgement, a physiological discovery of modern times had been overestimated, and above all dealt with in extravagant language. The next night I dreamed a sentence which clearly referred to this article: '*That is a really norekdal style.*' At first I had difficulty in analysing this word-formation; there was little doubt that it was created in parodic imitation of the superlatives 'colossa*l*' and 'pyramida*l*'; but it was not easy to say where it came from. Finally I broke down the monster into the two names '*Nora*' and '*Ekdal*' from two well-known dramas by Ibsen.* I had previously read a newspaper article about Ibsen by the same author whose latest opus I had criticized in this way in my dream.

II

One of my patients recounted a short dream to me which ended in a nonsensical word-combination. She is with her husband at some peasant celebration and then says: '*That will end in a general Maistollmütz.*' It is accompanied in her dream by the obscure thought that it is a pudding made of maize, a kind of polenta. The analysis broke the word down into *Mais* [maize]—*toll* [crazy]—*mannstoll* [man-crazy]—*Olmütz,** all of them recognizable as remnants from a conversation at table. Hidden behind *Mais*, as well as an allusion to the recently opened Jubilee Exhibition,* were the words: *Meissen* (a figurine of *Meissen* porcelain representing a bird); *Miss* (her relative's English governess had travelled to *Olmütz*); *mies*=nasty, miserable, used in Jewish slang in jest; and a long chain of ideas and connections started off from each separate syllable of this lump of a word.

III

A young man had his door-bell set ringing late in the evening by an acquaintance handing in a visiting-card. That night he has this dream: *a workman is waiting late at night to put the room-telephone*

[*Zimmertelegraph*] *to rights. After he has gone, it still goes on ringing, not with one continuous ring but only intermittently. The servant fetches the man back, and he says: 'It's odd how even people who are tutelrein don't know how to deal with this kind of thing.'*

As we see, the unimportant occasion for the dream refers only to one element in it. It only becomes significant once it has attached itself to an earlier experience of the dreamer's, just as slight in itself, which he has endowed with the significance of a proxy. As a boy living with his father, when drowsy with sleep he once spilt a glass of water on the floor so that the cable of the room-telephone was soaked and the *continuous ringing* disturbed his father's sleep. As the continuous ringing correlates to getting wet, the *intermittent ringing* is then used to stand for *drops falling*. But the word '*tutelrein*' can be analysed along three lines, aiming at three kinds of dream-material: '*Tutel*' =*Curatel*, which means guardianship; *Tutel* (perhaps '*Tuttel*') is a vulgar term for a woman's breast, and the component '*rein*' [clean] takes over the first syllables of '*Zimmertelegraph*' to form '*zimmerrein*' ['house-trained'], which has a great deal to do with wetting the floor, and in addition echoes a name present in the dreamer's family.[5]

IV

In a fairly long, chaotic dream of my own, which is apparently centred on a journey by ship, it happens that the next landing-station is called *Hearsing* and the one after that *Fliess*. This latter is the name of my friend in B.,* which has often been the goal of my journeys. But *Hearsing* is made up of the place-names of our local railway line in Vienna, which end so frequently in-*ing*: *Hietzing*,

---

[5] We employ the same analysis and synthesis of syllables—truly a syllabic chemistry—in inventing all kinds of witticisms when we are awake. 'What is the cheapest way of acquiring silver [*Silber*]? You go to an avenue of silver poplars [*Silberpappeln*], order them to be silent, then the '*Pappeln*' [gossiping] will stop and the silver is free.' The first reader* and critic of this book made the objection—which will probably be repeated by those who follow him—that 'the dreamer often appears too witty'. That is correct, as long as it refers only to the dreamer; it only involves disapproval if it is meant to apply to the interpreter too. In real, waking life I can make little claim to the description 'witty'; if my dreams appear witty, that is not because of my disposition, but on account of the peculiar psychological conditions under which the dream is worked out, and it is closely connected with the theory of Wit and the Comic. The dream is made witty because the straight and nearest way to express its thoughts is barred to it; it is made witty of necessity. My readers can be assured that my patients' dreams produce an impression just as witty (at least forced-witty)—or even more so—than mine.

Liesing, Mödling (Medelitz, 'meae deliciae' in its old name, that is, 'my delight' [*meine Freud'*]), combined with the English *hearsay*, which indicates slander, and sets up the connection with the unimportant daytime initiation of the dream, a poem in the *Fliegende Blätter** about a slanderous dwarf 'Sagter Hatergesagt' [Sez-he He-sed]. By connecting the final syllable '-*ing*' to the name *Fliess* one gets '*Vlissingen*', in reality the port in the sea-journey where my brother puts in when he comes to visit us from England. But the English name of *Vlissingen* is *Flushing*, which is the same as blushing, and recalls the woman patient I am treating who suffers from a 'blushing-anxiety'; it also reminds me of a recent publication on this neurosis by Bechterew which caused me feelings of annoyance.

V

Another time I had a dream made up of two separate parts. The first is the word '*Autodidasker*', which I recall vividly; the other is identical with a brief and innocuous fantasy I entertained some days before, to the effect that when next I see Professor N., I have to say: 'The patient I last consulted you about really does suffer only from a neurosis, just as you surmised.' Now not only does the new coinage '*Autodidasker*' have to satisfy the requirement that it should contain or represent a compromise-meaning, this meaning should also relate coherently to my intention, repeated from waking life, to give Professor N. that satisfaction.

Now *Autodidasker* breaks down easily into *Autor* [author], *Autodidakt* [self-taught] and *Lasker*,* which is also associated with the name *Lassalle*.* The first of these words leads to the—this time significant—occasion for the dream. I had brought my wife several volumes by a well-known author who is a friend of my brother's and who comes, so I have heard, from the same village as I do (J. J. David).* One evening she talked to me about the profound impression made on her by the sad and moving story of a wasted talent in one of David's novellas, and our conversation then turned to the signs of talent we perceived in our own children. Influenced by what she had just been reading, she expressed her concern about the children, and I consoled her with the remark that dangers of this sort are just the kind that can be averted by education and upbringing. That night my train of thought continued, took up my wife's worries, and wove all kinds of things into them. An observation the writer had made to my brother with regard to getting married showed my thoughts a side-path which made it possible to represent them in my dream. This path led to Breslau,* where a lady who was a very close friend of ours had got married. In Breslau I found examples in *Lasker* and *Lassalle* for my concern about wasting one's life for a woman, which formed the heart of my dream-thoughts. The two enabled me to represent both kinds of this disastrous influence at the same time.[6] 'Cherchez la femme', the phrase summing up these thoughts, leads me, though in a different sense, to my brother, who is still unmarried, and who is called *Alexander*. Now I note that *Alex*, our shortened form of his name, sounds almost like *Lasker* back-to-front, and that an impulse from this must have shared in effectively directing my thoughts to the roundabout route via Breslau.

However, my games with names and syllables in this dream contain a further meaning. They stand for the wish that my brother should enjoy a happy family life, and they do in the following way. In the novel of an artist's life, *L'Œuvre*,* whose subject-matter must have suggested itself to my dream-thoughts, it is well known that the writer has portrayed himself and his own family happiness in certain episodes, appearing in this role under the name of *Sandoz*. He probably reached this change of name along the following route. If we reverse *Zola* (as children like to do), we get *Aloz*. That was probably not sufficiently disguised for him; so he replaced the syllable *Al*, which also introduces the name *Al*exander, by the third syllable of that name, *sand*, and that is how *Sandoz* came about. And it is in much the same way that my *Autodidasker* was made.

My fantasy of telling Professor N. that the patient we had both seen only suffered from a neurosis entered my dream in the following way. Shortly before the end of my working year I acquired a patient who utterly baffled my diagnostic skills. A severe organic complaint, perhaps some change to the spinal cord, suggested itself, but was not to be demonstrated. It would have been tempting to diagnose a neurosis, which would have brought an end to all my difficulties, were it not that the sexual case-history, without which I refuse to diagnose a neurosis, was so energetically rejected by my

---

[6] *Lasker* died of progressive paralysis, that is, as the consequence of an infection (lues) caught from a woman; *Lassalle*, it is well known, died in a duel fought on account of a lady.

patient. Not knowing what to do, I turned to the physician whom I revere most deeply for his humanity (as do others) and to whose authority I most readily defer. He listened to my doubts, said they were justified, and then said: 'Keep the man under further observation; it will be a neurosis.' As I know that he does not share my views on the aetiology of neuroses, I did not contradict him, but neither did I hide my scepticism. A few days later I told my patient that I did not know how to treat him, and advised him to turn to someone else. Then to my great surprise he began to ask me to forgive him for lying to me; he was so ashamed, and then he revealed to me that very item of sexual aetiology which I had expected, and which I needed if I was to assume a neurosis. It was a great relief to me, but at the same time a source of embarrassment; I had to admit that my adviser, not thrown off course by requiring a case-history, had seen more correctly. I intended to tell him, when I saw him again—to tell him that he was right and I was wrong.

Now this is just what I am doing in my dream. But what sort of a wish-fulfilment is it supposed to be if I admit I am wrong? That is just what I do wish. I would like to be wrong in my worries and fears, or rather, I would like my wife, whose fears I have taken over into my dream, to be wrong. The theme associated with being right or wrong in the dream is not too far away from the one which is really interesting for the dream-thoughts. The same alternatives—organic or psychological damage caused by a woman—or rather, by sexuality: tabetic paralysis or neurosis. The way *Lassalle* met his end is connected more loosely to the latter.

Professor N. plays a part in this tightly knit (and, when carefully interpreted, quite transparent) dream, not only on account of this analogy, nor of my wish to be wrong, nor yet on account of his further connections with Breslau and with the family of our friend who married there—but also because of the following little occurrence which followed our consultation. After he had finished his professional task with that speculation, he turned his interest to personal matters. 'How many children do you have now?' 'Six.'—A dubious, respectful gesture.—'Girls? Boys?' 'Three of each. They are my pride and my wealth.' 'Now take care, the girls are no problem, but bringing up boys can have its difficulties later.' I rejoined that they had been quite well-behaved so far. Clearly this second diagnosis pleased me just as little as his earlier judgement that my patient only had a neurosis. These two impressions, then, are connected by proximity, being experienced all at once. In taking the story of the neurosis into my dream, I am substituting it for our conversation about bringing up children, which reveals still further connections with the dream-thoughts, as it touches so closely on my wife's worries as she later expressed them. Thus, even my anxiety that N. might be right in his remarks about the difficulties in bringing up boys makes its way into the dream-content by hiding behind the representation of my wish that I was wrong to nurse such fears. The same fantasy functions unaltered to represent the two opposite sides of the alternative.

These verbal distortions in our dreams are very like those familiar to us from paranoia, but which are also present in hysteria and obsessive ideas. The linguistic tricks of children, who at certain times really do treat words as if they were objects, inventing new languages and artificial word-combinations, are in this respect the common source for dreams and for the psychoneuroses.

Where the dream contains speech expressly distinct from thoughts, the rule applies without exception that the words spoken in the dream derive from words remembered in the dream-material. The words spoken are either retained intact or are slightly altered in expression; frequently they are a patchwork of various utterances remembered from the day. In this process the actual words remain the same, but their sense is altered to yield a different meaning, or multiple meanings. Speech in dreams often functions merely as an allusion to an event which was accompanied by the words remembered.

(b) *The Work of Displacement*

While we were collecting examples of dream-condensation, another relationship, probably no less significant, must already have caught our attention. We could not fail to observe that the elements pushing to the fore in the dream-content as essential components certainly did not play the same part in the dream-thoughts. As a corollary, this statement can also be reversed. What is clearly essential in the content of the dream-thoughts does not need to be represented in the dream itself at all. The dream, one might say, is *centred differently*; its content is ordered around a centre made up of elements other than the dream-thoughts. Thus, for example, the centre of the dream-content in the dream of the botanical monograph is clearly the element 'botanical'; the dream-thoughts, on the other hand, are concerned with complications and conflicts arising from obligations incurred by services between colleagues; thereafter they focus on the charge that I am giving up too much for the sake of my hobbies— and the element 'botanical' has no place at all here in the heart of the dream-thoughts, unless it is loosely related to it by contrast, for botany had never been one of my favourite subjects. In my patient's Sappho dream, *climbing up and down, being up above and down below* are made to be its centre; but in fact the dream deals with sexual relations with persons of the *lower* orders, so that only one of the elements in the dream-thoughts seems to have entered the dream-content, but then to an undue extent. Similarly, though it is true that cruelty reappears as a factor in the content of the may-beetles dream, which is about the relations of sexuality to cruelty, it does so in a connection of a different kind and without any reference to sexuality, that is, it is torn from its context and recast in a different, unfamiliar form. Again, in the dream of my uncle the meaning of the yellow beard that forms its centre seems to bear no relation to the ambitious wishes we have acknowledged to be the heart of the dream-thoughts. Dreams of this kind give the impression of *displacement* with good reason. In complete contrast to these examples, the dream of Irma's injection shows that in the formation of a dream individual elements are also able to retain the place they occupy in the dream-thoughts. When we first recognize this new relation, which is entirely variable in meaning, between dream-thoughts and dream-content, it is likely to fill us with astonishment. If in the course of some normal psychical process we find one idea being singled out from many others and becoming particularly vivid in our consciousness, we usually regard this success as proof that it has been accorded the especially high psychical value (a certain degree of interest) which is its due. But now we discover that this value accorded to particular elements in the dream-thoughts is not retained or not taken into account in forming a dream. After all, there is no doubt as to which are the most valuable elements in the dream-thoughts; our judgement needs no help to tell us. But in dream-formation these essential elements, charged though they are with intense interest, are dealt with as if they were of little value, and instead their place is taken in the dream by other elements which certainly had little value in the dream-thoughts. At first this gives the impression that the psychical intensity[7] of the particular ideas was not taken into consideration at all in their selection for the dream, but only the varying nature and degree of their determination. What enters the dream, one might think, is not what is important in the dream-thoughts, but what appears frequently and variously in them. However, this assumption will not take our understanding of dream-formation much further, as from the outset it leaves no room for thinking that these two factors in selecting elements for the dream—multiple determination and inherent value—must necessarily work along the same lines to produce the same meaning. It supposes that the ideas which are the most important in the dream-thoughts are likely to be the ones that recur in them most often, for the particular dream-thoughts radiate from them as it were from a centre. And yet the dream can reject these elements, even though they are emphasized so intensely and reinforced so variously, and it can take up into its content other elements which are characterized by the second quality, inherent value, alone.

To solve this problem we shall make use of another impression we had when we were examining the over-determination of the dream-content. Perhaps a number of my readers have already made their own judgement that this over-determination of the dream-elements is not a remarkable discovery at all, as it is quite self-evident. After all, the analysis starts out from the dream-elements and registers all the ideas that are associated with them; no wonder, then, that in the thought-material acquired in this way these are the very elements to emerge with particular frequency. I doubt if I could accept this objection, but I shall put into words something that sounds rather like it: among the thoughts brought to light in the analysis there are many which are more remote from the heart of the dream, standing out like artificial elements interpolated for some purpose. Their purpose is easy to discover; these are the very ones that set up the connection, often forced and far-fetched, between the dream-content and the dream-thoughts, and if these elements were eliminated from the analysis, the components of the dream would lose not

---

[7] The psychical intensity, value, weight of interest, of an idea is of course to be kept separate from the sensory intensity of its representation.

only their over-determination by the dream-thoughts, but any adequate determination by them at all. This leads us to the conclusion that very probably the multiple determination which decides the selection of elements for the dream is not always a primary factor in forming it, but often a secondary result of some power at work in the psyche as yet unknown to us. All the same, over-determination must be an important factor for the entry of particular elements into the dream, for we can observe that it is produced in some profusion in cases where it arises with some assistance from the dream-material.

The thought suggests itself that a psychical power is operative in the dream-work which on the one hand strips the psychically valuable elements of their intensity, and on the other creates new values *by way of over-determination* out of elements of low value; it is the new values that then reach the dream-content. If this is what happens, then *a transference and displacement of the psychical intensity* of the individual elements has taken place; as a consequence, the difference between the texts of the dream-content and the dream-thoughts makes its appearance. The process we are assuming here is *the* essential part of the dream-work; it has earned the name of *dream-displacement*. *Dream-displacement* and *dream-condensation* are the two foremen in charge of the dream-work, and we may put the shaping of our dreams down mainly to their activity.

It is also easy for us, I think, to recognize the psychical power which manifests itself in the facts of dream-displacement. The result of this displacement is that the dream-content no longer looks the same as the heart of the dream-thoughts, that the dream reproduces only a distortion of the dream-wish present in the unconscious. But dream-distortion is already familiar to us; we traced it back to the censorship exercised by one psychical agency in our mental life against another. Dream-displacement is one of the main means of bringing this distortion about. *Is fecit cui profuit.** We may assume that dream-displacement comes about through the influence of that censorship, the censorship of endopsychic defence.

The way in which these factors—displacement, condensation, and over-determination—interact in the process of dream-formation, and the question of which becomes dominant and which secondary, are things we shall set aside for later inquiries. For the moment we can state a second condition which the elements reaching the dream have to fulfil: *they should have evaded the censorship set up by resistance.* But from now on in interpreting dreams we propose to take account of dream-distortion as an indubitable fact.

(c) *The Means of Representation in Dreams*

Besides the two factors of dream-*condensation* and dream-*displacement* which we discovered were at work in the transformation of latent thought-material into the manifest dream-content, in pursuing our inquiry we shall encounter two further conditions which undoubtedly have an influence on the selection of material reaching the dream. But before continuing, even at the risk of appearing to pause on our way, I would like to look for the first time at what goes on in the course of interpreting a dream. If I am not deceived, the best way of explaining this clearly and ensuring it is proof against any objections would be for me to take one particular dream as a model, work out its interpretation, as I did in Chapter II with the dream of Irma's injection, but then to put together the dream-thoughts I have uncovered and from them reconstruct the process by which the dream was formed, that is, to complete the analysis of the dream by its synthesis. I have carried out this work on many examples for my own instruction; but I am unable to use them here because I am prevented by a number of considerations regarding the psychical material which most fair-minded people would approve of. These considerations were less troublesome when analysing dreams, for the analysis did not need to be complete, and retained its value even if it took us only a little way into the fabric of the dreams. But for their synthesis, the only way I knew for it to be convincing was for it to be complete. I could only give a complete synthesis of the dreams belonging to people unknown to the reading public. And as the means of doing so is only available to me from my patients, that is, from neurotics, this part of my account of dreams will have to be postponed until—in some other place—I am in a position to take the psychological explanation of neuroses to the point where it is possible to make the connection to our topic.

I know from my attempts at synthesizing dreams out of the dream-thoughts that the material emerging in the course of interpretation varies in value. One part of it is made up of the essential dream-thoughts, that is, those which completely replace the dream and would be sufficient by themselves to take its place, if the dream were not subject to censorship. The other part can be summed up under the name of '*collaterals*'; taken all together, they represent the paths along which the real wish rising up from the dream-thoughts is translated into the wish expressed in the dream. One group of these collaterals consists of associations to the real dream-thoughts, corresponding in my scheme to displacements from the essential onto the trivial. A second group comprises those thoughts which make combinations from among these materials, once trivial but now turned into important items by the displacement, and which lead from these to the dream-content. A third group, finally, contains the thought-combinations and ideas occurring to us which enable us to come upon the intermediate collaterals in the course of interpreting the dream-content; but it is not the case that *all of these ideas and combinations together should necessarily* have been involved in the formation of the dream.

At this point we are interested solely in the essential dream-thoughts. These mostly reveal themselves to be a complex of thoughts and memories with the most complicated structure, having all the features of the trains of thought familiar to us from waking life. Quite often they are lines of thought starting out from more than one centre, but not without their points of contact; almost invariably one train of thought is accompanied by its contradictory opposite, associatively linked to it by contrast.

Of course, the individual parts of this complicated structure stand in the most various logical relations to one another. They form foreground and background, digressions and explanations, they set terms and conduct proofs and raise objections. Then, when the entire mass of these dream-thoughts is subject to the pressure of the dream-work, and the pieces are whirled about, broken up, and pushed up against one another, rather like ice-floes surging down a river, the question arises: what has become of the bonds of logic which had previously given the structure its form? What kind of representation does the dream give to 'when', 'because', 'just as', 'although', 'either–or', and all the other relational terms without which we can understand neither sentences nor speech?

Our first answer must be that the dream has no means at its disposal among the dream-thoughts of representing these logical relations. Mostly it disregards all these terms and takes over only the factual substance of the dream-thoughts to work upon. It is left to the interpretation of the dream to re-establish the connections which the dream-work has destroyed.

This inability to express such relations must be due to the nature of the psychical material which goes to make the dream. After all, the fine arts, painting and sculpture, are subject to a similar limitation in comparison with literature, which can make use of speech. Here too the cause of the incapacity lies in the material which both arts use as their medium of expression. Before painting came to recognize the laws of expression applying to it, it used to go to some lengths to make up for this disadvantage. In ancient pictures we read scrolls issuing from the mouths of painted figures, reproducing in writing the spoken words the painter despaired of representing pictorially.

It may be that an objection will be raised at this point, disputing the dream's inability to represent logical relations. True, there are dreams where the most complicated intellectual operations go on, reasoning and counter-reasoning, chopping logic and drawing analogies. But here too appearances are deceptive. If we go further into the interpretation of dreams of this kind, we will learn that this is all *dream-material, not the representation of intellectual activity in the dream.* The ostensible thinking in the dream reproduces the *subject-matter* of the dream-thoughts, not the *relations of the dream-thoughts to one another*; and establishing such relations is what constitutes thinking. I shall offer some examples of this. However, the easiest thing is to make the point that everything spoken in dreams and expressly identified as such is always an—unaltered or only slightly modified—reproduction of words which are also present in the recollected material of the dream-thoughts. Words spoken are often only an allusion to an event retained in the dream-thoughts; the meaning of the dream is something quite different.

However, I do not dispute that work of critical thinking, which does not simply repeat material from the dream-thoughts, also has a share in forming the dream. I shall have to elucidate the influence exercised by this factor at the end of the present discussion. It will then emerge that this work of thinking is not produced by the dream-thoughts, but by the dream, which in some sense has already been completed.

For the moment, then, let us continue to accept that dreams do not have a particular way of representing logical relations between dream-thoughts. Where, for example, a contradiction is present in a dream, it is either a contradiction to the dream or a contradiction from the content of one of the dream-thoughts; the contradiction in the dream corresponds to a contradiction *between* the dream-thoughts only in a very indirectly mediated way.

But just as painting finally succeeded in finding a way of expressing at least the intention of the words spoken by the figures represented—tenderness, menace, warning, and the like—by a different means from fluttering scrolls, so it has emerged that it is possible for the dream to take into account particular logical relations between its dream-thoughts by suitably modifying its distinctive mode of representation. We may learn that different dreams take them into consideration to a different extent. One dream will disregard the logical coherence of its material entirely, while another will try to suggest it as fully as possible. In this respect dreams depart to a varying extent from the text they have before them to work upon. By the way, dreams show a similar variability in the way they behave towards the temporal sequence of the dream-thoughts, if the sequence is set up in the unconscious (as it is, for example, in the dream of Irma's injection).

What means, then, is the dream-work able to use to indicate these relations, which are so difficult to represent, in the dream-thoughts? I shall attempt to list them one by one.

First of all, the dream does justice to the connection undeniably existing between all the pieces of the dream-thoughts by concentrating them into the unified representation of a situation or an event. It renders *logical connections* in terms of *simultaneity*; in doing so, it proceeds like the painter who assembles all the philosophers or poets to present a picture of the School of Athens* or of Parnassus, for though they never gathered in one hall or on one mountain-top, they surely form a community in our thoughts.

The dream continues this method of representation in its details. Whenever it shows two elements close together, this is a guarantee that there is a particularly intimate relation between their equivalents in the dream-thoughts. It is not unlike what happens in our system of writing: *ab* means that both letters should be spoken as one syllable; *a* and *b* with a space between is a sign that *a* is to be read as the last letter of one word and *b* as the first of another. Accordingly, the combinations in the dream are not formed of random, completely disparate elements from the dream-material, but from ones which are also intimately related in the dream-thoughts.

To represent *causal relations* the dream has two procedures which, in essentials, amount to the same thing. When the dream-thoughts run something like: 'because this was so and so, then such and such was bound to happen', the dream's main way of representing this is to present the subordinate clause as an introductory dream and then add the main clause as the main dream. If I have interpreted aright this sequence can also be reversed, but the main clause will always correspond to the main part of the dream.

A patient of mine once gave me a beautiful example of this way of representing causality. I shall give a full account of her dream later. It consisted of a short prologue and a very elaborate part, with a very strong thematic centre, which might be entitled: 'Told by the Flowers'. The preliminary dream went like this: *She is going into the kitchen to the two maidservants and scolding them for not having finished preparing 'the bite to eat'. As she does so she sees a lot of crude kitchenware turned on end to dry off and piled in a heap on top of one another. The two maids go to fetch water, and to do so it is as if they have to wade into a river coming up as far as the house or into the yard.*

Then the main dream followed, introduced like this: *she is climbing down from high up over curiously shaped railings, glad that her dress does not catch on anything, etc.* The dream-prologue refers to the lady's parental house. It is likely that she has often heard the words in the kitchen from her mother. The piles of coarse crockery derive from the modest hardware shop in the same building. The second part of the dream contains an allusion to her father, who used to chase after servant-girls and caught a fatal illness during a flood—the house stood very near the riverbank. The thought hiding behind this preliminary dream, then, is: because I come from this house, from such modest and disagreeable circumstances. The main dream takes up the same thought, presenting it transformed by wish-fulfilment: I am of high degree; that is, rather: because I am of such low degree, my life has been such and such.

As far as I can see, a division of the dream into two unequal parts does not always signify a causal relation between the thoughts in both parts. It often seems as if the same material were being presented in the two dreams from different points of view; or the two dreams have arisen from separate centres in the dream-material, overlapping in content in such a way that what is the centre of one dream may play a part in the other as an allusion, and the other way round. In a certain number of dreams, however, the division into a shorter introductory dream and a longer dream following it does in fact signify a causal relation between the two parts. The second method of representing causal relations is employed where the material is meagre; it operates by transforming one image in the dream, whether a person or a thing, into another. We can seriously maintain that this connection is a causal one only in cases where we actually see this transformation happening; not where we merely observe that the one person or thing has now taken the place of the other. I said that the two methods of representing causal relations amounted to the same thing: in both cases *causation* is represented by *succession*, in the first case by one dream following another; in the second by the immediate transformation of one image into another. Admittedly, in most cases the causal relation is not represented at all, but submits to the inevitable one-after-the-other of the elements, inevitable even in the working of our dreams.

The dream has no way at all of expressing the alternative 'either . . . or'. It usually takes up the two options into one context as if they had equal rights. The dream of Irma's injection contains a classic example. Its latent thoughts clearly state: it is not my fault that Irma continues to suffer pain; the blame is to be ascribed *either* to her resistance to accepting my solution *or* to the unfavourable sexual conditions under which she lives, which I cannot change, *or* the nature of her pain is not hysterical at all, but organic. However, the dream presents all three of these all-but mutually exclusive possibilities and has no difficulty in adding the dream-wish as a fourth explanation. The 'either . . . or' was then introduced into the interconnections of the dream-thoughts by me after I had interpreted the dream.

However, where a dreamer wants to use an 'either . . . or' in recounting a dream: 'it was either a garden or a living-room, etc.', what is present in the dream-thoughts is not an alternative but an 'and', a simple addition tacked on. With this 'either . . . or' we are mostly describing a still insoluble characteristic in a dream-element: its haziness. The rule for interpretation in this case is: the separate options of the apparent alternative are to be treated as equal and linked by 'and'. For example, I dream that after waiting for a long time in vain for the address of my friend, who is staying in Italy, I receive a telegram giving me this address. I see it printed in blue on the paper slip of the telegram; the first word is blurred, something like:

> *via,*
> or   *villa,* the second clearly: *Sezerno.*
> or even (*casa*).

The second word, which sounds like an Italian name and reminds me of our etymological discussions, also expresses my annoyance that he should have kept the place where he is staying *secret* for so long; but in the analysis it can be seen that each one of the three items suggested as alternative possibilities for the first word offers an independent and equally valid starting-point for the chain of thoughts.

The night before my father was buried* I had a dream of a printed panel, a placard or notice nailed up, rather like the notices forbidding smoking in railway waiting-rooms. Written on it is either:

> *You are requested to close your eyes.*

or

> *You are requested to keep an eye closed.*

which I am used to representing in the following form:

> *You are requested to keep* $\genfrac{}{}{0pt}{}{your}{an}$ *eye(s) closed*

Each of the two versions has its particular meaning and leads the dream-interpretation along particular paths. I had arranged for the ceremony to be as simple as possible, because I knew what the departed thought about such events. However, other members of the family did not approve of such puritan simplicity; they considered it would let us down in front of the funeral guests. That is why one phrase in the dream makes the request to 'close an eye', that is, to be forbearing, or 'turn a blind eye'. In this case it is particularly easy to grasp the meaning of the haziness we have described as expressing an 'either . . . or'. The dream-work has not been successful in producing for the dream-thoughts a unified form of words which will also carry two meanings. The two main lines of thought have already separated in the dream-content.

Alternatives are difficult to represent, and in some cases they are expressed by the division of the dream into two halves of equal length.

The dream has a very striking way of dealing with the category of *opposites* and *contradictions*. This is simply disregarded. To the dream 'No' does not seem to exist. In particular, it prefers to draw opposites together into a unity or to represent them as one. Indeed, it also takes the liberty of representing some random element by its wished-for opposite, so that at first one cannot tell which of the possible poles is meant positively or negatively in the dream-thoughts. In one of the dreams just referred to, whose preliminary we have already interpreted ('because I am of such low degree'), the dreamer is climbing over a railing. As she does so, she is holding a branch of blossom in her hands. What this image brings to her mind is how the angel in pictures of the Annunciation (she herself is called Maria) carries a tall lily, and how the girls dressed in white walk in the Corpus Christi procession when the streets are decked with green branches. From these ideas it is quite certain that the blossoming branch in her dream alludes to sexual innocence. But the branch is covered with red blossoms, each one resembling a camellia. By the end of the way she has taken, her dream continues, the blossoms are rather faded; this is followed by unmistakable allusions to her period. Thus the same branch, which is carried as if it were a lily and borne by an innocent maiden, is at the same time an allusion to the *dame aux camélias*,* who always wore a white camellia, as we know, but wore a red one at the time of her period. The same blossoming branch ('des Mädchens Blüthen' ['the maiden's blossoms'] in Goethe's poem*) represents both sexual innocence and its opposite. The same dream, too, which expresses her joy at going through life immaculate, in some places allows the opposite train of thought—that she has been guilty of various sins against sexual purity (in childhood, that is)—to shimmer through. In analysing the dream we found it easy to distinguish the two trains of thought from each other; of these, the consolatory one seems to lie in a surface stratum, the reproachful one much deeper; both directly contradict each other, while their equal but opposite elements have come to be represented by the self-same dream-elements.

There is only one of the logical relations to benefit—to a very great extent—from the mechanism of dream-formation. It is the relation of similarity, congruence, or convergence, the *just like*, which dreams have the most various means of expressing better than anything else. Indeed, the mergers, or cases of 'just like' present in the dream-material constitute the basis for the formation of the dream, and a considerable part of the dream-work consists of creating new mergers of this kind, if those already present are prevented from entering the dream by the censorship of resistance. Finding representations for the relation of similarity is aided by the dream-work's activity of condensation.

In general, dreams represent *similarity, congruence, having features in common* by concentration into a *unity*, which is either already present in the dream-material or newly formed. The first case can be called an *identification*, the second a *composite formation*. Identification is applied when personages are involved; *composite formation* in cases where objects are the material to be unified, though composites can also be generated by personages. Places are often treated like persons.

In identification, only one of the figures linked by some common factor gets to be represented in the dream-content, while the other figure or figures seem to be suppressed. However, this one figure goes through all the relationships and situations which are generated both by the cover-figure itself and by the figure it covers. In composite formations that include persons, the dream-image will already contain features belonging to the figures individually but not shared by them, so that when these features are combined, a new unity, a composite figure, is certain to appear. The composite itself can be brought about in various ways. Either the figure in the dream takes its name from one of the persons it refers to—we know then that such and such a person is intended, rather as we know such things when awake—while its visual appearance belongs to the other person; or the dream-image is composed of visual features which in real life are distributed between both. Instead of being represented by visual features, the second person's share can also be rendered by the gestures we ascribe to him, the words we have him speak, or the situation we place him in. In this last instance the sharp distinction between identification and the formation of composite figures begins to get blurred.

The common quality or thing that justifies—that is, occasions—the merging of the two persons can be represented in the dream, or it can be absent. As a rule it is this very identification or formation of a composite figure that serves to make such representation of this common factor superfluous. Instead of repeating: *A* is hostile towards me, but so is *B*, I form a composite figure of *A* and *B* in my dream, or I imagine *A* performing the kind of action which does not belong to him, but which we know to be characteristic of *B*. The dream-figure obtained in this way encounters me in my dream in some new connection, and the circumstance that it signifies both *A* and *B* justifies me in entering what the two have in common, that is, their hostility towards me, into the appropriate place in the dream-interpretation. In this way I can often achieve an extraordinary degree of condensation in the dream-content; I do not need to make a direct representation of a complicated set of circumstances relating to a person, if I have found someone else to associate with him who has the same claim on some of those circumstances. It is easy to see the extent to which using identification as a means of representation can also serve to circumvent the censorship set up by resistance, which creates such harsh conditions for the dream-work. It may be that the impulse towards censorship is to be found in the very ideas associated in the dream-material with the one person; so then I find a second person who also has connections with the offensive material, but only with a part of it. This contact at a point where censorship is operative now entitles me to form a composite figure characterized by unimportant features from both persons. Being free of censorship, this composite figure is now fit to be taken up into the dream-content, and by making use of condensation in my dream I have satisfied the requirements of the dream-censorship.

Where a feature common to the two figures is also represented in the dream, this is usually a hint to look for some other, hidden common feature which the censorship has made impossible to represent. A displacement with regard to the shared feature has taken place here, to some extent in order to facilitate its representation. The presence in my dream of a composite figure having unimportant shared features allows me to infer that a different common feature, one by no means unimportant, is present in the dream-thoughts.

Accordingly, identification, or the formation of composite figures, serves different purposes: first, to represent a feature both persons have in common; secondly, to represent a *displaced* common feature; but thirdly, to find expression for a common feature that is merely *wished for*. Since wishing it to be the case that two people have something in common is often the same as *exchanging* them, this relation too is expressed in the dream by identification. In the dream of Irma's injection, I wish to exchange this patient for another, that is, I wish that the other were my patient, as Irma is; the dream takes account of this wish in showing me a figure who is called Irma, but who is examined in a posture in which I have only had occasion to see the other. In the dream of my uncle, this exchange is made into the centre of the dream; I identify myself with the minister by treating and judging my colleagues no better than he does.

It has been my experience that every dream without exception deals with oneself. Dreams are absolutely self-centred. Where a strange figure, not my self, appears in the dream-content, I can assume without hesitation that my self is concealed behind that figure. I can add to my self. At other times when my self appears in the dream, its situation tells me that another person is concealed behind it by a process of identification. The dream should then remind me to transfer something attached to this figure to myself, that is, the hidden thing we have in common. There are also dreams in which my self appears together with other figures, which again, once the identification is resolved into its components, reveal themselves to be my self. These identifications then allow me to associate my self with certain ideas, whose entry the censorship has stepped in to prevent. Thus I can represent my self in a dream in many ways, directly, or by means of identification with other figures. Several identifications of this kind make it possible for a tremendous wealth of dream-thoughts to be condensed.[8]

Identifications of localities bearing their own names can be resolved into their constituents even more transparently than those of persons, because in these cases there is no disturbance from the overweening self. In one of my Rome-dreams (p. 150), the place I am visiting is called *Rome*; I am astonished at the number of German placards on a streetcorner. This is a wish-fulfilment which makes me

---

[8] If I am in doubt as to which of the figures in my dream is concealing my self, I keep to the following rule: the figure in the dream which is subject to some affect, which I sense in my sleep, is the one that conceals my self.

promptly think of *Prague*; the wish may derive from a nationalistic German period of my youth. At the time I had the dream, a meeting in *Prague* with my friend was in prospect. So the identification of Rome and Prague can be explained by a wished-for common factor: I would prefer to join my friend in *Rome* than in *Prague*, and for this meeting I would rather exchange *Prague* for *Rome*.

The possibility of creating composite formations is high among the features which often give dreams their fantastic character, as they import into the dream-content elements which could never have been the objects of our perception. The psychical process of forming composites in a dream is clearly the same as when we imagine or depict a centaur or a dragon when we are awake. The distinction is only that when we create fantastic figures while we are awake, the decisive thing is what impression we intend the new figment itself to make, whereas the composite formation in the dream is determined by a factor lying outside its figuration, the feature common to them in the dream-thoughts. Composite formations in dreams can be executed in many different ways. The simplest represents only the characteristics of the one thing, and this representation is accompanied by knowing that it also applies to another object. A more careful technique combines features from both objects into a new image, and as it does so it makes skilful use of similarities between the two objects drawn more or less from real life. The new formation can turn out to be an utter absurdity or even be a great success as a fantasy, depending on the wit and the subject-matter that go into composing it. If the objects that are to be condensed into a unity are too disparate, the dream-work is often content to create a composite formation with a more distinct centre, to which less distinct determinant factors attach themselves. It is as if in this case fusion into one image has not been successful; the two representations overlap and produce something like a competition between the visual images. If we wanted to demonstrate how a concept is formed out of many separate perceptions, we might do it by representing them like this in a drawing.

Of course, dreams are swarming with composite formations of this kind; I have already given some examples in the dreams I have analysed so far; I shall now add some more. In the dream on p. 240, in which the patient's life is 'told by the flowers', in flowery, that is, euphemistic style, the dream-self is carrying a branch of blossom in her hand. This, as we have learned, signifies both innocence and sexual sinfulness at the same time. In addition, the way the blossoms grow on the branch recalls *cherry* blossom; the blossoms themselves, taken singly, are *camellias*, so that the whole gives the impression of an *exotic* plant. The factor the elements in this composite formation have in common emerges from the dream-thoughts. The blossoming branch is put together from allusions to gifts, which moved her, or were supposed to move her, to yield to persuasion. In childhood the cherries, in later years the spray of camellias; the exoticism is an allusion to a much-travelled botanist who tried to win her favour with a drawing of flowers. Another patient created an intermediate thing in her dream out of seaside *bathing-huts, water closets*, and the *attic rooms* of our urban dwelling-houses. The first two elements share a reference to the naked body and exposure in a state of undress; by combining this with the third element, we may infer that (in her childhood) the attic too had been the scene of an exposure. Another dreamed that her elder brother promised to treat her to caviare, and that afterwards this brother's legs were covered in *black beads of caviare*. The element of *contagion* in the moral sense and the memory of a *rash* in her childhood, which made her legs appear covered with *red* spots rather than *black*, have combined with the beads of caviare into a new concept, that of '*what she got from her brother*'. Parts of the human body are treated in this dream like objects, as they are in other dreams.

I stated earlier that the dream has no means of expressing the relation of contradiction, or of the opposite to a statement, that is: 'No.' I shall now set about contradicting this statement for the first time. It is possible to represent one group of these cases we can sum up as 'opposites' simply by identification, as we have seen; that is, the opposite can be associated with an exchange, a replacement. I have given frequent examples of this. Another group of opposites, coming roughly under the category of '*vice versa*', '*on the contrary*', comes to be represented in the dream in the following remarkable, one might almost say witty, way. The 'vice versa' does not reach the content of the dream as itself, but makes its presence in the material known by representing a closely related piece of the already formed dream-content—retrospectively, as it were—*in reverse*. It is easier to illustrate the process than describe it. In the pleasant dream of 'up and down', the dream represents climbing in reverse, just as it represents the original model in the dream-thoughts, Daudet's introductory scene where Sappho is presented, by its opposite; movement in the dream is difficult at first and then easier, whereas in the scene in the novel the climb is easy at first and later becomes increasingly difficult. 'Above' and 'below' as they relate to the brother are also represented in the dream the other way round. This indicates that there is a relation of reversal or opposition existing in the dream-thoughts between two parts of the subject-matter, which we discovered when we found that in the dreamer's childhood fantasy he was carried by his nurse, the reverse of the way the hero carried his beloved in the novel. My dream of Goethe's attack on Herr M. (p. 280) also contains a 'vice versa' of this kind which has to be corrected before it becomes possible to interpret the dream. In my dream Goethe attacked a young man, Herr M.; in real life, as the dream-thoughts retained it, my friend, a man of some importance, was attacked by an unknown young writer. In my dream I calculate from the year of Goethe's death* onwards; in real life the calculation started from the year the paralysis-sufferer was born. The thought that was decisive for the dream-material turns out to be a contradiction to the idea that Goethe should be treated as if he were a madman. 'Vice versa,' says my dream, 'if you don't understand that book, it's you who are feeble-minded, not the author.' All these dreams of reversal, it seems to me, also imply the derogatory phrase 'seeing the *wrong side* of someone' (the reversal relating to the brother in the Sappho dream).

If we want to pursue the relationships between dream-content and dream-thoughts further, it is best at this stage if we set out from the dream itself and ask: what is the significance of certain formal characteristics in the representation of dreams as they relate to the dream-thoughts? Foremost among these formal characteristics which cannot but strike us in dreams are the differences in sensory intensity among the individual dream-constructions, and the variations in the degree of distinctness among particular parts of the dream or among entire dreams when compared with one another. The differences in sensory intensity run the gamut from a clarity of contour which one is inclined—though with no warrant for it—to judge greater than that of reality, down to an infuriating haziness which we declare is characteristic of dreams because it does not fully compare with any of the degrees of imprecision we occasionally perceive in objects in real life. Moreover, we usually describe an impression received from an indistinct object in our dream as 'fleeting', while the clearer dream-images, we think, have stood up to our perception of them for some little time. Now the question is: what conditions in the dream-material give rise to these variations in vividness among different parts of the dream-content?

At this point we must first take some steps to counter certain almost inevitable expectations. Since real sensations experienced during sleep can also belong to the material of the dream, one is likely to assume that these elements in the dream, or elements deriving from them, will stand out in the dream-content with particular intensity, or conversely that what strikes us as particularly vivid in the dream can be put down to real sensations of this kind made in our sleep. But my experience has never confirmed this. It is not correct that the elements in the dream that are the offspring of real impressions during sleep (nervous stimuli) will be more remarkable for their vividness than others that have their origin in memories. Reality does not count as a factor in determining the intensity of dream-images.

Moreover, one might still expect that the sensory intensity (the vividness) of the individual dream-images has some relation to the psychical intensity of the elements in the dream-thoughts corresponding to them. In the latter, degree of intensity coincides with degree of psychical value; the most intense and vivid elements are simply the most significant, and these form the centre of the dream-thoughts. Now we know, it is true, that these are the very elements which the censorship most prevents from entering the dream-content. All the same it could be that their nearest offspring, acting as their proxy, carry a higher degree of intensity, though, being only derivative, without necessarily forming the centre of the dream-representation. However, comparative observation of dream and dream-material will destroy this expectation too. The intensity of the elements in the dream-material has nothing to do with the intensity of the elements in the dream; between the two a total '*transvaluation of all psychical values*'* does in fact take place. It is often solely in the fleeting breath of a dream-element hidden by more powerful images that we are able to discover a direct descendant of what held such powerful sway in the dream-thoughts.

The intensity of the elements in the dream proves to be deter-mined in a different way, that is, by two factors independent of each other. At first it is easy to see that those elements acting as the means of expression for the wish-fulfilment are represented with particular intensity. But then we learn from analysis that it is the most vivid elements of the dream that also generate the most trains of thought, that the most vivid are at the same time the best-determined. It does not alter the sense if we reformulate that last empirical statement as follows: the greatest intensity is shown by those elements in the dream which required the fullest and most complex *work of conden-sation* for their formation. We may anticipate that it will be possible to express this condition and the other condition of wish-fulfilment in one single formula.

I would like to prevent the problem I have just been dealing with—the causes of the greater or lesser intensity or distinctness of particular elements in a dream—from being confused with a different one concerning the variations in clarity to be found among entire dreams or sections of dreams. In the first, the opposites are clarity and haziness; in the second, clarity and confusion. It is evident, of course, that the rise and fall of the qualities on both scales occur in tandem. A part of the dream that appears clear to us usually contains intense elements; an unclear dream, on the contrary, is put together from less intense elements. Nevertheless, the scale from apparently clear to indistinct presents a far more complicated problem than the one presented by fluctuations in the vividness of the dream-elements; indeed, at this stage it is not possible to discuss it, for reasons I shall develop later. In a few individual cases one notes with some surprise that the impression of clarity or indistinctness made by a dream is not in the least significant for its structure, but has its origin in the dream-material as one of its components. In this con-nection I recall a dream of mine which on waking appeared to me to be so particularly well-structured, complete, and clear that, still drowsy as I was, I proposed to admit a new category of dreams which were not subject to the mechanism of condensation and displace-ment, but might be described as 'fantasies during sleep'. Closer scrutiny revealed that this rare dream displayed the same gaps and fissures in its structure as any other; so I gave up the category of dream-fantasies. However, the content of the dream was, in essence, that I was propounding to my friend* a difficult and long-sought theory of bisexuality, and it was due to the wish-fulfilling power of the dream that this theory—which the dream did not give, by the way—appeared so clear and complete to us. What I had taken to be a judgement on the finished dream was a part—and indeed the essential part—of the dream-content. You might say that the dream-work was encroaching on my first waking thoughts, conveying to me in the guise of a *judgement on* the dream that part of the dream-material it had failed to represent exactly *in it*. I once came upon the exact counterpart to this dream in a patient who did not want to tell her dream at all at first, although it belonged in the analysis, 'because it is so indistinct and confused'. Finally, protesting repeatedly that she could not vouch with certainty for her account, she gave it: several figures occurred in the dream, herself, her husband, and her father, and it was as if she did not know whether her husband was her father or who her father really was, or something like that. From combining this dream with the ideas occurring to her during the consultation, it emerged that her dream is about the pretty ordinary story of a maid-servant who had to confess that she is expecting a child and has to hear doubts as to 'who the father (of the child) really is'.[9] Here the lack of clarity shown by the dream was also a part of the material that initiated the dream. A part of this content had been represented in the dream's *form*. In my experience, one very rarely arrives at a situation like this one, where it is possible to interpret the clarity or confusion of the dream in terms of certainty or doubt present in its subject-matter. This qualitative scale from clarity to confusion is essentially dependent on the operation of the factor in dream-formation which I have so far left undiscussed, but which I shall be obliged to reveal later on.

In many of the dreams which stay for a stretch firmly within a certain situation and scene, interruptions occur which are described by the following words: 'But then it is as if at the same time it were a different place, and such and such happened there.' This kind of interruption to the main action of the dream—which can be resumed after a while—turns out to be a subordinate clause, an interpolated thought. The conditional in the dream-thoughts is represented in the dream by simultaneity ('if' = 'when').

---

[9] Accompanying hysterical symptoms: absence of her periods and great ill humour, this patient's main affliction.

What is the meaning of the sensation of inhibited movement, so close to anxiety, which appears so often in dreams? We want to move forward and cannot budge, we want to get something done and constantly come upon obstacles. The railway train is about to leave and we are unable to catch it; we raise our hand to avenge some insult and it fails us, and so on. We have already met this sensation in our discussion of exhibition-dreams, but we have not yet made a serious attempt to interpret it. It is convenient but inadequate to answer that motor paralysis occurs in sleep, making its presence felt in the said sensation. We are justified in asking: 'Then why do we not dream of inhibited movement all the time?', and in expecting that this sensation, which can always be summoned up in sleep, will be used for some representational purpose and will only be roused by a need for representation present in the dream-material.

This not-being-able-to-get-something-done does not always appear in dreams as a sensation, but also simply as a part of the dream-content. One such case is particularly suitable for explaining the significance of this item in our dreams. I will give a shortened version of a dream in which I appear accused of dishonesty. *The location is a jumble of a private clinic and several other places. A servant appears, summoning me to an examination.* In the dream I know that something has been missed, and that the examination is taking place because I am suspected of having appropriated what was lost. The analysis shows that 'examination' is to be taken as ambiguous, and includes 'medical examination'. Conscious of my innocence and of my function as consultant in this place, I accompany the servant unperturbed. At a doorway we are received by another servant, who says, pointing to me: 'You've brought* him? *But he's a decent man.' Then I enter a large hall, without the servant, where there are machines standing, and which reminds me of an Inferno with its diabolical punishments. Strung up on one apparatus I see a colleague who might have had every reason to be concerned about me; but he ignores me. Then I am told I can go now. I can't find my hat, and so I still can't go.*

The wish-fulfilment in the dream is obviously that I am acknowledged to be an honest man and allowed to go; so there must be all sorts of material in the dream-thoughts containing the contrary. Being allowed to go is the sign of my absolution; so if the ending of the dream introduces an occurrence that prevents me from going, the implication is that the suppressed contradictory material is using this feature to assert itself. So not finding my hat means: 'You're not an honest man after all.' Not-being-able-to-carry-something-out in this dream is an *expression of the contrary*, a '*No*'; hence, this qualifies my earlier claim that dreams are unable to express a negation.[10]

In other dreams, where not-being-able-to-move occurs as a sensation, not merely as a situation, the same contradiction is more powerfully expressed by this sensation of motor inhibition, as an impulse of willing opposed by a counter-willing. That is, the sensation of motor inhibition represents a *conflict of wills*. We shall hear later that this selfsame motor paralysis in sleep is one of the fundamental conditions of psychical activity while dreaming. Now the impulse that is transferred along the paths of motor activity is of course the will, and the fact that we are certain to feel this impulse inhibited while we are asleep is what makes the whole process so very appropriate for representing the *willing* and the '*No*' that opposes it. My explanation of anxiety makes it easy to grasp why the sensation of inhibited will is so close to anxiety and why it is combined with it so often in our dreams. Anxiety is an impulse of the libido, proceeding from the unconscious and inhibited by the preconscious. So in those dreams where the sensation of inhibition is combined with anxiety, it must be a matter of an impulse of willing which was once capable of developing libido, a matter of sexual stirrings.

(d) *Regard for Representability*

So far we have been occupied with examining how the dream represents relations between the dream-thoughts, but in doing so we frequently returned to the broader topic of the general nature of the changes undergone by the dream-material for the purposes of dream-formation. Now we know that the dream-material, largely divested

---

[10] In the complete analysis, an association with a childhood experience emerges by way of the following chain: 'The Moor has done his duty. The Moor *can go*.'* And then the joking question: 'How old is the Moor, when he has done his duty? One year old, for then he can walk/go.' (They tell me I had such a mop of black hair when I was born that my young mother declared I was a little Moor.)—Not being able to find my hat is an experience from the dream-day carrying many meanings. Our housemaid, a genius at putting things away, had hidden it.—This ending to my dream also conceals a rejection of sad thoughts of death: 'it will be a long time still before I have done my duty; I must not go yet.'—Birth and death, as in the dream of Goethe and the paralytic patient, which took place shortly before (p. 280).

of its logical relations, undergoes a concentration, while at the same time displacements of intensity among its elements necessarily bring about a psychical transvaluation of this material. The displacements we were considering turned out to be substitutions of one particular idea by another somehow closely associated with it; and they were useful in condensation, for in this way, instead of two elements, an intermediate factor common to them both gained entry to the dream. We have not yet mentioned another kind of displacement. But we learn from our analyses that there is such a thing, and that it makes its presence known in a *transposition in the words used to express* the thought concerned. In both cases it is a matter of displacement along a chain of associations, but the same procedure takes place in different psychical spheres, and the result of this displacement is that in one case one element is replaced by another, while in the other one element exchanges its verbal formulation for another.

This second kind of displacement occurring in the formation of dreams is not only of great theoretical interest; it is also particularly well suited to explain the appearance of fantastic absurdity in which dreams disguise themselves. As a rule, the displacement follows the direction taken when a colourless and abstract expression of the dream-thought is exchanged for a pictorial and concrete one. The advantage, and thus the intention of the substitution, is obvious. For the dream, what is pictorial is *capable of representation*, can be integrated into a situation where an abstract expression would cause similar difficulties for the dream-representation to those a political leading article, say, would make for an illustrated news-magazine. But not only representability has to gain from this exchange; the several interests of condensation and the censorship are able to do so too. Once the abstract, unusable thought is transformed into a pictorial language, the contacts and identities which the dream-work requires—and will create where they are not present—come about between this new expression and the rest of the dream-material more easily than before, for language has developed in such a way that the concrete words of every language are far richer in associations than its conceptual terms. One can imagine that a good bit of the intermediary work in the process of dream-formation takes place in this way—by appropriate linguistic transformation of the individual thoughts—for it aims at reducing the separate dream-thoughts to the most economical and unified expression possible in the dream. In the process one thought, whose expression perhaps for other reasons is fixed, will, in the way it distributes and selects, affect the expressive possibilities of another thought, and it may be that it does this from the outset, working as a poet does. If a poem is to rhyme, the second rhyming line is bound by two conditions; it has to express its due meaning, and it must find the same sound as the first rhyming line. The best poems, I suppose, are those where we do not notice the intention to find the rhyme, but where from the outset each thought has induced the other to choose the verbal expression that with a little adaptation will allow the rhyme to emerge.

In some cases this exchange of expression serves condensation by an even shorter route, by finding a form of words which, being ambiguous, will permit more than one dream-thought to be expressed. In this way the entire field of verbal punning is available for the dream-work to use. We should not be astonished at the role allotted to the word in dream-formation. You might say that the word, being the point of convergence for many kinds of ideas, is predestined for ambiguity; and the neuroses (obsessive ideas, phobias) take advantage of the word in their condensations and disguises no less brazenly than dreams. It is easy to show that dream-distortion too benefits from this displacement of expression. We are indeed misled if one ambiguous word is used instead of two unambiguous ones; and replacing our everyday, sober mode of expression by a pictorial one bars our understanding, particularly as the dream never states whether the elements it presents are to be interpreted literally or in a transferred sense, or whether they should be referred to the dream-material directly or via the mediation of interpolated phrases. I have already given several examples from dreams of representations which are only held together by the ambiguity of their expression ('Her mouth is wide open', in the injection-dream; 'I still can't go', in the last dream quoted, p. 253) and so on. I shall now relate a dream where the pictorial representation of abstract thoughts play a considerable part in its analysis. The distinction between this kind of interpretation and interpretation by means of symbolism can still be sharply defined; in symbolic dream-interpretation the key to the symbolization is arbitrarily chosen by the dream-interpreter; in our instances of verbal disguise these keys are generally known and given by established linguistic usage. If one has the right idea on the right occasion it is possible to resolve dreams of this kind wholly or piecemeal, even without recourse to what the dreamer has to say.

A lady with whom I am on friendly terms dreams: *She is at the opera. It is a performance of Wagner, which has gone on until 7.45 in the morning. In the stalls and the pit there are tables where people are eating and drinking. Her cousin, just back home from his honeymoon, is sitting at one of these tables with his young wife; nearby, an aristocrat. It is said about the latter that the young woman brought him something back from her honeymoon, quite openly, rather as one might bring a hat back from a honeymoon. There is a tall tower in the middle of the stalls, with a platform at the top surrounded by iron bars. The conductor is up there on high, wearing the features of Hans Richter;* he is constantly running round behind the bars, sweating frightfully, and from this position he is conducting the orchestra, which is ranged below around the base of the tower. She herself is sitting with a friend* (a lady of my acquaintance) *in a box. Her younger sister makes to pass her a large lump of coal from the stalls, giving as her reason that she really didn't know that it would take so long and by now she must be bitterly cold. (Rather as if the boxes had to be heated during the long performance.)*

The dream is nonsensical enough, to be sure, though on the other hand it is skilfully made to suggest a situation. The tower in the middle of the stalls from which the conductor directs the orchestra; above all, the coal her sister passes up to her! I deliberately did not ask for an analysis of this dream; having some knowledge of the personal relations of the dreamer, I succeeded in interpreting parts of it without her aid. I knew that she had had much sympathy for a musician whose career had been interrupted by mental illness. So I decided to take the tower in the stalls literally. Then it emerged that the man she had wished to see in Hans Richter's place in her dream *towered high above* the other members of the orchestra. This tower can be described as a *composite formation made by apposition*; with its lower part it represents the man's greatness; with the bars at the top, behind which he is running round like a prisoner or an animal in a cage (allusion to the unhappy man's name*), it represents what later befell him. Something like '*Narrenturm*' ['Tower of Fools']* might be the word in which both thoughts could coincide.

After this revealed the dream's mode of representation, it was possible to attempt to resolve the second apparent absurdity, the one involving the coals her sister passes up to her, by using the same key. 'Coals' was bound to signify 'secret love'.

> *Kein Feuer*, keine *Kohle*
> kann brennen so heiß
> als wie *heimliche Liebe*,
> von der niemand was weiß.*

> [*No fire*, no *coal*
> Can burn as hot
> As a *secret love*
> Which the world knows not.]

She herself and her friend were *left sitting* [i.e. unmarried]; her younger sister, who still had prospects of marrying, passes the coals up to her 'because she really didn't know *that it would take so long*'. What would not take so long is not stated in the dream. If we were telling a story we would fill the gap with: 'the performance'. In the dream we may consider the sentence as it stands, declare it is ambiguous, and add: 'before she got married'. The interpretation 'secret love' is then supported by the reference to the cousin sitting in the stalls with his wife, and by the *open love affair* fabricated about the wife. The dream is dominated by the oppositions set up between secret and open love, the fire of her own love and the young wife's coldness. In both parts of the dream, by the way, we have '*someone high up*' as a composite formulation referring to both the aristocrat and the musician who raised such high hopes.

In the course of the foregoing discussions we have at last disclosed a third factor whose part in the transformation of dream-thoughts into dream-content is not to be underestimated: *regard for the representability of the peculiar psychical material used by the dream*. That is, usually, representability in visual images. Of the various subsidiary connections to the essential dream-thoughts, preference is given to the one allowing visual representation, and the dream-work does not flinch from the effort of first recasting the recalcitrant material, for instance, into a different verbal form, even if the formulation is more unusual, just as long as it makes representation possible and puts an end to the psychological distress of the pent-up activity of the thoughts. This process of pouring the thought-content into a different mould, however, can at the same time be employed for the work of condensation and create associations with another thought which would otherwise not be available. This other thought itself may— perhaps in order to meet the first halfway—have previously altered its original expression.

In view of the part played by verbal jokes, quotations, songs, and proverbs in the mental life of the educated, it would be entirely in accordance with expectation if disguises of this kind were used very frequently indeed in representing dream-thoughts. For example, what do carts signify in a dream, when each one is filled with a different vegetable? It is the wishful opposite of 'Kraut und Rüben' [cabbages and turnips], that is, 'all of a muddle', and accordingly stands for 'disorder'. I was surprised that this dream has only once been related to me. There is only a small range of subject-matter for which a universally applicable dream-symbolism has developed, on the basis of generally known allusions and verbal substitutions. Dreams, by the way, share a good deal of this symbolism with psychoneuroses, legends, and popular customs.

Indeed, looking at it more closely, one has to acknowledge that with this kind of substitution the dream-work is not doing anything original at all. To achieve its aims—in this case, representability free of censorship—it is simply walking the ways already laid down before it in unconscious thinking; it gives preference to those transformations of repressed material which are also allowed to reach consciousness in the guise of witticisms and allusions, and which fill all the fantasies of neurotics. At this point we suddenly gain an understanding of Scherner's dream-interpretations, with their nucleus of truth which I have defended elsewhere. Our preoccupation in our imaginations with our own bodies is by no means peculiar only to dreams, nor characteristic of these alone. My analyses have shown me that it is a regular occurrence in the unconscious thinking of neurotics, and can be traced back to the sexual curiosity which youths or maidens growing up develop about the genitals of the other sex, but also about their own. But, as Scherner and Volkelt emphasize quite correctly, the house is not the only sphere of representations used to symbolize the body, whether in dreams or in the unconscious fantasizing of neurosis. I am acquainted with patients who have, it is true, preserved the architectonic symbolism of the body and the genitals (though of course sexual interest extends far beyond the external genitals); to them, pillars and columns signify legs (as in the *Song of Songs**); every gateway reminds them of one of the body's orifices ('hole'); every water-supply pipe of the urinary apparatus; and so on. But the spheres of ideas belonging to plant life or to the kitchen are just as readily chosen as a hiding-place for sexual images. In the first case the ground has been abundantly prepared by linguistic usage, the deposit of fantasy-comparisons from the oldest of ancient times (the Lord's 'vineyard', the 'seed', the maiden's 'garden'* in the *Song of Songs*). Apparently innocuous allusions to the daily tasks of the kitchen let us think and dream the nastiest as well as the most intimate details of sexual life, and the symptoms of hysteria become simply uninterpretable if we forget that sexual symbolism can conceal itself behind the unremarkable things of everyday life as its best hiding-place. There is sound sexual meaning to it when neurotic children cannot bear the sight of blood or raw meat, or throw up on eating eggs and pasta, or when the natural human fear of snakes is monstrously intensified in the neurotic; and wherever neurosis makes use of this kind of disguise, it is walking the way that all mankind once travelled in ancient cultural eras, whose existence, beneath only a little debris, is still attested today by linguistic usage, superstition, and custom.

At this point I shall include the promised flower-dream of a patient, where I will draw attention to everything with a sexual interpretation. After this beautiful dream was interpreted, the dreamer liked it no longer.

(a) Introductory dream: *She goes into the kitchen to the two maid-servants and scolds them for not having finished preparing 'the bite to eat', and as she does so she sees so much crockery turned up on end to dry, crude crockery in piles.* Later addition: *the two maids go to fetch water, and as they do it is as if they are wading into a river which is rising right up to the house or into the yard.*[11]

(b) Main dream:[12] *She is climbing down from high up*[13] *over curious railings or fences, which are combined into large diamond shapes made up of interwoven fencing in small squares.*[14] *It is really not made for climbing; she has constant trouble in finding a foothold, and is glad that her dress*

---

[11] For the interpretation of this introductory dream as 'causal', see p. 240.

[12] The course of her life.

[13] High birth. Wishful opposite to the introductory dream.

[14] Composite formation combining two localities: the attic, as it was called, of her father's house, where she played with her brother, who was the object of her later fantasies, and the farm belonging to the wicked uncle who used to tease her.

doesn't catch on anything, so that as she is walking she remains decent.[15] *As she goes she is carrying a **large branch** in her hand,*[16] *actually like a tree, thickly covered with **red blossoms, branched and spreading.***[17] *The idea of cherry-blossoms is present, but they look like **camellias** in full bloom, which, however, do not grow on trees. As she goes down, she has at first **one**, the suddenly **two**, and then again **one**.*[18] *As she gets to the bottom, the lower **blossoms are already rather fallen.** Now that she has reached the bottom, she sees a manservant who is, she might almost say, combing a tree just like hers, that is, he is ruffling **thick tufts of hair** hanging down from it like moss. Other workmen have cut down **branches** of this kind from a **garden** and thrown them onto the **street** where they are **lying around**, so that **many people take them.** But she asks whether it's all right, whether she too **can take one** for herself.*[19] *In the garden a young **man** is standing* (someone she knows, a foreigner), *and she approaches him to ask whether she can transplant such **branches to her own garden.***[20] *He embraces her, but she struggles, and asks him what he is thinking of, and whether he thinks it is permitted to embrace her like that. He says there is nothing wrong, it is allowed.*[21] *He then declares he is ready to go with her into the **other garden** to show her how to plant it, and says something to her that she doesn't quite understand: 'anyway, I need three metres—*(later she says 'square metres') *or three fathom cords of ground.' It was as if in return for being helpful he would demand something of her, as if he intended to **be compensated in her garden**, or as if he wanted to **cheat on** some law, so that he would have an advantage and she come to no harm. She doesn't know whether he really showed her something then.*

I must mention yet another sphere of ideas which frequently serves to mask a sexual content in dreams, as it does in neurosis. I mean that involved in a *change of dwelling*. Moving out of an apartment can easily be replaced by *taking off* [*one's clothes*],* that is, by an

---

[15] Wishful opposite of a real recollection from her uncle's farm that she used to expose herself while asleep.

[16] Like the one carried by the angel in the Annunciation, a tall lily.

[17] For the explanation of this composite formation, see p. 240: innocence, period, *la dame aux camélias*.

[18] Indicating the number of figures serving her fantasies.

[19] Whether she could also pull one down,* that is masturbate.

[20] The branch had by now taken over the function of proxy for the male genitals; it also, by the way, contains a very clear allusion to her family name.

[21] Refers, like the following, to precautions in marriage.

ambiguous word belonging to the sphere of ideas of dress. If the dream also contains a *lift*, then we recall that as a verb in English it also implies *to lift someone's clothes*.

Of course I have an excess of material of just this sort, but reporting it would take us too deep into a discussion of neurotic conditions. It all leads to the same conclusion, that we do not need to assume a specific symbolizing activity on the part of the psyche in the course of the dream-work. On the other hand, we may assume that the dream makes use of any symbolizations already present and waiting in unconscious thinking, because these satisfy the requirements of dream-formation better, both on account of their representability and also in most cases on account of their freedom from censorship.

(e) *Examples: Calculating and Speaking in Dreams*

Before I put the fourth factor controlling the formation of dreams in its due place, I will give some examples from my dream collection; some are able to illustrate the interaction of the three factors we are already familiar with; some to present belated evidence for certain unsupported assertions, or draw irrefutable conclusions from them. Indeed, in the foregoing account of the dream-work I have found it very difficult to prove my results by using examples. The instances I used to illustrate particular propositions only have any value as evidence in the context of a dream-interpretation; torn out of this frame of reference they lose their beauty, and a dream-interpretation that only skims the surface soon becomes so broad that it makes it easy to lose the thread of the argument it is supposed to be illustrating. I hope this reason of art will serve as my excuse for stringing together all sorts of examples whose only connection is that they relate to the text of the preceding section.

First, a few examples of particularly curious or unusual modes of representation in dreams. A lady's dream goes like this: *a maid-servant is standing on the ladder as if to clean the windows, and she has a chimpanzee and a gorilla–cat* (later corrected to: *angora cat*) *with her. She throws the animals onto the dreamer; the chimpanzee cuddles up to the dreamer, and that is most disgusting.* This dream has realized its intention by very simple means, by taking a turn of phrase literally and representing it as its wording says. 'Monkey' and the names of animals in general are pejoratives, insults, and the situation in the dream says just that: '*throwing insults around*'. This collection will shortly give further examples of the use of this simple trick in the dream-work.

Another dream proceeds in a similar way: *a woman with a child who has a strikingly malformed skull; she has heard it said of this child that he became like this on account of the way he was lying in his mother's womb. The doctor says it might be possible to give the skull a better shape by compressing it, but that would damage the brain. She thinks: as it's a boy, it will do him less damage.* This dream contains the concrete representation of the abstract concept: '*impressions of child-hood*', which the dreamer has heard in the explanations of her therapy.

The dream-work strikes out on a rather different path in the following example. The dream includes the memory of an excursion to the Hilmteich* near Graz: *it is dreadful weather outside; a miserable hotel, with water dripping down the walls, the beds are damp.* (This last bit of the content is less direct in the dream than I have put it.) The dream signifies '*superfluous*'. The abstraction present in the dream-thoughts has first, quite forcibly, been made ambiguous, perhaps replaced by 'overflowing' or by 'fluid' and 'superfluous', and then successfully represented by a number of similar impressions. Water outside, water inside on the walls, water in the form of damp in the beds, all fluid and *super*fluous.*

It would be a separate task to collect modes of representation of this kind and arrange them according to the principles they are based upon.

The dream-work often succeeds in representing very recalcitrant material, such as proper names, by a forced use of very remote associations. In one of my dreams, *I was given a task to do by my old professor, Brücke. I am preparing a slide, and I pick something out of it that looks like crumpled silver paper.* (More of this dream later.) The idea attaching to it, which occurs to me with some difficulty, is 'Stanniol' [silver foil], and then I realize that what I am alluding to is the name *Stannius*, which is the name of the author of a treatise on the nervous system of fishes which I once regarded with awe. The first scientific task my teacher gave me did actually involve the ner-vous system of a fish, the Ammocoetes.* Clearly, the picture-puzzle could do nothing with this name.

We can learn a great deal from the numerals and calculations occurring in dreams about what the dream-work consists of and how it plays around with its material, the dream-thoughts. Superstitions regard dreaming of numbers as particularly auspicious, so I will produce a few examples from my collection.

I

From the dream of a lady, shortly before bringing her therapy to an end:

She wants to pay for something; her daughter takes 3 fl. 65 kr.* from her purse; but she says: what are you doing? It only costs 21 kr. This bit of the dream was clear to me on account of the dreamer's circumstances, without any further enlightenment from her. The lady was a foreigner who had found a place for her daughter in a Viennese educational establishment and was able to continue under my treatment for as long as her daughter remained in Vienna. In three weeks' time the school year would come to an end, and with that her therapy would end too. On the day before her dream, the principal of the seminary had put it to her that she might like to decide to keep the child there for a further year. She had clearly continued this suggestion in her own mind to the point of thinking that in that case she would also be able to extend her treatment for another year. Now this is what the dream is referring to, for a year equals *365* days and the three weeks to the end of the school year and of her treatment can be replaced by *21* days (though not by that number of consultations). The numerals that were present early in the dream-thoughts were allotted a cash value in the dream, though the meaning this expressed was nothing more profound than 'time is money'.* It is true, *365* Kreuzer make *3 Gulden 65 Kreuzer*. The very small sums appearing in the dream are obviously a wish-fulfilment; her wish reduced the costs of both her treatment and the year's education at the seminary.

II

The numerals in another dream lead to more complicated associations. A young lady, married for a number of years, learns that an acquaintance of hers, Elise L., who is almost the same age as she is, has just got engaged. Soon afterwards she dreams: *she is sitting with her husband in the theatre; one side of the stalls is entirely empty. Her husband tells her that Elise L. and her fiancé had also wanted to go, but* had only got very bad seats, *3 for 1 fl. 50 kr.*, and of course they couldn't take those. In her opinion, that was no hard luck.

Where do the *1 fl. 50 kr.* come from? From an intrinsically trivial occasion from the day before. Her sister-in-law had been given *150 fl.* as a present by her husband, and was in a hurry to spend it, using it to buy some jewellery. Let us note that 150 fl. is *100* times 1 fl. 50 kr. Where does the *3* for the theatre seats come from? Only one association emerges for that: the engaged girl is younger than she is by that number of months—three. When we pursued the question of what the dream meant by presenting one side of the stalls as empty, we found its solution. It is an allusion, unchanged, to a little occurrence that gave her husband good reason to tease her. She had wanted to go to one of the performances advertised at the theatre for that week, and to be on the safe side she bought tickets several days beforehand, which meant she had to pay an advance-booking fee. When they arrived in the theatre they discovered that one side of the auditorium was almost empty; she had no need *to be in such a hurry.*

I shall now replace the dream with the dream-thoughts. 'It was *nonsense* to marry so early; *I had no need to be in such a hurry*; I can see from Elise L.'s example that I would still have got a husband, indeed one *a hundred times* better (husband, dear one),* if I had only *waited* (opposite to her sister-in-law's *hurry*). I could have bought *three* such husbands for the money (her dowry)!' We note that the numbers in this dream have altered in meaning and context far more than in the one just discussed. The dream's work of transformation and distortion has been more elaborate here, which we interpret as indicating that these dream-thoughts had a particularly high degree of resistance to overcome from within the psyche. We should also not overlook an absurd element in the dream-content, that is, that *two* people are supposed to occupy *three* seats. We will be encroaching on the interpretation of absurdity in dreams when we note that in content this absurd detail is meant to represent the most emphatic of the dream-thoughts: it was *nonsense* to marry so early. The number 3, referring to a quite unimportant comparison between the two persons (the difference of 3 months in their ages), is then skilfully employed to produce the nonsense required for the dream. The reduction of the real-life 150 fl. to 1 fl. 50 kr. is the equivalent of the *low value* ascribed to the husband (or dear one) in the dreamer's suppressed thoughts.

III

Another example shows us the arithmetic of dreams which has brought them into such disrepute. A man dreams: *he is sitting in the home of the B's* (a family he used to know) *and says, 'It was nonsense that you didn't give me Mali.' Then he asks the girl, 'How old are you, then?' Her reply: 'I was born in 1882.'—'Ah, then you are 28 years old.'*

As the dream took place in 1898, it is clear that the reckoning is wrong, and the dreamer's weakness in arithmetic might admit comparison with the paralytic patient's inadequacies, if it did not allow of a different possible explanation. My patient is one of the sort whose thoughts can never let go of any woman they happen to see. For some months the patient who regularly followed him into my consulting-room was a young lady whom he would encounter and ask after frequently, meaning to be entirely courteous in his behaviour towards her. She it was whose age he reckoned to be *28*. So much to explain the result of the ostensible calculation. However, *1882* was the year when he had married. He could not resist also getting into conversation with the two other female persons he met in my apartment, the two maidservants, by no means young, who used to open the door to him in turn, and when he did not find them very forthcoming, he explained to himself that they probably found him a '*settled*' elderly gentleman.

If we put these examples together with similar ones (to follow later), we may say: the dream-work is not doing arithmetic at all, it is not getting it either right or wrong; it is only putting together in the form of a calculation numerals occurring in the dream-thoughts which can be used as allusions to material resistant to representation. In doing so, it treats the numerals in exactly the same way as it does all other ideas, as it does names and speech which can be recognized as verbal presentations—that is, as material for expressing its intentions.

For the dream-work is also incapable of creating speech. However meaningful or irrational speech and reply in dreams may appear, the analysis tells us every time that in presenting them the dream has taken only fragments of speech spoken or heard in real life and dealt with them quite arbitrarily. It has not only torn them out of context and broken them up, accepting one bit and rejecting another, but often makes new combinations out of them, so that an apparently coherent speech in the dream will break down into three or four fragments in the analysis. In giving the words this new use, the dream has often departed from the meaning they had in the dream-thoughts, and discovered an entirely different meaning in the wording. On closer scrutiny it is possible to distinguish more distinct, compact elements in the dream-speech from others which function as connectives and have probably been filled in in the same way as we fill in missing letters and syllables when we are reading. Speech in dreams has something of the structure of breccia, in which larger fragments of various materials are bound together by a solidified matrix.

Strictly, it is true, this description applies only to those utterances in dreams which have something of the sensory quality of real speech, and can be described as 'speaking'. The others, which are not, as it were, felt, that is, heard as speech or uttered as speech (which are not accompanied by any acoustic or motor reinforcement in the dream, that is), are simply thoughts, appearing just as they do in our thought-activity when awake and passing unaltered into many of our dreams. Our reading-matter also seems to offer a full-flowing source, though hard to pursue, for the unimportant speech-material in our dreams. But everything that stands out conspicuously, in whatever way, submits to being traced back to speech pronounced in words we have ourselves uttered or heard in real life.

We have already found examples of the derivation of dream-utterances of this kind, which were made with other ends in mind. For example, in the 'innocuous market-dream' of p. 140, in which the words '*that's no longer available*' are used to identify me with the butcher, while a part of another speech, '*I don't recognize that, I won't have it*', really fulfils the task of making the dream innocuous. On the day before her dream, in fact, our dreamer had rebuked her cook for some impertinence with the words: '*I don't recognize that, behave yourself properly,*' and then she took the unimportant first part of this speech into her dream, in order to use it as an allusion to the later part, which would have fitted very well into the fantasy lying at the basis of the dream, but would also have revealed it.

A similar example, standing for many, which, indeed, all produce the same result:

A large yard, in which dead bodies are being burnt. He says: I'm going on. I can't bear the sight of it. (Not distinct as speech.) *Then he meets two butcher's boys, and asks: 'Well, did it taste good?' One of them answers: 'No, it didn't.' As if it were human flesh.*

The innocuous occasion for this dream is as follows: after their evening meal he paid a visit with his wife to their neighbours, good folk, but by no means *appetizing*. The hospitable old lady was just eating her supper, and *pressed* him (men have a joking compound word for it, with a sexual meaning) to taste some. He declined, he wasn't hungry any more. 'Oh, *go on*, you can manage it,' or words to that effect. So he has to taste it, and praises what she offered. '*That tastes good*.' Later, alone with his wife, he grumbles at the way his neighbour pushed herself on him, as well as at the quality of the food he had to taste. 'I can't bear the sight of it,' which was not definitely spoken even in his dream, is a thought referring to the physical charms of the lady who invited him to share her meal, and might be translated to mean that he has no desire to gaze on them.

The analysis of another dream will turn out to be more instructive. I shall relate it at this point on account of the very distinct speech forming its centre, but I shall not explain it until I deal with affects in dreams. My dream is very clear: *I have gone at night into Brücke's laboratory, and hearing a gentle knocking at the door I open it to* (the late) *Professor Fleischl, who comes in with several strangers and after a few words sits down at a table.* This is followed by a second dream: *My friend Fl. has come to Vienna inconspicuously; I encounter him in the street in conversation with my* (late) *friend P.,* and I walk with them to some place where they are sitting opposite each other as though at a small table, with myself to the fore at the narrow end at the little table. Fl. is telling us about his sister, and says: 'In three-quarters of an hour she was dead', and then something like: 'that is the threshold [Schwele]'.* As P. does not understand him, Fl. turns to me and asks me how much of his concerns I have told P. Then, overcome by quite remarkable affect, I try to tell Fl. that P. (can't know anything at all, of course, because he) is no longer among the living. But what I say, noticing the error myself, is:* **Non vixit.** *Then I give P. a penetrating look; beneath my gaze he becomes pale, hazy; his eyes become sick and blue—and finally he dissolves away. This makes me unusually glad, and I understand then that Ernst Fleischl too was an apparition, a* revenant, *and I find it perfectly possible for a figure of that kind to persist for only as long as it pleases us, and that it can be removed by someone else's wish.*

This beautiful dream includes so many of the puzzling characteristics of dream-content: criticism operating within the dream itself, so that I notice my mistake of saying '*Non vixit*' instead of '*non vivit*';* sitting at ease in the company of the dead, who are declared to be dead by the dream itself; the absurdity of the conclusion I draw from this and the great satisfaction it gives me—so that I would 'gladly give my life' to offer a full solution to these riddles. But, in reality I am incapable of doing what in fact I do in my dream: sacrificing my regard for persons dear to me to my ambition. However, any disguise would ruin the dream's meaning—which I know very well. So I shall content myself with selecting some elements from the dream to interpret, first here and then at a later point.

The scene in which I annihilate P. with a glance forms the centre of the dream. As I do so, his eyes become strangely and uncannily blue, and then he dissolves away. This scene is a remarkable imitation of one I really experienced. I was a demonstrator at the Physiological Institute and had the early shift. Brücke had learned that on a few occasions I had arrived late at the students' laboratory. One day he came on the dot of opening-time and waited for me. What he said to me was brief and to the point; but the words did not matter. What was overwhelming were his terrible blue eyes and the glance he gave me; I dissolved away before it, like P. in my dream, but to my relief P. had exchanged roles with me. Anyone who can recall those wonderful eyes of the master's, still beautiful in extreme old age, and anyone who ever saw his wrath, will have no difficulty in sharing the affects of the young sinner of long ago.

For a long time, however, I just could not find a source for the '*Non vixit*' with which I pass that sentence in my dream, until I recalled that the two words were so strongly distinct in my dream not because they were heard or called, but because they were seen. Then I knew straight away where they came from. On the pedestal of the Monument* to Emperor Joseph II in the Hofburg in Vienna the beautiful words can be read:

> Saluti patriae *vixit*
> *non* diu sed totus.

From this inscription I had picked out what was suited to the one, hostile, set of thoughts in my dream-thoughts, and was meant to say: 'The fellow hasn't any right at all to interrupt. After all, he's dead.' And then I could not help remembering that I had had the dream a few days after the memorial to Fleischl had been unveiled in the university arcades, and that while I was there I had seen Brücke's memorial once again, and (in my unconscious) must have reflected with regret that my friend P., with his great talents and undivided devotion to science, had been robbed by his all too early death of his well-founded claim to a memorial in these halls. So I raised this monument to my friend in my dream; his first name was *Josef*.[22]

According to the rules of dream-interpretation, I would still have no justification for replacing the *non vivit*, which I need, by the *non vixit* that my memory of the Joseph memorial puts at my disposal. This must have been made possible by the contribution of another element in the dream-thoughts. It tells me to pay some attention to the fact that the scene in my dream is the meeting-place for two currents of thought towards my friend P., a hostile one and an affectionate one, the first one on the surface, the second hidden, which both contrive to be represented in the same words '*Non vixit*'. Because he has rendered great services to science, I raise a monument to him; but because he has been guilty of a malevolent wish (expressed at the end of the dream), I annihilate him. I have just formed a sentence there with a very distinctive pattern, and in doing so I must have been influenced by some model. But where is a similar antithesis to be found, placing two opposing reactions to the same person in parallel, each of which has a claim to be fully justified and yet has no wish to disturb the other? In one place only, but a deeply impressive one for the reader: in Brutus' justificatory speech* in Shakespeare's *Julius Caesar*. 'As Caesar loved me, I weep for him; as he was fortunate, I rejoice at it; as he was valiant, I honour him; but, as he was ambitious, I slew him.' Does this not show the same sentence-construction and antithetical thinking as the dream-thoughts I have uncovered? So I am playing the part of Brutus in my dream. If only I could find another, confirmatory trace of this surprising parallel connection in the dream-content! I think it could be the following: my friend Fl. comes to Vienna in *July*. This detail has no support at all in real life. To my knowledge my friend has never been in Vienna in the month of *July*. But the month of *July* was named after *Julius Caesar*, and so might very well represent the

---

22 As a contribution to over-determination: my excuse for arriving late was that after working long into the night it was a long way from the *Kaiser-Josefstraße* to the Währingerstraße.

allusion I am looking for to the mediating thought that I am playing the role of Brutus.

Remarkably, I did once actually play Brutus. I performed the scene between Brutus and Caesar from Schiller's *Poems** before an audience of children. This was as a fourteen-year-old boy, together with my nephew, one year older than I, who had come to visit us from England—another *revenant*—for it was the playmate of my earliest childhood years who surfaced again with his return. Until I was almost four we had been inseparable, had loved each other and fought each other; and this childhood relationship has been decisive, as I have already suggested, for all my later feelings for companions of my own age. Since then my nephew John has had very many incarnations, bringing him back to life with now one side of his nature and now the other, as it is ineradicably fixed in my unconscious memory. He must have treated me very badly on occasion, and I must have shown courage towards my tyrant, for a little speech in my own justification has often been recounted to me, in which I defended myself when my father—his grandfather—called me to account: 'Why are you hitting John?' In the language of a child not yet two, it went: '*I hit him cos he hit me.*' It must be this childhood scene that turned the *non vivit* into *non vixit*, for in the language of later childhood 'hitting' is known by a word sounding just like *vixit*: *wichsen*; the dream-work is not above making use of connections of this sort. As for the hostility towards my friend P., which had so little cause in real life, he was my superior in many respects and therefore a suitable candidate to be a new edition of my playmate, so it certainly goes back to my complicated infantile relationship to John.

So I shall return to this dream again.

(f) *Absurd Dreams. Intellectual Performance in Dreams*

In our dream-interpretations so far we have come upon the element of *absurdity* so often that we are reluctant to put off any longer our investigation into where it comes from and what it means. Indeed, we recall that it was the absurdity of dreams which gave the opponents of their serious study one of their main arguments for regarding them as nothing but the meaningless products of a reduced and fragmented mental activity.

I shall begin with some examples in which the absurdity of the dream-content is only ostensible, disappearing as we go deeper into the meaning of the dream. They are dreams concerning—by chance, one might think at first—a dead father.

I

The dream of a patient who lost his father six years ago:

A great misfortune has befallen his father. He was travelling on the night train. There was a derailment. The seats collapsed, his head was jammed cross-wise between them. Then he sees him lying in bed, with a vertical wound just above his left eyebrow. He wonders that his father should have come to grief like this, for after all he is dead (he adds as he tells his story). *His eyes are so bright.*

According to the prevailing view of dreams, the content of this dream should be explained as follows: while he was imagining the accident to his father, the dreamer at first forgot that his father had been in the grave for years; as the dream proceeds, this memory is roused and causes him to be astonished at his own dream even as he is dreaming. However, analysis teaches us that it is quite unnecessary to look for explanations of this kind. The dreamer had ordered a bust of his father from a sculptor, and had first cast eyes on it two days before the dream. This is what seems to him to have *come to grief*. The sculptor has never seen his father, and is working from photographs in front of him. On the day before the dream, the devoted son sent an old family servant to the studio to see whether he too would pass the same judgement on the marble head, that is, that it turned out too narrow *in the cross-section* between the temples. Now follows the material from his memory that has contributed to the construction of this dream. When his father was troubled by business worries or family difficulties, he was in the habit of pressing both hands to his temples, as if his head had expanded and he wanted to press it together.—As a four-year-old child our dreamer was present when a pistol, which happened to be loaded, went off and blackened his father's eyes (*his eyes are so bright*).—When his father was alive, in his thoughtful or sad moods there was a deep vertical furrow to be seen in the place where the dream shows a wound. The substitution of a wound for this furrow points to the second occasion for the dream. The dreamer had taken a photograph of his little daughter; he had dropped the plate, and when he picked it up it showed a crack that ran like a vertical furrow across the little girl's forehead, reach-

ing down to her eyebrow. At this, he could not hold off his supersti-
tious forebodings, for the day before his mother died the photographic plate with her picture on it had cracked.

The absurdity of this dream is thus simply the consequence of a
slipshod way we have of using words, making no distinction between
a bust or photograph of a person and the person himself. We are all
used to saying: 'Don't you think it's hit your father off?' Of course,
the appearance of absurdity in this dream would have been easy to
avoid. If it is admissible to judge so soon after learning of only one
dream, one might say that this appearance of absurdity is permitted
or intentional.

II

A second, very similar example from my own dreams (I lost my
father in 1896):

*After his death my father played a part in Magyar politics, united
them politically* (I see a small, indistinct picture showing this): *a
crowd of people, as though in the Reichstag; one person standing on one or
on two chairs* [Stühlen], *others around him. I recall how like Garibaldi**
*he looked on his deathbed, and I am glad that this promise did come true
after all.*

That is surely absurd enough. I dreamed it at a time when *obstruction* from Parliament had thrown Hungary into a state of disorder,*
and the country was in the throes of the crisis from which it was
rescued by Kálmán Széll. The trifling circumstance that the scene in
the dream is made up of such small pictures is not without significance for elucidating this element. Usually the way dreams represent
our thoughts visually is in images that give the impression of being
more or less life-size; but the image in my dream is the reproduction
of a woodcut bound into the text of an illustrated history of Austria,
representing Maria Theresa* at the Reichstag in Pressburg; the famous scene of 'Moriamur pro rege nostro'.[23] Like Maria Theresa in the
picture, in my dream my father is standing surrounded by the crowd.
But he is standing on one or two chairs—so he is the *chairman*, or

[23] I do not recall the author or the work where I found a dream mentioned which was
swarming with unusually tiny figures, and whose source turned out to be an etching by
Jacques Callot* which the dreamer had been looking at during the day. Certainly Callot's
etchings contain a tremendous number of very small figures; one set of them deals with
the horrors of the Thirty Years War.

presiding judge [*Stuhlrichter*]. (He has *united* them. The intermediary here is the saying: 'We will not need a *judge*.') His resemblance on his deathbed to Garibaldi is something all those of us present did in fact remark. He had a *post-mortem* rise in temperature, his cheeks grew more and more flushed ... involuntarily, we continue: 'Und hinter ihm, in wesenlosem Scheine lag, was uns alle bändigt, das Gemeine'* [And behind him, mere empty appearance, lay what confines us all, the common and mean].

These exalted thoughts act as a warning that the very thing we shall encounter is 'vulgarity'. The '*post-mortem*' describing the rise in temperature corresponds to the words '*after his death*' in the dream-content. The most painful part of my father's suffering was the complete paralysis of the intestine (*obstruction*) during his last weeks. All sorts of disrespectful thoughts attach themselves to this. I recall one of my contemporaries, who lost his father when he was still a schoolboy—which moved me, deeply stirred by his loss, to offer him my friendship. He once told me mockingly about the grief of a relative whose father had died in the street and was brought home, only for the family to find when they undressed the corpse that in the moment of death or *post mortem* his bowels had emptied of stools. It distressed the daughter so deeply that this nasty detail could not but spoil her remembrance of her father. With this we have got through to the wish embodying itself in this dream. '*To be a pure and great presence to one's children after one's death*'—who would not wish for that? What has become of the absurdity of this dream? It appeared absurd only because the dream gave a faithful representation of a perfectly admissible turn of phrase, whose components combine to produce between them the sort of absurdity which usually goes unremarked by us. Here too we cannot dismiss the impression that the appearance of absurdity is intentional, created on purpose.

III

In the example I am about to offer, I am able to catch the dream-work in the act of intentionally fabricating an absurdity which the material itself offers no occasion for. It comes from the dream suggested to me by my meeting with Count Thun before my holiday journey. *I am riding [fahre] in a hansom-cab and I tell the driver to drive me [fahren] to a railway station. 'Of course, I can't drive [fahren]* *with you on the railway line itself'*, I say, after he raised an objection, as *if I had tired him out, although it is as if I had already driven [gefahren] with him on a stretch which one usually travels [fährt] by train.* Analysis provides this confused and nonsensical story with the following explanation: that day I had taken a hansom-cab which was meant to take me to a remote street in Dornbach. However, the cab-driver did not know the way, and, as these good folk do, he drove on and on until I noticed it and showed him the way, not sparing him a few scornful remarks. There is a train of thought spinning from this coachman to the aristocrat I shall meet later. For the moment just the pointer that one thing about the aristocracy we middle-class plebeians notice is how they prefer to take the driver's seat themselves. Count Thun himself certainly drives the Austrian state coach. However, the next sentence in the dream refers to my brother, whom I also identify with the cab-driver. This year I had called off our journey to Italy together ('*I can't drive with you on the railway line itself*'), and this refusal was a way of punishing him for his usual complaint that I normally *tire him out* on these journeys (which reaches the dream unchanged) in expecting him to make too many changes of place and take in too much in one day. That evening my brother had accompanied me to the station, but he jumped out at the Westbahnhof local railway station to take the local train to Purkersdorf.* I had remarked to him that he could go on with me a while longer if he did not take the local train, but took the main-line train from the Westbahnhof as far as Purkersdorf. Some of this entered the dream, where I am riding in the *cab* along a stretch which *one usually travels by train.* In reality it was the other way round (and '*Umgekehrt ist auch gefahren*' ['Travelling in the other direction is still travelling']); I had said to my brother: 'You can travel in my company in the main-line train along the same stretch as you're going to take the local.' I set up the entire confusion in the dream by saying 'cab' in it instead of 'local', which then of course serves very nicely to condense the figures of the cabby and my brother. Then I tease out some nonsense in the dream which this explanation seems scarcely fit to disentangle, and which virtually contradicts something I had said earlier ('I can't drive with you on the railway line itself'). As I have no need at all to mix the local train up with the cab, I must have shaped the entire puzzling tale in my dream intentionally.

But what was my intention? We shall now learn what absurdity in dreams signifies, and the motives that allow it entry or create it. The solution to the mystery in the present case is as follows: I need an absurdity and something incomprehensible in my dream in connection with the element *fahren*,* because in my dream-thoughts there is a certain judgement demanding to be represented. One evening, at the house of that hospitable and witty lady who appears in another scene of the same dream as a 'housekeeper', I had heard two riddles which I could not solve. As my fellow-guests were already familiar with them, I cut a rather ridiculous figure in my unsuccessful efforts to solve them. They involved two puns on *Nachkommen* [those who come after, descendants, following after] and *Vorfahren* [those who go before, forebears, travelling or driving ahead of]:

> Der Herr befiehlt's,
> Der Kutscher thut's.
> Ein jeder hat's,
> Im Grabe ruht's. (*Vorfahren.*)

[The master commands it,
The driver does it,
Everyone has it,
It lies in the grave. (*To go/drive
ahead, those who go before, i.e. forebears*)]

It was confusing, too, that half of the second riddle was identical with the first:

> Der Herr befiehlt's,
> Der Kutscher thut's.
> Nicht Jeder hat's,
> In der Wiege ruht's. (*Nachkommen.*)

[The master commands it,
The driver does it.
Not everyone has it,
It lies in the cradle. (*To drive after, those
who come after, i.e. children, descendants.*)]

Now when I saw Count Thun *driving ahead* so imperiously, and I got into my Figaro-mood, judging it to be the only merit of these grandees that they had taken the trouble to be born* (that they were *Nachkommen*/descendants), these two riddles became intermediary thoughts for the dream-work. As it is easy to mix up aristocrats with coachmen, and as it used to be the custom in our part of the world to address the coachman as 'brother-in-law',* the work of condensation was able to draw my brother into the same representative figure. But the dream-thought at work behind it runs: *It's nonsense to be proud of one's forebears. I prefer to be a forebear myself, an ancestor.* On account of this judgement: 'It's nonsense', hence the nonsense in my dream. This now probably solves the last riddle left in this obscure part of the dream, where I dreamed that I had already *driven before* [*vorher gefahren*] with the cabby, that is, already *driven ahead* [*vorgefahren*] with him.

Dreams are made absurd, then, when one of the elements in the dream-thoughts contains the judgement 'that is nonsense'; when one of the dreamer's unconscious trains of thought is motivated by criticism and mockery. In this way the absurd becomes one of the means used by the dream-work to express contradiction, like its reversal of the relation between dream-thought and dream-content, like its exploitation of feelings of motor inhibition. But the absurd in dreams is not just to be translated by a simple 'No'; rather, it is meant to reproduce the dream-thoughts' disposition to laugh or mock at the same time as contradicting. The dream-work only provides something ridiculous if it is motivated by this intention. Once again it is transforming *part of the latent content into a manifest form.*[24]

Actually we have already met a convincing example of this kind of meaning in an absurd dream: the dream I interpreted without analysis of the Wagner performance that lasted till a quarter to eight in the morning, when the orchestra was conducted from a tower, etc. (p. 297). Clearly it means: this is a demented world and a deranged society. The deserving don't get their due, and the ones who don't care get it all—by which she means her own fate in comparison with

---

[24] That is, the dream is parodying the thought it labels as ridiculous by creating something ridiculous associated with it. This is how Heine* sets about it when he wants to mock the King of Bavaria's bad verse. He does so in even worse:

> Herr Ludwig ist ein großer Poet,
> Und singt er, so stürzet Apollo
> Vor ihm auf die Knie und bittet und fleht,
> Halt ein, ich werde sonst toll, oh!
> This Ludwig's a poet of renown;
> When he sings out one of of his lays, he
> Has Apollo begging on bended knees:
> 'Stop, stop! you're driving me crazy!'

her cousin's.—It is also far from accidental that our first examples of the absurdity of dreams should concern a dead father. The conditions for creating absurdity in dreams are to be found typically together here. The authority that characterizes the father provoked the child's criticism early on; the strict demands he made caused the child to keep a keen eye open for his father's every weakness; but the filial devotion which surrounds the father's person in our thoughts, especially after his death, only intensifies the censorship which prevents any expression of this criticism from becoming conscious.

IV

Another absurd dream about my dead father.

I receive a communication from the district council of the town where I was born relating to payment of costs for hospital accommodation in 1851, necessary on account of a seizure suffered in my house. I make fun of it, for in the first place, in 1851 I wasn't born, and in the second, my father, to whom it possibly refers, is already dead. I go in to him in the next room and tell him about it. To my surprise he remembers that once in 1851 he was drunk and had to be locked up or detained. It was when he was working for the firm of T . . . 'So you used to drink, too?' I ask. 'Did you get married soon afterwards?' I calculate that I was actually born in 1856, which seems to me to follow right after it.

In the light of the foregoing discussion, we can only translate this dream's blatant display of its absurdities as the sign of a particularly bitter and passionate polemic in the dream-thoughts. However, we are all the more astonished when we confirm that in this dream the polemic is quite open, and the father is identified as the figure who is made the butt of the mockery. Openness of this kind seems to contradict our assumptions about the part played by censorship in the dream-work. But it is a help to our understanding that the figure of my father is only a stand-in here, and that the dispute is actually carried on with someone else who only makes an appearance in the dream in a single allusion. While dreams usually deal with rebellion against other figures behind whom the father is hiding, here the pattern is reversed; the father is turned into a straw man to cover others, and that is why the dream is free to divert itself so undisguisedly with his otherwise sacrosanct figure, because the certain knowledge is also involved that it is not he who is meant. This is to be learned from what occasioned the dream. It happened, in fact, after I had heard that an older colleague, whose judgement was regarded as irreproachable, had expressed his disapproval and astonishment that one of my patients was continuing his psychoanalytic work with me into its *fifth year*. The introductory sentences of the dream indicate in transparent guise that for a time this colleague took over the duties that my father was no longer able to fulfil (*payment of costs, hospital accommodation*); and when the ties of our friendship began to loosen, I fell into the same conflict of feelings as the role and earlier achievements of the father provoke in the case of dissension between father and son. My dream-thoughts are defending themselves bitterly against the charge that *I am not getting on faster*, which then extends from the treatment of this patient to other things too. Does he know anyone who can do it any faster? Doesn't he know that conditions of this kind are otherwise absolutely incurable and last a lifetime? What are *four to five years* compared with the length of a whole life, especially when the burden of the patient's existence has been made so much lighter during treatment?

The mark of absurdity is produced in this dream largely by stringing sentences from different parts of the dream-thoughts next to one another without any intermediary transition. In this way the sentence: *I go in to him in the next room* abandons the theme which gave rise to the previous sentences and faithfully reproduces the circumstances when I informed my father of my own, independent, engagement. The sentence wants to remind me of the noble selflessness the old man showed then, and to contrast it with the behaviour of someone else, a new figure. I note at this point that this is why the dream is free to mock my father, because in the dream-thoughts he is fully acknowledged and held up as a model to others. It is in the nature of all censorship that in speaking of forbidden things one is permitted to say things that are not true sooner than the truth. The next sentence my father remembers, *that once he was drunk and so had to be locked up*, no longer contains anything referring to him in real life. The figure he is covering here is the great Meynert,* no less, whose footsteps I followed with such great reverence and whose behaviour towards me after a short period of favour suddenly changed to undisguised hostility. The dream reminds me of something he told me himself: that as a young man he had once been addicted to *using chloroform as an intoxicant* and so had had to *spend time in an institution*; the dream also reminds me of a second experience with him shortly before his end. I had conducted a bitter literary dispute with him on the subject of male hysteria, which he denied existed, and when I visited him in his last illness and asked how he was, he lingered over the description of his condition, and closed with the words: 'You know, I was always one of the finest cases of male hysteria.' This is how he admitted to my satisfaction *and to my astonishment* what he had obstinately struggled against for so long. However, my basis for being able to conceal Meynert behind my father in this scene in my dream is not the analogy I discovered between the two figures, but the brief, though entirely adequate, representation of a conditional clause in the dream-thoughts. In full, it goes like this: All right, if I were second generation, the son of a professor or Hofrat, then I would certainly *have got on faster*. In my dream I actually make my father a Hofrat and professor. The grossest and most disturbing absurdity in the dream is to be found in its treatment of the year *1851*, which does not seem to be at all different to me from *1856*, *as if the difference of five years meant nothing at all*. But that was the very thing that was meant to emerge from the dream-thoughts and find expression. *Four to five years*—that is the length of time I enjoyed the support of the colleague I mentioned at the outset; but it is also the length of time I made my fiancée wait to get married; and also the length of time, by a chance coincidence promptly exploited by the dream-thoughts, that I am now making the patient I am closest to wait to be completely cured. '*What are five years?*' my dream-thoughts ask. '*That's no time at all to me. It's just not an issue.* I have time enough ahead of me, and just as that finally came good, despite your lack of faith, so will this too.' Besides, the number *51*, detached from the century, is determined in yet another way, actually with the opposite meaning; it also occurs in this sense several times in the dream. 51 is the age when a man appears to be particularly vulnerable,* when I have seen colleagues die suddenly, among them one who had waited a long time but died a few days after being appointed professor.

V

Another absurd dream, which plays games with numerals.

One of my acquaintances, Herr M., has been attacked in an essay by no less a person than Goethe, with quite unjustifiable passion, we all think. Naturally, Herr M. is annihilated by this attack. He complains *bitterly about it in company at table; but his reverence for Goethe has not suffered, despite this personal experience. I try to throw some light on the chronological pattern, which strikes me as improbable. Goethe died in 1832; as his attack must naturally have taken place earlier, Herr M. was a very young man then. It seems plausible to me that he was eighteen years old. But I am not sure what year we are in at present, and in this way the entire calculation is plunged into darkness. The attack, by the way, is included in Goethe's well-known essay 'On Nature'.**

We shall soon find a means of justifying the nonsense in this dream. Herr M., whom I know from his *company at table*, recently asked me to examine his brother, who was showing signs of *paralytic insanity*. He was right in his surmise. During this visit a distressing thing happened: without any cause the sick man *exposed* his brother by alluding in conversation to the *exploits of the brother's youth*. I had asked the patient the date of his birth, and repeatedly got him to do small calculations to test his failure of memory—tests, by the way, which he still passed quite well. I already note that in my dream I am behaving like a sufferer from paralysis. (*I am not sure what year we are in.*) Other material in the dream comes from another recent source. The editor of a medical journal, a friend of mine, had published an extremely unkind, '*annihilating*' criticism in his paper of the latest book by my Berlin friend Fl., written by a very *youthful* reviewer not fit to pass judgement. I believed I had a right to intervene and took the editor to task. He deeply regretted having accepted the review, but would not promise to print a correction. At this I broke off my connection with the journal, and in my letter of resignation stressed my expectation *that our personal relations would not suffer from this occurrence.* The third source of the dream is the story, then still fresh in my mind, told me by a patient of how her brother succumbed to psychological illness, breaking into a frenzy with the cry '*Nature, Nature*'.* His doctors were of the opinion that the cry derived from reading that beautiful *essay of Goethe's* and was an indication that he had been overworking at his studies in natural philosophy. I preferred to think of the sexual sense which even the less educated among us imply when they speak of 'Nature', and the fact that the unhappy young man mutilated himself in the genitals at least did not suggest I was wrong. He was *eighteen years old* when his attack broke out.

If I also add that my friend's book, so harshly criticized ('One wonders whether it is the author who is crazy, or oneself', another critic had said), deals with the *chronological patterns of life*, and even traces Goethe's long life back to the multiple of a biologically significant numeral, then it is easy to see that in my dream I am putting myself in the place of my friend. (*I try to throw some light on the chronological pattern.*) But I am behaving like a sufferer from paralysis, and the dream is revelling in its absurdity. That means, then, that the dream-thoughts are saying with irony: '*Naturally*, he is the fool, the madman, and you are the people of genius, who understand things better. But what if it were the other way round?' And this *reversal* is represented in the dream-content in quantity, for example, when *Goethe* attacks the young man, which is absurd, while even today a very young man could easily attack the immortal *Goethe*; and when I count forward from *the year of Goethe's death*, while I have my paralytic patient count forward from the *year of his birth*.

However, I have also promised to demonstrate that there is no dream that is not prompted by egoistic motives. Consequently, I must justify making my friend's cause my own in this dream, and putting myself in his place. It is not enough to call on the critical convictions of my waking mind for this. Now the story of the eighteen-year-old sufferer, and the different interpretations of his cry of 'Nature', allude to the position I have taken contrary to the majority of physicians in maintaining that the psychoneuroses have a sexual aetiology. I can say to myself: 'Just like your friend, that is how you will fare at the hands of the critics, indeed, you have already done so to some extent.' And now I am free to replace the 'he' of the dream-thoughts by a 'we'. 'Yes, you are right, we two are the fools.' I am reminded vigorously that 'mea res agitur'* by the reference to Goethe's incomparably beautiful little essay, for it was hearing this essay read at a popular lecture that decided me, when I was still an unsettled school-leaver, to study the natural sciences.

VI

I have not yet fulfilled my promise to analyse another dream in which my self does not occur to show that it, too, is egoistic. I mentioned a short dream on p. 207, in which Professor L. says: 'My son, the myope* . . .', and noted that it was only the preliminary dream to another, in which I have a part to play. Here is the missing main dream, which offers us an absurd and incomprehensible word-formation which needs explaining:

On account of some events in the city of Rome, it is necessary for the children to flee the city, which does in fact happen. The setting is then outside a gate, a double gate in the ancient style (the Porta Romana in Siena, as I know as I am dreaming). I am sitting on the edge of a fountain, very sorrowful, almost weeping. A female figure—an attendant, a nun—brings the two boys out and hands them over to their father—but I am not he. The older of the two is quite clearly my eldest son; I can't see the other's face. The woman who is bringing the boy wants him to kiss her goodbye. Her distinguishing feature is her red nose. The boy refuses her the kiss, but, giving her his hand in farewell, says: Auf Geseres, and to the two of us (or to one of us) he says: Auf Ungeseres. I have an idea that the latter indicates a preference.

This dream is built on a tangle of thoughts prompted by a play I had seen in the theatre, *Das neue Ghetto* [*The New Ghetto*].* The Jewish question, concern for my children's future, who cannot be given a fatherland of their own, concern about bringing them up in such a way that they can grow up able to move freely from place to place, these are easy to recognize in the relevant dream-thoughts.

'*By the waters of Babylon we sat down and wept.*'*—Like Rome, Siena is famous for its beautiful fountains; for Rome I have to find some substitute in my dream (see p. 148) among the places familiar to me. Not far from the Porta Romana in Siena we saw a large, brightly lit house. We learned that it was the *manicomio*, the lunatic asylum. Shortly before I had the dream I heard that someone who shared my religion had had to give up his hard-won position at a state asylum.

Our interest is roused by the spoken words: *Auf Geseres*, at a point in the situation retained in the dream where one should expect: *Auf Wiedersehen*; and by its quite nonsensical opposite: *Auf Ungeseres*.

Geseres, according to the information I have gathered from the scribes, is a genuine Hebrew word, deriving from the verb *goiser* and best rendered by 'suffering imposed upon one, destiny'. From its use in Jewish slang, one might suppose the word meant 'weeping and wailing'. *Ungeseres* is my very own word-formation, and first catches my attention, though to begin with I also have no idea what to do with it. The little remark at the end of the dream, that *Ungeseres* indicates some preference over *Geseres*, opens the gates to my ideas, and so to my understanding. After all, we find a similar preference between kinds of caviare: *unsalted* caviare is more highly regarded than *salted*. Caviare to the general,* 'great expectations': this conceals a joking allusion to one of the members of my household, younger than I, who will one day, I hope, take the future of my children into her care. It fits well with this that another member of my household, our good nanny, should be recognizable as the attendant (or nun) in the dream. However, there is an intermediary transition missing between the pair *salted–unsalted* and *Geseres–Ungeseres*. It is to be found in the pair *'leavened–unleavened'*; in their *flight* from Egypt, the children of Israel had no time to allow their dough to rise, and in memory of this they still eat unleavened bread* at Easter to this day. This is where I can accommodate the sudden idea that came to me during this part of the analysis. I remembered how we took a walk last *Easter* in the streets of Breslau, a town we did not know, my Berlin friend and I. A little girl asked me the way to a certain street; I had to make my excuses that I didn't know, and I then remarked to my friend: 'I hope in later life the little girl has a keener eye in her choice of persons to guide her.' Shortly afterwards I caught sight of a physician's plate: 'Dr *Herodes*, consulting hours . . .' I remarked: 'I hope our colleague is not actually a children's specialist.' My friend had meantime been expounding his ideas on the biological significance of *bilateral symmetry* to me, and had introduced a sentence with: 'If we just had one eye in the middle of our forehead like the *Cyclops* . . .' That leads now to the words spoken by the professor in the preliminary dream: *My son, the myope*. And this has led me to the main source for *Geseres*. Many years ago, when this son of Professor L.'s, who is today an independent thinker, was still *sitting on the school benches*, he suffered from an eye complaint which the doctor declared was a matter of some concern. In his opinion, as long as it remained *on the one side* it was of no significance, but if it were to pass over to the *other eye*, it would be serious. The trouble in the one eye cleared up without leaving any damage; shortly afterwards, however, signs of the infection really did appear in the other. The terrified mother sent for the doctor at once to come out to the solitude of her country lodgings. *'What sort of a "Geseres" are you kicking up?'* he hectored. 'If it has got better *on the one side*, it'll get better *on the other*.' And so it did.

And now its connection with me and mine. The *school bench* on which the son of Professor L. acquired his earliest wisdom passed as a gift from the boy's mother into the possession of my eldest son, the son, that is, I had speak the words of farewell in my dream. One of the wishes attached to this transference is now easy to guess. This school bench is also by its construction intended to protect the child from becoming *short-sighted* and *one-sided*. Hence the *myope* in my dream (and behind it *Cyclops*) and the discussion of *bilaterality*. My concern about one-sidedness has more than one meaning; as well as meaning physical one-sidedness, it can refer to intellectual development. Indeed, does it not seem that the craziness of the scene in the dream is a contradiction of these very concerns? After the child has spoken his words of farewell *to the one side*, he calls its very opposite *to the other side*, as if to set up a balance. *He is acting, as it might be, in observance of bilateral symmetry!*

Thus, dreams are often at their most profound when they appear at their craziest. Through the ages, those who had something to say and could not say it without risk would gladly don the fool's cap. The listener who was the target of the forbidden speech was prepared to tolerate it, as long as he could laugh and flatter himself with the view that the uncomfortable truths were obviously uttered by a fool. The Prince in the play who has to pretend to be a fool is behaving just as the dream does in reality, and so we can declare of the dream what Hamlet says of himself, as he replaces his true circumstances with his witty and unintelligible word-games: 'I am but mad north-north-west: when the wind is southerly, I know a hawk from a hand-saw.'[25]*

I have solved the problem of absurdity in dreams, then, to the point where we can say: the dream-thoughts are never absurd—at least not the dream-thoughts behind the dreams of sane and sensible people; and the dream-work produces absurd dreams or dreams with single absurd elements when criticism, mockery, and scorn are present in the dream-thoughts and waiting to be represented in its forms of expression. The important thing now is for me to show that the dream-work consists simply and solely of the interaction of the three

---

[25] This dream is also a good example of the generally valid proposition that the dreams of the same night, even if they are remembered separately, have grown from the ground of the same dream-thoughts. Incidentally, the dream-situation in which I have my children flee the city of Rome is distorted by a retrospective association with an analogous event that occurred in my childhood. Its meaning is that I am envious of relatives who took the opportunity many years ago to move their children to the soil of another country.

factors I have mentioned—and of a fourth I have yet to discuss; and to show that all it does is produce a translation of the dream-thoughts, while observing the four prescribed conditions; and to show that to ask whether the psyche is operating in the dream with all its mental capacities in action or only some of them is to put the wrong question and miss the real state of affairs. However, there are plenty of dreams containing judgements: they criticize, they acknowledge, they show astonishment at a single element in their content, they attempt explanations and set up arguments, so I must use selected examples to dispose of the objections arising from occurrences such as these.

My rejoinder is this: *everything in our dreams that ostensibly looks like the activity of the function of judgement is not to be understood as, say, an act of thinking on the part of the dream-work; rather, it belongs to the material of the dream-thoughts and has passed from there as a ready-made structure into the manifest dream-content.* For the moment, I can go one further. Even a good part of the judgements we make about our dreams as we remember them *after waking*, and the feelings summoned up in us as we reproduce them, belong to the latent dream-content and should be included in the interpretation of the dream.

I

I have already given a striking example illustrating this. A patient is reluctant to tell her dream, because it is *too unclear*. She has seen a figure in her dream and does not know *whether it was her husband or her father*. Then there follows a second part of the dream with a rubbish bin [Misttrügerl] in it, to which the following recollection is attached. As a young housewife she once mentioned jokingly to a young relative who was visiting that the next thing she had to do was get a new bin for the rubbish. The next morning one was sent to her, full of lilies of the valley. This part of the dream is a representation of the saying: 'It didn't grow on my own rubbish-heap.'* If we complete the analysis, we will find that a story she heard in her youth continued to leave its trace in the dream-thoughts: a girl had a baby, but *was quite unclear who the father was*. So the dream-representation is encroaching on her waking thoughts here, and causing the place of one element in the dream-thoughts to be taken by a waking judgement passed on the dream as a whole.

II

A similar case: one of my patients has a dream that strikes him as interesting, for immediately on waking he says to himself: *I must tell that to the doctor.* The dream is analysed and yields the clearest allusions to an affair he began in the course of his treatment, which he had decided *to tell me nothing about.*

III

A third example from my own dreams:

I am walking to the hospital with P. through a neighbourhood with houses and gardens. As we do so, the thought occurs that I have seen this neighbourhood in dreams several times before. I don't know my way around it very well; he shows me a path going across a corner to a restaurant (saloon, not garden); I ask there after Frau Doni and I learn that she is living in the back in a little room with three children. I go in that direction and before I get there I meet an indistinct figure with my two small daughters; then I take them with me after I have been standing with them a while. A kind of criticism of my wife for having left them there.

Then, when I wake, I feel a great *satisfaction*, which I explain as my expectation that I shall now learn from the analysis what is the meaning of: *I have already dreamed of this before.*[26] However, the analysis tells me nothing of the sort; it only shows me that my satisfaction belongs to the latent dream-content and not to my judgement about the dream. *It is the satisfaction that in my marriage I have had children.* P. is someone whom I accompanied for a while on the same path in life and who has gone much further than I have, socially and materially, but whose marriage has remained childless. The two occasions for the dream will serve instead of demonstration by a complete analysis. The previous day I read the obituary notice in the newspaper of *Frau Dona A . . . y* (which I turned into *Doni*), who had died in *childbed.* My wife told me that the departed had been looked after by the same midwife who had attended her when she had our two youngest. The name *Dona* occurred to me, for I had met it shortly before for the first time in an English novel. The other occasion for the dream is its date; it was the night before the birthday of my eldest boy, who has, it seems, a talent for poetry.

[26] A topic on which a long-drawn-out discussion has developed in the most recent issues of the *Revue Philosophique* (paramnesia in dreams).

IV

I am left with the same satisfaction after I wake from the absurd dream about my father playing a part in Magyar politics after his death; it is motivated by the continued feeling that accompanied the last sentence of the dream: *I recall how like Garibaldi he looked on his deathbed, and I am glad that this promise did come true after all. (Added on to this a continuation I have forgotten.)* From the analysis I am now able to fill in what belongs in this gap in my dream. It is a reference to my second son, whose first name I chose after a great figure in history* who had attracted me powerfully when I was a boy, particularly following my stay in England. All through the year when we were expecting him I had it in mind to use just this name, if it should be a son, and, *with great satisfaction*, I welcomed him with it the moment he was born. It is not difficult to see how the vaulting ambition which the father has suppressed is transferred in his thoughts onto his children. Indeed, it is not inconceivable that this is one of the ways by which such suppression, with which our life constrains us, comes about. The little boy earned his right of entry into the interconnections of this dream because he had the same accident—easily forgivable in a child or someone dying—of soiling his clothes. Compare the allusion to 'stools' and the dream-wish: 'To be a *pure and great* presence to one's children.'

V

If I am now to select expressions of judgement which are confined to the dream itself, and do not continue into our waking thoughts nor transfer themselves to them, it will be much easier for me to make use of dreams which I have already related with another aim in mind. The dream of Goethe and his attack on Herr M. seems to contain a large number of acts of judgement. '*I am trying to throw a little light on the the chronology, which strikes me as improbable.*' Does that not look like criticism of the nonsense that Goethe is supposed to have made a literary attack on a young man of my acquaintance? '*It seems plausible to me* that he was eighteen years old.' But that sounds like the result of an admittedly feeble-minded calculation; and '*I am not sure what year we are in*' would be an example of uncertainty or doubt in dreams.

However, I know from my analysis of this dream that the wording of these acts of judgement, ostensibly made only in the course of the dream, admits of another meaning which makes them indispensable for the dream-interpretation, and at the same time avoids any absurdity. With the sentence: '*I am trying to throw some light on the chronological pattern*' I am putting myself in the place of my friend, who really is trying to throw light on the chronological ordering of life. The sentence here loses its significance as a judgement passed on the nonsense of the preceding sentences. The interpolation '*it strikes me as improbable*' belongs with the later '*it seems plausible to me*'. I used more or less the same words in replying to the lady who told me of her brother's medical history: '*It seems to me unlikely* that his cry of "Nature, Nature" had anything to do with Goethe; *it is much more plausible to me* that it had the sexual significance familiar to you.' Now a judgement is certainly being passed here, though not in the dream but in reality, prompted by something the dream-thoughts had remembered and employed. The dream-content makes this judgement its own, just as it does any other fragment of the dream-thoughts.

The number *18*, with which the judgement in the dream is absurdly associated, still retains a trace of the context from which the real judgement was torn. Finally, my doubt that '*I am not sure what year we are in*' is meant simply to bring about my identification with the paralytic patient, for it was my examination of him that offered this one foothold for it.

In breaking down these apparent acts of judgement in the dream, we should remind ourselves of the rule for dream-interpretation given at the outset: we should regard the interconnectedness of the dream-components composed by the dream as inessential and illusory, and set it aside, for each individual dream-element should be traced back to its own source. The dream is a conglomerate which, for purposes of investigation, has to be broken up into fragments once more. However, on the other hand we should bear in mind that a psychical force is expressed in dreams which creates this apparent coherence, that is, it subjects the material produced by the dream-work to *a secondary revision*. We have expressions of that power here before us, which we will assess later as the fourth of the factors involved in the formation of dreams.

VI

I shall look for other examples of judgements made in dreams I have already related. In the absurd dream of the communication from the district council, I ask: '*Did you get married soon afterwards?*' *I calculate that I was of course born in 1856, which seems to me to follow straight after.* That is dressed up in the form of a line of reasoning towards a conclusion. My father married in 1851, soon after his attack; I am the eldest, born in 1856; so it all fits. We know that this is a false conclusion, effected in the interests of wish-fulfilment, and that the dominant sentence in the dream-thoughts is: '*four or five years, that is no time at all, it doesn't count.*' But the dream-thoughts give a different determination to every step in this line of reasoning towards a conclusion, in content and in form: it is my client, whose patience over five years my colleague is complaining about, who intends to get married as soon as his treatment is over. The way I treat my father in the dream recalls an *interrogation* or an *examination*, which reminds me of a university professor at Admissions who was in the habit of taking a complete military list of particulars: 'Date of birth?' '1856.'—'Patre?' The student would reply giving the father's first name with a Latin ending, and we students assumed that the high official *drew conclusions** from the first name of the father which he might not have been able to draw from the first name of the student being admitted. Accordingly, *drawing a conclusion* in the dream would be only a repetition of the *drawing a conclusion* that appears as a piece of material in the dream-thoughts. This tells us something new. If a conclusion occurs in the dream-content, it is certain to have come from the dream-thoughts; but it may be contained in these as a piece of remembered material or it can act as a logical connective to link a sequence of dream-thoughts. In each case a conclusion drawn in the dream represents a conclusion drawn in the dream-thoughts.[27]

This is a suitable point to continue the analysis of the dream. A memory of the Register of University Students (drawn up in Latin in my time) attaches itself to the professor's interrogation. And also to the course of my studies. The *five years* prescribed for the study of

---

[27] These results qualify my earlier account of the representation of logical relations (p. 237) on some points. That describes how the dream-work behaves generally, but does not take account of its subtlest and most scrupulous feats.

medicine were once again too few for me. I worked on unconcerned for some years more, and the circle of my acquaintances thought I was wasting my time, and doubted that I would be *finished*. Then I made a *quick* decision to take my examinations, and I was finished after all; *in spite of the postponement*. A fresh reinforcement for my dream-thoughts, which make up my defiant reply to my critics. 'And even though you wouldn't believe it, because I've taken my time over it: I shall finish, you'll see; I shall come to a conclusion after all. That is often the way it goes.'

The section at the beginning of the same dream contains some sentences which undeniably have the characteristics of argumentation. And this argumentation is not even absurd. It could just as easily belong to our thinking when we are awake. *In my dream I make fun of the communication from the district council, for in the first place, in 1851 I was not yet born, and in the second place, my father, to whom it possibly refers, is already dead.* Both propositions are not only intrinsically correct, but they also correspond completely to the arguments I would use in real life if I were to receive a communication of that kind. We know from our earlier analysis (p. 278) that this dream grew on the ground of dream-thoughts that were deeply embittered and full of scorn; if we assume that, in addition, the motives for censorship were also very strong, we will understand that the dream-work had every cause to create *an indisputable refutation of an absurd demand* after the model contained in the dream-thoughts. However, the analysis shows us that it is not for the dream-work to create this simulacrum freely; rather, it is obliged to use material from the dream-thoughts for it. It is as though an algebraic equation, in addition to the numbers, contained a plus and a minus sign for indicating a higher power or a root, and as though someone were to copy down this equation blindly, transferring the operative signs as well as the numerals into his copy and jumbling both sorts up together. The two arguments can be traced back to the following material. I find it distressing to think that many of the premises at the basis of my psychological solution to the psychoneuroses will produce incredulity and laughter once I have published them. That being the case, I have to maintain that impressions from their second year of life, sometimes even from their first, leave lasting traces in the emotional life of those who go on to fall ill; and these impressions, though much distorted and exaggerated in memory, can present us with the first and most fundamental reason for a hysterical symptom. When I find a suitable point to explain this to my patients, they are in the habit of parodying this newly acquired insight, declaring they are ready to look for memories from the time when they were *not yet in the land of the living*. I would also expect a similar reception if I revealed the unsuspected role played by the *father* in the earliest stirrings of sexuality in neurotic women (see the discussion on p. 198). And yet it is my well-founded conviction that both are true. In support of this, I have in mind particular examples where the father died when the child was very young, and where later, otherwise inexplicable occurrences prove that the child had indeed preserved memories of the figure who vanished from her life so soon. I know that both assertions are based upon *conclusions* whose validity will be disputed. It is thus a great achievement of wish-fulfilment when the very material of *these conclusions*, which I fear will be attacked, is used by the dream-work to establish *conclusions* that are indisputable.

VII

At the beginning of a dream that I have so far only touched upon, there is an explicit utterance of astonishment at its theme as it emerges.

My old professor Brücke must have given me some task to do, **strangely enough** *it has to do with dissecting my own lower torso, pelvis, and legs, which I can see in front of me as though I were in the dissecting room, but without feeling the lack of these limbs from my body, nor finding it at all gruesome. Louise N. is standing by and is helping me with the work. The pelvis has been eviscerated; one moment one has a view of it from above, the next a view from below, merging into each other. Thick, flesh-coloured tubercles are to be seen (which while I am still dreaming make me think of haemorrhoids). Also, something lying over it, looking like crumpled silver paper,*[28] *had to be carefully picked out. Then I was once again in possession of my legs and made my way through the city, but (out of tiredness) I took a cab. To my astonishment the cab drove in through the gateway of a house which opened up to it and let it pass along a passage which twisted at the end and finally led out into the open again.*[29]

---

[28] Silver foil [*Stanniol*]. Allusion to *Stannius, Nervensystem der Fische*, see p. 263.

[29] The location is the entrance hall of my apartment-building, where the children's prams belonging to the tenants are kept; but it is over-determined in several other respects.

Finally, I wandered through changing landscapes with an Alpine guide who was carrying my things. He carried me for a stretch out of consideration for my weary legs. The ground was swampy; we walked along the edge; people were sitting on the ground, like Red Indians or Gypsies, among them a girl. Just beforehand I had been moving on the slippery ground unaided, constantly surprised that I could manage so well after the dissection. At last we came to a little wooden house with an open window at the end. The guide set me down there and laid two wooden planks, which were standing ready, on the windowsill so as to bridge the chasm that had to be crossed from the window. This really filled me with fear for my legs. However, instead of the crossing I was expecting, I saw two grown men lying on wooden benches along the walls of the hut, and something like two children asleep next to them. As if not the planks, but the children, were to make the crossing possible. I wake with thoughts full of terror.

Anyone who has once acquired a proper impression of the sheer scope of condensation in dreams can easily imagine how many pages a detailed analysis of this dream must fill. Fortunately for the interconnections I shall borrow only the one example of surprise in dreams, which makes its presence known in that interpolated 'strangely enough'. I shall explain the occasion for the dream. It is a visit by that lady, Louise N., who is also helping me in my work in the dream. 'Lend me something to read.' I offer her *She** by Rider Haggard. 'A *strange* book, but full of hidden meaning,' I explain to her; 'the eternal-feminine,* the immortality of our emotions—' Then she interrupts me: 'I've read it. Haven't you anything of your own?'—'No, my own immortal works haven't been written yet.' 'Well, when can we expect what you call your latest insights,' she asked rather sarcastically, 'the ones you promise we too will find readable?' Now, when I come to think about it, I note that someone else is speaking through her to warn me, and I am silent. I think of the effort of self-conquest it is costing me to publish just my work on dreams, in which I am obliged to surrender so much of my innermost self. 'Das Beste, was Du wissen kannst, darfst Du den Buben doch nicht sagen'* [The best that you can know you cannot tell the children]. The task set me in the dream of *dissecting my own body, then, is the self-analysis* involved in relating my dreams. Old *Brücke* deserves to appear in this context; as early as my first years of scientific work it happened that I put a finding aside until his energetic urging made me publish it. But the further thoughts developing out of my conversation with Louise N. go too deep to become conscious; they are diverted by way of the material that was awakened incidentally in my mind by the mention of Rider Haggard's *She*. It is to this book, and to a second by the same author, *Heart of the World*,* that the judgement *strangely enough* refers, and many elements in the dream are taken from these two novels of fantasy. The swampy ground over which I am carried and the chasm to be crossed over planks we had brought with us come from *She*; the Red Indians, the girl, and the wooden house from *Heart of the World*. In both novels a woman is the guide; both of them are about a perilous journey, in *She* it is an adventurous way into the unexplored and scarcely trodden.* My weary legs, as I see from a note I made at the time of the dream, are a real sensation from those days. Their equivalent was probably a mood of weariness and the doubtful question: 'How far will my legs still carry me?' In *She*, the adventure ends when the guide, instead of leading herself and the others into immortality, goes to her death in the mysterious central fire. Fear of something like this had unmistakably stirred in my dream-thoughts. The *wooden house* is undoubtedly also the *coffin*, that is, the grave. But in its representation of this most undesirable of all thoughts by a wish-fulfilment the dream has achieved its masterpiece. In fact, I was once in a grave, but that was in an excavated Etruscan grave near Orvieto, a narrow chamber with two stone benches along the walls, on which the skeletons of two grown men were lying. The interior of the wooden house in my dream looks exactly like that, only with the stone replaced by wood. The dream seems to be saying: 'If you are to tarry in the grave, then let it be the Etruscan one'—and by making this underhand substitution, it transforms the most melancholy of expectations into a very desirable one. Unfortunately, as we shall hear, it can only change the imaginary idea accompanying the affect into its opposite, not always the affect itself as well. This is why I wake up with thoughts full of *terror*, after another idea has compelled my dream to represent it: that perhaps the children will achieve what was denied their father. This is yet another allusion to that strange novel in which one person's identity is preserved throughout a sequence of generations across 2000 years.

VIII

In the interconnections set up in another dream there is a similar expression of surprise at what is experienced in it, but this time it is linked to such a striking, far-fetched, and almost witty attempt at an explanation that I could not resist subjecting the entire dream to analysis just for its sake. I am travelling overnight from the 18th to the 19th of July on the line south of Vienna, and in my sleep I hear the shout: *'Hollthurn in ten minutes!' At once I think of holothurians*—a museum of natural history—and that this is a place where brave men defended themselves unsuccessfully against the power of their reigning princes.—Of course, the Counter-Reformation in Austria!—as though it were a place in Styria or the Tyrol. Now I can see a little museum indistinctly, where the remains or the acquisitions of these men are preserved. I would like to get down from the train, but I hesitate. There are women with fruit standing on the platform; they are crouched on the ground, holding their baskets out so invitingly.—I delayed, uncertain whether we still had time, and now we are still at a standstill.—All of a sudden I am in a different compartment, where the leather upholstery and the seats are so narrow that one's back bumps directly against the back of the seat.*[30] *I am surprised at this, but of course it is possible that I could have changed trains while I was still asleep. Several people, including an English brother and sister; a distinct row of books in a bookcase against the wall. I can see 'Wealth of Nations',* 'Matter and Motion'* (by Maxwell), thick books bound in brown linen. The man asks his sister about a book by Schiller,* whether she has forgotten it. One moment it looks as if the books are mine, the next as if they are theirs. I would like to intervene in the conversation to confirm or support—* —I wake up, my whole body sweating, because all the windows are closed. The train is stopping at *Marburg*.

As I am writing this down, a bit of the dream comes to mind which my memory wanted to pass over. *I say* [in English] *to the brother and sister of a certain work: 'It is from . . .', but I correct myself: 'It is by . . .* The man remarks to his sister: 'Did you hear? He said it correctly.'*

The dream begins with the name of the station, which must have

---

[30] This description is incomprehensible to myself too, but I am following the principle of reproducing the dream in the words that occurred to me as I wrote them down. The wording itself is part of the representation by the dream.

woken me up, though only partially. I replace this name, which is *Marburg*, by *Hollthurn*. That it was *Marburg* I heard the first, or perhaps the second time it was called is proved by the reference to *Schiller* in the dream, who of course was born in *Marburg*, though not the one in Styria. Now I was travelling on this occasion in very unpleasant circumstances, despite going first class. The train was overfull; in the compartment I had encountered a gentleman and a lady who seemed very superior persons and did not have the courtesy, or did not think it worth taking the trouble, to conceal in any way their displeasure at the interloper. My polite greeting was not returned; although husband and wife were sitting side by side (their backs to the engine), before my eyes the wife hurried to secure the window-seat opposite her with an umbrella; the doors were shut at once; demonstrative remarks exchanged about opening the windows. They could, no doubt, tell my need for fresh air straight away. It was a hot night, and the air in the totally closed compartment soon grew stifling. In my experience, such inconsiderate and intrusive behaviour is the mark of people who have not paid for their tickets, or who are only travelling half-fare. When the guard arrived and I produced my dearly bought ticket, there sounded from the lady's mouth, unapproachable and like a threat: 'My husband has an authorization.' She was a formidable figure, with ill-tempered features, in age not far from the decline of feminine beauty; her husband never uttered a word, he sat there without moving. I attempted to sleep. In my dream I take a terrible revenge on my disagreeable travelling companions; one would not guess what insults and humiliations are hidden behind the torn fragments of the first half of my dream. After this need was satisfied, the second wish asserted itself: to change compartments. Dreams change their scene so often without any protest being made at the transformation, so it would not have been in the least remarkable if I had promptly replaced my travelling companions with more pleasant ones from my memory. But here we have a case where something objected to the change of scene and thought it necessary to explain it. How did I suddenly get into a different compartment? I certainly couldn't remember having changed it. There was only one explanation: *I must have left the carriage while I was still asleep*, a rare occurrence, but instances of it are certainly known to neuropathologists. We know of persons who have embarked upon railway journeys in a hazy state without revealing any sign of their abnormal condition until they come to completely at some station on their way and are then astonished at the gap in their memory. So while I am still dreaming, I declare my case to be one of *automatisme ambulatoire*.

The analysis allows us to find a different solution. That attempt at an explanation, which amazes me when I had to ascribe it to the dream-work, is not original, but copied from the neurosis of one of my patients. I have already told the story elsewhere of a highly cultivated and, in real life, tender-hearted man, who, shortly before the death of his parents, began to accuse himself of murderous desires, and now suffered from the precautionary measures he was obliged to take as a safeguard against them. It was a case of severe obsessive ideas, while maintaining total insight. At first he took a dislike to walking down the street because of his compulsion to account to himself for the disappearance of all the people he met; if someone suddenly took evasive action to get away from his persecuting glance, he was left with the distressing feeling, and the thought that he might possibly have done away with him. There was a 'Cain-fantasy' behind it, among other things, for 'all men are brothers'. As this task was impossible to fulfil, he gave up going out for a walk and spent his life incarcerated within his four walls. But the newspapers constantly brought to his room news of murders that had taken place outside, and his conscience would plant doubts in his mind that he might be the murderer they were looking for. The certainty that he had definitely not left his apartment for weeks protected him for a while against these accusations, until one day the possibility occurred to him that *he could have left the building in a state of unconsciousness* and could have committed the murder in that way without knowing anything about it. From then on he locked the house door, gave the key to his old housekeeper, and forbade her insistently to let it come into his hands, even if he demanded it.

That is the source of my attempt at explaining that I changed carriages in a state of unconsciousness—it was transferred ready-made into my dream from material in the dream-thoughts and is obviously intended to be used by the dream as a means of identifying me with the figure of that patient. My memory of him was prompted in me by obvious association. A few weeks before I had made my last overnight journey with this man. He was cured, and was accompanying me to the provinces to attend his relatives, who had called on my services; we had a compartment to ourselves; we had all the windows open right through the night, and for as long as I was awake we enjoyed an excellent conversation. I knew that hostile impulses towards his father, dating from his childhood, in connection with sexuality, had been the root of his illness. So by identifying myself with him, I wanted to admit something analogous in myself. Indeed, the second scene in my dream actually dissolves into a riotous fantasy that the reason for the stand-offish behaviour of my two elderly travelling companions towards me is that my arrival disturbed the amorous exchanges they intended for the night. But this fantasy goes back to an early scene in my childhood when the child, driven no doubt by sexual curiosity, goes into his parents' bedroom and is driven from it by the father's mighty command.

It is superfluous to heap up further examples. They all would simply confirm what we have learnt from those already given: that an act of judgement in a dream is only a repetition of a model from the dream-thoughts. A repetition that is mostly out of place and introduced in an inappropriate context, but occasionally, as our last examples show, so cleverly employed that at first it is possible to have the impression of independent thinking. From this point we can turn our attention to that psychical activity which does not, it is true, seem to have a regular share in the formation of dreams, but where it does, endeavours to blend dream-elements of disparate origins into a dream that is meaningful and free of contradictions. However, before we do so we feel it is still imperative that we should first consider the expressions of affect that make their appearance in dreams, and compare these with the affects revealed by analysis in the dream-thoughts.

(g) *Affects in Dreams*

A shrewd remark of Stricker's has made us aware that the dream's expressions of affect will not allow us to dismiss them as contemptuously as we shake off its content once we are awake. 'If I dream I am frightened of robbers, the robbers are certainly imaginary, but the fear is real', and it is just the same when I dream I am happy. Our feeling testifies that the affects we live through in dreams are by no means inferior to the affects of similar intensity we feel when we are awake; and it is with the affects it contains, far more strongly than with the imagined ideas it contains, that the dream stakes its claim to be accepted as one of the real, formative, experiences of our soul. Now when we are awake we are unable to give these dream-affects their proper place, because the only way we know of assessing the psychical importance of an affect is from its connection with certain imagined ideas contained in the dream. If the affect and the content of ideas do not match in kind or intensity, then our waking judgement does not know what to make of it all.

We have always found it surprising that in our dreams the imagined ideas of the content are not attended by the effect upon our emotions that we would expect they would inevitably have in our waking thought. Strümpell said that ideas are stripped of their psychical values in dreams. However, there are plenty of dreams in which the opposite occurs: an intense expression of affect will make its appearance accompanying a content that does not seem to offer any occasion for the release of affect. I dream I am in a frightful, dangerous, repulsive situation, but I feel no fear or revulsion at all; at other times, on the contrary, I am filled with horror at something harmless, and with delight at something childish.

This puzzle will vanish, perhaps more suddenly and completely than any other presented by our dreams, once we pass from the manifest to the latent dream-content. We will not have to bother about explaining it, because it no longer exists. Analysis teaches us *that the imagined ideas in the dream-content have undergone displacements and substitutions, while the affects have remained in place unaltered.* No wonder that the ideas of the content, transformed as they are by dream-distortion, no longer match the unchanged affect; but no further astonishment either, once the analysis has put the right content in its former place.

Let us consider a psychical complex which has been subject to the influence of the censorship set up by resistance; the affects are that part of the complex which are most proof against the censorship, indeed, they are the only part that can give us a pointer towards filling the gaps. This is revealed in the psychoneuroses even more clearly than in dreams. In psychoneuroses the affect is always right, at least in its nature; although, of course, its intensity is increased by displacements of neurotic attention. If the sufferer from hysteria wonders that he is driven to fear a little thing so much, or the man with obsessive delusions wonders that such a distressing accusation should grow out of a trifle, both are misled, because they are taking the imagined idea—the little thing, the trifle—to be the essential thing, and they will be defending themselves in vain if they take these imagined ideas as a starting-point for their thinking. Psychoanalysis then puts them on the right track by acknowledging that, on the contrary, their affect is justified, and by looking for the idea relevant to it, which has been repressed and replaced by another. The assumption is that release of affect and content of imagined ideas do not form that indissoluble organic unity we usually treat them as being; rather, that both parts have been soldered onto each other in such a way that they can be separated by analysis. Dream-interpretation shows that this is in fact the case.

First of all I shall give an example where the analysis explains the apparent absence of affect accompanying the kind of imagined ideas in the dream-content which should have compelled its release.

I

She sees three lions in a desert. One of them is laughing, but she is not afraid of them. She must have run away from them, though, for she makes to climb a tree, but she discovers her cousin, a woman who is a teacher of French, already up there, etc.

The analysis brings the following material to bear: the unimportant occasion for the dream is a sentence from her English exercise, 'the mane is the lion's ornament'. Her father had a beard that framed his face like a *mane*. Her teacher of English is called *Miss Lyons*. An acquaintance sent her *Loewe's* ballads* [*Loewe*=lion]. These are her three lions, then; why should she be afraid of them?—She has read a story in which a Negro who has roused the others to revolt is hunted with hounds, and clambers up a tree to save himself. There follow, in a most playful spirit, remembered fragments, such as, 'Instructions on how to catch lions' from *Fliegende Blätter*: 'Take one desert and pass it through a sieve; the lions will be left in the sieve.' Then the very amusing, but rather improper, story of the official who is asked why he doesn't try harder to get into his boss's favour, and who replied that he has already tried crawling into it, but his immediate superior was already *up there*. The material all becomes intelligible when we learn that on the day of the dream the lady had been paid a formal visit by her husband's superior. He was very polite to her, kissed her hand, and *she was not at all afraid of him*, although he was such a big shot [in German idiom, 'ein großes Tier'=a big animal], and was much *lionized* in her country. So this lion can be compared to the lion in *A Midsummer Night's Dream*, who reveals himself to be Snug, the Joiner;* and all the lions we are not afraid of in our dreams are just like that.

II

For my second example I shall take the dream of the girl who saw her sister's little son lying dead in his coffin but, I add now, did not feel any grief or sadness at the sight. We know from the analysis why not. The dream only disguised her wish to see the man she loved again; the affect must have taken its tone from the wish, and not from its disguise. Hence, there was no reason at all for sadness.

In a number of dreams, the affect at least still keeps some contact with those ideas in the content which have taken the place of the right one. What happens then resembles what we learned of acts of judgement in dreams. If an important conclusion is drawn in the dream-thoughts, then the dream will also contain one; but it is possible that the conclusion in the dream has been displaced onto quite different material. Not infrequently this displacement takes place according to the principle of contraries.

I shall explain this last possibility in the following example of a dream which I have subjected to the most exhaustive analysis.

III

A palace on the sea. Later it does not lie directly on the edge of the sea, but on a narrow canal leading into the sea. A certain Herr P. is the governor. I am standing with him in a great reception room with three windows, and in front of them projecting walls rise like castle battlements. I have been assigned to the occupying force, perhaps as a volunteer naval officer. We are afraid of the imminent arrival of enemy warships, as we are in a state of war. Herr P. intends to leave; he gives me instructions about what is to be done if what we fear does happen. His ailing wife is with the children in the vulnerable palace. When the bombardment begins, the great hall is to be cleared. He is breathing heavily and makes to go away; I detain him, and ask how I can get news to him if necessary. He says something in reply, but then immediately falls down dead. I have probably overstrained him needlessly with my questions.

After his death, which doesn't make any further impression on me, thoughts about whether the widow will stay in the palace, whether I should report his death to headquarters and, as next in command, take over the direction of the palace. Then I am standing at the window, scrutinizing the ships as they pass; they are merchant ships, roaring past rapidly on the dark water, some of them with several funnels, others with bulging decks (which are very like the railway station buildings in the preliminary dream, not given here). *Then my brother is standing next to me and we are both looking out of the window on to the canal. One ship makes us start in alarm and call: The warship is coming. But it turns out that only the same ships already familiar to me are returning. Now there is a small ship passing by, oddly truncated, so that it ends at its broadest point; on deck there are some curious things to be seen, rather like cups or cans. We call as with one voice: 'That is the breakfast-ship.'*

The rapid movement of the ships, the deep, dark blue of the water, the brown smoke from the funnels—all this together creates a very tense and gloomy impression.

The localities in this dream are put together from several journeys to the Adriatic (Miramare,* Duino, Venice, Aquileia). A short, but enjoyable, Easter trip to Aquileia with my brother a few weeks before the dream was still fresh in my memory. *The naval war* between America and Spain,* too, and the worry attached to it for the fate of my relatives living in America, have a part in it. The operation of affect makes its presence felt in two places in this dream. In one place, an affect that might have been expected is absent; it is expressly emphasized that the governor's death makes no impression on me; in another place, where I think I see the warship, *I am filled with alarm*, and while I am asleep I feel all the sensations of terror. This well-constructed dream has accommodated affects in such a way that any noticeable contradiction is avoided. After all, there is no reason why I should be filled with alarm at the governor's death, and it is probably quite right that as commander of the palace I should be alarmed at the sight of the warship. However, the analysis points out that Herr P. is only a substitute for my own self (in my dream I am his substitute). I am the governor who suddenly dies. My dream-thoughts are concerned with the future of my relatives after my un-timely death. This is the only distressing thought among them. The fear, which in my dream is soldered onto the sight of the warship, must have been detached from there and relocated here. On the contrary, analysis shows quite the reverse: that the region in the dream-thoughts from which the warship is taken is filled with the most cheerful reminiscences. It was the previous year in Venice; it was an enchantingly beautiful day and we were standing at the windows of our room on the Riva Schiavoni, looking at the blue lagoon where there was more movement than usual to be seen on that day. English ships were expected and were to be given a ceremonial welcome, when suddenly my wife cried out, as joyfully as a child: '*The English warship is coming!*' In my dream I am filled with alarm at the same words; once again we see that speech in dreams derives from speech in real life. I shall shortly show that even the element 'English' in these words was not lost to the dream-work. Between my dream-thoughts and the dream-content, then, I am turning joyfulness into alarm, and I need only suggest that with this transformation itself I am giving expression to a part of the *latent* dream-content. However, this example demonstrates that the dream-work is free to detach the occasion for an affect from its connections in the dream-thoughts and place it anywhere else in the dream-content.

I shall take the incidental opportunity to make a closer analysis of the *breakfast-ship*, whose appearance brings the rationally sustained situation of the dream to such a nonsensical conclusion. If I look more keenly at the object in my dream, it occurs to me in retrospect that it was black, and being truncated where it was widest, it bore a great similarity at this end to an object that had interested us in the museums in Etruscan cities. This was a rectangular tray of black pottery, with two handles, on which objects like coffee-cups or tea-cups were standing, not unlike a modern *breakfast table service*. When we enquired, we were told that it was for the toilette of an Etruscan lady, with bowls for holding make-up and face-powder on it; and we joked with each other that it wouldn't be a bad idea to take something like that back as a present for our wives. So the object in the dream means *en toilette wearing black* [schwarze Toilette], being in mourning, and it is a direct allusion to someone's death. With the other end, the object in my dream is a reminder of the barque [Nachen], from the root νέκυς, as my linguist friend informed me, on which the body was laid in ancient times and given up to the sea for burial. This provides a connecting-thread for the reason why in my dream the ships return.

Quiet, in the rescued boat, to the harbour the old man returns.*

It is the return after shipwreck; indeed, the breakfast-ship looks as if it is broken off at its broadest point. But where does the name 'breakfast'-ship come from? This is where the 'English' element, which we kept in reserve from the warships, is put to use. *Breakfast* in English means *breaking one's fast*. *Breaking* belongs to shipwreck [Schiff*bruch*] again, and *fasting* is connected to the black toilette.

However, only the name of this breakfast-ship was newly coined by my dream. The thing itself existed, and reminds me of one of the most enjoyable hours of our recent journey. Mistrusting the cooking in Aquileia, we had brought food with us from Görz* and bought a bottle of excellent Istrian wine in Aquileia; and while the little post steamer made its way slowly along the Canale delle Mee into the empty stretch of lagoons towards Grado,* as the only passengers we took our breakfast on deck in the most cheerful mood, enjoying it as we had rarely enjoyed a breakfast before. So that was the *breakfast-ship*, and it is precisely the memory of this good cheer and enjoyment of life behind which the dream is concealing the most grievous thoughts of an unknown and uneasy future.

This detachment of the affects from the masses of imagined ideas which have given rise to them is the most striking thing that happens to them in the formation of a dream, but it is neither the only change, nor the most essential, that they undergo on their way from the dream-thoughts to the manifest dream. If one compares the affects in the dream-thoughts with those in the dream, one thing becomes clear at once: where there is an affect present in the dream, it is also present in the dream-thoughts, but not the other way round. In general, the dream has fewer and weaker affects than the psychical material from which, as adapted, it has emerged. When I have reconstructed the dream-thoughts, I can see how the most intense emotions of the psyche are invariably fighting to assert themselves, mainly in a struggle with others sharply opposed to them. If I then look back at the dream, I often find it colourless, lacking in any intense tonality of feeling. The dream-work does not only reduce the content of my thinking to the level of triviality, but often mutes the tonality of its feeling as well. I could say that the dream-work brings about a *suppression of the affects*. Let us take the dream of the botanical monograph, for example. What corresponds to it in my thinking is a passionate and emotional plea for my freedom to act as I do and arrange my life in the way that seems right to me and me alone. The dream that emerged from that sounds trivial: I have written a monograph; it is lying in front of me; it has coloured plates; there are dried plants attached to each specimen. It is like the stillness of a field strewn with corpses, with no trace remaining of the battle that once raged.

It is possible for it to work out differently, and for vivid expressions of affect to enter the dream itself; but let us first remain with the indisputable fact that so many dreams appear superficial, even trivial, whereas we cannot enter into the dream-thoughts without being deeply moved.

This is not the place to give a full theoretical explanation of this suppression of affect in the course of the dream-work; it would require us to go into the theory of affects and the mechanism of repression very thoroughly as the premiss of our argument. I will mention only two ideas at this point. I am compelled—on other grounds—to imagine the release of affect as a centrifugal process, directed towards the body's interior, analogous to the working of innervation in our motor and secretory processes. Just as in a state of sleep the transmission of motor impulses to the outside world appears suspended, so it is also possible that the centrifugal arousal of affects brought about by unconscious thinking could be hindered during sleep. If so, the stirrings of affect that come about as the dream-thoughts run their course would essentially be weak; and so those reaching the dream would be no stronger either. According to this line of thinking, the 'suppression of affects' would not be an achievement of the dream-work at all, but a consequence of the state of sleep. This may be so, but it cannot be the whole story. We must also remind ourselves that every dream of any greater complexity has also turned out to be the result of a compromise between two contesting powers in the psyche. On the one hand, the thoughts forming the wish have to struggle against the opposition of a censoring agency; on the other, we have often seen that in the process of unconscious thinking itself, each and every train of thought was yoked together with its contradictory opposite. As all these trains of thought have the potential for affect, by and large we will hardly go wrong if we conceive the suppression of affect as a consequence of the inhibition exercised by the opposites on each other and by the censorship on both as it suppresses their efforts. *Inhibition of affect would then be the second achievement of the dream-censorship, as dream-distortion was its first.*

I shall include an example of a dream where the muted tone of feeling in the dream-content can be explained by the oppositions present in the dream-thoughts. I am obliged to relate the following short dream, which every reader will read with some revulsion.

IV

A hill, and on this something like an outdoor privy; a very long bench, at its end a large hole for the privy. The back edge is all covered with piles of faeces of all sizes and degrees of freshness. Behind the bench some bushes. I urinate onto the bench; a long stream of urine washes it all clear, the pats of excrement detach themselves easily and drop into the opening. As if at the end there were still some left.

Why did I feel no disgust at this dream?

Because, as the analysis will show, the most agreeable and satisfying thoughts had a share in bringing it about. In the analysis the *Augean stables,** cleared by Hercules, came to my mind at once. I am this Hercules. The hill and the bushes belong in Aussee, where my children are staying at present. I have discovered the aetiology of neuroses in childhood, and thus I have protected my own children from becoming ill. The bench (except for the hole, of course) is a faithful imitation of a piece of furniture given to me as a present by a devoted lady patient. It reminds me of how much my patients honour me. Indeed, even the museum of human excrement is capable of a heart-warming interpretation. However much it disgusts me, in my dream it is a recollection of the beautiful land of Italy, where in the little towns, as well we know, the WCs are not appointed differently. The stream of urine which washes everything clean is an unmistakable allusion to greatness. That is how Gulliver* puts out the great conflagration in Lilliput; though by doing so, it is true, he attracts the displeasure of the smallest of queens. But Gargantua* too, Master Rabelais's superman, takes this revenge on the people of Paris by aiming his stream of urine at the town as he rides towards Notre Dame. Only yesterday I was turning the pages of Garnier's illustrations to Rabelais before going to sleep. And, curiously, another proof that I am the superman! The platform of Notre Dame was my favourite spot in Paris; I used to climb the church towers among the monsters and gargoyles. The speedy disappearance of all the excrement alludes to the motto: *Flavit et dissipati sunt,** which one day I shall use as a heading for the chapter on the therapy of hysteria.

And now for the operative occasion of the dream. It had been a hot summer afternoon; that evening I had given my lecture on the connection between hysteria and the perversions, and everything I could say displeased me utterly and seemed to me to be empty of all value. I was tired, had not a trace of pleasure in my arduous work, yearned to be away from this grubbing about in human dirt, longed for my children, and then for the beauties of Italy. In this mood I went from the lecture hall to a café to have a modest snack in the fresh air, having lost any pleasure in eating. But one of my audience came along with me; he asked if he might sit with me while I drank my coffee and choked down my roll, and began his flatteries. How much he had learned from me, how he now looked at everything with different eyes, how I had cleared the *Augean stable* of errors and prejudices in the theory of neuroses; in short, that I was a very great man. My mood was out of tune with his eulogy; I struggled with my disgust; went home earlier to get rid of him; read a few pages of Rabelais before going to bed, and read a novella by C. F. Meyer, *Die Leiden eines Knaben** [*A Boy's Sufferings*].

It was from this material that the dream emerged. Meyer's novella added the memory of scenes from childhood (compare the final image in the dream of Count Thun). The day's mood of disgust and dissatisfaction persisted in the dream to the extent that it was able to provide almost all the material for the dream-content. But in the night, the opposite mood of powerful and even excessive self-aggrandisement came to life and subsumed the first. The dream-content was obliged to find a form for itself that enabled it to use the same material to express both my delusion of inferiority and my overestimation of myself. This compromise-formation resulted in an ambiguous dream, but also in a muted tonality of feeling, as the opposites were inhibiting each other.

According to the theory of wish-fulfilment, this dream could not have come about if the opposite, megalomaniac train of thought, which—though suppressed—had a tonality of pleasure, had not come to join the thoughts of disgust. For distressing things are not to be represented in dreams; what we find distressing in our daytime thoughts can earn its entry into our dreams only if it will at the same time offer itself as a disguise for a wish-fulfilment.

The dream-work can also do something else with the affects of the dream-thoughts besides admitting them or reducing them to zero. It can *turn them into their opposite.* We have already learned the rule for interpretation that every element in a dream can also represent its opposite as well as itself. One never knows in advance whether to assume the one or the other; only the context will decide. An inkling of this state of affairs has clearly entered popular consciousness; dream-books often proceed on the principle of contrast when inter- preting dreams. The intimate associative connection which in our thinking tethers the idea of a thing to that of its opposite makes this kind of transformation into the contrary possible. Like every other displacement it serves the purposes of the censorship, but it is also frequently the work of wish-fulfilment, for after all, wish-fulfilment is nothing but the replacement of a disagreeable thing by its oppos- ite. Thus, just like our ideas of things, the affects of the dream- thoughts can also appear in the dream turned into their opposites, and it is probable that this transformation of an affect into its oppos- ite is the work of the dream-censorship. The *suppression of affect* and the *transformation of affect into its opposite*, of course, also have their functions in our social life, which gave us the ready analogy to dream- censorship; above all, they serve *dissimulation*. If I am in conversation with someone I should treat with solicitude, when all the while I would like to say something hostile to him, it is almost more import- ant for me to hide any expressive display of my affect than to moder- ate the wording of my thoughts. If I speak to him in words that are not impolite, but accompany what I say with a glance or gesture of hate, the effect I produce on that person is not much different from the one I would make if I had callously flung my contempt in his face. That is why the censorship bids me above all to suppress my affects, and, if I am a master of pretence, I will simulate the contrary affect, smile where I would rage, seem tender where I would destroy.

We are already familiar with an excellent example of the trans- formation of an affect into its opposite in the service of the censor- ship. In the dream of 'Uncle's beard' I feel great affection for my friend R., whereas and because the dream-thoughts are calling him a numbskull. This example of the transformation of affects into their opposite gave us our first clue to the existence of a dream-censorship. We also do not need to assume here that the dream-work creates a contrary affect of this sort wholly from scratch; it usually finds it ready and waiting in the material of the dream-thoughts and merely intensifies it with the psychical force of motives of defence until it becomes the predominant factor in forming the dream. In the dream of my uncle I have just mentioned, the contrary affect of affection probably has its source in my infancy (as the continuation of the dream suggests), for, from the special nature of my earliest childhood experiences (see the analysis on p. 271), the relationship between uncle and nephew has for me become the source of all my friendships and all my hatreds.

Certain suitable syntheses of fully analysed dreams will give us a good overview of these complicated processes of subsuming, diminishing, and turning into opposites which are the means by which the affects of the dream-thoughts finally turn into the affects in the dream. I will deal here with a few examples in which some of the instances I have discussed actually occur.

V

In the dream of the strange task my old professor Brücke gave me of dissecting my own pelvis, *I notice in the dream itself the absence of any appropriate feeling of horror.* Now this is wish-fulfilment in more than one sense. The dissection signifies the self-analysis that I am accomplishing, as it were, by publishing my dream-book, though in real life I have found it so embarrassing and painful that I have postponed printing the finished manuscript for more than a year. Now the wish is stirring that I should get over this sense of delay, which is why I do not feel any horror [Ger. *Grauen*, earlier rendered by the adjective 'gruesome'; homophone of *grauen*=to grow grey] in my dream. I would gladly notice the absence of *grauen* in the other sense; I am getting really grey; and this grey/*Grau* in my hair also reminds me not to delay any longer. Indeed, we know that at the end of the dream the thought reaches representation that I would have to leave it to the children to reach the goal of this difficult journey.

In the two dreams that transfer the expression of satisfaction to the moments immediately upon waking, this satisfaction is motivated in the one instance by the expectation that I shall now find out the meaning of 'I have dreamed of that before', and actually refers to the birth of my first children; in the other instance it is motivated by the conviction that 'what has been proclaimed by a sign' will now come to pass, and this is the same satisfaction that I felt when I welcomed my second son in his due time. In these cases the same affects persist in the dream as prevail in the dream-thoughts, but no dream works quite as simply as that. If we go a little deeper into the two analyses, we will learn that this satisfaction, which is not subject to censorship, draws added power from another source which does have the censorship to fear, and is charged with an affect that would certainly arouse opposition if it did not cover itself with the comparable affect of satisfaction, admissible and from an acceptable source, creeping in behind its back, as it were. Unfortunately I cannot demonstrate this from the example of this dream itself, but an instance from another field will make my meaning clear. I propose the following case: suppose there were someone near me whom I hate, so that I am moved by a strong feeling of joy when something happens to him. But my sense of morality does not give way to this emotion; I do not dare to utter my malediction, and when something he is not to blame for befalls him, I suppress my satisfaction and force myself to utter words and thoughts of commiseration. We have all found ourselves in such a position. But suppose the hated person does something wrong and gets into well-deserved trouble. Then I may give free rein to my satisfaction that he has been justly punished, and I express my agreement with many others who have no such axe to grind. However, I can observe that my satisfaction turns out to be more intense than the others'; it has been reinforced from the source of my hatred, which until now has been prevented by my inner censorship from releasing its affect; but under the changed circumstances it is no longer hindered from doing so. This case applies to society in general, when persons who are disliked, or members of an unwelcome minority, make themselves culpable in some way. Their punishment then is not usually commensurate with the wrong they have done, but with the wrong plus the ill will directed against them, which until now has been ineffective. Those carrying out the punishment are committing an injustice, there is no doubt about that; but their awareness of it is hindered by the satisfaction they get from the suspension of a long-held suppression within them. In cases like this, it is true the affect is justified in its nature, but not in its degree; and the self-criticism which can rest easy on the one issue only too readily avoids scrutinizing the second. Once the doors are opened, more people will force their way through than it was originally intended to admit.

It is a striking feature of the neurotic character that causes with affective potential give rise to an affect in the neurotic which is justified in its quality, but in quantity exceeds all measure. It can be explained in the following way—insofar as it admits of a psychological explanation at all. The excess derives from sources of affect that have remained unconscious and have so far been suppressed, and which are able to set up an associative connection with the real cause, while the desired route for their release is opened up by the irreproachable and admissible source of affect. This makes us aware that we should not focus exclusively on the relation of reciprocal inhibition between the suppressed and the suppressing agencies in the psyche. Just as much attention should be paid to those cases where both agencies work together and reinforce each other to bring about a pathological effect. Let us now apply these suggestions on the mechanics of the psyche to understanding how affects manifest themselves in dreams. A satisfaction that makes its presence known in the dream, and of course is promptly to be found in its place in the dream-thoughts, is not always fully explained by this evidence alone. As a rule, one would have to look in the dream-thoughts for a second source for it, one which is under pressure from the censorship. Under this pressure the source would have given rise, not to the affect of satisfaction, but rather to its opposite; however, the presence of the first source enables this second source to free its affect of satisfaction from repression and allow it to join with the satisfaction from the first source and reinforce it. In this way the affects in the dream appear to be made up of many tributaries flowing into them, and to be over-determined in respect of the material in the dream-thoughts. *Sources of affect which can give rise to the same affect come together in the process of dream-work to produce it.*

We get a little insight into these complicated circumstances from the analysis of the beautiful dream that has '*Non vixit*' as its centre (see p. 268). In this dream there are two places in the manifest content where expressions of affect of a different nature are condensed. Hostile and distressing emotions (in the dream itself it says 'overcome by quite remarkable affect') overlap at the point where I annihilate my friend and rival with the two words. At the end of the dream I am unusually glad and I make a positive judgement about a possibility I would recognize as absurd when awake, that there are in fact such things as *revenants*, which can be banished merely by wishing them away.

I have not yet related the occasion for this dream. It is of the essence, and leads us deep into understanding it. I received news from my friend in Berlin (whom I have identified by the initial Fl.) that he was to undergo an operation, and that relatives of his living in Vienna would let me know further how he fared. The first news after the operation was not satisfactory, and left me worried. Most of all I would have liked to travel to Berlin and see him myself, but just at that time I was suffering from a painful complaint which made every movement a torment. Now I learn from the dream-thoughts that I feared for the life of my dear friend. His only sister, whom I had not met, had died young after the briefest of illnesses, as I knew. (In my dream: *Fl. is telling us about his sister and says: in three-quarters of an hour she was dead.*) I must have imagined that his own nature was not much more resilient, and got the idea that in the end I would be making the journey in response to far worse news—and would arrive too *late*, which would cause me to reproach myself for ever.[31] This rebuke for coming too late has become the centre of the dream, but it has represented itself by a scene in which it is Brücke, the revered master of my student years, who rebukes me with a terrible glance from his blue eyes. It will soon emerge what brought about this shift of scene; the dream is unable to reproduce the scene in the way I experienced it. It is true, it gives the blue eyes to the other figure, but it gives the annihilating role to me, a reversal which is obviously the work of wish-fulfilment. My concern for my friend's life, my self-reproach that I am not making the journey to see him, my shame (he came to Vienna—to me—*inconspicuously*), my need to regard my illness as my excuse, all this goes into composing the storm of feeling that I felt distinctly in my sleep, and which rages in that region of the dream-thoughts.

However, there was something else about the occasion for the dream that had the completely opposite effect upon me. When I was given the adverse news of the first days after the operation, I was also

---

[31] It is this fantasy from the unconscious dream-thoughts that imperiously demands *non vivit* instead of *non vixit*. 'You have come too late. He is no longer alive.' It is noted on p. 269 that the manifest situation of the dream also aims for *non vivit*.

warned not to speak to anyone about the entire matter, which I found insulting, because it was premised on an unnecessary mistrust of my discretion. Of course I knew that this did not come from my friend, but I was hurt and embarrassed by the hidden rebuke, because it was—not entirely unjustified. Only a rebuke that 'has something in it' will sting, will have the power to stir our feelings, not the other sort, as we know. Not with regard to my friend, it is true, but once before, when I was much younger, in the case of two friends who both—to my honour—wanted to call me by that name, I quite unnecessarily babbled out something the one had said about the other. Nor have I forgotten the reproaches I got to hear then. One of the two friends between whom I played disturber of the peace was Professor *Fleischl*; the other can be replaced by his first name, *Josef*, which was also the name of my friend and rival P.* who appeared in the dream.

As evidence in the dream for the charge that I cannot keep anything to myself there are the elements *inconspicuous* and Fl.'s question, *how much of his concerns have I told P.?* However, it is the intervention of this memory that transposes the rebuke of coming too late from the present to my time in Brücke's laboratory. And in replacing the second figure in the annihilation-scene of the dream by someone called *Josef*, I make this scene represent not only the rebuke that I have come too late, but also the charge more strongly affected by repression: that I cannot keep a secret. The dream's work of condensation and displacement, as well as the motives for it, are evident here.

However, my petty present-day annoyance at the warning not to reveal anything is reinforced from sources flowing in the depths, and thus augmented, it swells to a torrent of hostile feelings towards persons who in real life are dear to me. The source providing the reinforcement flows at the infantile level. I have already related how my warm friendships and my enmities with my contemporaries go back to the company I kept as a child with my nephew, one year older than I. In our relations he had the upper hand; I learned to defend myself early; we were inseparable from each other; we loved each other; in between, so our elders tell me, we fought and—*told tales on each other*. All my friends are in some sense incarnations of this first figure, 'who came before my clouded gaze so long ago',* *revenants*. My nephew himself came back to visit as an adolescent, and then we

performed Caesar and Brutus together. An intimate friend and a
hated foe have always been necessary to my emotional life; I have
always been able to create for myself fresh embodiments of both, and
not infrequently my childhood ideal went so far that friend and foe
coincided in the same person—no longer at the same time, of course,
or switching repeatedly from one to the other, which was probably
the case in my earliest childhood years.

At this point I do not intend to pursue the way in which, given
such circumstances, a recent occasion for affect is able to hark back
to one from infancy, in order to use it as a substitute for itself to
produce the affect. It belongs to the psychology of unconscious
thinking, and would have its proper place in a psychological explanation of the neuroses. Let us assume for purposes of interpreting
the dream that a memory from childhood or one created in fantasy
presents itself, with something like the following content: the two
children start quarrelling over some object—exactly what, we can
leave open, although the recollection, or the illusory recollection, has
something quite definite in mind;—each one of them maintains that
he *came sooner*, that is, he has first claim on it; a fight develops; might
is right; the dream suggests that I could have known I was in the
wrong (*I notice my mistake*); but this time I am the stronger; I hold
the field; the defeated combatant hurries to my father, his grandfather; tells on me, and I defend myself with the words familiar from
my father's account: *I hit him because he hit me.* Thus, this memory,
or more probably fantasy, which forces its way into my mind in the
course of the analysis—without further evidence, I myself don't
know how—is a central part of the dream-thoughts, gathering the
affects prevailing there in the same way as a fountain-bowl collects
the waters streaming into it. From here the dream-thoughts flow
along the following channels: it serves you right that you have to get
out of the way for me; why did you want to get me out of the way?
I don't need you, I'll find someone else to play with, etc. Then the
channels open up along which these thoughts return and flow into
the dream-representation again. I must have charged my dead friend
Josef with some such 'Ôte-toi que je m'y mette'* at the time. He had
followed in my footsteps in Brücke's laboratory, but promotion there
was slow and difficult. Neither of the two assistants showed signs
of moving. The young scientists were growing impatient. My friend,
who knew he did not have many years to live, and who had no

obligations to the man ahead of him from any bonds of intimacy, was on occasion loud in expressing his impatience. As the member of staff ahead of him was a very sick man, the wish to get him out of the way, besides implying 'by promotion', also admitted an odious secondary meaning. Some years earlier I had naturally felt the same wish even more strongly to take up a position that had been vacated. Wherever there are hierarchies and promotions to be found in the world, the way is clear for wishes requiring suppression. Not even at the bed of his sick father can Shakespeare's Prince Hal* avoid the temptation of trying on the crown to see how it suits him. But, as one might expect, my dream punishes Josef, not me, for this ruthless wish.[32]

'As he was ambitious, I slew him.'* As he could not wait for the other to get out of the way for him, the dream got him out of the way. I nurse these thoughts right after attending the unveiling of the memorial to the other at the university. So one part of the satisfaction I felt in my dream can be interpreted as: a just punishment; it serves you right.

At my friend's funeral, a young man made the apparently unsuitable remark that the speaker addressed us as though the world could not go on without this one human being. He was protesting as a truthful person whose grief was offended by exaggeration. But my dream-thoughts connect with what he said: no one is really irreplaceable; how many I have already accompanied to the grave; but I am still alive, I have outlived them all, I hold the field. Such a thought, in the moment when I fear I shall not meet my friend again among the living when I make the journey to see him, allows the interpretation to unfold in only one way: once again I am glad to outlive someone; glad that it is not *I* who am dead, but *he*; that I hold the field as I did then in the fantasy of that childhood scene. This satisfaction, deriving from an infantile level, that I hold the field accounts for the greater share of the affect taken up into the dream. I am delighted that I am the survivor, I express it with the naive egoism of the married couple in the anecdote: 'If one of us dies, I'll go and live in Paris.' In my expectations, it goes without saying that I am not the one.

---

[32] It will have been noticed that the name of *Josef* plays such a large part in my dreams (see the dream of my uncle). In my dreams it is particularly easy for me to conceal my self behind figures with this name, for *Joseph* was also the name of the well-known *dream-interpreter* in the Bible.

One cannot deny that it requires arduous self-conquest to interpret and report one's own dreams. The interpreter has to expose himself as the only villain among all the noble figures who share his life. So I find it quite understandable that the *revenants* should only exist for as long as one wants them to, and that they can be removed at a wish. That is, of course, what my friend Josef was punished for. However, the *revenants* form the sequence of incarnations of my childhood friend; so I am also satisfied that I have replaced this figure over and over again, and a replacement will soon turn up for the one I am now about to lose. No one is irreplaceable.

But what has become of the dream-censorship in this? Why doesn't it raise the strongest objections to this grossly selfish train of thought, and transform the satisfaction clinging to it into grave unpleasure? I think it is because other, unobjectionable trains of thought about the same figures also end in satisfaction, and cover with their affect the one from the forbidden infantile source. In another stratum of my thoughts, I said to myself at that solemn unveiling of the memorial: I have lost so many dear friends, one through death, another when our friendship broke up; it is good, all the same, that I have found a replacement for them and gained this one friend who means more to me than the others could; and now, at the age when it is no longer easy to make new friendships, I shall hold him close for ever. I can transfer my satisfaction at having found this substitute for my lost friends into my dream undisturbed, but the hostile satisfaction from the infantile source slips in behind it too. Certainly, infantile tenderness helps to reinforce my present-day, justified affection; but infantile hatred, too, has made its way into the dream-representation.

In addition, however, the dream contains a distinct allusion to another train of thought which is allowed to end in satisfaction. After long waiting, my friend had shortly before had a baby daughter. I know how much he had mourned the early loss of his sister, and I wrote to him that he would transfer to this child the love he felt for his sister. At last this little girl would make him forget his irreplaceable loss.

So this sequence, too, again links on to the intermediary thoughts of the latent dream-content, from which the paths diverge in opposite directions: no one is irreplaceable. Look, only *revenants*; everyone we have lost returns to us. And now the associative bonds between the contradictory components of the dream-thoughts are drawn closer by the chance circumstance that my friend's little daughter has the same name as my own little playfellow, who was the same age as I was, the sister of my oldest friend and rival. I heard the name 'Pauline' with *satisfaction*, and as an allusion to this coincidence, I substituted one Josef for another Josef in my dream, and found it impossible to suppress the same initial sound in the names Fleischl and Fl. This becomes the starting-point then for a line of thought to the naming of my own children. I insisted that their names should not be chosen according to fashion, but should be in remembrance of persons dear to us. Their names turn the children into *revenants*. And finally, is having children not the only access any of us has to *immortality*?

I shall only add a few more remarks from another angle on affects in dreams. It is possible for a tendency to an affect—what we call a mood—to be present in the sleeper's psyche as the dominant element and then for it to share in determining the dream. This mood can proceed from the experiences and thoughts of the day; it can have somatic origins; in both cases they will be accompanied by the trains of thought appropriate to them. As far as the formation of dreams is concerned, it does not matter whether the content of imagined ideas in the dream-thoughts is the primary determinant of the tendency to affect, or whether it is itself aroused secondarily by the sleeper's emotional disposition, which can be explained by its somatic basis. In all cases, dream-formation operates under restriction: it can only represent a wish-fulfilment, and it is only from the wish that it can draw its psychic energy. The currently active mood will be treated in the same way as active sensation during sleep (see p. 181), which is either ignored, or reinterpreted as a wish-fulfilment. Moods of distress in sleep become the driving forces of the dream as they arouse energetic wishes which the dream is intended to fulfil. The material they cling to is worked over until it becomes usable as an expression for fulfilling them. The more intense and dominant the mood of distress is as an element in the dream-thoughts, the more certain it is that the most strongly suppressed wishes will use this opportunity to get themselves represented. For unpleasure, which they usually have to generate for themselves, is already present and active, so they discover that the most difficult part of their efforts to become represented has already been done. And this discussion touches once again on the problem of anxiety-dreams, which will turn out to be the borderline case for dreams and their functioning.

(h)* *Secondary Revision*

Let us at last raise the subject of the fourth factor in the formation of dreams.

If we continue our examination of the dream-content in the way we have been doing, by referring occurrences that strike us as noticeable in the dream-content back to their origins, we will come upon elements which will need an entirely fresh assumption to explain them. I have in mind those instances where the dreamer is astonished or annoyed as he dreamed, or where he recoiled—in fact from part of the dream-content itself. Most of these stirrings of criticism in our dreams are not aimed at the dream-content but, as I have shown from suitable examples, they turn out to be parts of the dream-material taken over into the dream and put to appropriate use there. However, some criticism in a dream refuses to be accommodated by a derivation of this kind; it is not possible to find its correlate in the dream-material. What is the meaning, for instance, of the criticism we meet quite frequently in a dream: 'After all, it's only a dream'? This is a real criticism of the dream, of the sort I could make when awake. Quite often, too, it is just the forerunner of our waking; more frequently it is itself preceded by a feeling of distress which is put to rest by telling ourselves that we are dreaming. However, the thought: 'After all, it's only a dream' while we are still dreaming has the same intention as the one Helen of Troy* gives it on the open stage in Offenbach's comic opera; it wants to reduce the significance of what has just been experienced and help to make what follows bearable. It serves to lull to sleep a certain agency, which might have every cause to stir at the given moment and forbid the continuation of the dream—or scene. But it is more convenient to go on sleeping and endure the dream 'because it's only a dream after all'. As I see it, the scornful criticism, 'after all, it's only a dream', occurs in the dream when the censorship, which never falls entirely asleep, feels caught unawares by the dream that has already been admitted. It is too late to suppress it; accordingly, the censorship responds with this comment to the anxiety or feeling of distress aroused by the dream. It is an expression of the *esprit d'escalier* on the part of the psychical censorship.

However, this example offers indisputable proof that not everything contained in the dream comes from the dream-thoughts, but rather that a function of the psyche indistinguishable from our waking thoughts can make some contribution to the dream-content. Now the question is whether this is wholly exceptional, or whether the psychical agency which usually only functions as censorship may claim to have a regular share in the formation of dreams.

We are bound to decide unhesitatingly for the latter. There is no doubt that the censoring agency, whose influence we have so far observed only in restrictions and omissions in the dream-content, is also responsible for interpolations and additions. These interpolations are often easy to recognize; they are announced timidly, introduced with an 'as if', are not in themselves particularly vivid, and they are always to be found in places where they can function to link two bits of the dream-content or set up a connection between two parts of the dream. The memory retains them less easily than the true offspring of the dream-material; if the dream is forgotten, they are the first to vanish, and I have the strong suspicion that our frequent complaint that we have dreamed so much but forgotten most of it and retained only fragments is due to the prompt disappearance of just these cementing thoughts. In a complete analysis these interpolations sometimes betray themselves because no material relating to them is to be found in the dream-thoughts. However, on closer scrutiny I have to say that this case occurs less frequently; still, these connecting thoughts do on the whole allow us to trace them back to material in the dream-thoughts, but material which was not able, either on its own account or by virtue of its over-determination, to claim admittance into the dream. It would seem that the psychical function in dream-formation we are now considering will make the effort to produce new creations only in extreme cases; as long as possible, it will turn to account whatever it is able to select as being suitable from the dream-material.

What marks this part of the dream-work out and exposes it to view is its purpose. This function proceeds rather as the poet* maliciously declares philosophers do: with its snippets and scraps it patches the gaps in the dream's structure. The result of its labours is that the dream loses its appearance of absurdity and incoherence, and approaches the pattern of an intelligible experience. But its labours are not always crowned with total success. In this way, dreams come about which might appear perfectly logical and rational; they start out from a plausible situation, continue it through changes free of contradictions, and bring it—though this happens less often—to an unsurprising conclusion. These dreams have gone through a very deep and thorough working-over from this function of the psyche which resembles waking thought; they seem to make sense, but this sense is also furthest from the real meaning of the dream. If we analyse them, we are convinced that here the secondary revision of the dream has played around with the material most freely, and retained the relations in it least. These are dreams that have already been interpreted, you might say, before we submit them to interpretation when we are awake. There are other dreams where this purposeful revision has only partially succeeded; coherence seems to be in control up to a point, then the dream becomes non-sensical or confused, and then perhaps for the second time in its course it goes on to make ostensible sense. In other dreams the revision has given up entirely; we are helpless in the face of a mean-ingless heap of fragmentary material.

I would not like to declare out of hand that this fourth shaping power has no capacity to contribute something new to the dream, for after all, it will soon appear that we are acquainted with it, indeed, it is the only one among our four dream-composers we are already familiar with. However, it is certainly the case that its influence, like that of the others, is manifested mainly in the preference and choice it makes from already-formed psychical material in the dream-thoughts. There is only one case where it is largely spared its work of building a façade onto the dream, as it were, and that is if such a structure is already present in the material of the dream-thoughts, ready and waiting to be used. The element in the dream-thoughts I have in mind I usually call a *fantasy*; it will avoid misunderstandings, perhaps, if I identify the *daydream*[33] as its equivalent in waking life. The part played by this element in the life of the psyche has not yet been fully recognized or revealed; M. Benedikt has made a start, and a very promising one, it seems to me, with his assessment. The significance of the daydream has not escaped the unerring insight of

---

[33] *Rêve, petit roman*—daydream, story.*

the poets; Alphonse Daudet's description of the daydreams of one of the minor figures in his *Nabab** is widely known. The study of the psychoneuroses leads to the surprising insight that these fantasies or daydreams are the immediate predecessors of hysterical symptoms—at least of a large number of them; hysterical symptoms cling not to the memories themselves but only to the fantasies constructed on the basis of the memories. The frequent occurrence of conscious fantasies during the day draws our attention to these formations; but just as conscious fantasies of this kind exist, there are also plenty of unconscious ones which cannot but remain unconscious because of their content and their origin in repressed material. If we immerse ourselves more deeply in the nature of these daytime fantasies, we find that they are quite justifiably called by the same name that we give to the productions of our thinking at night: *dreams*. They share certain essential characteristics with our nighttime dreams; investigating them could actually have opened up for us the best and nearest access to understanding dreams.

Like dreams, they are wish-fulfilments; like dreams, they are based in large part on our infantile experiences; like dreams they enjoy a certain relaxation of the censorship for their creations. If we go in pursuit of their structure, we become aware of how the wishful motive at work in their production and the material from which they are constructed are thrown into confusion, rearranged, and composed into a new whole. Their relation to the childhood memories they go back to is rather like the relation of many of the baroque palaces in Rome to the ancient ruins whose stones and pillars have provided the material for building in more modern forms.

In the 'secondary revision' exercised on the dream-content which we have ascribed to our fourth shaping factor, we find the same activity as the one that expresses itself freely and unconfined by other influences in the creation of daydreams. We might say without further ado that our fourth factor attempts to shape *something like a daydream* out of the material available to it. But in cases where a daydream of this sort is already formed in the web of the dream-thoughts, this factor in the dream-work will for preference take over the daydream and aim for it to enter the dream-content. There are such dreams consisting only of the repetition of a daytime fantasy, for example, the dream of the boy that he was riding in the war-chariot with the heroes of the Trojan War. In my *Autodidasker* dream, the second part of the dream at least is a faithful repetition of a daytime fantasy, innocuous in itself, about my relations with Professor N. The fantasy already present more frequently forms only a part of the dream, or only a part of it gets through to the dream-content; this is due to the complicated conditions the dream has to satisfy as it emerges. Then the fantasy is usually treated like any other component of the latent material; but once in the dream it is often still recognizable as a whole. In my own dreams there are often parts that stand out, making a different impression from the rest. They appear fluent, more coherent, but also more evanescent than other parts of the same dream; I know these are unconscious fantasies entering my dream as a coherent part of it, but I have never succeeded in pinning any of them down. For the rest, these fantasies, like all the other components of the dream-thoughts, are jostled up against one another, they are condensed, they overlay one another and the like; but there are transitional instances between those cases where they are free to form the dream-content, or at least the dream-façade, almost without alteration, and those at the opposite end of the range where they are represented in the dream-content only by one of their elements, or by some remote allusion to one of them. Obviously what befalls the fantasies in the dream-thoughts will depend crucially on any advantages they may have to offer against the demands of the censorship and the pressures towards condensation.

In choosing my examples for interpretation, I have as far as possible steered clear of dreams in which unconscious fantasies have played a relatively important part, because the introduction of this element of the psyche would have required lengthy explanations of the psychology of unconscious thinking. Nevertheless, I cannot entirely avoid discussing 'fantasies' in the present context, as they frequently enter the dream fully fledged, and even more frequently shimmer clearly through it. I would perhaps mention just one more dream, which appears to be made up of two different fantasies, opposites, but overlapping each other in certain places; one of these is superficial, the other becomes, as it were, the interpretation of the first.

The dream—the only one I have no careful notes for—runs roughly as follows: the dreamer—a young bachelor—is sitting in his regular inn, which looks as it usually does; several people appear on the scene to take him away, among them one who makes to arrest him. He says to his companions at table: 'I'll pay later. I'll be back.' But they smile and sneer: 'We've heard that before. That's what they all say.' One guest calls after him: 'There's someone else on his way out!' He is then led into a small room where he finds a woman with a child in her arms. One of his escorts says: 'This is Herr Müller.' A commissioner, or some other kind of official, turns the pages of a pack of notes or papers, repeating as he does so: 'Müller, Müller, Müller.' Finally, he asks him a question, which he answers with 'Yes'. He then looks round for the woman, and notices that she has grown a large beard.

The two components here are easy to distinguish. The superficial one is a *fantasy of being arrested*, and seems to be freshly formed by the dream-work. But behind it, material that has been slightly adapted by the dream-work comes into view: the *fantasy of getting married*, and the features that both could have in common once again stand out with particular clarity, as in one of Galton's composite photographs. The promise made by the young man, still a bachelor so far, that he will come back to his regular place at table, the scepticism of his drinking fellows, who joke from long experience, 'There's someone else on his way out (to get married)', these items make good sense in the other reading as well. So does the answer 'Yes' that he gives the official. Leafing through a pile of papers and repeating the same name the while correspond to a minor, but recognizable feature of marriage celebrations, that is, reading out the telegrams of congratulation arriving in piles, which are, of course, all addressed to the same name. With the personal appearance of the bride in this dream, the marriage-fantasy has even triumphed over the fantasy of being arrested which covers it. I was able to clear up the bride's beard at the end of the dream by making an inquiry—we did not get as far as an analysis. The day before, the dreamer had crossed the road with a friend who was just as averse to marriage as he was, and the friend had drawn his attention to a pretty brunette coming towards them. However, the friend had remarked: 'Fine, if only these women didn't grow beards like their fathers as they get older.'

Naturally, there are plenty of elements in this dream where dream-distortion has been at work more deeply and thoroughly. It may be that the words 'I'll pay later' refer to the way he fears his father-in-law might behave with regard to the dowry. Obviously all sorts of doubts are holding the dreamer back from relaxing and enjoying his marriage-fantasy. One of these doubts—that with marriage he will lose his freedom—was embodied in the transformation of the scene into an arrest.

If we return to our proposition that the dream-work is happy to make use of a fantasy already present and available instead of putting a new one together out of the material in the dream-thoughts, this insight may perhaps solve one of the most interesting puzzles offered by dreams. On page 24, I related a dream of Maury's [48], who was struck on the back of his neck by a board and woke from a long dream, a complete novel, set in the time of the French Revolution. As the claim is made that the dream was coherent, and its explanation is ascribed wholly to the stimulus that woke the sleeper, one quite out of his ken, all we seem to be left with is the one assumption that the entire dream, in all its profusion, must have been composed and set in train in the brief space of time between the moment the board fell onto the vertebra of Maury's nape and his waking up on account of the blow. We would not dare to ascribe such speed to the activity of our waking thoughts, so this might lead us to grant that the dream-work has the advantage of remarkable acceleration as the dream unfolds.

This conclusion quickly became popular, but recent authorities (Le Lorrain [45], Egger [20], and others) have raised strong objections to it. Partly they are sceptical of the accuracy of Maury's account of his dream, partly they are trying to prove that our speed of thinking in waking life is no less than that of our dreams, whose feats need not be played down. The discussion raises questions of principle whose answers seem to me to be still very far away. But I must confess that I do not find the arguments—Egger's, for example—convincing, especially his objections to Maury's guillotine dream. I would suggest the following explanation for this dream: would it be so very unlikely that Maury's dream might represent a fantasy which was preserved ready-made for years in his memory and was roused—I would say *alluded to*—when he responded to the stimulus that woke him? To start with, this disposes of the whole difficulty of composing such a long story with all its details in the extremely short space of time available to the dreamer; it is already composed. If the board had struck the back of Maury's neck while he was awake, there would have been room for a thought such as: 'that is just as if I were being guillotined.' But since he was struck while he was asleep, the dream-work quickly made use of the stimulus reaching it to produce a wish-fulfilment, *as if* it were thinking (this is to be taken entirely in a figurative sense): 'This is a good opportunity to make the wishful fantasy from my reading of yore come true.' It seems beyond dispute to me that the romance he dreamed is just the sort an adolescent habitually makes up under the influence of powerful and exciting impressions. Who would not have felt gripped—especially if you were French, and a historian of culture—by descriptions from the Reign of Terror, when the nobility, men and women, the flower of the nation, showed how one could die with a serene spirit, and kept their sharp wit and delicate manners up to their fatal departure from this life? How attractive to fantasize that you are a young man in their midst, kissing your lady's hand as you bid her farewell, and climbing the scaffold unafraid! Or, if ambition was the main motive for the fantasy, to imagine yourself into the figure of one of those mighty individuals who, by the power of their thoughts and their blazing eloquence alone, rule the city at the time when the heart of humanity is throbbing there; who out of conviction send thousands of human beings to their deaths as they pave the way for the transformation of Europe; who, even as they do so, know that their own heads are not safe, and that one day they will lay them beneath the knife of the guillotine! To do so perhaps in the role of the Girondistes,* or the heroic Danton?* That Maury's fantasy was motivated by ambition seems to be suggested by the feature retained in his memory: 'accompanied by an enormous crowd'.

However, this fantasy, completed long ago, does not even need to be run through; it is enough if it is, as it were, 'touched on'. This is what I mean: if a few bars of music are quoted (as they are in *Don Giovanni**), and someone says 'That's from Mozart's *Marriage of Figaro*', then all of a sudden I am overwhelmed by a surge of memories and I cannot for the moment bring particular ones to consciousness. The stimulus-word acts as a breaching-place in my memory through which a whole mass of recollections are set in motion all at the same time. It need not be any different in our unconscious thinking. The stimulus to waking rouses the psychical breaching-place, which opens up access to the entire guillotine-fantasy. But this will not run its full course while the fantasist is still asleep, only when he remembers it on waking up. Once awake, he remembers all the details of the fantasy that was touched on as a whole in his dream. But he has no means of being certain that he is remembering something he has really dreamed. The same explanation—that it is a question of ready-made fantasies roused in their entirety by the stimulus to waking—can be applied to other dreams dependent on a stimulus to waking, for example, Napoleon's dream of a battle just before the infernal machine went off. I do not want to assert that all dreams upon waking admit of this explanation, or that the general problem of acceleration in the course of the dream can be disposed of in this way.

We are now at the stage where we cannot avoid dealing with the relationship of this secondary revision of the dream-content to the other factors governing the dream-work. Does the process go something like this: the dream-forming factors—the efforts of condensation, the compulsion to escape the censorship, and regard for representability by the psychical means available to dreams—first form a provisional content out of the material given, and then this is reshaped retrospectively until it answers the requirements of a second agency as best it can? This is hardly likely. We should rather assume that the requirements set by this factor make one of the conditions the dream has to satisfy, and that this condition will operate by selecting from the broad mass of material in the dream-thoughts, enabling them to enter the dream, that is, it will function just as the factors of condensation, the censorship set up by resistance, and representability do. However, of the four conditions we have identified for the formation of dreams, this most recent one is in any case the one whose requirements appear to be the least compelling for the dream. It is highly likely that our identification of this psychical function, which performs what we have called the secondary revision of the dream-content, with the operation of our waking thought, arises from the following consideration: our waking (preconscious) thought behaves towards whatever random material presents itself to our perception in the same way as the function in question behaves towards the dream-content. It comes naturally to it to create order out of such material, to set up relations and locate it where we can expect an intelligible context. But this is probably going too far. The reason we are fooled by conjurers' tricks is because they rely on this intellectual habit of ours. In our efforts to make a coherent and intelligible whole of the sensory impressions presenting themselves to us, we often make the oddest mistakes or even falsify the truth of the material before us. The proofs of this are too widely known to need further demonstration. We read over misprints that spoil the sense, and create an illusion of the correct word. One editor of a widely read French journal is said to have dared to bet that in the course of printing he would have 'from the front' or 'from behind' slipped into every sentence of a long article without one of his readers noticing. He won the bet. Reading a newspaper some years ago, I was struck by an amusing example of making the wrong connection. After that sitting of the French Chamber of Deputies when Dupuy's* brave words 'La séance continue' put an end to the alarm caused by the explosion when an anarchist's bomb was thrown into the Chamber, visitors to the gallery were questioned as witnesses about their impressions of the assassination attempt. Among them were two visitors up from the provinces; one of them said he had certainly heard an explosion right after the end of a speech, but had thought it was the custom in Parliament to fire a shot whenever a speaker had finished. The other, who had probably heard several speakers already, made the same judgement, but with the variation that shots of this kind were made as a commendation, and only happened after particularly successful speeches.

It is probable, then, that the agency requiring the dream-content to be intelligible is none other than our normal thinking; it subjects it to a first interpretation, and by doing so brings about its complete misunderstanding. For our interpretation, it remains mandatory in all cases to pay no attention to the ostensible coherence of a dream, as having a suspect source, and to take the same route back to the dream-material, whether the dream is lucid or confused.

As we do so, however, we recall from our earlier discussion (p. 251) what it is that the qualitative scale from confusion to clarity essentially depends upon. The parts of the dream that appear clear to us are the ones where the secondary revision was able to accomplish something; in the other parts, which seem confused, the powers of this ability failed. As the confused parts of the dream are also very often less vivid and distinctive, we may draw the conclusion that the secondary dream-work is also to be held responsible for some contribution to the intensity of sensuous realization in particular elements of the dream.

If I am to look anywhere for something comparable to the definitive formation of a dream when normal thinking has a share in shaping it, the only things that come to mind are those puzzling inscriptions with which the *Fliegende Blätter* used to entertain its readers for so long. They set up the expectation that a certain sentence—in dialect for the contrast and with as comical a meaning as possible—contained a Latin inscription. To do this, the letters of the words are torn out of their proper order as syllables and rearranged. Now and again a genuine Latin word will come about, in other parts we think we can see abbreviations of such words, and in other parts of the inscription again we are willing to be taken in by the meaninglessness of solitary letters, assuming that the passages are apparently weathered, or that there are gaps in the inscription. If we don't want to be taken in by the joke, we have to ignore all the requirements for an inscription, keep our eye on the letters, and, without troubling about the required arrangement, put them together to make words in our mother-tongue.

I shall now set about summing up this lengthy discussion of the dream-work. We were confronted with the question of whether the psyche applies all its powers without any restrictions to the formation of dreams, or whether it employs only a fragment of them, inhibited in capability. Our investigations lead us to reject the terms of this question entirely, as inappropriate to the situation. Indeed, if we were to reply on the same terrain as the question, we should have to answer both views in the affirmative, even though as opposites they appear to be mutually exclusive. The work of the psyche in the formation of dreams can be broken down into two tasks: it generates the dream-thoughts, and it transforms them into the dream-content. The dream-thoughts are entirely reasonable, and are formed with all the expense of psychical energy we are capable of; they belong to that dimension of our thinking which has not become conscious, and from which, by some transposition, our conscious thoughts also arise. However many unanswered questions and puzzles the dream-thoughts raise, all the same these puzzles do not have any particular relation to dreams, and do not merit treatment among the problems of dreams. On the other hand, the other task of transforming the unconscious thoughts into the dream-content is peculiar to the life of dreams and characteristic of it. This is the true dream-work, and it is far more remote from the model of waking thought than even the most determined belittlers of the psyche's feats of dream-formation have thought. It is not that it is more negligent, more unreasonable, more forgetful, more incomplete, say, than waking thought; it is qualitatively something completely different from it, and so at first not comparable to it. It does not think, calculate, judge in any way at all; it confines itself to reshaping. It can be described exhaustively if we keep our eye on the conditions which its product has to satisfy. Above all, this product—the dream—has to be removed from the influence of the *censorship*, and for this purpose the dream-work makes use of the *displacement of psychical intensities* to the point of a transvaluation of all psychical values; thoughts are to be reproduced exclusively or predominantly in terms of the material provided by visual and aural memory-traces, and this requires the dream-work to *take account of representability*, which it does by setting up new displacements. Greater intensities than the dream-thoughts have at their disposal at night are (probably) to be created, and this purpose is served by the ample *condensation* undertaken with the elements of the dream-thoughts. Little account is taken of the logical relations in the thought-material; they are ultimately given a hidden representation in particular *formal* features of the dreams. The affects of the dream-thoughts are subject to lesser modifications than the imagined ideas of their content are. As a rule they are suppressed; where they are retained, they are separated from their ideas and combined with affects of a similar tonality. Only one part of the dream-work, the revisions, variable in extent, made by our partially roused waking thought, conforms to the conception our authorities would apply to the entire activity of dream-formation.

THE PSYCHOLOGY OF THE DREAM-PROCESSES

Among the dreams I have learned of through others, there is one that now has very special claims on our attention. It was told me by a patient who had heard it herself in a lecture on dreams; its actual source remains unknown to me. However, its content made an impression on the lady, for she very soon 'copy-dreamed' it, that is, repeated elements of the dream in a dream of her own, using this transference to express a point of resemblance to it.

The prior conditions for this model dream are as follows: for days and nights a father has been watching at his child's sickbed. After the child's death, he lies down to rest in a room nearby, but leaves the doors open so that he can look from his bedroom into the room where the child's body is laid out, surrounded by tall candles. An old man has been set to keep watch, sitting near the body and murmuring prayers. After a few hours' sleep, the father dreams *that the child is standing at his bedside, grasps him by the arm and whispers to him reproachfully, 'Father, can't you see that I am burning?'* He wakes up, notices a bright light coming from the room where the body is lying, hurries over, and finds the old attendant fallen asleep, the shroud and an arm of the beloved body burnt by a lighted candle that had fallen across it.

The explanation of this touching dream is simple enough, and was also given correctly by the lecturer, so my patient informed me. The bright light came through the open doors and fell on the father's eyes, leading him to draw the same conclusion as he would have made if he had been awake: that a fire had started when a candle fell over near the body. Perhaps the father had carried into his sleep the worry that the aged attendant might not be up to his job.

We too would find nothing to alter in this interpretation, unless it were to add the condition that the content of the dream must be over-determined, and that what the child said must have been put together from words he had really used in life in a context of events that were important to the father. Such as the complaint 'I'm burning'—of his feverishness when he died, and the words: 'Father, can't you see?' on some other occasion unknown to us, but charged with deep affect.

However, after we have acknowledged this dream to be a meaningful occurrence with a proper place in the context of what was going on in the father's psyche, we might well wonder that under such circumstances a dream came about at all, when it was advisable to wake up as quickly as possible. We will notice then that this dream too is not without its wish-fulfilment. In the dream the dead child behaves as if he were alive, he warns his father himself, he comes up to his bed and tugs him by the arm, just as he probably did in that memory from which the dream took the first bit of what the child said. Now, it was for the sake of this wish-fulfilment that the father prolonged his sleep for a moment. He gave the dream a prior claim over his waking reflection because it was able to show him the child alive again. If he had woken first and then drawn the conclusion that took him into the room where the child's body was lying, he would have shortened the child's life by this one moment, as it were.

There can be no doubt which distinctive feature of this little dream has captured our interest. So far we have mainly been concerned with probing after the hidden meaning of dreams, the route we should take to discover it, and the means the dream-work has employed to hide it. And now we come upon this dream, which offers no problems of interpretation, whose meaning is given undisguised, and we note that it still retains the essential characteristics that distinguish a dream sharply from our waking thought and rouse our need for explanation. Only when we have got rid of everything that has to do with the work of interpretation can we see how incomplete our psychology of dreams still is.

But before we take our thoughts along this new path, let us pause and look back, to see whether on our journey so far we have not left anything important unremarked. For we must be clear in our minds: the stretch of our way that makes for easy going lies behind us. Until now, if I am not much mistaken, all the paths we have trodden have led us into the light, to enlightenment and to full understanding; from the moment we propose to go more deeply into the psyche's inner processes of dreaming, all our ways lead into the dark. It is impossible for us to get as far as *explaining* the dream as a psychical process, for explaining means tracing back to what is already known, and at present the psychological knowledge does not exist that we could use as an explanatory framework for what we have been able to deduce from our psychological scrutiny of dreams. On the contrary, we shall be obliged to put forward a set of new assumptions touching speculatively on the structure of the psychical apparatus and the play of forces active in it, though we must take care not to spin them out too far beyond their first logical links, for if we do, their worth will vanish into uncertainty. Even if we make no errors of deduction, and take account of all the logical possibilities, there is still the threat that our calculations will go utterly wrong because the elements we start from are probably incomplete. There is no possibility of acquiring any information about—or at least of accounting for—how the instrument of our psyche is constructed or how it operates, from even the most careful examination of the dream or of any other psychical attainment *by itself*; for this, we will have to compare a number of the psyche's functions and from this study compile the requirements that turn out to be constants among them all. As we do so, the psychological assumptions that we draw from our analysis of dream-processes will have to wait at the station, as it were, until they have caught the connection to the results of other investigations attempting to reach the heart of the same problem from another point of attack.

(a) *Forgetting in Dreams*

I suggest, then, that we should first turn to a topic that raises an objection we have so far disregarded, but which is apt to cut the ground from under our efforts at dream-interpretation. We have heard the charge from more than one side that we do not have any actual knowledge of the dream we are proposing to interpret, or, more correctly, we have no guarantee that we know it in the way it really happened (compare p. 40). What we remember of the dream, and what we practise our arts of interpretation upon, is first of all damaged by the inaccuracy of our memory, which seems to be particularly incapable of retaining the dream, and in fact has probably lost the most important part of its content. Indeed, when we want to pay attention to our dreams, we so often find that we have cause to complain that we dreamed much more, but unfortunately we cannot remember any more than this one fragment, and even that seems to us curiously uncertain. Secondly, everything suggests that our memory not only reproduces the dream incompletely and inaccurately, but also falsifies it. Just as on the one hand one may doubt whether the dream really was as incoherent and confused as we relate it, so on the other hand it is possible to query whether it was as coherent as we relate it, whether in attempting to reproduce it we are not filling gaps—which may indeed be there or have been created by our forgetting—with arbitrarily chosen new material, decorating, tidying up, rounding off our dream, so that any judgement as to what its real content was is rendered impossible. Indeed, we found one authority (Spitta [64]) surmising that any kind of order or coherence in the dream at all is imposed upon it only when we attempt to recall it. In this way, we are in danger of having the very object whose value we have undertaken to assess wrested from our hands.

In our interpretations so far we have not listened to these warnings. Indeed, we have found the smallest, the most inconspicuous, the most uncertain components of the dream's content demanding interpretation no less audibly than its distinct and securely retained elements. In the dream of Irma's injection, there are the words: 'I *quickly* summon Dr. M.', and we assumed that even this extra little item would not have got into the dream if it did not admit of a particular derivation. In this way we arrived at the story of that unfortunate patient to whose bedside I 'quickly' summoned my older colleague. In the ostensibly absurd dream that treats the difference between 51 and 56 as a *quantité négligeable*, the number 51 was mentioned several times. Instead of taking this for granted or finding it unimportant, we inferred from it a second train of thought in the latent dream-content which led us to the number 51, and the trace we then pursued further led us to our fear that the age of 51 sets a limit to our life, all in sharpest contrast to a dominant trait of thought which was lavish in its grandiose expenditure of the days of our years. In the *Non vixit* dream there was the inconspicuous little insertion, which at first I did not notice: '*As P. doesn't understand him, Fl. asks me etc.*'. When the interpretation then came to a halt, I went back to these words and discovered the route from them to the childhood fantasy that makes its entrance into the dream-thoughts as an intermediary junction-point. It happened via the poet's lines:

Selten habt Ihr mich *verstanden*,
Selten auch verstand ich Euch,
Nur wenn wir im *Koth* uns fanden
So verstanden wir uns gleich!*

Seldom did you understand me,
Nor I you, in all the past;
Only when in filth we land, we
Understand each other fast.   (tr. Hal Draper)

Examples from every analysis could confirm how it is precisely the slightest features of a dream that are indispensable for its interpretation, and how long the delay in completing the task drags out if we notice these things only late in the day. In interpreting dreams, we paid equal attention to every nuance of the verbal form in which the dream before us was expressed; indeed, if we were presented with nonsensical or inadequate wording, as if the effort to translate the dream into the right version had not succeeded, we heeded these faults of expression as well. In short, what in the opinion of our authorities is supposed to be an arbitrary improvisation, concocted when at a loss, we have been treating like a sacred text. This contradiction needs explaining.

The explanation is in our favour, though without putting the other writers in the wrong. From the point of view of our newly gained insights into the origins of dreams, the contradictions are reconciled in their entirety. It is correct that we garble the dream in our attempt to reproduce it; in this distortion we meet again what we have called the secondary—and often misleading—revision of the dream by the agency of normal thinking. But this distortion is itself nothing but a part of the revision which the dream-thoughts regularly* undergo as a consequence of the censorship. In this regard, the authorities have senses or seen that part of the dream-distortion is at work in the manifest dream; this is of little use to us, for we know that a much more far-reaching work of distortion, less easy to grasp, has already chosen the dream, motivated by the hidden dream-thoughts. The authorities are wrong only in regarding the modifications the dream undergoes when remembered and put into words as being arbitrary, impossible to interpret further, and so very likely to put us on the wrong track in understanding the dreams. They underestimate the factor of determination in matters of the psyche. Nothing is arbitrary there. It can be shown quite generally that a second train of thought will promptly take over the determination of an element left undetermined by the first. For example, I try to think of a number quite at random; it is not possible; the number that occurs to me is unambiguously and necessarily determined by thoughts within me that may well be quite remote from my present intention. The changes the dream goes through as we edit it when awake are just as far from being arbitrary. They are still linked by association to the content they replace, and they serve to point us the way to this content, which may itself in turn be the proxy for another.

When I am analysing their dreams with my patients I am in the habit of putting this assertion to the test, never without success, in the following way. If the account of a dream appears difficult for me to understand at first, I ask its narrator to repeat it. He rarely does so in the same words. But the passages where he has altered his narrative are the ones revealed to me as the weak spots in the dream's disguise; they serve me as the embroidered sign on Siegfried's cloak* served Hagen. That is where the dream-interpretation can make a start. The narrator has been warned that I intend to take particular care in solving the dream; so under the pressure of resistance, he quickly protects the weak spots in the dream's disguise by replacing a revealing expression by one more remote. In this way he draws my attention to the expression he has dropped. From the trouble taken to defend the dream against being solved, I am able to infer how much care has gone into weaving the dream its cloak.

The authorities are less justified in devoting so much space to our doubts as we judge our accounts of dreams. For these doubts have no intellectual warrant; our memory has no guarantees at all, and yet we bow more often than is objectively justified to the compulsion to believe what it says. Our doubts about the correct reproduction of a dream, or particular items in a dream, are again only the offspring of the dream-censorship, our resistance to the possibility that the dream-thoughts might penetrate into consciousness. This resistance does not always come to an end with the displacements and substitutions it has carried out, it still clings to what has been allowed through in the form of doubts. We fail to recognize this doubt the more readily because it takes care never to attack intense elements in the dream, merely weak or indistinct ones. But by now we already know that between dream-thoughts and dream a total transvaluation of all psychical values has taken place; distortion was only made possible by the withdrawal of value, it invariably expresses itself in this way, and is sometimes content to leave it at that. If in addition some doubt comes and attaches to an indistinct element in the dream-content, we are able to follow this pointer and recognize the doubt as being a more direct descendant of one of the outlawed dream-thoughts. It is like the situation after a great upheaval in one of the republics of the Ancient World or the Renaissance. The powerful dynasties who once ruled are now banished, all the high positions are occupied by upstarts; in the city only utterly impoverished and powerless relatives or supporters of the overthrown powers are tolerated. But even these do not enjoy full civil rights and are mistrustfully kept under surveillance. In our case, the place of mistrust in the example is taken by doubt. That is why, when analysing a dream, I insist that any scale indicating degrees of certainty should be abandoned entirely, and the slightest possibility that something of one sort or another might have occurred in the dream should be treated as being absolutely definite. As long as anyone has not decided to let go of the question of certainty when tracing an element from the dream, the analysis will come to a standstill until he has. If the analysand dismisses the element in question as unimportant, the psychical effect will be that the involuntary ideas behind the element will not attempt to enter his head. An effect of this kind is not really a matter of course; it would not be absurd for someone to say: I am not certain whether this or that was contained in my dream, but the following comes to mind in relation to it. No one ever does say this, and it is this very effect of doubt which disturbs the analysis and unmasks it as the offspring and instrument of psychical resistance. Psychoanalysis is right to be mistrustful. One of its rules runs: *whatever disturbs the continuation of the work of analysis is a resistance*.

Forgetting dreams, too, will remain inexplicable unless we also include the power of the psychical censorship in our explanation of it. The feeling that we have dreamed a great deal in the night and only retained a little of it may have a different meaning in a number of cases, perhaps that the dream-work has palpably gone on right through the night and only left the one brief dream behind. In other cases, it is impossible to doubt the fact that after we wake we increasingly forget our dreams. We often forget them despite strenuous efforts to remember them. However, it is my view that just as we invariably overestimate the scope of this forgetting, we also over-estimate how much our knowledge of our dreams 'loses from their fragmentary and piecemeal nature. Everything we have lost in for-getting the dream-content can often be retrieved by the analysis; in a fair number of cases at least, it is possible to start from a single remaining shard and recover, if not the dream—but after all, that is not the important thing—then the dream-thoughts, all of them. It requires some effort of attention and self-overcoming on our part in the course of the analysis; that is all, but it does indicate that the act of forgetting the dream was not without a hostile purpose.

We are provided with convincing proof that forgetting our dreams is purposeful, serving the ends of psychical resistance,[1] when we observe a preliminary stage of forgetting in the course of certain analyses. It quite often happens that suddenly, in the middle of the work of interpretation, there comes to the surface a part of the dream that has been left out, but is described as forgotten until that moment. This part of the dream, rescued from oblivion, is always the most important part; it lies along the shortest route towards solving the dream and for that reason was most liable to be resisted. Among the examples of dreams I have included in the course of this treatise, there happens to be one where I have to interpolate a bit of dream-content retrospectively. It is my travelling-dream, the one that takes revenge on the lady who was my disagreeable travelling-companion,* which I have left almost uninterpreted, partly on account of its grossly indecent content. The omitted part runs: *I say [in English] about a book by Schiller: 'It is from . . .' but correct myself, noticing the error myself: 'It is by . . .' At that the man observes to his sister: 'He did say it correctly.'*

Self-correction in dreams, which seemed so marvellous to many of our authorities, probably does not require our attention. As the model for the linguistic error in this dream I shall rather point to one in my memory. I was seventeen years old,* making my first visit to England, and I spent a whole day on the shore of the Irish Sea. I was naturally lost in pleasure gathering the sea-creatures left behind by the tide, and I was just occupied with a starfish (the dream begins with *Hollthurn—holothurians* [sea-slugs]) when a charming little girl

---

[1] On the subject of intention in forgetting, compare my essay 'Über den psychischen Mechanismus der Vergeßlichkeit' ['The Physical Mechanism of Forgetfulness'], in the *Monatschrift für Psychiatrie und Neurologie*, 1898 [SE iii. 289].

came up to me and asked, 'Is it a starfish? Is it alive?' I replied, 'Yes, *he* is alive', but was then embarrassed at the inaccuracy, and repeated the sentence correctly. Instead of the linguistic error I made then, the dream replaces it by another, which is just as easy for a speaker of German to make. '*Das Buch ist von Schiller*' should not be translated as 'the book is from Schiller', but as 'by ...' The dream-work makes this substitution because the matching sound of '*from*' creates a splendid condensation with the German adjective '*fromm*' ['pious']—and from all we have heard of the dream-work's intentions and of its ruthlessness in choosing its means, we should no longer be amazed that it should do so. But what does this innocuous memory of the seashore have to say in the context of my dream? It uses the most innocent example possible to elucidate my misuse of an article designating *gender*, introducing *gender and sex (he)* where it does not belong. This is of course one of the keys to solving the dream. Anyone who has heard where the title of the book *Matter and Motion* comes from (*Molière* in *Le Malade Imaginaire*: La *matière* est-elle laudable?*—a *motion* of the bowels) will be able to complete the interpretation himself.

I can, by the way, settle the question of adducing proof that forgetting dreams is to a large extent the work of resistance with a demonstration *ad oculos*. A patient tells me he has had a dream, but has forgotten it without a trace; at that stage it is simply counted as not having happened. We continue our work, I come upon a resistance, make something clear to the patient, by persuasion and pressure help him to reconcile himself to some unpleasant thought, and no sooner has this succeeded than he cries: 'Now I remember what it was I dreamed.' The same resistance that disturbed him in the day's work of analysis also made him forget his dream. By overcoming this resistance, I have coaxed the dream back into memory.

Similarly, a patient who has reached a certain point in the work of analysis is able to remember a dream that occurred three, four, or more days before, but which meantime has been reposing in oblivion.

An experience I had in the course of writing this manuscript is an indication that dreams are just as unforgotten as other acts of the psyche, and that in this respect too, in their persistence in the memory, they are the full equal of the psyche's other feats. I had kept notes of plenty of my own dreams which for some reason at the time I could only subject to a very incomplete interpretation, or to none at

all. Now, one to two years later, I have made the attempt to interpret
some of them, intending to use them as material to illustrate my
assertions. The attempts were successful in every case; indeed, I
would even say the interpretation went along more easily such a long
time later than it did at the time when the dreams were still fresh in
my experience. I would suggest that a possible explanation for this
lies in the fact that meantime I have gone beyond a number of
resistances within myself which were disturbing me then. In making
these retrospective interpretations, I compared the results I had at
the time in tracing the dream-thoughts with my current, mostly far
richer, results, and discovered the earlier ones present unchanged
among the new ones. I cut short any astonishment at this when I
reflected that, after all, it has long been my practice to have my
patients interpret dreams they sometimes tell me dating from earlier
years, as though they were dreams from the previous night, according to the same method and with the same success. When I come to
discuss anxiety-dreams, I shall report two examples of belated
dream-interpretation of this kind. When I made this experiment
for the first time, I was led by the justified expectation that in this
respect too the dream would behave just like a neurotic symptom.
For when treating a psychoneurotic, a hysteric, say, psychoanalytic-
ally, I have to find an explanation for the earliest symptoms of
his complaint, long ago mastered and done with, as well as for the
current symptoms that brought him to me; and I find it far easier to
solve the former problem than the present, urgent, task. As early as
my *Studies on Hysteria*,* published in 1895, I was able to give the
explanation for the first hysterical attack which a woman of over
forty suffered at the age of fourteen.

In a looser sequence, I should like to add some further observations on the interpretation of dreams, which will perhaps provide
some orientation for the reader who wants to check my account by
working on his own dreams.

No one would expect the interpretation of his dreams to fall into
his lap without any effort. It needs practice just to become aware of
endoptic phenomena and other sensations normally out of range of
our attention, although there is no psychical motive to baulk at these
perceptions. It is considerably more difficult to get hold of 'involuntary ideas'. Anyone wanting to do this will have to fulfil the conditions this treatise has raised, and in following the rules it has given,

he must take pains to restrain any criticism, any prejudice, any bias of affect or intellect during the work of analysis. He will bear in mind the precept Claude Bernard* proposed for the experimenter in the physiological laboratory: 'Travailler comme une bête', that is, to work as doggedly as a beast, but also with as little concern about the results. Anyone following this advice will no longer find the task difficult. However, interpreting a dream is not always accomplished at one fell swoop; quite often one's interpretive powers feel at the end of their tether after pursuing a chain of ideas, when the dream ceases to say anything more that day; then it is as well to break off and return to the work of analysis another day. Then a different bit of the dream-content will draw attention to itself, and one gains access to a fresh stratum of the dream-thoughts. This procedure might be called 'fractional' dream-interpretation.

The most difficult thing is to persuade the beginner in dream-interpretation to recognize the fact that his task is not over when he has a complete interpretation of a dream in his hands, one that is meaningful and coherent, and enlightens him about all the elements in the dream-content. Besides this, it is possible that there is an overarching interpretation of the dream which has escaped him. It is really not easy to get an idea of the wealth of unconscious trains of thought in our thinking, all struggling for expression, nor to believe how clever the dream-work is in its polysemous mode of expression, killing seven flies at one blow, like the Little Tailor* in the fairy-tale, as it were. The reader will always be inclined to accuse the author of overloading every rift with ore; but anyone who has gained experience of interpretation himself will have learned better.

The question whether every dream is amenable to interpretation is to be answered by 'No'. It should not be forgotten that the interpreter has against him those same psychical powers that are responsible for the distortion in the dream. In this way it becomes a contest of relative strength whether one's intellectual interest, capacity for self-overcoming, psychological insight, and practice in the interpretation of dreams can master the inner resistances. For a stretch it is always possible, enough at least to be convinced that the dream is a meaningful formation, and mostly, also, to acquire an inkling of that meaning. Very often a dream following hard on the heels of the one we are interpreting will enable us to establish a reading we have assumed for the first, and to carry it further. A whole set of dreams, carrying on for weeks or months, often rests on common ground, and is to be interpreted in its interrelations. In cases where we have a sequence of dreams, it can often be noticed how one dream will take for its centre what the next only alludes to on the periphery, and the other way round, so that the two complement each other for purposes of interpretation as well. I have already used examples to show how the various dreams of the same night are quite regularly to be treated as a whole.

The best-interpreted dreams often have a passage that has to be left in the dark, because we notice in the course of interpretation that a knot of dream-thoughts shows itself just there, refusing to be unravelled, but also making no further contribution to the dream-content. This is the dream's navel, and the place beneath which lies the Unknown. Indeed, the dream-thoughts we come upon as we interpret cannot in general but remain without closure, spinning out on all sides into the web-like fabric of our thoughts. Out of a denser patch in this tissue the dream-wish then arises like a mushroom from its mycelium.

Let us return to the facts about forgetting dreams. For we have omitted to draw one important conclusion from them. If our waking life shows the unmistakable intention of forgetting the dream that was formed at night, either as a whole immediately after we wake, or bit by bit in the course of the day, and if we identify the main party to this forgetting as our psychical resistance to the dream—which has already done its utmost to the dream in the night—then the question arises, what has actually enabled the dream to be formed at all in face of this resistance? Let us take the most glaring case, when our waking life does away with the dream as though it had never happened. In this case, if we take the play of psychical forces into account, we would have to say that the dream would not have come into existence at all if the resistance had held sway at night as it does by day. Our conclusion is that during the night it has lost a part of its power; we know it has not been entirely suspended, for we have demonstrated the distorting part it plays in forming the dream. But we are aware of the possibility that it has been reduced at night, that this lowering of resistance makes the formation of dreams possible; and thus it is easy to understand how, once restored to full force on waking, it promptly gets rid of what it had to admit while it was weak. Indeed, descriptive psychology instructs us that the main condition for the formation of dreams is the sleeping state of the psyche; so we can now add the explanation: *the state of sleep makes the formation of dreams possible by reducing the endopsychic censorship.*

It is certainly tempting to regard this conclusion as the only one it is possible to draw from the facts about forgetting dreams, and to develop further inferences from it about the ratio of energy between sleeping and waking. However, let us pause here for the moment. Once we have immersed ourselves rather more deeply in the psychology of dreams, we will learn that there are still other ways of imagining how the formation of dreams is made possible. It might also be possible to evade the resistance to bringing the dream-thoughts into consciousness without the resistance being abated. It is also plausible that the state of sleep helps to bring about both the factors favourable to the formation of dreams at the same time, that is, the reduction of resistance as well as its evasion. Let us break off here, and pick up the thread a little later.

There is another set of objections to our procedure in interpreting dreams which we must now deal with. Of course we proceed by abandoning all the purposive ideas that normally dominate our reflections, concentrating on one particular element in the dream, and then noting what involuntary thoughts it calls up in us. Then we take up the next component in the dream-content, go through the same work with this one, and allow ourselves to be carried along by our thoughts with no care for the direction in which they are moving, even though they take us, as they say, all over the shop. We do so in the confident expectation that in the end, without any intrusion on our part, we shall come upon the dream-thought that gave rise to the dream. The objection made in criticism of this procedure runs more or less as follows: there is nothing wonderful about getting from one particular element in a dream to anywhere at all. *Something or other* can be linked by association to every idea; the only remarkable thing is that by this aimless and arbitrary drift of thoughts you are supposed to arrive straight at the dream-thoughts. That is probably a self-deception; you trace the train of associations from the one element until you note that for some reason it breaks off; if you take up a second element, it is only natural that the original openness of association should now undergo a certain limitation. You still have the earlier chain of thoughts in mind and so, when analysing the second imagined idea from the dream, thoughts come to mind which also have something in common with the earlier chain. Then you imagine you have found a thought which represents a junction-point between two dream-elements. As you allow yourself every liberty in combining thoughts, really excluding only the transitions from one idea to another that are operative in normal thinking, ultimately it is not difficult to take a sequence of 'intermediary thoughts' and concoct something you call the dream-thoughts, claiming with no warrant, as they are completely unknown, that these are the psychical replacement of the dream. But it is all arbitrary, a clever-seeming exploitation of sheer chance. And the person who subjects himself to this useless labour can take any old dream and along these lines conjure up any old interpretation.

If we are really presented with such objections, we can defend ourselves by referring to the impression our dream-interpretations make, to the surprising combinations with other dream-elements that emerge in the course of tracing particular imagined ideas, and to the unlikelihood that something that covers the dream as exhaustively and illuminatingly as one of our interpretations could be reached in any other way than by following the traces of psychical connections set up earlier. We could also justify ourselves by pointing out that our procedure when interpreting dreams is identical with our method in treating hysterical symptoms, where we do have a guarantee that the method is correct in the appearance and disappearance of symptoms in their place, that is, where our reading of the text is supported by the interpolated illustrations. However, there is no reason for us to avoid the problem of how it should be possible that, by tracing a chain of thoughts spinning out arbitrarily and aimlessly, we can reach a pre-existent destination, for though we cannot solve this problem, we are in a position to dispose of it completely.

For it is demonstrably wrong to say that we are being borne along an aimless flow of ideas when we relax our reflectiveness and let the involuntary ideas come to the surface, as we do when we are interpreting dreams. It can be shown that the only purposive ideas we are able to relinquish are the ones known to us, and the moment these cease, unknown—or, as we would loosely say, unconscious— purposive ideas take over and then determine the course taken by the involuntary ideas. There is no way that our own influence on the life of our psyche can bring about a kind of thinking without purposive ideas; nor am I acquainted with any state of psychical disorder that might do so. In this respect the psychiatrists have dispensed with the stability of the psyche's interconnected structure much too soon. I know that an uncontrolled flow of thoughts with no purposeful ideas is not present in hysteria or paranoia, just as it is not to be found in the formation or the solution of dreams. It may be that it does not occur at all in the endogenous psychical illness; even the delirious fantasies of the mad, according to Leuret's brilliant surmise, are meaningful, and are only unintelligible to us because of what they have left out. I have received the same conviction on the occasions I have had for observation myself. The delirious fantasies are the work of a censorship that no longer bothers to hide its supremacy, and instead of sharing in the creation of an inoffensive version, it ruthlessly deletes what it objects to—leaving the remainder incoherent. This censorship proceeds just like the Russian newspaper censorship at the borders; it allows foreign journals to come into the hands of the readers under its protection only when passages are heavily blacked out.

It may be that the free play of ideas along a random chain of associations is present in destructive organic processes of the brain; what is regarded as such in the psychoneuroses can be explained in every case by the effect of censorship on a sequence of thoughts thrust into the foreground by still hidden purposive ideas. It has been regarded as an unmistakable sign of associations without any purposive ideas if the imagined ideas (or images) coming to the surface appear to be connected to one another by the links of what we call superficial associations, that is, by assonance, verbal ambiguity, coincidence in time without any relation in meaning, all the associations we permit ourselves in jokes and word-play. This characteristic applies to the thought-connections that lead us from the elements in the dream-content to the collaterals and from these to the actual dream-thoughts; we have found examples of this in a number of dream-analyses, which were bound to arouse our surprise. No connection was too loose, no joke too bad to form the bridge from one thought to another. But we are not far from a true understanding of such indulgence. *Whenever one psychical element is connected with another by an offensive or superficial association, there also exists a proper and deeper link between the two, which is subject to the resistance of the censorship.*

The pressure of censorship, not the suspension of purposive ideas, is the real reason for the predominance of superficial associations. In the representation, the superficial associations replace the deep associations when the censorship has made the latter's normal connecting routes impassable. It is as if something causing a general traffic hold-up, a flood, for example, has made the broad highways in the mountains impassable; the traffic is kept going along steep and difficult footpaths, normally trodden only by the huntsman.

We can distinguish two cases here, though they are essentially one. In the first instance the censorship is aimed only at the connection between two thoughts which, when taken separately, are not subject to its disapproval. In this case, the two thoughts enter consciousness severally, one after the other; their connection remains hidden; instead, however, some superficial link between them occurs to us, which we would not otherwise have thought of, and which as a rule begins at a different corner of the complex of ideas from the place where the suppressed, but essential connection starts out. Alternatively, in the second case both thoughts are subject to the censorship in their own right, on account of their content; then neither appears in its proper form, but in some modified, substitute guise, and the two substitute thoughts are chosen in such a way that the superficial association between them reproduces the essential connection between the thoughts they have replaced. *In both these cases, under pressure from the censorship, a displacement has taken place from a normal association, to be taken seriously, to one that is superficial and seemingly absurd.*

Knowing of these displacements, we are quite confident in also relying on superficial associations in the course of interpreting dreams.[2]

The two propositions—that when conscious purposive ideas are relinquished, command over the flow of ideas passes to hidden purposive ideas; and that superficial associations are only displaced substitutes for deeper suppressed associations—are most fully used

---

[2] Of course the same considerations also apply to cases when the superficial associations are exposed in the dream-content, as they are, for example, in the two dreams related by Maury (p. 51: *pélerinage—Pelletier—pelle*; *Kilometre—Kilogramme—Gilolo—Lobelia—Lopez—Lotto*). I know from my work with neurotics which reminiscence it is that prefers this kind of representation. It is from looking up the encyclopaedia (all reference works) at the time of puberty, when their curiosity is roused, that most young people have satisfied their need for an explanation of the riddle of sexuality.

by psychoanalysis in the treatment of neuroses; indeed, the two propositions become the fundamental pillars of its technique. When I bid a patient relax all his reflectiveness, and tell me whatever comes into his mind then, I am relying on the premiss that he cannot let go of the purposive ideas behind the treatment, and I consider I am justified in concluding that the seemingly most harmless and wayward things he tells me are related to his illness. Another purposive idea, which the patient has no inkling of, is the idea of my own person. Accordingly, a complete account of this procedure, as well as a thorough proof of both explanations, properly belongs in a presentation of psychoanalytic technique as a method of therapy. At this stage we have come to one of those points of contact where we have in principle left the subject of dream-interpretation.

Only one conclusion left from these objections is correct, and that is that we do not need to ascribe all the ideas that come to mind in the course of interpretation to the dream-work of the night as well. Of course, as we interpret when we are awake, we are taking a path leading back from the dream-elements to the dream-thoughts. The dream-work took the opposite way, and it is highly unlikely that these paths are passable in both directions. What emerges is rather that by day we create passageways via fresh thought-associations which reach the intermediary thoughts and the dream-thoughts now in one place, now in another. We can see how the fresh thought-material of the day pushes into the interpretive trains of associations, probably also forcing the intensified resistance which has set in since the night to find new and more remote detours. The number and kind of the collaterals that we spin out by day, however, is psychologically quite insignificant, as long as it leads us along the path to the dream-thoughts we are looking for.

(b) *Regression*

But now that we have guarded ourselves against these objections, or at least indicated where our weapons of defence are resting, we can no longer put off broaching the psychological investigations for which we have long been arming ourselves. Let us sum up the main results of our inquiry so far. Dreams are fully paid-up psychical acts; their driving-force is a wish in need of fulfilment; their unrecognizability as wishes, and their many oddities and absurdities, derive from the influence of the psychical censorship which they have gone through in the course of their formation; as well as the compulsion to escape this censorship, the following factors have shared in forming them: the compulsion to condense the psychical material, regard for representability in visual or other sensory images, and—though not invariably—regard for a rational and intelligible appearance for the dream's structure. From each of these propositions, the way leads on to psychological postulates and conjectures. The reciprocal relationship between the wish as motive and the four conditions, as well as their relations among themselves, is still to be investigated, and the place of dreams in the interconnected life of the psyche is still to be located.

We placed a dream at the head of this chapter to remind us of the puzzles that still remain to be solved. We had no difficulty in interpreting this dream of the burning child, even though it was not told as completely as we would have it. We asked ourselves why the father should have dreamed at all, instead of waking up, and we recognized that one motive for the dream was the wish to imagine the child alive. Another wish also had a part in this, as we shall see from a later discussion. At first, then, it was for the sake of the wish-fulfilment that the processes of thought were transformed into a dream during sleep.

If we reverse this process, there is only one characteristic left that distinguishes the two kinds of psychical occurrence from each other. The dream-thought would have gone like this: 'I can see a light coming from the room where the body is lying. Perhaps a candle has fallen over, and the child is burning!' The dream reproduces the result of this reflection unaltered, but represented in a situation that is immediate and to be apprehended with the senses as if it were a waking experience. But that is the most distinctive and striking characteristic of dreaming in general; a thought—as a rule the wishful thought—is objectified in the dream, represented or, as we imagine, experienced as a scene.

Now how are we to explain this characteristic peculiarity of the dream-work, or, to put it less ambitiously, to find a place for it in the interconnections of the psychical processes?

If we look more closely, we are likely to notice that two distinctive characteristics, almost independent of each other, are perceptible in the dream in the form in which it appears. One is representation in terms of an immediate situation, with no 'perhaps' about it; the other is the transposition of the thought into visual images and into speech.

The transformation undergone by the dream-thoughts when the expectation they express is put in the present tense may not appear very striking in this particular dream. This is related to the curious, actually secondary role of wish-fulfilment in this dream. Let us take another dream, where the wish in the dream is not separated from the waking thoughts continued into it, for example, the dream of Irma's injection. The dream-thought that reaches representation here is an optative: if only Otto were to blame for Irma's illness! The dream represses the optative and replaces it by a simple present: Yes, Otto is to blame for Irma's illness. This, then, is the first of the transformations that even a dream with no distortions performs with the dream-thoughts. However, we shall not linger long over this first peculiarity shown by dreams. We can settle it by referring to conscious fantasies, to daydreams, which treat their content of imagined ideas in the same way. When Daudet's M. Joyeuse* wanders idle and unemployed through the streets of Paris while his daughters are obliged to believe he is sitting in his office holding down a job, he daydreams of the chance events that are to help him towards a patron and a position, likewise in the present tense. The dream, then, uses the present in the same way, and with the same justification, as the daydream does. The present is the tense in which the dream is represented as fulfilled.

However, only the second characteristic is peculiar to the dream as distinct from the daydream: its content of imagined ideas is not framed as thoughts, but transformed into sensory images which we believe in, and which we think we are actually experiencing. Let us add at once that not all dreams display this transformation of imagined idea into sensory image; there are dreams consisting only of thoughts, which we would not dispute were still essentially dreams. My dream '*Autodidasker*—the daytime fantasy with Professor N.' is one of this kind, which had elements intruding into it which were hardly more sensory than if I had thought up its content by day. Also, in every dream of any length there are elements that have not shared the sensory transformation, but are simply thought or known in the way we are used to thinking or knowing them when awake. At this point let us further bear in mind that this kind of transformation of ideas into sensory images does not only characterize dreams, but also hallucinations, the visions that appear independently in states of health, say, or as the symptoms of psychoneuroses. In short, no aspect of the relation we are investigating here is an exclusive one; nevertheless, it remains the case that this characteristic of dreams, where it occurs, seems to us the one that is the most remarkable, so that the life of dreams seems unthinkable without it. However, to understand it will require far-reaching discussion.

Among all the observations on the theory of dreams to be found among the authorities, I would like to draw attention to one as offering a valuable starting-point. In his *Psychophysik* (Vol. II, p. 520) the great G. T. Fechner [25]* speculates, in a discussion devoted to dreams, that *the theatre where our dreams are enacted is a different one from the scene of action where our ideas are generated in waking life*. This is the only assumption that will enable us to understand the peculiar characteristics of the dream-life.

The idea it puts at our disposal is that of *location in the psyche*. Let us put aside entirely the fact that the psychical apparatus we are dealing with here is also familiar to us as an anatomical specimen; and let us take care to avoid being tempted to define the psychical location in broadly anatomical terms. We shall remain on psychological terrain, bearing in mind only to follow the requirement that we should think of the instrument serving the functions of the psyche as acting like a composite microscope, say, or a photographic apparatus. The psychical location then corresponds to a place within this apparatus where one of the preliminary stages of the image comes about. In the microscope and telescope, as we know, these are partly hypothetical locations, places where no tangible component of the apparatus is sited. There is no need, I think, to apologize for the inadequacy of this figure, nor of all the others like it. These metaphors are only meant to support us in the attempt to make the complexity of the psyche's achievements intelligible by analysing the apparatus into its components and ascribing particular functions to particular parts of it. To my knowledge, this is the first time anyone has ventured to conjecture from this kind of analysis how the instrument of the psyche is composed. It seems harmless enough to me. In my view, we may give free rein to our speculations as long as we keep our judgement cool as we do so, and do not mistake the scaffolding for the building. Since all we need on first approaching something unknown is the support of some provisional ideas, let us begin by turning to the crudest and most tangible hypotheses.

Let us, then, imagine the psychical apparatus as a composite instrument, whose parts we shall call *agencies* or, to put it more concretely, *systems*. In doing so, we raise the expectation that these systems may be in a constant spatial orientation towards one another, rather as the various systems of lenses in a telescope are located one behind the other. Strictly speaking, we do not need to assume a real spatial arrangement for the psychical systems. It is sufficient if a firm sequence can be set up by establishing that in certain psychical processes the systems go through a definite temporal sequence in their arousal. This sequence may undergo alteration in other processes; let us, for preference, leave this possibility open. From now on, for the sake of brevity, we shall refer to the component parts of the apparatus as 'ψ-systems'.

Now the first thing that strikes us about this apparatus composed of ψ-systems is that it has a direction. All our psychical activity starts from (internal or external) stimuli and ends in innervations. Accordingly, we shall ascribe to the apparatus one sensory and one motor end; at the sensory end a system is located for receiving our sense-perceptions; at the motor end there is another which opens the floodgates to motor activity. The psychical process generally runs its course from the perceptual end to the motor end. The most general diagram for the psychical apparatus, then, would look as in Figure 1.

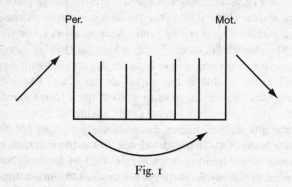

Fig. 1

But that does no more than fulfil a requirement long familiar to us, that the psychical apparatus must be constructed like a reflex apparatus. The reflexive process is still the model of all psychical performance too.

We now have a reason to hypothesize the first appearance of a differentiation at the sensory end. A trace of the perceptions impinging upon us remains in our psychical apparatus, and this we can call a '*memory-trace*'. Indeed, we call the function relating to this memory-trace our 'memory'. If we are serious about intending to link psychical processes to systems, then the memory-trace can only consist in permanent alterations to the elements of the systems. Now there are difficulties about this, as pointed out elsewhere,* if one and the same system on the one hand wants to preserve faithfully any alterations to its elements, and on the other is still supposed to encounter new occasions for change with fresh receptivity. According to the principle guiding our experiment, we shall distribute these two activities between different systems. We assume that an outermost system of the apparatus is the receptor for the perceptual stimuli, but that it does not retain anything of them, that is, it has no memory; we assume too that behind this system there is a second one that transforms the momentary excitation of the first into permanent traces. If so, this would be the diagram of our psychical apparatus (Fig. 2).

Per.   Mot.

Mem. Mem.´ Mem.˝

Fig. 2

We know that there is something else we retain permanently from the perceptions impinging upon the *Per* system. besides their content. Our perceptions also turn out to be linked to one another in our memory, above all if they occurred at the same time. We call this fact *association*. Now it is clear that if the *Per*.-system has no memory at all, it cannot retain the traces for association either; the particular

Per.-elements would be intolerably obstructed in their function if some remnant of an earlier link were to assert itself against a fresh perception. So we must assume, rather, that the basis for association is the memory-system. If so, the fact of association then consists of a process where, as a consequence of reductions in resistance and of pathways set up from one of the *Mem.*-elements, the excitation is passed on to one *Mem.*-element rather than another.

If we go into it further, it becomes necessary to assume not one but several *Mem.*-systems of this kind, in which the same excitation, passed on by the *Per.*-elements, is fixed permanently in several different ways. In any case, the first of these *Mem.*-systems will contain the permanent association brought about by coincidence in time; in the more remote *Mem.*-systems the same stimulus-material will be arranged according to other kinds of coincidence, so that relations of similarity, say, and other kinds, would be represented by these later systems. Of course, there would be little point in trying to put the psychical significance of a system of this kind into words. Its character would lie in its intimate relation to elements in the raw material of memory, that is—if we wanted to point towards a more far-reaching theory—it would lie in the gradations of conductive resistance in the transmission of excitations to these elements.

This would be a suitable point to intervene with a remark of a general nature, which may perhaps indicate something significant. The *Per.*-system, which has no capacity to retain changes, that is, has no memory, offers our consciousness the entire range and variety of sensory qualities. Contrariwise, our memories, not excepting those most deeply imprinted, are essentially unconscious. They can be made conscious; but there is no doubt that they can deploy all their influence in the unconscious state. Indeed, what we call our character rests upon memory-traces of impressions made on us; in fact, it is the very impressions that had the greatest influence upon us, from our earliest youth, that hardly ever become conscious. But if memories do become conscious, they do not display any sensory quality, or only a very slight one in comparison with our perceptions. If it could be confirmed *that in the ψ-systems, memory and quality in our consciousness are mutually exclusive*, then a most promising insight into the conditions governing the excitation of neurones is opened up for us.

What we have been assuming so far about the composition of the psychical apparatus at its sensory end has been done without considering dreams or any psychological explanations that might derive from them. However, dreams provide the proof for our knowledge of another part of the apparatus. We have seen that it was impossible for us to explain the formation of dreams if we did not venture the hypothesis that there were two psychical agencies, and that one of these subjected the other to criticism, with the consequence that the second was excluded from becoming conscious.

The criticizing agency, we decided, entertained closer relations to consciousness than the criticized. It stands between the latter and consciousness like a protective screen. We also found some grounds for identifying the criticizing agency with the one that guides our waking life and decides our voluntary and conscious doings. If we follow our hypothetical pattern, then, and replace these agencies by systems, then the insight just mentioned shifts the criticizing system to the motor end. We will now introduce the two systems into our diagram (Fig. 3), expressing their relation to consciousness in the names we give them.

Fig. 3

The last of the systems at the motor end we shall call the *Preconscious*, to indicate that the processes of excitation going on in it are able to reach consciousness without further hindrance, as long as certain further conditions are satisfied, for example, that they should have reached a certain intensity, attracted a certain share of the function we have to call attention, and the like. At the same time, it holds the key to our voluntary motor actions. The system behind it we call the *Unconscious*, because it has no access to consciousness *except by way of the Preconscious*, while its processes of arousal have to put up with alterations to them as they make their passage through.

In which of these systems, then, shall we place the impulsion to form dreams? For the sake of simplification, in the *Uncon.*-system. True, we shall hear in later discussions that this is not entirely correct, and that the formation of dreams is bound to start out from dream-thoughts belonging to the preconscious system. However, we shall also learn, when we come to discuss the dream-wish, that the motive force of the dream is contributed by the *Uncon.* On account of this factor, let us assume that the unconscious system is the starting-point for the formation of dreams. Like all other thoughts in process of formation, the dream aroused here will express the urge to move on into the *Precon.*, and from there to gain access to consciousness.

Experience tells us that, for the dream-thoughts in daytime, this route leading through the Preconscious to consciousness is blocked by the censorship of resistance. At night they are able to make their own way to consciousness; but the questions arise, what path do they take, and what changes enable them to take it? If the dream-thoughts were enabled to do this because the resistance on guard at the border between Unconscious and Preconscious is reduced at night, then we would have dreams made of the material of our imagined ideas which would not display the hallucinatory characteristics we are interested in at present.

The reduction of the censorship between the two systems *Uncon.* and *Precon.*, then, can only explain the formation of such dreams as *Autodidasker*, but not such dreams as the one of the *burning child*, which we put as a problem at the beginning of these investigations.

We can only describe what goes on in a hallucinatory dream by saying: the excitation takes a *retrogressive* route. Instead of moving towards the motor end of the apparatus, it moves towards the sensory end, and finally reaches the system of perceptions. If we call the direction in which psychical processes move from the unconscious when we are awake the *progressive* direction, then we may say of dreams that they have a *regressive* character.

In that case, this regression is certainly one of the most important psychological features characterizing the process of dreaming; but we must not forget that it does not only characterize dreams. Intentional remembering, too, and other processes that are part of our normal thinking correspond to a backward direction taken in the psychical apparatus, starting from a complex act generating imagined ideas and moving back to the raw material of the memory-traces at its basis. When we are awake, however, this backward reach never stretches further than the remembered images; it is unable to produce the hallucinatory vividness of perceptual images. Why is this different in dreams? When we discussed the work of condensation in dreams, we could not avoid the assumption that the intensities attaching to imagined ideas are transferred in their entirety from one idea to another by the dream-work. It is probably this modification in the normal psychical processes that makes it possible to charge the *Per.*-system with energy in the contrary direction, starting out from the thoughts and going all the way to the height of sensory vividness.

I hope we are far from deceiving ourselves about the importance—or otherwise—of these reflections. All we have done is give a name to an inexplicable phenomenon. We call it regression when an idea transforms itself in dreams back into the sensory image from which it once, at some time, emerged. But this step too needs to be justified. Why find a name, if it does not teach us anything new? Now it is my view that the name 'regression' is useful insofar as it connects a fact familiar to us to the scheme of a psychical apparatus characterized by its tending in a certain direction. This is the point where for the first time it has been worthwhile to have set up such a scheme. For it is only with the help of this scheme that we will be able to understand another characteristic of dream-formation without considering the problem anew. If we regard the process of dreaming as a regression within our hypothetical psychical apparatus, this explains without further ado the empirically established fact that all the logical relations between the dream-thoughts are lost in the course of the dream-work, or only expressed with difficulty. According to our diagram, these intellectual relations are not located in the first *Mem.*-systems, but are contained in those lying further to the right, and except for the perceptual images, they are bound to lose their specific form of expression in the course of regression. *In the course of regression, the close-knit web of dream-thoughts is unravelled into its raw material.*

What changes make this regression, impossible by day, possible in our dreams? We will leave it to conjectures on this point. It must, I suppose, be a matter of changes in the degree of energy charging the particular systems, making them more suitable, or less, as paths for the excitation to travel; but in every apparatus of that kind the same effect on the path of the excitation could be brought about by more than one kind of modification. One thinks at once, of course, of the state of sleep, and of the changes in energy-charge that it produces at the sensory end of the apparatus. By day there is a continuous current from the ψ-system of the *Per.* to acts of motion; at night it comes to an end, and would no longer be able to prevent the current of excitation from flowing back in the reverse direction. This would be the 'withdrawal from the external world' which is supposed, in the theory of some authorities (see p. 44), to explain the psychological nature of dreams. Meantime, in explaining regression in dreams we shall have to take into consideration those other regressions that come about in waking states and that are pathological. In these forms, of course, what I have just said is of no help at all. Regression occurs in spite of the uninterrupted sensory current flowing in a progressive direction.

For the hallucinations of hysteria and paranoia, and the visions of people of sound mind, I can offer the explanation that they do in fact correspond to regressions, that is, that they are thoughts transformed into images, and that the only thoughts to undergo this transformation are those that have intimate connections with suppressed or still unconscious memories. For example, one of my youngest patients suffering from hysteria, a boy of twelve years old, is prevented from sleeping by '*green faces with red eyes*', which fill him with horror. The source of this apparition is the memory, suppressed but once conscious, of a boy he saw very often four years ago, and who offered him a repellent embodiment of a number of children's bad habits, among them masturbation, which my patient accused himself in retrospect of having committed. His mama had remarked at the time that the badly behaved boy had a *greenish* colour to his face and *red* (that is, *red-rimmed*) eyes. Hence the terrifying ghoul, which, by the way, is only intended to remind him of another prediction of his mother's, that boys like that become weakminded, cannot learn anything at school, and die young. Our little patient makes part of the prophecy come true; he makes no progress at school, and, as he shows on being questioned about the ideas involuntarily entering his mind, he is terribly frightened of the second part. However, after a short time his treatment has brought the successful result that he is able to sleep, is losing his fears, and is finishing his school year with an excellent report.

At this point I can add the resolution of a vision which a forty-year-old patient with hysteria told me from her days of good health. One morning she opens her eyes and sees her brother in the room, but, as she knows, he is in a lunatic asylum. Her little son is asleep in the bed next to her. So that the child should not be *frightened* and *suffer convulsions* when he sees his *uncle*, she draws the *sheet* over him, and then the apparition vanishes. The vision is a reworking of a childhood memory of the lady's, which was conscious, it is true, but was most intimately related to all the unconscious materials in her psyche. Her nurse had told her that her mother, who died early (my patient was only eighteen months old when her mother died), had suffered from epileptic or hysterical *convulsions*, in fact, ever since a fright she had when her brother (my patient's *uncle*) appeared to her as a ghost with a *sheet* over his head. The vision contains the same elements as the memory: the brother's apparition, the sheet, the fright, and its effect. However, these elements are arranged in a different context and transferred to other figures. The obvious motive for the vision, the thought it replaces, is the worry that her little son, who has such a close physical resemblance to his uncle, could share the same fate.

The two examples I have quoted are not entirely free from all connection with the state of sleep, and so they are perhaps not wholly suitable for making the proof I need them for. I refer, then, to my analysis of a patient suffering from hallucinatory paranoia,[3] and to the results of my still unpublished studies of the psychology of the psychoneuroses, to reinforce my argument that in these cases of thoughts regressively back-transformed, one should not overlook the influence of a suppressed or unconscious memory, most often one from infancy. This memory draws the idea connected to it and denied expression by the censorship into the regression, as it were, which is the form of representation in which it has its own psychical presence. I may quote one result from my *Studies on Hysteria*, that when we are successful in bringing the scenes from childhood (whether they are recollections or fantasies) into consciousness, they are seen as hallucinations, and only cast off this character when they are communicated. It is also widely known that even in people who do not normally have a visual memory, their earliest childhood

[3] 'Weitere Bemerkungen über die Abwehr-Neurosenpsychosen' ['Further Remarks on the Neuropsychoses of Defence']. *Neurologisches Centralblatt*, 1896, Nr. 10 [SE iii. 159].

recollections are characterized by a sensory vividness that is retained and persists into later years.

If we recall the part played in the dream-thoughts by infantile experiences or by fantasies based upon them, and bear in mind how often bits of them resurface in the dream-content, and how the dream-wishes themselves are often derived from them, then we will not reject the probability that in the dream, too, the transformation of thoughts into images may also be the consequence of the *attraction* that their memory, represented now in visual terms and aiming for revival, exercises on the thoughts cut off from consciousness and struggling for expression. According to this view, the dream could also be described as *the substitute for the scene from infancy, altered by transferring the scene onto recent experiences*. The scene from infancy cannot be renewed; it has to be satisfied with its return as a dream.

One of the hypotheses put forward by Scherner and his disciples is made superfluous when we point out the significance of infantile scenes (or of their repetition in fantasies) as, to some extent, a model for the dream-content. Scherner assumes a condition of 'visual stimulus', or excitation within the organ of sight, when the visual elements of dreams are particularly vivid or profuse. There is no need for us to object to this assumption if all we are doing is confirming that a condition of excitation of this kind applies simply to the perceptual system of the organ of sight; but we shall argue that this condition of excitation is a renewal of a visual stimulus that once actually happened, brought alert by the memory of it. I have at hand a good example from my own experience of this kind of influence from an infantile recollection; my own dreams have in general fewer sensory elements than I have to reckon with in the dreams of others; but in the most beautiful and vivid dream I have had in recent years, it is easy for me to trace the hallucinatory clarity of the dream-content back to the sensory qualities of recent impressions. I mentioned a dream on p. 301, in which the deep blue colour of the water, the brown colour of the smoke from the ships' funnels, and the dark brown and red of the buildings I saw left a profound impression on me. If any dream was to be interpreted in terms of visual stimulus, then it was this one. And what had put the organ of my sight into this stimulated state? A recent impression, which joined with a number of earlier ones. The colours I saw were first of all the colours of the building-blocks which the children had been playing with on the day before my dream, putting up a wonderful edifice for me to admire. They had the same dark red for the big bricks, and the blue and the brown for the small ones. This was joined by impressions of colour from my last Italian journey, the lovely blue of the Isonzo and the lagoons, and the brown of the Carso.* The beautiful colours in my dream were only a repetition of what I saw in recollection.

Let us sum up what we have learned about the peculiar ability of the dream to recast the content of its imaginary ideas into sensory images. We have not explained this characteristic of the dream-work by tracing it back to known laws of psychology, say; rather, we have picked it out because it is a pointer towards unknown conditions, and we have distinguished it by calling it a 'regressive' characteristic. It was our view that wherever it occurs, this regression is probably an effect of resistance, as it pits itself against the entry of the dream-thought into consciousness along the normal way, as well as being an effect of the attraction exercised on it at the same time by the presence of strong sensory memories. It may be that in dreams regression is made easier as, in addition, the progressive current flowing from the sensory organs during the day also ceases; in other forms of regression, the absence of this auxiliary factor has to be made up for by a reinforcement of other motives for regression. Let us not forget to note also that in these cases of pathological regression, as in dreams, the process of transmitting energy may well be different from that of regression in normal psychical life, as it enables the perceptual system to carry a full hallucinatory charge. What we described when we analysed the dream-work as 'having regard to representability', we might perhaps relate to the *selective attraction* exercised by the scenes in our visual memory which the dream-thoughts have touched upon.

It may be that we ourselves have not found this first part of our psychological study of dreams particularly satisfactory. Let us console ourselves that of necessity, we are building out into the dark. If we have not gone entirely astray, we are bound to come upon another point of attack in approximately the same region, where we shall then, it may be, find our way more surely.

(c) *On Wish-Fulfilment*

The dream of the burning child at the head of this chapter offers a welcome occasion to assess the difficulties encountered by the theory of wish-fulfilment. We have all certainly heard with some surprise that the dream is supposed to be nothing but a wish-fulfilment, and not only because this seems to be contradicted by anxiety-dreams. For after hearing the first explanation claim that behind dreams there are concealed meaning and psychical value, we would hardly have expected such a straightforward definition of what this meaning might be. According to Aristotle's correct, but meagre definition, the dream is a process of thinking continued into sleep—insofar as one is sleeping. Now if by day our thinking can create such a variety of psychical acts—judgements, inferences, refutations, intentions, and the like—why should it have to limit itself solely to producing wishes? Are there not plenty of dreams that render a different kind of psychical act in an altered form—a care or concern, for example—and is not the father's particularly transparent dream at the head of this chapter one just of this kind? In his concern, he concludes from the light striking his eye, even though he is asleep, that a candle has fallen over and might have set fire to the body; he transforms this inference into a dream by clothing it in a meaningful situation and putting it into the present. What part does wish-fulfilment play in this, and are we not misjudging the predominance of the thought in it, continuing from waking life or aroused by the fresh sense-impression?

That is all perfectly correct, and it compels us to go more closely into both the part played by wish-fulfilment in dreams, and the significance of waking thoughts as they continue into sleep.

Wish-fulfilment itself has already made us distinguish two groups of dreams. We have found dreams that openly professed that they were wish-fulfilments; others where the wish-fulfilment was unrecognizable, and often hidden by all the devices of the dream-work. These latter, we saw, were performed by the dream-censorship. The wishful dreams that were undistorted we found were mainly children's dreams; short, frank wishful dreams *appeared*—I emphasize this proviso—to occur in adults too.

We may now ask where the wish realized in the dream comes from. But when we ask 'where from?', what are our points of reference, contrast and differentiation? In my view, the contrast is between the life of the day as it has entered consciousness, and a psychical activity which has remained unconscious and can only make itself felt at night. In this light, I can identify three possible sources for a wish. (1) It can have been aroused in the course of the day, but on account of external circumstances left unappeased; if so, there emerges at night a frank and unappeased wish. (2) It can have surfaced during the day, but have been rejected; if so, there emerges an unappeased but suppressed wish. Or (3), it can have no connection to the life of the day, and belong to those wishes that only stir within us at night, arising from what has been suppressed. If we apply our scheme of the psychical apparatus, we will locate a wish of the first kind in the *Precon.*-system; we assume of the second kind of wish that it has been driven from the *Precon.*-system back into the *Uncon.*, and persists only there, if at all; and we believe that the wishful impulse of the third kind is not capable of going beyond the borders of the *Uncon.*-system at all. Now, do wishes from these different sources have the same value for dreams—do they have the same power to initiate a dream?

A survey of the dreams available to us to answer this question reminds us first of all to add a fourth source for the wishes in dreams: the wishful impulses that become activated at night (e.g. responses to the stimulus of thirst, or sexual need). Once we do so, it seems probable that the origin of the dream-wish makes no difference to its capacity to initiate a dream. I recall the little girl's dream, which continued the trip across the lake interrupted in the daytime, as well as the other children's dreams quoted in the same context. They are explained by an unfulfilled, but unsuppressed daytime wish. Examples of a wish suppressed by day and breaking out at night can be pointed out in vast numbers; I could add a very simple instance here. A lady with some taste for mockery had a younger friend who had become engaged; throughout the day she would answer the questions of acquaintances—whether she knew her friend's fiancé and what she thought of him—with unqualified praise; in doing so she silenced her judgement, for she would have liked to tell the truth: *you could buy him for ten a penny*.* At night she dreams that the same questions are put to her, and she replies with the tradesman's phrase: *for repeat orders, just give the number*. Finally, we have learned from a great many analyses that in all dreams subject to distortion, the wish comes from the unconscious and is imperceptible by day. It seems at first, then, that in the formation of dreams all wishes have the same value and the same power.

I am not able to prove here that the situation is actually quite different from this, but I am very much inclined to assume a stricter determination for dream-wishes. Of course, the children's dreams leave no room for doubt that a wish left unsatisfied by day can initiate a dream. But we should not forget that this is a child's wish, with the peculiar strength of infantile experience. I am very doubtful whether the unfulfilled daytime wish of an adult is sufficient to create a dream. It seems to me rather that, as our thinking takes progressive control over the life of our impulses in creating or retaining intense wishes, such as children experience, we renounce them more and more, giving them up as good for nothing. It may be that individual differences hold good here, one type of person preserving infantile psychical processes longer than another—just as, indeed, differences of this kind also apply to the weakening of a mode of imagination that originally was strongly visual. But in general, I believe, the wish left unfulfilled from the day is not strong enough in adults to create a dream. I readily grant that a wishful impulse coming from the conscious will contribute towards arousing the dream, but probably no more than that. The dream would not arise if the preconscious wish had no other source where it could get reinforcement.

That source is the Unconscious. *I imagine that the conscious wish becomes the initiator of a dream only if it succeeds in wakening an unconscious wish consonant with it, and drawing reinforcement from this.* Following indications from the psychoanalysis of neuroses, I consider that these unconscious wishes are always alive, ready at all times to seek out expression if the opportunity offers, always ready to ally themselves with some impulse from the conscious, and to transfer their own great intensity to the less intense charge of the conscious impulse.[4] It is then bound to appear as if the conscious wish alone were realized in the dream; however, one striking little thing about the form taken by the dream will act as a pointer to the track of the powerful accomplice from the Unconscious. These wishes of our Unconscious, ever stirring, never dying—immortal,

[4] They share this characteristic of indestructibility with other really unconscious psychical acts, i.e. acts that belong to the *Uncon.*-system only. These are paths laid down once and for all, which are never out of use, and which, whenever an unconscious excitation recharges them, always act as a conduction-route to discharge the process of arousal. To use a comparison: their only kind of annihilation is that of the shades in the underworld of the *Odyssey*—who waken to new life once they have drunk blood. The processes dependent on the preconscious system are destructible in a quite different sense. The psychotherapy of neuroses is based on this distinction.

one might say—remind us of the legendary Titans whose shoulders from time immemorial bore the great mountain-masses laden upon them by the victorious gods, which even now still quake from time to time from the convulsions of their limbs—these repressed wishes, I say, themselves have infantile origins, as we learned from our investigations into the psychology of neuroses. I would therefore like to dismiss the statement I made earlier that it does not matter what the origin of the wish behind the dream might be, and replace it by another one as follows: *the wish represented in the dream has to be an infantile one.* In adults, then, it comes from the *Uncon.*; in children, where there is as yet no division or censorship between *Precon.* and *Uncon.*, or where this is only gradually being established, it is an unfulfilled, unrepressed wish from waking life. I know this intuition cannot be demonstrated universally; but I maintain that it can be demonstrated frequently, even in cases where one might not have suspected it, and that it is not to be generally refuted.

As far as the formation of dreams is concerned, then, I shall let the wishful impulses arising from conscious waking life take a backseat. The only function I will grant them is possibly to provide material for active sensations during sleep (cf. p. 176). I shall stay on the course laid down by this line of thought when I now consider the other psychical stimuli remaining from the life of the day which are not wishes. It is possible for us to put a provisional end to the energy charges of our waking life when we decide to go to sleep. Anyone who can do that well is a good sleeper; Napoleon I is supposed to have been a model of this kind. It is not always successful and not always complete. Problems needing to be settled, cares tormenting us, impressions overwhelming us continue the activity of our thoughts into our sleep too, and keep psychical processes going in the system we have called the Preconscious. If we want to classify these stirrings of thought that continue into sleep, we can set up the following groups: (1) what has been left unfinished by some chance delay during the day; (2) what has been left unsettled, unsolved by some failure of our powers of thought; (3) what has been rejected and suppressed by day. These are joined by the powerful fourth group, which has been stirred in our *Uncon.* by the work of the Preconscious in the course of the day; and finally we can add the fifth group: the unimportant—and hence unresolved—impressions of the day.

There is no need to underestimate the psychical intensities that these remains of the day introduce into the condition of sleep, especially from the group of unresolved problems. It is certain that these impulses are still struggling for expression at night too, and we may assume just as surely that the state of sleep makes it impossible for the usual process of excitation to continue in the Preconscious, ceasing as it becomes conscious. Insofar as we are able in the normal way to be conscious of our thinking processes at night too, we are simply not asleep. What kind of change in the *Precon.* system is brought about by the state of sleep, I cannot say; but there is no doubt that the psychological characteristic of sleep is to be looked for essentially in the changes of energy charge in this system, which also controls access to our power of movement, which is paralysed in sleep. Against this, there is nothing I know of in the psychology of dreams that bids us assume that sleep is anything but a secondary factor in bringing about changes in the *Uncon.* system. No other way is left, then, for the night-time excitation in the *Precon.* than the one the wishful impulses from the *Uncon.* take; it has to look to the *Uncon.* for reinforcement and join in following the detours of the unconscious excitations. However, what is the attitude of the preconscious remains of the day towards the dream? There is no doubt that they enter the dream in quantity, and make use of the dream-content to make their presence felt by the consciousness, even at night; indeed, on occasion they dominate the dream-content, compelling it to continue the work of the day; it is also certain that the remains of the day can just as easily be characterized by other things besides wishes; but even so, it is very instructive, and for the theory of wish-fulfilment quite decisive, to see what condition they have to accept to gain entry into the dream.

Let us take one of our earlier examples, for example, the dream that had my friend Otto appear with the symptoms of Basedow's disease (p. 207). During the day my thoughts were troubled on account of Otto's appearance, and the disquiet worried me deeply, like everything touching this person. It also pursued me, I assume, into my sleep. Probably I wanted to find out what was the matter with him. At night, this concern found expression in the dream I have related; in the first place, its content was nonsensical, and in the second, it did not correspond to any wish-fulfilment. However, I began to investigate where this inappropriate expression of the concern I had felt in the day came from, and in the course of analysis I discovered a connection by which I identified him with a certain Baron L., and myself on the other hand with Professor R. There was only one explanation for why I was obliged to choose this particular substitute for my daytime thought. In my *Uncon.*, I must always have been prepared to identify with Professor R., for this was the fulfilment of one of my immortal childhood wishes, my rage for greatness. Ugly thoughts towards my friend, which I would certainly repudiate by day, had exploited the opportunity to slip into the representation and become part of it, but my daytime worry, too, had also found some sort of expression by means of a substitute in the dream-content. The daytime thought, which was not in itself a wish, but on the contrary a worry, was obliged to find some route to a connection to an infantile wish, one now unconscious and suppressed. The wish then enabled the worry to 'originate', though duly dressed up, in consciousness. The more dominating this worry was, the more violent the yoking required could be; there was no need for any connection at all to exist between the content of the wish and the content of the worry, nor was there any in our example.

I am now able to give a precise account of the significance of the unconscious wish for dreams. I grant that there is an entire group of dreams which are *initiated* mainly, or even exclusively, by the remains of the day, and I think that even my wish to become a professor extraordinarius at long last could have allowed me to sleep in peace that night, if my disquiet about my friend's health had not still been stirring from the day. But even so, this worry would still not have produced a dream; the *driving-force* that the dream needed had to be contributed by a wish; it was up to the worry to find a wish for itself that would act as the driving-force of the dream. To put it in the form of a comparison: the daytime thought might possibly play the part of *entrepreneur* for the dream; but the entrepreneur who has the idea, as we say, and the will to translate it into action, still cannot do anything without capital; he needs a *capitalist* to take on the expenses, and the capitalist in this case, who contributes the psychical expenditure for the dream, is always and unfailingly, whatever the daytime thought may be, *a wish from the Unconscious*.

On other occasions the capitalist is himself the entrepreneur; in dreams, indeed, that is the more usual case. An unconscious wish has been aroused by the day's work, and it now creates the dream. All the other situations possible in the economic circumstances I have just suggested as an example also have their parallels in the procedures of the dream; the entrepreneur is in a position to contribute a small amount of capital himself; several entrepreneurs might turn to the same capitalist; several capitalists might club together and provide what the entrepreneurs require. Likewise, there are also dreams that are supported by more than one wish, and there are further variations of a similar kind, which can easily be reviewed, and are of no more interest to us. We shall only later be in a position to fill any gaps there may be in this account of the dream-wish.

The *tertium comparationis** of the analogies I have been drawing— the appropriate amount made available—can be used with finer differentiation to elucidate the structure of the dream. In most dreams it is possible to recognize a centre endowed with particularly strong sensory intensity, as I described on p. 232. As a rule this is the direct representation of the wish-fulfilment, for if we put the displacements of the dream-work into reverse, we find the psychical intensity of the elements in the dream-thoughts replaced by the sensory intensity of the elements in the dream-content. The elements in the neighbourhood of the wish-fulfilment often have nothing to do with its meaning; rather, they turn out to be the offspring of distressing thoughts going against the grain of the wish. However, from their often-contrived connection with the element at the centre, enough intensity has rubbed off on them to give them the potential for representation. In this way the wish-fulfilment's power of representation is diffused across a certain contextual sphere, and within this all the elements, even the weakest, are enabled to arrive at representation. In dreams driven by several wishes, it is easy to distinguish the spheres of the particular wish-fulfilments from one another, and often to read the gaps in the dreams as border-zones as well.

Although these observations have limited the significance of the remains of the day for the dream, it is still worth our while to pay some further attention to them. After all, they must be a necessary ingredient in forming the dream, if we are surprised at the fact that every dream shows some link to a recent impression of the day, often of the most trifling sort, as part of its content. We have not yet been able (p. 139) to understand the necessity for this added ingredient to the dream-mélange. And we will only do so if we hold fast to the part played by the unconscious wish and then turn to the psychology of neuroses for information. There we learn that an unconscious idea as such is incapable of entering the Preconscious, and that it is only able to effect any expression by attaching itself to an innocuous idea already present in the Preconscious; it transfers its intensity onto this, concealing itself behind it. This is the fact of *transference*, which contains the explanation for so many striking occurrences in the inner life of neurotics. The transference can leave the idea from the Preconscious unchanged, giving it an undeservedly great intensity; alternatively, it can forcibly modify the idea from the Preconscious by the content of the idea transferring from the Unconscious. Forgive my liking for analogies from everyday life, but I am tempted to say that the situation of the repressed idea resembles that of an American dentist in our own dear country, who may not practise his profession unless he makes use of a formally qualified doctor as his ostensible brass plate or cover before the law. And just as it is not exactly the doctors with most work of their own who enter these alliances with the dental technicians, in the operations of the psyche it is not those preconscious or conscious ideas which have attracted ample attention to themselves in the Preconscious that are elected to cover a repressed idea. For choice, to spin its web of connections around them, the Unconscious actually prefers preconscious impressions and ideas that have either been ignored as unimportant, or, if considered, have promptly been rejected. It is a well-known proposition of association theory, empirically confirmed, that ideas which have set up an intimate connection with one aspect, will keep aloof, as it were, from entire groups of new connections; I once attempted to base a theory of hysterical paralysis on this proposition.

If we assume that the same need for transference by repressed ideas as we recognized in analysing neuroses also holds good in dreams, this will explain at one blow two of the puzzles we have encountered in dreams: that every analysis of a dream is able to draw attention to the interweaving of a recent impression; and that this recent element is often of the most trifling sort. We can add to this what we have already learned elsewhere: that these recent and trifling elements reach the dream-content so frequently as substitutes for the earliest and oldest of our dream-thoughts, because they also have the least to fear from the censorship set up by resistance. However, while freedom from censorship only explains the preference for the trivial elements, the constant occurrence of recent elements reveals the need for transference. The demand of the repressed for material that is as yet free of associations is satisfied by both groups of impressions, the trivial because they have not given any occasion for a wide range of connections, and the recent because there has not been time for it.

Thus we can see that the remains of the day, to which we may now give credit for the trivial impressions, not only borrow something from the *Uncon.* when they get a share in forming a dream—that is, the driving-force at the disposal of the repressed wish—but they also have something indispensable to offer the Unconscious, the point of attachment it needs for transference. If we wanted to go more deeply into the inner processes at this point, we would have to cast a brighter light on the play of excitations between Preconscious and Unconscious—indeed, the study of the psychoneuroses presses us to do so, but dreams simply do not offer any support for it.

Just one further remark on the remains of the day. There is no doubt that they are the real disturbers of sleep, not dreams, which endeavour rather to guard our sleep. We shall come back to this later.

We have up until now been pursuing the wish behind the dream, we have derived it from the field of the *Uncon.*, and analysed its relationship to the remains of the day, which for their part may be wishes or psychical impulses of any other kind, or simply recent impressions. In this way we made room for the claims that can be made for the importance of our multifarious waking thought in forming dreams. It would not even be impossible to use this train of reasoning as the basis for explaining those extreme cases in which the dream continues the work of the day and brings an unsolved problem of our waking life to a happy conclusion. We only lack an example of the kind where analysis would reveal the infantile or repressed source of the wish that, when called upon, so successfully reinforced the efforts of preconscious activity. However, we have not come a single step closer to solving the puzzle of why all the Unconscious is able to offer in sleep is the driving-force to produce a wish-fulfilment. The answer to this question is bound to shed light on the psychical nature of wishing; it will be given with the aid of our schematic picture of the psychical apparatus.

We have no doubt that this apparatus too only reached its present perfection by way of a long development. Let us attempt to transpose it back to an earlier stage of its functioning. Hypotheses requiring a different kind of substantiation tell us that at first the apparatus aimed to maintain itself as far as possible without stimulus, and so in its earliest structure it assumed the scheme of the reflexive apparatus, which enabled it to discharge at once in motor activity any sensory excitation reaching it from outside. But this simple function is disturbed by the exigencies of life; it is to these that the apparatus also owes the impulsion to further development. The exigencies of life first approach it in the form of the great bodily needs. The excitation caused by internal need will seek some discharge into a motor activity we might describe as an 'internal change' or an 'expression of emotion'. A hungry child will cry or flail about helplessly. However, the situation remains unaltered, for the excitation coming from an internal need is not consistent with an intermittent force but with one that is continuously in operation. A change can only take place if in some way—for the child, if someone else comes to its aid—the *experience of satisfaction* is felt, annulling the internal stimulus. An essential component of this experience is the appearance of a certain perception (of food, in our example); from now on its remembered image will remain associated with the trace left in the memory by the excitation aroused by the need. The next time this need appears, an impulse in the psyche will arise, thanks to the association created, which will invest the remembered image with that perception and evoke the perception itself; what it really wants, then, is to restore the situation of its original satisfaction. An impulse of this kind is what we call a wish; the reappearance of the perception is the fulfilment of the wish; and when the perception is fully charged with the excitation roused by the need, that is the shortest path to the wish-fulfilment. There is nothing to hinder us from assuming a primitive state of the psychical apparatus when this path really was taken in this way, and when wishing ended in hallucinating. This earliest activity of the psyche, then, aims at a *perceptual identity*, that is, at a repetition of the perception linked to the satisfaction of the need.

Bitter experience of life must have modified this primitive thought-activity into a more adaptable, secondary one. Elsewhere, the creation of a perceptual identity on the short, regressive path within the apparatus does not have the same result as when the same perception is charged from outside. The satisfaction does not set in;

the need goes on. To make the internal charge equivalent to the external, it must be constantly kept going—which does actually happen in hallucinatory psychoses and hunger-fantasies, whose only psychical feat is *that they hold on to* the desired object. To put the psychical force to more purposefully adapted use, it is necessary to halt the process of complete regression so that it does not go beyond the remembered image; then it can set off from the remembered image to seek out other paths, which will finally lead to creating the desired perceptual identity from the direction of the external world. This inhibition, as well as the consequent diversion of the excitation, is a function of a second system governing voluntary movement, that is, coming into operation only once movement is used to carry out purposes that have already been remembered beforehand. Still, all the complicated activity of thought spinning out from the remembered image to the creation of perceptual identity by the external world only represents the *long way round to wish-fulfilment*[5] which experience has made necessary. Thought, after all, is nothing but a substitute for an hallucinatory wish, and to say that the dream is a wish-fulfilment is self-evident, for nothing but a wish is capable of putting our psychical apparatus to work. The dream, which fulfils its wishes along short, regressive paths, has preserved for us a mere sample of the psychical apparatus's *primary*—discarded—way of functioning, discarded, that is, as inexpedient. It seems banished to the night, though it once governed our waking, when the life of the psyche was still young and helpless, rather as we find the primitive adult weapons, the bow and arrow, which the human race has laid aside, in the nursery still. *Dreaming is a part of the—surmounted—childhood life of the psyche.* In the psychoses, these primary ways of functioning in the psychical apparatus, which are normally suppressed in waking life, will come forcibly into their own again, and then reveal how incapable they are of satisfying our needs with regard to the external world.

Clearly, the unconscious wishful impulses also seek to assert themselves by day as well, and we learn from the fact of transference as well as from the psychoses that they are striving by way of the

---

[5] Le Lorrain [45] rightly praises the wish-fulfilling function of the dream: 'Sans fatigue sérieuse, sans être obligé de recourir à cette lutte opiniâtre et longue qui use et corrode les jouissances poursuivies' ['Without major fatigue, without the obligation to resume that stubborn struggle which wears out and spoils the pursued delights'].

preconscious system to get through to consciousness and take control of movement. It is the censorship between *Uncon.* and *Precon.*, then, which dreams really compel us to assume, that we must acknowledge and honour as the guardian of our mental health. Now, is it not imprudent of this guardian to reduce his activity at night, allowing the suppressed impulses of the *Uncon.* to find expression, and making hallucinatory regression possible again? I do not think so, for when the critical guardian takes his rest—and we have evidence in any case that his slumber is not deep—he also closes the gateway to movement. Whatever impulses from the normally inhibited *Uncon.* may go rampaging upon the scene, they can be left to their own devices, they remain harmless, because they are unable to set the motor apparatus going, which is the only thing whose impact can change the external world. The state of sleep ensures the safety of the stronghold to be guarded. The situation is less harmless if the displacement of forces is brought about not by the relaxation at night of the critical censorship's expenditure of energy, but by its pathological reduction, or by a pathological reinforcement of the unconscious excitations, while the Preconscious is still charged with energy and the gates to movement are open. Then the guardian is overwhelmed, the unconscious excitations overcome the *Precon.*, and from there they take control of what we say and do, or forcibly bring about hallucinatory regression, and direct the course of the apparatus, which was not intended for them, by virtue of the attraction exercised by perceptions on the distribution of our psychical energy. We call this condition psychosis.

This puts us well on the way to building further on our psychological scaffolding, which we left at the point where we had included the two systems *Uncon.* and *Precon.* But we still have reasons enough to linger with our assessment of the wish as the sole psychical driving-force of the dream. We have accepted the explanation that the dream is always a wish-fulfilment because it is a creation of the *Uncon.*-system, whose only aim is wish-fulfilment, and which has at its disposal only the forces of the wishful impulses. Now if we want, even for a moment longer, to maintain our right to start out from the interpretation of dreams on very wide-ranging psychological speculations, we are under an obligation to show that we can use them to locate the dream in a context of interconnecting which can also include other psychological formations. If a system of the

Uncon.—or for the sake of discussion, something analogous to it—does exist, then the dream cannot be its only expression; every dream may well be a wish-fulfilment, but there must be other forms of abnormal wish-fulfilments besides dreams. And really, the theory of all psychoneurotic symptoms culminates in the proposition *that they too have to be conceived as wish-fulfilments of the Unconscious.* Our explanation makes the dream only the first item in a series which is of great significance to the psychiatrist, for understanding it would mean being able to solve the psychological part of the psychiatrist's work. However, the other items in this series of wish-fulfilments, for instance, hysterical symptoms, have one essential characteristic that I have not yet encountered in dreams. For I know from investigations I have alluded to frequently in the course of this treatise that for a hysterical symptom to be formed, both currents of our psychical life must come together. The symptom is not merely the expression of an unconscious wish realized; another wish from the Preconscious has to join it, realized by the same symptom, so that the symptom is determined *at least* doubly, once from each of the conflicting systems. As in the dream, there is no limit set to any further over-determination. The determinant that does not come from the *Uncon.* is, as far as I can see, invariably a train of thought reacting to the unconscious wish, for example, self-punishment. In general, then, I can say that *a hysterical symptom only comes into being when two opposing wish-fulfilments, each with its source in a different psychical system, are in a position to coincide in one expression.* Examples would be of little use here, for only a complete exposé of the complications present would be convincing. So I shall leave it at the assertion, and only offer an example as an illustration, not for any value it may have as evidence. A patient's hysterical vomiting, then, turned out on the one hand to be the fulfilment of an unconscious fantasy from her years of puberty—the wish, in fact, to be constantly pregnant and have countless children; later this was expanded to: by as many men as possible. A powerful defensive reaction had set in against this unbridled wish. However, as the patient was in danger of losing her fine figure and her good looks through this vomiting, so that no man would take a fancy to her, her symptom was also perfectly acceptable to her self-punishing train of thought, and so, being admissible to both sides, it could be realized. It is the same manner of dealing with a wish-fulfilment as it pleased the Parthian queen to use against the triumvir Crassus.* She thought he went on the campaign for love of gold; so she had molten gold poured down the throat of his dead body. 'Now you've got what you wished for.' Until now, all we know of the dream is that it expresses a wish-fulfilment of the Unconscious; it seems that the dominant preconscious system tolerates this, once it has imposed certain distortions upon the dream. In general, one cannot actually demonstrate a train of thought opposed to the dream-wish that is also, like its adversary, realized in the dream. We come across some signs of reaction-formations in our analyses of dreams, but only now and again, for example, my affection for my friend R. in the dream of my uncle (p. 109). However, the missing ingredient from the Preconscious can be discovered elsewhere. After undergoing all sorts of distortions, the dream is free to express a wish from the *Uncon.*, while the dominant system has withdrawn into the *wish to sleep*, realizing it by the changes it is able to bring about in the charges of energy within the apparatus of the psyche, and finally holding on to it for as long as sleep lasts.[6]

This firmly held wish of the Preconscious to sleep generally has the effect of making it easier for dreams to be formed. Let us consider the dream of the father who was led by the light coming from the dead child's room to conclude that the body might have caught fire. We have indicated that one of the psychical forces deciding that the father should draw this conclusion rather than be woken up by the light was the wish to prolong the life of the child imagined in the dream by just that moment. Other wishes arising from what has been repressed are likely to escape us, because we are not in a position to analyse this dream. But we may in addition take the father's need of sleep to be its second driving-force; just as the dream prolongs the child's life, the father's sleep too is lengthened by a moment. Let the dream go on, was his motivation, otherwise I shall have to wake up. As it does in this dream, the wish to sleep lends its support to the unconscious wish in all other dreams. On p. 99 we gave an account of dreams that presented themselves frankly as dreams of convenience. Actually, all dreams can lay claim to this description. The effectiveness of the wish to go on sleeping can be seen most easily in the dreams we have when we are woken up, as they adapt the external sensory stimulus in such a way that it is compatible with

---

[6] I have taken this idea from Liébault's theory of sleep; it is to him we are indebted for the revival of research into hypnosis in our time.

continuing sleep, and weave it into a dream to remove the demands it might make as a reminder of the outside world. However, this wish must also have a share in making possible all those other dreams that can only attempt to wake us up by disturbing our state of sleep from within. What the *Precon.* often says to our consciousness when the dream goes too far, is: 'Don't worry! Go on sleeping. After all, it's only a dream.' Even though this is never uttered aloud, it is a good general description of the attitude of the dominant activity of our psyche towards dreams. I am bound to draw the conclusion *that, throughout the entire state of sleep, we know just as certainly that we are dreaming as we know that we are asleep*. We do not have to pay any attention to the objection that our consciousness is never directed to the one item—the knowledge that we are asleep—and that it attends to the other—the knowledge that we are dreaming—only on particular occasions, when the censorship feels as if it has been caught unawares.

(d) *Arousal by Dreams. The Function of Dreams. Anxiety-Dreams*

Knowing as we do now that throughout the night the Preconscious is set on the wish to sleep, we can pursue the process of dreaming with greater understanding. But let us first summarize what we know about it so far. We would say, then, that a residue from the day is left from our waking activity, and that its charge of energy does not completely withdraw at night; alternatively, our waking activity has stirred one of our unconscious wishes during the day; or again, both may happen together—we have already discussed several possibilities in this respect. Either the unconscious wish has already been making its way towards the day's remnants in the course of the day, or this may not happen until the state of sleep sets in, when the wish brings about a transference onto them. A wish then emerges which has been transferred onto the recent material; alternatively, the suppressed recent wish has been revivified by reinforcement from the Unconscious. Its intention is to make its way into consciousness along the normal route taken by thought-processes via the *Precon.* But it comes up against the censorship—which still persists—and is now subject to its influence. At this stage it takes the distorted form for which the way was already prepared by its transference onto recent events. Up to this point it is on the way to becoming something similar to an obsessive idea or illusion or the like, that is, a thought reinforced by the transference and distorted in its expression by the censorship. However, the state of sleep does not allow the Preconscious to penetrate any further; probably the system has protected itself against penetration by reducing its excitations. The process of dreaming, then, takes the route of regression opened up by this characteristic of the state of sleep, and as it does so it follows the attraction exercised on it by groups of memories, some of which are only charged with visual intensity, not translated into the terms of the later systems. On the way to regression, it acquires representability. We shall deal with the question of compression later. The process of dreaming has now travelled the second stretch of its zigzag course. The first part extended progressively from the unconscious scenes or fantasies to the Preconscious; the second part moves from the borders of censorship on towards the perceptions again. However, once a dream-process has become the content of a perception, it has, you might say, evaded the obstacles placed on it in the *Precon.* by the censorship and the state of sleep. It is now able to draw attention to itself and be noticed by consciousness. For consciousness, which we regard as a sensory organ for the apprehension of psychical qualities, can be aroused from two locations when we are awake. First and foremost from the periphery of the whole apparatus, the perceptual system; besides this, from the excitations of pleasure and unpleasure which are the only psychical quality to emerge from the transfers of energy within the apparatus. All the other processes in the ψ-system, even those in the *Precon.*, lack any psychical quality, and so they are not an object of consciousness, in so far as they do not provide pleasure or unpleasure for our perception. We shall have to assume that *these releases of pleasure and of unpleasure automatically regulate the processes of energy-charging*. However, in order to make more fine-tuned performance possible, it later turned out to be necessary to shape the course of ideas so that it was more independent of signs of unpleasure. To this end, the *Precon.* system needed qualities of its own, able to attract consciousness, and it most probably acquired them by setting up the connection between preconscious processes and the memory-system of linguistic signs—which was itself not without qualities. Through this system's qualities, consciousness, which previously was only a sensory organ for perceptions, now also becomes the sensory organ for part of our thinking processes. There are now, as it were, two sensory surfaces, one turned towards processes of perceiving, the other towards processes of thinking.

I have to assume that the state of sleep makes the sensory surface of consciousness that is turned towards the *Precon.* far less susceptible to excitation than the surface turned towards the *Per.*-systems. Of course, there is also a purpose to giving up interest in thought-processes at night. Nothing is supposed to happen in our thinking; the *Precon.* wants to sleep. However, once the dream has become a perception, it is able to use the qualities it has now acquired to arouse consciousness. This excitation of the senses achieves what it is its function to achieve; it makes a part of the energy-charge available in the *Precon.* pay attention to what is arousing it. So it has to be admitted, then, that the dream always *arouses* us, it sets in action part of the force at rest in the *Precon.* The dream then undergoes what we have described as secondary revision, which takes account of coherence and intelligibility. That is to say, it treats the dream like any other perceptual content: its ideas are subjected to the same expectations, that is, insofar as its subject-matter allows. As for the direction taken by the course of this third part of the dream-process, it is again a progressive one.

To avoid misunderstandings, a word about the temporal characteristics of these dream-processes is probably called for. A very attractive line of thought was put forward by Goblot [29], which was obviously set off by the puzzle presented in Maury's guillotine dream: he attempts to show that dreams take up only the time of the transitional period between sleeping and waking. Waking up takes time; the dream occurs in this time. In this view, the last image of the dream was so strong that it forced the sleeper to wake up. In reality, the image was so strong only because with it we were already so close to waking. 'Un rêve c'est un réveil qui commence.'*

Dugas [18] has already emphasized that Goblot has to throw out a great deal of factual material to make his thesis generally valid. There are also dreams from which we do not wake, for example, many where we dream that we are dreaming. From our knowledge of the dream-work, we cannot possibly agree that it only lasts for the period of waking. On the contrary, it must be more likely that the first part of the dream-work is already beginning during the day, when it is still governed by the Preconscious. The second part of the dream-work—the changes imposed by the censorship, the attraction exercised by the unconscious scenes, the breakthrough to perception—probably goes on throughout the night, and to that extent we may always be right when we claim we have been dreaming all night long, even though we are unable to say what. However, I do not believe that the processes of the dream really follow the temporal sequence we have been describing: first the presence of the transferred dream-wish, then the distortion by the censorship, and after that the shift in the direction of regression, etc. We have had to construct this kind of sequence in describing it; in reality it is much more likely to be a matter of simultaneously trying out this or that path, a toing and froing of excitations until finally they accumulate in the way most suitable for the one lasting constellation to emerge. Some experiences of my own lead me to think that the dream-work often needs more than a day and a night to deliver its results, though if that is so, the extraordinary art shown in constructing the dream loses its wonder. Even the consideration it gives to intelligibility as a perceptual event can, in my opinion, come into effect before the dream has attracted consciousness to itself. On the other hand, from then on the process is accelerated, for after all, the dream now goes through the same treatment as anything else perceived. It is like a firework that has been hours in the preparation, and then blazes up in a moment.

Either the dream-process is enabled by the dream-work, quite independently of the time or the depth of sleep, to gain enough intensity to attract consciousness to itself and rouse the Preconscious; or its intensity is not sufficient for this, and it has to remain at the ready until it attracts attention—which becomes more mobile then—immediately before waking. Most dreams appear to operate with relatively low psychical intensities, for they are waiting until it is time to wake. But this also explains how we are, as a rule, aware of something we have dreamed if we are suddenly jolted out of deep sleep. Just as when we wake up naturally, the first thing we see is the perceptual content created by the dream-work, and next after that what is given by the outside world.

However, greater theoretical interest applies to the dreams that are able to wake us up in the midst of our sleep. If we bear in mind its efficacy demonstrable everywhere else, we may well ask why the dream, that is, the fulfilment of the unconscious wish, is still left with the power to disturb sleep, that is, the fulfilment of the preconscious wish. The cause must lie in their energy relations, of which we have no knowledge. If we did, we would probably find that letting the dream run on, and expending a certain detached attention on it, represents a saving of energy in contrast to keeping the Unconscious within the same bounds at night as during the day. Our experience shows that dreaming, even if it interrupts our sleep several times in one night, is compatible with sleep. We wake up for a moment, and go back to sleep again at once. It is as if we were brushing away a fly in our sleep; we wake up *ad hoc*. When we go back to sleep, we have removed the disturbance. Fulfilling the wish to sleep, as familiar examples of nurses' sleep and the like show us, can be combined with a certain expenditure of attention in a specific direction.

However, at this point an objection which is based on better knowledge of unconscious processes demands a hearing. We have described even unconscious wishes as being constantly alive and active. Nevertheless, during the day they are not strong enough to make themselves audible. But in the state of sleep, if the unconscious wish has had the power to form a dream and arouse the Preconscious with it, why does this power seep away once we are aware of the dream? Rather, should not the dream renew itself constantly, just as the disturbing fly is fond of coming back again and again to the spot it was driven away from? What right had we to assert that dreams get rid of any disturbance to our sleep?

It is quite correct that the unconscious wishes always remain alive and active. They represent paths that are always passable, whenever a quantity of excitation makes use of them. It is even the salient feature of unconscious processes that they are indestructible. In the Unconscious, nothing is brought to an end, nothing is past or forgotten. We get the strongest impression of this from the study of neuroses, especially of hysteria. The unconscious path of thoughts, leading to discharge in an attack, can be travelled again at once, if sufficient excitation has accumulated. An injury experienced thirty years ago, once it has gained access to the unconscious sources of affect, will continue throughout all those thirty years to act just like a recent one. Whenever the memory of it is touched, it comes to life again charged with excitation, which is then discharged in a motor attack. It is just here that psychotherapy can intervene. Its job is to deal with the unconscious processes, settling them and making it possible to forget them. In fact, what we are inclined to regard as self-evident, and to explain by the primary influence of time on the remnants of memory in the psyche, by waning memories and the low intensity of fading impressions, are in reality secondary changes which have come about by hard labour. It is the Preconscious that does this work, and the only route that psychotherapy can take is to subdue the *Uncon.* to the authority of the *Precon.*

For a particular unconscious process of excitation, then, there are two outcomes. On the one hand, it is left to itself; if so, it will finally break out somewhere and for this once it will discharge its excitation in movement. Alternatively, it succumbs to the influence of the Preconscious, which *binds* the excitation, instead of *venting* it. *But it is the latter that takes place in the process of dreaming.* The charge of energy coming from the Preconscious towards the dream (which has now become perceptual) because it has been diverted there by the excitation of consciousness, binds the unconscious excitation of the dream and neutralizes its capacity to disturb. If the dreamer wakes for a moment, he really has brushed away the fly that threatened to disturb his sleep. We can now have some idea that it really was more convenient and more economical to let the unconscious wish run its course, opening up its path to regression so that it can form a dream, and then to deal with the dream, binding it by a small expenditure of preconscious work, than to keep a tight rein on the Unconscious throughout the entire time spent asleep as well as waking. It was, of course, to be expected that even if dreaming was not originally a process with a purpose, it would have found itself a function within the play of forces in the psyche. We can now see what that function is. Dreaming has taken on the task of bringing the excitation of the *Uncon.*, which was left free, back under the control of the Preconscious. In doing so, it discharges the excitation of the *Uncon.*, acts as a safety-valve for it, and at the same time ensures the sleep of the Preconscious in exchange for a small expenditure of waking activity. In this way it presents itself as a compromise, just like all the other psychical formations in the series it belongs to, serving both systems at the same time as it fulfils the wishes of both, in so far as they are compatible with each other. A glance at Robert's 'excretion theory' explained on p. 66 indicates that we have to admit this authority was right on the main question of the function of dreams, though we part company from him in our assumptions and in our assessment of the dream-process.

The qualification, *insofar as the wishes are compatible with each other*, suggests possible cases where the function of a dream may miscarry. The process of dreaming is first admitted as a wish-fulfilment of the Unconscious; if this attempted wish-fulfilment gives such a violent jolt to the Preconscious that it can no longer preserve its repose, the dream has broken the compromise, and no longer fulfils the other part of its task. If this happens, it is interrupted at once and replaced by a fully wakened state. In this case too, it is not actually the fault of the dream if, though normally the guardian of sleep, it has to appear as its disturber, and this need not make us doubt its fitness for its purpose. This is not the only instance in the organism where a useful arrangement becomes useless and disturbing as soon as there is some change in the conditions under which it comes into being; in these cases the disturbance at least serves the new purpose of signalling the change and summoning up the organization's regulatory means against it. I have in mind, of course, the case of anxiety-dreams, and—so as not to appear to be avoiding this evidence against the theory of wish-fulfilment, wherever I come upon it—I propose to approach an explanation of anxiety-dreams, at least with some suggestions.

By now we no longer regard it as a contradiction that a psychical process producing anxiety can still, for that reason, be a wish-fulfilment. We are able to explain it to ourselves as follows: the wish belongs to one system, the *Uncon.*, while the system of the *Precon.* has rejected and suppressed this wish. Even in cases of complete psychical well-being, the *Uncon.* is not totally subject to the *Precon.*; the measure of this suppression indicates the degree of our psychical normality. The symptoms of neurosis show us that the two systems are in conflict with each other; they are the compromise results of the conflict, putting a provisional end to it. On the one hand they enable the *Uncon.* to find an outlet for the discharge of its excitation, act as a sally-port for it, and on the other, they still offer the *Precon.* the possibility of having some control over the *Uncon.* It is instructive, for example, to consider the significance of a hysterical phobia or of agoraphobia. Say that a neurotic is incapable of crossing the road alone, which we rightly describe as a 'symptom'. Suppose we then nullify this symptom by forcing him to perform the action he believes he cannot take. If we do, it results in an attack of anxiety, as, indeed, an attack of anxiety in the street has often become the occasion for agoraphobia to set in. In this way we learn that the symptom has been created in order to prevent the outbreak of anxiety; the phobia is situated like a frontier stronghold against the anxiety.

We will not be able to take our account further without looking at the part played by the affects in these processes, which can only be done incompletely at this point. So let us propose that the suppression of the *Uncon.* is necessary above all because, if left to itself, the course of ideas in the *Uncon.* would develop an affect which was originally characterized by pleasure but, since undergoing the process of *repression*, is characterized by unpleasure. The aim of the suppression—but also its consequence—is to prevent this development of unpleasure. The suppression extends as far as the content of the ideas in the *Uncon.*, because the release of unpleasure could take off from there. This proposition is based on a quite specific assumption about the nature of the development of affect, which it regards as being accomplished by the motor or secretory systems, seeing the key to its innervation as located in the imagined ideas of the *Uncon.* These ideas are strangled, as it were, by the *Precon.*'s control of them, and inhibited from transmitting the impulses developing the affect. If this charge of energy from the *Precon.* stops, then the danger is that the unconscious excitations will release an affect, which—as a consequence of its earlier suppression—can only be felt as unpleasure, as anxiety.

This danger is let loose if the dream-process is allowed to run its course. The conditions for its realization are if repressions have taken place and if the suppressed wishful impulses are able to become sufficiently strong—conditions, in fact, which are entirely outside the psychological framework of dream-formation. If it were not that our topic is connected to that of the development of anxiety by this one factor—the freeing of the *Uncon.* during sleep—I could dispense with discussing anxiety-dreams and spare myself all the obscurities attaching to them.

The theory of anxiety-dreams, as I have already said many times, belongs to the psychology of neuroses. We have nothing further to do with it now that we have indicated the place where it touches our topic, which is the process of dreaming. There is just one more thing I can do. As I have maintained that neurotic anxiety arises from sexual sources, I can submit anxiety-dreams to analysis to point out the sexual material in their dream-thoughts.

I have good reasons to refrain from using any of the examples which my neurotic patients offer me in plenty, and I shall give preference to anxiety-dreams from young persons.

I have no longer had a real anxiety-dream myself for decades. I remember one from my seventh or eighth year, which I submitted to interpretation some thirty years later. It was very vivid, and it showed me *my beloved mother with a distinctively tranquil, sleeping expression on her face, who was being carried into the room by two (or three) people with birds' beaks, and laid on the bed*. I woke up crying and screaming, and disturbed my parents' sleep. The—curiously draped—elongated figures with the birds' beaks I had taken from the illustrations to *Philippson's* edition of the Bible;* I believe they were gods with falcons' heads from an Egyptian tomb relief. Besides this, the analysis provided me with the memory of a badly behaved boy, our caretaker's son, who used to play with us children in the field in front of the house, and I rather think he was called *Philipp*. I have the feeling as though it was from this boy that I first heard the vulgar word for sexual intercourse for which the educated substitute a Latinate word, 'coition', but which is characterized clearly enough by the choice of falcons' heads.* I must have guessed the sexual meaning of the word from the face of my experienced mentor. The expression on my mother's face in the dream was copied from the sight of my grandfather, whom I had seen snoring in a coma a few days before his death. So the interpretation in the secondary revision of the dream must have been that my mother *is dying*—the *tomb* relief also chimes with this. I woke up in this state of anxiety, and did not stop until I had wakened my parents. I remember I calmed down all of a sudden when I saw my mother, as though I needed the reassurance: so she is not dead, after all. But this secondary interpretation of the dream already happened under the influence of the anxiety released. Not that I was anxious because I had dreamed that my mother was dying; but I interpreted the dream in its preconscious version in this way because I was already under the power of anxiety. But the anxiety could be traced back by way of repression to a dark, obviously sexual desire which had found an appropriate expression in the visual content of the dream.

A twenty-seven-year-old man, who has been very ill for a year, dreamed several times between the ages of eleven and thirteen with feelings of great anxiety, *that a man with a hatchet was coming after him; he wants to run, but feels as if he is paralysed and cannot move from the spot.* That is probably a good model of a very common anxiety-dream, beyond any sexual suspicion. In the course of analysis, the dreamer at first comes upon a—chronologically later—story of his uncle, who was attacked in the street at night by a suspicious individual, and he makes his own inference from this that he might have heard of a similar experience at the time of the dream. The hatchet rouses the recollection that at the time he once hurt himself with a hatchet when he was chopping kindling. Then he comes directly upon his relationship with his younger brother, whom he used to maltreat and knock about, and he remembers one occasion particularly when he kicked him in the head with his boot, so that the boy bled and his mother exclaimed: 'I'm afraid he'll kill him one day.' While he seems fixed on the topic of violence, another memory from his ninth year suddenly surfaces. His parents had come home late and went to bed, while he pretended to be asleep, and he heard a panting and other sounds that seemed uncanny to him, and he could also guess at the position of the two in bed. His further thoughts show that he had set up an analogy between this relationship of his parents' and his own to his younger brother. He subsumed what happened between his parents under the concept: *violence and fighting.* As proof of this conception he noticed that there was often *blood in his mother's bed.*

It is, I would say, a matter of everyday experience that the sexual intercourse of adults seems uncanny to the children who observe it, and arouses anxiety in them. I have explained this anxiety as a matter of sexual excitation which their understanding cannot cope with; probably it also gets repudiated because the parents are involved in it, and so it is transformed into anxiety. At an earlier period of life the stirrings of sexuality felt towards the parent of the opposite sex do not yet meet with repression, and express themselves freely, as we have heard (p. 197).

I would have no doubts about applying the same explanation to the night-time attacks of anxiety accompanied by hallucinations (the *pavor nocturnus*) suffered so often by children. There too it can only be a matter of stirrings of sexuality which are not understood, and rejected. A record of them would probably also indicate a temporal periodicity, for sexual libido can be intensified as much by arousal from chance impressions as by the spontaneous, intermittent processes of development.

I lack the empirical material needed to carry this explanation through to the end. On the other hand, the paediatricians seem to lack the one point of view that would allow them to understand the entire series of phenomena from the somatic as well as the psychical aspect. As a comic example of how close one can get to an understanding of such cases, and then, blinded by the blinkers of medical mythology, walk right past it, I would like to quote a case I found in Debacker's [17] thesis of 1881 on *pavor nocturnus* (p. 66).

A thirteen-year-old boy in poor health began to become timid and dreamy; his sleep became restless, and was broken almost once every week by a bad attack of anxiety with hallucinations. His memory of these dreams was always very distinct. He was able to relate that the devil had shouted at him: 'Now we've got you, now we've got you,' and then there was a smell of sulphur and brimstone, and the fire burned his skin. He would wake from this dream in terror, but at first was not able to cry out until he had found his voice, and he was heard to say distinctly: 'No, no, not me, I haven't done anything,' or: 'Please, don't. I'll never do it again.' Sometimes he would also say: 'Albert didn't do that.' Later he avoided getting undressed 'because the fire would only get him if he was undressed'. In the middle of these dreams of the devil, which put his health in danger, he was sent to the country, where he recovered in the course of eighteen months, and then, when he was fifteen years old, he once confessed: 'Je n'osais pas l'avouer, mais j'éprouvais continuellement des picotements et des surexcitations aux *parties*;[7] à la fin, cela m'énervait tant que plusieurs fois, j'ai pensé me jeter par la fenêtre du dortoir.'*

It is probably not difficult to guess: (1) that in earlier years the boy masturbated, probably denied it, and was threatened with heavy punishments for his bad habit. (His admission: 'Je ne le ferai plus'; his denial: 'Albert n'a jamais fait cela'); (2) that in the turmoil of puberty, the temptation to masturbate was aroused again with the tickling in his genitals; but that now (3) a repressive struggle broke out within him, suppressing the libido and transforming it into an

---

[7] My italics; but in any case not to be misunderstood.

anxiety which resumed retroactively the punishments he had once been threatened with.

By contrast, let us hear the conclusions drawn by our authority (p. 69). 'We may conclude from these observations that (1) the influence of puberty on a boy of weakened heath can produce a condition of great weakness, and that it can go as far as *a very considerable cerebral anaemia.*[8]

'(2) This cerebral anaemia produces a change in the character, demonomanic hallucinations and states of intense anxiety at night, and perhaps also by day.

'(3) The demonomania and the boy's self-accusations derive from the effects of his religious education, which influenced him as a child.

'(4) As the consequence of a fairly long stay in the country, physical exercise, and the return of his strength at the end of puberty, all the phenomena disappeared.

'(5) Perhaps one may ascribe the child's predisposition to this cerebral condition to heredity and to his father's earlier syphilis.'

The final word: 'Nous avons fait entrer cette observation dans le cadre des délires apyrétiques d'inanition, car c'est à l'ischémie cérébrale que nous rattachons cet état particulier.'*

(e) *Primary and Secondary Process. Repression*

In venturing further into the psychology of dream-processes, I have taken on a difficult task to which my expository skills, also, are scarcely equal. To express the simultaneity of such complicated interrelationships in terms of linear sequence in my description of them, while ensuring that each proposition I put forward does not appear to be based on prior assumptions, is likely to be too much for my powers. It is brought home to me now that in giving an account of the psychology of dreams I am not able to follow the historical development of my insights. My perspective on dreams was given me by my previous work on the psychology of neuroses, which I ought not to use as a point of reference here, although I shall have to do so again and again as I proceed in the opposite direction, starting out from dreams with the intention of making the connection to the

---

[8] My italics.

psychology of neuroses. I am aware of all the difficulties this will cause the reader, but I do not know how to avoid them.

Dissatisfied as I am by this state of affairs, I am happy to linger on a different aspect which seems to me to increase the value of my labours. As the introduction to my first chapter has indicated, I found a topic dominated by the sharpest contradictions among the opinions of the authorities. Our own treatment of the problems raised by dreams has found room for most of these contradictions. We ourselves had to argue decisively against only two of the views raised: that the dream has no meaning, and that it is a somatic process; but otherwise we were able to acknowledge that all these mutually contradictory opinions were right on some point in these complicated interrelationships, and to demonstrate that they had discovered something that was correct. By exposing the hidden dream-thoughts, we have confirmed in general that the dream does continue the motivation and interests of waking life, for dream-thoughts are engaged only with what seems to be important and of great interest to us. Dreams are never concerned with trivia. But we have also admitted the opposite, that dreams will also pick up the rejected trifles of the day, and will not make a major interest of the day their own until this has to some extent withdrawn from the work of our waking hours. We found this held good for the dream-content, which expresses the dream-thoughts in a form altered by distortion. For reasons to do with the mechanics of association, we said, the process of dreaming more readily takes possession of fresh or unimportant representations for its material, which have not yet been requisitioned by our waking thought; and for reasons of censorship, the process of dreaming transfers psychical intensity from what is important, but also objectionable, onto what is insignificant. The hypermnesia of dreams and their command of childhood material have become the two pillars on which our theory rests; our theory of dreams has ascribed to wishes deriving from childhood the part of indispensable moving-force in the formation of dreams. Of course it would not occur to us to doubt the importance, experimentally demonstrated, of external sensory stimuli during sleep, but we have given this material the same place relative to the dream-wish as we have the remnants of thought left over from the work of the day. We do not need to dispute that the dream interprets the objective sensory stimulus as if it were an illusion; but where the authorities left the motive for this interpretation uncertain, we have put it in. The interpretation occurs in such a way that the object perceived is deprived of its power to disturb our sleep and becomes available for purposes of wish-fulfilment. It is true, we do not accept that subject-ive states of excitation in the sensory organs occurring during sleep are a particular source of dreams, though this appears to have been demonstrated by Trumbull Ladd [40]. However, we are able to explain them as a regressive revival of memories operating behind the dream. Internal organic sensations, too, which are seized on as the key point in explaining dreams, also retain their function in our conception, but with a more modest scope. In our view, these sensations—of falling, floating, being inhibited—represent material available at all times for the dream-work to use to express the dream-thoughts whenever it needs to.

That the process of dreaming is rapid and momentary appears to us to be true of the perception by consciousness of the ready-made dream-content; but we have found it more likely that the preliminary parts of the dream-process take a slow, drifting course. With regard to the puzzle of a dream-content abounding in ideas but concen-trated into the briefest moment, we were able to add that these are cases where the dream admits structures ready-made and already present in the life of the psyche. We agreed that dreams are distorted and deformed by memory, but we found this no obstacle, for this is only the last, manifest part of a work of distortion operative from the start of the process of dream-formation. In the embittered, seem-ingly irreconcilable dispute over whether our inner life sleeps at night or still has all its capacities at its disposal as it does by day, we were able to say that both sides were right, but that neither of them was entirely right. We were able to discover in the dream-thoughts proof of highly complicated intellectual performance, operating with almost all the instrumentation of the psychical apparatus; but it still cannot be denied that these dream-thoughts originated in the day-time, and it is essential to assume that there is such a thing as a state of sleep for the inner life. This is how even the theory of partial sleep came into its own; but the state of sleep, we found, is not character-ized by the disintegration of psychical interconnections, but by the focus on the wish to sleep by the psychical system in control of the day. Withdrawal of attention from the external world, too, retained its importance in our conception of the dream; although it is not the only factor, it helps to make the regressive nature of representation in dreams possible. There is no disputing that voluntary direction of the course of ideas is abandoned; but this does not mean that the life of the psyche becomes purposeless, for we have heard that once the voluntary purposes are relinquished, involuntary purposes take control. We have not only acknowledged the existence of loose associative connections in dreams, but we have given them a much wider scope than could have been suspected; however, we discovered that they were only imposed substitutes for other—proper and meaningful—associations. Certainly, we too called the dream absurd; but we learned from examples how clever the dream is when it is pretending to be absurd. We do not disagree on the functions that have been ascribed to the dream. That the dream, like a safety-valve, allows the psyche to let off steam; and that, as Robert puts it, by imagining it in the dream, all sorts of harmful stuff is rendered harmless—this not only coincides exactly with our theory of the dream's double wish-fulfilment, but it becomes more intelligible in our theory than in Robert's, even in its formulation. The psyche's revelling in the free play of its capacities can also be found in our theory, in the way preconscious activity allows the dream to run on. The 'return of our inner life to the embryonic point of view in dreams', and the words of Havelock Ellis [23], 'an archaic world of vast emotions and imperfect thought', appear to be happy anticipations of our own argument, which has *primitive* ways of working, suppressed by day, taking part in the formation of dreams; and like Delage [15], we regard 'the *suppressed*' as the motive force of dreaming.

We have fully recognized the part Scherner ascribes to the dream-imagination, as well as Scherner's own interpretations, but we have had to allocate them, as it were, a different place in the problem. It is not that the dream forms the imagination, but that the unconscious activity of the imagination has the greatest share in the formation of the dream-thoughts. We are still indebted to Scherner for drawing our attention to the source of dream-thoughts; but almost everything that he ascribes to the dream-work is to be put down to the activity of the Unconscious during the day, which provides the spur for dreams no less than for neurotic symptoms. We had to distinguish the dream-work from this activity as something quite different and far more specific. Finally, we have certainly not given up the relation between dreams and disorders of the psyche; rather, we have set it more firmly on a fresh basis.

What is new in our theory of dreams acts as a kind of greater whole, holding the most various and contradictory conclusions of our authors together and including them in our structure, with many of them altered and only a few entirely rejected. But our building too is still incomplete. Quite apart from the many uncertainties we have brought upon ourselves by advancing into the darkness of psychology, there is also a fresh contradiction that seems to weigh upon us. On the one hand, we had the dream-thoughts come about by means of completely normal mental activity, but on the other, we discovered a number of quite abnormal thought-processes among the dream-thoughts, and we made our way from them to the dream-content; we then go over them again in our interpretation of the dream. Everything we have called the 'dream-work' appears to depart so far from psychical processes we know to be rational, that the harshest judgement passed by our authors on the low psychical performance of dreaming cannot fail to seem perfectly right and proper.

At this point it may be that we will gain aid and enlightenment only by advancing still further. I will single out one of the constellations leading to the formation of dreams:

We have learned that the dream takes the place of a number of thoughts that come from the life of the day and are connected in a perfectly logical way. This removes any doubts that these thoughts have their origin in our normal mental life. All the characteristics we admire in our thought-processes, and which mark them out as complicated feats of a high order, can also be found in the dream-thoughts. But there is no need to assume that this intellectual work is accomplished during sleep—that would throw our idea of the psychical state of sleep, firmly held so far, into dire confusion. Rather, these thoughts could very well come from the day, and from their first prompting could have gone on unnoticed by our consciousness, and could already have been completed when we fell asleep. If we are to gather anything from this situation, it is at most *that the most complicated feats of thinking are possible without the participation of consciousness*—which in any case we were bound to learn from every psychoanalysis of a hysteric or person with obsessional ideas. These dream-thoughts are in themselves certainly not incapable of becoming conscious; if they have not become conscious to us in the course of the day, there may be several reasons for it. Becoming conscious is connected with the application of a particular psychical function, attention, which it seems is used only in a particular quantity, and this latter may be diverted from the train of thought in question by other aims. Another way in which such trains of thought can be withheld from consciousness is the following: we know from our conscious reflection that when we are paying attention, we are pursuing a definite path. If, as we go along this path, we come upon an idea that does not stand up to criticism, we break off; we let the charge of our attention drop. Now it seems that the train of thought we embarked on and abandoned can carry on spinning itself out, even though our attention is no longer turned to it, provided that the process does not reach a particularly high intensity at any point, forcing attention onto it. A train of thought may be rejected at the beginning, probably consciously, by a judgement that it is wrong, or useless for the present purpose of the act of thinking, so it is possible that this is the reason why it will continue, unnoticed by consciousness, until we fall asleep.

Let us sum up: we call a train of thought of this kind *preconscious*; we regard it as completely rational, and it can just as readily be one that has been merely neglected as one that has been interrupted or suppressed. Let us also state outright how we visualize the course that a train of ideas follows. We believe that, starting from a purposive idea, a certain amount of excitation that we call 'charging energy' is displaced along paths of association selected by this purposive idea. A 'neglected' train of thought has not received such a charge of energy; a 'suppressed' or 'rejected' train of thought has had it withdrawn; both are left to their own excitations. A train of thought that has been purposively charged will, under certain circumstances, be capable of attracting the attention of consciousness to itself, and via this mediating agency it will then receive a '*supercharge*'. We shall have to explain our assumptions about the nature and function of consciousness a little later.

A train of thought set going in the Preconscious in this way can die down of its own accord or it can hold its own. We envisage the first outcome as occurring if the energy of the train of thought has been diffused in all the associative directions leading out from it, putting the entire chain into a state of excitation that lasts for a while, but then fades away as the excitation needing discharge is transformed into a quiescent charge. If this first outcome does occur, the process has no further significance for the formation of dreams. However, there are other purposive ideas lurking in our Preconscious which come from the sources of our unconscious and ever-active wishes. These can take over the excitation in the sphere of thoughts left to themselves, set up a connection between these and the unconscious wish, *transfer* to them the energy belonging to the unconscious wish, and from now on the neglected or suppressed train of thought is in a position to hold its own, though this reinforcement does not give it any right to be admitted to consciousness. We may say that the train of thought, preconscious until now, has been *drawn into the Unconscious*.

Other constellations leading to the formation of a dream might be, if from the start the preconscious train of thought were linked with the unconscious wish and for that reason came up against rejection from the dominant purposive charge; or if an unconscious wish became active from other (perhaps somatic) causes, and were to look for a transference onto the psychical residues that are not charged by the *Precon.* and do not come halfway to meet it. All three cases have the same result in the end: a train of thought comes about in the Preconscious, deserted by the preconscious energy-charge, but receiving one from the unconscious wish.

From then on the train of thought undergoes a series of transformations which we no longer recognize as normal psychical processes, and which produces a disconcerting result, a psychopathological formation. Let us single them out and put them together.

(1) The intensities of the individual ideas in their total amount become capable of discharge and pass over from one idea to another, so that individual ideas are formed which are invested with great intensity. With the frequent repetition of this process, the intensity of an entire train of thought can finally be concentrated in a single one of its elements. This is the fact of *compression* or *condensation* which we got to know in the course of the dream-work. It is condensation that is mainly to blame for the disconcerting impression made by dreams, for we are quite unfamiliar with anything analogous to it in our normal inner life accessible to consciousness. Here too we have ideas possessing great psychical significance as points of intersection or as the final result of entire chains of thought, but

their importance is not expressed by any characteristic obviously discernible to internal perception; the importance of the idea in this respect does not make what is presented in it any more intense. However, in the process of condensation all the psychical inter-connections are converted into the *intensity* of the ideational content. It is the same as if I were having a book printed, and had a word I regarded as overwhelmingly important for understanding the text printed in italics or bold. In speaking, I would pronounce the word loudly and slowly and with emphasis. The first comparison takes us directly to one of the examples borrowed from the dream-work (*Trimethylamine* in the dream of Irma's injection). Art historians remind us that the oldest historical sculptures follow a similar prin-ciple to express the rank of the personages represented by their size in the sculpture. The king is represented as two or three times bigger than his entourage or his vanquished enemy. A sculpture from the Roman period will make use of more subtle means for the same purpose. It will place the figure of the Emperor in the middle, show him raised high, devote particular care to the modelling of his figure, lay his enemies at his feet, but no longer have him appear as a giant among dwarfs. Meanwhile, the bow the inferior makes to his superior among ourselves today is still a late echo of that ancient principle of representation.

The direction taken by the condensations in the dream is pre-scribed on the one hand by the rational preconscious relations of the dream-thoughts, on the other by the attraction of the visual memories in the Unconscious. The work of condensation aims to produce those intensities required to break through to the perceptual systems.

(2) Again, intermediary ideas, rather like compromises (see the numerous examples), are created by the mobility with which these intensities can be freely transferred, also in the service of condensa-tion. This is something equally unheard of in the normal processing of ideas, where what matters most is the selection and retention of the 'right' element among them. By contrast, composite and com-promise formations occur with extraordinary frequency when we are searching for the words to express preconscious thoughts; these are described as varieties of 'slips of the tongue'.

(3) The ideas that transpose their intensities from one to the other have the *loosest relations* to one another, and are linked by associations of a kind scorned by our normal thinking and left to be exploited for

comic effect. In particular, verbal associations based on punning and similarities of sound are regarded as being equal in value to the others.

(4) Thoughts contradicting each other do not aim to cancel each other out, but persist side by side, often combining *as if there were no contradiction* into products of condensation, or they form compromises which we would never forgive our logical thinking for committing, but often approve of in our actions.

These are some of the most striking of the abnormal processes which the dream-thoughts, having previously had a rational form, undergo in the course of the dream-work. As we see, what chiefly characterizes them is the importance attached to making the charge of energy mobile and *capable of discharge*; the content and the proper meaning of the psychical elements carrying the charge become unimportant. One might still suppose that condensation and the formation of compromises take place only to help to bring about regression, if it is a matter of transforming thoughts into images. However, the analysis—and still more clearly the synthesis—of dreams that dispense with any regression to images, for example, the dream '*Autodidasker*—conversation with Professor N.', reveal the same processes of displacement and condensation as the rest.

Thus, we cannot deny the insight that two essentially different psychical processes play a part in forming dreams; the one creates perfectly rational dream-thoughts, just as valid as normal thinking; the other treats these in a most disconcerting, irrational manner. We have already isolated the second in Chapter VI as the true dream-work. What have we to say now about the origins of this second psychical process?

We could not give an answer at this point if we had not already gone some way into the psychology of neuroses, particularly of hysteria. From this we learn that the same irrational psychical processes—and others I have not enumerated—control the production of hysterical symptoms. In hysteria too we first discover a set of completely rational thoughts, entirely equal in validity to our conscious thoughts; but we are unable to find out anything about their existence in this form and can only reconstruct them in retrospect. If they make their way through to our perceptions at some place, we see from our analysis of the symptoms formed that these normal thoughts have undergone abnormal treatment, and *by means of condensation and compromise-formation, by way of superficial associations under cover of contradictions, and possibly along the path of regression, they have been transposed into the symptoms.* Given this total identity between the characteristics of the dream-work and the psychical activity whose outcome is psychoneurotic symptoms, we consider we are justified in carrying over to dreams the conclusions that hysteria forces us to draw.

From the theory of hysteria we take the following proposition: *a normal train of thought is subject to this kind of abnormal treatment only if an unconscious wish originating in infancy and in a state of repression has been transferred to it.* It is for the sake of this proposition that we have built our theory of the dream on the assumption that the wish motivating the dream always originates from the Unconscious—which, as we have admitted, cannot be proved to be universally applicable, though it cannot be disproved either. But to be able to say what '*repression*' is, a name we have played with so often, we will have to go on building our psychological scaffolding for a while longer.

We gave our attention to the fiction of a primitive psychical apparatus whose activity was regulated by the attempt to avoid the build-up of excitation and maintain itself as free of excitation as possible. That is why it was constructed along the lines of a reflex apparatus; the power of movement, which first of all provides a route to changes within the body, was the path of discharge at its disposal. We then discussed the psychical consequences of the experience of satisfaction, and in doing so, we could already have included our second assumption, that a build-up of excitation—following various modalities which need not concern us here—is felt as unpleasure, and puts the apparatus into action in order to restore the experience of satisfaction in which the reduction of excitation is felt as pleasure. A current of this kind in the apparatus, starting out from unpleasure and aiming for pleasure, we call a wish; we said that only a wish can set the apparatus in motion, and that the course of excitation in it is automatically regulated by the perceptions of pleasure and unpleasure. The first wishing was perhaps a hallucinatory charging of the memory of satisfaction. However, this hallucination, if it was not to be retained to the point of exhaustion, turned out to be no good at bringing about the cessation of the need, and hence the pleasure, bound up with the satisfaction.

This made a second activity—in our terms, the activity of a second system—necessary, which did not allow the memory-charge to get as far as perception and from there to bind the forces of the psyche, but diverts the excitation caused by the need along a detour; by way of voluntary movement, this indirect route ultimately alters the external world in such a way that a real perception of the object of satisfaction can come about. Up to this point we have been following our schematic plan of the psychical apparatus; the two systems are the germ of what we have put in place as the *Uncon.* and *Precon.* in the fully developed apparatus.

To be able to alter the external world effectively by movement, it is necessary to build up a large number of experiences in the memory-systems and to have a variety of firmly fixed associations that are summoned up in this memory-material by different purposive ideas. Let us now take our assumptions further. The activity of the second system, multifariously feeling its way, emitting charges of energy, withdrawing again, on the one hand needs to have all the memory-material freely at its disposal; on the other, it would be an unnecessary expense of effort if it were to send vast quantities of energy-charge along particular paths of thought, which would then discharge uselessly and reduce the quantity needed for altering the external world. I postulate, then, that it is for the sake of efficiency that the second system manages to keep the greater part of the energy-charges quiescent, and uses only a smaller part for displacement. The mechanics of these processes is quite unknown to me; anyone wanting to take these ideas seriously would have to look for analogies to them in physics and find a way of visualizing the process of movement as it occurs in the excitation of neurones. But I do maintain that the activity of the first ψ-system is directed towards *the free discharge of quantities of excitation*; and that the second system *inhibits* this discharge by emitting its own energy-charges, transforming the charge into a quiescent one and probably raising its level. I am assuming, then, that the discharge of excitation as governed by the second system is linked to quite different mechanical conditions from those present when governed by the first. Once the second system has ended its exploratory thought-activity, it also suspends its activity of inhibiting and damming the excitations, allowing them to be discharged in movement.

Some interesting thoughts arise if we look at the relation of this inhibition of discharge by the second system to regulation by the unpleasure principle. Let us consider the counterpart to the primary experience of satisfaction, the *experience of an external shock*. Suppose a perceptual stimulus, the source of an excitation of pain, impinges on the primitive apparatus. If so, this will be expressed in spasmodic movements until one of them removes the apparatus from the perception and at the same time from the pain; if the perception reappears, this process will promptly be repeated (as a movement of flight, say), until the perception has disappeared once more. But in this situation no inclination will remain to recharge the perception of the source of pain with hallucinatory, or any other kind of intensity. Rather, if this painful memory-image is aroused in some way, there will be an inclination in the primary apparatus to abandon it at once, for after all, any overflow of its excitation would call up unpleasure (or, more precisely, would begin to call it up). Turning away from the memory, which is only a repetition of the earlier flight from the perception, is made easier because, unlike the perception, the memory does not possess enough quality to excite consciousness and in this way attract a fresh charge of energy. This effortless and regular way the psychical process has of turning away from the memory of what was once painful offers us the model and the first example of *psychical repression*. It is widely recognized how much of this avoidance of what is painful—ostrich tactics—is still demonstrably to be found in the inner life of normal adults.

As a consequence of the unpleasure principle, then, the first ψ-system is utterly incapable of taking anything unpleasant into the context of its thoughts. All the system can do is wish. If this were to remain so, it would hamper the thinking-activity of the second system, which needs to have at its disposal all the memories laid down in experience. Two paths are now possible. Either the work of the second system frees itself completely from the unpleasure principle, and continues on its own way without bothering about the unpleasure roused by a memory; or it can charge the unpleasurable memory in such a way that the release of unpleasure is avoided. We can reject the first possibility, for the unpleasure principle is patently the regulator for the course of excitation in the second system. This leaves us with the second possibility: that this system is able to charge memories in such a way that they inhibit discharge, and thus also inhibit any discharge—comparable to the inhibition of a motor innervation—in the direction of the development of unpleasure. We have, then, two points of departure—the account taken of both the unpleasure principle and the principle of the least expenditure of innervation—leading us to the hypothesis that charging by the second system also represents an inhibition on the discharge of excitation. But let us hold on to the thought—it is the key to the theory of repression—*that the second system can only charge an idea if it is in a position to inhibit the development of unpleasure issuing from it.* Anything that might perhaps escape this inhibition would also be inaccessible to the second system, and as a consequence of the unpleasure principle would promptly be dropped. However, the inhibition of the unpleasure need not be total; the beginnings of unpleasure must be allowed, for they give the second system some indication of the nature of the memory and perhaps of its unsuitability for the purpose intended by the thinking-process.

I shall now give the name of *primary process* to the psychical process which the first system alone allows; and the one resulting from the inhibition imposed by the second system I shall call the *secondary process*. There is another point where I can show why the second system is bound to act as a corrective to the primary process. The primary process aims to discharge excitation in order to set up a *perceptual identity*, using the amount of excitation accumulated in this way to do so; the secondary process has abandoned this intention and taken up another in its place—to set up a *thought-identity*. All thinking is only a roundabout way from the memory of a satisfaction, adopted as its purposive idea, to an identical charge of the same memory, which, it is intended, will be regained by way of motor experiences. Thinking must interest itself in the connecting paths between ideas without allowing itself to be led astray by their intensities. But it is clear that condensations of ideas, intermediary and compromise-formations, are an obstacle to attaining this goal of identity; by replacing one idea with another, they diverge from the path that led on from the first. So in secondary thinking, processes of this kind are carefully avoided. It is also easy to see that the unpleasure principle also puts difficulties in the way of the thinking process in its pursuit of thought-identity, though otherwise the principle offers it very important clues. Thinking, then, must move towards freeing itself more and more from the exclusive regulation of the unpleasure principle, and towards limiting the development of affect by thought-activity to the minimum that can still function as a signal. This finer differentiation of functioning is meant to be achieved by a fresh supercharge, mediated by consciousness. But we are well aware that this is rarely a complete success, even in the most normal inner life, and that our thinking always remains vulnerable to falsification by interference from the unpleasure principle.

But this is not the flaw in the efficient functioning of our psychical apparatus that makes it possible for thoughts, which present themselves as the products of secondary thought-activity, to fall victim to the primary psychical process ('primary psychical process' is now the formula we can use to describe the activity that leads to dreams and to hysterical symptoms). Inefficiency arises from the encounter of two factors from our evolutionary history: the one devolves entirely onto the psychical apparatus, and has exercised a crucial influence on the relations between the two systems. But the other comes into its own fitfully, introducing driving-forces of organic origin into the inner life. Both have their origins in infancy, and are the deposit of the changes that our psychical and somatic organism has gone through since the time of childhood.

When I called a process in the psychical apparatus a *primary* one, it was not only with an eye to its place in a hierarchy or to its efficiency, but rather because in choosing this name I also wanted to include some reference to time. It is true, a psychical apparatus that would only possess the primary process does not to our knowledge exist, and to that extent it is a theoretical fiction; but we do know as a fact that the primary processes are present as a given from the start, while the secondary processes only develop gradually in the course of our life; they inhibit and overlay the primary processes, perhaps not attaining complete control over them until the prime of life. As a consequence of this belated entry of the secondary processes, the heart of our being, made of the unconscious wishful impulses, cannot be comprehended or inhibited by the Preconscious, whose function is restricted once and for all to indicating the most convenient paths to the wishful impulses from the Unconscious. These unconscious wishes exert a compulsion on all the psyche's later aims and efforts, which have to adapt themselves to this pressure, or labour to divert it, redirecting it to higher aims. As a further consequence of this belated appearance, a wide field of memory-material also remains inaccessible to preconscious charging.

Now among these wishful impulses originating in our infancy, which cannot be destroyed or inhibited, there are also some whose fulfilment is a contradiction to the purposive ideas pursued by secondary thinking. The fulfilment of these wishes would no longer produce an affect of pleasure, but of unpleasure, *and it is this very transformation of affect that makes up the nature of what we call 'repression'*. How a transformation of this kind occurs, what paths it takes, what motive forces drive it—these questions make up the problem of repression, which we need only touch upon here. It is enough for us to hold on to the idea that a transformation of affect of this sort occurs in the course of our development (we only have to think of the emergence in a child's life of disgust, which was absent at the start), and that it is linked to the activity of the second system. The memories that are the starting-point for the unconscious wish to summon the release of affect, were never accessible to the *Precon.*; that is why the release of the affect belonging to them cannot be inhibited either. Precisely because of this emergence of affect, these ideas are now inaccessible even from the preconscious thoughts onto which they have transferred their wishful force. On the contrary, the unpleasure principle takes over, and causes the *Precon.* to turn away from these transference-thoughts. These are left to themselves, 'repressed', and so it is that the presence of a store of infantile memories, unavailable to the *Precon.* from the start, becomes the prerequisite for repression.

In the most favourable cases, the production of unpleasure comes to an end as soon as the energy-charge is withdrawn from the transferred thoughts in the *Precon.* This successful result indicates that the intervention of the unpleasure principle has been effective. However, it is a different matter if the repressed unconscious wish experiences an organic reinforcement, which it lends to its transference-thoughts; doing so puts them in a position to attempt to force their way through with their excitation, even if they have lost their energy-charge from the *Precon.* A defensive struggle ensues, in which the *Precon.* reinforces the opposition to the repressed thoughts; there follows a breakthrough of the transference-thoughts, which are the vehicle of the unconscious wish, into some form of compromise by forming a symptom. But from the moment the repressed thoughts are powerfully charged with the unconscious wishful excitation, and on the other hand have been deserted by their preconscious charge, they are subject to the primary process, and their only aim is motor discharge or, if the way is open, hallucinatory revival of the desired perceptual identity. Earlier, we found empirically that the irrational processes we described only unfold with thoughts that are in a state of repression. Now we are able to understand yet another part of these relationships. These irrational processes are the *primary* ones in the psychical apparatus; they always make an appearance wherever imagined ideas are deserted by their preconscious charge and left to themselves, when they can be invested with the uninhibited energy of the Unconscious as it strives for discharge. There are, in addition, some other observations to support the view that these processes which I have called irrational are not falsifications of normal processes, not intellectual errors, but modes of activity of the psychical apparatus that are free of inhibition. Thus we can see that the shift from preconscious excitation to motor action follows the same processes, and that the attachment of preconscious imagined ideas to words can easily show the very same displacements and confusions which we normally ascribe to inattention. Finally, evidence of the increase in work that becomes necessary with the inhibition of these primary modes of functioning comes from the fact that we produce a comic effect, a surplus to be discharged in laughter, if we let these modes of functioning in our thinking force their way into consciousness.

The theory of the psychoneuroses maintains with absolute certainty that only wishful impulses from infancy that are sexual in nature and have been subject to repression (transformation of affect) are capable of revival in later periods of development, whether as a consequence of the individual's sexual constitution—which, of course, developed out of an original bisexuality—or as a consequence of unfavourable influences on his sex-life; if this is the case, they will provide the driving-force for the formation of all psychoneurotic symptoms. It is only by introducing these sexual forces that the demonstrable gaps in the theory of repression can be filled. I will leave it an open question whether sexual and infantile factors should also be required for the theory of dreams; I leave this theory unfinished at this point, for I have already taken a step beyond what can be demonstrated by assuming that dream-wishes always originate in the Unconscious.[9] Nor will I go any further in my investiga-

---

[9] Here as elsewhere, there are gaps in my treatment of the topic which I have left intentionally, because to fill them would require on the one hand too much effort, and on the other reliance on material alien to dreams. Thus, for example, I have avoided indicat-

tion into what makes the difference between the interplay of psychical forces in the formation of dreams and in the formation of hysterical symptoms; after all, we do not have accurate enough knowledge of one of the two objects of comparison. But there is another point which I regard as very important, and I will preface it by confessing that it is only for the sake of this point that I have included my entire discussion of the two psychical systems, with their modes of activity and repression. For it is not now a matter of whether my conception of these is halfway correct, or—easily possible in such difficult matters—whether it is skewed and incomplete. However much the interpretation of the psychical censorship and of the rational and the abnormal revisions of the dream-content may change, it will still hold good that processes of this kind are active in the formation of dreams, and are in essentials most closely analogous to the processes identified in the formation of hysterical symptoms. Now the dream is not a pathological phenomenon; it does not presuppose a disturbance of the psychical equilibrium; it does not leave any reduction in efficiency behind it. The objection that my own dreams and the dreams of my neurotic patients do not allow any conclusions to be drawn about the dreams of normal persons may well be dismissed without consideration. So when we argue from the phenomena to the forces driving them, we are recognizing that the psychical mechanism which the neurosis makes use of is not first created by a pathological disorder attacking the inner life, but is already present

---

ing whether I attach different meanings to the word 'suppressed' [*unterdrückt*] and the word 'repressed' [*verdrängt*]. I only need to make it clear that the latter emphasizes its affiliation to the Unconscious more strongly than the former. I have not gone into the closely related* problem of why the dream-thoughts undergo distortion by the censorship, even in cases where they give up their progressive movement towards consciousness and opt for the path of regression—and further such omissions. What I was chiefly concerned to do was to give some impression of those problems we are led towards by further analysis of the dream-work, and to indicate the other topics such analysis encounters on its way. I have not always found it easy to decide where to break off from pursuing them.—The fact that I have not dealt exhaustively with the part played by sexual ideas in dreams, and have avoided interpreting dreams with an obviously sexual content, has a particular reason, which may not coincide with the reader's expectations. It is utterly foreign to my opinions and the theoretical views I put forward in neuropathology to regard the sexual life as a shameful thing which neither physician nor scientist should be concerned with. And, in my opinion, the moral indignation that moved the translator of Artemidorus of Daldis [2] to withhold the chapter on sexual dreams from the reader is ridiculous. What decided me was solely the realization that in explaining sexual dreams I would have to become deeply involved in the still unsolved problems of perversion and bisexuality, and so I kept this material for another occasion.

in the normal structure of the psychical apparatus. The two psychical systems, the censorship on the transit between them, the inhibition and overlaying of one activity by the other, the relations of both to consciousness—or whatever a more correct interpretation of the actual circumstances may have to offer instead of these—all these belong to the normal structure of our psychical instrument, and dreams show us one of the ways leading to an understanding of that structure. If we are content with a minimum of completely guaranteed new knowledge, we will be able to say that dreams prove to us *that what is suppressed continues to exist in normal persons too, and remains capable of psychical functioning.* The dream itself is one of the expressions of what is suppressed; in theory, this is so in all cases; palpably and empirically it is so at least in a great number of instances, and these, in fact, display the striking characteristics of the dream-life at their clearest. In waking life, what is suppressed in the psyche is thwarted in its attempts at expression by the *removal of contradictions by their opposite** and cut off from internal perception; at night, and in the power of compromise-formations, it finds ways and means of forcing its way into consciousness.

*Flectere si nequeo superos, Acheronta movebo.**

By pursuing the analysis of dreams, we can get a little further in our understanding of how this most marvellous and mysterious instrument is composed; true, it is only a little further, but it is a beginning, enabling us to push on further in their analysis, starting from other formations which have to be described as pathological. For illnesses— at least those that are rightly called functional—do not have the destruction of this apparatus or the creation of new splittings within it for their precondition; they are to be explained *dynamically* by the strengthening and weakening of the components in the interplay of forces, so many of whose effects are hidden while they are functioning normally. I hope to show elsewhere how the composition of the apparatus out of the two agencies also allows a finer differentiation in normal functioning too, which would not be possible for one only.[10]

---

[10] Dreams are not the only phenomenon allowing us to base psychopathology on psychology. In a short series of articles, not yet completed, in the *Monatschrift für Psychiatrie und Neurologie* ('The Psychical Mechanism of Forgetfulness', 1898 [SE iii, 289]; 'Screen Memories' [SE iii, 301]) I attempt to interpret a number of everyday psychical phenomena in support of the same insight.

(f) *The Unconscious and Consciousness. Reality*

If we look more closely, it is not the existence of two systems near the motor end of the apparatus, but the existence of two different processes of excitation and two modes of its discharge that were suggested by our psychological discussions in the previous section. For us it would scarcely matter, for we must always be prepared to drop our provisional assumptions if we think we are in a position to replace them with something else closer to the unknown reality. Let us now try to correct some notions which could become misleading if we view the two systems in the crudest and most immediate sense as two locations within the psychical apparatus, notions that have left their mark in the terms 'repressing', or 'pushing back', and 'pushing through'. So when we say that an unconscious thought is aiming to be carried over into the Preconscious so that it can then push through to consciousness, we do not mean that a second thought is supposed to be formed in a new place, like a copy with the original existing concurrently with it. And as for pushing through to consciousness, let us also take care to detach it from any idea of a change of place. When we say a preconscious thought is pushed back and repressed, and then taken over by the Unconscious, we might be tempted by these images drawn from the sphere of ideas about battles for territory to assume that a constellation in one locality of the psyche is really being dissolved and replaced by a new one in the other locality. Instead of these metaphors, let us say what seems to correspond more closely to the real state of affairs: that a charge of energy is invested in a particular constellation, or is withdrawn from it, so that the psychical structure comes under the control of an agency, or is removed from it. Again, we are replacing a topographical mode of representation here by a dynamic one. What is mobile, it seems to us, is not the psychical formation, but rather its innervation.

All the same, I think it is useful and justifiable to keep this graphic way of representing the two systems. We will avoid any misuse of this mode of representation if we remind ourselves that ideas, thoughts, psychical formations generally are not to be located in organic elements of the nervous system at all, but, as it were, *between them*, where resistances and accesses form their corresponding correlatives. Everything that can become the object of our inner perception is *virtual*, like the image in the telescope made by the passage of light-rays. However, we are justified in assuming that the systems—which are not of a psychical nature themselves and will never be accessible to our psychical perception—are like the telescope lenses that create the image. If we continue this comparison, the censorship between the two systems would correspond to the refraction of a ray of light as it passes over into a new medium.

Up to now we have been psychologizing off our own bat. It is time to take a look at the theoretical opinions dominating contemporary psychology and examine how they relate to our propositions. The question of the Unconscious in psychology is, in Lipps's[11] forceful words, not so much a psychological question as *the* question of psychology. As long as psychology settled this question with the merely verbal explanation that 'the Psychical' was simply 'the Conscious', and 'unconscious psychical processes' were palpable nonsense, the door was closed to any psychological evaluation of the observations a physician was able to gain from abnormal psychical states. The physician and the philosopher will only meet when both recognize that 'unconscious psychical processes' is 'the most appropriate and considered expression for a well-established fact'. All the physician can do is to dismiss with a shrug of the shoulders the assertion that 'consciousness is the definitive characteristic of what is psychical', perhaps assuming, if his respect for the philosopher's remarks is still strong enough, that they have not been dealing with the same object nor pursuing the same science. For even one single perceptive observation of the inner life of a neurotic, one single analysis of a dream, is bound to urge upon him the unshakable conviction that it is possible for the most complicated and logical thought-processes, which cannot after all be denied the name of psychical processes, to occur without arousing the person's consciousness. Certainly, the physician does not learn of these unconscious processes until they have exercised some effect upon consciousness that can be communicated or observed. But this effect upon consciousness can display a psychical character that is wholly at variance with the unconscious process, so that it is impossible for our internal perception to recognize the one as a substitute for the

[11] 'The Concept of the Unconscious in Psychology', Lecture held at the Third International Congress for Psychology in Munich, 1897.

other. The physician must maintain his right to use an *inferential method* to make his way from the effect on consciousness to the unconscious psychical process; on his way he learns that the effect on consciousness is only a remote psychical effect of the unconscious process, and that the latter has not become conscious as such; also that it was present and in operation without revealing itself to consciousness in any way.

The essential preliminary to true insight into the psyche's way of working is to get away from overestimating the attribute of consciousness. The Unconscious must, as Lipps puts it, be assumed to be the general basis of the life of the psyche. The Unconscious is the greater sphere that includes the smaller sphere of the Conscious; everything conscious has a prior stage that is unconscious, whereas the Unconscious can remain at this stage and still claim to have the full value of a psychical function. The Unconscious is the true reality of the psyche, *its inner nature just as unknown to us as the reality of the external world, and just as imperfectly revealed by the data of consciousness as the external world is by the information received from our sensory organs.*

Now that the old antithesis between conscious life and the life of dreams as the psychical Unconscious has been put in place, a number of the problems of dreams, which were still profoundly engaging the earlier authors, have been removed. So many feats performed in dreams which made them marvel are now no longer to be credited to dreams, but to unconscious thinking, which is also active by day. If, as Scherner says, dreams seem to play with a symbolizing representation of the body, this is the feat of certain unconscious fantasies, which probably arise in response to sexual impulses, and are expressed not only in dreams but also in hysterical phobias and other symptoms. If a dream continues the work of the day and completes it, and even has valuable ideas and brings them to light, all we have to do is simply divest it of its dream-disguise as being the achievement of the dream-work and a sign of assistance from the dark powers in the depths of our soul (cf. the Devil in Tartini's* sonata dream). The intellectual feat itself is due to the same psychical powers that achieve all such feats during the day. We are probably far too much inclined to overestimate the conscious character even of intellectual or artistic production. However, from what some highly productive people, such as Goethe and

Helmholtz* tell us, we learn rather that the new and essential elements of their creations came into their mind suddenly and entered their perception almost complete. There is nothing odd about the contribution of consciousness in other instances where the efforts of all the mental powers were required. But it is the much-abused privilege of consciousness that, wherever it has a share, it conceals from us all the other activities of the psyche.

It is scarcely worth proposing the historical significance of dreams as a particular topic. Cases where a dream caused some commander to undertake a great enterprise whose success changed the course of history only present a new problem if we treat the dream as an alien force in contrast to other, more familiar psychical powers; but no longer if we regard the dream as a form of expression for impulses which are hampered by resistance by day, but are able to draw reinforcements from deep sources of excitation by night. But the respect ancient peoples paid to dreams is a tribute, based on a true psychological intimation, to the untamed, indestructible elements in the human soul, the *daemonic* powers* that produce the dream-wish and that we rediscover in our Unconscious.

I say '*in our Unconscious*' deliberately, for what we have given this name to is not identical with the Unconscious of the philosophers, not even with the Unconscious as Lipps conceives it. To the philosophers, it is simply meant to denote the opposite of the conscious. Lipps goes further and tells us that everything psychical is present in an unconscious state, and some of that is also present in a state of consciousness. But it is not as evidence for *this* proposition that we have called on the phenomena of dreams and the formation of hysterical symptoms; observation of our everyday life alone is enough to establish it beyond any doubt. The new thing we have learned from our analysis of psychopathological formations, indeed, from the first of the series, the dream, is that the Unconscious—that is, the essential nature of the psyche—occurs as the function of two separate systems, and does so in normal psychical life. Thus there are *two kinds of Unconscious* which, we find, the psychologists have not yet distinguished. Both are unconscious as psychology understands the term; but in our conception, the one we have called *Uncon.* is also *incapable of reaching consciousness*, whereas we have called the other *Precon.* because, although it is true it has to keep to certain rules, and may have to submit to a fresh censorship, its excitations are able to reach consciousness—still without taking account of the

Uncon.-system. The fact that, in order to reach consciousness, the excitations have to make their way through an immutable sequence of agencies, which we discovered from the changes imposed by the censorship they exercised, enabled us to set up a spatial analogy. We described the relations of the two systems to each other and to consciousness by saying that the *Precon.*-system stood like a partition-screen between the *Uncon.*-system and consciousness. The *Precon.*-system did not only block access to consciousness, we said, it also governed access to voluntary movement and directed the transmission of a mobile energy-charge, a part of which is familiar to us in the form of attention.

We also have to distance ourselves from the distinction between *supraconsciousness* and *subconsciousness* which has become so popular in recent literature on the psychoneuroses, as this above all seems to emphasize that what is psychical and what is conscious enjoy equal status.

What role is left in our account for once-omnipotent consciousness, which hid everything else from sight? No more than *that of a sensory organ for perceiving psychical qualities*. In accordance with the ideas at the basis of our attempted scheme, we can only conceive conscious perception as a function peculiar to a particular system, to which we may appropriately give the abbreviation *Con*. We conceive this system to be similar in its mechanical characteristics to the perception-system *Per.*, that is, susceptible to excitation by qualities and incapable of retaining any trace of alteration, that is, without memory. The psychical apparatus, which is turned towards the external world with the sensory organ of the *Per.*-systems, is itself the external world for the sensory organ of the *Con.*, which has its teleological justification in this state of affairs. Here again we encounter the principle of a series of agencies that seems to govern the structure of the apparatus. The excitatory material flows to the sensory organ of the *Con.* from two directions: from the *Per.*-system, where its excitation, determined by the qualities, probably undergoes fresh revision until it becomes a conscious sensation; and from within the apparatus itself, where the quantitative processes are felt qualitatively as the series pleasure–unpleasure, once they have achieved certain alterations.

Those philosophers who became aware that rational and highly composed thought-formations are possible even without a contribution from consciousness then had difficulties in ascribing any function to consciousness; it seemed to them to be a needless mirror-image of the completed psychical process. We are rescued from this embarrassment by the analogy between our *Con.*-system and the perceptual systems, for we can see that perception by our sensory organs has the result of directing a charge of attention towards the paths where the approaching sensory excitation is spread; the qualitative excitation of the *Per.*-system serves to regulate the discharge of the mobile quantity in the psychical apparatus. We can claim the same function for the overlying sensory organ of the *Con.*-system. In perceiving new qualities, it makes a new contribution to directing the mobile quantities of energy-charge, and to distributing them suitably. By its perception of pleasure and unpleasure, it influences the course of the energy-charges within the psychical apparatus, which otherwise operates unconsciously and by means of displacement of quantities. It is probable that at first the displacement of energy-charge is regulated automatically by the unpleasure principle, but it is quite possible that consciousness of these qualities adds a second, and finer, regulation, which can even be at odds with the first, completing the efficiency of the apparatus by enabling it, quite contrary to its original disposition, to submit even what is connected with the release of unpleasure to the processes of energy-charge and revision. We learn from the psychology of neuroses that a major part in the functioning of the apparatus is assigned to this regulation by the qualitative excitations of the sensory organs. The automatic domination of the primary unpleasure principle and the restriction of efficiency this involves are broken by the processes of sensory regulation, which are themselves automatic actions. We learn that repression, which originally served a purpose but nevertheless ends in a harmful loss of inhibition and inner control, is more easily brought to bear on memories than on perceptions, because they cannot receive any additional energy-charge from the excitation of the psychical sensory organ. If a thought to be fended off does not enter consciousness on the one hand because it is subject to repression, it can at other times only be repressed because it has been withdrawn from conscious perception for other reasons. These are the hints we make use of in our therapy to reverse the course of repressions that have already taken place.

From a teleological standpoint, the value of a supercharge of energy, which is produced by the regulatory influence of the *Con.* sensory organ on the mobile quantities, cannot be better demonstrated than by its ability to create a new series of qualities and thereby a new regulatory process—which is what constitutes the superiority of human beings over animals. For thought-processes are in themselves without quality, apart from the pleasurable and unpleasurable excitations accompanying them, which, as possible disturbances to thought, are after all meant to be kept within bounds. In order to invest them with some quality, they are associated in human beings with verbal memories, whose residual quality is sufficient to attract the attention of consciousness to them, which will then invest the thinking with a fresh charge of mobile energy.

We can only gain an overall view of the problems of consciousness in all their variety when we analyse hysterical thought-processes. When we do, we have the impression that the charge passing from the Preconscious to consciousness is also associated with a censorship similar to the censorship between *Uncon.* and *Precon.* This censorship too only sets in when a certain quantitative limit is reached, so that less intense thought-formations escape it. All the possible cases in which thoughts refuse to enter consciousness, or force their way into it only under limitations, are to be found together within the framework of psychoneurotic phenomena; they all point to the intimate reciprocal relationship between censorship and consciousness. I will close these psychological reflections with a report of two examples that illustrate this.

A consultation last year took me to an intelligent and unembarrassed-looking girl. Her style of dressing is disconcerting; where women's clothes are normally attended to down to the last pleat, one of her stockings is hanging down and two buttons of her blouse are open. She complains about having pains in one leg, and exposes her calf without being asked. But her main complaint, in her own words, is: *she has a feeling in her body as if something were sticking in it that is moving to and fro and shaking her through and through. When that happens, her whole body seems to grow stiff.* My colleague, also present, catches my eye; he has no difficulty in understanding her complaint. It seems remarkable to both of us that the patient's mother seems to make nothing of it, though she must have found herself repeatedly in the situation that her daughter is describing. The girl herself has no idea of the meaning of what she is saying; if she had, she would not utter it. In her case, the censorship has been successfully obscured, so that a fantasy that would otherwise remain in the Preconscious is admitted into consciousness under the seemingly innocuous mask of a complaint.

Another example. I begin the psychoanalytic treatment of a fourteen-year-old boy suffering from *tic convulsif*, hysterical vomiting, headaches, and the like by assuring him that when he closes his eyes he will see images, or ideas will come into his mind which he should tell me. He answers in images. The last impression he had before he came to me is revived visually in his memory. He had been playing a board game with his uncle, and now sees the board in front of him. He considers various positions that are favourable or unfavourable, moves that one should not make. Then he sees a dagger lying on the board, an object which his father owns, but which his imagination has removed onto the board. Then there is a sickle on the board, then it is joined by a scythe, and now the image of an old farmer makes its appearance, mowing the grass in front of the boy's faraway home with a scythe. After a few days I came to understand this sequence of images. Unhappy family circumstances have upset the boy. A harsh, irascible father, constantly quarrelling with his mother, with a method of bringing up his son by threats; his father's divorce of his gentle, tender mother; the remarriage of his father, who brought a young woman home one day to be his new mama. It was in the first days after this happened that the fourteen-year-old's illness broke out. The suppressed rage against his father composed those images into intelligible allusions. A recollection from mythology provided the material. The sickle is the one Zeus used to castrate his father, the scythe and the image of the farmer represent Cronos, the violent old man who devours his children, and on whom Zeus takes such unfilial revenge. The father's marriage was an occasion to throw back at him the accusations and threats which the boy had previously heard from him because he had been *playing* with his genitals (the board game; the forbidden moves; the dagger one can use to kill). In this case, it is long-repressed memories and their unconscious offspring that have slipped into consciousness by the roundabout routes opened up to them in the form of *apparently meaningless images*.

I would, then, look for the theoretical value of an interest in dreams in the contributions it makes to our psychological knowledge and in the start it makes towards our understanding of the psycho-neuroses. Who can guess how important a thorough acquaintance with the structure and functions of a psychical apparatus may become, when even the present-day state of our knowledge enables our therapies to have a fortunate influence on the essentially curable forms of psychoneuroses? And what of the practical value of this interest, I hear it asked, for our knowledge of the psyche, and for the revelation of hidden character traits in the individual? Do not the unconscious impulses revealed in dreams possess the value of real forces in our inner life? Is the ethical significance of our suppressed wishes to be treated as an unconsidered trifle, for just as they create dreams, they may one day create other things?

I do not feel justified in answering these questions. My thoughts have not pursued the problem of dreams under this aspect. I only think that, in any case, the Roman Emperor was wrong to have his subject put to death because he dreamed he had murdered his Emperor. He should have been concerned first with what the dream meant; most likely it was not the same as it appeared to be. And even if a dream with a different tenor had this treasonable meaning, it would still be fitting for us to bear Plato's observation in mind, that the virtuous man is content to dream what the wicked man actually does. In my view, then, it is best to absolve dreams. Whether we should ascribe *reality* to unconscious wishes, I cannot say. Of course we cannot grant it to any of the transitional or intermediary thoughts. Looking at these unconscious wishes reduced to their ultimate, their truest expression, we must bear in mind that what has psychical reality too can have more than just one form of existence.* To answer our practical need to judge men's characters, their actions and consciously uttered opinions are mostly sufficient. Actions, above all, deserve to be put in the forefront, for many impulses which have forced their way through to consciousness are still often annulled by real forces in our inner life before they have issued in action; indeed, that is why they often do not encounter any psychical obstacle on their way, because the Unconscious is certain they will be prevented at another point. It is still instructive in any case to get to know the much-disturbed soil on which our virtues proudly grow. The complexity of a human character, moved dynamically this way and that, can very seldom be resolved by deciding between simple alternatives, as our superannuated morality would have it.

And what of the value of dreams for our knowledge of the future? Of course that is out of the question. Instead, one should rather ask: for our knowledge of the past. For in every sense, dreams come from the past. It is true, the ancient belief that dreams show us the future is not entirely without some truth. For by representing a wish as fulfilled, a dream does indeed take us into the future; but this future, taken by the dreamer to be in the present, is shaped by the indestructible wish into the image of that past.

FREUD'S BIBLIOGRAPHY*

1. **Aristotle.** *Ueber Träume und Traumdeutungen.* Trans. by Bender.
2. **Artemidorus.** *Symbolik der Träume.* Trans. by Friedrich S. Krauss. Vienna 1881.
3. **Benini, V.** 'La memoria e la durata dei sogni'. *Rivista italiana di filosofia.* XIIa. 1898.
4. **Binz, C.** *Ueber den Traum.* Bonn 1878.
5. **Börner, J.** *Das Alpdrücken, seine Begründung und Verhütung.* Würzburg 1855.
6. **Bradley, F. H.** 'On the failure of movement in dream'. *Mind.* III. 1894.
7. **Brander, R.** *Der Schlaf und das Traumleben.* Leipzig 1884.
8. **Burdach, K. F.** *Die Physiologie als Erfahrungswissenschaft,* vol. III. 3rd edn. 1826–32.
9. **Büchsenschütz, B.** *Traum und Traumdeutung im Alterthum.* Berlin 1868.
10. **Chaslin, P.** 'Du rôle du rêve dans l'évolution du délire'. Thesis, Paris 1887.
11. **Chabaneix, P.** *Physiologie cerebrale: Le subconscient chez les artistes, les savants et les écrivains.* Paris 1897.
12. **Calkins, Mary Whiton.** 'Statistics of dreams'. *Amer. J. of Psychology.* V. 1893.
13. **Clavière.** 'La rapidité de la pensée dans le rêve'. *Revue philosophique.* XLIII. 1897.
14. **Dandolo, G.** *La coscienza nel sonno.* Padua 1889.
15. **Delage, Yves.** 'Une théorie du rêve'. *Revue industrielle,* II. 1891.
16. **Delboeuf, J.** *Le sommeil et les rêves.* Paris 1885.
17. **Debacker, F.** 'Des hallucinations et terreurs nocturnes des enfants'. Thesis, Paris 1881.
18. **Dugas, L.** 'Le souvenir du rêve'. *Revue philosophique.* XLIV. 1897.
19. —— 'Le sommeil et la cérébration inconsciente durant le sommeil'. *Revue philosophique.* XLIII. 1897.
20. **Egger, V.** 'La durée apparente des rêves'. *Revue philosophique.* XL. 1895.
21. —— 'Le souvenir dans le rêve'. *Revue philosophique.* XLVI. 1898.
22. **Ellis, Havelock.** 'On dreaming of the dead'. *The Psychological Review.* II, No. 5. September 1895.
23. —— 'The stuff that dreams are made of'. *Appleton's Popular Science Monthly.* LIV. April 1899.

24. **Ellis, Havelock.** 'A note on hypnagogic paramnesia'. *Mind*. VI. 1897.

25. **Fechner, G. T.** *Elemente der Psychophysik.* 2nd edn. 2 vols. Leipzig 1889.

26. **Fichte, I. H.** *Psychologie. Die Lehre vom bewussten Geiste des Menschen.* 2 vols. Part I. Leipzig 1864.

27. **Giessler, M.** *Aus den Tiefen des Traumlebens.* Halle 1890.

28. —— *Die physiologischen Beziehungen der Traumvorgänge.* Halle 1896.

29. **Goblot, E.** 'Sur le souvenir des rêves'. *Revue philosophique.* XLII. 1896.

30. **Graffunder, P. C.** *Traum und Traumdeutung.* 1894.

31. **Griesinger, W.** *Pathologie und Therapie der psychischen Krankheiten.* 3rd edn. Stuttgart 1871.

32. **Haffner, P.** 'Schlafen und Träumen'. *Frankfurter zeitgemässe Brochüren.* Vol. 5, no. 10. 1884.

33. **Hallam, F. and S. Weed.** 'A study of the dream consciousness'. *Amer. J. of Psychology.* VII. 1896.

34. **Hervey de Saint-Denys, Marquis d'.** *Les rêves et les moyens de les diriger.* Paris 1867. (anonym.)

35. **Hildebrandt, F. W.** *Der Traum und seine Verwerthung für's Leben.* Leipzig 1875.

36. **Jessen, P.** *Versuch einer wissenschaftlichen Begründung der Psychologie.* Berlin 1855.

37. **Jodl, F.** *Lehrbuch der Psychologie.* Stuttgart 1896.

38. **Kant, J.** *Anthropologie in pragmatischer Hinsicht.* Kirchmann edn. Leipzig 1880.

39. **Krauss, A.** 'Der Sinn im Wahnsinn'. *Allgemeine Zeitschrift für Psychiatrie.* XV and XVI. 1858–9.

40. **Ladd, G. T.** 'Contribution to the psychology of visual dreams'. *Mind.* I. 1892.

41. **Leidesdorf, M.** *Das Traumleben.* Vienna 1880.—*Sammlung der 'Alma Mater'.*

42. **Lemoine, A.** *Du sommeil au point de vue physiologique et psychologique.* Paris 1855.

43. **Liébeault, A.** *Le sommeil provoqué et les états analogues.* Paris 1889.

44. **Lipps, T.** *Grundthatsachen des Seelenlebens.* Bonn 1883.

45. **Le Lorrain, J.** 'Le rêve'. *Revue philosophique.* XL. 1895.

46. **Maudsley, H.** *Physiology and the Pathology of Mind.* 2nd edn. London 1868.

47. **Maury, A.** 'Nouvelles observations sur les analogies des phénomènes du rêve et de l'aliénation mentale'. *Annales méd. psych.* 1855.

48. —— *Le sommeil et les rêves.* Paris 1878.

49. **Moreau, J.** 'De l'identité de l'état de rêve et de folie'. *Annales méd. psych.* I. 1855.

50. **Nelson, J.** 'A study of dreams'. *Amer. J. of Psychology.* I, 1888.

51. **Pilcz, A.** 'Ueber eine gewisse Gesetzmäßigkeit in den Träumen'. Author's abstract in *Monatsschrift für Psychologie und Neurologie.* V. 1899.

52. **Pfaff, E. R.** *Das Traumleben und seine Deutung nach den Principien der Araber, Perser, Griechen, Indier und Aegypter.* Leipzig 1868.

53. **Purkinje, J. E.** 'Wachen, Schlaf, Traum und verwandte Zustände', in Wagner's *Handwörterbuch der Physiologie.* vol. 3. Braunschweig 1846.

54. **Radestock, P.** *Schlaf und Traum.* Leipzig 1879.

55. **Robert, W.** *Der Traum als Naturnothwendigkeit erklärt.* Hamburg 1886.

56. **Sanctis, Sante de.** 'Les maladies mentales et les rêves'. Extrait des *Annales de la Societé de médecine de Gand.* LXXVI. 1897.

57. —— 'Sui rapporti d'identità, di somiglianza, di analogia e di equiva- lenza fra sogno e pazzia'. *Rivista quindicinale di Psicologia, Psichia- tria, Neuropatologia.* 15 Nov. 1897.

58. **Scherner, K. A.** *Das Leben des Traums.* Berlin 1861.

59. **Scholz, F.** *Schlaf und Traum.* Leipzig 1887.

60. **Schopenhauer, A.** 'Versuch über das Geistersehen und was damit zusammenhängt'. *Parerga und Paralipomena*, 2nd edn. Berlin, vol. I, 1862.

61. **Schleiermacher, F.** *Psychologie, Gesammelte Werke*, ed. L. George. vol. VI, pt. 3. Berlin 1862.

62. **Siebeck, H.** *Das Traumleben der Seele.* Berlin 1877.

63. **Simon, M.** *Le monde des rêves.* Paris 1888. Bibliothèque scientifique contemporaine.

64. **Spitta, H.** *Die Schlaf- und Traumzustände der menschlichen Seele.* 2nd edn., Tübingen 1892.

65. **Stumpf, E. J. G.** *Der Traum und seine Deutung.* Leipzig 1899.

66. **Strümpell, L.** *Die Natur und Entstehung der Träume.* Leipzig 1877.

67. **Tannery, M. P.** 'Sur la mémoire dans le rêve'. *Revue philosophique.* XLV. 1898.

68. **Tissié, P.** *Les rêves, physiologie et pathologie.* Paris 1898. Bibliothèque de philosophie contemporaine.

69. **Titchener, E. B.** 'Taste dreams'. *Amer. J. of Psychology.* VI. 1895.

70. **Thomayer, S.** 'Sur la signification de quelques rêves'. *Revue neu- rologique.* No. 5, 1897.

71. **Vignoli, T.** *Von den Träumen, Illusionen und Hallucinationen.* Inter- nationale wissenschaftliche Bibliothek. Vol. 47.

72. **Volkelt, J.** *Die Traum-phantasie.* Stuttgart 1875.

73. **Vold, J. Mourly.** *Expériences sur les rêves et en particulier sur ceux d'origine musculaire et optique.* Christiania 1896. Report in *Revue philosophique.* XLII. 1896.

74. ——*Einige Experimente über Gesichtsbilder im Traum.* Report on Third international Congress for Psychology in Munich, *Zeitschrift für Psychol. Sinnesorgane.* XIII. 1897.

75. **Weygandt, W.** *Entstehung der Träume.* Leipzig 1893.

76. **Wundt, W.** *Grundzüge der physiologischen Psychologie.* 2 vols. 2nd edn. 1880.

77. **Stricker, S.** *Studien über das Bewusstsein.* Vienna 1879.

78. —— *Studien über die Association der Vorstellungen.* Vienna 1883.

POSTSCRIPT

Only as I was correcting the final proofs in September 1899, I learned of a short work, *Induktive Untersuchungen über die Fundementalgesetze der psychischen Phenomene* [*Inductive Investigations into the Fundamental Laws of Psychical Phenomena*] by Dr C. Ruths, 1898, announcing a larger work on the analysis of dreams. From what the author has indicated, I may expect that on many points his results will agree with mine.

EXPLANATORY NOTES

Any annotator of *The Interpretation of Dreams* owes a great debt to Alexander Grinstein, who in his book *On Sigmund Freud's Dreams* (Detroit, 1968) has tenaciously pursued many of the literary and other allusions and summarized some of the lesser-known books to which Freud refers. Much of the historical material is elucidated by William McGrath in *Freud's Discovery of Pycho-analysis* (Ithaca, NY, 1986).

1 [Epigraph] *'Flectere si . . . movebo'*: Virgil, *Aeneid* vii. 313: 'If Heaven I cannot bend, then Hell I will arouse.' Freud took this motto, not directly from Virgil, but from a political text by Ferdinand Lassalle (1825–64) on the Austro–Italian War of 1859.

7 *Aristotle*: Greek philosopher (384–322 BC). The number in square brackets following the title refers to the entry in Freud's original Bibliography (pp. 413–16).

8 *Schelling*: Friedrich Wilhelm Joseph Schelling (1775–1854), a leading post-Kantian philosopher, established himself with his early treatise *On the World-Soul* (1798) as an exponent of 'Naturphilosophie' which sought to understand the natural world as the harmonious expression of an indwelling spiritual force.

10 *. . . ou fait*: 'We dream about what we have seen, said, desired, or done.'

Xerxes: this story is told by Herodotus (*c*.490–425 BC) in Book VII of his *Histories*. The King of Persia, Xerxes, when preparing to invade Greece, was terrified by ominous dreams. His counsellor Artabanus told him: you say that you're being haunted by a dream figure, the emissary of some god, who refuses to let you cancel the expedition. In actual fact, though, dreams don't come from the gods, my son. I have lived many more years than you, so I can explain what these dreams are that drift into us. The visions that occur to us in dreams are, more often than not, the things we have been concerned about during the day. And, you see, we have been extremely occupied with this expedition for some days now.' (Trans. Robin Waterfield, Oxford World Classics edn. (Oxford, 1998), 413–14).

11 *Lucretius*: Titus Lucretius Carus (*c*.100–*c*.55 BC), author of the philosophical poem *On the Nature of the Universe*, devoted to explaining the universe in purely natural terms without need for gods. Quotation from iv. 962 ff.:

> And those pursuits which most we love to follow,
> The things in which just now we have been engaged,
> The mind being thus the more intent upon them,
> These are most oft the substance of our dreams.

Lawyers argue their cases and make laws,
Generals fight battles, leading troops to war . . .

(trans. Ronald Melville, Oxford World's Classics edn. (Oxford, 1999), 127).

11 *Cicero*: Marcus Tullius Cicero (106–43 BC), Roman orator and states-man. *De divinatione* ('On Divination', composed *c*.44 BC) is a dialogue undermining belief in predicting the future by dreams, augury, or other forms of divination. Quotation: 'It is chiefly the remains of those things we have thought about or done during the day that are moved and agitated in our souls.'

14 *Scaliger*: Julius Caesar Scaliger (1484–1558) and his son Joseph Justus Scaliger (1540–1609), important classical scholars.

19 *. . . au jour*: 'That every impression, even the most insignificant, leaves an unalterable trace, indefinitely capable of reappearing.'

23 *June days of 1848*: the suppression of a revolutionary uprising in Paris.

24 *infernal machine*: an explosive device used in warfare.

the Tagliamento: a river in Friuli in northern Italy; Napoleon had this dream when, as commander-in-chief of French forces under the Directory, he fought a campaign against the Austrians in Lombardy, which was then under Austrian rule.

Robespierre . . . Fouquier-Tinville: Maximilien de Robespierre (1753–94) and Jean-Paul Marat (1763–93), leaders of the French Revolution; Antoine-Quentin Fouquier-Tinville (1746–95), public prosecutor during the Reign of Terror.

25 *. . . exclusive*: 'a certain affinity, but which is not unique or exclusive'.

27 *Gulliver's Travels*: in this satire (1726) by Jonathan Swift (1667–1745), Gulliver's second voyage takes him to the giants of Brobdingnag, his fourth to the intelligent and virtuous horses (Houyhnhnms) who keep humans (Yahoos) as domestic animals.

32 *Schopenhauer*: Arthur Schopenhauer (1788–1860), the philosopher of pessimism and author of *The World as Will and Idea* (1819) and *Parerga and Paralipomena* (1851). The latter includes 'Versuch über das Geistersehen und was damit zusammenhängt' ('Essay on Seeing Spirits and Related Matters'), to which Freud is referring.

37 *. . . de dehors*: 'Dreams of purely psychic origin do not exist . . . the thoughts of our dreams come to us from outside . . .'

41 *'. . . bonnes methodes'*: '. . . the observation of dreams involves special difficulties, and the only way to avoid all errors in such a case is to set down on paper without the least delay whatever one has just felt and noticed; otherwise partial or complete forgetfulness takes over; total forgetfulness is not important; but partial forgetting is treacherous; for if one sets out straight away to recount what is not forgotten, one is

tempted to use the imagination to complete the fragments provided by memory . . . one becomes an artist unwittingly, and the narrative, periodically repeated, imposes itself on its author's own belief, and in all good faith he presents it as authenticated fact, duly established in accordance with proper technique . . .'

42 *'a dream came to me'* . . . *'I dreamed'*: the impersonal formulation in German is 'mir hat geträumt', as distinct from the form with the active subject, 'ich habe geträumt' (J.C.).

48 *'. . . absurdité'*: 'there are no absolutely rational dreams, which do not contain some incoherence, anachronism, absurdity.'

'. . . spirituel': 'The dream is the anarchy of the psyche, the emotions, and the mind, it is the play of functions that are left to their own devices, acting without control and without purpose; in the dream the mind is a spiritual automaton.'

'. . . somniare': 'Nothing can be imagined that is so absurd, so incoherent, or so bizarre that we are not able to dream it.'

49 *Charles XII. . . Pultava*: at the battle of Poltava in 1709, Russian forces inflicted a massive though not final defeat on the ambitious Swedish king Charles XII (1682–1718).

'. . . et raisonnante': 'The production of these images, which in the waking man are usually the product of the will, is the intellectual equivalent of those movements, in the sphere of motility, which are to be seen in cases of chorea and paralytic illnesses . . . a whole series of degradations of the thinking and reasoning faculty.'

51 *'. . . idées'*: '(1) a spontaneous and, as it were, automatic mental action; (2) a perverse and irregular association of ideas.'

52 *'. . . irraison pur'*: 'The dream is neither wholly unreasonable nor wholly irrational.'

'. . . les anges': 'In sleep, apart from perception all the mental faculties—intelligence, imagination, memory, will, morality—remain essentially intact; only they apply themselves to imaginary and unstable objects. The dreamer is an actor who plays at will fools and wise men, executioners and victims, dwarfs and giants, devils and angels.'

53 *'. . . du fait présent'*: 'The Marquis d'Hervey allows the intelligence, during sleep, all of its liberty of action and attention, and seems to think that sleep consists only in the shutting-off of the senses, their separation from the external world; so that according to his view the sleeping man is hardly different from the man who lets his mind wander while closing off his senses; the only difference marking off ordinary thinking from that of the dreamer is that the latter's ideas take on a visible, objective form which could be mistaken for that which is caused by external objects; memory takes on the appearance of an actual event.'

53 '... *l'éveillé*': 'there is a further and most important distinction, in that the intellectual faculties of the sleeper do not have the same stability that they have in the man who is awake.'

54 *Schubert*: Gotthilf Heinrich Schubert (1780–1860), a physician who helped to popularize Schelling's 'Naturphilosophie' and strongly influenced later Romantic writers through his *Views of the Night-Side of the Natural Sciences* (1808) and *The Symbolism of Dreams* (1814).

the younger Fichte: Immanuel Hermann Fichte (1796–1879), son and editor of the philosopher Johann Gottlieb Fichte, and himself a noted philosopher and theologian. Freud quotes from his *Psychologie* (1864).

57 *Kant's categorical imperative*: formulated in Kant's *Groundwork of the Metaphysics of Morals* (1785) and developed in his *Critique of Practical Reason* (1788), this is the moral injunction to act only according to principles which one thinks universally binding.

59 ... *is a murderer*: 1 John 3: 15.

... *evil thoughts*: Matthew 15: 19.

60 *Kant*: editors have been unable to find this passage in the *Anthropologie* (1804). In the section headed 'On involuntary poetry in a healthy state, i.e. on the dream', Kant follows the Enlightenment tendency to explain dreams by physiological stimuli. Elsewhere Kant describes dreams disparagingly as 'nothing but wild and distasteful chimeras' in which 'ideas of the imagination are tossed together with those of the external senses': *Dreams of a Spirit-Seer* (1766).

'... *vengono dinanzi*': 'Some of our desires which we believed had been suppressed and extinguished for a time are reawakened; old, dead passions come back to life; things and people we never think about appear before us.'

62 '... *à réfouler*': 'It is our inclinations which speak and make us act, without conscience holding us back, although sometimes it gives us warning. I have my faults and wicked inclinations; while awake, I try to struggle against them and usually manage not to give way to them. But in my dreams I always give way, or to put it better, I act according to their commands, without fear or remorse ... Clearly the visions which appear before my mind and constitute the dream are suggested to me by the impulses whose effects I feel, and which my absent willpower does not try to suppress.'

'*En rêve ... dans le rêve*'. 'In dreaming man is revealed to himself in all his nakedness and native wretchedness. As soon as he suspends the exercise of his will he becomes the plaything of all the passions from which, when awake, he is defended by conscience, his sense of honour, and fear ... In dreaming, it is above all the instinctive man who is revealed ... Man returns, so to speak, to the state of nature when he dreams; but the less his mind has been influenced by acquired ideas, the more it is still under the influence of inclinations that clash with them in the dream.'

65 *Mephisto*: in the scene 'Faust's study (I)' in Goethe's *Faust, Part One* (1808), the devil Mephistopheles complains: 'The earth, | The air, the water, all give birth: | It germinates a thousandfold, | In dry or wet, in hot or cold!' (trans. David Luke, Oxford World's Classics edn. (Oxford, 1987); all subsequent quotations are from this version).

68 '. . . *odieuse*': 'If they were deeply in love they almost never dreamed about one another before marriage or during the honeymoon; and if they had erotic dreams they were of being unfaithful with some indifferent or unattractive person.'

    . . . *ressorts tendus*: 'so many wound-up springs'.

69 '. . . *le sommeil*': 'In short, the dream is the product of the mind wandering without purpose and direction, fastening in turn upon such thoughts as have retained enough strength to put themselves in its way and arrest its course, establishing connections between them, sometimes weak and unclear, sometimes strong and tighter, according to the degree to which the brain's activity is more or less impaired by sleep.'

    . . . *to the grave*': quotation from the novel *Heinrich von Ofterdingen* (1802) by Novalis (pseudonym of Friedrich von Hardenberg, 1772– 1801), where the poet Heinrich defends dreams against his sceptical father. Heinrich's mild plea does not fit the extraordinary symbolic, prophetic, and erotic dream that he himself has just experienced.

74 . . . *de la folie*: 'the real determining cause of the madness'.

79 *Artemidorus*: Artemidorus of Daldis in Asia Minor (second century AD) wrote a treatise on dreams in five books entitled *Oneirocritica*, considering how to interpret them as predictions of the future.

84 '. . . *problème obscure*': 'Any psychologist is obliged to confess even his failings if he thinks he can thus cast light on some obscure problem.'

    Irma: Anna Hammerschlag, daughter of Freud's Hebrew teacher Samuel Hammerschlag, and a close friend of Freud's wife Martha; in 1885 she married Rudolf Lichtheim of Breslau, son of a neurologist who was a long-standing friend of Freud's associate Josef Breuer. Her brother Paul married Breuer's daughter Bertha in 1893. This illustrates the close web of professional and family ties within the acculturated Jewish community to which Freud belonged.

    Otto: Dr Oskar Rie (1863–1931), a lifelong friend of Freud's, paediatrician to his children.

85 *Dr M.*: Josef Breuer (1842–1925), Freud's close colleague for some ten years and collaborator on the *Studies on Hysteria* (1895). By the late 1890s their friendship had cooled and Freud had transferred his devotion to Fliess; hence Breuer figures here as a blunderer.

    Leopold: Ludwig Rosenberg, a paediatrician, colleague and friend of Freud's. He and his brother-in-law Oskar Rie belonged to the group which met in Freud's house to play the card-game Tarock every Saturday evening from the 1890s till the death of the fourth player, Professor Leopold Königstein, in 1924.

88 *1885*: a mistake for 1884, when Freud published his first study of cocaine. The friend who abused it was Ernst Fleischl von Marxow (1846–91); see Introduction, p. xxiv.

90 *Inspector Bräsig and his friend Karl*: characters from the Low German dialect novel *Ut mine Stromtid* ('From my Time as a Farm Manager', 1862–74) by Fritz Reuter (1810–74), who was popular for his Dickensian humour. There is an English version entitled *An Old Story of my Farming Days*, translated by M. W. MacDowall, 3 vols. (London, 1878). In *On Sigmund Freud's Dreams* Grinstein gives a plot summary (pp. 33–6) and relates it to Freud's associations (pp. 37–40).

91 *dysentery . . . diphtheria*: the German 'Dysenterie' and 'Diphtherie' are closer in sound than their English equivalents (J.C.).

93 *another friend*: Wilhelm Fliess (see Introduction, pp. xxiii–xxiv).

100 *A young colleague*: Rudi Kaufmann, Josef Breuer's nephew; see Freud's letter to Fliess, 4 March 1895.

101 *Alphonse Daudet . . . Prévost*: French novelists: Alphonse Daudet (1840–97), now best remembered for *Lettres de mon moulin* (1869); Paul Bourget (1852–1935), author of *Le Disciple* (1889); Marcel Prévost (1862–1941), whose many novels include *L'Automne d'une femme* (1893).

102 *Aussee . . . Hallstatt*: Aussee is a popular Alpine holiday resort, with salt-baths, in Styria. Hallstatt is a village on a lake in the Salzkammergut, some 12 miles from Ischl (mentioned below).

the Dachstein: a mountain massif south of Hallstatt, rising to 2,995 metres (9,827 feet).

vale of E[s]cher: correctly Echerntal, a wooded valley with waterfalls near Hallstatt. The atmosphere of this holiday is best conveyed by Baedeker: 'The Waldbach-Strub (2060 ft.), in the well-wooded Echern-Thal, 1 hr. to the S .W. of Hallstatt, is precipitated in three leaps from a height of 330 ft. through a cleft in the rocks. The Schleier Fall, of about equal height, descends into the same abyss. Both are insignificant in dry seasons. A picturesque path [*Malersteig*] leads along the Waldbach from Croallo's Inn (halfway through the Echern-Thal) to the Lahn and back to Hallstatt.'

lodge: 'Hütte', a word whose semantic range, from 'cottage' via 'cabin' to 'shack' or 'kennel', makes it difficult to translate: here it means a building which, having originally been a cabin providing refuge for climbers, has developed into a modest hotel.

103 *Dornbach*: a village in the Vienna Woods, immediately west of Vienna. Again, Baedeker supplies the atmosphere: 'The chief attraction here is the Park of Prince Schwarzenberg, through which a road ascends from the tramway terminus to the (3 M[iles]) Hameau, or Holländer Dörfel

(1515 ft.; Inn), a fine point of view ... From the Holländer Dörfel a
pleasant path leads in ¾ hr. to the Sofien-Alpe (1595 ft.; Inn), which may
also be reached direct in 1¼ hr. by a picturesque path from Neuwaldegg
via the Rohrer-Hütte (Inn).'

106 ... *with which you have been pleased to draw attention to yourself of late*:
later editions tone down the criticism of the 'unjustified generalizations' to '... die sich zum Glück leicht zurückweisen läßt': Strachey:
'... though fortunately one which it is easy to disprove' (J.C.).

108 *professor extraordinarius*: a professor who is not among the established
professors ('Ordinarien') and does not share their administrative and
supervisory duties.

considerations of religion: a euphemistic reference to anti-Semitism.

109 *Uncle Josef ... sad one*: Josef Freud, Freud's paternal uncle, was
imprisoned in 1866 for dealing in counterfeit roubles; Freud's father may
have been implicated as well.

110 *Galton*: Sir Francis Galton (1822–1911), British scientist, anthropologist,
and eugenicist, who believed that both physical and mental traits were
inherited. His composite photographs were intended to bring out the
basic anthropological type represented by various individuals.

111 *infected*: the first edition has 'Infection', seemingly a mistake for 'Injection'; Strachey translates as 'injected'.

112 *'Das Beste ... sagen'*: words spoken by Mephistopheles in the scene
'Faust's Study (II)' of Goethe's *Faust, Part One*. In his many quotations
from *Faust*, Freud shows especial fondness for the words of the devilish
tempter Mephisto, the 'Spirit of Perpetual Negation' who cynically
questions the high-flown aspirations of the hero—a model for Freud's
analysis of unconscious motives? This qualifies the widespread view, put
forward by Thomas Mann among others, that Freud identified with the
overweening ambitions of Faust. Also quoted on p. 293.

115 *Goethe*: the poem 'Totality' (*c*.1814) runs in full:

> Ein Kavalier von Kopf und Herz
> Ist überall willkommen;
> Er hat mit feinem Witz und Scherz
> Manch Weibchen eingenommen;
> Doch wenn's ihm fehlt an Faust und Kraft,
> Wer mag ihn dann beschützen?
> Und wenn er keinen Hintern hat,
> Wie mag der Edle sitzen?

['A Cavalier in head and heart is welcome everywhere; with his refined
wit and jests, he's turned many a woman's head; but if he lacks a powerful fist, then who wants to protect him? And if he hasn't a backside, how
can the lord be seated?'] The title 'Totality' refers to the need for perfection in all bodily parts.

116 *Bernheim*: Hippolyte Bernheim (1840–1919), a leading medical hypnotist, whom Freud visited at Nancy in 1889 in order to study his methods.

123 *Lenau*: Nikolaus Lenau (pseudonym of Nikolaus Franz Niembsch, Edler von Strehlenau, 1802–50), Austrian poet of *Weltschmerz* (cosmic suffering). His poem 'Das tote Glück' ('Dead Happiness') seems to be about infanticide; it could imply abortion, but not contraception.

128 *Böcklin*: Arnold Böcklin (1827-1901), Swiss painter; Freud may be thinking of his *The Island of the Dead* (1880).

Dreyfus: in 1894 Captain Alfred Dreyfus, a Jewish officer with French Military Intelligence, was found guilty of spying for Germany and sent to the penal settlement of Devil's Island in the West Indies; in 1897 evidence suggesting his innocence was brought to light and led to the Dreyfus Affair which divided French society.

129 *Berlin friend*: Fliess.

134 *in Hamlet*: I. v. 129–30.

135 *Hänschen Schlau*: one of the epigrams written in the 1750s by Gotthold Ephraim Lessing (1729–81) runs:

> 'Es ist doch sonderbar bestellt',
> Sprach Hänschen Schlau zu Vetter Fritzen,
> 'Daß nur die Reichen in der Welt
> 'Das meiste Geld besitzen.'

['It's really very odd,' said Jacky Sly to Cousin Fred, 'that only the rich people in the world have most of the money.']

141 *a certain kind of carelessness*: i.e. appearing in public with one's fly unbuttoned.

'I won't take it' . . . *dream-content*: the translation unavoidably disguises the overlap between 'Das nehm ich nicht' ('I won't have it') and 'Benehmen Sie sich anständig' ('Behave properly').

143 *Apollo candles* . . . : the missing words are supposed to be 'and masturbates'.

146 *Nansen*: Fridtjof Nansen (1861–1930), Norwegian explorer, who in 1893–6 explored the Arctic Ocean in a ship, the *Fram*, that was specially designed to be lifted, not crushed, by ice-floes. Nansen was also a scientist, and on returning from his expedition was made professor of zoology at the University of Christiania (Oslo).

division of the Chinese Empire: especially between 1897 and 1900, Germany sought to acquire territory and influence in the vulnerable Chinese Empire.

148 *Prater*: a park north-east of the centre of Vienna, popular for its restaurants and puppet-theatres.

Bourgeois Ministry: 'Bürgerministerium'. In 1868 the Emperor Franz Joseph appointed a cabinet led by the liberally inclined aristocrat Prince

'Carlos' Auersperg and consisting mainly of middle-class ministers such as Eduard Herbst (Justice), Karl Giskra (Interior), and Johann Nepomuk Berger (without portfolio; succeeded in 1871 by Joseph Unger).

satchel: an allusion to Napoleon's alleged remark, 'Every French soldier carries in his cartridge-pouch the baton of a marshal of France', indicating that in his army any gifted soldier could reach the highest rank. In fact the saying was uttered by Napoleon's adversary Louis XVIII in an address to cadets in 1819.

Rome: on Freud's long-inhibited desire to visit Rome, see Ernest Jones, *Sigmund Freud: Life and Work* (London, 1953–7), ii. 17–21.

149 *Lübeck*: a North German port near Hamburg, where Freud's wife came from.

Gleichenberg: a popular holiday resort near Graz in Styria, overlooked by an old castle on a high crag.

Karlsbad: now Karlovy vary, a town in the narrow valley of the River Tepl, still a popular resort; in Freud's day, according to Baedeker, it attracted over 30,000 visitors a year, many of them seeking relief from liver complaints in the local mineral springs.

150 *not be a very comfortable place for Germans*: because of the growing strength of Czech nationalism. From the 1880s on, figures recording the growth of the Czech-speaking population and the decline of the German speakers were officially displayed outside the Prague city hall in order to hearten Czechs. Tensions exploded in the anti-German riots of December 1897.

in my seventeenth year: Freud revisited Freiberg (Příbor), his birthplace, in August and September 1872, when he was sixteen. On the accuracy or otherwise of his recollection, see Jones, *Freud*, i. 35–6.

one of our classic writers: in 1925 Freud identified this writer as the humorous Romantic author Jean Paul Friedrich Richter (1763–1825).

Winckelmann: Johann Joachim Winckelmann (1717–68), a Prussian schoolteacher, who went to Rome in 1755, became librarian to Cardinal Albani, and wrote an epoch-making history of classical art.

Hannibal: Carthaginian general (247–182 BC) who fought against the Romans in the Second Punic War, defeating them at Lake Trasimene (217 BC) and elsewhere, and conquering the South Italian province of Campania.

151 *Hasdrubal*: Freud here confuses Hannibal's brother Hasdrubal with his father Hamilcar Barca. He corrected this mistake in later editions and commented on it in *The Psychopathology of Everyday Life*, ch. 10.

Thiers: Adolphe Thiers (1797–1877), French historian and statesman, author of *Histoire du consulat et de l'empire* (1845–62).

Masséna: André Masséna (1758–1817), later duc de Rivoli, one of Napoleon's outstanding generals; widely though wrongly supposed to be a Jew called Menasse or Manasseh.

155 *Graben*: a major shopping street in the centre of Vienna.

157 *Pélagie*: Grinstein has identified this novel as *Hypatia* (1853) by Charles Kingsley (1819–75). Set in early Christian Alexandria, it has as hero the monk Philammon who admires the learned pagan Hypatia but is attracted to the courtesan Pelagia, who is really his sister.

158 *you owe Nature a death*: probably an inaccurate recollection of Shakespeare's *1 Henry IV*, v. i. 126: 'thou owest God a death.' Freud uses the same misquotation in his letter to Fliess of 6 February 1899.

159 *Brücke*: Freud's teacher Ernst Brücke (1819–92).

'. . . *gelüsten'*: from the dialogue between Mephisto and the student in the scene 'Faust's Study (II)' of Goethe's *Faust, Part One*.

Fleischl: see note to p. 88 above.

Spalato: Spalato (stress on first syllable), now Split in Croatia, was then an important town of some 20,000 inhabitants in the Austrian crownland of Dalmatia.

Stettenheim: Julius Stettenheim (1831–1916), Jewish journalist and satirist, active in Hamburg and Berlin.

160 '*Der Du . . . Kothe'*: quotation from Part II (1812) of Goethe's autobiography *Aus meinem Leben: Dichtung und Wahrheit* (*From my Life: Poetry and Truth*, 1811–33), Book 10: on receiving a letter in mock-classical verse from his friend Johann Gottfried Herder (1744–1803), requesting the loan of a book and punning on Goethe, *Goten* (Goths) and *Kot* (excrement), Goethe was understandably offended; he reflects: 'It was certainly indelicate to permit himself this joke on my name; for a person's own name is not like a cloak that merely hangs upon him and can be tugged and twitched, but a perfectly fitting garment, indeed like his own skin, that has grown around him, and cannot be scraped and flayed without doing him an injury.'

'*So seid . . . Staub'*: from Goethe's play *Iphigenie auf Tauris* (1787), II. ii. Iphigenie says this on learning how many Greek heroes have perished in the siege of Troy. The line helps to introduce the ambiguity, crucial for the action, between 'divine image' as a statue of a god and as a description of a human being made in the gods' image.

Cattaro: Cattaro (stress on first syllable), now Kotor in Croatia, southeast of Dubrovnik; then an Austrian naval base and fortress town near the frontier with Montenegro.

Ischl: a fashionable spa and holiday resort in the Salzkammergut, southeast of Salzburg, where the Emperor generally resided from July to September.

Count Thun: Count Franz Anton Thun (1847–1916), a member of a great feudal family in Bohemia, who became Prime Minister of Austria in March 1898 and made concessions to the Czechs which only inflamed further the nationalism of the Germans; he resigned in October 1899.

161 *The Marriage of Figaro*: *Le Nozze di Figaro*, opera by Mozart with libretto by Lorenzo da Ponte, first produced in Vienna in 1786; based on the seemingly subversive comedy *La Folle Journee ou Le Mariage de Figaro* (*The Crazy Day or The Marriage of Figaro*, 1781) by Pierre-Augustin Caron de Beaumarchais (1732–99).

162 *Taaffe*: Count Eduard Taaffe (1833–95) became Prime Minister of Austria in 1879 and continued till 1893; the remaining Liberals soon left his government and entered opposition, leaving the 'Iron Ring' of conservative, clerical, and pro-Slav politicians. Taaffe's premiership thus marks the end of the Liberal era in Austria.

Krems or Znaim: *Krems*, an old town on the Danube above Vienna. *Znaim*, a town in Moravia, now Znojmo in the Czech Republic, just across the Austrian border.

Graz: one of the main cities in Austria, capital of Styria.

163 *the Wachau*: a picturesque stretch of the Danube above Vienna, where the river flows through a narrow rocky defile, extending from Melk to Krems.

Emmersdorf: a village in the Wachau, famous for its late-medieval church.

Fischhof: Adolf Fischhof (1816–93), a doctor, who was among the leaders of the 1848 Revolution in Vienna, later a respected leader of Austrian Liberalism.

'Fifty years ago': Grinstein (p. 104) suggests this refers to Tennyson's poem 'The Roses on the Terrace', beginning 'Rose, on this terrace fifty years ago', which links up with Freud's later reference to the Wars of the Roses.

a fellow-student: Heinrich Braun (1854–1927), a converted Jew, later a prominent Socialist politician in Germany. See Freud's letter to his widow Julie Braun-Vogelstein, October 1927 (in *Letters 1873–1939*, ed. Ernst L. Freud (London, 1961)). As she was Braun's fourth wife, Freud seems to be comparing him with Henry VIII in respect of sexual energy as well as resistance to authority.

aristocrat: identified by McGrath as Robert Edler von Siebenrock.

white and red roses: *3 Henry VI*, I. i.

164 *A colleague*: Victor Adler (1852–1918), founder of the Austrian Social Democratic Party, and brother-in-law of Heinrich Braun. Adler said that Freud, despite his radicalism, would imitate the Prodigal Son by returning to his father's house (see Luke 15). 'Adler' is the German word for 'eagle'.

Zola's Germinal: Émile Zola (1840–1902); *Germinal* (1885) recounts a miners' strike in northern France. The title refers to the seventh month in the French Revolutionary calendar. These associations may explain its substitution for *La Terre* (*Earth*, 1887).

165 *Flavit et dissipati sunt*: 'He blew and they were destroyed.'

165 *incontinentia alvi*: physical incontinence.

Grillparzer: Franz Grillparzer (1791–1872), Austrian dramatist; in his tragedy *Des Meeres und der Liebe Wellen* (1831) the repressive uncle of the priestess Hero ensures that the lamp, which is intended to guide her lover Leander as he swims across the Hellespont to her tower, is blown out, so that Leander perishes.

166 *Rabelais*: François Rabelais (*c*.1483–1553); in his *Gargantua* (1534), ch. 17, the giant Gargantua visits Paris: 'Then smiling, he untied his fair braguette, and drawing out his mentul into the open air, he so bitterly all-to-bepissed them, that he drowned two hundred and sixty thousand four hundred and eighteen, besides the women and little children' (Urquhart's translation).

167 *Odhin's Consolation*: *Odhins Trost*, a novel (1880) by Felix Dahn (1834–1912), the prolific author of once-popular historical and legendary novels about the early Germanic past.

La Terre: the old peasant Fouan is maltreated by his brutal son.

Panizza: the Munich satirist Oskar Panizza (1853–1921) wrote the scandalous play *Das Liebeskonzil* (*The Council of Love*, 1895), set during the Renaissance: a decrepit God decides to punish humanity for its vices by commissioning the Devil to invent syphilis and beget an irresistible woman to infect mankind, beginning with the Pope.

179 *Sunday rider*: in a letter to Fliess of 7 July 1898, Freud writes, referring to an enclosed essay: 'It completely follows the dictates of the unconscious, on the well-known principle of Itzig, the Sunday rider. "Itzig, where are you going?" "Do I know? Ask the horse."'

181 *Arcole*: Napoleon Bonaparte defeated Austrian troops at Arcola (the usual form of the name) in northern Italy on 16 November 1796. He became First Consul by his *coup d'état* of 18 Brumaire (= 9 November) 1799.

'the nightingale': 'Wilt thou be gone? It is not yet full day. | It was the nightingale and not the lark | That pierced the fear-full hollow of thine ear': Juliet in *Romeo and Juliet*, III. v. 1–3.

187 *Andersen*: Hans Christian Andersen (1805–75), Danish writer of fairy-tales.

Fulda: Ludwig Fulda (1862–1939), in his day a very popular German dramatist. *Der Talisman* (1893) dramatizes the story of the Emperor's new clothes. The 'talisman' of the title is explained as the courage of truth ('der Mut der Wahrheit').

188 *... sexual life and the work of culture begins*: how closely Freud conceived the two in the development of culture is indicated by his use of a singular verb for a plural subject here, perpetuated in later editions (J.C.).

190 *Keller's ... man's eternal nature*: at the beginning of Book VI of Homer's *Odyssey*, the shipwrecked Odysseus is found washed up on the shore of Phaeacia by the king's daughter Nausicaa. The great Swiss novelist Gott-

fried Keller (1819–90) wrote as his masterpiece *Der grüne Heinrich* (2 versions, 1854–5 and 1879–80). Heinrich Lee, the hero, receives this advice from his art teacher Römer, and it is doubly confirmed, first when Römer dies in misery and insanity in Paris, and later when Heinrich, having studied art unsuccessfully in Munich, returns home destitute.

192 *the Odyssey*: in Book XI of the *Odyssey*, Odysseus summons up the souls of the dead by sacrificing sheep and giving their blood to the souls to drink.

195 *angel-maker*: this word (*Engelmacherin*) is also the vulgar term for an abortionist.

196 *'. . . no traveller returns'*: *Hamlet*, III. i.81–2.

197 *Fourth Commandment*: the commandment 'Honour thy father and thy mother' is for Freud the fourth, as it is in both the Catholic and Lutheran Churches, adopting the division established by St Augustine, whereas the Reformed Churches and the Church of England count this as the fifth, following the order in Exodus 20 rather than that in Deuteronomy 5.

201 *Oedipus*: the protagonist of the plays *Oedipus the King* and *Oedipus at Colonus* by Sophocles (496–406 BC).

. . . far-distant crime: trans. E. F. Watling (Harmondsworth, 1964), 28. Subsequent quotations are from this version.

202 *later tragedies of fate*: Freud is referring to a genre of early nineteenth-century German dramas where a curse is worked out; an example is *Die Ahnfrau* (*The Ancestress*, 1817), a popular but immature play by Grillparzer.

204 *'sicklied o'er . . . thought'*: *Hamlet*, III. i. 87. Goethe's interpretation of *Hamlet* occurs in his novel *Wilhelm Meisters Lehrjahre* (*Wilhelm Meister's Apprenticeship*, 1795–6): Shakespeare intended to portray 'the effects of a great action laid upon a soul unfit for the performance of it'; Hamlet's is 'a lovely, pure and most moral nature, [which] without the strength of nerve which forms a hero, sinks beneath a burden which it cannot bear and must not cast away' (Book IV, ch. 13, in Thomas Carlyle's translation).

Brandes: the Danish critic Georg Brandes (1842–1927), internationally famous in his day, published *William Shakespeare* in German in 1896.

Hamnet: the Stratford parish register records the death of Shakespeare's son Hamnet, aged eleven, on 11 August 1596. The burial of John Shakespeare, the dramatist's father, is recorded on 8 September 1601. *Hamlet* is entered in the Stationer's Register on 26 July 1602 and said to have been 'lately acted by the Lord Chamberlain his servants'; the Oxford editors believe that Shakespeare wrote it in about 1600 and revised it later. Brandes's conjecture thus looks unlikely.

'Macbeth . . . childlessness': see the (unjustly ridiculed) discussion of this subject in A. C. Bradley, *Shakespearean Tragedy* (1904), note EE.

206 *Dr Lecher*: Dr Otto Lecher, Liberal member of the parliamentary opposition, delivered a speech lasting twelve hours on 28–9 October 1897
against the government's support for the use of Czech in schools and
offices in Bohemia and Moravia. Lecher himself represented Brünn, now
Brno, in Moravia.

207 *'My son, the myope'*: this dream is more fully analysed in the section on
'Absurd Dreams' in Chapter VI. The German words *'Myop'* and
'Cyclop' resemble each other more closely in sound than the corre-
sponding English 'myope' and 'cyclops' (p. 284) (J.C.).

   Basedow's disease: a swelling of the thyroid gland in the throat, producing
   a goitre or *struma* (mentioned below), along with the symptoms described
   here.

208 *Basedow*: Johann Bernhard Basedow (1723–90), educational reformer
who founded the Philanthropinum at Dessau; a friend of Goethe, mentioned in the poem 'Diner zu Koblenz' ('Dinner at Koblenz', 1774).

210 *'dies irae, dies illa'*: from the medieval hymn by Thomas of Celano beginning 'That day of wrath, that day will dissolve the world into ashes',
anticipating the Day of Judgement when 'even the righteous will barely
be saved'. Three verses are familiar from being quoted in the 'Cathedral'
scene of *Faust I*.

216 *'Ein Tritt . . . schlägt'*: another quotation from the dialogue between
Mephisto and the student in the scene 'Faust's Study (II)' of *Faust, Part
One*.

218 *dyspnoea*: difficulty in breathing.

   Sappho: a novel (1884) by Daudet (see note to p. 101) about a young
   man's relationship with a courtesan known as 'Sappho' after the Greek
   woman poet, having once posed for a sculpture of her; for a plot summary see Grinstein, pp. 257–60.

   Von Stufe zu Stufe: a play, first performed in 1869 or earlier, by the
   German actor and director Hugo Müller; *Rund um Wien* has not yet been
   traced. I owe this information to W. E. Yates.

219 *Uhland*: Ludwig Uhland (1787–1862), late-Romantic poet, author especially of ballads.

   'Einst hatt' ich . . . trägt': from the 'Walpurgis Night' scene of *Faust, Part
   One*, where Faust almost succumbs to erotic temptation before having an
   involuntary vision of Gretchen, the lover whom he has abandoned.

221 *may-beetles*: Maikäfer. The exact English rendering is 'cockchafer', but
the dream-interpretation requires a reference to 'May' ('She was born
in *May* and had been married in *May*, p. 222), so 'may-beetles' is
preferred (J.C.).

222 *Adam Bede*: a novel (1859) by George Eliot (pseudonym of Mary Ann
Evans, 1819–80), in which the pretty but foolish Hetty Sorrel is seduced
by Arthur Donnithorne, while the noble-hearted workman Adam Bede
marries the plain but admirable Methodist preacher Dinah Morris.

Maupassant: Guy de Maupassant (1850–93), some of whose fiction featuring prostitution (*La Maison Tellier*, 1881) or adultery (*Bel-Ami*, 1885) might well be thought immoral.

Le Nabab: Daudet's *Le Nabab* (1877), a novel sketching Paris life in the Second Empire, focusing on a politician and financier who has made a fortune in Egypt and who attaches himself to the duc de Mora.

The Magic Flute: opera by Mozart with libretto by Emmanuel Schikaneder, first produced in Vienna in 1791. The words quoted are spoken by the wise Sarastro to his adoptive daughter Pamina.

223 *Das Käthchen von Heilbronn*: a play (1810) by Heinrich von Kleist (1777–1811), in which the heroine, of humble birth, is devotedly and at last successfully in love with a nobleman. In Act IV, scene ii, Käthchen speaks to the Count in her sleep and reveals his previously unconscious awareness that he loves her: 'You are as much in love with me as a beetle.' In the first edition, Freud transposed the words to: 'Verliebt ja bist Du wir ein Käfer mir.' 'Beetle' (*Käfer*) was a regional term of endearment (I owe this information to Mrs Hilda Brown).

Tannhäuser: Wagner's opera, first performed in 1845. Freud misquotes the Pope's condemnation of Tannhäuser, which begins: 'Hast du so böse Lust geteilt' ('If you have shared such foul desire'): Tannhäuser, having succumbed to the pagan sensuality of Venus, seeks absolution from the Pope but is told he can no more be absolved than the Pope's staff can blossom; the self-sacrifice of the saintly Elisabeth brings about this miracle, destroys Venus, and redeems Tannhäuser.

Penthesilea: a tragedy by Kleist, written in 1807, published in 1808; the heroine, an Amazon queen prone to violent mood-swings, feels belittled by her lover Achilles, sets her dogs on him, and devours his flesh.

225 *Propylea*: a propylaeum in Greek architecture is a porch supported by columns at the entrance to a sacred enclosure, such as the entrance-hall of the Acropolis in Athens; the name 'Propyl(a)ea' is also given to neo-classical works like the monumental gateways in Munich, completed in 1862.

227 *Ibsen*: Nora is the heroine of *A Doll's House* (1879) and the Ekdal family feature in *The Wild Duck* (1884), both by Henrik Ibsen (1828–1906).

Olmütz: now Olomouc, then an important garrison town of some 20,000 inhabitants in Moravia.

Jubilee Exhibition: in 1898, marking the fiftieth anniversary of the accession of the Emperor Franz Joseph.

228 *The first reader*: Wilhelm Fliess. Freud inserted this footnote in response to an objection by Fliess (see letter of 11 September 1899); the analogy between dreams and witticisms was to be explored in *Jokes and their Relation to the Unconscious*.

B.: Berlin.

229 *Fliegende Blätter*: a much-read German comic paper.

Lasker: Eduard Lasker (1829–84), a leading German politician of Jewish origin who helped to found the National Liberal Party.

Lassalle: Ferdinand Lassalle (1825–64), German Socialist politician, son of a Jewish businessman; killed in a duel.

J. J. David: Jakob Julius David (1859–1906), born, like Freud, in Moravia, though at Weisskirchen; he was brought up nearby at Fulnek, close to the boundary with Austrian Silesia. David was well known at this time for realistic stories of village life.

230 *Breslau*: now Wrocław in Poland; then the capital of the German province of Silesia.

L'Œuvre: Zola's *L'Œuvre* ('The Work [of Art]', 1886), a novel about artists whose hero, Claude Lantier, is based on Zola's friend Paul Cézanne; Zola himself appears as the novelist Pierre Sandoz.

235 *Is fecit cui profuit*: a legal maxim: 'he who profited from it, did it.'

239 *School of Athens*: a fresco by Raphael (Raffaello Sanzio, 1483–1520) painted between 1509 and 1511 in the Vatican.

242 *the night before my father was buried*: in a letter to Fliess of 2 November 1896, Freud says this dream took place the night after the funeral.

243 *dame aux camélias*: the play *La Dame aux camélias* (*The Lady with the Camellias*, 1852) by Alexandre Dumas *fils* (1824–95), best known as the source of Verdi's opera *La Traviata* (1853).

Goethe's poem: 'Der Müllerin Verrat' ('The Treachery of the Miller's Daughter', 1798), a ballad in which a lover, himself a two-timer, complains of how his girlfriend has betrayed their love to her family.

249 *Goethe's death*: in 1832.

250 *transvaluation of all psychical values*: borrowed from a phrase often used by Friedrich Nietzsche (1844–1900), e.g. in *The Genealogy of Morals* (1887), where Nietzsche announces that he is preparing a work called *The Will to Power: An Attempt at a Transvaluation of all Values* (Part 3, sec. 27). A book under this title was compiled from his notebooks by his friend Peter Gast and his sister Elisabeth Förster-Nietzsche and published posthumously in 1901.

251 *my friend*: Fliess. For his theory of bisexuality, see the Introduction, pp. xxiii–xxiv.

253 *. . . summoning me to an examination*: the German 'Untersuchung' doubles the meanings of '(medical) examination' and '(legal) investigation' here (J.C.).

254 *'The Moor has done his duty . . .'*: from Schiller's play *Fiesco* (1784), III. iv; the conspirator Fiesco dismisses his Moorish servant and accomplice, Muley Hassan, with what the latter considers ingratitude. (German *gehen* can mean both 'go' and 'walk' (J.C.).)

257 *Hans Richter*: conductor (1843–1916); an assistant to Wagner, he conducted the premiere of the *Ring* at Bayreuth in 1876; he often conducted in London, and was conductor of the Hallé Orchestra in Manchester from 1900 to 1911.

the unhappy man's name: given in a 1925 addition as Hugo Wolf (1860–1903), the composer whose works include the opera *Der Corregidor* (1896) and many songs to words by Goethe, Mörike, and Eichendorff. As music critic for the Vienna *Salonblatt*, 1884–7, he was a passionate Wagnerian and opponent of Brahms. In 1897 he suffered a mental breakdown; after a brief and illusory recovery, he was sent in December 1898 to an asylum where he stayed until his death.

Tower of Fools: 'Narrenturm', an old term for a lunatic asylum.

258 *'Kein Feuer, keine Kohle ... weiß'*: an anonymous folk-song, of which a version entitled 'Heimlicher Liebe Pein' ('The Pain of Secret Love') is in the famous German collection *Des Knaben Wunderhorn* (*The Boy's Magic Horn*, 1806–8), compiled by Achim von Arnim and Clemens Brentano.

259 *Song of Songs*: 5: 15, 'His legs are as pillars of marble, set upon sockets of fine gold.'

260 *garden*: Song of Songs 4: 12: 'A garden shut up is my sister, my bride.'

261 *pull one down*: in German, 'sich einen herunterreißen'.

... *clothes*: *ausziehen*, a pun, condensing the meanings of 'moving out (of a house)' and 'taking off (one's clothes)'. This paragraph was omitted in subsequent editions (J.C.).

263 *the Hilmteich*: a large pond, with boats for hire and a restaurant nearby, just outside Graz.

fluid and superfluous: Überflüssig = superfluous; *überfließend* = overflowing; *flüssig* = fluid; *über'flüssig* = super'fluous: the alliterative and punning connections are glaring in German, less apparent in English (J.C.).

Ammocoetes: Freud's short paper on the roots of the nerves in the spine of the *Ammocoetes* was published in the proceedings of the Vienna Academy of Sciences in 1877.

264 *3 fl. 65 kr.*: fl. = Florin or Gulden; kr. = Kreuzer. This is the old currency before Austria adopted the gold standard in 1892, whereupon the Gulden was replaced by the Krone at the rate of 2 Kronen to one old Gulden. Twelve Gulden would correspond roughly to one pound sterling.

'time is money': in English in the original.

265 ... *dear one*: Schatz, a term of endearment, literally 'treasure', so establishing a link with buying jewellery and with the value of the husband in the dream (J.C.).

268 *Fl. ... P.*: Fliess, and Josef Paneth (1857–90), Freud's friend, colleague, and successor at the Vienna Institute of Physiology.

threshold: Freud uses a non-existent and unintelligible word, *Schwele*, which sounds like *schwelen* ('to smoulder') or *Schwelle* ('threshold').

269 *Non vixit*: 'he has not lived'; *non vivit*: 'he is not alive'.

Monument: the monument to the Emperor Joseph II (reigned with his mother Maria Theresa from 1765, and alone from 1780 to his death in 1790), Austria's Enlightened despot. An equestrian statue of him by Zauner stands on the Josefsplatz adjacent to the Hofburg (the Imperial residence in the centre of Vienna). The inscription means: 'He lived for his country's good, not long, but entirely.' Freud noted in 1925 that it actually read 'Saluti publicae . . .', 'for the public good'.

270 *Brutus' justificatory speech*: *Julius Caesar*, III. ii. 282–4.

271 *Schiller's Poems*: the poem comes from Schiller's play *Die Räuber* (*The Robbers*, 1781), IV. v, where the hero Karl Moor sings it accompanying himself on the lute.

273 *Garibaldi*: Giuseppe Garibaldi (1807–82), Italian patriot and republican, who contributed to his country's unification by conquering Naples and Sicily with his guerrilla Redshirts.

state of disorder: the Hungarian political crisis in 1898–9 was initiated by the fall of Count Badeni's government in Austria in November 1897: proponents of Hungarian independence sought to replace Hungary's customs union with the Austrian half of the Dual Monarchy by a separate tariff on exports, and refused to accept the compromise worked out by the Prime Minister Baron Bámffy; his successor Kálmán Széll formed a coalition which governed from 1899 to 1903.

Maria Theresa: Empress of Austria from 1740 to 1780. When Frederick the Great of Prussia invaded the Austrian province of Silesia in 1740, the young Empress appealed for Hungarian help at the Diet of Pressburg (now Bratislava) in 1741. The response was 'We will die for our ruler'.

274 *'Und hinter ihm . . . Gemeine'*: from Goethe's poem 'Epilog zu Schillers "Glocke"' (1815).

273 *Callot*: Jacques Callot (1592–1635) made many etchings of courtiers, beggars, and hunchbacks, and recorded the horrors of the Thirty Years War in his series *Les Grandes Misères de la guerre* (1633), partly inspired by the French invasion of Lorraine.

275 *Purkersdorf*: a small town some 8 miles west of Vienna, on the main railway line.

276 *. . . the element 'fahren'*: *fahren* (to go, travel) is a basic semantic unit used in a wide variety of compounds, seen in Freud's punning on 'Vorfahren'. He uses the word itself frequently in the account of his dreams (J.C.).

taken the trouble to be born: a quotation from Beaumarchais's *Le Mariage de Figaro* (see note to p. 161): 'Because you are a great lord, you believe yourself to be a great genius! . . . You took the trouble to be born, and that is all.'

277 *brother-in-law*: an example of this usage with which Freud would have been familiar is found in Goethe's early poem 'An Schwager Kronos' ('To the Coachman Kronos'), written during a journey by coach in 1774.

Heine: from 'Lobgesang auf König Ludwig' by Heinrich Heine (1797–1856), one of Freud's favourite writers (translation from Hal Draper, *The Complete Poems of Heinrich Heine: A Modern English Version* (OUP, 1982), 539). The poem, published in February 1844 in Karl Marx's *Deutsch-Französische Jahrbücher*, is aimed at the reactionary King Ludwig I of Bavaria. On Freud's use of Heine, see Sander L. Gilman, 'Freud reads Heine reads Freud', in Mark H. Gelber (ed.), *The Jewish Reception of Heinrich Heine* (Tübingen, 1992), 77–94.

279 *Meynert*: Theodor Meynert (1833–92), Professor of Psychiatry at the University of Vienna.

280 *'51 is the age ... vulnerable'*: this alludes to Wilhelm Fliess's efforts to find significant periodicities and a 'chronological pattern' in life' (p. 282) based on combinations of 28 and 23 (= 51). See Introduction, pp. xxiii–xxiv. On the harsh review mentioned on p. 281, see Frank Sulloway, *Freud: Biologist of the Mind*, 2nd edn. (Cambridge, Mass., and London, 1992), 144.

281 *'On Nature'*: this essay, long attributed to Goethe, was in fact written by his acquaintance, the Swiss clergyman G. C. Tobler, who visited Goethe in Weimar in 1781, conversed with him about natural science and natural theology, and published the product of these discussions in the *Tiefurt Journal* in the winter of 1782–3.

'Nature, Nature': this sounds very like the young Goethe: see his essay 'On Shakespeare's Birthday' (1773): 'And so I cry "Nature, nature! nothing so natural as Shakespeare's people."'

282 *mea res agitur*: 'this concerns me'.

my son the myope: see note to p. 207.

283 *The New Ghetto*: a play by the Zionist leader Theodor Herzl (1860–1904), in which an upright Jewish lawyer, ostensibly assimilated to Gentile society, finds himself rejected and confined to an invisible (hence 'new') ghetto. The importance of this play for Freud was first explored by Peter Loewenberg in 'A Hidden Zionist Theme in Freud's "My Son, the Myops" Dream', *Journal of the History of Ideas*, 31 (1970), 129–32, and is developed by McGrath, pp. 236–44.

'By the waters of Babylon ... wept': Psalm 137.

284 *'Caviare to the general'*: *Hamlet*, II. ii. 437.

unleavened bread: see Exodus 12: 17.

285 *'I am but mad ... hand-saw'*: *Hamlet*, II. ii. 379.

286 *'... rubbish-heap'*: 'rubbish' here is *Mist*, literally, 'dung'. To condense 'Misttrügerl' and 'Nicht auf meinem eigenen *Mist* gewachsen' plausibly, the English is more genteel than the German (J.C.).

288 *a great figure in history*: Freud named his second son Oliver after Oliver Cromwell (1599–1658), Lord Protector of England from 1653 to 1658.

290 *drew conclusions*: presumably about the student's Jewish origins.

293 *She*: the novel (1887) by H. Rider Haggard (1856–1925); its entrancing heroine, the queen of a lost Central African kingdom, has survived without ageing for 2000 years.

'*the eternal feminine*': the last words of Goethe's *Faust, Part Two* are: 'das Ewig-Weibliche | Zieht uns hinan'—'Eternal Womanhood | Draws us on high'.

'*Das Beste . . . sagen*': see note to p. 112.

294 *Heart of the World*: a novel (1896) by Rider Haggard centring on a hidden Mexican city where the Aztec priesthood survives, and on a heart-shaped stone whose two halves, when reunited, are expected to enable the Aztecs to reconquer Mexico; this prophecy is frustrated by a sexual conflict. For a plot summary, see Grinstein, pp. 404–11.

'*into the unexplored and scarcely trodden*': a hidden allusion also to Faust's descent to the Mothers in order to reanimate Helen of Troy: 'A path untrodden | Which none may tread; a way to the forbidden, | The unmoved, the inexorable' (*Faust, Part Two*, 'A Dark Gallery').

295 *holothurians*: sea-slugs.

Wealth of Nations: in full *An Enquiry into the Nature and Causes of the Wealth of Nations* (1776), a famous book on economics by Adam Smith (1723–90).

Matter and Motion: a book on physics (1877) by James Clerk Maxwell (1831–79).

Schiller: Friedrich Schiller (1759–1805), the dramatist and philosopher, was born not in Marburg (in Central Germany) but in Marbach am Neckar near Stuttgart. The Austrian town of Marburg is near Graz.

'*It is from*' . . . '*It is by*': in English in the original. (The German word *von* can mean either 'from' or 'by', according to context (J.C.).)

300 *Loewe's ballads*: Carl Loewe (1796–1869) composed many ballads which long remained popular as family entertainment.

301 *Snug, the Joiner*: see *A Midsummer Night's Dream*, v. i. 221.

302 *Miramare*: near Trieste on the Adriatic, has a chateau which once belonged to the Emperor Maximilian of Mexico. Nearby are the castle of Duino, later famous as the place where Rilke began the *Duino Elegies* in 1914, and the remains of the Roman city of Aquileia.

'*naval war between America and Spain*': in 1898. McGrath, pp. 256–8, relates this dream to contemporary events and points out that the conflict between democratic America and Roman Catholic Spain formed a parallel in Freud's imagination to the conflict between Hannibal and Rome.

304 '*Quiet . . . returns*': from one of Schiller's epigrams, 'Erwartung und Erfülmlung' ('Expectation and Fulfilment'): 'In den Ozean schifft mit tausend Masten der Jüngling, | Still, auf gerettetem Boot, treibt in den Hafen der Greis' ('The youth launches into the ocean with a thousand masts, | Quiet, in the rescued boat, to the harbour the old man returns').

Görz: now Gorizia in north-eastern Italy.

Grado: a small fishing port and tourist resort on the Adriatic.

306 *the Augean stables*: the fifth of Hercules' ten labours was to clean out many years' accumulation of dung from the cattle-yard belonging to King Augeias, who owned many hundreds of cattle; he did this by diverting two rivers to run through the yard.

Gulliver: see Swift, *Gulliver's Travels*, 'A Voyage to Lilliput', ch. 5.

Gargantua: see note to p. 166.

307 *Flavit . . . sunt*: see note to p. 165.

Die Leiden eines Knaben: a story (1883) by Conrad Ferdinand Meyer (1825–98) about a boy at the court of Louis XIV suffering under the strict and uncongenial educational regime of the Jesuits.

313 *P.*: Josef Paneth; see note to p. 268.

'*at whom . . . ago*': 'Die früh sich einst dem trüben Blick gezeigt' from the prefatory poem to *Faust, Part One*, 'Zueignung' ('Dedication'), in which Goethe reflects on his lifelong preoccupation with this work.

314 '*Ôte-toi que je m'y mette*': 'Come out so that I may have your place' (a sexual double entendre).

315 *Prince Hal*: see 2 *Henry IV*, IV.v.

'*As he was ambitious . . . him*': from the speech in which Brutus justifies killing Caesar in *Julius Caesar*, III. ii. 27.

318 *(h)*: wrongly labelled '(g)' in the first edition, a small instance of the hasty proof-reading that characterizes the volume (J.C.).

Helen of Troy: *La Belle Hélène*, operetta by the German-French Jacques Offenbach (1819–80), first produced in 1864; from the love-duet between Helen and Paris in Act II.

319 *the poet*: Heine in no. 58 of the 'Homecoming' section of the *Book of Songs* (1827), translated as follows by Hal Draper:

> Life and the world's too fragmented for me!
> A German professor can give me the key.
> He puts life in order with skill magisterial,
> Builds a rational system for better or worse;
> With nightcap and dressing-gown scraps as material
> He chinks up the holes in the Universe.

320 *daydream, story*: in English in the original (J.C.).

321 *Nabab*: see note to p. 222.

325 *Girondistes*: properly Girondins, a radical faction in the French Revolution, named after the Gironde region from which three of their leaders came; tried and guillotined in October 1793.

Danton: Georges Danton (1759–94), revolutionary leader.

325 *Don Giovanni*: opera by Mozart, first performed in Prague in 1787. Freud is referring to the banquet scene in the final act.

327 *Dupuy*: Charles-Alexandre Dupuy (1851–1923), French politician, elected President of the Chamber of Deputies on 5 December 1893; during his first week in office an anarchist, Auguste Vaillant, threw a bomb at him, whereupon Dupuy said calmly: 'The session continues, gentlemen.' It was during his period as Prime Minister of France (May 1894 to January 1895) that Captain Dreyfus was exiled to Devil's Island.

334 *Selten . . . gleich: Heine*: no. 78 of 'The Homecoming' (cf. note to p. 319).

regularly: an under-translation. Freud does not in fact use *'regelmäßig'* here, but *'gesetzmäßig'*, i.e. as governed by laws (which he has been working out in his dream-book). However, to spell out this passing claim in the text would be to over-translate, so the translator makes things easy for herself (J.C.).

335 *the embroidered sign on Siegfried's cloak served Hagen*: in the *Nibelungenlied* (written *c.*1200), the sign marks the single vulnerable spot on Siegfried's body and enables Hagen to murder him.

337 *. . . the lady who was my disagreeable travelling-companion*: in the 1st edition Freud reserves his animus for the lady alone; in later editions he applies it to her and her husband: 'two disagreeable fellow-travellers' (Strachey) (J.C.).

seventeen years old: changed in later editions to 'nineteen'. Freud first visited Britain in 1875, when he stayed with relatives in Manchester.

338 *'La matière est-elle laudable?'*: i.e. is the patient's stool normal?— Molière, *Le Malade imaginaire* (*The Hypochondriac*, 1673).

339 *Studies on Hysteria*: Freud is referring to 'Frau Cäcilie M.', whose story is told as part of the fifth case-history in the *Studies on Hysteria* and in an extended footnote to the second. Born Baroness Anna von Todesco in 1847, she married the Jewish banker Leopold, Baron von Lieben, in 1872; her mother belonged to the wealthy Gomperz family. These and other connections deterred Freud from recounting her case in full detail, although she was his patient for over five years, from 1888 (possibly 1887) to the autumn of 1893. She died in 1900.

340 *Claude Bernard*: French physiologist (1813–78).

Little Tailor: the hero of the tale 'The Brave Little Tailor' in the Grimms' *Tales* (1815); he shows his valour by killing seven flies at a stroke.

348 *M. Joyeuse*: from Daudet's *Le Nabab* (see note to p. 222 above).

349 *Fechner*: Gustav Theodor Fechner (1801–87) developed the Romantic philosophy of nature in a number of works including *Elements of Psychophysics* (1860).

351 *as pointed out elsewhere*: by Josef Breuer in the *Studies on Hysteria*, in a footnote to Section I of the theoretical essay he contributed.

359 *Carso*: described by Baedeker as 'an inhospitable and dreary plain, strewn with blocks of limestone, called the Karst (Ital. *Carso*, Slav. *Kras*), which extends from Fiume to Gorizia'.

361 *You could buy him for ten a penny*: more literally, the German 'Er ist ein Duzendmensch' would yield 'his sort are turned out by the dozen'. But for once, 'established linguistic usage' in English offers a serviceable equivalent for the commercial idiom (J.C.).

362 *Odyssey*: see note to p. 192.

366 *tertium comparationis*: the third item to which two others are compared.

373 *Crassus*: Marcus Licinius Crassus (d. 53 BC), a wealthy Roman politician, general, and property-owner. This anecdote is told by the historian Dio Cassius (AD 150–235). I owe this information to Nicholas Purcell.

376 *. . . qui commence*: 'A dream is the beginning of waking.'

382 *Philippson's edition of the Bible*: an edition of the Old Testament in Hebrew and German. The pictures described here, illustrating Deuteronomy 4, are reproduced in McGrath, pp. 41, 43.

   . . . falcons' heads: *Vogel* = bird: in interpreting the dream, Freud relates it to *vögeln* (slang) = to fuck (J.C.).

384 *'Je n'osais . . . dortoir'*: 'I didn't dare admit it, but I kept having prickly feelings and overexcitations in my *parts*; finally it got on my nerves so much that I thought several times of throwing myself out of the dormitory window.'

385 *'Nous avons . . . particulier'*: 'We have classified this observation among the apyretic deliria proceeding from inanition, for we attribute this particular state to cerebral ischaemia.' 'Ischaemia' is a deficiency in the supply of blood to any organ.

401 *closely related*: the first edition has *nahe liegende*; SA, *naheliegende*; Strachey, 'obvious'. I have translated the words as they occur— meaningfully—in the first edition. The later text, as established, may be evidence of rethinking or the correction of a misprint (J.C.).

402 *removal . . . opposite*: see p. xliv, n. 8.

   'Flectere . . . movebo': see note to p. 1, above.

405 *Tartini*: the composer Giuseppe Tartini (1692–1770) wrote a sonata known as the 'Trillo del Diavolo' ('The Devil's Trill') in 1714; it is said that he dreamed of selling his soul to the Devil, who then played him this sonata, and on waking he wrote down what he could remember.

   Helmholtz: Hermann von Helmholtz (1821–94; ennobled in 1882), wide-ranging German scientist who made major advances in both physics and physiology; in the latter, his measurements of nervous stimuli enabled him to establish a strictly material and quantitative physiology. This approach, associated with the 'Helmholtz School', was transmitted to the young Freud via his teacher Brücke.

406 *daemonic powers*: this tenacious German concept was formulated by
Goethe in a famous passage in Book 20 of his autobiography *Dichtung
und Wahrheit* (*Poetry and Truth*): 'He [the young Goethe] believed that
in Nature, both living and lifeless, animate and inanimate, he had discovered something which manifested itself only in contradictions and
therefore could not be grasped by any concept, far less by a word. It was
not divine, for it seemed devoid of reason; not human, for it had no
intellect; not devilish, for it was beneficent; not angelic, for it often displayed malice [*Schadenfreude*]. It seemed like chance, for it showed no
regularity; it resembled Providence, for it revealed interconnections. It
seemed able to penetrate all the limits imposed on us; it seemed to deal as
it pleased with the necessary elements of our existence; it contracted time
and extended space. It seemed to enjoy only the impossible and to spurn
the possible with contempt. To this being, which seemed to intervene
among all others, separating and uniting them, I applied the term "daemonic", following the example of the ancients and of those who had
perceived something similar.'

411 *. . . we must bear in mind that what has psychical reality too can have more
than just one form of existence*: this is a concluding proposition which
Freud revised and varied considerably for later editions. First edition:
'. . . so muß man sich wohl erinnern, daß auch dem psychisch Realen
mehr als nur eine Existenzform zukommt.' This was modified successively in the 1914 and 1919 editions to: '. . . so muß man wohl sagen, daß
die *psychische* Realität eine besondere Existenzform ist, welche mit der
materiellen Realität nicht verwechselt werden soll', and followed by a
further paragraph developing the distinction. Strachey: '. . . we shall
have to conclude, no doubt, that *psychical* reality is a particular form of
existence not to be confused with *material* reality. . . .' (J.C.).

413 *Freud's Bibliography*: These are the texts and references listed by Freud
at the end of the first edition. As they originally included a number of
errors, they have been minimally adjusted according to the corrections
made by Angela Richards for the SE volume and, in her train, by the
editors of *Die Traumdeutung*, vol. ii of Sigmund Freud, *Studienausgabe*
[*der gesammelten Werke*], 10 vols. and supplementary vol. (Frankfurt am
Main, S. Fischer Verlag, 1969–75) (J.C.).

INDEX OF DREAMS

Note. The name or description of the dreamer is to be found in brackets after the dream.

GENERAL INDEX

Note. Information to be found in footnotes is indicated by n. after the page number. Information from notes at the end of the book is entered under the page number.

SAMBURU

Contents

Foreword by Wilfred Thesiger

The Samburu are a proud warrior-race of cattle-owning pastoralists, akin to the famous Maasai. They dwell in the Highlands of Northern Kenya, but their land was never a part of the 'White Highlands' previously inhabited by European settlers and ranchers. It lay in the Northern Frontier District and a special pass was required, even for a few years after independence, before anyone other than a government official could enter any part of the NFD. In consequence, the Samburu were virtually isolated from the rest of Kenya, and were barely aware of events and changes occurring in the rest of the country. Even today Samburuland is still a remote area, as yet spared the impact of mass tourism, such as occurs on the coast and in the Masai Mara. Conservative by nature, the Samburu still cherish and retain the customs and ceremonies of their ancestors, unlike most tribes in Kenya who today have largely abandoned theirs. This will eventually occur among the Samburu, the inevitable consequence of widespread education, a drift to the towns, a great increase in public transport and more contact with newspapers, radio and even television.

Much has been written about the Maasai, but almost nothing about the Samburu. Now fortunately we have Nigel Pavitt's book, which deals with their environment and every aspect of their lives. No other book about them has previously been published which combines meticulous and hitherto unrecorded accounts of fascinating customs and ceremonies, with such exceptional illustrations.

Paul Spencer, who worked for several years as an anthropologist among them in the late fifties, wrote a book *The Samburu*; despite my interest in the subject, I found it almost unreadable. I was astonished that he dismissed circumcision in a few paragraphs. The operation is performed in a unique manner and the attendant ceremonies are the most important in the lives of the Samburu.

The very structure of the tribe is based on their system of age grades, which separate boys from warriors, and warriors from elders. Every fifteen years or so a new age-set is instituted. Then boys from fourteen years of age to men perhaps twenty-four years old, who however still rank as boys till they have been circumcised, are operated on in public, and woe betide any of them who flinch or utter a sound. Eventually, after more ceremonies, the initiates take over as warriors, while their predecessors become junior elders.

SAMBURU

Foreword by Wilfred Thesiger

NIGEL PAVITT

A John Macrae Book
HENRY HOLT AND COMPANY
NEW YORK

North Horr

LAKE TURKANA

South Island

Loiengalani

Mount Kulal
6354'

TURKANA

RENDILLE

Marsabit

2°North

Ol Doinyo Mara
6780'

Mount Ngʼiro
9030'

Tum

South Horr

Lava

Ilaut
8313'

Baragoi

Elbarta plains

Ndoto Mountains
8650'

Lesirikan

Nguruhit

Baio

Laisamis

Marti

Latakwen

MILGIS LUGGA

SEIYA LUGGA

GREAT RIFT VALLEY

Morijo

Parsaloi

Ol Doinyo Lenkiyieu
(Mathews Range)

Lodosoit

Porro
8304'

Losiolo

Lorroki forest

Kirisia Hills

Ngilai

Serolevi

MARALAL

POKOT

Warges
8820'

Wamba

Sabachi
(Lololokwi)
6500'

Kisima

Lorroki plateau

Lodungokwe

Archers Post

WUASO NGʼIRO RIVER

Suguta Marmar

Kirimun

Nyahururu

Samburu Game Reserve

Buffalo Springs Game Reserve

ISIOLO

Nanyuki

SUDAN

ETHIOPIA

L. TURKANA

UGANDA

KENYA

SOMALIA

Maralal

L. Victoria

Kisumu
Nakuru

Mount Kenya

Equator

NAIROBI

SOMALIA

Mount Kilimanjaro

TANZANIA

Indian Ocean

MOMBASA

Legend:

SAMBURU DISTRICT
MAIN ROADS
OTHER ROADS
MOUNTAINS
RIVERS
SEASONAL RIVERS
SAMBURU SEASONAL GRAZING GROUNDS
GAME RESERVES

SCALE:-1:1,000,000

20 10 0 20 40 60 80 Kilometres
10 5 0 10 20 30 40 50 Miles

SAMBURU

I was present when new age-sets were introduced in 1960, in 1976 and in 1990; on the last two occasions I was involved to some extent in the proceedings, owing to my close relationship with the families of certain initiates; as a result I began to understand the importance to them of these rituals and ceremonies. On one occasion a sophisticated Samburu official turned to me and said in English, 'You will never realize what this means to us. No other event in our lives is of comparable importance.'

Until I read Nigel Pavitt's book, I had assumed that I was familiar, from personal observation, with the details of these initiation ceremonies; only then did I realize how much I had overlooked, and these are only some of the ceremonies with which he deals.

Nigel Pavitt arrived in Kenya in 1955 to do his National Service with the King's African Rifles. He then remained on with the KAR as a regular officer and, after independence, served with the Kenya Army until 1967. He first encountered Samburu serving in the ranks and felt an instinctive liking for them, which increased to admiration after he had witnessed their bravery during operations against Somali outlaws on the northern frontier. Since then he has lived continuously in Kenya and has spent as much time as possible among the Samburu. His easy manner, his patience, his genuine interest in their tribal life and his obvious regard for individuals have earned him universal respect. This has enabled him to interest them in his enquiries and gain their co-operation and assistance; it has also enabled him to take whatever photographs he wished without hindrance. It is by no means easy to overcome their reluctance to be photographed.

At first sight, this book may appear to be just another collection of photographs on the people of Kenya, but anyone who reads the detailed and to me absorbing text will see how carefully they have been selected to illustrate it. It is Nigel Pavitt's tribute to the Samburu. With the changes now taking place among them, such a book can never be produced again.

Wilfred Thesiger
Maralal, 1991

The Land and the People

Samburu District, an area of some 8,000 square miles where the majority of the Samburu people live, lies in northern Kenya between the Equator and three degrees north of it, to the south west of Lake Turkana and north of the Wuaso Ng'iro River. Its landscape is one of great diversity and beauty. The tremendous force generated by tectonic movements in the Earth's crust, which formed the Great Rift Valley a thousand million years ago, resulted in an extensive area of upland plateau rising to a height of 8,000 feet. Here, close to the administrative centre of Maralal, the rainfall averages more than thirty inches a year and to the casual observer the vegetation is more temperate than tropical. It is the only place in the entire district where climate and soil are suited to large-scale agricultural enterprises. For the past ten years, wheat farming has been undertaken by tenant farmers from other parts of Kenya. The Samburu, whose life revolves round cattle, have always disliked tilling the land.

The landscape changes abruptly beyond the plateau. At Losiolo, just forty-five minutes' drive out of Maralal if there has been no rain, the golden wheat fields end without warning as the rich arable land tumbles 3,000 feet into a stark valley below. This is arguably the finest view in Kenya of the Great Rift Valley, a system of deep trenches and troughs that cut a swath across the Middle East and Africa. It is at its most dramatic between the Ethiopian Highlands and southern Tanzania, where it is characterized by straight parallel sides and the sharpness of its vertical walls. Standing at Losiolo, on the edge of the eastern wall of the eastern branch of Earth's most formidable fracture, with a strong breeze blowing, is an exhilarating experience. The land stretches westwards as far as the eye can see to the white, natron-encrusted soils of the Suguta Valley, with the mountain ranges beyond shimmering in the heat. This low-lying country is awesome – a scarred and forbidding spectacle of contorted rocks and jagged lava riven by deep gorges where erosion over the millennia has left an indelible mark. The temperature here rarely falls below ninety degrees Fahrenheit and permanent water is scarce. There are no access roads and the inhabitants are understandably few.

The sudden change from grassland to forest on the eastern side of the plateau cannot be explained by rainfall alone, so another reason must be sought. It is possible that fire has been an influencing factor or it may simply be a change in the soil structure itself. The Lorroki Forest has a direct bearing on the rainfall pattern over this central region; it also acts as a vital water catchment area, giving life to herdsmen in the semi-arid scrublands away to the east. It is an open forest composed mainly of magnificent podocarpus trees – relatives of the yew family – and juniper or cedar trees (*Juniper procera*), festooned with long strands of pale green lichen which give them an eerie appearance in the early morning mist. At lower altitudes, olive (*Olea africana*) and croton trees (*Croton megalocarpus*) grow in abundance. This forest is a haven for elephants and buffaloes, and for numerous species of birds and butterflies.

A young man herds his family's cattle high in the Ndoto Mountains, which rise to over 8,600 feet; they are bounded by semi-desert. The correct name for the range is Ol doinyo Loondoto, 'the mountain of small smooth stones or pebbles'. Here, in the rivers and seasonal watercourses, the Samburu collect the most perfect stones with which to play the age-old game of *bau*, which they call *ntotoi*.

Most of the other isolated mountains and ranges in the district are more than 500 million years old and, like the highlands, were created by inflections in the Earth's crust during the formation of the Great Rift Valley. One notable exception is Mount Kulal, which is of recent volcanic origin. Although it lies in neighbouring Marsabit District, it is inhabited by the Samburu. Its activity subsided barely two million years ago, by which time early man was already living on the shores of Lake Turkana, a short distance to the west. In an ocean of semi-desert, these mountains are oases of tranquil beauty where fresh mountain streams and plunging waterfalls cut through forested gorges to the barren lands below. Quite apart from the beneficial influence they have on the climate, they provide dry-weather pasture for cattle and firewood for those who live close by.

Over the years the sleepy frontier town of Maralal has doubled in size to about 30,000 people and the exclusive club, intended principally for the colonial administrators, has given way to a tourist hotel, but the easy-going atmosphere is essentially the same. The two main streets are often dusty, sometimes muddy, depending on the season, and are lined with shops built of juniper wood interspersed with bars. Some of the bars are simple, one-roomed affairs with light-hearted paintings on the walls. In each, the barman is protected from drunken customers by an expanded metal cage from where beer and single-tot sachets of spirits are served. The streets are bordered with ornamental pepper trees where people foregather and while away the day. The pace is slow in Maralal. There is no need for anyone to exert himself to complete something when it could easily be accomplished the following day or even the day after that. Occasionally I catch a glimpse of a *matatu*, a local taxi, with 'No hurry in Africa' painted in bold letters on the back. At times it can be disconcertingly true! Newspapers arrive a day late *if* someone remembers to put them on the bus. Otherwise, the radio keeps people informed of newsworthy events which could just as well be happening on another planet for all the effect they have on the place.

Before independence in 1963, Samburu was one of the districts of northern Kenya that were closed to foreigners of African as well as European descent; without a special permit issued by the administration, it was impossible to go there. Being in the army, I was fortunately exempted from all this red tape. However well-intentioned the controls may have been at the time, they resulted in the benign neglect of the inhabitants. For many reasons this suited the Samburu, who were pleased to be left alone. Traditionalists in a world of change, they preferred to live their lives free from alien influences and external pressures. In some ways this is still so. However, their isolation has left them behind other parts of the country in terms of education, agricultural development and the provision of social services. Only now are changes gradually being felt. Many Samburu of the younger generations realize they must adapt to new ways if the tribe is to progress; but few want to see their rich cultural heritage disappear overnight, only to be replaced by another with what they consider to be inferior values. It is unfortunate that people who cling to age-old customs and resist change are so often misunderstood. Sometimes this resistance to new ideas is written off as sheer backwardness, but the truth is they have been taught by experience over many centuries that the way of life they have evolved is the one best suited to their harsh environment. Clothes are most certainly one aspect of this and have nothing whatsoever to do with morality, as some prudish sects would make us believe. Shirts and trousers are a highly uncomfortable form of dress in which to herd cattle under the blazing sun of an arid region; in these conditions the loincloth is much more practical.

The Samburu form part of the Maa-speaking peoples of whom the Maasai are the best known. They speak dialect with a quicker manner of speech than the Maasai, but ninety-five words out of every hundred are common to both tongues. The remainder of their vocabulary is polyglot, highlighting the diverse origins of some of the clans. It is believed beyond reasonable doubt that the large majority of Samburu were once a minor branch of the Laikipiak Maasai who were renowned for their belligerence. Others were breakaway groups from the neighbouring Rendille, Turkana and Borana tribes.

The name 'Samburu' is of Maasai origin and tends to confirm that in the remote past the Samburu were hunters and honey-gatherers rather than large-scale stock-owners. A *samburr* is a traditional leather bag peculiar to them, for carrying meat and honey on their backs; hence their generally accepted name. In conversation with another, however, the Samburu will always call themselves 'L'oikop'. This again is a name of Maasai origin which was used in a derogatory way by other Maasai clans to describe their despicable relatives, the Laikipiak. Literally, it meant 'those who kill one another' (or murder people of their own tribe). The Laikipiak Maasai could hardly have objected to the accuracy of that descriptive name but why the Samburu persist in using it, notwithstanding their origins, remains a mystery. Some elders claim that it is a corruption of *kopok*, 'the ones who are left behind' (from a fight with the enemy); others say it is *loopok* 'the survivors'. Both seem more plausible than L'oikop, but these explanations are not widely known. In 1888 Count Samuel Teleki von Szek, a Hungarian nobleman, and Lieutenant Ludwig von Höhnel, an Austrian naval officer, were the first Europeans to come into contact with the Samburu at South Horr, during their epic journey to the shores of Lake Turkana. They were told the tribesmen were called *L'oibor kineji* (von Höhnel recorded the name as 'Burkeneji') 'the owners of the white goats'. Either the travellers were misled into recording inaccurate information or, as was so often the case, their question may not have been understood properly by their interpreters.

To trace the history of a people like the Samburu is extremely difficult beyond a period of about one hundred years. Oral traditions rapidly become interwoven with mythology to the point where it is almost impossible to differentiate the two. They are believed to have their origins in the Sudan, and share certain customs with the tribes living there, such as removing the two lower incisors, using spittle as a blessing and adopting a one-legged stance. Nevertheless, the ancient Egyptians were the first to practise circumcision and while their methods were dissimilar to the Samburu's, there are accounts of mass circumcisions and men holding the backs of the initiates which are reflected in the Samburu practices of today. This may be an indication that the forefathers of the Samburu had contact with peoples of the Nile Basin, possibly in the kingdom of Cush, which flourished until the fourth century AD. They migrated up the Nile with other Maa-speaking peoples during the fifteenth century. Some of the oldest men alive today claim the tribe came from Parkaba, others talk about Oto, which has taken on the meaning 'the faraway place'. It is said that their land was wrested from the Galla, a powerful race who live mainly in southern Ethiopia.

Throughout the nineteenth century the Samburu were constantly on the move, due in part to adverse climatic conditions or disease and in part to numerous acts of aggression against them.

At the beginning of that period, the Samburu were living near Lake Baringo, where they were allied to the Jamus who still live beside this lake and have close kinship ties with a section of the Lmasula, the largest of the eight Samburu clans. They lacked the cohesion and political structure of an identifiable race until they were forced to unite or perish by the sword of the barbaric Turkana, who about this time were pushing south east from their territory west of Lake Turkana. The Turkana had a reputation of being fierce fighters and greedy for cattle and camels, but the initial brief contacts between the two tribes were not apparently unfriendly. Either out of deference to their fighting skills or to emulate an appearance that was markedly different to their own, the *moran* (a colloquial name for 'warriors', from the Samburu word *lmuran*) adopted the elaborate Turkana hairstyle of plastering the crowns and backs of their heads with blue clay. This fashion lasted about fourteen years, by which time the Samburu had suffered a reversal at the hands of the ruthless newcomers and migrated north to their former homeland with their *moran* resplendent once more in traditional ochred braids. The Samburu use ochre extensively as a body decoration; it is a red mineral which is ground to a powder and mixed with animal fat to the consistency of greasepaint.

The era between 1840 and 1860 is looked upon by the Samburu as an outstanding period in their history. The *moran* of that time wrested Mount Ng'iro (spelt 'Nyiru' on modern maps) and Mount Kulal from the Galla, whose burial mounds can be seen in many areas, and Marsabit Mountain from the Laikipiak Maasai. These valuable acquisitions enabled them to increase their herds and embark on further expansion, to the pastures along the eastern shores of Lake Turkana as far north as Chew Bahir (formerly Lake Stefanie). Not all those who were vanquished retreated to other lands. Many families were spared and assimilated with the Samburu to such an extent that a number of clans can trace their origins back to them. This is especially so of the Lmasula clan, who have inalienable rights over Mount Ng'iro, the principal seat of Nkai, the god of the Samburu; many important ceremonies are performed there. The only cloud on the horizon during this period of comparative peace and sustained prosperity were the Turkana who, by now, had reached the southern end of Lake Turkana and were menacing herdsmen on the Elbarta Plains. Since the cattle-owning Samburu and camel-owning Rendille had forged a close alliance which exists to this day, they were able to contain the threat for a while. At first sight, the collaboration by two tribes who are culturally, linguistically and economically dissimilar seems surprising. However, they are bound together by strong bonds of friendship fostered by inter-migration and inter-marriage over countless generations. Possibly one third of all Samburu are ultimately of Rendille descent.

As so often happens in Africa, peace and prosperity did not last long; bloodshed and turmoil came suddenly in their wake. The Turkana had consolidated their gains by the last quarter of the nineteenth century and with renewed vigour, marched up the eastern side of Lake Turkana, plundering the Samburu herds as they went. Unfortunately for the Samburu, this scourge occurred at a time when they had been weakened by the spread of smallpox from Abyssinia and their cattle were dying of rinderpest in what turned out to be the worst outbreak ever of its kind. They were forced to take refuge in their mountainous strongholds and give up their pastures north of Mount Kulal. In doing so, they hoped to rebuild their herds to the point where they could resume their nomadic lifestyle. However, many families were destitute after losing all their stock and dispersed among the neighbouring tribes, where they took to hunting, honey-gathering and fishing to avert starvation. Some of them – perhaps out of shame – never rejoined the Samburu.

Every disaster has a silver lining and this series of catastrophes was no exception. No sooner had the Samburu been driven from their pastures than a combined force of warriors from the Purko and Kisongo sections of the Maasai crushed the Laikipiak Maasai in a decisive battle near Nakuru. This took place in the late 1880s. Until then, the Laikipiak had been very troublesome indeed. They had consistently fought other sections of the Maasai, wreaking havoc everywhere they went. This time their defeat was so total that they ceased to exist as a separate race. A few survivors did regroup in a vain attempt to recover a part of their former territory, but were repulsed. By good fortune this left the highly prized grasslands of the Lorroki Plateau a no-man's-land; the Samburu, who had always laid claim to the area, re-established themselves and returned there with their remaining herds. With nowhere to go and insufficient livestock to live off, many of the Laikipiak Maasai also took to hunting; others were given refuge by the Samburu, though few Samburu families acknowledge descent from the survivors of this rout.

The Purko Maasai did the Samburu one more good turn at the beginning of this century. As a reprisal for isolated stock raids, they dealt the Turkana a devastating blow on the Elbarta Plains, close to modern Baragoi. This gave the Samburu a much-needed breathing space to regroup and foster their herds.

When the British appeared on the scene at the end of the nineteenth century to administer their fledgling protectorate, Emperor Menelik's armies in Abyssinia were causing the Borana, one of the Galla tribes, to flee south across the border to avoid persecution. They reached what is now the Marsabit District of Kenya. Armed with a motley assortment of guns, they inflicted severe injury on the Samburu and defeated a significant, tough remnant of Laikipiak Maasai on Marsabit Mountain. For a time the British chose to ignore the Northern Frontier altogether, having neither the personnel to be stationed in this desert fastness nor a road network for easy access to it. The decision to administer the region was taken in 1909 when two half-companies of the King's African Rifles established stations at Marsabit and Moyale. Within a year the Marsabit garrison was moved to Loiengalani in an effort to protect the Samburu from highly mobile mounted bands of well-armed Abyssinian marauders, who were bent on enslaving the local populace and indiscriminately killing the game. It took the askaris three weeks to reach there from Nairobi – a journey which can now be completed in two days – but once they were operational, the situation gradually improved.

About this time the Samburu were evicted from Marsabit Mountain, ostensibly because the administration could not protect them there. Be that as it may, the British did at least help the Samburu to settle an old score with the Turkana. Their warriors were allowed to join a punitive expedition of the King's African Rifles which rounded up large numbers of Turkana stock as a lesson to the tribesmen for their flagrant lawlessness.

It was only when the boundaries of the Samburu became sacrosanct under colonial rule that they were able to settle down in peace and multiply. The entire Northern Frontier District, known as the NFD, came under the military in 1921 and for the first time the Samburu were given a properly defined district of their own with its headquarters at Barsaloi. Until now, they had been loosely administered from Marsabit and Archers Post. Many inconsistent changes took place in the succeeding years. Barsaloi was closed down in 1929 and it was not until 1934 that Maralal was chosen as the site for a new headquarters. That lasted only a year, for in 1935 the district was merged with Laikipia District and Maralal was down-graded to a sub-station. There was more to this move than meets the eye. Being the heartland of large-scale European ranches, Laikipia District was in the firm control of a powerful settler lobby whose members had for some years cast covetous eyes on the Lorroki Plateau. They alleged, without any justification, that the Maasai had been cleared from the area to make way for them. Such was the force of their arguments that the issue was brought before the Kenya Land Commission of 1933 which ruled in favour of the Samburu. But this was not the end of the affair.

The Commission also considered measures to restrict stock levels on the Lorroki Plateau to the carrying capacity of the land. This was the beginning of an imposed system of grazing schemes which was not abandoned until 1962. Of all the actions taken by the colonial administrators, the grazing schemes were hated; they were also perhaps the most despised and the most flouted. The biggest obstacle District Commissioners experienced in realizing their potential benefit to the community was that they were never posted to the district for long enough to carry through a coherent policy which had the support of the tribal elders. One elder I know who was a well-respected senior chief for forty years told me, 'Our cattle would have been finished had the scheme been implemented strictly and we abided by its rules. We were forced to send our surplus herds to the low country to circumvent them. We all loathed the concept and when it was abolished in 1962, we burnt our stock permits to celebrate.' Thirty years on, the issue still rankles and the condition of the grasslands is far worse.

As pastoralists, the Samburu have an emotional and economic commitment to their stock to the virtual exclusion of anything else. Cattle represent a man's wealth and give him a social standing in his community which nothing else can do; without them, he cannot marry or participate in his obligatory age-set ceremonies. A man's herd will provide the basic food needs of his family – milk either drunk fresh or curdled like yoghurt, butter fat or ghee, and blood drawn from the jugular of a cow which can be drunk on its own or diluted with a little milk. Oxen are seldom slaughtered except to celebrate important occasions; cows are never killed because it is through them that the owner can increase the size of his herd. A man will rate the well-being of his herd almost as highly as that of his children. He will know the temperament of each animal, its foibles and above all its distinctive markings. Ask a wealthy stockman how many cows he owns and he will probably have no idea, but he will know instinctively if one is missing and will be able to describe it in precise detail. Each animal will be branded with the individual marks of a particular section or clan and its ears will be cut in a special way to identify the owner's family. No Samburu would ever steal a cow from a clansman but other stock-owners used to be fair game. Cattle-raiding was a major pre-occupation of the warriors, who treated it like any other dangerous sport. It released their pent-up frustrations while adding to the size of their families' herds. For fifty years they targeted European-owned ranches to the fury of the settler community and unfriendly neighbouring tribes to whom they became a major nuisance. Only after independence was cattle-rustling treated seriously and offenders given heavy prison sentences.

While sheep and goats are not accorded the same importance as cattle, they are nevertheless an asset of considerable value. They survive drought and are a very useful source of inexpensive meat. Goats are much preferred to sheep and on the whole are better suited to the semi-arid conditions of the low country where browse is abundant and grass is scarce; they breed much faster, too. The camel is gaining in importance for much the same reasons as the goat; it is also a prolific provider of milk. The Samburu do not have a tradition of keeping camels but the progressive deterioration of the grass structure in many of their grazing areas is forcing them to adapt. This process will undoubtedly accelerate as the camel proves its economic worth over other types of stock.

The elders in their prayers bless 'the eight skins of the L'oikop', a term used to signify that the Samburu are divided into eight distinct clans. To these must be added a ninth, the Ltorobo clan, whose members follow the Samburu lifestyle, but are always considered apart from the rest. The Wandorobo inhabit several mountain ranges in the district, earning a livelihood gathering honey and occasionally hunting game. Contrary to old beliefs, they are not in Samburu District a separate race of primitive people. Their status has much more to do with economics than ethnic origin. The Samburu recognize this by calling any of their people who do not own livestock, *ltorobo*. Many of them can trace their ancestry to the Borana and Laikipiak Maasai who, as I mentioned earlier, resorted to hunting after they were defeated in battle and had their livestock removed from them. A number of Dorobo families have acquired cattle again over the years, but they tend to remain closely associated with their traditional hunting grounds. The Lmasula clan is larger than all the other Samburu clans combined and plays a dominant role in the ritual ceremonies of the tribe. Its size is mainly due to the liberal policy of the clan elders in welcoming migrants who marry into the clan without much fuss. As such, the clan is not of very pure stock – a fact which some of the smaller clans are not slow to point out. Being so big, the Lmasula clan is itself divided into eight sections. No man may marry into his own clan or, if he is a Lmasula, into his own section of the clan. These constraints are designed to prevent inbreeding.

Immediately a male of the tribe is circumcised, he joins an age-set which is composed of all the young men who are initiated within a period of about fourteen years. He will maintain a close affinity with the members of it until he dies. Girls do not have any age-set grouping; they pass through two stages of life, namely *girlhood* and *womanhood*, whereas men pass through three. These are *boyhood* (from birth to adolescence) when they are not members of an age-set, *moranhood* (from circumcision to marriage) when they are warriors and *elderhood* (from marriage until death). Customarily, there is only one age-set of *moran* at any one time, but when young boys are circumcised into a new one, there will be a period of transition lasting about five years when two age-sets will be responsible for the defence of the tribe. Although they will both be *moran*, they will not call each other so. The senior *moran* will call their juniors 'Ero', meaning 'boy', and in reply, the juniors will call their seniors 'Apaiya', a term of respect for someone who belongs to an older age-set.

Samburu society is polygamous and the elders are loth to be specific about the number of wives, children and even cattle they have. Population estimates of varying reliability were undertaken by government officials before the first definitive nationwide census was conducted in 1962. Two others have followed; not everyone was counted in the most recent one, held in 1989, so the statistics will be misleading if ever they are published. Since independence in 1963, the Samburu have increased by 3.5% per annum but the trend is now more rapidly upward. I believe that they presently number 125,000 and by the turn of the century could reach 200,000 strong. The consequences of this increase will be very formidable, especially in years of drought.

Almost three quarters of the population live in or around the mountainous or upland plateau regions of the district where life is less severe than in the low-lying areas. The rest of the people tend their stock in the semi-arid scrublands. Here, the harsh environment makes agriculture impossible, but livestock thrives, as the soil is rich in mineral salts and endemic diseases are few. Unencumbered by possessions, the herdsmen lead a semi-nomadic way of life, following the rains and seeking out the best pastures over a large tract of land. As the broken country gets lower, it becomes drier, hotter and even more barren. In the north, these tough conditions are made doubly worse by ridge after ridge of jagged lava which are buffeted relentlessly by high winds. The rainfall is scanty and unpredictable; when it does rain, however, it can often be sudden and very violent. Watercourses gush in brown torrents for a few hours before baking dry again in the blistering heat. In years of plenty, the land is covered with a profusion of plants, the acacia thorn trees burst outrageously into blossom and wild flowers of infinite beauty bloom for a day, then quickly fade away. This is a time when the normal grim struggle the stock-owners experience to keep their cattle and small stock alive retreats for a while.

Sometimes nature is not so benevolent. Roughly every seven years the rains fail and the countryside is scorched and shrivelled until the colours are burnt uniformly brown. All able-bodied men lend a hand at the wells and pray they will not run dry. The skills of the stockmen are now tested to the limit. Being browsers, goats and camels will generally survive a bad drought without too much attention, a fact which underscores their economic importance to the Samburu. In contrast, cattle will invariably succumb to the rigours of famine – nature's way of culling stock which has outgrown the carrying capacity of the grasslands. It can be ruthless, indiscriminate and very unjust. During the last serious drought, in 1984, tens of thousands of cattle died. At the time, most people did not believe that the herds would recover, but they have been proved wrong. The Samburu consciously overstock in favourable times. They are unswerving in the belief that the more cows they own, the better their chances are of having at least a few survivors after a prolonged drought. When a money economy did not exist, this attitude was understandable. Today, cash from the sale of stock in times of plenty would buy others in times of need, and solve many of the problems caused by the degradation of the land.

The Samburu live in harmony with nature, and wild animals are accepted as part of the scene even though they can be very troublesome indeed. Buffaloes and elephants are dangerous to human life and cause extensive damage to crops, lions and leopards prey on their stock, while the numerous herds of zebra on the Lorroki Plateau compete for scarce grazing and water in times of drought. The Samburu Game Reserve in the south of the district is a unique sanctuary for wildlife. Here can be seen large herds of elephants watering in the Wuaso Ng'iro River and species of animals whose habitat is restricted to the semi-arid regions of the north – reticulated giraffe, Grevy's zebra, gerenuk and *Oryx beisa* to name but a few. Elephants and rhinos were once numerous throughout the district, but the depredations of well-armed poachers from across the

Somali border have taken their toll. While elephants can still be found in a number of places and seem to be on the increase again, rhinos are confined to a small area in the Mathews Range where they are guarded night and day. Of all the waterholes I have visited in Kenya, the one at the lodge in Maralal has the greatest number of wild animals coming to it at the right time of year. Lucky visitors may also catch a glimpse of a leopard from a hide in the lodge grounds.

Over the years, there have been a number of well-meaning projects aimed at improving the living standards of the people. They have almost all failed. All too often, aid donors introduce schemes which their experts deem appropriate without involving the local inhabitants, who know all about the environment and their needs. Some of the most successful and beneficial projects in the district were started by missionaries, the Catholic mission hospital at Wamba being an outstanding example. However, it does seem to a layman that there is a tendency among certain religious orders to spend lavishly on grandiose churches in order to save souls, rather than on programmes that would actually save people's lives.

Great emphasis has been given to education since 1963. Then, there were only a handful of schools in the district; now there are dozens, ranging from nursery level to high schools. Examination results in some of them are impressive. Approximately 50% of all eligible boys attend school for a while, but the percentage drops to nearer fifteen when it comes to girls, many of whom leave prematurely to get married. Since there is a constant need for children to tend their families' livestock, the likelihood of every child going to school in the foreseeable future is remote. Given the right encouragement, the educated youth can improve the living standards of their people by introducing better methods of animal husbandry and bringing progress to their homes. Unfortunately, it does not always happen this way. Once they have had their eyes opened to the consumer society of this materialistic world, many of them, not unnaturally, covet a different lifestyle. Unable to resist the temptation, they drift to cities and towns in search of non-existent work and quickly fall into a cultural vacuum. Away from tribal discipline for the first time in their lives, the next step in becoming a social misfit is all too short.

When two Samburu meet, they will never pass without greeting one another. They will say who they are, where they are from and what they are going to do. They will always enquire after the health of the animals and children, and ask if there has been any rain. There are no secrets; everybody knows exactly what everyone else is doing. Traditional values and norms of behaviour were evolved by the forefathers of the tribe over hundreds of years. They were designed to unite the people in the face of terrible odds. Since there were no chiefs or hereditary leaders, the elders strictly enforced discipline to a point where there were no petty criminals and no murderers. Moreover, if disputes arose within a family or clan, they would meet to decide how best to settle them. The younger generation accepted their word as law, partly out of respect for the age-grade system in which elders were venerated and partly out of a very real fear of their powerful curse. To this day, a *moran* can be asked by an elder to go to a distant place to deliver a message or collect a cow and he may not refuse even if he has never seen the man before. Nevertheless, cracks have started to appear in their rigid code of ethics. Some young men now drink and smoke, a privilege previously reserved for the elders; others decry their traditions as being outmoded. The tribe has reached a crossroads and the elders, bewildered by the pace of change, are faltering, uncertain which route to take. For the moment, tradition prevails.

OVERLEAF: Dawn breaks over the foothills of Ol doinyo Lenkiyieu, 'the mountains of the fatty chest meat of an ox' – so named by the Samburu because important age-set ceremonies were customarily held there.

One of the few permanent streams having its source on Mount Ng'iro, whose peaks rise to a height of 9,030 feet. Ng'iro is revered by the Samburu as a sacred mountain and many important ceremonies are held on its summit. The Samburu reason that even if Nkai, their god, is invisible, he has to be somewhere physical. There can be no better place for him to rest than on the highest mountain in the district. Lambs are sometimes sacrificed in the caves there.

Two young men pause in a typically relaxed pose, leaning on their spears with their sticks and clubs between their crossed legs. The Samburu walk great distances with a characteristic loping stride.

OPPOSITE: The Milgis is the largest seasonal river in Samburu District – a lifeline for stock-owners living in the low-lying country east of the Kirisia Hills.

The herds of zebra roaming the Lorroki Plateau, south of Maralal, are fearless – a manifestation of the Samburu herdsmen living in harmony with nature. In the dry weather, both cattle and zebra water in the shallow pans which usually dry up before the rains fall again.

The Great Rift Valley, more than 4,000 miles long and in
places 5,000 feet deep, stretches from the Lebanon to Mozambique.
It is the most dramatic feature of its kind on earth.
One of the finest views of it in Kenya can be seen at Losiolo,
a short drive from the administrative centre of Maralal.

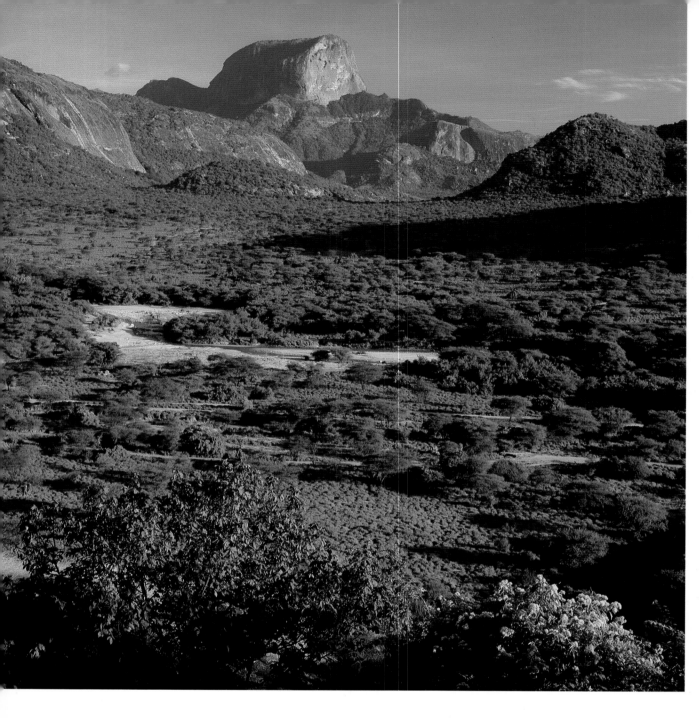

Poi, a massive lump of hard granatoid rock, is a startling monument to the tremendous force generated by movements in the earth's crust millions of years ago. Situated on the eastern side of the Ndoto Mountains, it lies close to the important waterholes at Ilaut.

Dominating the landscape to the north of the Samburu Game Reserve is Ol doinyo Sabachi – more commonly but incorrectly known as Mount Lololokwi. The name 'Lololokwi' originates from the Laikipiak Maasai whose territory it once was. They called the impressive feature Ol doinyo Lomanlokwe, 'the mountain with the round head'. Noted for the sheer granatoid gneiss of its southern face, the mountain rises to a height of 6,200 feet and has permanent water and a small forest on top. Every year, the Samburu graze their cattle there in the dry weather. Climbing the mountain for the first time, I came face to face with a rhino on the narrow stock path to the top. It was immediately obvious who had the right of way!

Blanket-clad elders congregate outside a *manyatta* at the foothills of the Ndoto Mountains. The elders rule on all important aspects of customary law and will remain in conference until they have reached a consensus of opinion.

A young boy plays with his toy bow and arrow. The small tuft of hair on the back of his head is not an unusual style for boys of his age.

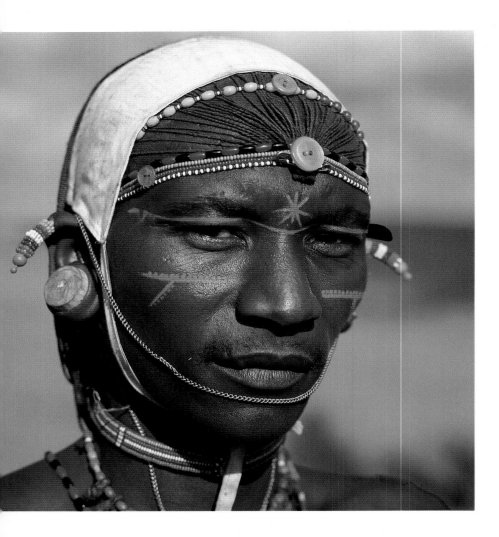

The warriors of the tribe are unmistakably ostentatious in their dress.
This young man has put wooden earplugs in his pierced earlobes.
The small cloth over part of his ochred hair keeps his braids in place.

The *mporro* is a necklace which is worn exclusively by married women. A long time ago, it was made of strands from giraffes' tails. Nowadays, the fibres of doum palm fronds (*Hyphaene coriacea*) make do. The large red beads are seeds. This woman's colourful beaded earrings are backed with leather. They were once very fashionable but are rarely seen today.

The Family

A Samburu settlement is known as a *nkang'* or, more colloquially, a *manyatta*. Typically, it will be sited in open country, often some distance from permanent water, and will consist of six or more houses built in a rough circle with an open space in the centre. The houses will be surrounded by a thorn or brushwood fence with each stock-owner having an individual gateway through it. There are no hard and fast rules as to who will live together in the same *manyatta*. Most families will be related but there will always be one or two elders who are just close friends of the same age-set and clan as the others. The composition of settlements is likely to change from one season to the next with the younger members of families departing in the dry weather to graze the herds on the distant pastures. They will remain there in temporary stock camps until the rains fall again.

There is a collective spirit among families who live together in the same *manyatta*. While they are nominally independent economically, they co-operate closely with one another and divide their manpower if a family does not have adequate to cope on its own. Despite the advantages of being a member of a large settlement, most stock-owners prefer a smaller unit, as the grasslands close to the *manyatta* will not be exhausted so quickly. The state of the grasslands also determines how far away the people of one *manyatta* will live from their neighbours. They can be as little as half a mile apart on the Lorroki Plateau or several miles in the semi-arid regions.

Women are entirely responsible for building and repairing the houses, which need constant attention during the rains. The style of traditional houses varies slightly depending on the availability of wood. Some have cedar walls and a curved roof; others have a lattice framework on top of which are laid small branches with foliage, covered all over with a thick coating of dung. In the low country, the framework is more likely to be covered with hides and mats. The houses are rectangular in shape with rounded corners and stand about five feet high. They have no doors or windows, only a single opening for an entrance, and are dark inside. A small passage partitioned by donkey pack-frames leads past an area where firewood is stacked and the newborn calves are tethered at night, to the hearth in the middle of the house. The fire must never be allowed to die out. On one side of the hearth are the raised sleeping quarters of the warriors and their friends; on the opposite side, a smaller area for the woman of the house and her young children. If she has no circumcised children, the accommodation will not be divided and the family will sleep together.

Situated a short distance behind each house will be the stock pens in which the family's sheep and goats are kept at night. There will also be two small enclosures nearby, one to coop up the kids and lambs, and the other to protect the calves. Cattle will usually be left to intermingle in the open spaces after evening milking, as long as the herd bulls do not have a tendency to fight.

Marriage is the turning point in a girl's life. She leaves home when she is about fifteen and enters a world where she is a complete stranger. She may not even know her husband, let alone his relatives and the elders of his clan. Somewhere in these unfamiliar surroundings, however, she will probably find succour from a woman who once belonged to her own clan. She cannot count on the support of her parents unless she is in dire need; nor may she see their home again for several years. In time, she will grow accustomed to her new life and come to regard her husband's clan as her own. Most girls consider themselves fortunate to marry a young man. They dread the prospect of being given away to an elder and becoming the second or third wife of his household; but in this they have no say. On the other hand, there is an *esprit de corps* among wives of a polygamous marriage who can gang up against their husband and get their own way. Each wife has a house and a herd of her own, built up from the cattle she is given by her husband on marriage, and the women are at pains to become friends rather than rivals. The senior wife is always in charge; when she gives an order, the others must obey.

There is no birth control among married Samburu. Every parent wishes to have as many children as possible, for it stabilizes a marriage. The more there are of them, the more propitious the family is thought to be. Infant mortality has been reduced considerably in recent years, due to the improvements in government medical services and the efforts of a few missionary orders which assist with health care. The result is a rapid increase in the population with the average polygamous family today having at least ten children. The effects of this on the traditional cattle economy are likely to be serious in years to come, for more mouths require more cattle to feed them, yet the herds will not multiply at the same rate. There will also be greater demands for cattle to celebrate ceremonial occasions and to provide bridewealth prior to a marriage.

A mother gives birth at home whenever possible, attended by other married women who assist delivery. The umbilical cord is placed across one of the father's right sandals – or the mother's if the baby is a girl – and cut with a knife. A husband does not attend the birth of his children and takes little interest in what he considers to be a woman's affair. If he is away from home when his wife gives birth to a son, she must give him a heifer from her herd to add to his own. Normally, one would have thought that it would be the other way round but, no, the wife is at fault for having a baby boy in his absence! No one could care less if the child is a girl.

There are two ceremonies when a child is born. The first, called *lkupoket*, takes place on the day of the birth. A kid, whose fleece must be of uniform colour, is killed beside the entrance to the house and the mother of the newborn will drink a little of its blood, but may not partake of the meat. Other women – friends and relatives – feast on the meat and afterwards scatter the remains of the blood mixed with the contents of the animal's stomach round the perimeter of the *manyatta*. Whatever is left over after that is put on the top right-hand corner of the mother's house. Meanwhile, the bones and the grass upon which the kid was slaughtered will be collected and burnt outside the house for fear of witchcraft.

A baby boy will be given a male calf by his father as the foundation of his herd. Blood will be drawn from its jugular on four consecutive days, diluted with milk and given to the mother. It is a symbolic replacement of the blood she lost during labour and will be her only nourishment for this period. If the child is a girl, the calf will be an unserved heifer, but it will remain the property of her father when she grows up. By watching the proceedings, the family will know the sex of the newborn child. Friends and relatives who call later to see the mother tend to avoid asking the obvious question of whether the baby is a boy or a girl; rather, they enquire after the calf and discover for themselves the sex of the child.

The father will not go near his wife's house until four days after the birth of the child when the second ceremony, called *lbuutan*, is customarily held. If the family so desires, this ritual can be postponed for several months, even years, to avoid having to kill another animal. The only stipulation is that it must be performed before the child is circumcised.

An ox or sometimes a sheep – but never a goat – is slaughtered outside the mother's house. The left side of the animal is given to the elders to eat, while part of the right side is cooked by elderly women for the mother and themselves. That evening, the ribs and right hind leg of the ox are roasted by the elders and shared with other guests of the family. Uncircumcised youths returning from herding will be given the heart. Only the warriors and their girlfriends are strictly prohibited from eating any of this meat.

The following day, the mother will peg out the skin on the ground to dry it in the sun. Next, she will scrape it and oil it to make it supple so that the child can use it as a sleeping mat until he or she grows up and leaves home.

In some parts of Africa, twins are anathema and will be killed at birth. In the distant past, this was true of the Samburu when they were the first-born of a family. Nowadays, husbands are delighted when their wives give birth to twins. There is a belief that snakes came into the world as twins; consequently, snakes and twins are the best of friends. Twins never harm a snake; if one enters their home, they will offer it a little milk or tobacco. They claim to have the power to order a snake to bite somebody they dislike; moreover, if one bites a friend of theirs, they will spit on the fang marks to neutralize the venom. Fortunately, I have never had occasion to call on their help!

A woman's interests revolve narrowly round her family. If she has a child or two yet fails to become pregnant again for some while, she will affix to her hair long strands of light blue and pale green beads which will hang down her back as a good omen for pregnancy. Old women will advise her on the best months for wearing the beads but August is often favoured. If she then conceives, she will continue to wear the beads until she gives birth or the child is weaned. Otherwise, they are usually worn for a month at a time and the process repeated periodically for three to four years. If she still fails to have more children, the family will give up hope and burn in the hearth of her home the leaves and bark of a cedar tree mixed with lichen, though the reason for this custom is not clear.

The relationship between a man and his wives is never an easy one. The enormous difference in their ages can lead to tension, especially over the inevitable uncertainty of a woman's promiscuity with younger men. Although she is allowed a discreet sexual relationship with men of her husband's age-set, a wife must be careful not to associate with the warriors of the tribe, who are likely to be nearer her own age. They may not even enter her home until such time as her eldest son has been circumcised and is a *moran* in his own right. Only then does she receive the consideration and the respect reserved for older women, but this does not allow her to play any part in tribal affairs. Women's liberty is far from being realized among Samburu women who are resigned to a subordinate role. A wife is a costly investment for a man and he has no wish to see her emancipated. She is there to bring up the children, maintain and occasionally move the home, help with the livestock, milk the cows, carry heavy loads of firewood from the forests and look after the donkeys which she uses to fetch water about every other day. Her life is a grind, yet she has the satisfaction of her children and the respect she can command in the community if they are brought up well.

The mother of a woman's husband plays an important role in raising the children and in doing so moulds their characters for adult life. She will tell them stories about the history of the tribe and instruct them in the way they must behave. Samburu childhood spans a comparatively short period of time. From about the age of six, children will start to shepherd the small stock and look after the calves. As boys grow up, they learn to sing to their cows, praising the virtues of the bulls of the herd. This is the beginning of a strong attachment they have for cattle which will never desert them. Meanwhile their sisters will mind their baby brothers and sisters, and take an interest in the home. They join in dances but have little time to play games, which are generally associated with animals – both domestic and wild – and the warriors whom they idolize.

Divorce is uncommon among the Samburu although a woman who is maltreated or whose husband is a drunkard may run away to her parents. If she has children, she will almost certainly be brought back home. If she refuses, she will lose all right to them and may never see them again. If there are no children from the marriage, the man will demand back the bridewealth he paid to her parents to annul the union. A husband will have no compunction in beating his wife with a thin whip if he thinks that she deserves it. Unjustified punishment, however, is frowned upon by the elders, who may intercede on her behalf. In this case, the man must respect their views and be less harsh.

There are considerable social barriers between men and women and there are conflicting interests, too, over the ownership and disposal of cattle. A husband may unashamedly exploit his wives' herds to his own advantage, though this can have the effect of uniting the family against him: his sons' interests are best served by protecting their mother's herds. A woman depends on her sons to look after her in old age, although she ultimately becomes the responsibility of the last-born who will inherit her herd. Their herds and their wives and children are her security. She will have an honoured position in their households where she can be a unifying factor after all her children have married and left home. A woman who has no sons is at a tremendous disadvantage; in old age, she will have to rely on a son-in-law for her needs, but such a relationship can never be the same. It is hardly surprising, then, that both men and women crave baby boys.

When a husband dies, his widows are not allowed to remarry. The elders of the clan will assemble some time after his death to kill an ox at a ceremony called *sikiria*. The purpose of this is to bless the widows and appoint a part-time consort to help them bear more children in their late husband's name. There is no prior consultation about this with the women; as in other matters affecting their well-being, they have no say. The consort will already have a wife and family of his own, but he will not refuse the decision of the elders. Besides, there are no financial implications to the appointment and he can visit the women as frequently or infrequently as he likes.

OVERLEAF: Samburu settlements are called *Nkang'* or, more colloquially, *manyatta*. A typical one will consist of six or more houses built in a rough circle with an open space in the centre. The houses are surrounded by a thorn or brushwood fence to prevent the livestock straying and marauding predators getting in. Nothing is more important to a Samburu than his cattle. They represent his wealth and standing in the community. He will rate their well-being almost as highly as that of his own children.

41

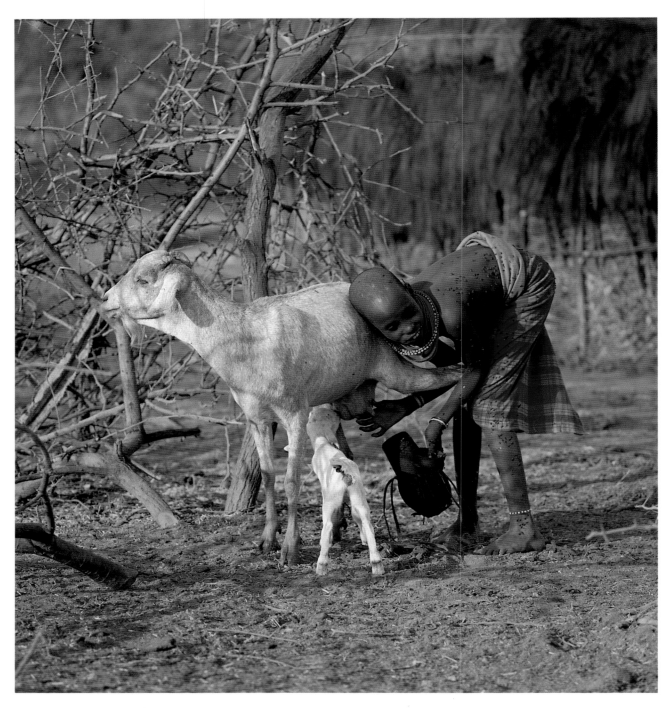

A young girl milking a nanny goat into a gourd-like container
made of wood. Only women and children deign to milk goats,
although everyone will drink the milk.

A woman milks a camel at a *manyatta* in the dry country close to Latakwen.
The proximity of the calf helps to stimulate the flow of milk. Baby camels
have a wool-like texture to their coats which they lose after six months.

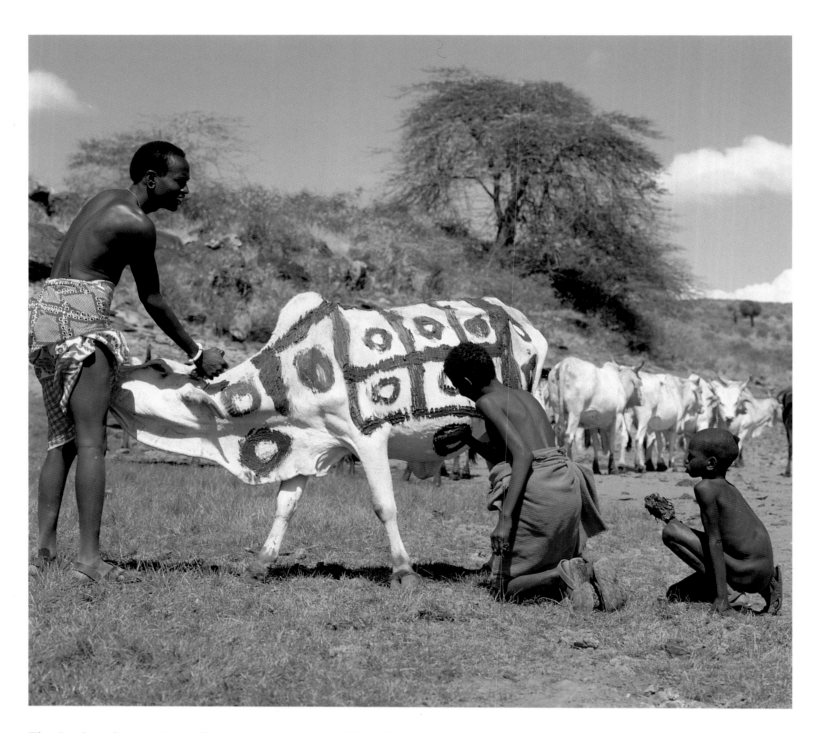

The Samburu have a close affinity with their cattle. When the warriors herd them, they will frequently sing to them, praising the bull of the herd. Boys love to decorate their favourite animals with mud or clay when they take them to salt licks.

From an early age, children of both sexes tend their family's flocks of sheep and goats. They help to look after the lambs and lend a hand at milking time.

The status of this woman is easily identified by her ornaments. The traditional *mporro* necklace, the simple metal earrings and the coils of mild steel wire wound round her right forearm immediately confirm that she is married.

Mothers carry their babies in bright cotton material tied round their waists or slung on their backs with a knot over one shoulder. Their upper forearms are often covered in coils of brass wire, wound so tightly that they may restrict the movement of the arm and weaken the biceps.

A Samburu house stands about five feet high; its construction reflects the semi-nomadic lifestyle of the people. Building materials depend on the availability of timber. Away from the forested areas, foliage is laid over a carefully made framework of brushwood which is then thickly plastered with a mixture of cow dung and mud.

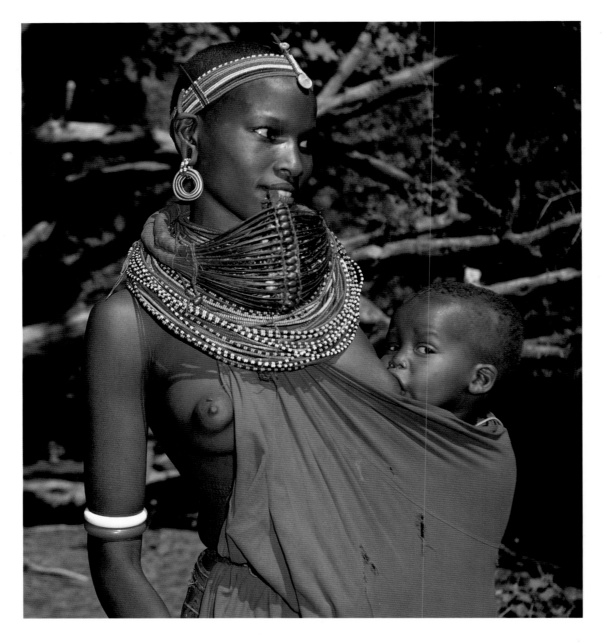

A young woman suckles her baby son. This was the first child of her arranged marriage as the third wife of a man almost forty years her senior.

In places where water is scarce, it is not unusual for a mother or girls from her husband's family to wash babies by squirting them with water from their mouths.

In the drier regions of the district, mats made from wild sisal fibres (*Sansevieria*) are used in preference to dung. Before the women weave them, the *Sansevieria* leaves are buried for a week and then pounded to remove the fibres.

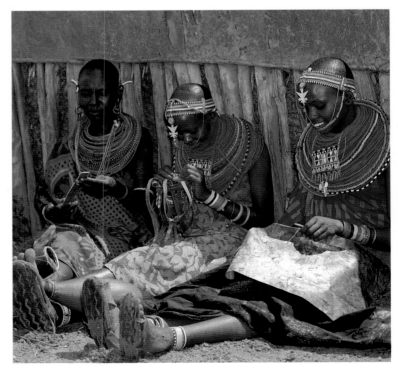

A mother and her two unmarried daughters busy themselves making a leather carrier for a new milk gourd and sewing a goatskin cloak which will be worn by the woman's son several weeks before his circumcision.

Women are responsible for the hewing of wood and drawing of water. The loads they carry would make most strong men groan under their weight. Fire is a potent symbol of life; the fire in the hearth of a house must never be allowed to die out. For this reason, forests in the district are receding each year.

OVERLEAF: Everyone is happy when the long dry season is broken by heavy cloudbursts. These young boys steal a few minutes from herding to enjoy a mud slide at a nearby water pan.

A child washes in a stock trough, hand-carved from the wood of a *Commiphora* tree. Young children customarily wear single strands of beads round their necks and waists. This small boy also has a metal bell tied to his right leg in case he is separated from his mother in the thick riverine bush which lines the Milgis *lugga*.

To avoid disturbing the mud which has settled in the bottom of a sand scrape, a young boy kneels to quench his thirst in the Seiya *lugga*. The Seiya, in flood, is one of the most dangerous rivers in the country. Hardly a year passes by without a vehicle getting stuck in the quicksand and being swept away.

Young boys compete with each other to throw a light spear through a hoop. By the time they are grown up and become warriors, they can be devastatingly accurate.

Wrestling is a favourite pastime of young boys. Their necklaces of green beads show that they are not yet old enough to be circumcised.

As is the case in many countries of the world, donkeys and camels are the beasts of burden. They carry chattels, water, newborn animals in panniers and, not infrequently, young children and old people.

In both these pictures, the basic structures of a house are being transported. The curved sticks will be tied together in the shape of an igloo and covered with skins or woven mats to form a temporary shelter in a stock camp.

gum, gave away twenty of his thirty cows over a period of six weeks. He was not angry about this, but hoped God would recognize his sacrifice and reward him in other ways.

As the day for circumcision draws closer, a fat ox is killed and eaten by the initiates, while their mothers reduce its fatty tissue to liquid form and rub it into their sons' black cloaks. Some hours later, the boys are blessed as they leave the *lorora*, led by a select group of junior elders to certain traditional places as far apart as Marsabit and Baringo to gather sticks and staves for their bows, arrows and clubs; these are cut from a tree of the *Commiphora* family, *Boswellia neglecta*. Gum, *naing'ure*, used later to tip these arrows, *lbaa*, and weight the clubs, is extracted from the same tree which grows abundantly in arid country, especially in the hills close to South Horr. At other times, the gum is chewed by women and children, used to relieve headaches by placing it near a fire and inhaling the fumes, or as a cure for 'flu by boiling it in milk and tea.

While the boys search for gum, the elders kindle a fire using firesticks and friction. This seemingly insignificant act is of major consequence, for it brings the new age-set firmly under their control. From that moment they become the 'firestick elders' to the new generation. They supervise the boys' passage through *moranhood* and have the power of a potent curse to discipline them or curb their excesses. Since fathers would be unwilling to curse their sons, it is normal for the firestick elders to belong to an age-set which is junior to the fathers. Indeed, youths are never circumcised into an age-set less than three below their fathers' unless there are mitigating circumstances and the firestick elders have considered favourably the merits of the case.

A round trip as much as two hundred miles over six or seven days is not unusual to collect gum; only the weak or sick are excused the journey, in which case their brothers must go instead. On return to the *lorora*, singing the *lebarta*, the boys urge the elders in song to finalize the arrangements for their circumcision quickly. This may still be several days, even weeks, away. Circumcisors are few and far between and the elders may have to wait patiently to secure the services of a good one. By that time the moon phase may be inauspicious for the ceremony. Generally, boys will only be circumcised from two days after a new moon until the beginning of the last quarter. Any even number of days after the sighting of the new moon is considered more propitious than the odd days. Sometimes, when everything seems to be settled, a further delay may occur if one of the boys has not yet arrived. Since the Samburu have a custom that requires full brothers and sisters to be circumcised in the order of their birth, the absence of the eldest son can prevent others in the family undergoing the rites. I have witnessed traumatic scenes because of this. On other occasions, disputes between elders can lead to friction and a threat to curse the initiates if the wishes of an individual are ignored.

About this time, the firestick elders call all the boys together and demand that they reveal if they have on any occasion had sexual intercourse with a circumcised woman – this is strictly forbidden for an uncircumcised boy. The truth is extracted from them through the threat of a curse and those who lie are said to die. Fathers are very angry if their sons have slept with a circumcised woman because in that case they are obliged to give a heifer to the man who holds the boy's shoulders during his circumcision, lest that man may also die.

At last the circumcisor arrives at the *lorora* and the date of the ceremony is set. The sharp instruments of every household – pangas and axes – are blessed individually on ox hides by pouring milk over them. These hides must be from animals which have been killed rather than those dying of natural causes. At the conclusion of the ritual, the boys are also blessed before setting out in a group to fetch water from a source that never dries up. Many boys from Maralal and the Lorroki Plateau go to Kisima, where crystal-clear water bubbles up between rocks from the bowels of the earth. Each carries a new gourd-shaped container made by his mother from hollowed-out wood. In it is a little milk which he will pour into the spring before refilling the container with milky water. He must collect four small pebbles, drop them into the container and then pluck a bunch of marsh grass to tie to its carrying straps. The boys will also tie grass through the shoulder-knots of their black capes after they have daubed the right side of their bodies with white clay. The importance attached to milk and grass as a blessing is directly related to the Samburu's strong affinity with their cattle. When they return to the *lorora*, they will sing the *lebarta* for a while and disperse.

As the boys enter the perimeter fence through their own stock gateways, their mothers fling a little milk at their feet to bless them. Each mother will then prepare a bed-like structure, two feet or so off the ground, on the right-hand side near the entrance to her house; her son will lie on this after his ordeal. Later, she will shave his head, first wetting his hair with a mixture of milk and water which she pours into the bowl of a traditional four-legged wooden stool. Afterwards, all the hair will be collected carefully and put on the stool.

Most boys are circumcised at first light the next day, but there are some families – possibly 20% in all – who customarily circumcise in the afternoon. It is generally recognized that these boys have to display a lot of courage. After a period of feverish activity in the hot sun, the operation can be most painful, with the initiates tending to lose more blood than do their companions in the early morning.

In the same way that some Christian boys may have two godfathers, a Samburu boy will have two sponsors who help him at this time and attend to him at his circumcision, one holding his shoulders and the other his right leg. Upon the successful conclusion of the rites, he will treat them as close relatives and call them the equivalent of 'uncle'. He may never again address them by their real names. The sponsors measure the boy for sandals, cutting them from the ox hide which was blessed that morning and upon which he will sit while he is being circumcised. As he puts them on, his mother will hang his *nchipi* round her neck or waist and wear it until the *lmuget loolbaa*, the ceremony of the arrows, takes place a month later. Every scrap of severed leather must be picked up and put on the stool with the boy's hair. His mother will then take it into her house and tip it on to his newly constructed bed, beneath his ox hide.

The sponsors will also help to slaughter a ram. A small flap of skin from its forehead is first removed and tied to the middle finger of the boy's right hand. The ram is then carefully skinned since the initiate must sit on a wet sheepskin during his operation. This practice is not universal, however, for some clans – most notably those whose origins stem from the neighbouring Rendille tribe – place a white stone underneath the ox hide instead. After the operation is over, the stone is immediately removed and hidden by the boy's father to prevent the possibility of its being used for sorcery.

Now it is the turn of the boys due for circumcision that afternoon to rush off to the nearby grazing grounds to bring home the herds – no boy can be circumcised unless his family's cattle are in the *lorora*. The animals are driven at a fast trot and boys display courage by jumping on the backs of their bulls as they thunder towards the narrow stock ways. Stories of valour in this wild-west setting abound, but I have yet to witness such a spectacle myself.

Boys wait their turn patiently outside their mothers' houses for the circumcisor to arrive. He operates on the sons of the most senior family in the *lorora* first and moves in a clockwise direction. Most families have their children circumcised at the entrance to their homes, but others by tradition perform the ritual at their stock gateway into the *lorora*. This is so of the families whose ancestors came from the Rendille.

The boys I have watched appear remarkably composed, often singing the *lebarta* as if nothing was about to happen to them. This is more than can be said for the *moran*, who worry about the conduct of their brothers to such an extent that they work themselves up into a frenzy, quivering all over – the effect of hysterical over-stimulation which is often the first sign of an uncontrollable fit. Tears shed by initiates at this time are not associated with cowardice but rather are an expression of nervous excitement at the lack of confidence shown in them. Even their own brothers, fearing they may flinch, may try to hit them with a stick unless forcibly restrained by their friends.

The choice of a circumcisor or *lakitoni* is vitally important; the best ones are in great demand and not always available. Many are Samburu living close to Mount Ng'iro, but others may come from far away. An accomplished *lakitoni* can circumcise a boy in a minute. After retracting the foreskin, he cuts off all the inner skin attached to the glans. Then, pulling the foreskin forward, he makes a small slit in the top of the prepuce, about half an inch from the end, and forces the glans through it. This has the effect of leaving the end of the foreskin as a pendant, called a tie, beneath the penis. The circumcisor's double-bladed knife is made by the blacksmiths of the tribe, razor-sharp to start with but rather blunt towards the end of a morning's work. I watched one circumcisor sharpening his knife on his calf; while his leg looked as tough as old leather, the effect could hardly have been the same! This same man was drunk by the afternoon and in no fit state to operate, but nobody dared to intervene. The boys must have suffered unnecessarily but no one showed fear.

Basic hygiene is negligible and I would expect major improvements on the present crude methods before the next age-set is opened in the year 2004 – if for no other reason than the fear of spreading Aids. Mercifully, this has not been a problem among the Samburu, but the dangers are very real. One must give credit to the experienced *lakitoni*, for one seldom hears of initiates being taken to hospital due to loss of blood, although complications do occasionally set in. Very few boys are circumcised in hospital, both they and their fathers preferring the prestige associated with the traditional rites. Schoolmasters, university students, soldiers and policemen were among those I saw returning home to undergo the knife. These older boys, being more developed, suffer the most pain, yet instances of cowardice are extremely rare; I heard of only three in 1990 out of an estimated 10,000 boys. This is about half as many again as were circumcised in 1976, when the initiation of the previous age-set took place.

Should an initiate show any sign of fear while he is being circumcised, his family's cattle would be driven out of the *lorora* straight through the perimeter fence. The boy would be severely beaten and years ago could even have been killed because of the shame he brought on his family and the rest of the clan. Throughout his life, he would be regarded as a coward and marriage would be almost impossible, except to a divorcee. His relatives would be ostracized for a while, ashes and dung would be rubbed on his mother's head and in future no one would go through the low entrance to her house other than bottom first. The dread of a boy flinching must weigh very heavily on the minds of the family as the time for circumcision draws near. Family honour is at stake, yet it is bad manners to betray one's inner feelings in public. At the approach of the circumcisor, tension and excitement mount and the boy's family get more wrought up.

The boy's sponsors lay out his ox hide at the entrance to his mother's house and place the sheepskin pad on top of it. His black cloak is removed and then his sandals as he stands naked on his ox hide. The mixture of milk and water is poured over his head, whereupon he collapses on to the sheepskin in a sitting position, his outstretched legs apart. One sponsor, wearing a woman's skin apron over his right shoulder, wraps the black cloak round the boy's chest and squats, holding his shoulders firmly, while the other sponsor holds his right thigh. His left leg can be held by a close relative, but this is not obligatory. The boy looks stoically ahead, his face expressionless, his eyes a distant glassy stare. Not a muscle twitches on his body; he could be hypnotized or under an anaesthetic for all the signs of pain he shows.

Within a minute the operation is over. Milk and water are poured over the circumcisor's bloody knife as he moves swiftly on to his next patient. He has earned himself a fee of two hundred shillings or one goat, and two shillings for the knife; the fee escalates in line with the value of a goat. At 12,000 shillings an hour, his job is arguably the most lucrative in the country, but he will have to wait for the turn of the century to reap the same rewards again. By the time he has circumcised three age-sets, he is forced to retire.

I have already mentioned that full brothers and sisters must be circumcised in the order of their birth. For a girl this is normally a preliminary to her marriage. However, when she has an elder and a younger brother who are due to be circumcised in a *lorora*, she will have to be circumcised there, even if there are no immediate prospects of betrothal. As soon as her elder brother has been circumcised and carried into his mother's house, the men move back and women surround the girl at the entrance to the house. Once she is safely indoors, her younger brother will be led out and the crowd of men will surge forward as the women disperse.

Immediately a boy has been circumcised, he will sing the *lebarta*, imploring his father to give him a cow. As he sings, his sponsors replace his sandals and gently carry him on his ox hide into his mother's house where he is laid on his couch to rest for a while. The sponsors and the *moran* of the family then draw blood from the jugular of an ox and mix it with milk for the boy to drink. After the first sip, he will spit four times on his own stomach as a blessing. Should anyone be in great agony after his operation, some families will tie donkey droppings to the underside of the roof, above the boy's head. This is believed to relieve pain. Any blood spilt on the ox hide during or after the operation must not be mopped up until the following day when the fathers help their sons to wash in a little warm water. This is the last occasion a boy may wash or even clean his teeth with water until the end of the *lmuget loolbaa*, the ceremony of the arrows, a month later.

Meanwhile, preparations will be going on at the *lorora* for the majority of the boys who will be circumcised the following day. Tension remains high and everyone is restless. The kudu-horn trumpet is blown at frequent intervals and the boys sing almost continuously throughout the night. Circumcision starts at first light, when it is almost impossible to see properly what is going on. It will last about two hours, depending on the number of boys in the *lorora* and the expertise of the *lakitoni* with his knife. No cattle are allowed out to graze until every boy has undergone the ritual. The procedures are identical to those I have already described. At their conclusion, women are despatched to cut the branches of two different types of tree which are stuck upright on either side of the entrance to the house as an indication that a member of the household has been circumcised. In forested areas the branches of olive and cedar trees are favoured, but other species such as acacia will be used in the semi-arid regions.

During the morning, groups of four or more elders will visit each home where circumcision has taken place to bless the household. For every child circumcised, the proud father will tie a strip of lion skin, *munken*, below each knee, hang two copper-wire ornaments normally worn by women and called *urauri* in his pierced earlobes and place a string of pale green beads round his head. As he sits on his four-legged stool at the entrance to his home, one of the elders will smear his forehead and hair with butter fat from a small wooden container held by his wife, who must be in the company of another woman. As this is done, a prayer is muttered aloud by the elders. The wife will also give everyone present a small dab of butter to rub on their hands. The elders then go into the house and, in turn, throw four pinches of tobacco into the embers of the fire while chanting another prayer to Nkai. At the end of this ritual, each elder is given a little chewing tobacco as a gift from the household.

Groups of women will also visit every household later in the day to drink tea and eat some meat. They must bring a present of milk and leave with a little tobacco. They will smear their beads with the remains of the butter fat and with considerable amusement sing a short circumcision song at the entrance to the home, referring to the lecherous intentions of impotent old men.

As soon as a boy has washed himself the day after his ordeal, his sponsors will prepare his bows and arrows, using the special sticks gathered on the long journey to collect gum. The arrows will be eight in number, each tipped with a round blob of gum. The remainder of the gum will be put on a stave which looks rather like, and is used as, a club. The sponsors also help to fit his new head-dress. Two black ostrich feathers are fastened on either side of a narrow band of plaited palm fibre which fits tightly round his forehead like a sweat band. Hanging down from the back of the band are four strings of beads – normally a combination of two colours depending on the boy's clan. I have seen dark blue, pale green and white ostrich-shell beads. They terminate at the shoulder blades in bead-like seeds or wood carved in the shape of a bead. Inevitably, there are exceptions to this rule. Some clans do not allow their boys to wear ostrich feathers and others forbid them to shoot birds, which is the main pre-occupation of the *laibartak*, the new initiates, for the next month or so. The obligatory and distinguishing mark of any newly circumcised boy is, however, the women's copper earrings he wears in his ears.

The *laibartak* are subject to various prohibitions and restrictions after they have been circumcised. We already know that they are not allowed to wash for a month; instead they smear themselves with fat. Nor are they allowed to drink water for two weeks. They may not stay outside their *lorora* or a *manyatta* after sunset, but must sleep either in their mother's house or at the home of a clansman; they may not hold a knife or a sharp instrument for fear of hurting themselves; since they are still technically unclean, they may not pick up food with their fingers, meat being eaten with the aid of sharp sticks; they may not break the bones of animals they eat; they may not climb trees or wade rivers; they may not kill anything, however small, other than birds; and they may not quarrel with anyone, since to do so is believed to leave them argumentative for the rest of their lives. Within days of their circumcision, they start to visit nearby *manyattas* again, singing the *lebarta* and demanding a sheep to eat. Mutton with lots of fat is their main diet at this time and no one will refuse them a reasonable request.

As a boy recovers from his operation, he travels farther afield, hunting birds with his bow and four blunt arrows. The other arrows are kept in reserve in case he loses one and may be given away at a later date. The only species of birds that may not be killed are, not unreasonably, the larger ones such as eagles, vultures, crows and doves, and for unexplained reasons small seed-eaters and the attractive blue-eared glossy starling. When a bird is killed, it is carefully skinned without using a knife, stuffed with dry grass and attached to the boy's head-band by means of its beak. A bird which has had its head shot off accidentally cannot be used. The enthusiastic hunter can collect a dozen or more skins; other boys may resort to guile and trap theirs. If a *moran* kills a bird and gives it to a boy, they will call each other *nkwenyi* as a mark of friendship. Similarly, if someone is given an arrow by a boy, they will call each other *mpirian* for a while. The *laibartak* also chase girls, shooting arrows at their legs. A girl can ransom herself by handing over a bead with which the boy will decorate the gum on his club. With two consecutive years of good rainfall in Samburu District in the late 1980s the 'shooting season' of 1990 should have only a temporary effect on the birdlife. I estimate that 100,000 birds were killed for ritual purposes, the majority being sparrows, weavers, barbets, bee-eaters and starlings.

At the end of a month hunting birds, the wounds of the *laibartak* should have healed and they are ready to move to a new stage in their progress towards becoming full warriors of the tribe.

Circumcision ceremonies take place in purpose-built encampments, called *lorora*, which can be large enough to house two hundred families. They are generally occupied for two to three months before being burnt to the ground. The women are responsible for building and repairing the houses, which are sited in a rough circle round a perimeter fence of thorn scrub or brushwood.

Uncircumcised boys are considered to be children, whatever their age. They have no standing in the tribe and do not belong to an age-set. They style their hair in an unmistakable 'pudding bowl' and often rub charcoal and fat into it. Several weeks before their initiation, they change their hairstyle to a circular tuft on the back of their shaven skulls. At this time, they will wear the *nchipi*, a distinctive decoration of every boy who participates in the ritual. Fastened to a leather thong which passes through the boy's pierced ears are eight strings of blue or blue and white beads hanging down the back of his neck. Each string terminates at the small of the back in a large bronze-coloured wing cover of a torpedo-shaped beetle, *Sterocera hildebrandti*.

OVERLEAF: The initiates must wear charcoal-blackened cloaks which are made by their mothers from three goatskins. They gather frequently to sing the *lebarta*, a circumcision song with a slow, haunting melody whose words are ad-libbed to suit the occasion. It is held to be a particularly potent form of collective inducement and is said to give encouragement to the initiates to withstand pain.

THIS SPREAD AND OVERLEAF: With tension mounting in the days leading up to circumcision, it is not unusual for some of the initiates to break down under the strain. They succumb to hysterical and often violent outbursts and have to be forcibly restrained. These fits are known to the Samburu as *ndokuna*.

The mothers of the initiates rub animal fat into their sons' cloaks, shortly before the boys set out on an arduous journey to collect sticks, staves and gum, which will later be made into bows, arrows and clubs.

The initiates beg animals from the nearby stock-owners and eat huge amounts of meat in the weeks before they are circumcised. They retreat to the bush to roast oxen on open charcoal fires, keeping well out of sight of women.

Clad in their black cloaks, the initiates leave the *lorora* in an organized band, led by a select group of junior elders to traditional places in search of trees of the *Commiphora* family, *Bowellia neglecta*, which grow abundantly in the arid regions of the district. The journey may take them a week or more. On their return to the *lorora*, singing the *lebarta*, with their sticks, staves and gum over one shoulder, they are blessed before dispersing to their parents' homes.

The day before a circumcision ceremony, the sharp instruments of every household – such as *pangas* and axes – will be blessed by the elders of the *lorora*, who pour a little milk over them as they intone a blessing. These instruments will be laid out on the ox hides upon which the boys will be circumcised.

OVERLEAF: When all the sharp instruments of the *lorora* have been blessed, the initiates set out in a group to draw water from a source that never dries up. Each boy will carry a new gourd-shaped container made by his mother from hollowed-out wood. Kisima, situated on the Lorroki Plateau some twelve miles from Maralal town, is a favoured place. Here, the boys pluck bunches of marsh grass to tie to their gourds and through the knots of their black cloaks.

Another traditional form of adornment is daubing the
right sides of the face and body with white clay.

Some families have a tradition of placing a white stone underneath their sons' ox hides, although the majority of boys will sit on a wet sheepskin when they are circumcised. A ram is slaughtered for this purpose and a small flap of skin is cut from the forehead before it is skinned. The initiate will wear this flap on the middle finger of his right hand as a ring.

After the initiates have collected water and returned to their *lorora*, their mothers shave them. Their hair will first be wetted with the water they brought back mixed in the bowl of a traditional four-legged stool with a little milk. Afterwards, all the hair will be placed carefully on the stool and, later, taken into their mothers' houses where it will be scattered on top of the boys' newly constructed beds. This woman has already put her son's *nchipi* round her neck. She will wear it for a month.

New sandals are made for every initiate by cutting a small piece of leather from the ox hide upon which the boy will be circumcised. He must wear them until the conclusion of the *lmuget loolbaa*, the ceremony of the arrows, a month later.

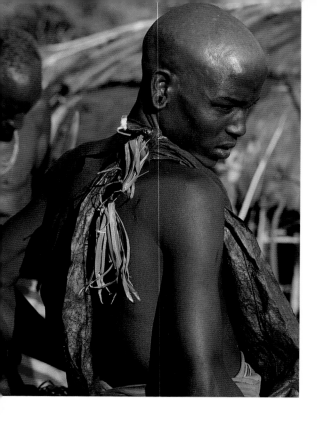

An initiate keenly watches the activities of his ritual helpers as the time for his circumcision draws closer.

Boys whose families customarily circumcise their children in the afternoon rush off to the nearby grazing grounds to drive their fathers' cattle home. No boy may undergo the ritual unless his family's livestock is penned in the *lorora*.

The ritual helpers of two initiates slaughter and skin the rams
in readiness for the boys' circumcision. The demands on a family's
cattle and small stock are very heavy at this time.

In the early morning, a father leads his son to the entrance to his home to await the arrival of the circumcisor.

Lemoloi is an expert circumcisor who lives on Mount Ng'iro, in the north of the district. He belongs to the Lmarraato clan – a small clan renowned for its skill with the knife. He is seen here stropping his knife made by the blacksmiths of the tribe.

A boy's sponsors lay out his ox hide at the entrance to his mother's house and place a sheepskin – folded in the form of a pad – on top of it. His black cloak is removed and then his sandals as he stands naked waiting his turn with the circumcisor. A mixture of milk and water is poured over his shaven head as a blessing.

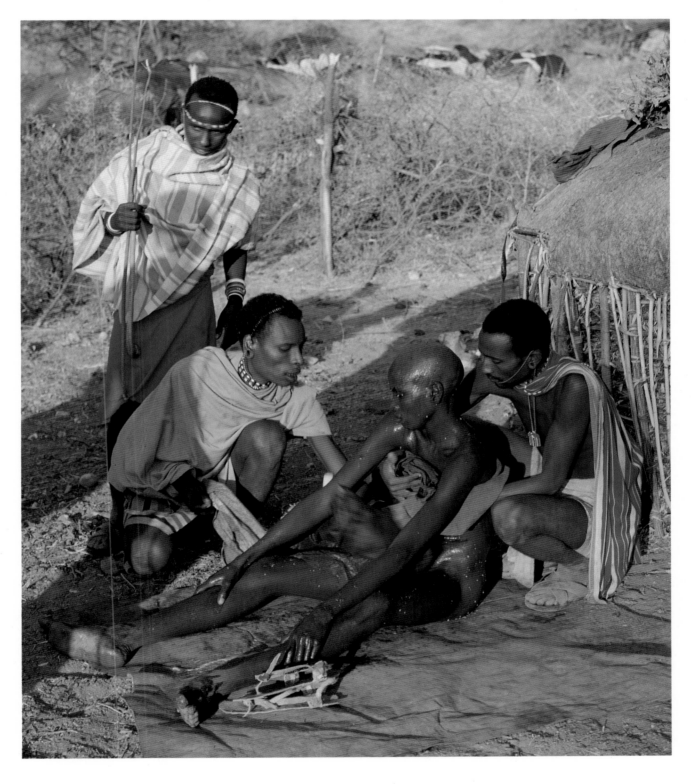

The boy then sits on the sheepskin pad, his outstretched legs apart. One of his sponsors squats, holding his shoulders, while the other grasps his right thigh. The boy looks calmly ahead, not twitching a muscle or blinking an eyelid.

Within a minute, the operation is over and the circumcisor moves swiftly on to his next customer.
Brave boys immediately burst into song, imploring their fathers to give them a cow.
As a boy sings the *lebarta*, his sponsors replace his sandals and gently carry him on his
ox hide into his mother's house where he will be laid to rest on his couch for a while.

A boy's sponsors will now draw blood from an ox by tying a rope tourniquet round the animal's neck and piercing the jugular with a short, sharp arrow. Two or three pints can be drawn from a healthy steer, which will not be bled again for more than a month.

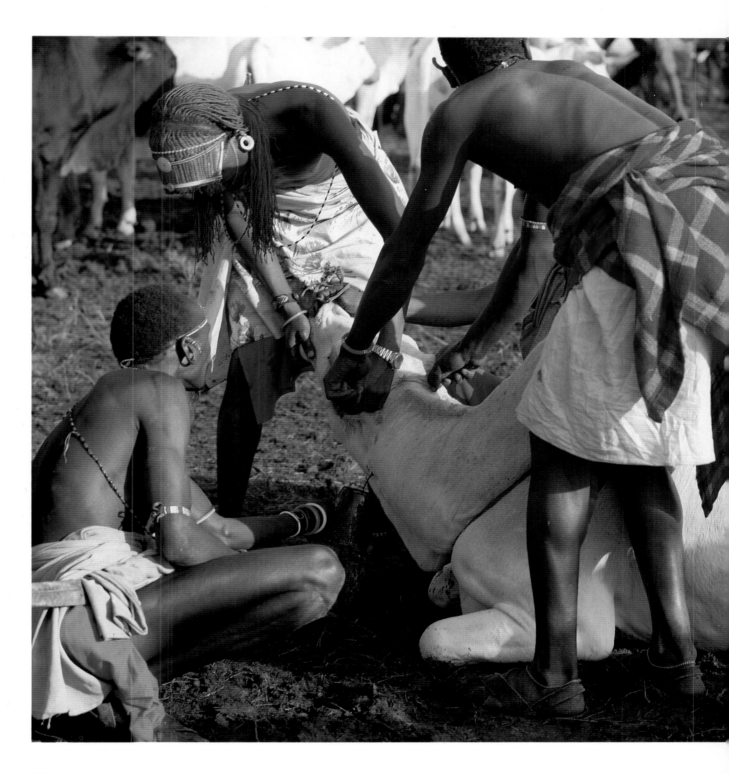

When the tourniquet is released, dung is rubbed into the wound and as the animal stands up, someone gives it a good hard hit on its ribs with the flat of the hand to make it jerk its head back. This is said to stop the flow of blood. The blood drawn at this time is given to the boy to drink as a symbolic replacement for the blood he has lost during his operation.

The day after a boy has been circumcised, he will hang in his pierced earlobes copper earrings that are normally worn by married women. His sponsors will make him a new head-dress of ostrich feathers fastened to a narrow band of plaited fibre which fits tightly round his forehead like a sweat-band. Hanging from the back of the band are four strings of beads terminating in bead-like seeds or wood carved in the shape of a bead.

Later, a 'firestick elder' – one of the elders responsible for the ceremonial proceedings – will smear his forehead and hair with butter fat from a wooden jar held by his wife.

For each son who is initiated into the warrior age-set, a proud father ties a strip of lion skin below his knees, hangs two copper ornaments which are normally worn by women in his pierced earlobes and places a string of pale green beads round his head.

For a month or so after circumcision, boys spend their time shooting birds with a bow and four blunt arrows. When a bird is killed, it is skinned without the use of a knife, stuffed with dry grass and attached to the boy's head-band by means of its beak. An enthusiastic hunter can collect more than a dozen skins. The initiates may also shoot their arrows at the legs of young girls who ransom themselves by giving the boy a bead to stick in the gum on the end of his club.

As the boys' wounds heal, their dancing becomes more energetic. Before long, they imitate the dances of the warriors which, hitherto, they have been forbidden to perform.

The Lmuget Ceremonies

A man will participate in five *lmuget* ceremonies during his passage through *moranhood*. Each ceremony will mark a change in his status, some having more significance than others. The climax to every *lmuget* is the moment when the participants slaughter their oxen or, if they are from a poor family, their goats, for a great feast. Hence the reason for naming these ceremonies *lmuget* – 'the death of many cattle in one place'.

All *lmuget* ceremonies take place in specially built encampments, also called *lorora*, where members of the same age-set and the same clan gather together. A separate enclosure commonly known as the *lmuget* is built a short distance from the main *lorora* for each of the last three ceremonies. This is where the warriors eat, sleep, dance and entertain their girlfriends. They are forced to live outside the mainstream of society due to the prohibitions imposed on them, such as eating in front of married women.

The phase of the moon will determine the start of the celebrations which will normally be between the fourth and the nineteenth day after the sighting of a new moon. As during circumcision, even days are considered more propitious than odd days.

Since many of the features of the *lmuget* ceremonies are similar to each other, I shall only describe in detail the ritual of the first, the *lmuget loolbaa*.

Lmuget Loolbaa

The *lmuget loolbaa* – the ceremony of the arrows – is sometimes also called *lmuget lenkwueny* – the ceremony of the birds. It is the most important of all the *lmuget* ceremonies and the most elaborate. At its conclusion, an initiate becomes a *moran*. The ceremony takes place almost a month after a boy has been circumcised and may be spread over two to four days, depending on the size of the *lorora* and the number of oxen to be slaughtered there. I attended one at Porro, north of Maralal, where fifty-one oxen were killed on the first day. On such occasions, brothers will generally kill their oxen on consecutive days to avoid a surfeit of meat in their family on one day alone.

During the ceremony, the initiate's father will wear a woman's leather apron over his right shoulder, women's copper earrings and strips of lion skin below his knees as garters, in the same way as he had done after his son's circumcision. Likewise, each initiate will be assisted by two family friends, who are likely to be retiring *moran*. They will become more or less like bond brothers to him and thenceforth he will call them *nkiyeu*, after a strip of meat used in the ceremony, never again by their real names. Should he do so inadvertently, he will be fined a heifer. Since this is another way of enlarging family ties which can prove useful later in life, the two helpers will not be the same people who attended a boy during his circumcision.

In the early morning of the day chosen by the firestick elders for the ceremony, each boy and his ritual helpers will lead an ox out of the *lorora* with a leather thong tied to its right hind leg. The boy will also bring with him a brand from his mother's house to start a small fire close to where his ox will be killed. This will be in a clearing about a hundred yards from the *lorora*, following the same order of a family's lineage in the clan as that adopted during circumcision. Sometimes the elders will insist on the oxen being killed in a line, at other times in a circle exactly similar to the order of the houses in the *lorora*.

Having thrown the ox to the ground, one of the boy's helpers, wearing a woman's leather apron over his right shoulder, will plunge a brand new knife into the vertebrae at the base of its skull to sever the spinal cord. Grass is then stuffed into this hole and a little in the animal's mouth. Next, a large fold of skin is carefully cut from the neck to form a receptacle and the jugular is pierced to allow the blood to flow freely and collect in it. A gourd is filled with this blood, which is stirred vigorously to remove the clotting agents. The boy and his helpers will then drink the rest of it while it is still warm, straight from the fold of skin.

The helpers cut two strips of hide from the chest and underbelly of the ox, which will be made into garters and worn by the boy below his knees until the late afternoon. As they skin and butcher the animal, the boy goes off to cut piles of foliage upon which the meat will be laid. The cuts from the left side of the beast will be placed separately from those of the right side. Only the marrow from the leg bones may be eaten at this stage: the rest of the meat is already bespoken.

The boy may be helped by his friends to dig two shallow trenches which will follow the same order and pattern as that used for killing the oxen. They will be just out of sight of the *lorora* and the place where the animals were slain. Each will be about two feet wide, four feet long and one foot deep. They will be dug roughly three to four feet apart and will be oriented towards a holy mountain. Everyone is aware how the meat is apportioned, so there is never a quarrel over its division, however unfair this might appear to an outsider. Some of the least appetizing parts of an ox – the head, stomach, neck, tail, hooves and offal – are reserved for women and small children. As this meat is left unattended for a while, it will be covered with the hide to prevent vultures swooping low to steal it. Beside the hide will be the leather thong used earlier in the day but now freshly oiled with animal fat, and the gourd of blood, which will be later diluted with milk and enjoyed by the women and children.

The sponsors at the time of the boy's circumcision are entitled to special cuts of meat at this and all his future *lmuget* ceremonies. The man who held his back receives the rear half of the fillet and backbone; the man who held his right leg, a portion of the animal's right rump. The elders are given one side of the rib cage, the left rump and the whole of the left front leg, but not the shoulder. The *moran* and the initiates enjoy the lion's share of the carcass including the chest, right front leg and shoulder, one side of the rib cage and most of the meat from the right hind leg; part of this hind leg will be given to the uncircumcised youths, who will grill it over a separate fire. Last but not least are the teenage girls, who will play an important role in a warrior's life over the next few years. In the evening, the initiates – who will have become the new *moran* – will roast for them the front portion of the fillet and backbone, and the left shoulder.

After gathering firewood, the boy will make a blazing fire in both his trenches from the small fire that he had kept alight beside his ox. When they have died down to glowing embers, he will lay in parallel lines over each of them eight green roasting sticks which he had cut from the nearby bush. He and his helpers will partake of the meat reserved for the warriors and roast it over the coals in the right trench, while the cuts for the elders will be cooked over the left trench. As this is in progress, the mothers of the initiates and other women come to collect their meat, which they will carry away in traditional *samburr* leather bags to cook at home. They will wear round their necks and dangling from their copper earrings the head-dresses and birds which their sons left behind in the *lorora* that morning. It is rather sad that except for this brief appearance, this is the end of the head-dresses which have taken so much skill and care to put together; they are finally discarded and trampled under foot by the family's cattle returning from pasture that evening.

The elders take no part in roasting their meat. They will keep their distance, relaxing in the shade and chatting, until their portions are piled high in front of them. Likewise, uninvited visitors arriving during the ceremony in the expectation of being fed, will also sit to one side in the company of other people from their own age-set.

When the meat is cooked, the initiate and his two helpers gather under a pre-selected tree. The boy collects sprigs of four different types of foliage which will vary according to the locality but where possible will include cedar and olive trees. He gives them to one of his helpers who places a strip of fatty meat from the chest of the ox to protrude between them. This meat is called *nkiyeu*, which is why the initiates call their helpers that name. The other helper then takes the bundle and with the boy sitting on the ground, holds it out to him. The initiate touches the meat with his lips and spits on his stomach as a token blessing. This is repeated four times. Next, the helper gently brushes the bundle against the right side of the boy's brow, down the side of his face, neck and shoulder, down the arm to where his hand clasps his knee and on down to his foot. This is also repeated four times, whereupon they change places and the initiate does the same to the *moran*. I have seen boys of the blacksmiths' clan place their knives on top of the foliage but this practice is not widespread. After the ritual has been completed, the helper again holds the strip of fatty meat to the boy's mouth and he bites off and swallows four pieces of it. The rest is eaten by others. Urged on by the shouts of his friends and onlookers, the initiate next tries to break a hip bone of his ox with one blow from his knobkerrie. If he fails after three attempts, his helpers will complete the task for him. Once this would have been regarded as a disgrace, but now it would merely be the source of some amusement.

While the elders and the *moran* feast, the initiate and his two helpers go to the *lorora* to give the boy's mother a portion of the left rump in which his ritual knife will be stuck. The party must pass through the family's own stock entrance and may not enter the *lorora* unless the boy's mother is at home. His second visit to her later that afternoon is a momentous one. He takes her the top part of the left hip bone which he broke earlier on and presents it with the words, 'Mother, this is the food I was eating when I was young. I am returning it to you. Never give me food again.' He and his helpers will then drink a little milk mixed with the water he collected the previous day. From that moment until he becomes a junior elder, the boy will not eat at home again. On his subsequent visits he may only take milk or tea as long as he is in the company of another warrior of his own age-set. He may no longer be seen eating by married women nor touch the food they have cooked. Henceforth, his life will revolve round his age-mates, who customarily live on meat, blood and milk in the bush, though maize meal has become an important part of the diet today. This taboo can cause problems in a modern society. Schoolboys can be forced to become boarders rather than day scholars to overcome the difficulty of having to cook their own food when they return home each evening. Others leave school altogether to enjoy their new-found freedom, for this is the first time in their lives that they can associate freely with teenage girls.

The initiate will be shaved by his mother in the same manner as before his circumcision. Afterwards, he will discard his black cloak in her home and with his father's help, smear himself all over with red ochre before donning a new white loincloth and rubber tyre sandals. In earlier times, he would have been given a new goatskin cape, oiled but not black, and a pair of rawhide sandals. Next, sitting on a stool at the entrance to his mother's house, he will shoot off his arrows along the ground towards a crowd of admiring children who scramble to collect them as souvenirs. He will keep the bow, however, since it will come in useful later to bleed cattle. Now that he has thrown away his arrows, he is a warrior – a *moran* – at long last. His mother can remove the *nchipi* – the distinctive head-dress of uncircumcised boys – which she has worn as a necklace or tied round her waist for a month. In the weeks that follow, she will make from it a double string of blue and white beads, which she will wear looped through her earrings to signify that she has a son who is a warrior of the tribe. Some of the other beads worn by him after circumcision will be used by his mother to decorate a gourd-like container in which she will keep milk especially for him on his infrequent visits home.

Almost immediately, the new *moran* foregather and sing and dance the songs of the warriors. As night falls, they collect again near the roasting pits and sing a song abusing women to the accompaniment of a kudu-horn trumpet which is blown incessantly. This song is openly obscene and will not be sung on any other occasion. When the girls come out of the *lorora* to dance, the new warriors tell them in song that they wish to sleep with them that night. These direct overtures are not taken too seriously, although the girls do respond encouragingly by praising the young braves belonging to their section of the clan. After an interlude to enjoy their roast meat, singing will start again and carry on at an increasing tempo until exhaustion overcomes them in the early hours of the morning. The senior *moran* will be on hand to maintain discipline and drill the new *moran* in their dance routines.

The time has now come for the mothers of the *moran* to dismantle the couches they built in their houses just prior to their sons' circumcision. All the material used in making them, as well as their sons' hair and the scraps of severed leather left over from the boys' sandals, will be burnt outside their homes. Following this, the mothers shave their husbands' heads and are in turn shaved by their female relatives. Two days later, the new *moran* can wash themselves at last. Early in the morning they head for the nearest stream or waterhole to rid themselves of a month's grime. For the first time in their lives, they will decorate themselves with a mixture of red ochre and animal fat and adorn themselves with beaded necklaces and other ornaments which will have been begged or borrowed from their helpers and the senior *moran*. Some will even borrow a spear from a friend; others will have to sell a goat to pay the local blacksmith to make one.

The transformation from initiate to *moran* is a striking one. It does not take a boy long to exert his new authority, especially over women. Within twenty-four hours of the end of this ceremony, I have witnessed a new *moran* giving harsh orders to his mother, who instantly obeyed them.

Lmuget Lewatanta

The *lmuget lewatanta*, the ceremony of the roasting sticks, ideally takes place a month after the *lmuget loolbaa*. There is a tendency these days, however, to perform both ceremonies together, even combining them as one. The *lmuget lewatanta* is the least important of all the *lmuget* ceremonies. The main reason for it being held at all is to keep the newly initiated *moran* under the control of the firestick elders for a further month so that they can be instructed in their responsibilities and how to behave.

The climax to this *lmuget*, like all others, is the ritual killing of oxen. While roasting is in progress, the *moran* are asked by the firestick elders to stand to the left or the right of their roasting pits. There are no hard and fast rules about this; everyone is at liberty to stand on whichever side he pleases, although it is usual for brothers to choose alternate sides. Little importance is attached to this division, which may have been created in years gone by to split the standing army of *moran* quickly into two forces.

Special care has to be taken to prevent the roasting sticks being burnt, for when the meat is cooked, the *moran* must gather them all up and arrange them upright against a prominent tree – preferably a species of olive, podo or cedar – where they will never be touched again. A short while later, the elders will blow the kudu-horn trumpet to summon all the *moran* to where these sticks have been laid. Here, they will be given a final address of indeterminable length before being blessed as the warriors of the tribe. Henceforth, they will look after their clan's livestock and be responsible for recovering it after stock raids.

Shortly after the next new moon, the families in the *lorora* will disperse to their *manyattas* and the women will burn the houses to the ground.

Lmuget Lenkarna

It is customary for the *lmuget lenkarna*, the ceremony of the name, to be held about five years after the *lmuget lewatanta*. It is the most important ceremony next to the *lmuget loolbaa* and a new *lorora* will be built and occupied for about two months. This is the occasion when the *moran* from the junior age-set assume full responsibility for the defence of the tribe, since the men from the age-set one senior to them will have all married and settled down to a more sedentary life as junior elders.

Several months before the start of this *lmuget*, each of the eight Samburu clans appoints a ritual leader, known as *launoni*, from the age-set of the *moran*. The elders from all the different clans will congregate on Mount Ng'iro to choose the families from which these leaders should come. Their decision is not open for discussion; once a family has been nominated, the elders from it will meet in secret session to select the best candidate they can find. The ritual leader chosen by the Lmasula clan is automatically appointed to the position of head *launoni*.

Sometimes a *moran* will object to being made a *launoni*. In this case, he will be coerced into accepting the appointment which in the end he cannot refuse. His initial resistance to the office is associated with the fact that he must settle down to premature elderhood, which may be distasteful to him as it means giving up the glamorous life of the *moran*. Once all the *launoni* have resigned themselves to their new role, they will journey to the top of Mount Ng'iro to see their clan elders, who will present each of them with a sheepskin cape, similar to those worn by women. They must wear these over their right shoulders until the end of the *lmuget* ceremony, which will normally take place about two months later.

Since their office is one of considerable ritual importance and no harm must befall them until their marriage, they will be provided with a body-guard of *moran* to accompany them wherever they go. They no longer involve themselves in petty disputes with their age-mates nor sleep in their houses, or vice versa, since they are now like fathers to them. They have the power to curse the *moran* if the need arises, call meetings which every *moran* must attend and summon them to arms in times of conflict. No one from their age-set will disobey their command.

The ritual leaders will be the first in their clans to kill two oxen at the start of the *lmuget lenkarna*, which will last up to four days. This is the signal for everyone else to follow suit, but not many *moran* these days will slaughter two oxen. Most will be content with an ox and a goat, while those from poor families will make do with two goats. The firestick elders are again in charge of the proceedings and on this occasion will kindle a fire at the killing ground outside each *lorora*, using traditional firesticks from which all the fires in the roasting pits will be lit. The reason for this ritual is that a new age-set name will be bestowed on the warriors, having been chosen for them by the Lmasula elders on Mount Ng'iro in consultation with their *launoni*.

At the conclusion of this ceremony, the head *launoni* will visit all eight Lmasula sections of his clan in turn; he will be given nine cows by each of them. This nucleus herd may be augmented at the next *lmuget* ceremony and so his wealth will increase.

Lmuget Lelaingoni

The *lmuget lelaingoni*, the ceremony of the bull, will be performed roughly six years after the *lmuget lenkarna*. One or two months before it takes place, the firestick elders meet to select a *moran* from the Lmasula clan to kill a white bull, known as *laingoni*, on the top of Mount Ng'iro, Warges or the Kirisia Hills; the exact location depends on where the chosen *moran* lives. The bull is presented by the head *launoni* from his herd and is killed by suffocating it on the ground. Its meat is divided among all the age-sets in the usual way. The firestick elders will be present for the occasion and will light a fire to roast the meat using their traditional firesticks. This symbolizes the closing of the age-set. No more boys may thenceforth be circumcised into it.

After the *moran* have killed their oxen to celebrate the *lmuget*, they are permitted to marry. However, they are generally careful to avoid doing so before the *launoni* of their clan, who customarily marries soon after this ceremony. If anyone does marry before his *launoni*, he is fined a heifer. As this is a means whereby the *launoni* can enlarge their herds, they will take the trouble to visit the members of their clan throughout the district at the conclusion of the ceremony, to check for themselves who has married before time.

Lmuget Lekule E Mbene

The *lmuget lekule e mbene*, the ceremony of the milk and leaves, is the last of the *lmuget* ceremonies and will be performed several years after the next age-set has been circumcised, at a time when the cattle are fat and healthy after a season of good rains. This may be as much as twenty-five years after the circumcision of the participants. The date is fairly flexible as long as it has been completed well before the initiation of the age-set two junior to them, for which the participants will become the firestick elders. By the time it takes place, the *launoni* and possibly the entire age-set will be married. One peculiarity of this *lmuget* is that no man from another age-set may sleep in the *lorora* at night.

The evening before the first oxen are killed, the participants will be called by the elders to the *naapo*, the central meeting place in the *lorora*. Each man will bring with him some milk and sit round the *naapo* in order of seniority. The elders will then give them a final blessing before they all drink their milk.

The ceremony will be spread over two to four days and each man will kill a fat ox on which to feast. Their wives collect their share of the meat in the customary manner and return to their homes, where they boil up the fatty tissue to reduce it to a liquid. As their husbands enter the *lorora* towards evening, singing, they will hand them a gourd of curdled milk mixed with the fat of the slain oxen. The men will drink this in front of their wives and from then on will not be restricted from eating food in front of married women. This marks another turning point in their lives, because henceforth they will be treated as elders in all respects.

It is possible – and nowadays very common – for a married man to seek dispensation and eat his wife's food before this *lmuget*. To do so, he has to slaughter a fat ram outside his house in the presence of respected senior elders and friends of his own age-set in a ceremony called *lminong'*. The fat from the animal must be reduced to a liquid by his wife and sipped by all those present. The husband will then be given a little meat to eat in front of his wife, and his mother if she is still alive. As he swallows it, the old men will bless him and give permission for him to partake of his wife's food. The rest of the meat is enjoyed by the others.

OVERLEAF: The *lmuget loolbaa*, the ceremony of the arrows, takes place one month after the initiates have been circumcised. It starts at daybreak when each boy – assisted by his two chosen helpers – leads an ox out of the *lorora* to a pre-selected open space where it will be slaughtered for a great feast. I have seen as many as fifty-one oxen killed in a morning. The helpers butcher the animals in a special way with meat from the left side of the carcass being kept separate from the cuts of the right side.

Blood is a popular nourishing drink among the Samburu. When the warriors
slaughter an ox or one of their small stock, they will drink it while it is still
warm, straight from a fold of skin which is cut in the animal's neck.
Blood is richer in protein than either milk or meat and was advocated
as a cure for tuberculosis in Europe a century ago.

Once an ox has been thrown to the ground, one of the boy's helpers plunges a brand new knife, made
by the blacksmiths of the tribe, into the vertebrae at the base of its skull to sever the spinal cord.
The oxen are killed in the same order of a family's lineage in the clan as was adopted during circumcision.

While the oxen are being butchered, the initiates and their young brothers indulge in the marrow from the leg bones. This is a much sought-after delicacy.

The blood from each ox will be collected in a gourd and stirred vigorously to stop it coagulating. This blood will be kept for the enjoyment of the women and children later that day.

A young boy sucks marrow from the lower leg of a freshly slaughtered ox.

Every initiate must dig two roasting pits three or four feet apart and orientated towards a holy mountain. Afterwards, he cuts sixteen poles from nearby bushes and places eight of them over each pit. He and his helpers will roast their meat over the fire in the left-hand trench while the cuts for the elders will be prepared over the right trench.

The initiates' mothers collect their paltry portions of the oxen in traditional leather bags, called *samburr*, while their sons roast the best cuts a short distance away.

The mothers wear their sons' head-dresses for the occasion. This is the last time these are seen in public, for they are thrown away that evening and trampled under foot by the cattle returning to the *lorora* from pasture.

OPPOSITE: This is the first occasion an initiate is allowed to sound the kudu-horn trumpet. It is by no means easy to blow.

When all his meat has been roasted, an initiate will go to a pre-selected tree where one of his helpers will gently brush the fatty meat from the chest of his ox, which is sandwiched between the sprigs of four different trees or bushes, down the boy's face and the right side of his body to his foot. This ceremony is repeated four times.

Urged on by the shouts of his friends and the onlookers, the initiate next tries to break a hip bone of his ox with one blow from his knobkerrie. If he fails after three attempts, his helpers will complete the task for him.

Before dusk that day, he presents the broken bone to his mother with the words, 'Mother, this is the food I was eating when I was young. I am returning it to you. Never give me food again.'

127

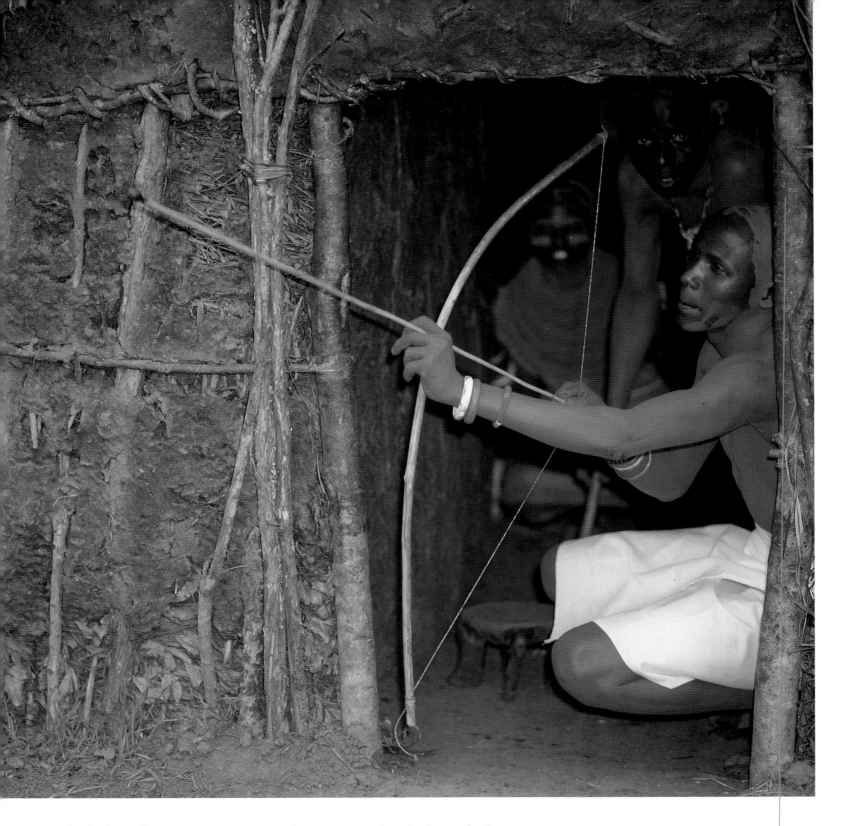

In the late afternoon, every initiate who participated in the *lmuget loolbaa* ceremony is shaved by his mother. Next, he will discard his black cloak and, helped by his father, smear himself all over with red ochre. Then, sitting on a stool at the entrance to his mother's house wearing a new white loincloth, he shoots his blunt arrows towards an admiring throng of children who scramble to retrieve them as souvenirs.

Now that the initiate is a warrior at last, he will go to the nearest stream or waterhole to wash off a month's grime. He then decorates himself with a mixture of red ochre and animal fat, and adorns himself with beads. The sudden change in his appearance is remarkable.

The Moran

Many people consider the warrior age-set an anachronism. That it will probably last until the twenty-first century is proof enough of the tenacity of the tribal elders in upholding time-honoured values and resisting change.

One can hardly call the young men 'warriors' today, even though they are still the potential task force of a warrior-oriented society in which *moranhood* is a supreme ideal. The last major skirmish took place about ten years ago when a large quantity of livestock was stolen by Turkana outlaws in the north of the district. Nowadays, the young bloods who seek adventure and excitement will probably join the armed forces, where the disciplined life and the possibility of conflict are more in keeping with their warlike traditions. I can vouch personally for several instances of their brave conduct under fire. As Adjutant of an infantry battalion of the Kenya Army, I vividly recall the courage of one young Samburu askari who was a member of a patrol that was ambushed by *shifta* insurgents from Somalia in the north of the country. The sustained and accurate firepower forced the soldiers to take cover, but not so the Samburu; on his own initiative, he made his way fearlessly towards the enemy, picking off the bandits one by one as he went. Wounded but not to be browbeaten, he routed them almost single-handed.

The art of traditional warfare is well known to the *moran* but remains largely unpractised. The Samburu preferred to fight on their own terms, avoiding the tactic of large-scale conflict in open country perfected by the Maasai more than a century ago. Every *moran* would carry two spears and a shield or a spear and a bow with a quiver of poisoned arrows. A man with two spears would only throw one before trying to retrieve it as he defended himself with the other. Their side arms included a razor-sharp double-bladed short sword, commonly called a *simi*, and a knobkerrie which has now given way to a decorated club weighted with a vicious assortment of steel nuts, fly-wheels or cogs. I have never seen a Samburu shield, for they were banned very many years ago by the colonial government as a punishment for the lawless ways of the tribesmen. They were made of buffalo hide and followed the Turkana style, being slimmer and somewhat lighter than the massive oval-shaped shields used by the Maasai. This enabled the *moran* to cover great distances at speed. They wore rhino-hide sandals in thorn scrub and over lava rocks, which gave them a tremendous advantage over enemies such as the Turkana, Pokot and Borana, who had scant protection from their more conventional rawhide sandals.

In general, raids were carried out on a limited scale with the aim of acquiring cattle. Before setting out, the *moran* would consult a *laibon* – a soothsayer and clairvoyant – and recruit other *moran* from their clan to join them. On returning home after a successful raid, the spoils would be divided among all the participants according to their personal achievements. This made the bravest *moran* conspicuous to the rest. In modern times, warriors merely act as a deterrent to stock rustlers from neighbouring tribes and defend their herds against marauding predators. This is possibly the only opportunity they now get to blood their spears; one senior *moran* I know claims to have impaled over one hundred buffalo on his, to prove his courage.

The *moran* are the most striking members of Samburu society and are inevitably attracted to young girls. For fourteen years, they enjoy a convivial and relatively undemanding life with a permissive sexual code. Most of them will at one time or another have a lover for whom they show their affection by lavishing beads on her. But this will not stop them sleeping with other girls when an opportunity occurs. There are two cardinal rules in this aura of promiscuity. No one may sleep with a circumcised woman which, put another way, means that married women are taboo; and a girl must never become pregnant, for to do so will bring disgrace to both families and prevent the culprit playing a proper role in his *lmuget* ceremonies. *Coitus interruptus* is the method adopted by a *moran* to avoid this, but if his girlfriend does conceive, the foetus will normally be aborted by traditional means. This can be achieved by feeding the girl on fat, after which experienced women induce a miscarriage by manipulating her abdomen.

Compared to the elders and young boys of the tribe, the *moran* are flamboyant in their dress and a constant focus of attention. Body decoration is not a refined art among them, although they frequently apply abstract designs in orange to their faces and red ochre to their heads, round their necks and over their shoulders, down to their breast bones in a V. They take infinite trouble to braid each other's long, ochred hair which can sometimes reach down to the waist. Above the forehead, the hair may be tied in a short bunch or fashioned in a fringe which looks rather like the sort of sunshade worn by tennis players. The *moran* insert round ivory plugs with holes in the centres in their pierced earlobes and loop loosely over their ears a small metal chain made of copper wire which acts as a chinstrap. Two long strings of beads are slung over their shoulders and across their chests like cross-straps, while numerous beaded necklaces and bracelets add a splash of colour to their singular appearance. It has been said that people who pay great attention to their hair do not, as a rule, care about clothes. This is true of the Samburu *moran*, whose attire at one time was dressed goatskins but is now a brightly coloured loincloth wrapped carelessly round the waist to leave exposed the right side of the body where the *simi* hangs from a leather belt. I am surprised they can withstand the cold in the mountainous regions of the district where I prefer to put on thick sweaters and huddle up beside a log fire!

Singing and dancing are a major form of relaxation which brings the *moran* in regular contact with the young girls of their clan. Although these gatherings release tensions, the *moran* will be on their guard to prevent their counterparts from another clan seducing their girls. This is a matter of honour and can be a recurrent source of irritation at well-attended dances. Singers of both sexes try to outwit each other, alluding in verse to worldly matters and inviting their partners to unravel conundrums with sexual overtones and double meanings. When the warriors sing on their own, they leap high in the air to a rhythmic beat, each attempting to outperform the other. Years ago, the prestige in rustling cattle was enormous. Often a girl would refuse to sing her lover's praises unless he stole a cow, thus directly contributing to stock raids and lawlessness. These days, many *moran* have turned their attention to cattle trading rather than stealing and have found it just as lucrative, albeit less exciting.

Sooner or later a girl is bound to be taken from the clan and married to an elder. When this happens, custom permits her lover and his close friends to attend the wedding and sing a song cursing the bridegroom and the bride's family for giving her away. This is little more than a show of bravado and no one takes it very seriously. The lover will not even demand back his beads.

At the end of the rains when the grass is lush, the *moran* free themselves from herding and roam the countryside or take to the forests to eat meat. Here, they may spend several months with their companions, each bringing an ox to slaughter for an indefinite feast. It is staggering how much meat they can eat; it will be roasted or boiled with the bark and roots of certain trees to produce a potent broth. I have always believed that the violent fits the warriors sometimes throw – they are akin to epileptic fits – are partly induced by the properties extracted from these roots. However, I am no longer convinced that this is the major cause; I have seen a number of uncircumcised boys under stress suffering the same symptoms, although not all of them had eaten meat in the forest with their elder brothers who were *moran*.

The Samburu call fits *ndokuna* and regard them as a sign of manliness. The *moran*, it seems, are predisposed to quivering and shaking, which under certain circumstances will lead to a fit. Shaking occurs when a person is under stress and may be looked upon as a release of nervous energy. It is an indication of the impulsive and highly strung temperament of the young men. When they settle down as elders later in life, these symptoms completely disappear. Some people may wonder, therefore, if this idiosyncrasy is simply a sham but I am in no doubt that it is not. Quite frequently a *moran* will recover from shaking but when this gives way to a fit, he must be forcibly restrained by two of his age-mates. I have seen instances of them running blindly through thorn fences and at one circumcision ceremony I attended, a young soldier on leave charged headlong into a cow and injured his neck. I had spoken to him only an hour earlier and he was very calm, but as the time drew near for his brother to be circumcised and tension mounted in the charged atmosphere, he broke down. Those to whom I have spoken claim their blood boils up inside them until they lose control of their senses – a form of nervous breakdown during which a person is not accountable for his actions.

Samburu district has no fencing or man-made boundaries. The wide open spaces of a virgin land are one of its great attractions. The *moran* drive their families' cattle to wherever the best grazing happens to be; if anyone tried to stop them, he would be roundly cursed. The Samburu have implicit faith in the efficacy of the curse, which was widely used by the elders to regulate grazing. In closing certain areas for a season or two by threatening to curse trespassers, they enabled the grass to regenerate and become valuable pasture in times of drought.

The breed of cattle they keep is generally known as Boran, a member of the African species *Bos africanus*, with a pronounced and heavy hump. These cattle have a high resistance to endemic diseases such as East Coast fever (a tick-borne disease), rinderpest and trypanosomiasis, which is caused by a bite from the tsetse fly. Despite this, disease still takes its toll. Other factors beyond a person's control, such as drought and stock thefts, can also affect the size of a herd regardless of the owner's skill.

In the dry season, the *moran* are a considerable asset to their families. They play an important role at waterholes, working long hours to satisfy the needs of their stock. They will also walk great distances with a distinctive, springy gait to seek out the best pastures and when necessary, establish a temporary grazing base far from home. On these occasions, they will be joined by young boys and occasionally a small sister to help shepherd the goats. Living in the bush can be hard when food is scarce, but as the rains fall anew, life quickly returns to the parched land. Soon the cows are in milk again and the pangs of hunger are no more.

There is little doubt that *moranhood* is the best period of a man's life. Fearless and arrogant, he is in his prime, doing largely what he likes. He abstains from alcohol and cigarettes but regularly takes snuff. Animal fat is an important constituent of his diet. He will also use it as a medicine, mixed with the powdered seeds of the *seketet* bush (*Myrsine africana*), to cure malaria, purge worms, heal wounds and relieve chest pains. His fat intake would give most Westerners a high enough cholesterol level to cause heart disease, but his exceptional fitness and active life counteract this. When research doctors carried out a random test on Maasai *moran*, who also eat a lot of fat, their cholesterol count was about 50% of the level found in the average American.

The *moran* enjoy the companionship of their fellow warriors who form a close-knit community, sharing almost everything and relying heavily on one another in their daily lives. '*Supa Murata*' – 'Greetings, fellow age-mate' – can often be heard ringing across the plains. They will never go anywhere without their spears, which are hand-crafted by the blacksmiths of the tribe in return for payment of one goat. Many of them still carry two spears, the Samburu version of a matched pair of sporting guns. Since no one may eat alone unless he has slaughtered an animal by himself in the bush, the *moran* will generally be seen moving about in pairs. Milk and tea are the only nourishment they may take in the presence of married woman, so a gourd of milk is invariably kept in the home of every woman who has a son belonging to the warriors' age-set.

The *moran* are privileged and pampered members of society and relish the attention showered on them. Even the elders who have the responsibility of curbing their excesses respect their independent spirit and think back nostalgically to the good times they had themselves.

When browse is scarce in the dry season, the warriors take pride in keeping their families' livestock fat and healthy. In the South Horr Valley, they climb to the tops of the acacia thorn trees, some thirty to forty feet high, to knock down the green seed-pods which are a favourite food of their goats.

Three warriors survey the surrounding countryside from a huge rock high up in the Kirisia Hills.

The Samburu warriors, or *moran*, are vain and proud. They take great trouble to braid each other's long, ochred hair; an elegant coiffure can take at least three days to complete. There are two styles: one with the braids at the front of the head fashioned in a protruding fringe rather like a sunshade; the other with the braids gathered together and tied in a bunch which is then decorated with a large button. A mixture of cow's urine and ashes is often rubbed into the hair first, as this makes it easier to braid.

The wooden head-rest is used as a pillow at night.

A small piece of flat wood has the same effect as a comb to straighten the braids of a warrior's coiffure.

Facial markings in orange are applied according to an individual's tastes. This warrior is evidently a twin since he is wearing two cowrie shells round his right wrist. His necklace of plaited grass also tells a story. It signifies that one of his cows rejected its calf at birth. No one except the warrior will milk or drink the milk of the cow until it nurtures the calf of its own volition.

OPPOSITE: Round ivory ear-ornaments are a traditional and distinctive decoration of the *moran*.

138

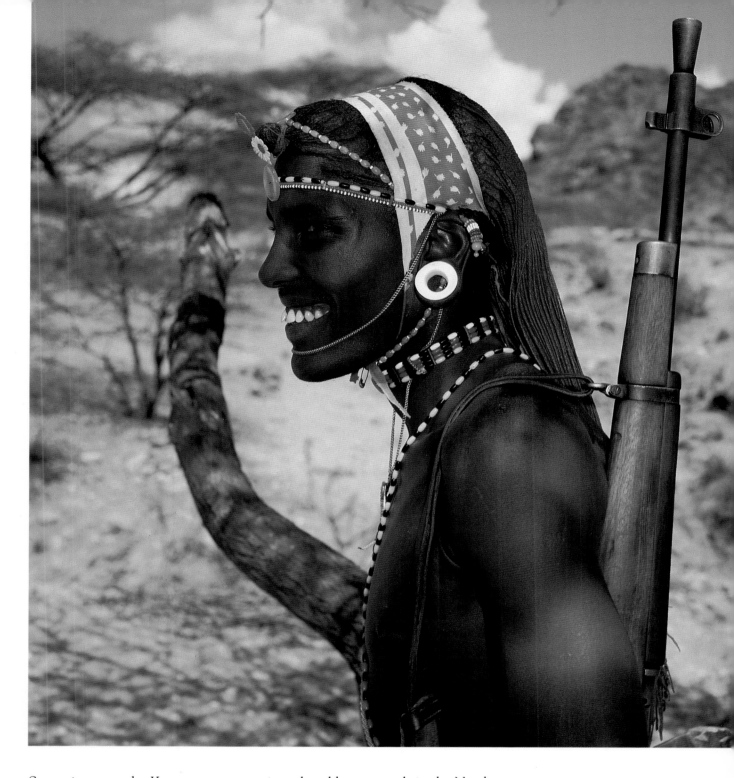

Some time ago, the Kenya government introduced home-guards in the Northern Frontier District to combat stock thefts and lawlessness. The scheme has been an unqualified success. I met this warrior the day that he was issued with an old service rifle. He was very excited to exchange his spear for a gun!

Years ago, every warrior grew his hair long; now, it is a matter of personal preference. If a close member of his family or a *moran* of his section of the clan dies, a warrior is obliged to cut all his hair off and throw it away in the bush.

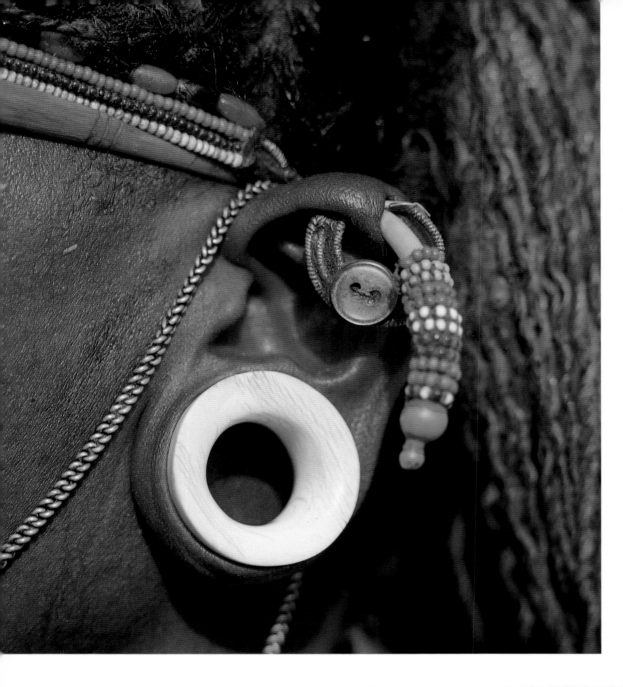

Boys have their ears pierced in two places when they are about eight years old. By the time they are grown up, they will have stretched their lobes to the correct size to fit their ivory ear-ornaments. They do this by putting bundles of dried grass stems, or a series of round wooden plugs of a gradually increasing diameter, in their lobes.

The *moran* adorn themselves with a multitude of brightly coloured beaded necklaces of differing shapes and sizes which are made by their girlfriends. The talon worn by the *moran* on the right was taken from a vulture.

OPPOSITE: The Samburu have a flair for adapting modern materials to traditional ornaments. Old ballpoint pens, plastic piping, rubber washers, spent cartridges and large buttons are all put to good use.

142

I took these photographs of two young brothers with intricate facial designs just three months after they had been initiated into *moranhood*.

Prior to becoming a junior elder, this senior *moran* has cut his hair short and given away most of his ornaments to the *moran* of the new generation. Even his ivory ear-plugs have been taken, so he has put dried grass stems in his lobes instead.

The *moran* are not allowed to eat food in the presence of women. Friends from the same clan will often take to the forests with an ox on which they will feast for several days.

The *moran* are prone to throwing fits in tense situations. They are similar to those suffered by epileptics and last about the same length of time. A person has to be forcibly restrained by at least two of his age-mates while he is incapacitated in this way.

Milgis *Lugga*

Lugga is a word heard throughout the northern regions of
Kenya. Of Somali origin, it means a seasonal watercourse.
The Milgis is the largest in Samburu District, rising in the
Kirisia Hills, above Maralal, before dissipating into
numerous small watercourses near the Kaisut Desert, some
one hundred miles to the east. It cuts an impressive divide
between the Ndoto Mountains and the Mathews Range.

For three months a year in the rainy season, water
gushes in raging brown torrents after violent cloudbursts,
as dangerous and fickle as any river in the country. Then,
as the countryside bakes dry in the scorching sun, the
water level drops dramatically. When the river dries up,
the last flows of water are apparent from the patterns of
flaked and curled mud.

Once the pools of water have finally dried up, the
Samburu dig wells along the watercourse. Water is never
too far from the surface and digging for it in the sandy
river bottom is a comparatively easy task. All able-bodied
men and teenage boys lend a hand to water the stock.

For more than six months each year, the Milgis is a
lifeline for the people living a semi-nomadic existence in
the low country east of the Kirisia Hills. Here, their
livestock thrives because of the natural mineral content of
the soil; endemic diseases are also few.

Important water-holes along the Milgis *lugga*. They are dug on a family or clan basis and may not be used by others without permission. In the height of the dry weather, the water table drops rapidly. In consequence, some wells away from the *lugga* have to be excavated to a great depth.

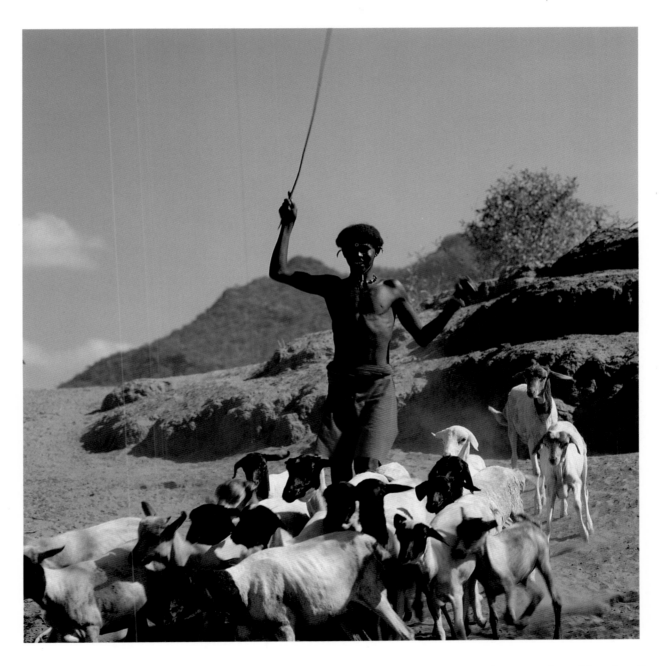

An uncircumcised youth with a typical 'pudding bowl' hairstyle drives his goats to a water-hole.

Girls and young children lend a hand to control their family's
small stock (sheep and goats) at the water-holes.

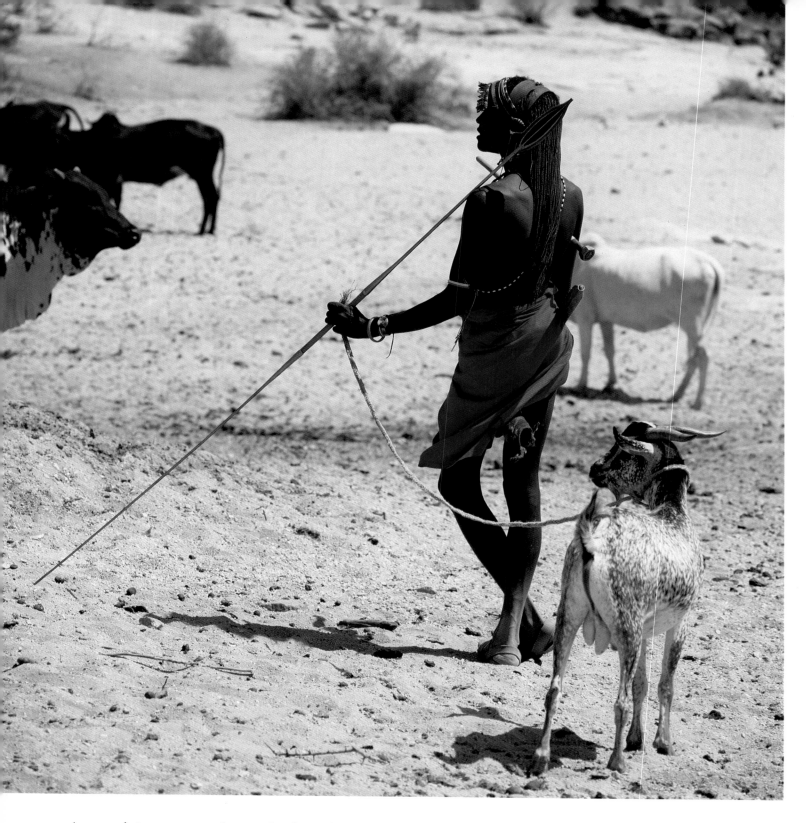

A *moran* brings a goat and a sun-dried goatskin to sell at a local market near Ngurunit. Goats are an important source of revenue to the Samburu. They are hardy animals and breed up to three times a year.

Camels at a water-hole along the Milgis *lugga*. They are steadily increasing in popularity among those Samburu families which trace their origins to the camel-owning Rendille – a neighbouring tribe which inhabits the semi-desert country to the north east of Samburu District.

Camels survive drought by eating forage which no other domestic animal can reach. They only require water every ten days to three weeks depending on the temperature and amount of moisture in the vegetation, and can be milked four times a day.

The deep wells at Ilaut on the north-eastern side of the Ndoto Mountains are a vital watering point close to the Kaisut Desert. They are used by both Samburu and Rendille stock-owners. Sometimes, seven men are needed to lift water to the troughs.

The *moran* chant as they pass their buckets to each other, without pause, in time with the tune. This man has tied his long braided hair on top of his head to keep it out of the way while he works.

The depth of a well is described by the number of men in a human chain who are needed to lift water to the troughs. This is a six-man well. It has to be re-excavated each year when the rains end. In the semi-arid regions of the district, cattle are watered every other day, whereas sheep and goats can last three days.

With his hair dishevelled, a *moran* pauses from the arduous task of watering his stock.

Homeward bound! A girl drives her family's flocks to the nearby grazing grounds after they have been watered by her elder brothers from wells along the Milgis *lugga*.
Without a large family, a man has considerable difficulty caring for his stock.

CHAPTER SIX

Girls and Marriage

Girls begin their training for motherhood at an early age by helping with the household chores and looking after their baby brothers and sisters. By the time they are six or seven years old they will tend the flocks of sheep and goats, and lend a hand at milking time. Their strict upbringing is in contrast to the lax discipline enjoyed by their brothers of the same age. They are taught to avoid familiarity with elders, even their own fathers. This makes it impossible for a man to be responsible for his daughter's education.

As soon as they start to take an interest in the opposite sex, their mothers will explain to them that the passionate feelings they may have towards certain men are irrelevant, for they will never be allowed to wed someone of their own choosing. A girl is not even consulted when the time comes for her to marry. She will have been conditioned to the notion that the bond of matrimony is not based on any physical attraction; rather, it is looked upon as a sound long-term investment by her family. To be a good wife, a girl must learn to show a sense of respect, be a loving mother and fulfil her household duties conscientiously. Almost any girl can be married off, but a well brought up daughter will be a source of pride to her father and give him standing in the community. He will have no difficulty marrying her into a good family to create a bond of friendship that should be of lasting benefit to him.

When a girl is still adolescent she will attend dances organized by the *moran* of her clan where she will become closely associated with their activities. Acutely aware that she must look her best at these gatherings, she will go to great lengths to groom herself by putting red ochre on her shaven head and round her neck, darkening her eyebrows with a mixture of charcoal and fat, painting designs in orange on her face, and rubbing fat on the beads of her necklaces to make them glisten in the sun. By doing so, she is likely to earn the praise of a young man. As time goes by, she will probably become his mistress and he her protector. They will stay together in the girl's house, known as *singira*, which is built near her mother's home. Their relationship, unlike marriage in later life, will be forged largely out of a physical and sexual attraction to each other. In the back of their minds, however, they know full well that their association has no future. Since both of them come from the same clan, marriage is forbidden. Over the years the *moran* will heap beads upon his lover until she barely has space to put another string round her neck. It becomes a matter of prestige and honour that she is faithful to him. If she is ever caught befriending another *moran*, he would immediately demand his beads back and seek someone else. There is also a likelihood that the *moran* from the opposing factions would fight.

When the warrior age-set receives permission to marry from the elders of the tribe, they will be between twenty-five and thirty-five years old. Each warrior will travel far and wide in search of a girl from a respectable family who must not be a member of his own section or clan. He may be helped in this by friends and relatives. It is even possible that he may rely on their advice and not set eyes on his prospective wife, who may be too young for immediate marriage. This will not stop his father negotiating with the girl's father a promise of betrothal at a later date. If all goes well, further meetings will be arranged over a period of months until the bridewealth, payable to the girl's father, is fixed – customarily seven cows, one of which will be in calf – and a date set for the wedding. The bride-to-be will be about fifteen years old at this time. Neither she nor her mother play a part in arranging the marriage. The traditional ceremony is complicated and possibly unique, with the ritual spread over three days. A week or so before it is due to take place, arrangements are put in hand to buy fat, ochre, sugar and presents for the bride's parents. It is usual for the ex-lover of the bride to provide the fat and ochre while the bridegroom is responsible for buying the rest.

The bridegroom and his best man will make themselves new ox-hide sandals before leaving the bridegroom's *manyatta* on the day preceding the wedding ceremony. Towards late afternoon, the two men, accompanied by the bridegroom's closest friends, will set out to drive the agreed number of cattle forming part of the bridewealth to the home of the bride's parents. The bridegroom will also take a ewe – which is known as *nkerr* – as a present for the bride's mother and a sheepskin to give to the woman who made the bride's wedding gown. They will sing as they enter the *manyatta* at dusk, through a stock entrance other than the one belonging to the bride's father, and will spend that night apart from her family.

At the first glimmer of dawn the next day, the bride's father, the bridegroom and his best man will adorn themselves with brass earrings which are customarily worn by married women and a single string of light green beads round their foreheads. They will also tie a strip of lion skin just below each knee and carry a tanned sheepskin and two sticks, one longer than the other. Meanwhile, the bride's mother will put on a goatskin cape, selected from a billy goat of uniform colour which was skinned and dried in a special way to leave a broad band of hair down the centre. Sewn on to this band are six cowrie shells set in pairs. Mother and daughter will go to the cattle pen where the mother will milk a chosen cow. During the milking, the bride will lean her head on her mother's back under the cape to symbolize that she was carried on her mother's back as a child and even now is not grown up. The milk, mixed with a little water, will be poured over her head before she is circumcised. The ritual is almost identical to that of the boys.

Circumcision – for girls, a clitorodectomy – takes place at the entrance to her mother's house which, by tradition, must face a holy mountain. One woman holds the girl's shoulders while another grasps her right leg as she sits on a cowhide. They are the girl's sponsors and become like her godmothers, extending the family's ties in a similar way. The circumcisor is invariably a skilled middle-aged woman from the Ltorobo clan.

While this is happening, the bridegroom and his friends drive the bridewealth and the ewe out of the *manyatta* and wait a short distance away. Once the bride is resting inside her mother's house at the end of her ordeal, they re-enter the *manyatta* through the stock entrance of the bride's father, where they are met by two old women from his family. The bridegroom will hand them the sheepskin and then the ewe; this will be tethered underneath the bride's couch until the wedding ceremony is over, when it will join her mother's flock. Thenceforth, the bridegroom will call his mother-in-law *pakerr* after the sheep he gave her, never again by her real name. He and his best man will also give the old women their sandals for safekeeping in the house of the bride's mother, since they must walk barefoot until they depart the following day. Lastly, they will temporarily exchange their sticks for one the women will offer each of them.

As day breaks, an ox of the bridewealth, earmarked as the wedding ox and known as *rikoret*, will be slaughtered just outside the bride's mother's house by the bridegroom plunging a knife into the vertebrae at the base of its skull to sever its spinal cord. Its meat is a feast for the elders and married women of the bride's family and friends, and not for the warriors or the bridegroom's party. While the animal is being skinned and butchered, women collect two long branches of a *seki* tree and, singing, position them upright on either side of the entrance to the mother's house to warn strangers to keep out. The *seki* is *Cordia ovalis*, commonly known as the sandpaper tree on account of its rough leaves, used by the warriors for polishing their ear ornaments. Depending on the locality of the *manyatta*, branches from other trees may be placed outside the house.

Next, blood is drawn from the jugular of a cow by a warrior and stirred vigorously in a gourd. He will add a little milk before bringing it to the entrance to the house, where the sponsor who held the girl's shoulders during circumcision will be standing. She will take the gourd from him and hand it to the bride's mother. The sponsor's daughter – or, if she has none, another young girl from the family – will be given the wooden stirrer which the warrior used to prevent the blood coagulating. The bride's mother will enter her house first, followed closely by the sponsor and her daughter. The young girl places the wooden stirrer in the roof above the hearth and makes her exit. The two women invite the bride to drink the concoction, even if it is only a sip.

The bride will in all probability remain indoors that day, attended by her mother and the sponsors, although she is at liberty to go outside and watch the dancing if she feels well enough. By mid-afternoon, all the invited guests will have foregathered to sing and dance in age-set groups and the festivities will continue until the early hours of the morning. The bridegroom and his best man will rest in the house of the bride's mother with the old woman and her daughter. They will not get much sleep, however, for they have to cook the fatty meat from the chest of the ox which will be eaten by the elders the following day.

About nine o'clock the next morning, the bride will dress in her wedding gown, made from three goatskins which are well oiled and smeared with red ochre. She will put on a necklace, known as *mporro*, made from the fibres of doum palm fronds and worn only by married women. She will wear on her wrists bracelets fashioned from coils of mild steel wire and through her pierced ears will hang a brass chain. Her earrings will be those specially worn by brides at marriage ceremonies, called *ltirriangani*, which she will remove later that evening.

Her mother will put in a *samburr* a gourd full of milk, a small wooden jar of butter fat and some blades of green grass as a blessing. As her daughter leaves home for the last time with it on her back, three women will be standing in line on the right-hand side of the entrance. Nearest will be the sponsor who held her right leg during her circumcision, next the bride's mother and farthest away the sponsor who held her shoulders. They will counsel her before she moves slowly towards the all-male guard of honour made up of her relatives and their friends. Her husband and his best man will be waiting there, having already been given back their sandals and their own two sticks.

The bridegroom will precede the best man and his bride through an arch of crossed sticks; this is the first time they will have been seen in public in close proximity to each other. The bride's father will position himself on the right of the guard of honour; if he is dead her eldest brother, so long as he has been circumcised, will take his place. As the bride passes her father, he will give her the longer of the two sticks he has carried throughout the ceremony and she will go with it to her new home. Its significance will be understood later.

As the bridal party walks slowly in single file away from the *manyatta*, the elders squat down for a final blessing before repairing to the house of the bride's mother, where they will drink the blood of the wedding ox mixed with broth and eat the meat that was prepared for them by the bridegroom the previous evening. The bridal party must reach the bridegroom's home that day, however far away it may be and however long it will take them to get there. At the start of their journey, in sight of the bride's home, they will stop on no less than four occasions, crouching for almost five minutes at a time. At each halt, the best man will offer the bride milk to drink from his own gourd, which she will often refuse. None of them is permitted to look back over their shoulders as they walk, except the best man in the event of the bride needing help. In the unlikely event of the bride looking back, it would be taken as a sign of an unstable marriage. The best man will assist her over obstacles, carry her across water, for she must not get her feet wet, and find a way round columns of *siafu*, safari ants, for it is an omen of bad luck to cross their paths. It is customary for the bride to rest a lot on the journey; she will also walk very slowly on the advice of her counsellors, who will have told her that she must not appear too eager to follow her husband home!

When they reach the entrance to the groom's *manyatta*, they will stop for a while to allow his immediate family to gather round and invite his bride into her new home, each promising her a gift of a cow. Even teenagers will make such an undertaking although their offering, of necessity, may only be a sheep or a goat.

The bridegroom's mother will make a symbolic presentation to the bride of a baby-in-arms or a girl up to three years old. This child may be her own or borrowed for the occasion from a close relative. Once in her mother-in-law's house, the bride will take off her *samburr*, give the child a little milk from her gourd and afterwards return it to its mother. Then all the other children in the *manyatta* will gather round her for a sip of the milk. When the bridegroom and his best man leave the house to select a sheep for slaughter, she will promise a young girl a string of her own beads in return for help the following day. This will also give the other women from the *manyatta* an opportunity to greet her. As night falls, she will be given the fat from the slaughtered animal mixed with curdled milk – her first proper nourishment after an exhausting day.

Around seven o'clock the next morning, the bridegroom will go to his family's cattle pen accompanied by his bride, his best man and the young girl who was promised beads in return for help the previous day. Here, they ceremonially mark the cattle which the husband will give his wife as her allotted herd. In some ways this is little more than a gesture, for she would not be allowed to take the animals with her if she ever decided to return to her parents' home. Nevertheless, these animals are the founding of a herd which she will build up for her sons' benefit. As long as the husband is rich enough to give his wife more than one cow, the second animal must be a bull. In all, he may be generous enough to offer her a quarter of his entire herd. The animals are selected and identified one at a time by each person present marking them on their backs with red ochre using long sticks. Once the owner has marked a beast, his best man will follow suit; next, the young girl with a stick borrowed from her parents and last of all the bride, whose father's stick is now put to good use. If the bride is pleased with her gifts, she will immediately open the stock gate to let the cows out to graze. On the other hand, if she is dissatisfied, she will refuse to open it until she has been promised another animal.

When the calves and the sheep and goats have been let out of their pens to graze, the newly weds and the best man will re-emerge from the bridegroom's parents' home and sit on the right of the entrance in the company of two old men. The bridegroom and his best man will remove their strips of lion skin, the brass earrings and strings of green beads they have worn for three days and place them on a traditional four-legged stool upon which blades of green grass have been laid. The bride's father will do likewise at his own home. The two old men will then pray for the couple and sprinkle milk on the stool.

Late that afternoon, as the cattle return from pasture, the bridegroom and his best man will place the tanned sheepskins they have been carrying since the start of the ceremony and the sticks used to mark the bride's cattle on the ground beside the stool. Next, the best man or an old woman of the bridegroom's family will shave a little hair from the bridegroom's and then the bride's temple and the hairline round their heads. This hair is put in the bowl of the stool and mixed with a little milk to signify that they have been united as one. The stool will then be placed at the head of the matrimonial bed while the sheepskins and sticks will be laid down on the right side of it, where they will remain for three to four days until removed by the bridegroom's mother. At the same time, the hair will be scattered in the house but the other accoutrements of the marriage ceremony will be returned to their rightful owners.

The marriage will not be consummated for some while. After three weeks or so, when the bride has healed, the bridegroom's mother will be told to sleep elsewhere, for the couple will not build a home of their own for at least another month. All the women in the *manyatta* will help with its construction which must be finished in a day.

The best man will remain a close friend of the family and custom allows him to sleep with the bride whenever her husband is away. If the bridegroom does not wish this, he will have to present the man with a heifer.

Sometimes, girls are circumcised without immediate prospects of marriage – if they have become pregnant accidentally or if a younger brother of theirs is due to be initiated into a new age-set. To signify their status after circumcision, they wear copper earrings and a plaited reed head-band. Hanging down their backs from the head-band will be two strands of light blue and two strands of pale green beads with seeds or beads tied to the ends.

A young girl of marriageable age in all her finery.

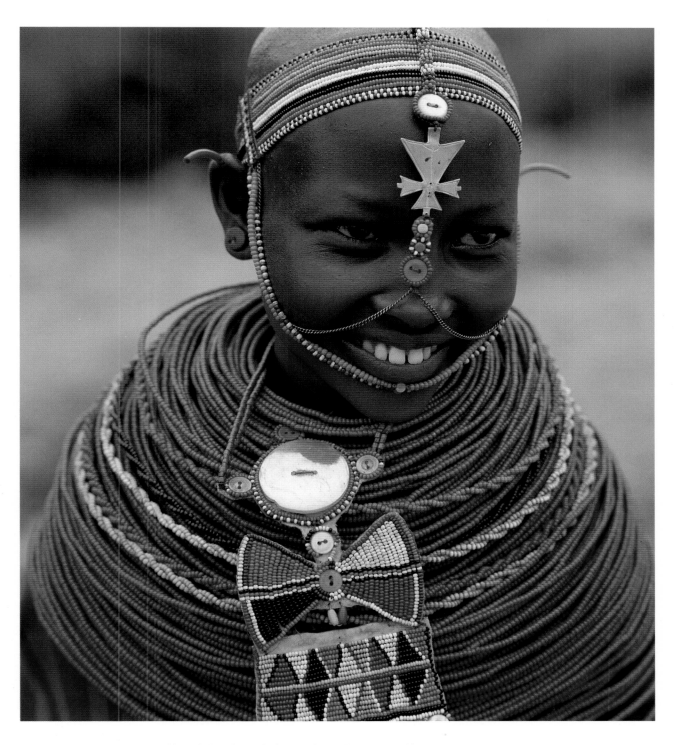

Girls are given strings of beads by their fathers when they are still young. As soon as
they are old enough to have lovers from the warrior age-set, they regularly receive
gifts from them. Over a period of years, their necklaces can smother them up to their necks.

Only the girls and the warriors of the tribe decorate their faces with abstract designs. The orange powder they use for this purpose is called 'blue'! This contradiction dates back to the years when they powdered a proprietary brand of clothes' whitener – 'Reckitt's Blue' – to decorate themselves. The beauty of the girl opposite has been enhanced by blackening her eyebrows with charcoal dust mixed with fat.

The evening before his wedding, the bridegroom will drive part of the bridewealth to the home of the bride's parents in the company of his best man and a few close friends.

The bridewealth varies from family to family, but is generally set at seven cows, one of which will be in calf. One or two of these animals will be handed over to the bride's father several weeks before the wedding. However, there will invariably be an undelivered balance which the bridegroom will hold on to for as long as possible.

The bridegroom will also present his future mother-in-law with a ewe which is called *nkerr*. From then on, he will call her *pakerr*, never again by her real name.

The bride is circumcised – which for girls means a clitorodectomy – at daybreak on her wedding day. Shortly after the ritual, blood is drawn from the jugular of an ox and brought by a warrior in a gourd to her mother's house. Here, it will be handed to the woman who held the girl's shoulders during the brief operation. The bride's mother wears a special goatskin cape, selected from a billy goat of uniform colour which has a broad band of hair left down the centre. This cape may never be used again for ritual purposes.

A group of warriors sing the opening song of the wedding celebrations, which is called *Baringoi*. They are joined by the bridegroom and his best man who are distinguishable from the rest by their copper earrings, normally worn by married women. They each carry a tanned sheepskin which is obligatory for them until the wedding is over.

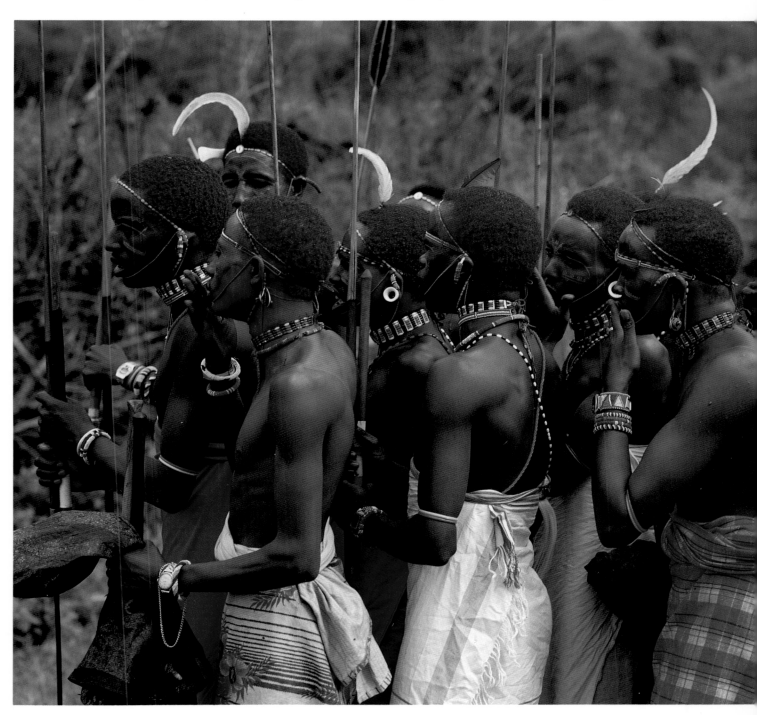

As his future wife rests after her ordeal on a couch in her mother's house, the bridegroom kills the wedding ox – known as *rikoret*. He does this as humanely as possible by plunging a knife into the vertebrae at the base of its skull to sever the spinal cord.

The bridegroom must wear garters made of lion skin; these feature prominently in Samburu culture. They may not be worn by a family which has had a relative or ancestor killed by a lion. Nor may they be used during a wedding if the bride became pregnant before her circumcision; likewise, if her father has murdered a person of his own tribe. In such cases, dried reeds are worn instead.

Weddings are wonderful opportunities for the *moran* and their girlfriends to get together. The first dances to be performed are always dances of display in which the girls are only spectators. Singing and dancing continue well into the night.

OVERLEAF: Married women will congregate and dance in separate groups. Red has always been their preferred colour, but yellow is now finding favour too.

In their dances, the warriors take it in turns to leap high in the air from a standing position without bending their knees. This is achieved by flexing their ankles in a seemingly effortless way.

The warriors often sing in a circle while the girls look on. Soloists ad-lib words to traditional tunes, praising the bravest *moran* or the bulls of their families' herds.

They also compete among themselves to see who can jump highest and continue longest without tiring.

Girls arch their backs and by thrusting out their chests flick their
necklaces up and down as they dance silently to the songs of the warriors.

The warriors do not carry their spears during the dances which require them to leap high in the air. The black pompoms on some of the spears are made from ostrich feathers. Sheathed spears with pompoms were once reckoned to be a sign of peace; these days, they are merely a decorative embellishment.

A bridegroom elaborately made up on his wedding day. Custom requires him to hang
in his pierced earlobes *urauri*, the copper earrings worn by married women.

In the early morning a day after the wedding ceremony, the elders gather to
form a guard of honour outside the *manyatta* of the bride's father. As they
incant a blessing with their sticks raised, the bridegroom, closely followed by
his best man and his bride, walks slowly down the two parallel lines and away
to his home. Once the wedding party is out of sight, the old men squat down
for prayers, beseeching Nkai to give the newly-weds health, happiness and a
large family. They will then repair to the house of the bride's parents to drink
the blood of the wedding ox mixed with broth and the fatty meat from the
chest of the ox which the bridegroom cooked for them the previous night.

At the start of their journey, in sight of the bride's home, the wedding party
will pause and squat down on four occasions. Only the best man is allowed to
look back over his shoulder should the bride be in need of help. The
bridegroom and his best man customarily carry two sticks and a tanned
sheepskin each. They also wear new leather sandals which they made
themselves specially for the journey to and from their home. They must reach
the bridegroom's *manyatta* in a day despite the bride's indisposition.

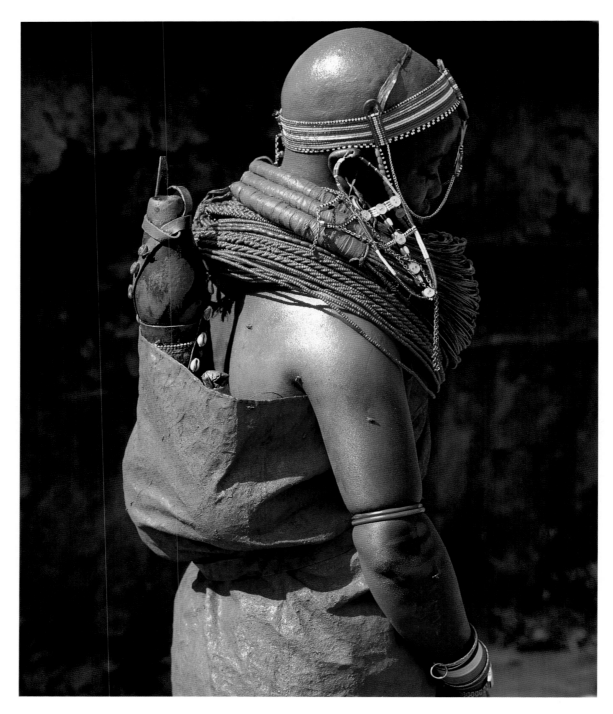

The bride waits pensively outside her new home until she is enticed in with promises of cattle. She is dressed in her wedding gown made of three goatskins which are well oiled and covered in red ochre. She carries on her back a gourd full of milk and a small wooden jar containing butter; these are her only presents from her parents and family. The large earrings she wears are called *ltirriangani*. They are only put on by brides and must be removed that evening inside her husband's home.

Still in their wedding finery, the married couple and their best man (on the left of the picture) relax on arrival at the home of the bridegroom's mother. The newly-weds will live there for a month or so until the women of the *manyatta* build them a home of their own.

Samburu elders are venerated by the other age-sets of the tribe. They are the sages who are consulted about tribal law, customs and practices. They meet regularly to discuss important issues or, socially, to pass the time of day.

CHAPTER SEVEN

The Elders

In contrast to the splendour of the *moran*, the appearance of the elders is exceptionally drab. Attractive beaded finery and red ochred locks give way to simple metal ornaments hanging from each ear, a brightly coloured blanket used as a wrap and an astonishing selection of unusual hats. Even the long burnished spear is replaced by a stick. However, the elders' looks belie the extent of their power, which can be wielded as a last resort through a potent curse. All forms of unexpected misfortune from disease among cattle to premature death are often ascribed to witchcraft or sorcery but failing those, a curse. The curse is not lightly used, nor is it uncommon; once it has been pronounced, it can only be removed by the guilty person offering his accuser a gift to secure his blessing. The Samburu claim that a curse will do no harm to an innocent man, but if it is justified it may lead to his death. Nkai is considered the supreme arbiter in such a situation because it is He who conferred on certain persons the power to curse. Most people believe strongly in its effectiveness. As such, it acts as a deterrent to malcontents and mischief-makers who are forced to conform to the norms of society and show respect. Even the haughty *moran* treat their firestick elders with deference, fearing a collective punishment or something a lot worse for gross indiscipline.

The blacksmiths' clan, the Lkunono, are considered by many to possess the most potent curse of all. It can be used individually or collectively depending on the circumstances. When I was in Maralal on one occasion, a circumcisor from the Lkunono was cursed by the clan elders for being too greedy. He had refused to circumcise boys at a small *lorora*, preferring to go straight to a larger one where he could earn more money. This behaviour was considered unworthy and mean. His punishment was that he could never again circumcise boys or make earrings, knives, arrow tips, spears or cattle brands. Since no Samburu would dream of buying articles made by a person with a curse, his livelihood had been brought to an abrupt end. Within days the circumcisor had apologized for his actions and begged forgiveness, to which the elders reluctantly agreed on condition that thenceforth he only charged half the normal fee for circumcising boys.

Another circumcisor living in the north of the district was also cursed for being too greedy. He had demanded more than double the customary fee. Within two weeks he was dead. This story was related to me to illustrate the power of the curse. The fact that the man had suffered a severe bout of cerebral malaria and that his death may have been pure coincidence was brushed aside. In the eyes of the Samburu, he had died unpropitiously away from home as a result of a curse.

Most men desire as many wives as they can afford but due to the nature of the age-grade system and the restrictions it imposes on the *moran*, they rarely marry before they are twenty-five years old and normally much later. By the time a person has enough cattle to be able to marry a second or third wife, he will probably be forty years older than his new bride. This can put the marriage under severe strain. The relationship between the elders and the *moran* over women is really no easier. On the one hand, the elders will make excuses to postpone for as long as possible the *lmuget lelaingoni*, the ceremony of the bull, after which the *moran* are permitted to marry. On the other hand, the *moran* resent the girls from their clan being taken from them for arranged marriages to old men when they themselves are not allowed to marry; they may become disruptive to the social order through a sense of frustration and annoyance. The elders recognize the attractions the *moran* have for their youthful wives and guard them jealously. This may be the underlying reason for the custom which prohibits the *moran* to eat in front of married women. Any wife caught committing adultery is given a sound thrashing and warned never to misbehave again. By the time the *moran* can finally marry, there are almost inevitably more of them than there are eligible young girls. This can again lead to frustration and a long wait until adolescent girls grow up and are old enough to leave home.

A man's generosity or his meanness are favourite topics of conversation. Generosity is a worthy trait and a man is respected for it; mean men are despised and command little standing in the community. It is customary for a host to give his friends or guests a share of whatever food or milk there is in the house to the point of self-denial. However, by doing so, he must be careful not to let his children go hungry. Anyone journeying far from home will automatically be housed and fed by a complete stranger, as long as he is of the same age-set and clan as his host. This hospitable way of entertaining has evolved from the hardships associated with nomadism but today's more severe economic pressures may have the effect of reducing this wonderfully friendly tradition.

Many senior elders spend much of their day sitting, squatting, lying or even dozing in the shade of a tree. It is amazing how they can find new topics to talk about all day, every day. When idle gossip turns into a serious discussion, one elder after another rises to his feet, always with a stick in his hand, to air his views eloquently. Everyone appears to be an accomplished orator and has something to say. My friends assure me that many speeches can be both boring and highly repetitive, which makes me feel better when I am frustrated by a lack of proper understanding of the Maa language.

All major decisions affecting a family or clan must be unanimous. Objections are discussed at length until a consensus of opinion is reached. This may take several days. If a man has very strong views and is unwilling to accede to the wishes of the majority, his lone voice can prevail. If he did this too often, however, he would be considered an unworthy man. On one occasion I visited a *lorora* at Lesirikan with my Samburu friends. We had been there a week earlier at the instance of the chief to deliver a circumcisor from South Horr. A loquacious elder objected to my presence, though, more probably, it was my camera he disliked. When this matter came up for discussion with the elders, I had their widespread support for having helped them find a circumcisor just when they wanted one. Realizing he had misjudged the prevailing mood, the man quickly withdrew his remarks and presented me with a goat as a conciliatory gesture. Since it would have been bad manners to have refused the gift, my friends and I feasted on it that evening with unconcealed delight.

Very old men do not normally take an active part in the elders' discussions. They are often asleep and oblivious to what is going on. Nevertheless, they are greatly respected as wise old men and may be consulted on difficult matters relating to customs and traditions. The oldest man present at a gathering will always be called upon to lead the blessing at the end of a debate. Everyone rises to their feet and faces the general direction of Mount Ng'iro as the old man waves his stick after his invocations. 'May Nkai look after you . . . May Nkai give you life . . . May Nkai give you cattle . . . May Nkai give you children . . .' and so on. The elders chant 'Nkai' after each invocation and as they do so loosely clench and immediately release the fists of both hands. At the end of the blessing, everyone present will spit three times into his right hand.

The Samburu have never had hereditary rulers; chiefs are merely an imposition of government to publicize and enforce official policy but have practically no voice on ceremonial occasions. Until his death, the most influential elder was Lesepen, an astrologer who had an uncanny knack of foretelling the future by gazing at the stars. His home was on the top of Mount Ng'iro, but when I met him in September 1990, his modest *manyatta* was tucked away among large boulders in the arid country to the west of the mountain. He was a frail old man of almost ninety years, in the autumn of his life. 'The stars control everything on earth,' he told me. 'I study both the morning and the evening stars but the evening star is the most important. It tells me everything that is happening in the world, especially events taking place around me in the bush. The morning star is not so powerful because it has been cursed by its mother, the sun.'

When I asked him who would take over from him, he answered, 'My father and my grandfather knew all about the stars. When I was a young boy before my circumcision, I used to help my father. Though young, I was well known, but as soon as I became a warrior, I stopped prophesying for a while. Now that I am old and sick, my sons will take my place. My eldest son is experienced but too talkative; my younger son is also very knowledgeable and does not say much. One of them will be like me. He will be the person to whom all the L'oikop [Samburu] will go to seek advice.' I was left in no doubt that the younger son would eventually take his place.

The Samburu are expert stockmen and take great pains to enlarge their herds of cattle over a period of many years. The social values placed on a big herd are very significant. It not only enables a man to have more wives, but it gives him a status in society which is lacking for someone who only owns sheep and goats.

The cattle given by a husband to his wife at the time of their marriage can be exploited by him in certain circumstances at a later date. For instance, when his wife's relatives seek additional gifts at regular intervals, which they are bound to do, he will in all probability give them an ox from her allotted herd rather than from his own. In this way, he prevails on his in-laws to be reasonable in their demands. At the same time, he protects his 'nucleus' herd, which he can build up or dispense to buy more wives.

By the time a man gets married, he should have enough cattle to make him self-reliant. His mother will have given him most of them, for she customarily shares her herd with her sons when they reach marriageable age. So long as the father is alive, however, all the cattle in the family will remain together as part of the old man's herd. When he dies, the eldest son of the first wife will inherit his nucleus herd. This son will give each of his brothers and half-brothers a gift of a heifer. His married brothers are now allowed to split their cattle from the main herd and become truly independent.

A woman's youngest son will inherit the unallocated portion of her herd when she dies. Girls inherit nothing from either parent because they are given cattle by their husbands when they marry. However inequitable these laws may seem to some people, they are accepted without question as fair by the Samburu.

The Samburu do not believe in life after death. Death is regarded as unpropitious at any time although a man or a woman who has reached old age, has a large family and many cattle, and dies at home is considered to be a little more fortunate than others. For them a ram is slaughtered and its fat is reduced to a liquid by boiling the fatty tissue. In the case of an old man, the eldest son of the family will pour some fat into his father's mouth followed by each son in turn, and the dead man is told to eat it. If the eldest son is away at the time, he must give a heifer to the next born, who acts on his behalf. The old man's personal ornaments will be covered in fat and divided equally among his sons. His right hand is then placed under his head and the body is wrapped in an ox hide and tied with a leather thong. As it is taken from the home in the direction of the setting sun to where it will be laid to rest, the eldest son will hold his father's head while the other sons carry his body in order of their age, with the youngest holding his feet. If there are insufficient sons to do this, the closest male relatives will be called in to help. The body will be lain on its right side with the head facing Mount Ng'iro under a thriving tree and everyone present will lay on top of it a branch from another tree, starting with the eldest son and ending with his mother and sisters. As the party returns to their *manyatta*, they will pause and squat down briefly on four separate occasions. They must not look back over their shoulders until they reach home.

The procedures are identical when an old woman dies except that she will be wrapped in a cowhide and her youngest son will hold her head as she is carried to her resting place. This has a direct bearing on the Samburu laws of inheritance. The only people who are entitled to be buried in a shallow grave are exceptionally old men and the *laibons*. Their bodies are covered with soil and stones to create a mound. When their friends and well-wishers pass by from time to time, they may throw more stones or branches on top of the mound as a token of remembrance and tell the deceased to lie in peace.

It is widely believed that anyone who dies without children has been cursed. The body will be thrown into the bush with his or her belongings and forgotten. This even applies to a *moran* who is killed in battle, although an ox – known as *lkishiret* – must be slaughtered by the family at a later date; none of the dead *moran*'s younger brothers can be circumcised until this has been done. This ritual is said to protect the boys from dying like him. The immediate relatives of a dead person must shave their heads, but when a *moran* dies, his fellow warriors in the same section of his clan must do likewise. They will throw their hair into the bush to signify it is dead like their comrade. If a *moran* shaves his head on any other occasion – for example, if he contracts a skin disease – his hair is kept in his mother's house.

The Samburu expect wild animals and vultures to eat their dead and a member of the family will check to ensure this has happened. If the body has not been devoured within two days, a goat will be killed beside it to attract scavengers, especially hyenas. An entire *manyatta* must move to a new site one 'moon' after a person has died in his own home. To avoid this inconvenience, there is a tendency to take very old or sick people to a shady spot outside the *manyatta* during the hours of daylight. When an infant dies, it is buried deep inside the house; that house must then be burnt and razed to the ground.

Although the attire of the elders is often drab in contrast with the warriors of the tribe, they love to wear an astonishing selection of unusual hats.

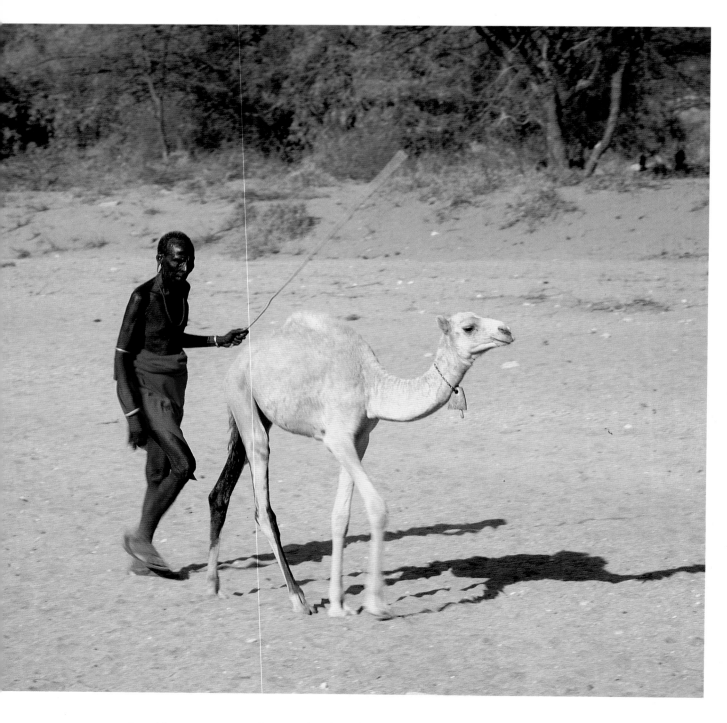

An old man, spare as the grasslands in his home area, drives
a young camel to his *manyatta* in the late afternoon.

Two men deep in conversation squat on their haunches outside a *manyatta*.

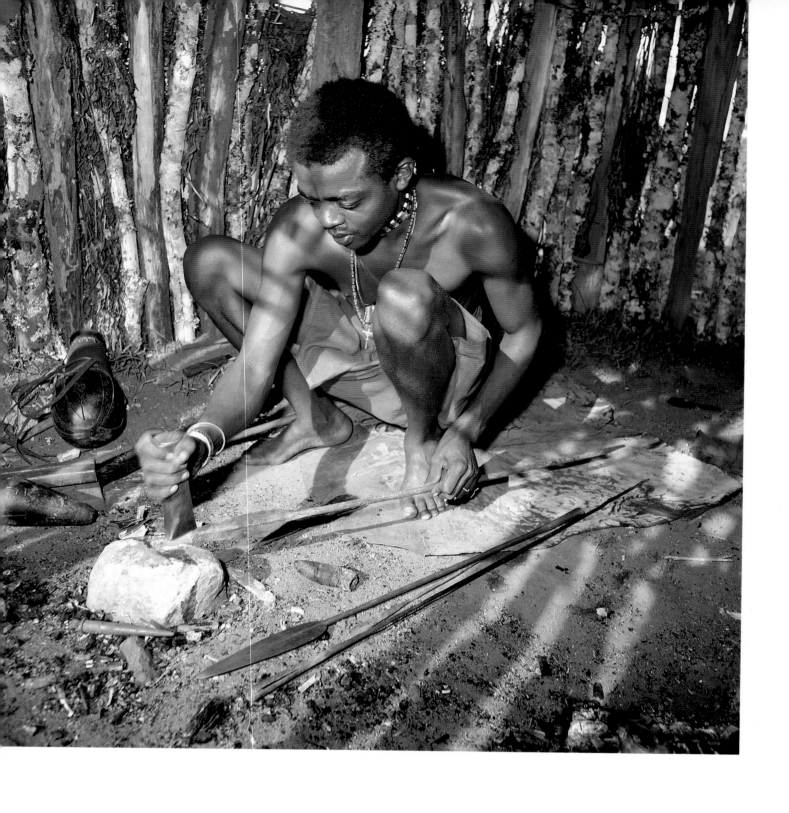

OPPOSITE: An elderly woman from the blacksmiths' clan, the *lkunono*, works the bellows while her son (above) fashions a spear from an iron rod. The bellows are made from goatskins; she will pump each one alternately to raise the heat in the charcoal fire. The skills of the blacksmiths are handed down from father to son. This young man will take two days to make a spear for which he will be paid a goat.

Potters are rare among the Samburu. This woman is one of a handful of experts, all of whom are female. She lives below Warges Mountain, near Wamba, but her source of clay is several miles distant to the east.
The women are members of the Ltorobo clan and can trace their origins to the Laikipiak Maasai.

This old woman is scraping a goatskin which has been pegged out on the ground and dried in the sun. She removes all the dried flakes of flesh and tissue to make it supple. Three skins are used to make a wedding dress. It is customary for the bridegroom to present a sheepskin to the woman who makes his bride's gown.

The Wandorobo are hunters and honey-gatherers who have an intimate knowledge of nature. This old man, Lepitei, is holding a leather bag – a *samburr* – in which he carries his honey. He can get more than a bagful from each hive in season by visiting them twice a month. He has exclusive traditional rights to a large forested area in the Mathews Range, close to the Ng'eng River. Here, he has about one hundred hives made from hollowed-out logs. His main problem is the damage caused to them by honey badgers, which are numerous.

There is a tradition that prevents some sections of the Samburu from quarrelling or drawing blood from one another. When boys from those sections are circumcised by a man who is part of the alliance, they must each give him two cowrie shells. He will reciprocate in kind.

Lemoloi, a well-known circumcisor, is seen here wearing 198 cowrie shells round his wrist. They were presented to him by the ninety-nine boys he had operated on over a two-day period in August 1990. The shells are worn for a week or so and then put away.

Lominchira was the oldest man living at Porro in 1990. Based on the age-grade system of the Samburu, I estimate that he was between eighty-five and ninety years old. He slept and rested a lot but could still walk several miles from home.

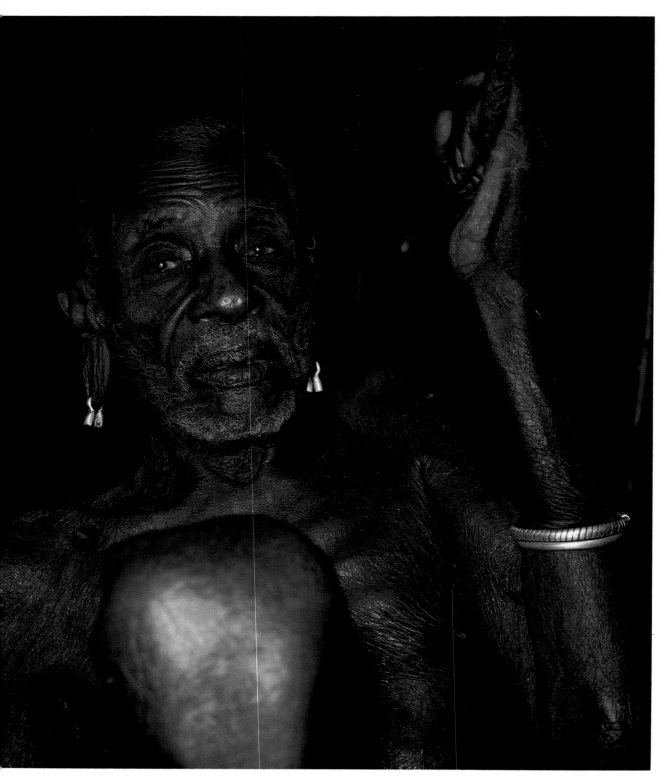

I took this photograph of Lesepen, the famous Samburu astrologer, two months before his death in November 1990. I found him a dignified but frail old man, in the autumn of his life. He was living frugally in the foothills of Mount Ng'iro, near Tum. In his heyday, Lesepen was the most respected and powerful elder of the tribe, advising on all ceremonial matters and foretelling future events. He is credited with saving many Samburu lives at the time of the *ngoroko* raids – a period of aggressive rustling by armed Turkana outlaws more than a decade ago.

Copper bracelets worn on the right wrist of a man are rarely seen today. They are a mark of valour – the equivalent of a Victoria Cross – awarded by the elders of the tribe. Those who wear them will have displayed outstanding courage and killed an enemy – in the case of this man, an armed Somali bandit with his spear.

The elders' ornaments are few – one or two beaded necklaces and simple metal earrings, often shaped like a bell.

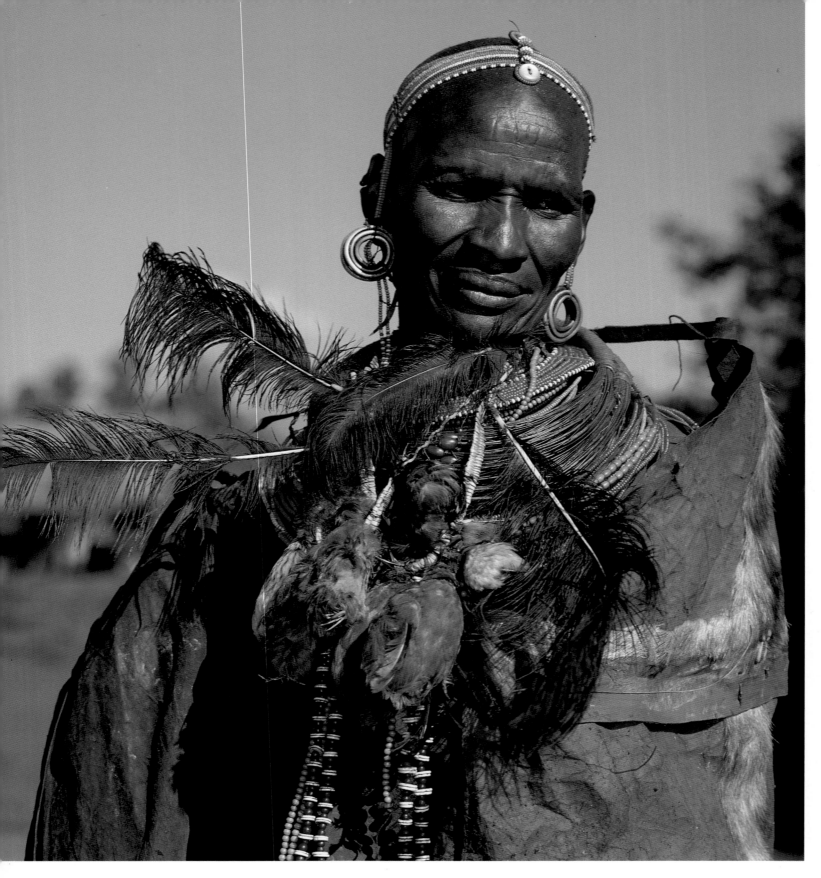

A woman wears a goatskin cape and her sons' bird head-dresses during the *lmuget loolbaa* ceremony.
She has two separate strings of blue and white beads hanging from her neck
which denote that two of her sons were circumcised and have become warriors of the tribe.

Women take great pride in wearing strings of navy blue and white beads which reveal to others the
number of sons they have borne who are warriors of the tribe. Each string is double, looped through the
right earring and has cowrie shells attached at one end. The woman opposite has three warrior sons.

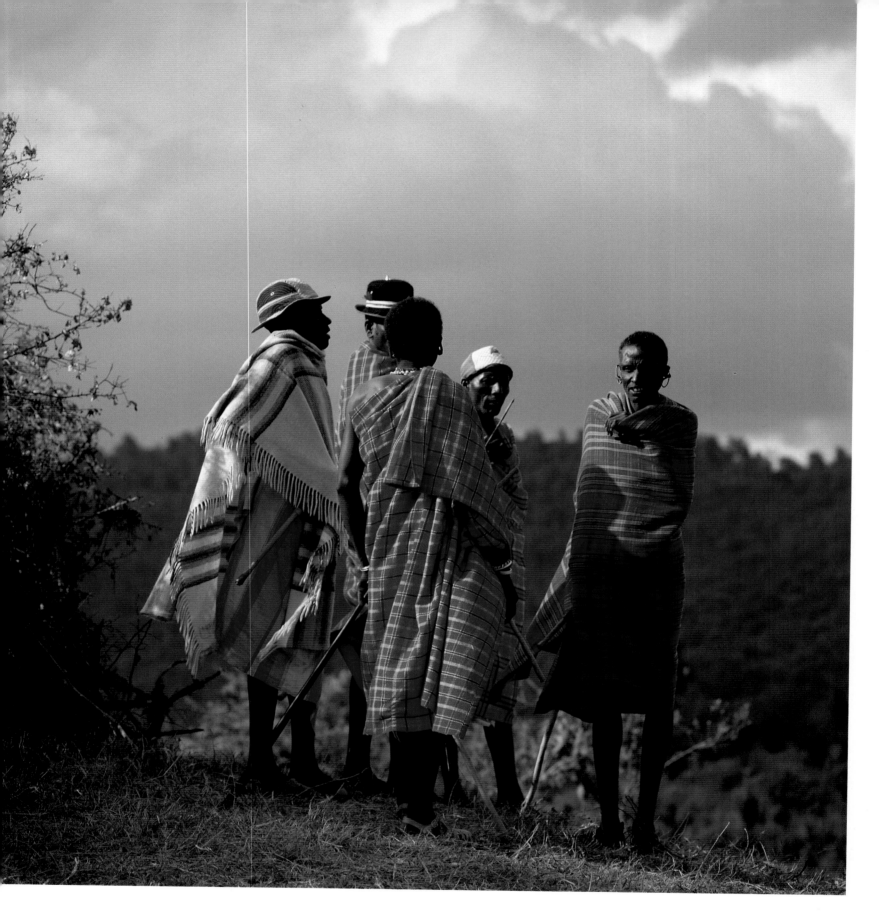

The status, prestige and influence of the elders are based on the number of cattle, wives and children they have. Their generosity in the community also affects their standing in the tribe. They wrap themselves in brightly coloured blankets; as with other aspects of tribal dress, red is the preferred colour.

An old man blows a kudu-horn trumpet during a *lmuget* ceremony. Only the elders or the *moran* are allowed to sound the horn on ceremonial occasions or, if an enemy is seen, to summon the warriors to battle.

The ancient game of *bau* is played in many regions of Africa. It is especially popular with Samburu elders who while away the hours of daylight pitting their skills against young and old. The wooden board is always placed on a hide. Women are not allowed to play this game.

This woman is almost ninety years old. Now frail and partially blind, she has never had a day's illness in her strenuous life.

Epilogue

Most traditional societies in Africa have undergone enormous change in the past fifty years. The few that have held out against the unrelenting pressures are either tribes that have been isolated from the outside world because of their remoteness or civil wars, or nomadic peoples living in a harsh desert environment where the introduction of a different lifestyle would spell disaster.

Samburu District is neither inaccessible nor desert, so it is not for geographical reasons that the pace of change has been slow. The principal cause lies with the attitude of the Samburu elders, most of whom have spent their entire lives close to home. They believe passionately in the superiority of their way of life and have never been tempted to embrace the modern world. Only recently have some changes become evident. The process of transformation from an age-old policy of isolationism will now gather momentum.

Progress does not require traditions to be cast aside. Changes made simply for the sake of them would do more harm than good. The Samburu need help to improve their lifestyle, not to destroy it. Their qualities of bravery, generosity, honesty and respect of the family should be preserved. The trouble is that different people view 'progress' in different ways; it is almost impossible to reconcile all shades of opinion. My interpretation of it will be at odds with that of the average school leaver who counts progress in the more materialistic aspects of stylish clothes, electronic goods and the glittering entertainment of the 'civilized' world. I view development in terms of projects that will uplift the living standards of the people.

The Samburu require considerable financial and material support to build dams and develop water catchment areas. Since almost half Kenya's land mass is semi-desert, it seems strange that the international aid agencies have not done more in this field. The storage of floodwaters from seasonal rivers would have a major impact on the economy of the region and benefit those living there.

The Samburu are skilled stockmen and deserve better veterinary services to combat endemic diseases. They need advice on how to improve the quality rather than the quantity of their livestock, but their temperamental aversion to selling it must be discouraged. This would stop the degradation of the grasslands. It would also bring the Samburu into the money economy of today, forcing them to place less reliance on cattle as the sole arbiter of a man's wealth. However, this departure from their tradition will only be achieved if the livestock marketing facilities in the district are greatly improved. Of late, a handful of Samburu have ventured into small businesses of their own. In the past, Somalis were the merchants and cattle-traders in the district; they provided a service and did themselves well.